STATE-DIRECTED DEVELOPMENT

Political Power and Industrialization in the Global Periphery

This study undertakes a comparative analysis of the state as an economic actor in developing countries. Why have some developing country states been more successful at facilitating industrialization than others? An answer to this question is developed by focusing on both patterns of state construction and patterns of state intervention aimed at promoting industrialization. Four countries are analyzed in detail – South Korea, Brazil, India, and Nigeria – over the twentieth century. The states in these countries varied from cohesive-capitalist (mainly in Korea but also in Brazil) to fragmented-multiclass (mainly in India but also in Brazil) to neo-patrimonial (mainly in Nigeria). It is argued that cohesive-capitalist states have been most effective at promoting industrialization and neo-patrimonial states the least. The performance of fragmented-multiclass states falls somewhere in the middle. After explaining in detail why this should be so, this study traces the origins of these different state types historically, emphasizing the role of different types of colonialisms in the process of state construction in the developing world.

Atul Kohli is the David K. E. Bruce Professor of International Affairs at Princeton University. He has written or edited nine books and has published some fifty articles. His most recent publications include *The Success of India's Democracy* (2002) and *States, Markets and Just Growth* (2003). He has held fellowships from the Russell Sage Foundation, the Ford Foundation, and the Social Science Research Council, New York.

Advance Praise for *State-Directed Development*

"Kohli's provocative book rehabilitates the state in face of claims that state sovereignty has declined as a result of globalization. Reviewing the comparative capacity of four states in this admirably grounded project he demonstrates that markets, liberty and security require a strong state. Bringing history back in, he argues that the differences in state capacity of Brazil, India, Nigeria and Korea have been shaped by their distinct colonial' experiences."

– Susanne Hoeber Rudolph, *University of Chicago*

"This book amounts to a head-on challenge to what John Stuart Mill once called 'the deep slumber of a decided opinion', the opinion that the developing country state should focus on alleviating poverty and providing a market-friendly framework for the private sector. Kohli argues that fast economic growth is unlikely without a more forceful kind of state intervention in support of investor profits, and he illuminates the institutional characteristics of the state that are likely to make such intervention effective or not. Subsequent research on the political economy of growth will have to take this as a touchstone."

– Robert Hunter Wade, *London School of Economics*

STATE-DIRECTED DEVELOPMENT

*Political Power and Industrialization
in the Global Periphery*

ATUL KOHLI
Princeton University

CAMBRIDGE
UNIVERSITY PRESS

CAMBRIDGE UNIVERSITY PRESS

Cambridge, New York, Melbourne, Madrid, Cape Town, Singapore, São Paulo

Cambridge University Press
40 West 20th Street, New York, NY 10011-4211, USA

www.cambridge.org
Information on this title: www.cambridge.org/9780521836708

First published 2004
Reprinted 2005

Printed in the United States of America

A catalog record for this publication is available from the British Library.

Library of Congress Cataloging in Publication Data

Kohli, Atul.
State-directed development : political power and industrialization in the
global periphery / Atul Kohli.
p. cm.
Includes bibliographical references and index.
ISBN 0-521-83670-0 (hb) – ISBN 0-521-54525-0 (pb)
1. Industrial policy – Developing countries.   2. Industrialization – Developing
countries.   3. Developing countries – Economic policy.   4. Developing
countries – Politics and government.   I. Title.
HD3616.D452.K64   2004
338.9′009172′4–dc22   2003069755

ISBN-13   978-0-521-83670-8 hardback
ISBN-10   0-521-83670-0 hardback

ISBN-13   978-0-521-54525-9 paperback
ISBN-10   0-521-54525-0 paperback

To
My Parents

Contents

vii

PART IV   DASHED EXPECTATIONS: NIGERIA

List of Tables and Figures

Tables

Figures

Acknowledgments

This book was a long time in the making, nearly a decade. A substantial portion of the research and writing was completed during three years of sabbatical leaves. My foremost thanks are thus to Princeton University for its generous leave policy. During the first of these sabbaticals in 1992–93 I was a visitor at the Economic Growth Center, Yale University; I would like to acknowledge the collegiality and support of Koichi Hamada, Gustav Ranis, and T. N. Srinivasan (then the director of the center). The Russell Sage Foundation in New York City offered me a fellowship during 1996–97, facilitating a full year away from teaching and administrative duties at Princeton. And finally, I was a visitor in 2001–2 at the Graduate Center, City University of New York. During that year, I appreciated friendship and conversations with Forrest Colburn, Mauricio Font, and Susan Woodward.

A number of colleagues with shared interests read the entire manuscript and gave me very useful suggestions. I would especially like to acknowledge the help of Thomas Callaghy, Andrew Coleman, Peter Evans, Patrick Heller, Ashutosh Varshney, and Meredith Woo-Cumings. Another set of colleagues read and commented on parts of the manuscript, both saving me subsequent embarrassment of mistaken facts and helping me to clarify or to modify the argument. These included Jeremy Adelman, Sheri Berman, Bruce Cumings, Carter Eckert, Neil Englehart, John Gerring, Stephan Haggard, Jeff Herbst, David Kang, Devesh Kapur, John P. Lewis, Pratap Mehta, Chung-In Moon, Gyan Prakash, Adam Przeworski, Susanne Rudolph, Anna Seleny, Robert Wade, John Waterbury, and Crawford Young. A discussion with my Princeton colleague Evan Lieberman was especially helpful in rethinking some conceptual categories.

I must also acknowledge the help of some graduate students at Princeton. Rina Agarwala, Vanya Krieckhaus, Erik Kuhonta, and Rani Mullen were not only able research assistants, but also insightful scholarly critics of one part of the manuscript or the other. In this role of an assistant and a critic, I would especially like to single out the important contribution of Maya Tudor in preparing tables and figures and for helping to bring the manuscript to conclusion. Other graduate students who read and provided useful written comments on parts of the study were Bruce Giley, Jaime Kirzner-Roberts, Elizabeth Kittrell, Ilan Nam, Sejin Oh, David Yang, and Min Ye. Finally, Kerry Griffin helped to complete the index.

The manuscript was ably copyedited by Ilene Cohen. To her, my sincere thanks. Peter Johnson provided useful ideas for the cover art. The prolonged interest that Lewis Bateman at Cambridge University Press maintained in this book provided needed encouragement. My most significant debt is to Edna Lloyd for typing and retyping numerous versions of the manuscript. I need not add, but I will add that Edna's cheerful cooperation was indispensable in bringing this project to completion.

Finally, I would like to note the help of loved ones. Marie Gottschalk and our daughter, Tara Kohli, provided all the warmth, distractions, and good cheer necessary for a balanced life while working on a long drawn-out project. My brother, sister, and their respective families remain an important part of my extended connections. This book is dedicated to my parents, Dr. Jai Dev and Pushpa Kohli, for years of love and support.

Introduction

States and Industrialization in the Global Periphery

Legitimate states that govern effectively and dynamic industrial economies are widely regarded today as the defining characteristics of a modern nation-state. Ever since Western countries developed such political economies a few centuries back, those left behind have sought to catch up. Among late developers, countries such as Japan and Russia avoided being colonialized by consolidating their respective states and adopting alternative strategies of industrialization, with varying results. The search for development among late-late-industrializers of Asia, Africa, and Latin America intensified mainly after the Second World War, when numerous activist states emerged as sovereign. It is clear from the vantage point of the end of the twentieth century that state-led development efforts have been more successful in some parts of the global periphery than in others. This book looks at the role states have played in fostering different rates and patterns of economic development, especially via deliberate industrialization.

States in most peripheral countries of Asia, Africa, and Latin America are important, active economic actors, engaged in varying patterns of state intervention. In some developing countries the state's economic role has come to be associated with both rapid industrial transformation and enhanced equity. In other cases, by contrast, governments and bureaucrats have pilfered the economic resources of their own societies, failing to stimulate economic growth and facilitating transfer of wealth into the hands of unproductive elites. In yet other cases, state intervention is associated with mixed outcomes: States have helped to solve some important economic problems, while ignoring other problems and creating new ones.

This study undertakes a comparative analysis of the state as an economic actor in developing countries. Why have some of these states been more successful at facilitating industrialization than others? This question really has two components: What features distinguish state intervention in the more successful cases from intervention in the less successful cases? and How does one explain varying state capacities to choose and implement economic decisions? The first question of patterns of state intervention focuses both on the state's policy choices and on its relationship with such key economic actors as business and labor. By contrast, the second question, concerning state capacities, looks to the institutional character of the state itself, an identity often assumed well before the political elite initiated deliberate industrialization. This book then is about patterns of state construction and patterns of state intervention aimed at promoting industrialization.

It is mainly an inductive study that seeks a general understanding of the state as an economic actor in developing countries via detailed analyses of four major developing countries of the twentieth century: South Korea, Brazil, India, and Nigeria (see Table 1 and Fig. 1, below). These cases provide a range of variation in state capacities to pursue economic transformation, from a fairly effective, growth-promoting state in South Korea to a rather ineffective and corrupt Nigerian state, with Brazil and India providing mixed cases. What helps to explain these variations? Indeed, this is a key puzzle in late-late-development.

The main argument of the book, drawn from comparative historical analysis of these four countries, is that the creation of effective states within the developing world has generally preceded the emergence of industrializing economies. This is because state intervention in support of investor profits has proved to be a precondition for industry to emerge and flourish among late-late-developers. Patterns of state authority, including how the politics of the state are organized and how state power is used, have decisively influenced the economic context within which private economic decisions are made. They are thus important, nay, critical, for understanding varying rates and patterns of industrialization. Patterns of state authority, in turn, often exhibit long-term continuities. Colonialism in the first half of the twentieth century, especially, was defining of the state institutions that emerged in developing countries, and that in turn molded their economies in the second half of the century.

I. Some Clarifications

The focus of this study requires, if not a justification, at least some preliminary clarifications. Three brief caveats are in order.

First, it is clear that development involves a lot more than economic growth and that variations in economic growth reflect more than underlying variations in industrial growth. Moreover, any study of the role of the state in industrialization must attend to issues of agricultural growth and income distribution. Nevertheless, the primary focus of this study is on the political and policy determinants of industrialization, because industrial growth is a key determinant of any country's overall economic growth, and economic growth remains a core element of any understanding of development.

Second, a central concern with the economic role of the state in development really does not require any justification. It is more than an idiosyncratic assertion to hold that states are important economic actors in developing countries and thus worthy of serious scholarly interest – even if rates of economic growth reflect a host of other factors. In this regard one can note numerous variables that influence a given country's economic performance over a specific period, including world economic conditions, resource endowments, differing starting points, demographic factors, national price regimes, patterns of savings, levels of technology, and entrepreneurship. For their part, however, historians of economic processes repeatedly emphasize the significance of institutions, especially the role of government. Lloyd Reynolds, for example, concluded his major study of economic growth in the "Third World" by observing that the analysis of underlying economic factors does not fully reveal the "mystery" of "sources of sustained growth." What is missing from the economic models, according to him, "can be labeled as political. Government matters."[1] W. Arthur Lewis similarly noted in a presidential address to the American Economic Association that one building block of any full understanding of "the engine of growth" would be "a theory of government, where government would appear to be as much the problem as the solution."[2] More recently, a number of scholars have gone further, suggesting that an activist state has been a key ingredient of rapid development, especially in parts of East Asia, and that, conversely, malfunctioning states have contributed heavily to developmental failures, say, in sub-Saharan Africa.[3] The prima facie case for a broad focus on state and development is thus strong.

---

[1] See Lloyd G. Reynolds, *Economic Growth in the Third World, 1850–1980* (New Haven, Conn.: Yale University Press, 1985), 413–14.

[2] W. Arthur Lewis, "The State of Development Theory," *American Economic Review* 5 (March 1984): 8.

[3] See, for example, Peter Evans, *Embedded Autonomy: State and Industrial Transformation* (Princeton, N.J.: Princeton University Press, 1995); Stephen Haggard, *Pathways from the Periphery: The Politics of Growth in the Newly Developing Countries* (Ithaca, N.Y.: Cornell University Press, 1990); Robert Wade, *Governing the Market: Economic Theory and the Role of Government in East Asian Industrialization* (Princeton, N.J.: Princeton University Press, 1990); and Alice Amsden, *Asia's Next Giant: South Korea and Late Industrialization* (New York: Oxford University Press, 1989). A recent assessment of this "developmental state" literature is Meredith Woo-Cumings, *The Developmental State* (Ithaca, N.Y.: Cornell University Press, 1999). For the role of the state in African cases, see Richard Sandbrook, *Politics of Africa's Economic Stagnation* (Cambridge: Cambridge University Press, 1985). A recent collection in which a group of economists emphasize the role of institutions in economic growth, including the role of public institutions, is Dani Rodrik, ed., *In Search of Prosperity: Analytic Narratives on Economic Growth* (Princeton, N.J.: Princeton University Press, 2003). This volume came to my attention only as the present study was going to press.

Finally, there is the issue of case selection: Why have Korea, Brazil, India, and Nigeria been chosen?[4] Two brief and preliminary justifications for case selection will suffice for now. First, these four are large and significant developing countries: Nigeria, for example, is the most populous country in sub-Saharan Africa, as is Brazil in South America (see Table 1, below).[5] Any meaningful generalizations about state and development would necessarily have to apply at least to these cases. Moreover, the general ideas developed below are actually examined against more cases than a focus on four countries may suggest. For example, detailed analysis of countries over time provides other cases within a single country, and some further check on propositions will be provided by examining them briefly against other cases, especially within each region. Thus, for example, I return in the conclusion to a consideration of how well the propositions developed with reference, say, to the Korean case apply to other successful East Asian cases or, similarly, the extent to which the propositions developed with reference to Nigeria help to explain other African failures. And second, as already noted, these four cases provide a range of variation – from effective state intervention in Korea to an ineffective state in Nigeria – that helps to frame the analytical puzzle: What explains such variation in developmental efficacy?

II. The Intellectual Context

As an investigation of both state construction and state intervention in the developing world, this study addresses several interrelated scholarly debates. One of the more heated debates concerns the role of states versus that of markets in the process of late-late-development. A less well developed debate that this study engages concerns how it came about that some parts of the developing world acquired more effective developmental states than did others.

The systematic political and economic study of developing countries began only after the Second World War and grew rapidly thereafter. For some two to three decades the organizing framework was to seek generalizations

---

4 Much can be said on this issue, and I return to some related concerns in due course, especially in the conclusion. Some basic development indicators of these four cases are summarized in Table 1.

5 Other ready candidates for inclusion on the grounds of "large" and "significant" would have been China, Indonesia, Turkey, Egypt, and Mexico. Given its communist past, China was too much of an "outlier"; the Chinese case is nevertheless important for a discussion of "state capacity" and I consider it briefly in the conclusion. Egypt has been so mired in regional conflicts that it is atypical. Indonesia, Turkey, and Mexico, however, were all worthy of inclusion. The main excuse for not including them is limited scholarly energy. One useful comparative analysis that goes over some of the same thematic concerns as this study but with reference to Mexico, Egypt, Turkey, and India is John Waterbury, *Exposed to Innumerable Delusions: Public Enterprise and State Power in Egypt, India, Mexico, and Turkey* (Cambridge: Cambridge University Press, 1993).

about the developing world as a whole, with an emphasis on determining how this world, the "Third World," was distinct from the one composed of the more advanced and industrialized political economies. This approach held as much for political scientists and sociologists associated with the modernization framework as it did for radical dependency critics and for economists trying to carve out a niche for economic development studies within economics. Thus modernization scholars worried about the prospects for stability and democracy in the developing world, dependency scholars examined why dependent political economies were not likely to replicate the dynamism associated with early capitalism, and economic development specialists often argued that market imperfections so prevalent in the developing world necessitated state intervention and import substitution.[6]

But this early development literature seldom asked why some developing economies performed better than others. This is because in an important sense, it was simply too early to ask this question in the 1950s and the 1960s, as only in the 1970s did the dramatic variations in performance across developing countries, especially in rates of industrialization, start to become apparent. Only from then on did these variations become a central concern for development scholars. By contrast, insofar as the earlier literature shed some light on these issues of comparative political economy, it was only indirect: Modernization literature could be construed as suggesting that variation in economic performance may have something to do with the role of regime type: democratic versus authoritarian; dependency literature proposed that the same variations may instead reflect greater or lesser dependency on global capitalism; and it was implicit in the economic development literature that varying economic performance was considered to reflect the relative success of the state's efforts to rectify market imperfections. These were important insights, some of which are incorporated into the empirical analyses below. We also revisit more specific hypotheses associated with these literatures in the conclusion. Suffice it to note for now that none of these earlier frameworks is up to the task at hand because they were not designed for the explicit purpose of developing sound political economy

---

[6] These are large bodies of literature and this is no place to discuss them. For one good review of the modernization literature, see Samuel Huntington, "The Change to Change," *Comparative Politics* 3 (April 1971): 3, 283–322. Dependency literature is well reviewed in Gabriel Palma, "Dependency: A Formal Theory of Underdevelopment or a Methodology for the Analysis of Concrete Situations of Underdevelopment?," *World Development* 6 (1978): 881–924. And the literature on economic development is usefully assessed in Albert O. Hirschman, "Rise and Decline of Development Economics," in Hirschman, *Essays in Trespassing: Economics to Politics and Beyond* (Cambridge: Cambridge University Press, 1981); and Paul Krugman, "Toward a Counter-Counter-Revolution in Development Theory," *World Bank Economic Review*, Supplement (Washington, D.C.: Proceedings of the World Bank Annual Conference on Development Economics, 1992, 1993).

explanations of variations in rates and patterns of economic development across the developing world.[7]

The political economy debate on why some parts of the developing world have had faster-growing economies than others polarized in the last two decades of the twentieth century around a more neoliberal, promarket position, on the one hand, and a statist argument, on the other hand. The promarket position emerged nearly hegemonic, especially among some economists and development policy practitioners.[8] For its part, the statist argument, often articulated by interdisciplinary scholars of development, provided a cogent scholarly dissent.[9] This book hopes to advance this debate further yet by developing the existing statist position, though not by adopting an aggressive antimarket positon. On the contrary, one of the themes of this study is that state intervention in rapid industrializers was often characterized by market-reinforcing behavior, understood in the sense of supporting profitability for private investors – and not as strengthening competitiveness or openness or, even less, as a state's self-limiting proclivity. The state versus market mind-set thus is simply not very helpful for understanding how the interaction of states and markets has served to produce a range of economic outcomes.

Two claims at the heart of the promarket position on economic development are examined. First, there is the outward-orientation claim, which suggests that greater openness and greater competitiveness in the economy generate higher rates of production growth via more efficient allocation of scarce resources. And second, the laissez-faire claim holds that state intervention in the economy necessarily generates distortions that hurt economic growth. Although the outward-orientation position is the more compelling of the two claims, it nonetheless requires a number of qualifications about the importance of state intervention for export promotion and about the problem of identifying the causal direction between exports and growth. Moreover, the preponderance of the evidence indicates that

[7] I have critiqued the modernization and dependency literatures for their neglect of the autonomous and varying role of the state in development and the development economics literature for assuming that states will play a "welfare maximizing" role without a good understanding of when and how states might take on such a role. See "Introduction," in Atul Kohli, ed., *The State and Development in Third World* (Princeton, N.J.: Princeton University Press, 1986); Atul Kohli, *The State and Poverty in India: The Politics of Reform* (Cambridge: Cambridge University Press, 1987), chap. 1; and Atul Kohli, "State, Society, and Development," in Ira Katznelson and Helen Milner, eds., *State of the Discipline* (New York: W. W. Norton, 2002), 84–117.

[8] See, for example, Anne Krueger, "The Political Economy of the Rent Seeking Society," *American Economic Review* 64 (1974): 291–303; Deepak Lal, *The Poverty of "Development" Economics*, Hobart Paperback no. 16 (London: Institute of Economic Affairs, 1983); and World Bank, *Development Report* (New York: Oxford University Press, 1991).

[9] Among others, see Wade, *Governing the Market*; Amsden, *Asia's Next Giant*; and Evans, *Embedded Autonomy*.

late-late-industrialization has always commenced under conditions of protection. As to the laissez-faire claim, there is a stunning lack of evidence for the proposition that less government facilitates more rapid industrialization in the developing world. On the contrary, the evidence shows that state intervention aimed at boosting investor profitability is strongly associated with rapid industrialization. This study investigates validity of these claims via detailed case materials, and the main findings – that there are serious doubts about these claims – are summarized in the conclusion.

The main dissent from the promarket position in contemporary development studies is offered by statist scholars who emphasize the constructive role played by state intervention in select, successful cases. This literature has carefully documented how numerous such state interventions – tariffs, subsidies, credit control, manpower training, technology promotion, and bureaucratic cooperation with the private sector and oversight – have contributed to industrialization and rapid growth, especially in East Asia. Other scholars have gone further, asking what sort of states are capable of such interventions and often emphasizing such variables as leadership priorities and/or the quality of bureaucracy.[10] The present study builds on this literature; indeed, it could not have been written without the foundation laid by these bold and original formulations. One argument that is central in this statist literature informs the thinking here as well – that successful state intervention often involves close cooperation between the state and private investors. At a popular level, this idea is often expressed in such characterization of East Asian political economies as "Korea Incorporated" or "Taiwan Incorporated." At a more scholarly level, the idea is expressed as "embedded autonomy" being a precondition for successful development, an idea that suggests not only close cooperation between the state and business but also a measure of insulation for the bureaucratic elite so as to minimize corruption and "state capture" by private interests.[11]

Although the present study builds on the statist literature, it also departs from that literature in important ways. First, this study is as interested in the question of why some parts of the developing world have acquired more effective states than others as it is in the more widely discussed question of what characterizes effective, developmental states and what exactly such states do to foster rapid industrialization. This shift in focus demands a more

---

[10] A highly influential early such study, not of a developing country, but on reinterpreting the Japanese experience, was Chalmers A. Johnson, *MITI and the Japanese Miracle: The Growth of Industrial Policy, 1925–1975* (Stanford, Calif.: Stanford University Press, 1982). The most significant recent contribution along these lines is Evans, *Embedded Autonomy*. See also the citations in n. 3.

[11] See Evans, *Embedded Autonomy*, passim but esp. chap. 1. There is some striking overlap between Evans's book and this one. However, as explained immediately below, differences in the questions posed, modes of analysis, and the underlying theoretical orientation also loom large.

historical orientation because the core character of these states was often
acquired long before they started intervening in the economy to promote
development. A comparative historical analysis, in turn, leads to a consideration of the role of varying types of colonialisms in molding different types
of states across the developing world. Second, this study, in examining issues of state effectiveness, is as concerned with the political organization
of the state as it is with bureaucratic capabilities. A central concern then is
with power, as distinct from competence or information. And finally, when
analyzing what exactly interventionist states do to promote rapid industrialization, I focus as much on issues of mobilizing basic factors of production as
on improving the efficient use of such factors via upgrading technology or
"learning by doing." This shift, too, leads to a more detailed consideration
of such issues as (1) the state's capacity to collect taxes and thus to make
public investments and (2) the state's role in disciplining the labor force.
In sum, the present study, while clearly a part of the scholarly statist dissent from the more neoclassical accounts of development, at the same time
departs from many existing statist accounts by providing a more historical
and political analysis of the state's role in both promoting and hindering
industrialization.

III. The Argument

Industrialization involves social change. While its narrow outcome is an
increase in industrial production from existing or new factories, a broader
set of societal changes have also generally accompanied, if not preceded,
industrial development. These include a situation of political stability, the
availability of experienced entrepreneurs and of a capable urban work force
and mobilizable capital, the emergence of a market for industrial goods, and
the presence of a growing body of technical knowledge. It is not surprising
that among the earliest, "spontaneous" industrializers, such as England, the
process occurred slowly, over centuries, and was "caused" not by any single
development but by the merging of several streams of underlying changes.
It was Gerschenkron who first argued persuasively that follower countries
within Europe did not reproduce England's "spontaneous" model. Instead,
he held, they needed a more organized initiative from banks or states to
help to generate "a movement on a broad front" to help industry to take
off by mobilizing capital, creating a work force, and facilitating technology
transfer.[12] What was true for late-developers within Europe or Japan was,
of course, doubly true for late-late-industrializers of the developing world.
Since the mid-twentieth century, states have sought to promote industry in
most countries of Asia, Africa, and Latin America. What is also clear from

[12] See Alexander Gerschenkron, *Economic Backwardness in Historical Perspective* (Cambridge:
Harvard University Press, 1962), esp. chap. 1.

the vantage point of the end of the century, however, is that this half-century of effort has seen considerably more success in some parts of the developing world than in others. Explaining these divergent pathways is the main task of this book.

Based on detailed comparative analysis of four countries that vary from success to failure, I argue that the way state power is organized and used has decisively influenced rates and patterns of industrialization in the global periphery. A core analytical task involves identifying different patterns of state authority and then tracing the impact of those variations on economic outcomes and probing the origins of the varying state types. The role of concentrated political power in helping states to set the agenda for their economies also needs to be understood. No quick summary of the argument can substitute for detailed empirical analysis. This is not only because the devil really is in the details but also because summary arguments may be more persuasive after digesting the empirical details. I return to the big picture again in the conclusion. At this time, it is useful to note four of the arguments underlying the book's comparative analysis.

State Types

Referring to ideal types, I identify three historical patterns of how state authority is organized and used in the developing world, neopatrimonial states, cohesive-capitalist states, and fragmented-multiclass states. Although these labels are less than fully satisfactory, they are better than most others in use. In any case, the focus ought to be more on the patterns described by the categories than on the labels themselves.

In addition to centralized and coercive control over a territory, a defining characteristic of all modern states is a well-established public arena that is both normatively and organizationally distinguishable from private interests and pursuits. Unfortunately, for a variety of historical reasons, this distinction between the public and the private realms was never well established in a number of developing country states, especially African states. As a result, a number of distorted states emerged with weakly centralized and barely legitimate authority structures, personalistic leaders unconstrained by norms or institutions, and bureaucracies of poor quality. These states are labeled here as neopatrimonial because, despite the façade of a modern state, public officeholders tend to treat public resources as their personal patrimony. These are therefore not really modern, rational-legal states. Whether organized as a nominal democracy or as a dictatorship, state-led development under the auspices of neopatrimonial states has often resulted in disaster, mainly because both public goals and capacities to pursue specific tasks in these settings have repeatedly been undermined by personal and narrow group interests. Of the cases analyzed in this study, Nigeria best exemplifies this ideal-typical tendency.

Cohesive-capitalist and fragmented-multiclass states are two of the other ideal-typical states to be found in the contemporary developing world. The more effective modern rational-legal states in the developing world tend to vary mainly along two dimensions: cohesion of state authority and the state's class commitments. Cohesion of authority is manifest at both the intraelite and the elite-mass levels, and variations in patterns of authority demarcate the more cohesive states from the more fragmented ones. Developing country states may also be narrowly committed to working with capitalists or may rest their power and goals on a more multiclass base.[13]

The cohesive-capitalist states, sometimes called developmental states, are situated opposite neopatrimonial states on the political effectiveness continuum.[14] These states are characterized by cohesive politics, that is, by centralized and purposive authority structures that often penetrate deep into the society. For a variety of historical reasons these states have tended to equate rapid economic growth with national security and thus defined it as a priority. In their pursuit of rapid growth, cohesive-capitalist states have carved out a number of identifiable links with society's major economic groups and devised efficacious political instruments. Especially notable among the social links is a close alliance with producer or capitalist groups. An important corollary of this political arrangement is a tight control over labor. The main political instrument of these states is, of course, a competent bureaucracy. Since a narrow elite alliance between the state and capital is difficult to hold together, politics within these units has often been repressive and authoritarian, with leaders often using ideological mobilization (e.g., nationalism and/or anticommunism) to win acceptance in the society. Cohesive-capitalist states in developing countries, such as in South Korea under Park Chung Hee and in Brazil during both Estado Novo and the military dictatorship, thus share some organizational and class characteristics with fascist states of interwar Europe and Japan.[15] (Obviously, however,

[13] Careful readers may wonder whether such other combinations as cohesive-multiclass and fragmented-capitalist are also possible. The short answer is yes, but generally not in the developing world. A well-organized social democracy, such as Sweden, may illustrate the cohesive-multiclass category, and the United States may be a good example of a fragmented-capitalist state. A fuller discussion of these state types is beyond the scope of this study, though some such issues are discussed in due course, especially in the conclusion.

[14] It will become clear in due course, especially in the section on Korea, why I prefer the concept of cohesive-capitalist states over "developmental states." Suffice it to note here that the idea that developmental states facilitate development strikes me as too obvious for both analytical and normative comfort. A label such as cohesive-capitalist states (in an earlier draft, I had used the term "neofascist states") instead both captures better a state's independent political characteristics – by which I mean the ideology, organization, and the underlying class alliances – and cautions observers to take note of the costs incurred by the type of "development" these states promote.

[15] Generalizing about "fascist-style regimes" during the interwar years, Claudio Segre notes that "within wide national variations, fascist states had certain characteristics and aspirations in

these states do not draw explicit comparisons with discredited fascism, and they tend to shy away from the politics of mass mobilization and ethnic cleansing.) For better or for worse, these states have also proved to be the most successful agents of deliberate state-led industrialization in peripheral countries.

In between the two extremes of political effectiveness defined by neopatrimonial states on the one end and cohesive-capitalist states on the other lie fragmented-multiclass states. Unlike neopatrimonial states, fragmented-multiclass states are real modern states. They command authority, and a public arena within them is often well enough established that leaders are held accountable for poor public policies and performance. Unlike in cohesive-capitalist states, however, public authority in these states tends to be more fragmented and to rest on a broader class alliance – meaning that these states are not in a position to define their goals as narrowly or to pursue them as effectively as are cohesive-capitalist states. Leaders of fragmented-multiclass states thus need to worry more about political support than do leaders of other types of developing country states. For example, they must typically pursue several goals simultaneously, as they seek to satisfy multiple constituencies. Industrialization and economic growth may be an important state goal, but it is only one among others: agricultural development, economic redistribution, welfare provision, and maintaining national sovereignty. Policy formulation and implementation, moreover, is often politicized, either because of intraelite conflicts or because state authority does not penetrate deep enough down in the society to incorporate and control the lower classes. When confronted by mobilized opposition, fragmented-multiclass states typically become obsessed with issues of legitimacy and often find themselves promising more than they can deliver. While not all fragmented-multiclass states are necessarily democracies, all developing country democracies with plebiscitarian politics and weak institutions constitute a special subset of fragmented-multiclass states. The cases of India and Brazil in several periods exemplify this type of state. Attempting to pursue a complex state-led agenda with limited state capacities, then, fragmented-multiclass states tend to be middling performers on numerous dimensions, including the promotion of industrialization and growth.

common. In their political systems, they created police states, one party systems led by a charismatic dictator. Their economic systems aimed to develop some form of national socialism. The government was to play an active role in controlling the economy, but unlike Marxian socialism, the state was not to take over the means of production. Fascist socialism was directed at the interests of the nation.... Fascism also aspired to some form of the corporatist state.... Fascist regimes mobilized and disciplined societies to transform themselves far more rapidly than would have been the case under a laissez-faire system." See his entry on "fascism" in *The Oxford Companion to Politics of the World* (New York: Oxford University Press, 2001), 274–76.

Neopatrimonial states and the two more modern, rational-legal types of states, namely, cohesive-capitalist and fragmented-multiclass states, are ideal types of developing country states and are not found in a pure form in any of the countries discussed below. Instead, countries in specific periods exhibit more of one tendency than another. When comparing and analyzing state types empirically, one generally needs to focus on some such state characteristics as leadership goals, degree of centralization of public authority, downward penetration of public authority, political organization of the mobilized political society, scope of state intervention in economy, and quality of the economic bureaucracy. It may be easy in an abstract fashion to suggest, as I have, that cohesive-capitalist states are characterized by the top leadership equating rapid economic growth with national security, a highly centralized and penetrating public authority, state-controlled political society (though in close alliance with capitalist groups), and a highly interventionist state, with a good quality economic bureaucracy. Neopatrimonial and fragmented-multiclass states have been similarly characterized in their pure form. Real historical records of actual countries, however, seldom reveal state types in their ideal-typical form; states instead tend more toward one set of characteristics than another, opening the way for more complex analyses.

State Types and Patterns of Industrialization

If authority structures in the developing world can be variously categorized as neopatrimonial, cohesive-capitalist, and fragmented-multiclass states, the first relevant question for this study concerns how these states influence economic outcomes. The nearly exclusive focus in the literature on appropriate policy choices is incomplete, even misleading. Policy choices matter, of course, but these choices must be explained. More important, the impact of the same policy applied in two different settings may vary because of the contextual differences, some of the more obvious being varying global conditions and different initial conditions of an economy. The import of these issues will become clear in due course, but now the contextual difference that deserves emphasis – because it is significant and generalizable across cases – concerns the varying political and institutional conditions in which economic policies are chosen and pursued.

More specifically, identifying variations in how states are organized and in the institutionalized relationship of the state to the private sector is key to understanding the relative effectiveness of state intervention in the economy. In the cases examined in this study, this relationship varies along a continuum stretching from considerable convergence in goals to mutual hostility between the state and the private sector. I argue that, other things being equal, the setting that has proved to be most conducive (i.e., serves as a necessary but not a sufficient condition) to rapid industrial growth in the developing world is one in which the state's near-exclusive commitment to high growth coincided with the profit-maximizing needs of private entrepreneurs. The narrow ruling coalition in these cases was a marriage of repression and profits, aimed at economic growth in the name of the nation. Cohesive-capitalist states have generally created such political economies. Turning their countries into state-guided corporations of sorts, they have tended to be the fastest growers in the developing world.

Growth-oriented cohesive-capitalist states pursued their commitment to high growth by developing trade and industry with well-designed, consistent, and thoroughly implemented state intervention. Specific policy measures varied but were generally aimed at easing supply-and-demand constraints faced by private entrepreneurs. Some of these interventions were direct, and others, indirect. On the supply side, for example, we find that cohesive-capitalist states helped to facilitate the availability of capital, labor, technology, and even entrepreneurship. Thus supply of capital was boosted at times by superior tax collection and public investment, at other times by using publicly controlled banks to direct credit to preferred private firms and sectors, and at yet other times by allowing inflation to shift resources from both agriculture and urban labor to private industrialists. Repression was also a key component in enabling private investors to have a ready supply of cheap, "flexible," and disciplined labor. Examples of less-direct interventions on the supply side include promotion of technology by investing in education and research and development and/or by bargaining with foreign firms to enable technology transfer.

On the demand side, too, cohesive-capitalist states have pursued a variety of policies to promote their growth commitment. These have included expansionist monetary and fiscal policies, and tariffs and exchange-rate policies aimed at boosting domestic demand. And when domestic demand was not sufficient, these states have just as readily adopted newer policies that shift the incentives in favor of export promotion or, more likely, that help to promote production for both domestic and foreign consumption.

There was thus significant variation in the specific policy measures undertaken by cohesive-capitalist states. Only some policies, such as labor discipline, necessitated a repressive state. But what most policies adopted by cohesive-capitalist states reflected instead was a single-minded and unyielding political commitment to growth, combined with a political realization that maximizing production requires assuring the profitability of efficient producers but not of inefficient ones. Sometimes this required getting prices right, but just as often it required "price distortions," such as undervaluing exchange rates, subsidizing exports, and holding wages back behind productivity gains. The central issue concerned the state's goals and capacities, expressed in the institutionalized relationship between the state and the private sector. Cohesive-capitalist states in successful industrializers have thus been pragmatically – and often ruthlessly – procapitalist, much more than they have been purely and ideologically promarket. Among the cases in this study, South Korea under Park Chung Hee and Brazil during Estado Novo and under military rule most clearly fit this political economy model.

Perfect coincidence between the goals of the state and those of private elites has been rare in the developing world, depending as it does on the difficult-to-acquire political precondition of cohesive state power and a narrow alliance between the state and the capital-owning elites. Instead, many ruling elites governed states with fragmented political institutions and defined the public good more broadly. The elites pursued (or, at least, debated) several crucial goals simultaneously: economic growth, redistribution, legitimacy, and national sovereignty. Policy intervention in these fragmented-multiclass states was aimed not only at promoting growth but also at enhancing legitimacy and short-term welfare provision.

Mixed political goals of fragmented-multiclass states had several consequences for choosing and pursuing development policies. First, ruling elites were less focused in these cases on assessing state intervention strictly from the vantage point of growth consequences. Diffuse goals, in turn, enabled various groups and individuals to capture state resources for short-term, consumption-oriented benefits. Second, the relationship of the state to the private sector in such contexts was considerably more complex than in cohesive-capitalist states, sometimes cooperative but just as often conflictual. And third, both policy making and implementation were more politicized, diluting their unidirectional effectiveness.

Fragmented-multiclass states are thus actually more "normal" than the other two ideal-typical cases being discussed here. But because the choice of economic strategy and of policy tools in these cases reflected the logic of both growth and politics, the institutional setting of fragmented-multiclass states was seldom conducive to achieving hypergrowth in industry. The case of India supports such a general contention, as do the cases of Brazil and South Korea in select periods.

Let us consider specific examples of the political economy dynamics of fragmented-multiclass states. Fragmented-multiclass states were neither more nor less interventionist than cohesive-capitalist states, but they were generally less effective at alleviating the supply-and-demand constraints faced by their investors. Again, for example, when it came to mobilizing capital in many fragmented-multiclass states, tax-collecting capacities were limited, public-spending priorities included numerous goals other than growth promotion, attempts to direct credit easily evolved into cronyism, and inflation as a tool of resource transfer could readily become a liability for political leaders concerned about their legitimacy. Periodic hostility on the part of the state elite toward private investors made the latter, both domestic and foreign, reluctant to invest. Repression of labor was also not a ready alternative in fragmented-multiclass states, thus making it difficult for investors to mobilize a cheap and docile labor force.

On the demand side, monetary and fiscal policies seldom reflected a consistent growth commitment but fluctuated instead with political cycles characterized by greater or lesser legitimacy. And finally, tariff and exchange-rate policies adopted to protect the national economy, and thus to promote demand for indigenous goods, often created powerful interest groups. As these groups were difficult to dislodge, fragmented-multiclass states found themselves more rigidly committed to a particular development path. In sum, fragmented-multiclass states, like cohesive-capitalist states, sought to promote industrialization, but they did so less effectively because their goals were more plural and their political capacities less developed. In other words, varying patterns of state authority decisively influenced developmental trajectories.

According to this line of argument, the worst setting for industrialization on the periphery was the states that had no clear public goals and whose leaders reduced the state to an arena for personal aggrandizement. These neopatrimonial states have unfortunately constituted a significant subset of the developing world. State intervention in these cases has often been motivated either by the need to build short-term political support via patronage or by personal greed – or sometimes by both. The relationship of the state and the private sector in such contexts has just as often been mutually corrupt: Political instability, inconsistent policies, and pilfering of public resources for personal and sectional gains have all hurt state-led efforts to promote industry and growth. The case of Nigeria provides a striking instance of such a development path, though elements of the same are also evident elsewhere.

We will see that neopatrimonial states, like cohesive-capitalist and fragmented-multiclass states, have also intervened heavily in their economies, but with disastrous results. Neopatrimonial states have often emerged in societies with weak private sectors, but instead of strengthening the private sector, these states have appropriated scarce economic resources and diverted them everywhere but toward productive investment. Inconsistent economic policies, failure to support indigenous capitalists, poor-quality but activist labor, and political instability have all reinforced the existing weakness of the national private sector in manufacturing and industry.

Given this profound weakness of domestic capitalism, neopatrimonial states have sought to undertake economic activities directly or invited foreign goods and producers to fill the vacuum. Given the states' nondevelopmental proclivities and organizational weakness, efforts to produce goods in the public sector have generally failed. The remaining alternative of importing goods or attracting foreign investment makes sense only if there are alternative sources of income and demand. For a country such as Nigeria, oil exports provided a ready source of income and demand, which was met by foreign goods and producers; this is less true for other neopatrimonial states. Commodity booms, however, seldom last forever. The political incapacity to anticipate such cycles, plan for them, and cut back on imports and public expenditures when circumstances so demand further aggravate the tragedies of commodity-dependent neopatrimonial states. Given such state weakness, the question remains, is there a way out of these repetitive cycles of developmental disasters in neopatrimonial states?

Patterns of State Construction

If goals and capacities of the state, especially as they are expressed in the institutionalized relationship of the state and the private sector, are important for understanding relative effectiveness of state intervention, the next logical, though historically prior question, concerns the origins of this variation itself. Why have some states succeeded in harnessing the energies of their private sectors to facilitate rapid industrialization, whereas others have created a mutually corrupt relationship, leading to waste and stagnation? Or, more specifically, why have some parts of the developing world ended up with cohesive-capitalist states, others with neopatrimonial states, and yet others, probably the majority, with fragmented-multiclass states? This question forces the analysis to take a more historical turn.

The first general observation concerning the roots of different state types is that states acquired some of their core characteristics well before they became activist states, ready to pursue deliberate industrialization. While this is demonstrated throughout this book via historical analysis, two theoretical observations as to why this should be so are offered here. First, institutions are social patterns that gel only over time; and once gelled, they often endure beyond the forces that brought them into being. Breakdowns and discontinuities in institutions are not uncommon, but these are often dramatic, requiring explanation. What also requires explanation is how institutions are established. By contrast, continuity is in the nature of institutions, as patterns that endure through a variety of underlying mechanisms such as internal order and shared norms, boundaries vis-à-vis the broader social context, socialization of new members, and support from the society in which they function.

What is true for societal institutions in general – and this is the second theoretical observation – is even more true for state institutions. States centralize coercion, and both state formation and basic changes in the state's authority structure often involve the use of significant organized power, if not organized coercion. Organizing power and coercion, however, are never easy. Not only do such efforts face opposition from existing centers of power with a vested interest in continuity, but they are also plagued by numerous problems such as mobilizing resources, accessing technology, and overcoming obstacles of collective action. Those responsible for constructing states must therefore possess a clear preponderance of power to impress their institutional design on national societies. Institutions of a modern state in the developing world have thus often originated by acts of coercion imposed by external powers, and, once founded, their basic patterns have just as often continued well beyond the intentions and interest of the founders.

Basic state forms in the developing world emerge and change mainly via a series of infrequent big bangs. Of course, it will become clear in due course that incremental changes, via the development of either new social classes or such new political forces as parties, are also very much part of an ongoing process of how the character of a state changes. Basic changes, however, by which I mean, say, the transformation of a neopatrimonial state into a cohesive-capitalist state or even into a fragmented-multiclass state, tend to be rare because such changes require decisive political intervention. Variations in the state's basic authority structures in the developing world can thus be seen as a product of three sets of competing influences capable of such decisive political intervention: colonialism, nationalist movements, and coercive politics of national armed forces.

The impact of colonialism on state formation was especially significant because most developing country states are the product of colonialism, and their respective forms were molded decisively by this encounter with more advanced political economies. Once established, core institutional characteristics acquired during colonial rule have also proved difficult to alter. Anticolonial nationalist movements were one potential organized force capable of altering the basic state forms inherited from colonialism. With only a few notable exceptions, however, such as India or the more revolutionary nationalists, such as in China or Vietnam, anticolonial nationalist movements in much of Asia and Africa were too superficial and/or fragmented to alter the inherited state forms decisively. More forceful actions to reorder the nature of state authority were taken instead by organized armed forces. But even armed intervention was rarely decisive in altering a state's developmental goals and capacities – either because the armed forces were internally divided or because they lacked civilian collaborators.

The significance of colonialism in constructing alternative state types thus looms large in this study. The study of the impact of colonialism on developing countries has often focused on economic matters. As important as this is, the relative neglect of political analysis has been unfortunate, for colonialism was first and foremost an act of political control, which led well-organized states with dynamic economies to establish supremacy over a variety of disorganized, poor peoples of Asia and Africa.[16] Economic exploitation was very much a part of colonialism, as was racial subjugation

[16] See, for example, D. K. Fieldhouse, *Colonialism, 1870–1945: An Introduction* (New York: St. Martin's Press, 1981).

and humiliation. All this was possible by means of direct political control, however varied the structures and processes of establishing that control. This variation occurred because the realities on the ground differed, in part because different colonizers brought different ideologies of rule with them and in part because the urgency, motive, and capacities of colonizers differed across place and time. The cumulative impact was that colonialism in some parts of the developing world laid the foundation for what would eventually emerge as cohesive-capitalist states, in other parts, as neopatrimonial states, and in yet other parts, as fragmented-multiclass states. Specific historical experiences of at least the two more extreme cases of Korea and Nigeria, briefly illustrated here, can help to clarify this general observation.

South Korea's cohesive-capitalist state, for example, originated during Japanese colonial rule, which differed in important respects from the colonialism of the European powers. As late developers, the Japanese made extensive use of state power for their own economic development, and they used the same state power to pry open and transform Korea within a relatively short period of time. The Japanese colonial impact was thus intense, brutal, and deeply architectonic. Three patterns of what eventually became South Korea's cohesive-capitalist, growth-promoting state originated in this period: A relatively corrupt and ineffective agrarian bureaucracy was transformed into a highly authoritarian and penetrating political organization; the state established close and working production-oriented alliances with the dominant classes; and a well-developed system of state control of the lower classes was created. Over time, as one would expect, these structures were battered by numerous new forces and some significant changes ensued. Nevertheless, the core state-class characteristics endured, eventually providing South Korea with a framework for the evolution of a high-growth political economy.

By contrast, British colonialism in Nigeria created a highly distorted state that readily evolved into a neopatrimonial and ineffective set of political organizations. Britain ruled Nigeria on the cheap, expending as little energy as possible. Within the shell of a modern colonial state and cloaked in the ideology of indirect rule, the British essentially utilized various "traditional" rulers to impose order. At its core, colonialism in Nigeria thus reinforced a pattern of patrimonial and personalistic rule that failed to centralize authority, to develop an effective civil service, and relatedly, to develop even such minimal political capacities as the ability to collect direct taxes. The public realm that came into being was barely demarcated from private and sectional interests in terms of both culture and organization. After the Second World War, when the colonial state's access to resources grew and the state became more and more involved in the economy, these distorted beginnings were further accentuated, as the state became further enmeshed in particularistic and personalistic networks. The political elite of sovereign Nigeria were never able to overcome the original deficiencies of state construction. They simply went from crisis to crisis, both controlling and wasting the society's scarce developmental resources.

The bald emphasis on colonialism as a determinant of state forms in the developing world needs to be qualified. Two types of qualifications in particular are called for. First, not all the cases examined below fully fit the argument. The Indian case, for example, more or less fits the argument but, of course, a popular and powerful nationalist movement was a critical influence on the development of the postcolonial state in that country. Nevertheless, Indian nationalists altered the inherited state less than often meets the eye, and the nature of India's nationalist movement was itself not unrelated to the character of British colonialism in India. By contrast, because formal colonialism ended rather early in Latin America, the argument does not readily apply to a country such as Brazil. Even in Brazil, however, colonialism and other external influences cast a long political shadow. For example, the power of landed oligarchs, a weak central government with a patrimonial bureaucracy, and the prevalence throughout the country of decentralized and despotic political units that rested on patronage and private use of force were characteristics acquired during the colonial period – characteristics that lingered for at least a century after decolonization and even beyond. This legacy was overcome, and even then only partially, in the 1930s. The cohesive-capitalist state of Brazil, moreover, both during Estado Novo (1937–45) and subsequently under military rule (1964–84), was dominated by a settler colonial elite and supported by the armed forces. It drew inspiration, if not direct support, from the outside, that is, from European fascist states in the 1930s and subsequently from the U.S.-supported anticommunist, national security doctrines.

The second type of qualification requires taking account of factors other than colonial impact in molding alternative types of authority structures in the developing world. Patterns of colonial rule, that is, were themselves influenced by varying local realities. More important, nationalist elite and military rulers have tinkered, sometimes even seriously, with the basic state structures they inherited. At a minimum, the size of the state has grown everywhere since activist states came to preside over the societies and economies of developing countries. The development of new social classes, especially of capital-owning groups, and the emergence of newly organized political movements have also influenced changes in the character of the state. Nevertheless, even as these issues must be taken into account, a central argument of this study is that state institutions inherited from the colonial past have proved to be "coins that do not readily melt."[17] Political and social

---

[17] While arguing against the economistic tendency to reduce political and social life to material forces, Schumpeter used this phrase to emphasize the "sticky" quality of institutions. See Joseph Schumpeter, *Capitalism, Socialism and Democracy* (New York: Harper and Brothers, 1947).

developments of the first half of the twentieth century were thus the mold
for the shape and the functioning of developing country states in the second
half of the century.

Power for Development

Power is the currency that states use to achieve their desired ends. Power
may be more or less legitimate, and it may be used positively as an incentive
or negatively as punishment or threat of punishment. The fact that some
states have been more successful than others at propelling industrialization
suggests that successful states possessed a greater degree of power to define
and pursue their goals. Which factors contribute to developmental power
in the hands of states is thus a theoretical theme that runs throughout
this volume, a set of concerns that may also be usefully summarized at the
outset.[18]

Political analysts often think of power in distributional terms: who has it
and who does not. Power in this way of thinking has a zero-sum quality, because, it is believed, the more power some have in society, the less others will
have. Given a liberal preference for a more even distribution of power, this
mode of conceptualizing power leads directly to comparisons of democracy
with authoritarian governments, with a marked normative preference for
the former over the latter. I share this normative preference and return to
some related issues in the conclusion. An exclusive emphasis on distribution
of power, however, is not very helpful analytically for understanding variations in state capacity to achieve economic goals, mainly because it detracts
attention from conceptualizing power as a resource that – like wealth – also
grows or withers. Some authoritarian governments are more efficacious at
wielding power than other authoritarian governments; the same may be true
of democratic states. State capacities thus do not vary as a simple function
of whether a government is more or less democratic. It is not surprising
that research efforts aimed at clarifying whether democratic governments
are better than authoritarian governments at facilitating economic growth
have remained largely inconclusive.[19]

A full understanding of why some states are more efficacious than others
at facilitating industrial transformation has to be centered around a concept
of power as a societal resource that varies in quantity and can thus grow or
decline. Efficacious states simply have more power at their disposal than

---

[18] Another study that addresses this general issue is Joel Migdal, *Strong Societies and Weak States:
State-Society Relations and State Capabilities in the Third World* (Princeton, N.J.: Princeton University Press, 1989). Migdal's concern with state efficacy is much broader than my interest
in industrial policy; in terms of analytical perspectives, my major quarrel with that insightful
book is its tendency to view power distribution as a zero-sum game between the state and
society.

[19] See, for example, Adam Przeworski and Fernando Limongi, "Political Regimes and Economic Growth," *Journal of Economic Perspectives* 7 (Summer 1993): 62–64.

less efficacious ones: Cohesive-capitalist states thus command a lot more power to define and pursue their goals than neopatrimonial states, with fragmented-multiclass states falling somewhere in between along the continuum. Key determinants of this variation in state power for development are organizational characteristics of state institutions, on the one hand, and the manner in which states craft their relations with social classes, especially producer classes, on the other hand.

Some states are simply more purposive and better organized than others. Some states also choose to work closely with their dominant classes, whereas others, facing a variety of pressures, maintain some distance. Maximum power to propel industrialization is generated when purposive, well-organized states work closely with producing classes. Under these circumstances – the circumstances of cohesive-capitalist states – coercive, organizational, mobilizational, and economic powers of a society are aggregated and can help to propel economic change. If one thinks of the process of industrialization as a chariot, one can imagine states and entrepreneurs as two horses that may pull it. The chariot will move rapidly if both horses are strong and if both pull in the same direction. When the two horses do not pull in the same direction – as is often the case in fragmented-multiclass states, where states and entrepreneurs sometimes work together, but just as often do not – society's power resources will be dissipated, and the chariot of industrialization will not move as rapidly and smoothly. And when both horses are feeble – the case of poorly formed neopatrimonial states with weak private sectors – power to propel economic change will be lacking and the economic chariot may not move very far at all.

Leaving the metaphor aside, among the deeper determinants of a state's political capacities are state ideology and organization, on the one hand, and the manner in which state power is grafted onto the social structure, on the other hand. Ideologies help to define leadership priorities, and these priorities, in turn, influence who is likely to support the state. State ideologies vary along a number of dimensions, including the degree to which it is production-oriented and the degree to which it is economically nationalist. As to patterns of political organization, levels of concentration at the apex and the downward penetration of public power vary across states, as do the skill levels and the professionalism of the bureaucracy. These variations are consequential for a state's capacity to get things done. And finally, how the state is connected to various interest-oriented economic groups also has an impact on a state's economic capacities. For example, interest-oriented organizations in open polities – such as political parties – may bring together narrow or broad coalitions and may be more or less institutionalized. In closed polities the state may have created well-organized corporatist groups, or interests may remain unorganized. Variations in underlying patterns of ideology, organization, and the state's relations with economic groups thus create numerous combinations leaving real-world states with varying

capacities to pursue economic development. In general, states with a narrow commitment to economic growth, a close alliance with capital-owning
groups, tight control over other interest groups from above, and well-
developed, professional bureaucracies tend to be more capable of defining
and implementing an agenda of industrial transformation.

The role of ideology, organization, and state-class links in influencing
state power for development can finally be clarified with reference to the
three ideal-typical states discussed above. A narrow commitment to rapid
economic development inclines cohesive-capitalist states to focus on a few
critical tasks and to work closely with producer groups. A competent bureaucracy is generally essential to pursue these political goals, as well as to cement
an alliance with business. Political and economic power thus reinforce each
other and help to move the society rapidly toward state-defined goals. As
noted above, a narrow alliance of state and business elites that hopes to
run a country as if it were a corporation is difficult to hold together, mainly
because others in society also demand representation. If left unchecked,
such demands require a state's attention and resources and detract from
its power to pursue its narrow growth goals. That is why cohesive-capitalist
states tend to be authoritarian, often reaching deep down into the society
to create well-structured interest groups and thereby to minimize political
opposition. Since corporatism may create only a quiescent exclusion and
thus may not add to the state's overall power, the more ambitious cohesive-
capitalist states even attempt controlled ideological mobilization of popular
groups – say, in the name of the nation – so as to also harness their energies to
pursue state goals. Viewed from a liberal standpoint, such cohesive-capitalist
states resemble fascist states of yore, and thus are not very desirable political forms. Nevertheless, it is these states that have succeeded in generating considerable power to pursue rapid industrialization in the developing
world.

Neopatrimonial states, by contrast, tend to have a weak sense of public
purpose, such that ideology does not play a very significant role. Pronounce-
ments of public goals are usually cloaks for the pursuit of personal and sectional interests. The organizational underpinning of neopatrimonial states
also tends to be underdeveloped: Much of politics tends to be preclass, interest groups are often not well organized, and public bureaucracies lack
competence and professionalism. Without a coherent ideology and effective organizations, neopatrimonial states lack developmental power and are
rarely capable of defining and pursuing economic goals. Such economic
growth as occurs in these settings therefore is likely to occur in spite of an
ineffective state, rather than as a result of state action. Economic resources
controlled by the state are instead likely to be put to corrupt use and end
up in the hands of elites for private consumption, leading to failed efforts
at state-led development.

Leaders of fragmented-multiclass states generally preside over states in
which power is not highly concentrated, usually not so much because of a

deliberate democratic design as because of weak political institutions that encourage intraelite divisions and limit a state's downward authoritative reach in the society. These leaders are generally also committed to a broad set of goals, and a variety of interest groups within these states make their demands known to the ruling elite. As noted above, given the competing goals they face, these legitimacy-sensitive elites work closely with business only on some issues and only some of the time. Since political and economic elites may often work at cross-purposes and since the demands of numerous other groups may also require attention, power resources of fragmented-multiclass states are often dissipated and there is an upper limit on how rapidly they can propel industrialization. Given continuous public scrutiny of leaders in such settings, however, there is also a lower limit on how corrupt and ineffective the elite can get. Within these upper and lower limits, the nature and the quality of public institutions can vary a fair amount, as can state performance. For example, institutions such as ruling political parties may be well organized, enabling elites to prioritize their goals and pursue them consistently. Public bureaucracies may also vary in their skills and professionalism, thus helping to account for further variation in a state's capacity to implement economic policies. While a variety of fragmented-multiclass states may be politically more desirable because, even when authoritarian, they are more responsive to the demands of their citizens, when it comes to state-led economic development, they command limited power resources and generally tend to be middling performers.

To sum up, this is a study that probes the role of the state as an economic actor in select developing countries by analyzing both the patterns of state construction and the patterns of state intervention aimed at promoting industrialization and economic growth. The central question throughout is how one can best understand the degree to which a state is developmentally effective. Since the states under consideration often acquired some of their core characteristics in the first half of the twentieth century, the time period under consideration for each country is generally the century as a whole. However, it is also important to note at the outset that this is not a study of the more "neoliberal" phase of development that many countries entered toward the end of the twentieth century. The analysis of each case thus concludes around the time period when these states embraced a more market-oriented development strategy. While the empirical accounts are aimed at developing general themes – themes that are introduced briefly above and that are discussed further in the conclusion – they are also meant to stand alone, providing a fairly full analytical story of individual countries within a coherent, comparative framework. The challenge of striking an appropriate balance between the generalizing frame of social science and the more specific individual histories is a perennial one. It will be up to the readers to decide how well that challenge has been met here, both in terms of getting individual country stories "right" and, more important, in terms of developing a persuasive general argument.

TABLE 1: *Some Relevant Indicators of Korea, Brazil, India, and Nigeria*

	Korea	Brazil	India	Nigeria
GDP per capita (Current PPP $)	15,074	7,446	2,388	859
Population (millions)	47	170	1016	127
Annual % growth in GDP per capita, 1950–2000	5.2	2.8	2.3	0.9
Gini coefficient	32 (1998)	61 (1998)	38 (1997)	51 (1997)
National poverty head count (population %)	N/A	17 (1990)	29 (2000)	34 (1993)
Adult illiteracy (% of population aged 15 and above)	2	13	43	36
Government expenditure (% of GDP, 1995)	14.6	18.6	14.2	Not known
Public investment (% of gross domestic investment, 1998)	27	19	30	Not known
Contribution of state-owned enterprises (% of GDP, 1990)	10	7	13	Not known

Source: World Bank, World Development Indicators. Data for 2000 unless otherwise noted.

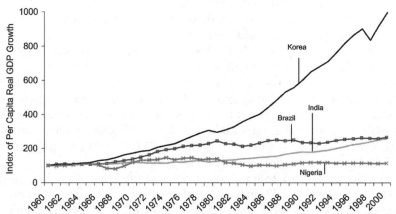

FIGURE 1: Pattern of per capita GDP growth: Korea, Brazil, India, and Nigeria, 1960–2000. *Note:* The data are taken from the World Bank's World Development Indicators. For the purposes of illustration, the data were transformed such that the 1960 GDP per capita of each country is represented as an index of 100. I would like to thank Evan Lieberman and Maya Tudor for their assistance with this figure.

PART I

GALLOPING AHEAD

Korea

As records of developing countries go, South Korea is one of the great economic success stories of the twentieth century. Starting from a war-destroyed,
improvised economy in the mid-1950s, South Korea industrialized rapidly
and in 1996 joined the "rich man's club," the Organization for Economic
Cooperation and Development. How did South Korea do it? The analyses
in the following three chapters emphasize the role of the state, while also
taking other variables into account. Chapter 1 looks back to the Japanese
colonial period in the first half of the last century for the origins of a modern, but nearly fascistic state that I label cohesive-capitalist, as well as for the
beginnings of productivity-based economic growth. The Rhee regime that
emerged in South Korea under American influence following the Second
World War is analyzed in Chapter 2. It is suggested that Rhee's preoccupa-
tion with political survival distracted him from attending to the economy
and contributed to a lackluster interregnum. By contrast, Park Chung Hee
reestablished continuity with the colonial period by rebuilding an authoritarian and penetrating colonial state, on the one hand, and by reestablishing
close links with Japan, on the other hand. Chapter 3 analyzes these critical
developments. I argue that South Korea's rapid industrialization under Park
Chung Hee and beyond is best understood by simultaneously focusing on
the roles played by a growth-oriented, cohesive-capitalist state and by neighboring Japan. The comparative and theoretical implications of this analysis
are discussed more fully in the conclusion of the study.

1

The Colonial Origins of a Modern Political Economy

The Japanese Lineage of Korea's Cohesive-Capitalist State

A full account of South Korea's economic dynamism in the second half of the twentieth century must begin with developments in the first half of the century. The argument is that the Japanese colonial influence on Korea, from 1905 to 1945, was important in shaping a modern political economy that later evolved into a high-growth path to development. Japanese colonialism differed in important respects from European colonialism. As late developers, the Japanese made extensive use of state power for their own economic development and then used the same state power to pry open and transform Korea in a relatively short period. The Japanese colonial impact was thus more intense, more brutal, and deeply architectonic in comparison with European colonialism. It also left Korea with three and a half decades of economic growth (the average annual growth rate in production was more than 3 percent). When judged against the standards of such other colonial economies as India and Nigeria (though not Brazil, which had also experienced significant economic growth by midcentury), the result was a relatively advanced level of industrialization.

More specifically, the colonial origins of three patterns that we now readily associate with the South Korean "model" are traced below. First, I discuss how the Korean state was transformed under Japanese influence from a relatively corrupt and ineffective agrarian bureaucracy into a highly authoritarian, penetrating organization, capable of controlling and transforming Korean society. This is followed by an analysis of a second pattern, namely, the new state's production-oriented alliances with the dominant classes, an alliance that buttressed the state's capacity both to control and to transform. Relatedly, it is also important to note the structural changes in the economy. Not only did the colonial economy experience steady growth and industrialization, but it also became rather heavily export-oriented, including exports of manufactured products. Finally, there was the third pattern, of brutal repression and systematic control of the lower classes in both the cities and the countryside. The cumulative impact of these state-class

27

configurations was to create a framework for the evolution of a high-growth political economy.

I. The Construction of a Colonial State

The Old Agrarian Bureaucracy

By the time the Japanese had gained decisive influence over Korea – about 1905, after the Japanese victory in the 1904 Russo-Japanese War – the old state within Chosòn was already in an advanced stage of disintegration. A brief review of the state-class links in late Chosòn, presented here, is essential for appreciating the changes ushered in by Japanese colonial power.[1] The Yi dynasty had provided Korea with continuous and, for the most part, stable rule for nearly five hundred years. In addition to providing centuries of geographic and political stability, Chosòn also shared in the socioeconomic progress characteristic of the region, especially of China. The court and the army were modeled along the lines of those in China; the ruling classes were versed in Chinese classics and, among them, arts and culture flourished; and the largely agricultural economy kept pace with such technological innovations as improved irrigation systems and methods of paddy cultivation. Even in the nineteenth century, therefore, a prolonged experience with territorial and political stability, elite literacy, and exposure to new technology distinguished Korea from many other parts of the world that we today call the developing world, including countries such as Brazil, India, and especially Nigeria.

At the same time, the very intricate state and class alliances that were responsible for this stability and progress, however, also became major constraints on successful adaptation to changing external pressures, especially in the second half of the nineteenth century. The clearest manifestation of the powerlessness of a centralized agrarian bureaucracy, for example, was the state's continued inability to collect taxes on agrarian incomes, especially from the powerful Yangban elite, Korea's landowning official class.[2] This ongoing problem, in turn, came to be associated with several problematic political trends. First, the state resorted to squeezing the peasantry

---

[1] The best book on the late Chosòn continues to be James Palais, *Politics and Policy in Traditional Korea* (Cambridge: Harvard University Press, 1975). For a differing account, see Ching Young Choe, *The Rule of the Taewon'gun, 1864–73: Restoration in Yi Korea* (Cambridge: Harvard University Press, 1972). A good overview is provided by Carter J. Eckert, Ki-baik Lee, Young Ick Lew, Michael Robinson, and Edward W. Wagner, *Korea Old and New: A History* (Seoul: Ilchokak Publishers for the Korea Institute, Harvard University, 1990), chaps. 8–14. For another useful but abbreviated account that helps to put traditional Korea in a comparative perspective vis-à-vis China and Japan, see John K. Fairbank, Edwin O. Reischauer, and Albert M. Craig, *East Asia: Tradition and Transformation* (Boston: Houghton Mifflin, 1978), chaps. 12 and 20.

[2] See Palais, *Politics and Policy in Traditional Korea*.

(e.g., by enacting corvée labor and military service), which encouraged brigandage and restiveness in the peasant population. Second, the state's limited resources exacerbated the competition and tensions in what was already a personalized and factionalized elite at the apex of the political pyramid. And finally, financial difficulties made it difficult to mobilize any serious military response to growing external pressures.

How does one explain powerlessness in a centralized polity? The leading historian of late Yi Korea, James Palais, traces the roots of this conundrum back to the manner in which the monarchy and the Korean officials-cum-aristocrats, the Yangban, mutually checked one another's powers. The power of the Yangban class rested in part on access to hereditary land wealth but also on a close identification with the centralized bureaucracy, which helped to secure socioeconomic privileges and additional wealth and power. Royal authority, in turn, was seldom all that great. Being under Chinese suzerainty, Korean emperors did not enjoy the "mandate of heaven" possessed by their Chinese counterparts. The recruitment of the aristocracy to the bureaucracy via the examination system also enabled landed power to be deeply embedded throughout the Korean state, checking the scope of royal authority vis-à-vis the Yangban.[3] This balance of power was a source of stability for several centuries. But as external pressures grew, along with a concomitant need for taxes and other socioeconomic resources, the balance also became a major constraint on the monarchy's power to initiate reforms. The agrarian bureaucracy, according to Palais, "could not solve the problem of creating adequate political authority for the achievement of national goals," making the Yi state simultaneously "centralized and weak."[4]

In addition to the limiting balance of power between the monarchy and the Yangban, other factors, too, contributed to the ineffectiveness of the Yi state. First, it was not merely the presence of a powerful land-controlling stratum in society that limited the state's capacity, because by contrast, the colonial state in Korea was able to carve out a different type of ruling alliance with the same landowning class. The key factor in Yi Korea was thus the direct control that landed groups exercised over state offices.[5] Second, the Korean monarchy remained to the very end highly personalistic and patrimonial. In the words of Bruce Cumings, the Korean monarchs were incapable of acting along "the modern distinction between public and

---

[3] For a discussion of how open or closed Korea's examination system may have been to the non-Seoul-based landed elite, see Edward W. Wagner, "The Ladder of Success in Yi Dynasty Korea," in James B. Palais, ed., *Occasional Papers on Korea*, no. 1 (Seattle: University of Washington, April 1974), 1–8. The prolonged study of Chinese classics that was necessary to succeed in the exams appears to have been a major impediment for those without an independent source of wealth. Nevertheless, there is evidence to indicate that some merit-based recruitment did occur below the highest levels.

[4] See Palais, *Politics and Policy in Traditional Korea*, esp. chaps. 1–4 and 14, quotes are from p. 5.

[5] See Fairbank et al., *East Asia*, esp. 307.

private realms" and thus incapable of designing state-led national goals of economic development.[6] Third, the ruling stratum below the monarch was highly factionalized,[7] making it difficult to initiate cohesive responses to growing challenges. And finally, the reach of the Yi state from the center to the periphery was rather limited. While provincial and county officials were directly appointed from Seoul, each county magistrate was responsible for governing nearly 40,000 people (there being some 330 magistrates for about 12 million Koreans).[8] Since these magistrates were rotated frequently, they were typically dependent on the well-entrenched Yangban elite for local governance. Moreover, the lower-level officials – below the magistrate – were not salaried but rather constituted a hereditary group of people who were allowed to collect and keep some local taxes as compensation for their services. These petty functionaries operated virtually as local czars, not easily influenced from above and responsible for the "venality and exploitation of the peasant population."[9]

In sum, the ineffectiveness of the Yi state was rooted in part in the pattern of state-class linkages and in part in the design of the state itself. A personalistic apex, a factionalized ruling stratum, and a limited downward reach of central authorities were all significant factors in the state's powerlessness. This state – weak from the inside and hemmed in by powerful social actors from the outside – contributed little to sustained economic progress.[10] Worse, when faced with growing security challenges and related fiscal crises,

---

[6] See Bruce Cumings, *The Origins of the Korean War: Liberation and the Emergence of Separate Regimes, 1945–1947* (Princeton, N.J.: Princeton University Press, 1979), 10.

[7] As I read the historical evidence, James B. Palais is probably correct in denying intraelite factionalism the central place in his analysis of the political problems of Yi Korea. See Palais, *Politics and Policy in Traditional Korea*, esp. the "Introduction." Nevertheless, most historical treatments document a deeply factionalized elite in Yi Korea. See, for example, Ki-baik Lee, in Eckert et al., *Korea Old and New*, where he concludes that "intra-bureaucratic strife" rendered "the decision making process dilatory and ineffective" (p. 110). Fairbank et al. also note in *East Asia* that factional struggles were "hereditary" and "endemic" in Yi Korea (p. 313). I therefore see no analytical conflict in suggesting factionalism as an additional debilitating trait.

[8] See Palais, *Politics and Policy in Traditional Korea*, chap. 2. Palais cites the figure of ten million for the Korean population in the mid-nineteenth century. Later research has revised this estimate upward.

[9] See Ki-baik Lee, in Eckert et al., *Korea Old and New*, 111.

[10] There is also some evidence from revisionist historians that late Yi Korea experienced a degree of economic dynamism but none to suggest that this was state-induced. Bruce Cumings cites the work of Korean historian Kim Yông-Sôp to suggest that pre-Japanese Korean agriculture was probably not stagnant. See Cumings, "The Legacy of Japanese Colonialism in Korea," in Ramon H. Myers and Mark R. Peattie, eds., *The Japanese Colonial Empire, 1895–1945* (Princeton, N.J.: Princeton University Press, 1984), 491. See also Susan S. Shin, "Some Aspects of Landlord-Tenant Relations in Yi Dynasty Korea," in James B. Palis and Margery D. Loang, eds., *Occasional Papers on Korea*, no. 3 (Seattle: University of Washington, June 1975), 49–88.

the Yi state turned on its own society, in rapacious and predatory fashion. Such a perspective appears to be the consensus of a number of historians and observers of the day: Programs of the Yi government became "embezzlement facilities for a rapacious officialdom";[11] "maladministration... of the native Yi dynasty had affected adversely the whole of Korean public service";[12] "one of the strongest and most fixed impressions made (during my travels to Korea) was that of the well-nigh hopeless corruption of Korean court";[13] and the Korean government "takes from the people directly and indirectly, everything that they earn over and above a bare subsistence, and gives them in return practically nothing."[14]

Since rapacious and ineffective states were common in the world of agrarian bureaucracies and indeed continue to be a common feature in parts of the contemporary developing world – especially in the case of Nigeria – one may genuinely wonder how Korea's "predatory" agrarian bureaucracy was transformed into what some may describe as a "developmental" state.[15] Or using my preferred language, how was an ineffective and rapacious patrimonial state transformed into a well-organized, cohesive, growth-promoting state? The impact of Japanese colonial power was decisive in altering both the nature of the Korean state and the relationship of this state to various social classes. The transformation of the state is discussed immediately below,

---

[11] Young Ick Lew, in Eckert et al., *Korea Old and New*, 179.

[12] Alleyne Ireland, *The New Korea* (New York: E. P. Dutton, 1926), 92.

[13] George Trumbull Ladd, *In Korea with Marquis Ito* (New York: Charles Scribner's Sons, 1908), 152. While this is a highly pro-Japanese, even prejudiced account, there is no reason not to make use of some of its more descriptive observations.

[14] The quote is from George Kennan, a friend of Theodore Roosevelt, who influenced Roosevelt's attitudes toward Korea. It was cited – though not approvingly – in Andrew J. Grajdanzev, *Modern Korea* (New York: John Dey, 1944), 35.

[15] I use quotation marks around the evocative concepts of "predatory" and "developmental" states to indicate my considerable discomfort in describing these states as such. As noted in the introduction, I avoid these concepts. "Predatory" is misleading because it creates a state-versus-society image; in reality, where "predation" prevails, the demarcation between the public and private realms tends to be not well established and political and economic elites often collude to squeeze and misuse a society's resources. "Developmental" is also misleading because the states so described are often not strictly developmental. For example, both the Japanese colonial state and the subsequent South Korean state under Park Chung Hee discussed in Chapter 3, while successful agents of economic transformation, were also to varying degrees rather brutal states. In turn, the normative calculus of evaluating a state that is simultaneously brutal and helps to promote economic growth is clearly complex. In any case, recent and useful contributions that discuss the concept of "developmental states" are Chalmers Johnson, "Political Institutions and Economic Performance: The Government-Business Relationship in Japan, South Korea and Taiwan," in Frederic C. Deyo, ed., *The Political Economy of the New Asian Industrialism* (Ithaca, N.Y.: Cornell University Press, 1987), 136–64; Peter Evans, "Predatory, Developmental and Other Apparatuses: A Comparative Political Economy Perspective on the Third World State," *Sociological Forum* 4 (Fall 1989): 561–87; and Meredith Woo-Cumings, ed., *Developmental State* (Ithaca, N.Y.: Cornell University Press, 1999).

and the changing relationship of the state to social classes is considered in subsequent sections.

Toward a Cohesive-Capitalist State

The Japanese military victory over the Russians in 1904 marked the emergence of Japan as the major regional power, a power that had been rising steadily since the Meiji restoration in the 1860s. Subsequently, Japan, with the acquiescence of Western powers, had a relatively free hand in Korea. Japanese motives in Korea, like the motives of all imperial powers, were mixed – they sought to control it politically and to transform it economically for their own advantage. Security concerns were probably dominant insofar as Korea had for some time already been an object of regional power competition.[16] Given the mercantilist nature of the Japanese political economy, however, there is little point in dwelling on the old debate about which was more important to an imperial power – security or economic interests. More than in the case of most other imperial powers, the Meiji oligarchs of Japan readily associated national power with national wealth and national wealth with overseas economic opportunities.[17]

Certain unique aspects of Japanese imperialism are at the heart of its colonial impact on Korea.[18] First, the Japanese themselves had barely escaped being imperialized. Further, Japan colonized neighboring states with whom it shared racial and cultural traits, not unlike if England had colonized a few continental states across the channel. Proximity meant that many more Japanese ended up playing a direct role in colonial rule, including a much larger role for the military and police, than was ever the case in most European overseas colonies. The near geographical contiguity and shared cultural and racial traits also implied that the Japanese could realistically consider their rule to be permanent, with the expectation of eventual full integration of the colonies into an expanded Japan. This possibility, in turn, influenced Japan's economic and political strategies in Korea, especially the Japanese-initiated industrialization of Korea, a strategy quite distinct from, say, what Great Britain pursued in India or Nigeria.

Furthermore, Japanese colonial strategy was deeply informed by its own successful domestic reform efforts following the Meiji restoration. In

---

[16] See Hilary Conroy, *The Japanese Seizure of Korea, 1868–1910* (Philadelphia: University of Pennsylvania Press, 1960).

[17] For a nuanced interpretation, see Peter Duus, "Economic Dimensions of Meiji Imperialism: The Case of Korea, 1895–1910," in Myers and Peattie, eds., *The Japanese Colonial Empire*, 128–63, esp. 132–33.

[18] For an excellent detailed discussion, see Mark R. Peattie, "Introduction," in Myers and Peattie, eds., *Japanese Colonial Empire*, 3–60. A more recent collection that came to my attention only as this book went to press is Gi-Wook Shin and Michael Robinson, eds., *Colonial Modernity in Korea* (Cambridge: Harvard-Hallym Series on Korean Studies, Harvard University Press, 2000).

Peattie's words, much of what Japan undertook in its colonies "was based upon Meiji experience in domestic reform."[19] Of all the colonizing nations, Japan stands out as nearly the only one with a successful record of deliberate, state-led political and economic transformation. By trial and error the Meiji oligarchs had designed a political economy that was well suited to the task of catching up with advanced Western powers. The essential elements of this political economy are well known and can be briefly reiterated: (1) the creation of a centralized state capable of controlling and transforming Japanese society, (2) deliberate state intervention aimed first at agricultural development and second at rapid industrial growth, and (3) production of a disciplined, obedient, and educated work force. It was this model of deliberate development, with its emphasis on state building and using state power to facilitate socioeconomic change, that inspired the Japanese colonizers.[20] This stands in striking contrast, say, to the British, who having created a private property regime, waited in vain for Bengali *zamindars* in India to turn into a sheep-farming gentry.

It is not surprising that the earliest Japanese efforts in Korea were focused on reforming the disintegrating Chosòn state in order to advance political control and economic transformation. A fair number of political reforms had thus in fact been put into place during 1905–10, especially 1907–9, even prior to the formal annexation of Korea in 1910. Subsequently, under very harsh authoritarian circumstances, a highly bureaucratized, deeply penetrating state was constructed in the decade 1910–20.

A key architect of the early 1907–9 reforms was the Meiji oligarch and the former Meiji-era premier of Japan, Ito Hirubumi, whose role helps us to trace the origins of the design of the new Korean state. As a young man Ito had been one of the handful of leaders who had led the Meiji "revolution" and who had subsequently participated in the reform efforts that followed the destruction of Tokugawa shogunate. Ito had traveled extensively in Europe and had been fascinated with Prussian bureaucracy as a model for Japan – the Prussian "model" as a route to Western rationality and modernity that did not entail "succumbing" to Anglo-American liberalism.[21] Within Japan in 1878, Ito "led the campaign to make the bureaucracy the absolutely unassailable base and center of political power in the state system." Subsequently, in 1881,

---

[19] See Peattie, "Introduction," in Myers and Peattie, eds., *Japanese Colonial Empire*, 29.

[20] Hyman Kublin has argued that Japanese "colonial doctrine" evolved in Formosa (later Taiwan) and was subsequently implemented in Korea (see Kublin, "The Evolution of Japanese Colonialism," *Comparative Studies in Society and History* 2 (October 1959): 67–84). This is true insofar as Formosa was colonized in 1895 and Korea in 1910. However, it is important to note that Kabo reforms in Korea (tried about 1895) and early experimentation in Formosa were simultaneous efforts, both probably a product of a single "colonial official mindset" in Japan – a product of Meiji Japan – with simultaneous political learning going on in both Korea and Formosa.

[21] See Jon Halliday, *A Political History of Japanese Capitalism* (New York: Pantheon, 1975), 37.

Ito helped to reorganize Tokyo University as a "school for government bureaucrats," and by 1887 "a basic civil service and entrance apprenticeship
based on the Prussian model was installed."[22] With this experience behind
him, Ito was appointed in the early 1900s to run the Korean protectorate,
with near-absolute powers as the resident-general or the "uncrowned King
of Korea." He was quite self-conscious about his task: "Korea can hardly
be called an organized state in the modern sense; I am trying to make
it such."[23]

Ito and his successors set about constructing a new Japanese-controlled
Korean state. The first task was to gain central control. With their superior military power, the Japanese in 1907 dismantled the Korean army,
repressed those who "mutinied," incorporated other army officers into a
Japanese-controlled gendarmerie, and forced the Korean monarch to ab-
dicate. Having captured the heart of the state, the colonial rulers sought
systematically to create a depersonalized "public arena" in which to spread
their power wide and deep, and to co-opt and/or repress native Korean political forces. For example, the patrimonial elements of the monarchial state
were destroyed early on and replaced by a cabinet-style government run by
Japanese bureaucrats.[24] Since the appointments of these and other lower-
level bureaucrats were governed by "elaborate rules and regulations which,
in the main follow[ed] the lines of the Imperial Japanese services," the
new Korean state quickly acquired a rational character.[25] Ex-post scholarly
accounts have characterized the Japanese colonial civil service as "outstanding," composed of "hard working and trusted cadre" who deserve "high
marks as a group."[26] Elements of the highly developed Japanese style of
bureaucratic government were thus transferred directly to Korea.

While other colonial powers in other parts of the world also created
a competent civil service (e.g., the British in India), the Japanese colonial project was qualitatively distinct in both the extent and the intensity
of its bureaucratic penetration. There were some 10,000 officials in the

---

[22] Ibid., 35–36. For a discussion of the development of the Prussian bureaucracy, especially
concerning the development of such traits as an espirit de corps, an ethos of public service,
a degree of insulation from aristocratic interests, a tight internal authority structure, and a
relative absence of corruption, see Hans Rosenberg, *Bureaucracy, Aristocracy, and Autocracy:
The Prussian Experience, 1660–1815* (Cambridge: Harvard University Press, 1958); and for
evolution of this bureaucracy in nineteenth-century Germany, see Gary Bonham, *Ideology
and Interests in the German State* (New York: Garland, 1991), esp. chaps. 2, 7, and 8.

[23] Both quotes are from Ladd, *In Korea with Marquis Ito*, 435 and 174, respectively.

[24] For details, see H.I.J.M.'s (His Imperial Japanese Majesty's) Residency General, *Annual Report
for 1907 on Reforms and Progress in Korea* (Seoul, 1908). While these colonial "annual reports"
must be taken with a grain of salt when it comes to the Japanese government's self-serving
evaluations, they are nevertheless a storehouse of enormous amounts of data.

[25] See Ireland, *The New Korea*, 104; also see H.I.J.M.'s Residency General, *The Second Annual
Report on Reforms and Progress in Korea (1908–1909)* (Seoul, 1909), 45.

[26] See Peattie, "Introduction," in Myers and Peattie, eds., *Japanese Colonial Empire*, 26.

Japanese-Korean government in 1910; by 1937 this number had reached 87,552. More than half of these government officials in 1937, or 52,270, were Japanese. Contrast this with the French in Vietnam (where, by the way, the presence of the French was already more significant than, say, that of the British in Nigeria), who ruled a colony of similar size with some 3,000 Frenchmen; in other words, there were nearly fifteen Japanese officials in Korea for every French administrator in Vietnam.[27] The presence of Korean bureaucrats, trained and employed by the Japanese, was also sizable: Nearly 40,000 Koreans qualified as government officials on the eve of the Second World War. While most of the Koreans did not occupy senior positions in the colonial government, there can be little doubt that they became an integral part of a highly bureaucratic form of government over the four decades of colonial rule. Moreover, during the Second World War, as the demand for Japanese officials grew elsewhere, many Koreans moved up in the bureaucratic hierarchy. This sizable cadre of Japanese-trained Korean bureaucrats virtually took over the day-to-day running of a truncated South Korea, first under American military government and eventually when a sovereign state was formed.

One further characteristic of the colonial government that needs to be underlined is the successful link the Japanese created between a highly concentrated power center in Seoul and a densely bureaucratized periphery. All bureaucracies face the problem of seeing to it that central commands are implemented by the officials at the bottom rung. This requires ensuring that lower-level officials are responsive mainly to those above them in the bureaucratic hierarchy, rather than to personal interests or to the interests of societal actors with whom they interact. The Japanese in Korea were quite aware of this problem and continued to experiment until they arrived at arrangements deemed satisfactory.

Of course, certain circumstances were helpful in establishing authority links between the center and the periphery: Ruling arrangements in Seoul were highly authoritarian – the power of the Japanese governors-general in both policy making and implementation was absolute. Nearly all of them were senior military men, and Korea was not a very large country in terms of both population and size (again, for example, note the contrast with the role of the British in India). The Japanese, however, took additional actions.[28] For example, when confronted with corrupt regional or local officials, the central authorities experimented – in line with "new" institutional

---

[27] The data are from Michael Robinson, in Eckert et al., *Korea Old and New*, 257.

[28] The following examples are taken from various reports on administration that the Japanese colonial government published regularly. See, for example, H.I.J.M's Residency General, *Annual Report for 1907*, 18–20; and Government-General of Chosen, *Annual Report on Reforms and Progress in Chosen (Korea)*, *1918–21* (Keijo [Seoul], 1921), chap. on "Local Administration."

economics – with paying these officials higher salaries, especially an "entertainment allowance," in the hope that, if more satisfied, they would do a more conscientious job. When this did not work, the colonial authorities centralized further, leaving local officials with even less discretion and subjecting them to more rules. In the early colonial period these officials were required to wear crisp uniforms, replete with swords, so as to set them apart from the average citizen. In this way symbolic politics was used to create a state-society or a public-private distinction and to convey the will of the state to the farthest reaches of society. When such efforts also failed to secure full compliance, Korean officials were replaced with the more compliant Japanese officials, at least until more suitable Koreans could be found for the job.

The Police Force

In addition to developing the civil bureaucracy, in the new Korean state the Japanese also helped to develop the state's essential arm: a well-organized police force. Once again, there is nothing unique about a colonial power developing a police force per se. Noteworthy in this instance, however, are both the extensive and the intensive nature of police supervision in colonial Korea. The colonial police force was designed along the lines of the Meiji police insofar as it was highly centralized and well disciplined and played a major role in social and economic reforms.[29] The police force in colonial Korea grew rapidly: from some 6,222 gendarmes and police in 1910 to 20,777 in 1922 to more than 60,000 in 1941.[30] One scholar suggests that at the height of the colonial rule, there were so many police that the lowest-level policeman knew "every man in the village."[31] While senior police officers tended to be Japanese, over half of the force was made up of Koreans, often of the lower class. These Koreans were trained by the Japanese in Korean police academies, established expressly for that purpose. Records indicate that there were ten to twenty applicants for every position,[32] suggesting a level of cooperation between Koreans and Japanese that probably pains the modern

---

[29] One scholar of Meiji Japan thus notes: "The police ... had operational responsibility for a bewildering variety of government programs and policies in addition to public safety, traffic control, and criminal investigation and apprehension. They enforced economic controls, discouraged unionism, inspected factories, censored publications, licensed commercial enterprises, arranged for public welfare aid, supervised druggists and publications, controlled public gatherings, managed flood control and fire prevention, maintained surveillance of people suspected of 'dangerous thoughts,' and did countless other things that brought government close to the daily life of every Japanese." See Robert M. Spaulding, Jr., "The Bureaucracy as a Political Force, 1920–45," in James William Morley, ed., *Dilemmas of Growth in Prewar Japan* (Princeton, N.J.: Princeton University Press, 1971), 36–37.

[30] See Robinson, in Eckert et al., *Korea Old and New*, 259.

[31] Ching-Chih Chen, "Police and Community Control Systems in the Empire," in Myers and Peattie, eds., *Japanese Colonial Empire*, 213–39, esp. 225.

[32] Ibid., 236.

Korean nationalist. Beyond formal training, the Japanese maintained very close supervision over their police force; during the period 1915–20, for example, about 2,000 policemen – or nearly one out of every ten – were sternly disciplined annually for violating police rules.[33]

This extensive and closely supervised police force, which penetrated every Korean village, performed numerous functions other than standard police duties of maintaining law and order. Police were also empowered with control over "politics, education, religion, morals, health and public welfare, and tax collection."[34] The police, who were outfitted in military uniforms, again replete with swords, also had summary powers to judge and punish minor offenders, including by whipping. Even in production, local police were known to have "compelled villages to switch from existing food crops" to cash crops and to adopt "new techniques" in rice production so as to facilitate exports to Japan. Moreover, as land surveys conducted during 1910–18 show, tenancy and conflicts over land increased, with local police "always interven[ing] in favor of landlords."[35] It is thus not surprising that even a Japanese observer was led to conclude that Terauchi Masatake (the first Japanese governor-general of Korea, following Ito and formal annexation) and his successors had transformed the "entire Korean peninsula into a military camp."[36]

One final aspect of the police role concerns the links between the police and local society via local elites. The police successfully utilized the proverbial carrot and stick to incorporate village elders and others into a ruling alliance. The police thus buttressed their already extensive powers by working with, rather than against, indigenous authority structures. So armed, the police used the knowledge and influence of the local elites to mold the behavior of average citizens in such diverse matters as "birth control, types of crops grown, count and movement of people, prevention of spread of diseases, mobilization of forced labor and ... report[ing] on transgressions."[37] The police and many local elites thus came to be despised by Koreans at large as collaborators. Unfortunately for Koreans, although many of the landed elite were indeed eventually eliminated as a political force (i.e., via

---

[33] Ibid., 236–39.

[34] Robinson in Eckert et al., *Korea Old and New,* 259.

[35] Ching-Chih Chen, "Police and Community Control Systems," 228–31. It is important to note that the extensive role of the police remained intact throughout the colonial period. For example, when Americans finally arrived in Korea after the Japanese surrender, they found (for example, in South Cholla province) that police departments were the biggest within the local bureaucracy, and within the police departments, "economic sections" of the police were important. See Grant E. Meade, *American Military Government in Korea* (New York: King's Crown Press, Columbia University, 1951), esp. 31.

[36] The quote is from Shakuo Shunjo and is cited in Ching-Chih Chen, "Police and Community Control Systems," 222, n. 26.

[37] Ibid., 226.

land reforms following the Korean War), much of the colonial police was incorporated directly into the new state structure of South Korea.

In sum, the personalized and factionalized Yi state, with its limited reach within society, came to be replaced by a cohesive colonial state, simultaneously oppressive and efficacious, with considerable capacity to penetrate and control the society. The core of this new cohesive state was a highly centralized apex with, first, near absolute powers of legislation and execution to set and implement "national" goals – and, second, pervasive, disciplined civil and police bureaucracies.

The Politics of the New State

The politics practiced by the new rulers added to the state's capacity to impose its will on the society. Except for a somewhat liberal interlude in the 1920s, the political practices of the Japanese colonial state in Korea were, for the most part, brutally authoritarian. This was especially so from 1930 onward, when Japan created its own version of fascism at home and exported it to its colonies. For example, Korean newspapers were either suspended or heavily censored, political protest was met with swift retribution, and political organizations and public gatherings were generally banned. Those professing Korean nationalist sentiments were either exiled or remained poorly organized. While latent and scattered sympathy for nationalists and communists endured throughout the colonial period, a coherent nationalist movement was never allowed to develop.[38] Further, Japanese used "thought police" to detect and eliminate active political dissidence and also developed a "spy system" to buttress the civil and police bureaucracy that was "probably better developed in Korea than anywhere [else] in the world."[39]

The colonial authorities were deliberate in their use of repression to instill fear in the minds of Koreans and thus to minimize dissent and reinforce bureaucratic control: To avoid "restlessness" in the "popular mind," government reports of the period declared that it was "essential" to "maintain unshakable the dignity of the government" and "to impress the people with the weight of the new regime."[40] When Koreans resisted, nonetheless, Governor-General Terauchi Masatake supposedly responded, "I will whip you with scorpions,"[41] and when the Koreans eventually succumbed, the gloating satisfaction is also obvious in official documents:

---

[38] See Chong-Sik Lee, *The Politics of Korean Nationalism* (Berkeley: University of California Press, 1963).

[39] See Grajdanzev, *Modern Korea*, 55.

[40] Government-General of Chosen, *Results of Three Years' Administration of Chosen since Annexation* (Seoul, 1914), 2–3.

[41] Quoted in Mark R. Peattie, "Introduction," in Myers and Peattie, *Japanese Colonial Empire*, 18.

"They have gradually yielded their obstinate prejudices and their disdainful attitude."[42]

In spite of the power and pervasiveness of the state the Japanese had created, it would be a mistake to believe that a thorough bureaucratic penetration and a politics of fear were their only instruments of rule. There is no doubt that bureaucratic growth enabled the new state to undertake many more activities that contributed to economic growth and that repression enabled the establishment of order, freeing the state elite to focus on other "developmental" matters. Nevertheless, bureaucratic and repressive power are seldom enough to elicit the measure of cooperation that is essential for generating economic dynamism. We must therefore also take note of other, nonrepressive instruments of rule that the new colonial state put to use.

First, a segment of the Korean political elite in the precolonial period was quite favorably inclined toward Japan.[43] These Koreans from the political class were incorporated both officially and unofficially into the new system of rule. Second, and relatedly, the colonial state forged numerous implicit and explicit alliances with the Korean propertied classes that turned out to be of critical long-term significance. For now I note that on the whole Korean monied groups – both the urban and rural – did not oppose colonial rule. Most of them benefited from this rule and generally went along – some even with enthusiasm – with the colonial project. And third, the Japanese undertook considerable expansion of education, facilitating propaganda and political resocialization. Whereas in 1910 nearly 10,000 students attended some sort of school, by 1941 this number was up to 1.7 million and the rate of literacy by 1945 was nearly 50 percent. The focus was on primary education and the curriculum was designed with the goal of raising "practical men able to meet the requirements of the state."[44]

---

[42] Government-General of Chosen, *Thriving Chosen: A Survey of Twenty-Five Years' Administration* (Seoul, 1935), 81.

[43] For example, when confronted with the fact of being left behind in the race to modernity, many Koreans had looked to Meiji Japan as a model for their own advancement; for better or for worse, therefore, "modernity" to many Koreans came to be represented by Japan. See Gregory Henderson, *Korea: The Politics of Vortex* (Cambridge: Harvard University Press, 1968), esp. 67. Moreover, some Korean elites, enamored with Japan, had participated in Japanese-supported Kabo reforms of 1895. Later, the pro-Japanese Korean organization Ilchin-hoe (Advancement Society) enjoyed considerable support between 1905 and 1910; for example, at its least popular phase in 1910, the Ilchin-hoe still enjoyed a membership of nearly 140,000 and had some 100 subsidiary organizations. See, for example, Vipin Chandra, "An Outline Study of the Ilchin-hoe (Advancement Society) of Korea," in James Palais, ed., *Occasional Papers on Korea*, no. 2 (Seattle: University of Washington, March 1974), 52.

[44] The quote is from official documents of the government-general and is taken from Ireland, *New Korea*, 190. For more recent scholarship that confirms these trends, see E. Patricia Tsurumi, "Colonial Education in Korea and Taiwan," in Myers and Peattie, eds., *Japanese Colonial Empire*, esp. 305, where the author notes that "by 1940 half of all Korean school-age children were attending elementary school."

To conclude this subsection, the Japanese in Korea replaced the decrepit Yi state with a powerful centralized state. This was no liberal state. It was more statist vis-à-vis Korean society and considerably more repressive than even the statist and illiberal Japanese political economy of the period. Central decision making was highly concentrated in the office of the governor-general, whose will, reflecting the imperial design and goals, was implemented via an extensive, well-designed, and disciplined bureaucracy. The new state also achieved considerable downward penetration: The civil and police bureaucracies both reached into society's nooks and crannies, while continuing to respond to central directives; Korean elites in the localities were incorporated into the ruling alliance; and when all else failed, there was the well-functioning intelligence service to buttress the state's supervisory role. While there will emerge in due course a fuller understanding of how power was generated in this system and the uses to which it was put, it should already be evident how the Japanese colonialists transformed a relatively ineffective agrarian bureaucracy into a cohesive state that could get things done.

II. The Colonial State, Propertied Classes, and Economic Change

The colonial state in Korea was a busy state. While pursuing the imperial interests of Japan, it evolved a full policy agenda, including the goal of Korea's economic transformation. The broad strategy of transformation was two-pronged: The state utilized its bureaucratic capacities to directly undertake numerous economic tasks, and, more important, the state involved propertied groups – both in the countryside and in the cities, and both Japanese and Koreans – in production-oriented alliances aimed at achieving sustained economic change. The result measured by the criteria of growth and industrialization (though not by such other criteria as human rights, national self-determination, and fair economic distribution) was a considerable success. And since success generally begets emulation and continuity, it is important to analyze the colonial economic strategy.

Two general observations are in order. First, while the governor-general in Korea possessed near absolute powers, he was nevertheless an agent of the Japanese imperial government. The colonial state in Korea thus pursued Japanese needs and interests, not Korean ones, which changed over time.[45] In broad brush strokes, during the early phase, say, the first decade of colonial rule, Japan treated Korea mainly as a strategic gain that could also be exploited in a fairly classic fashion: exchange of agricultural products for manufactured goods. Subsequently, as Japanese demand for food outpaced

---

[45] For one review of Japanese colonial economic policies, see Samuel Pao-San Ho, "Colonialism and Development: Korea, Taiwan, and Kwantung," in Myers and Peattie, eds., *Japanese Colonial Empire*, 347–86.

its own supply, the colonial state aggressively undertook measures to increase food production in Korea. Manufacturing was discouraged in this early phase, again in a fairly classic colonial fashion, to protect Japanese exports to Korea. Following the First World War, however, with swollen company profits, Japan sought opportunities for export of capital and thus relaxed restrictions against production of manufactured products in Korea. From here on Japan's colonial strategies started diverging from what Britain was doing at the same time in India and Nigeria.

The need to co-opt nationalistic pressures within Korea led the colonial state to involve certain prominent Korean businessmen in manufacturing. Aggressive industrialization of Korea occurred only in the 1930s. This was in part a result of Japan's strategy to cope with the depression (to create a protected, high-growth economy on an empire-wide scale) and in part a result of Japan's aggressive industrialization, again on an empire-wide scale, which reflected national power considerations.[46] Japan was able to switch its imperial policies in Korea frequently and decisively; this, in turn, underlined the highly centralized nature of authority within the Japanese-controlled Korean state, as well as that state's influence on the economy.

The second related observation concerns the pressures on the governor-general in Korea to pursue imperial interests while simultaneously running a cost-effective government. Historical documents of the time, especially the annual reports of the governor-general in Korea, make it clear that, among their various achievements, the colonial authorities in Korea wanted to emphasize their repeated efforts to enhance revenues and minimize expenditures, especially by rationalizing the bureaucracy.[47] Since any shortfall between revenues and expenditures within Korea had to be financed by the Japanese imperial government – and typically, there was a net revenue inflow from Japan to Korea – one presumes that firm pressure was exerted on respective governors-general to boost the cost efficiency of public services. The general point, then, is that, unlike many other governments, the colonial state in Korea did not operate with a soft budget constraint. On the contrary, there was constant pressure to economize, thereby hardening the budget constraint. The result was a significant, positive, trickle-down effect on the efficiency of the bureaucracy, including the economic bureaucracy.

Increased State Capacity

The increased capacity of the new colonial state in Korea to undertake economic tasks directly is evident early in the historical record, for example,

---

[46] See, for example, E. B. Schumpeter, *The Industrialization of Japan and Manchukuo, 1930–40* (New York: Macmillan, 1940), esp. chaps. 9–11, 21, 22, and the conclusion.

[47] The reference is to Government-General of Chosen, *Annual Report on Reforms and Progress in Chosen (Korea)* (Keijo [Seoul], published regularly – for the most part, annually – between 1910 and 1939). See, for example, the 1914 report, where repeated references are made in the opening chapter to "financial efficiency" and to the "economy of administration."

regarding state capacity to collect taxes. The old Yi state, one may recall, was incapable of extracting taxes from society, especially revenues from landowners. The contrasting performance of the colonial state is notable. Land revenue in 1905, the year Japanese influence in Korea began to grow, was some 4.9 million yen; by 1908 this had jumped to 6.5 million yen, or a real increase of some 30 percent in three years.[48] Subsequently, numerous other sources of revenue were added to that obtained from land – for example, railways, post office, and customs – and receipts from the ginseng monopoly and from such public undertakings as salt manufacture, coal mines, timber work, and printing bureaus. The jump in revenue intake was also remarkable: Whereas the total revenue in 1905 (land and other revenues) was 7.3 million yen, by 1911, one year after formal annexation, the total revenue intake was 24 million yen, or an increase of more than 300 percent.[49]

The factors that help to explain this increased state capacity were twofold. First, the colonial state, backed by its superior coercive power, broke the stranglehold of landowning groups on the Yi state, pensioning off the Yangban elite and replacing them with Japanese career bureaucrats. And second, the colonial elite utilized the newly created civil and police bureaucracies to collect taxes. Specifically, as early as 1906, thirty-six revenue-collection officers, again in full regalia of uniforms and swords, were posted throughout Korea to identify cultivated land, owners of the land, and the revenue due from the land.[50] While the rate of taxation on land was not increased, it was regularized. Additionally, uniformed revenue officers worked in conjunction with local police officers in the process of tax collection, lest anyone forget this newly established separation of state and society or the intrusive presence of the new cohesive state in society.

The successful land survey that the Japanese conducted in Korea between 1910 and 1918 similarly highlighted the efficacy of the new state. The Yi state had repeatedly discussed such a comprehensive land survey but never managed to carry it out; the bureaucratic capacity was absent, as was the power to confront land-controlling groups that wanted to hide the extent of their taxable lands. By contrast, the colonial state made an exhaustive land survey a priority. Over a period of eight years the Japanese invested some 30 million yen in the project (compared, say, with the total revenue intake of 24 million yen by the government-general in 1911). The survey "mapped all plots of land, classified it according to type, graded its productivity and

---

[48] The figures are from 1907 and 1908–9. The real increase was probably somewhat less because this simple calculation does not take account of increase in production, which, in any case, we know to have been relatively small in those years.

[49] The 1905 figure is from H.I.J.M's Residency General, *Annual Report*, 1907, and the 1911 figure is from Government-General of Chosen, *Annual Report*, 1910–11. While reliable data on inflation for these years are not readily available, there is no indication in government documents of huge price increases.

[50] Based on H.I.J.M.'s Residency General, *Annual Report* 1907, chap. 5 on "Public Finance."

established ownership."[51] While Japanese civil servants supervised the entire project, Korean landowners cooperated and eventually benefited; local land-investigation committees, for example, which were responsible for investigating the "ownership, location, boundaries and class of land," were composed of "land-owners themselves."[52] As a result of the survey, the colonial state secured a revenue base and, less obviously, enhanced its control over the Korean agrarian sector by bringing in the landowning classes as ruling partners. What the Korean landlords lost in terms of autonomy from and influence over the traditional Yi state, they made up first by securing new, Western-style, legal private property rights and later by gaining enhanced profits from land.[53] The relatively successful penetration by the Japanese colonial state of the agrarian periphery then stands out as a fairly unique display of state efficacy in the comparative history of colonialism, which, as will become clear repeatedly in this book, is replete instead with cases of "indirect power," that is, with indigenous landed elites maintaining significant control.

Over time the colonial state in Korea undertook numerous other projects of economic value. Though unable to provide a comprehensive discussion here, I wish to indicate some of the main areas.[54] First, the government-general invested heavily in infrastructure, so much so that Korea's roads and railways were among the finest that any developing country inherited from its colonial past. Second, as mentioned above, the Japanese invested significantly in Korean primary education. Given the long gestation period, however, the returns on this investment were probably reaped less by colonial Korea than by the two sovereign Koreas, which inherited a relatively literate labor force. Third, the colonial government ran a number of economic enterprises directly, for example, railways, communications, opium, salt, and tobacco. Judged by the regular financial contribution that these public undertakings made to public revenues, they were run relatively efficiently. And finally, the government-general played an important role in the overall process of capital accumulation.

A few other points also deserve mention. The currency and banking reforms that the new colonial state undertook early on led to a significant jump in private, institutional savings: For example, deposits in the Bank of Choson (Korea) doubled from some 18 million yen in 1911 to 37 million yen in 1913, and the number of depositors in the postal savings bank jumped from about 20,000 in 1909 to 420,000 in 1913.[55] Later in the course of

---

[51] See Robinson in Eckert et al., *Korea Old and New*, 265.

[52] Government General of Chosen, *Annual Report, 1911–12*, 13.

[53] See Robinson in Eckert et al., *Korea Old and New*, 266–67.

[54] For a full discussion, see Samuel Pao-San Ho, "Colonialism and Development," in Myers and Peattie, eds., *Japanese Colonial Empire*.

[55] The data are from Government General of Chosen, *Results of Three Years' Administration of Chosen since Annexation* (1914), 19.

colonial rule the government-general required Koreans to buy government bonds, which helped to finance the industrialization drive of the 1930s. While capital inflows from Japan remained the dominant source, local capital accumulation also increased considerably. Facts and figures aside, the general point again is this: The cohesive colonial state in Korea, even more than the Japanese Meiji state on which it was modeled, became heavily and directly involved in economic tasks and, judged strictly by economic criteria, performed these tasks rather effectively.

More significant than the state's direct economic role was the indirect role that led to the involvement of wealthy groups in productive activities. The mechanics of how these state-private sector alliances were created is important because similar arrangements were later central to South Korea's great economic success. The dynamics of change in both the agrarian and the industrial sectors thus deserve our attention.

The State and the Agrarian Sector

The colonial state restructured its relationship with the Korean landed classes. The highest Yangban elite who held office in the Yi state were pensioned off.[56] As career bureaucrats took over official functions, the landed class's direct control of the state weakened. The successful land survey further confirmed the supremacy of the new state, as the capacity of the landed classes to evade the reach of the state shrank in its wake. In return, however, the state was generous with the landowners, first, so as not to alienate them, and second, to induce them to be active partners in executing the state's goals. For example, the Japanese introduced a new legal code – based on the Meiji legal code – that created Western-style legal private property, thus securing the control of Korean landed groups over their land in perpetuity. While the Japanese in the process ended up owning significant amounts of agricultural land in Korea, most Koreans who controlled land prior to the arrival of the Japanese maintained and even expanded their landownership.[57] Moreover, many among the landed elite were incorporated into local governance, cooperating with and helping local agents of the state maintain control over villages. While students of colonialism often distinguish direct and indirect colonial rule, the Japanese political arrangements in Korea utilized both forms: Direct bureaucratic penetration was buttressed by the authority of local influentials. This arrangement also suggests that,

---

[56] For details, see Government General of Chosen, *Annual Report, 1910–11*, 18–19.

[57] The colonial government's own assessment is interesting. While lamenting the political opposition from educated Koreans, government documents of the period note: "People of the upper class having personally experienced imperial favor and being in a position to feel directly or indirectly the benefit of the new regime, seem to be contented with it." See Government General of Choson, *Results of Three Years' Administration*, 64. See also Robinson in Eckert et al., *Korea Old and New*, 266–67.

contrary to some recent arguments, the presence of a landowning class does not necessarily inhibit the formation of a powerful "developmental" state. Much depends on the specific relationship of the state and landowners.[58]

The Japanese colonial government periodically made significant efforts to boost agricultural production in Korea. Unlike Britain's main concern with commercial crops in its colonies, Japan focused on Korea's main food product, rice. The underlying motivation was Japan's own changing economic needs. Thus, prior to 1919 efforts to boost production were minimal, but following the rice shortage and related riots in Japan in 1918, a major plan was inaugurated to expand rice production in Korea. The success on this front contributed to "overproduction" such that all plans to increase rice production were canceled in 1933 in response to pressures from Japanese rice producers. Again, however, the war with China in 1938–39 created food shortages in Japan, and Korea was "resuscitated as a granary of the Empire."[59]

During the early phase the Japanese focused their efforts on land improvement, especially on irrigation, drainage, and reclamation of arable land. The resulting increase in production was not huge and resulted from both extensive and intensive efforts; for example, increase in rice production between 1910 and 1924 averaged around 1.5 percent per annum and land productivity in the same period improved at about 0.8 percent per annum.[60] Subsequently, when rapid increase in rice production became a goal, Korea's Japanese rulers utilized the knowledge acquired during the Meiji transformation and concentrated their efforts on spreading the use of improved seeds, fertilizer, and irrigation. The gains were significant: The percentage of paddy land using improved seed doubled between 1915 and 1940, reaching 85 percent; fertilizer input expanded ten times during the same period;[61] and between 1919 and 1938 land under irrigation increased annually by nearly 10 percent.[62] As a result, rice production between 1920 and 1935 grew at nearly 3 percent per annum and somewhere between one-half and two-thirds of this growth resulted from improvements in land

[58] Joel Migdal, for example, tends to view state capacity in agrarian societies as inversely related to the power of landowning and other traditional elites. See Migdal, *Strong Societies and Weak States: State-Society Relations and State Capabilities in the Third World* (Princeton, N.J.: Princeton University Press, 1988). Peter Evans makes a similar argument. See Evans, "Class, State and Dependence in East Asia: Lessons for Latin Americanists," in Fredric D. Deyo, ed., *The Political Economy of the New Asian Industrialism* (Ithaca, N.Y.: Cornell University Press, 1987), 203–26.

[59] For these policy swings and for the direct quote, see Grajdnazev, *Modern Korea*, 92–94.

[60] See Sang-Chul Suh, *Growth and Structural Changes in the Korean Economy*, 73, table 33.

[61] Ibid., 77, table 34.

[62] Grajdanzev, *Modern Korea*, 96–97. Some of the increase in irrigation may have come from private rather than public investments.

productivity.[63] The overall rate of increase in rice production per unit of land for the colonial period (1910–40) averaged on the order of 2 percent per annum. (Compare this, for example, with India's post–green revolution – say, 1970 to the present – rates of productivity increase in cereal production; they have been only a little higher than 2 percent per annum.) While some of these improvements may have been a spontaneous response to food shortages and higher prices in Japan, it is nevertheless difficult to imagine such a relatively quick increase in supply without significant public efforts, especially in providing new seeds and in facilitating the distribution of fertilizer.

It is a sad fact that increases in production in Korea did not lead to improvement in food consumption. The bulk of the additional production ended up in the export market, and imported goods did not become consumption items for the vast majority. As a well-documented study concludes, "Per capita use of food grains as a whole declined substantially after the early years of the colonial period." The same author points out that this disjuncture between production and consumption was a result of several causes but was due mainly to a combination of population growth and the absence of many nonagricultural opportunities, a situation that increased the burden on tenants and on small farmers.[64] Given the steady growth in production as consumption for the majority of the population declined and given the considerable inequality in landownership, it is likely that the incomes of landowning groups mushroomed. Other available evidence is consistent with this proposition: The rates of return on agricultural investment were very high for most of the period; income inequality widened; and there was rapid growth of small depositors in saving institutions. The general point is that Korean landowning groups prospered under colonial government, becoming part of an implicit but comfortable ruling alliance between a cohesive state and the property-owning elites.

Three other characteristics of the changing agrarian sector are noteworthy. First, Japanese corporations and entrepreneurs ended up owning large tracts of Korean agricultural land – anywhere from one-quarter to one-third of all the arable land. This was a result of a conscious government policy that began with the hope of attracting Japanese immigrants to Korea, but when that goal met with only limited success, Japanese corporations became heavily involved. Especially significant as a landowner was

---

[63] Sang-Chul Suh, *Growth and Structural Changes in the Korean Economy*, 73, table 33. See also Shigeru Ishikawa, *Economic Development in Asian Perspective* (Tokyo: Kinokuniya Bookstore, 1967), 84–109; and Ramon H. Myers and Yamada Suburo, "Agricultural Development in the Empire," in Myers and Peattie, eds., *Japanese Colonial Empire.*

[64] Sang-Chul Suh, *Growth and Structural Changes in the Korean Economy*, 86–87.

the infamous Oriental Development Company,[65] which, like most other Japanese landowners, leased lands to tenants, collected rents in kind, most often rice, and sold the rice back to Japan in the export market. The rate of return on such activities was high, higher than in Japan, and many a fortune was made.[66] From our standpoint, the direct involvement of the Japanese in Korean agriculture helps to explain two points: the mechanics of how the more advanced techniques of agricultural production were transferred from Japan to Korea and the mechanics underlying forced exports, whereby Japanese landowners sold rice grown in Korea back to Japan directly.

A second characteristic of the changing agrarian sector was its heavy export orientation. For example, while total Korean rice production during the colonial period nearly doubled, rice exports to Japan during the same period increased six times.[67] Additionally, while the overall economy of the Japanese Empire was protected, trading within the empire was relatively free of tariffs and other restrictions. Rapid growth of exports to the metropole with a more advanced agriculture thus points to an additional source – the quintessential source of competition – that must also have contributed to sustained improvements in agricultural productivity. And last, consider the geography of the changing agrarian scene. Given climatic conditions, rice production and Japanese ownership of Korean land were both more concentrated in the southern half of Korea, and the bulk of rice exports also originated in the South. Thus, the southern half of Korea developed a relatively productive agricultural sector during the colonial period.

To conclude this discussion on the changes in the agrarian sector, two developments of long-term consequence are striking. Most obvious is that a productive agriculture was a necessary component of rapid economic growth, first in colonial Korea and later, even more prominently, in sovereign South Korea. While many developing countries, such as Nigeria, are still attempting their agricultural revolution, and others, such as India, hailed their green revolution from the mid-1960s onward, Korea was already undergoing a biological revolution in agriculture in the first half of the twentieth century. Just before the Second World War rice yields in Korea were approaching

---

[65] See, for example, Karl Moskowitz, "The Creation of the Oriental Development Company: Japanese Illusions Meet Korean Reality," in James B. Palais, ed., *Occasional Papers on Korea*, no. 2 (Seattle: University of Washington, March 1974).

[66] For data on the comparative rates of return, see Sang-Chul Suh, *Growth and Structural Changes in the Korean Economy*, 85, table 39. It is also important to note that the process of securing rice for exports was quite coercive. So, for example, when American forces took control of southern Korea after the Second World War, they discovered that colonial police performed such economic functions as "collect[ing] the harvested rice for exports to Japan." See Grant Meade, *American Military Government in Korea* (New York: Columbia University, King's Crown Press, 1951), 31.

[67] Sang-Chul Suh, *Growth and Structural Changes in the Korean Economy*, 92, table 43.

Japanese yields, which were then among the highest in the world (if the U.S. yields in 1938 were 100, Japan's were 154, and Korea's were 111).[68] Rapid increase in agricultural production in turn provided both food and inputs to sustain an industrial drive, on the one hand, and yielded high incomes, on the other hand. A decade hence, after land reforms were implemented in South Korea, the productive agricultural base and related incomes also contributed to the emergence of a domestic market for manufactured goods.

The other less obvious legacy concerns the "model of development" that undergirded the agrarian transformation. Even more than Meiji Japan, the colonial state in Korea established itself as the key actor directing economic change. The state then employed various carrots and sticks to incorporate the propertied groups in a production-oriented alliance. A key focus of the state's efforts was on improving the technology of production, through better seeds, fertilizer, and irrigation. Even after decolonization, these efforts had left a legacy of a bureaucratic infrastructure that was adept at facilitating technology-intensive agricultural development. Moreover, public subsidies from the colonial state helped to improve the profitability of private producers, as well as productivity and production. This pattern of an alliance of the state and the propertied class, centered around technology and other public subsidies, would repeat itself in subsequent periods and in numerous other economic activities, especially in industry, to which I now turn.

The State and Industrialization

The extent of Korea's industrialization during the colonial phase was both considerable and nearly unique in the comparative history of colonialism: The average annual rate of growth in industry (including mining and manufacturing) during 1910–40 was nearly 10 percent; and by 1940, nearly 35 percent of the total commodity production originated in the industrial sector.[69] While analyzing the why and how of this experience, as well as its long-term significance, the main point is not that South Korea somehow inherited a relatively industrialized economy. It did not! A fair amount of the heavy industry was located in the north and significant industrial concentrations were destroyed during the Korean War. Nevertheless, a war-destroyed economy with an experience of rapid industrialization behind it is quite different from a tradition-bound, stagnating, agrarian economy. In the former

---

[68] See Grajdanzev, *Modern Korea*, 87. See also Shigeru Ishikawa, *Economic Development in Asian Perspective*, 95, charts 2–5.

[69] See Sang-Chul Suh, *Growth and Structural Change in the Korean Economy*, 38, table 11, and 46, tables 17 and 18. Note that the "commodity production" data do not include construction, trade, services, and public utilities that are generally included in the more conventional "national income" data; the latter for pre–Second World War Korea are not readily available.

the institutions and practices of industrialization – the knowledge and ideas associated with industrialization – continue to live on.[70]

The Japanese approach to Korea's industrialization went through three more or less distinct phases. During the first decade of colonial rule Japan sought to protect the Korean market as an outlet for Japanese manufactured goods. Rules and regulations were thus created to inhibit the start-up of new factories in Korea, whether by Japanese or by Korean entrepreneurs. The fact that annual growth rates in the manufacturing sector during this decade still averaged a respectable 7 percent reflected the very low starting base. This growth had several components. First, there were the new public sector investments in power, railways, and other infrastructure. The private sector growth originated mainly in food-processing industries – especially rice mills – that were initiated by Japanese migrants hoping to sell rice back to Japan. Exchanging Japanese manufactured goods for Korean rice and other primary products was, of course, the initial colonial policy. The government-general thus helped Japanese entrepreneurs start up these mills by providing financial and infrastructural support. And finally, some of this early growth also involved the participation of Koreans. For one, small-scale manufacturing did not require the permission of the government-general. Moreover, incomes of landowning Koreans had started to rise, and not all of their demands could be met by Japanese imports. Emulating the Japanese migrants, Koreans set up small industries often called "household industries" in Japanese colonial documents. These businesses typically employed ten to twenty workers in such areas as metals, dyeing, papermaking, ceramics, rubber shoes, knitted cotton socks, sake, and soy sauce. The number of such small factories increased from 151 in 1910 to 1900 in 1919, with 971 of these 1,900 factories owned by Koreans.[71]

The First World War transformed Japan from a debtor to a creditor country. With swollen company profits, the Japanese imperial government sought opportunities for Japanese capital overseas, including in Korea. As restrictions on manufacturing in Korea were lifted, a second phase in Korean

[70] This distinction can be sharpened by using the concepts of "idea gaps" and "object gaps" proposed in the "new" economic growth theory. Whereas the "object gap" refers to lack of concrete objects as factories that direct attention to savings, and investment bottlenecks in development, the "idea gap" refers to the knowledge base on which development rests. The "new" growth theory emphasizes (as did several old growth theories) the role of knowledge and technology in economic growth. See, for example, Paul Romer, "Idea Gaps and Object Gaps in Economic Development," *Journal of Monetary Economics* 32 (1993): 543–73. One may thus argue that in Korean colonial economic history, even if "objects" were destroyed during decolonization, the legacy of "ideas" was substantial.

[71] See Soon Won Park, "The Emergence of a Factory Labor Force in Colonial Korea: A Case Study of the Onoda Cement Factory," Ph.D. thesis, Harvard University, 1985, pp. 16–18. This thesis was subsequently published as a book that I have not consulted. See Soon Won Park, *Colonial Industrialization and Labor in Korea: The Onada Cement Factory*, Harvard-Hallym Series on Korean Studies (Cambridge: Harvard University Press, 2000).

industrialization began. But Japanese investors did not rush in. The competitive pressure from Japanese manufactured goods was considerable, and the government-general wanted to encourage complementarities rather than competition between Japanese exporting to Korea and Japanese investing in Korea. The colonial state supported a select few Japanese investors by helping them to choose their areas of investment, providing cheap land, raising capital for investment, guaranteeing initial profits via subsidies, and moving workers to out-of-the-way locations. As a result, major business groups, such as Mitsui and Mitsubishi, made the move into Korea, and others followed. The average annual rate of growth in industry during the 1920s was over 8 percent. A significant component of this was Japanese private investment in textiles; there was also some in processing of raw materials and some large-scale investment in mining, iron, steel, hydroelectric power, and even shipbuilding. The number of factories employing more than 50 workers jumped from 89 in 1922 to 230 in 1930.[72]

Korean participation in this second phase, while a distant second to the role of Japanese capital, was not insignificant. Relatively small-scale Korean household industries continued to mushroom. Their growth reflected several underlying trends: rising demand resulting from growing incomes of wealthy Koreans and Japanese in Korea, as well as economic growth in Japan; the role of Japanese factories as "Schumpeterian innovators" that were followed by a "cluster" of Korean imitators; and forward and backward linkages created by Japanese investments.[73] Moreover, after the Korean nationalist outburst in 1919, the colonial government liberalized its ruling strategy for several years and sought to co-opt some wealthy Korean businessmen. Enterprising Koreans with initial capital – often with roots in land wealth – were thus allowed to enter medium- to large-scale trade and manufacturing. Those willing to cooperate with the government-general were also provided credit, subsidies, and other public supports. Of the 230 factories that employed more than 50 workers in 1930, some 49 thus came to be Korean-owned.[74]

South Korean nationalist historiography often underestimates the level of cooperation between the Japanese colonial state and native Korean capital. Revisionist historians, however, have now documented its extensive nature.[75] In the words of Carter Eckert: "Korean capitalism ... came to enjoy its first

---

[72] Park, "The Emergence of a Factory Labor Force," 42.

[73] See, for example, Young-Iob Chung, "Japanese Investment in Korea, 1904–45," in Andrew Nahm, ed., *Korea under Japanese Colonial Rule* (Kalamazoo: Western Michigan University, Center for Korean Studies, 1973), 93.

[74] Soon Won Park, "Emergence of a Factory Labor Force in Colonial Korea," 42.

[75] See, for example, Carter J. Eckert, *Offspring of Empire: The Koch'ang Kims and the Colonial Origins of Korean Capitalism, 1876–1945* (Seattle: University of Washington Press, 1991); and Dennis McNamara, *The Colonial Origins of Korean Enterprise* (New York: Cambridge University Press, 1990).

flowering under Japanese rule and with official Japanese blessing."[76] Here then are the early origins of a cohesive-capitalist state. Major Korean chae-bols (big business groups), such as Kyongbang (the most prominent Korean group during the colonial period, having its beginning in textiles), Kongsin Hosiery, Paeksan Trading Company, Hwasin Department Store, and Mokpo Rubber Company, thus got their start during this period.[77]

During the 1930s and well into the Second World War, Korea underwent very rapid industrialization: The average annual rate of growth of industry was nearly 15 percent and a significant component of the new growth orig-inated in heavy industries, especially chemicals. Once again, government policies were the moving force behind these developments. As the Western world sank into the Great Depression and protected economies sprouted, Japan aggressively sought growth by creating an import-substituting econ-omy of sorts on an empirewide scale.[78] After annexing Manchuria in 1931, moreover, Korea became an advanced military supply base for the Japanese war effort in China. The Korean economy was thus developed by the colo-nial government as part and parcel of an empirewide strategy to promote rapid growth, with a potential war always in mind.

The development of hydroelectric power in northern Korea during the 1920s and the early 1930s had brought down the cost of electricity and thus lowered the barriers to starting new factories. Raw materials such as coal and iron ore were also concentrated in the same part of Korea, so transportation costs were kept down. With wages for workers nearly half of those in Japan and absolutely no labor protection laws, market conditions for investment in Korea, especially in northern Korea, were advantageous during the 1930s. There was also a "push" factor at work: The Japanese imperial government tightened control on Japanese industry within Japan, while giving business a freer hand elsewhere in the empire. Nevertheless, the direct involvement of the government-general in encouraging business into Korea was essential. The colonial state periodically laid out its industrial policy, indicating the preferred direction of economic change, especially, given the planning for war, where the government anticipated demand to grow. Moreover, government and business cooperated to the extent that

---

[76] Eckert, *Offspring of Empire*, 6. As one can readily imagine, this claim is rather controversial. For a good discussion of related historiographical debates and references to subsequent Korean scholarship that supports this claim, see Carter Eckert, "Economic Development under Japanese Colonial Rule," in *Cambridge History of Korea "Modern" Volume* (Cambridge: Cambridge University Press, forthcoming).

[77] The point here is not that these same groups subsequently facilitated Korea's export-led growth. Some contributed to this process, others failed, and other new ones emerged. The point here is, instead, that Korean capitalism as a "system" was being created under Japanese tutelage. I am indebted to Chung-in Moon's criticisms, which forced me to clarify this point.

[78] See, for example, Elizabeth Schumpeter, *The Industrialization of Japan and Manchukuo, 1930–40* (New York: Macmillan, 1940), esp. chaps. 21.2 and 22.2 by G. C. Allen.

the contours of corporate policy were "indirectly fixed" by the government's economic plans.[79] Another analyst notes that "adaptability to state economic priorities was a prerequisite for successful large-scale enterprise" in colonial Korea.[80]

The government-general utilized both economic and noneconomic instruments to ensure compliance with its preferred economic guidelines. First, the colonial state kept a "tight control on the colony's financial structure."[81] The government-general, for example, controlled the Choson Industrial Bank, which helped to finance new investments and which had controlling interests in a number of diverse industries. This was a critical issue for Korean investors, as they had no other independent source of credit. Even for Japanese zaibatsu (big business groups), who could raise some of their finances from corporate sources in Japan, cooperation with the state was important; for example, the government-general floated compulsory savings bonds within Korea as a way of helping Japanese companies to finance some of the gigantic investment projects (hydroelectric power and fertilizer plants) in northern Korea. Second, there were the perennial subsidies; one analyst estimates that these were on the order of 1 percent of "GNP" per year.[82] These were used selectively to promote the government's priorities. For example, the largest subsidy for a while went to Mitsubishi to encourage gold mining, to provide the gold needed by the Japanese imperial government to purchase such strategic imports from the United States as scrap iron, copper, and zinc.[83] The next largest subsidy was provided to producers of zinc and magnesium, products necessary for manufacturing airplanes. And so on.[84] Tax exemptions were similarly used judiciously to encourage and direct economic activity.

While it is difficult to assess the significance of noneconomic factors in this state-directed, state-business alliance, they are nevertheless worth noting. The governor-general would periodically exhort businessmen to eschew narrow "capitalistic profits and commercial self-interest" and to consider the economic "mission" of Korea from the standpoint of the "national economy." The direction of influence between the state and business is also nicely captured by the fact that both Japanese and Korean businessmen referred to the governor-general as *jifu* (a loving father), highlighting the

---

[79] See Eckert, *Offspring of Empire*, 73.

[80] McNamara, *Colonial Origins of Korean Enterprise*, 9.

[81] See Eckert, *Offspring of Empire*, 73. See also Jung-En Woo, *Race to the Swift: State and Finance in Korean Industrialization* (New York: Columbia University Press, 1991), chap. 2.

[82] Young-Iob Chung, "Japanese Investment in Korea, 1904–45," in Nahm, *Korea under Japanese Rule*, 91.

[83] There is a great self-congratulatory discussion of how Governor-General Ugaki thought of this scheme to provide subsidies for gold mining. See his speech in Government-General of Chosen, *Thriving Chosen*, 85–87.

[84] See Grajdanzev, *Modern Korea*, 138–40.

benevolent upper hand of the state. Again, in the words of Carter Eckert, businessmen were inextricably bound up with the policy-making process, and what they lost in "autonomy," they made up "magnificently" by way of "corporate profits."[85]

A few specific examples of government and business cooperation further illustrate the nature of this mutually convenient alliance represented by the cohesive-capitalist state. The example of government subsidies for Mitsubishi to encourage gold mining has already been noted. Mitsui was similarly granted the ginseng monopoly by the government-general in exchange for a healthy share of the sprawling profits as taxes on the monopoly. The interesting case of the smaller Onoda cement factory has been studied in detail.[86] The government-general's surveys discovered large limestone deposits in Korea, information that was passed on to cement manufacturers in Japan. The government-general also indicated its need for cement within Korea, thus encouraging Onoda to invest in Korea. Most important, the government-general laid the groundwork for Onoda's expansion by ordering provincial governors to buy cement from Onoda factories for all government construction projects during the agricultural expansion phase in the 1920s, and it regularly earmarked nearly 10 percent of the annual budget intended for agricultural production projects for purchase of this cement.

The cooperation between the government-general and colonial Korea's largest Japanese business group, Nihon Chisso, was so intertwined that it is difficult to tell where the public efforts ended and private efforts began. For example, the preliminary work for the construction of hydroelectric power plants – such as surveys, selection of location, and soil tests – was conducted by the government-general. The private resources of Nihon Chisso were then tapped, but, again, the government-general played a key role in the accumulation of capital by putting the services of the government-controlled Industrial Bank at the company's disposal and by floating savings bonds. The government further helped by moving workers from the south to the labor-scarce northern region, where power generators were to be located; it subsequently remained deeply involved in the pricing and distribution of electrical power. The government's yield from this collaboration was abundant cheap electricity in Korea, which, in turn, became the basis for rapid industrialization. For Nihon Chisso, hydroelectric power was only one of the company's numerous projects in Korea. The enormous goodwill it won from

---

[85] All the quotations in this paragraph are from Eckert, *Offspring of Empire*, 73–74. Note that the exhortations to businessmen began rather early under colonial rule. A government report of 1914 notes that the governor-general called business leaders to a party, explained the government's policies, and urged them not only to be concerned with profits, but also "to bear in mind the promotion of the interest of the state." See Government-General of Chosen, *Results of Three Years' Administration of Chosen since Annexation, 1914*, 13.

[86] See Soon Won Park, "Emergence of a Factory Labor Force in Colonial Korea," esp. 83–99.

the government-general subsequently translated into opportunities for expansion in a number of other lucrative fields, for example, nitrogen and fertilizer production.

Several of the larger Korean business groups also benefited from close cooperation with the government-general. New research has documented how the largest Korean business group, Kyongbang, financed its investments with the help of the government-general. The subsidies provided by the government between 1924 and 1935 added up to nearly "one fourth of the company's paid-up capital in 1935." Further, loans from the government-controlled Choson Industrial Bank were the main source of financing. Personal relationships of key actors helped to secure the bonds among Kyongbang, the Industrial Bank, and the government-general. The terms of the loans were very favorable, indicating a comfortable and close relationship between the colonial state and a Korean business group.[87] Other research similarly documents the close cooperation between the colonial state and the Min brothers in the field of banking and Pak Hung-Sik in commerce – ventures that eventually matured into such major Korean chaebols as the Hwasin Department Store.[88]

Within the framework of a war economy, the planned government-business cooperation became the basis of very rapid industrialization of Korea in the period 1930–45. During some years the rates of growth were breathtaking: Between 1936 and 1939, for example, industrial production more than doubled. By the early 1940s agricultural and industrial production were nearly at par (both providing some 40 percent of the national production); and by 1943 heavy industry accounted for nearly half of all industrial production.[89] Certain patterns within this overall economic transformation also deserve our attention, especially because they proved to be of long-term significance.

First, the colonial state preferred to work with large business groups. Following the Meiji model with a vengeance in Korea, the government-general aggressively encouraged the formation of large-scale business enterprises: Larger groups enjoyed preferred interest rates on credit, lower charges on electricity, direct price supports, and indirect subsidies such as lower transportation costs on government-controlled railways. Nearly two-thirds of the total production in the late 1930s was thus produced by only a handful of Japanese zaibatsu in Korea. Since the Korean family-centered but gigantic enterprises also came into their own under this regime, herein may lie the origin of chaebols.[90]

---

[87] See Eckert, *Offspring of Empire*, quote is from 84.

[88] McNamara, *Colonial Origins of Korean Enterprise*.

[89] See Soon Won Park, "Emergence of a Factory Labor Force in Colonial Korea," 51, tables 11 and 12.

[90] This theme is well developed in McNamara, *Colonial Origins of Korean Enterprise*, esp. 127–30.

A second pattern is also noteworthy, namely, that a significant stratum of Korean entrepreneurs emerged under colonial auspices. Many of these would go on to establish such major chaebols of modern South Korea as Samsung, Hyundai, and Lucky. It is misleading to compare the Korean presence with that of the Japanese mainly by the proportion of total private capital or of large enterprises owned by Koreans. Looked at that way, it appears minuscule.[91] In fact, however, a significant minority of firms – nearly 30 percent – were owned jointly by Koreans and Japanese. More important from the standpoint of the emergence of an entrepreneurial class was the scale of Korean participation by 1937: "There were 2,300 Korean run factories throughout the industrial spectrum, and about 160 of these establishments employed over 50 workers."[92] Since these figures are for all of Korea, and since it is fair to assume that most of these must have concentrated in the South after the communists took over the North, one may conclude with some confidence that colonialism left behind a considerable density of entrepreneurship in South Korea.

A third pattern concerns the geographical distribution of industry. Those wishing to deny continuities with the colonial period again point to the fact that much of the industry was located in the north and was thus not inherited by South Korea. Although this is partly true, insofar as the largest chemical and other heavy industries were indeed located in the northern provinces, a number of qualifications are called for. The chemical, metal, and electricity-generating industries, which were concentrated in the north, constituted 30, 8, and 2.2 percent, respectively, of the total industrial production in 1938,[93] for a total of some 40 percent. But nearly half of all industry was probably located in the south.[94] The nature of southern industries was also distinct, tending to be in such fields as food processing, textiles, machines and tools, and tobacco-related industries. By contrast, the industries in the north were highly capital-intensive, high-cost production units that were not well integrated into the local economy. Northern industries were much more likely to evolve into white elephants, requiring continuous and extensive maintenance and upgrading, rather than into nimble, labor-intensive exporters of consumer products.

The last pattern that needs to be noted concerns the deep ties that came to link the economy of colonial Korea with that of Japan. This pattern is, of course, not unique to Japan and Korea but rather tends to characterize many metropoles and their colonies. What is unique, however, is the degree

[91] This, for example, is the approach adopted in Sang-Chul Suh, *Growth and Structural Changes in the Korean Economy*.

[92] See Eckert, *Offspring of Empire*, 55.

[93] These and the subsequent facts concerning geographical distribution of industry are from Grajdanzev, *Modern Korea*, appendix 3.

[94] See, for example, Stephan Haggard, David Kang, and Chung-in Moon, "Japanese Colonialism and Korean Development: A Critique," *World Development* 25 (June 1997): table 6.

to which Korea was already an exporting economy and the degree to which it was already exporting manufactured products to Japan and other parts of the empire. The textile industry, for example, grew handsomely during the 1920s and the 1930s (averaging a growth rate of 10 percent per annum), and by 1940, some 37 percent of textiles produced in Korea were being exported, mainly to China and Manchuria.[95] If the average foreign trade ratio for a country of the size of Korea in 1938–39 was 0.24, Sang-Chul Suh estimates that Korea's foreign trade ratio in those years was around 0.54, suggesting that Korea was exporting twice as much as any other comparable economy. Moreover, 43 percent of these exports were manufactured goods.[96] How many other developing countries in the world emerged from colonialism with this type of an economic profile? Of note here is not only the structure of the economy that was inherited by South Korea, but also the psychological legacy: Whereas most developing countries emerged from the Second World War with a distrust of open economies – either because they associated openness with industrial stagnation (as in India and Nigeria) or because they associated import substitution with successful industrial growth (as in Brazil) – many South Korean elites, rather early on, came to associate an export orientation with a high-growth economy.

To sum up this section, the highly cohesive and disciplining state that the Japanese helped to construct in colonial Korea turned out to be an efficacious economic actor. The state utilized its bureaucratic capacities to undertake numerous economic tasks: collecting more taxes, building infrastructure, and undertaking production directly. More important, this highly purposive state made increasing production one of its priorities and incorporated property-owning classes into production-oriented alliances. These propertied classes were variously rewarded – especially with handsome profits – for cooperating with the state in fulfilling this economic agenda. The state, in turn, utilized numerous means – including promotion of technology, control over credit, subsidies, capital accumulation, and even noneconomic exhortations – to ensure compliance from both Korean and Japanese landlords and businessmen. The result was an economy successful at exporting manufactured goods. Revisionist historians have documented the development of a substantial stratum of Korean entrepreneurs who flourished from this cooperation with the state; and others then also sought larger government support so they too could reap such profits. This model of development – inspired by Meiji Japan and transformed in the colonial setting – eventually situated the state-directed economy with its state-capital alliance at the heart of the strategy of transformation.

---

[95] See Yung Bong Kim, "The Growth and Structural Change of Textile Industry," in Chong Kee Park, ed., *Macroeconomic and Industrial Development in Korea* (Seoul: Korea Development Institute, 1980), 202.

[96] See Sang-Chul Suh, *Growth and Structural Changes in the Korean Economy*, 120, table 58, and 121, table 58, respectively.

III. The Colonial State and the Lower Classes

The colonial authorities sought to transform Korea to meet Japanese imperial needs. Controlled involvement of the lower classes – peasants and workers – was essential for the success of this project; and both the colonial state and the propertied classes collaborated to ensure their compliance. While historical studies of lower classes in colonial Korea are meager, such scattered evidence as is currently available suggests that both peasants and workers derived few benefits from Korea's rapid economic transformation. From a political standpoint, the pervasive, highly repressive colonial state succeeded in imposing order on Korean society, thereby freeing up the cohesive state to focus its political energies on the pursuit of a narrow, production-oriented agenda. On the economic front, incomes and wages generally lagged behind productivity gains, facilitating higher profitability, savings, and investments. Moreover, since much of the growth was export-oriented, lagging incomes and limited mass demand did not constrain growth.

This repression and exclusion of the lower classes, so integral to the colonial political economy, continued well into the future, so it is important to analyze the structure and dynamics of the strategy. First, as far as trends in the colonial countryside were concerned, recall that precolonial Yi Korea was hardly a haven for the tenants, peasants, and others at the bottom of the social hierarchy. Yi Korea remained a slave society until the early nineteenth century. Although slavery then declined sharply throughout the century, it was the Japanese who actually abolished the practice. Further, the Korean rulers of the Yi state dealt with recurring fiscal crises by squeezing the peasantry, especially via indirect taxation, thus contributing to misery, rebellion, and brigandage. What the Japanese did in this situation was to rationalize the strategies of both extraction and control.

While well-organized gendarmes subdued pockets of open rebellion for quite some time, the bulk of the peasantry was systematically brought under the state's dominion. First, the legalization of private property in the hands of landlords and a regularization of land rents created a legitimate basis for tenancy as the modal relationship between tiller and landowner. Certainly, tenancy had been around in Korea for centuries, but it increased throughout the colonial period as the population grew, such that by the end of the period, nearly 70 percent of farming households worked under tenancy arrangements of one type or another.[97] And as most students of agrarian societies understand, this mode of production leaves the tenant population dependent on landowners. The situation is especially severe where tenants are not legally protected, where attempts to forge tenants' organizations are met with swift retribution, and where the weight of the state is mainly behind the landowners.

---

[97] See Robinson, in Eckert et al., *Korea Old and New*, 307.

The Japanese developed a twofold strategy for controlling the peasant population: direct and effective downward penetration of the state and incorporation of landowning or other influential local groups as ruling allies. To the best of my knowledge, there are no detailed studies available (at least not in English) as to how this system worked in practice, especially from the viewpoint of the peasant. As far as one can make out, sporadic peasant rebellion never died out, but overall the repressing ruling strategy was effective,[98] with control resting on a combination of direct and indirect rule. The traditional system of influence within villages, as well as of information flows, was buttressed by a well-organized bureaucracy: local police with uniforms and telephones; tax collectors, also uniformed; and an intelligence service that periodically prepared reports on various topics for the provincial and central governments.

The Korean working class originated under Japanese rule. While Korea was still largely an agrarian country in the 1940s with more than 70 percent of the population deriving its livelihood from agriculture, there was already by then a considerable working class. For example, where there had been fewer than 10,000 industrial workers in 1910, the population of such workers had reached 1.3 million by 1943.[99] Assuming a minimum family size of four, a good 20 percent of the population must have earned a living from industrial work. Moreover, another 15 percent of Koreans lived outside Korea elsewhere in the Japanese Empire; a significant minority worked as unskilled urban labor in Japan, and some were in Manchuria. Since many of the workers within Korea had been moved from the populated south to factories in the north, and since most of the Koreans working in the empire returned to Korea when the empire disintegrated, a significant minority of the population in colonial Korea experienced dislocation from its traditional social niche.[100]

The colonial state collaborated with both Japanese and Korean capitalists to devise the structures for controlling this working class. The broad framework was brutally simple: Attempts to create labor unions were prohibited; trespasses were met with severe retribution; and there were few, if any, laws to regulate the workplace and protect workers.[101] This antilabor stance of the Japanese-controlled cohesive-capitalist state of Korea was largely successful, even if the system did not eliminate all unionization attempts and

[98] For evidence on the nature and extent of lower-class restiveness, especially as expressed through the communist movement, see Robert Scalapino and Chong-Sik Lee, *Communism in Korea, Part I: The Movement* (Berkeley: University of California Press, 1972), esp. chap. 3.

[99] For details, see Soon Won Park, "Emergence of a Factory Labor Force in Colonial Korea," part 1.

[100] For a moving discussion of the human toll exacted by the large-scale movement of Koreans under Japanese rule, see Cumings, *Origins of the Korean War, 1945–1947*, chap. 2.

[101] See Grajdanzev, *Modern Korea*, 177–84, esp. 182.

strikes[102] – especially in the somewhat more liberal 1920s and again in the late 1930s, when a war economy increased the demand for labor and thus labor's bargaining power.

Within this broad framework, individual companies had a fairly free hand in setting management practices, at least until the war years, when the state actively involved itself in the control and mobilization of labor. Not surprisingly, Japanese companies such as the Onoda cement factory adopted a Japanese management style.[103] Japanese managers sought to create a skilled, disciplined, and hierarchically organized work force in exchange for job security and decent wages. These wages, often higher than earnings in both Korean-owned factories and in agriculture, nonetheless lagged behind the hefty gains in productivity. Young Korean peasants with little education were hired in their late teens and early twenties. They received on-the-job training and were occasionally sent to Japan for more specialized experience. Though punished severely for lack of punctuality or lack of diligence, they were also rewarded for loyalty and performance. And those who survived the various tests and hurdles were given assurances of job security, pensions, and other retirement benefits. The carrot-and-stick approach appears to have been successful: In this one case, at least, young Korean peasants were transformed over the course of a few decades into "Onoda men." Despite the fact that they were given second-class treatment in comparison with Japanese workers, they took pride in being skilled industrial workers in a Japanese company.

Since there is very little research available that does not depend on company documents, one has to be cautious in making judgments about how "satisfied" and "loyal" Korean workers really were. There was very little real increase in wages throughout this period of high growth. Moreover, when economic opportunities opened up during the hypergrowth of the 1930s, workers voted with their feet; the rate of turnover in the Onoda cement factory during the 1930s rose sharply, for example, as skilled workers took their skills wherever the wages were highest.[104] Most important, workers were prohibited from forming any organizations of their own, and such efforts on their part were met with dismissal, arrest, and a permanent police record. Industrial relations in colonial Korea were thus "absolutely one-sided," in favor of management.[105] Workers were closely supervised in factories that

---

[102] For details, see Soon Won Park, "Emergence of a Factory Labor Force in Colonial Korea," 60–80; Asagiri, "Korea: Labour Movement," *Labour Monthly* 11 (September 1929): 568–70; and Ta Chen, "The Labor Situation in Korea," *Monthly Labor Review* (November 1930): 26–36.

[103] The following account is based on the case study of the Onoda cement factory in Soon Won Park, "Emergence of a Factory Labor Force in Colonial Korea," esp. part 2, B, secs. 1, 4, 5, 9.

[104] Ibid., 142.

[105] Ibid.

were "very closed, isolated, and protected." The workplace was "closed to outsiders by a wire fence, the constant patrol of its guards and the availability of police protection in case of an incident." And finally, closing the state and company cooperation loop, the Japanese management "kept radical elements out by tight inspection and in doing this they were fully supported by government policy and a strong police posture."[106]

Conditions in Korean-owned factories were certainly no better and may have been worse. One case study of the largest Korean business house certainly supports this view.[107] For example, 80 percent of the workers at Kyongbong's textile mill were unmarried peasant girls in their late teens, some even recruited from tenant families who worked the lands owned by the mill owners. The factories operated round-the-clock, each girl working a grueling twelve-hour shift, with one forty-minute break. Since labor control was deemed essential, work was under "intense labor supervision." Discipline inside the factory was "severe" and extended to personal lives: All of the girls lived in dormitories within a factory compound and needed permission to leave the compound or to receive visitors. The system resembled "a low-security prison." Whenever labor conditions in this and other plants became turbulent, "strikes were repressed with the same energy as was used to repress communism." State "intimidation and force" were thus central to this relatively simple and "crude approach to social control."

During the war years, social controls on workers tightened as the state became directly involved in labor management. A *sampo* system was established, whereby "industrial patriotism clubs," involving employers and employees, were created for the purpose of increasing production. Workers' representatives, who were paid full-time salaries by employers, and employers formed associations that designed programs for "educating the workers, making the production process more efficient and preventing disputes among workers."[108]

In sum, a bureaucratic and penetrating cohesive state collaborated with property-owning groups in colonial Korea to create a repressive and exclusionary strategy for controlling the laboring classes. This strategy of control, moreover, was necessary for rapid economic transformation: Once the majority of the lower classes was subdued, the colonial state was free to concentrate its architectonic energies on the work of planning and pursuing economic transformation. Moreover, the political capacity to hold wage increases below productivity gains facilitated high profitability and thus continued investment and growth.

---

[106] Ibid., 184.

[107] The account in this paragraph is drawn from Eckert, *Offspring of Empire*, chap. 7.

[108] This quote and the materials in this paragraph are drawn from George E. Ogle, *South Korea: Dissent within the Economic Miracle* (London: Zed, 1990), 6.

To conclude this discussion on colonial Korea, if Korea at the turn of the twentieth century was a mini-China, by midcentury Japanese colonialism had transformed it into a mini-Japan. The element of truth in this statement is essential for understanding the subsequent high-growth political economy of South Korea. Japanese colonialism in Korea helped to establish a cohesive-capitalist state identifiable in terms of some basic state-society patterns that turned out to be of long-term significance. These patterns included a highly bureaucratized, penetrating, and architectonic state, a state-dominated alliance of state and property owners for production and profits, and repressive social control of the working classes. It is to the issue of how these patterns did or did not continue into subsequent periods that we now turn our attention.

2

The Rhee Interregnum

Saving South Korea for Cohesive Capitalism

The defeat of the Japanese in the Second World War opened the way to another traumatic phase in Korean history. As the Japanese hurriedly departed, Korean nationalism exploded, the country was divided into a communist north and an American-controlled south, and an externally aided civil war followed. All this is well known.[1] Syngman Rhee dominated South Korean politics during this period, especially following the end of the Korean War in 1953 and then prior to 1960, when he was forced out of power. I analyze in broad strokes those elements of the emerging South Korean state and society during the Rhee period that contributed significantly to longer-term economic development.

The argument advanced is that a systematic pursuit of economic growth was really not a regime priority in Syngman Rhee's Korea. The main concern of the United States in South Korea was the threat of communism and, relatedly, maintaining political and economic stability. While Rhee facilitated some of this, he was an autocratic ruler whose priorities included securing personal power, holding the northern communists and domestic opposition at bay, and maximizing U.S. aid to South Korea. South Korean political economy in the period, including a middling economic performance, was more a product of these forces and less a result of any coherent economic strategy.[2]

---

[1] Especially noteworthy here is the monumental two-volume study by Bruce Cumings, *The Origins of the Korean War*, vol. 1: *Liberation and the Emergence of Separate Regimes, 1945–1947*, and vol. 2: *The Roaring of the Cataract* (Princeton, N.J.: Princeton University Press, 1979 and 1990, respectively).

[2] Over the years some analysts have tended to juxtapose Rhee's "import substitution" against the more successful "export promotion" phase under Park Chung Hee. Among major political economy studies, one example of this intellectual tendency is Stephan Haggard, *Pathways from the Periphery: The Newly Industrializing Countries in the International System* (Ithaca, N.Y.: Cornell University Press 1991), esp. chap. 3. As I suggest below, such formulations are misleading insofar as they attribute too much purposiveness and coherence to Rhee's economic policies.

In spite of the economic neglect, a number of important developments during this period proved to be of long-term economic significance. First, some essential structures of the colonial state survived, including a pervasive, centralized civil bureaucracy and a penetrating, multifunctional police force. When a purposive authoritarian ruler, Park Chung Hee, replaced the personalistic Rhee, these inherited structures provided the building blocks of a more efficacious, cohesive-capitalist industrializing state. Second, a fairly dense entrepreneurial base was built up during this period. Some of these entrepreneurs got their start during the colonial period, others of the same vintage migrated from the north, and yet others emerged anew. Most of them benefited from (1) the sale of Japanese investments at rock-bottom prices, (2) U.S. aid and related war recovery, and (3) a modicum of economic protection. Third, land reforms eliminated large landowners as a political and economic force, with benign long-term consequences. Aside from contributing to improved agricultural productivity and equality, compensation received by landlords found its way back into the economy, especially into the rapid spread of education. Fourth, below the apex, leftist political forces were brutally put down during this period, freeing successive regimes to focus on narrower growth concerns in alliance with indigenous capitalists. And relatedly, labor was recorporatized in the Japanese fashion, facilitating discipline and enabling the regime and the producers to hold wages behind productivity growth.

I proceed by offering the following caveat: It would be a gross distortion of the historical facts to suggest or even to imply that developments during the Rhee interregnum were deliberately designed to pave the way toward the subsequent high-growth political economy. On the contrary, numerous events during the period moved in the opposite or even unrelated directions. Indeed, if there was any "logic" to the period, it was more cold war in nature than developmental. The account that follows, therefore, attempts to do some justice to the contrary pulls and pushes of history, while weaving together an argument that links the colonial political economy to the subsequent high-growth phase under Park Chung Hee. The challenge is to explain how elements of Japanese-style cohesive-capitalism survived within the cold war polity established by the United States.

I. Old State and New Politics

Having surrendered, the Japanese had three weeks to leave Korea before American forces took control south of the 38th parallel. Japanese central authority in Korea vanished rapidly, and, as often happens in such circumstances, Korean resentment toward both the Japanese and their Korean collaborators erupted. The interim government that the South Koreans formed – Korean People's Republic (KPR) – thus expressed the popular mood common to many postcolonial settings, namely, nationalistic, left-leaning, and anti-imperialistic.[3] Had this government and the political forces it represented ever consolidated, the Korean state would probably have evolved into more of a fragmented-multiclass state that put a higher premium on political legitimacy than on economic growth. As it was, however, the incoming Americans were suspicious of this motley crowd; they saw the KPR as dominated by elements of the Korean "riffraff," who were probably too close to "the communists." Since the main goal of the U.S. forces was to create a stable, pro-American regime, they dismissed the popular KPR and sought to work instead with Korean middle classes. The latter turned out to be mainly industrialists and landlords with some Western education and former colonial officials. Pitched against the popular forces, the politics of creating a pro-American order in South Korea thus became a politics of preserving the repressive state infrastructure inherited from the Japanese, on the one hand, and turning a blind eye to or even encouraging the emergence of a rightist autocracy, on the other hand.

The Colonial State Maintained

With the establishment of a pro-American political order as its central goal, the U.S. occupation force in South Korea chose to maintain the sprawling, repressive colonial bureaucracy. This posed a problem initially because a majority of the senior civil servants were Japanese. The political mood in "liberated" South Korea, however, was sharply anti-Japanese. When Americans asked senior Japanese officials to stay on to facilitate continuity, politicized Koreans were deeply offended. Some Japanese civil servants were then kept on as advisers, while Americans backtracked and quickly restaffed the colonial state structure with Koreans. This pattern of bureaucratic continuity – of Japanese-designed institutions staffed by Koreans – eventually came to characterize not only the civil service but also the police and the judiciary.

As noted in Chapter 1, Koreans staffed only 20 to 25 percent of the positions within the colonial civil service, many at intermediate and lower levels. During the Second World War, however, with Japanese personnel needed elsewhere, quite a few Korean officials had already moved up in the hierarchy. Americans quickly promoted other Koreans with the help of Japanese advisers and rebuilt the civil service. There was no shortage of talented Koreans, in part because the heart of the old colonial bureaucracy was located in Seoul: This "giant bureaucratic octopus" was now responsible for governing a truncated country.[4] Moreover, many senior Korean bureaucrats from the north migrated south and were absorbed into the

---

3 In addition to Cumings, *Origins of the Korean War*, vol. 1, see Gregory Henderson, *Korea: The Politics of the Vortex* (Cambridge: Harvard University Press, 1968), esp. 120; and Grant E. Meade, *American Military Government in Korea* (New York: King's Crown Press, 1951), esp. 62–63 and 72.

4 The phrase was coined by Bruce Cumings.

bureaucracy. In general, then, enough Koreans – who had legal training and who had passed the Japanese civil service exam and were subsequently trained in the colonial service – were available to staff the bureaucracy.[5] A firsthand account suggests that, even below the national level, "capable Koreans for the most important jobs proved not too difficult to find" and that by mid-1946 "Korean administrators . . . were in actual control of most of the government functions."[6]

The infrastructure of the colonial civil service, now staffed by Koreans, was thus maintained, and the die for long-term evolution of South Korean bureaucracy was cast. During the Korean War, this bureaucracy became more entrenched; it ran daily government, generally following Japanese precedents.[7] Subsequently, Rhee more or less maintained this structure. One student of Korean bureaucracy thus concludes that the Japanese-trained Korean bureaucrats "helped to implant the sinews of a basic legal and rational framework in administration," staving off what "might have become a hotbed for the unchecked spoils system of the inexperienced politicians."[8] Whether inexperienced or not, Rhee was a patronage-oriented leader who valued the personal loyalty of senior bureaucrats more than their professionalism. Moreover, positioning former colonial collaborators in visible senior positions was a political liability for him. These factors contributed to a fair amount of turnover in the upper echelons of the bureaucracy, such that had the Rhee style of leadership continued beyond 1960, it is conceivable that the professionalism of Korean bureaucracy could have been permanently damaged. However, since Rhee's hold on power was limited, this did not come to pass, and continuity with the colonial service survived. Data collected as late as 1968 – that is, twenty-three years after decolonization and eight years after Rhee's demise – documented that, of the 2,339 higher civil servants (including subsection chiefs and above), some 75 percent still had come out of the colonial civil service.[9]

During the Korean War these bureaucrats ran daily government and subsequently helped with the war recovery and with facilitating a modicum of stability. One area of the economy that was important to Rhee, however, and where the bureaucracy acted efficaciously was tax collection. Even in this early period South Korea was more dependent on direct taxes than were most other developing countries. Jones and Sakong thus estimate that, if the

[5] See Hahn-Been Lee, *Korea: Time, Change and Administration* (Honolulu: East-West Center Press, University of Hawaii, 1968), esp. 102.

[6] This is from an account of the South Cholla province by an American military officer who served there in 1946. See Meade, *American Military Government in Korea*, 72–89 and 8, respectively.

[7] See Lee, *Korea*, chap. 5, esp. 103 and 106.

[8] Ibid., 99.

[9] Based on data provided in Suk-Choon Cho, "The Bureaucracy," in Edward R. Wright, ed., *Korean Politics in Transition* (Seattle: University of Washington Press, 1975), 72–73.

share of direct taxes as a percentage of total taxes in economies similar to South Korea in the 1950s was around 25 percent, actual direct tax collected in South Korea was nearly 34 percent.[10] This is an important piece of evidence, for at least two reasons. First, collection of direct taxes challenges the capacity of even the most well-designed bureaucracies. Early success in Korea on this front underlines the point that the bureaucracy rebuilt on the Japanese colonial base was effective and available to be used if and when the political leadership so desired. Tax collection was important for Rhee; he did not meddle much with these departments and even retained Japanese-trained senior civil servants ("collaborators") as heads of related bureaus in order to facilitate tax collection.[11] And second, the fact that the Korean state could collect direct taxes relatively effectively also helps to explain why in subsequent periods Korea needed to depend less on taxing foreign trade for public revenue than did many other developing countries.

A similar pattern of continuity with the colonial state structure also came to characterize the police, in fact, even more so than in the case of the civil bureaucracy. The Americans needed an effective police to impose their own order. Once again, only 30 percent of the colonial police was made up of Koreans. Americans reopened old Japanese police academies and – with the help of Japanese advisers and after a course in mathematics and/or English – promoted Korean officials to senior positions.[12] The size of the police force grew over its already sizable colonial base, nearly doubling the intensity of police penetration within South Korea.[13] The continuity in personnel was remarkable: "As late as 1960 [the year Rhee was thrown out of power] those who had been with Japanese police constituted about 70 percent of the highest-ranking officers."[14]

In Rhee's hands the police continued to be a highly centralized and effective agent of control. They were present in all parts of the country, shared "close links to village heads and bureaucratic officials," and were "feared by the general population."[15] Moreover, the police constituted a "cohesive core" with their own "esprit de corps." They were generally "contemptuous" and "resentful" of their fellow Korean citizens and, like the Japanese, were committed to imposing order on what they deemed to be an "unruly"

---

[10] Leroy P. Jones and Il Sakong, *Government, Business and Entrepreneurship in Economic Development: The Korean Case* (Cambridge: Harvard University Press, 1980), table 20, p. 114.

[11] See Lee, *Korea*, chap. 5.

[12] See Robert K. Sawyer, *Military Advisors in Korea: KMAG in Peace and War* (Washington, D.C.: Office of the Chief of Military History, Department of the Army, 1962), esp. 9.

[13] See Cumings, *Origins of the Korean War*, vol. 1, p. 166.

[14] See Sung-Joo Han, *The Failure of Democracy in South Korea* (Berkeley: University of California Press, 1974), 11. See also John P. Lovell, "The Military and Politics in Postwar Korea," in Wright, ed., *Korean Politics in Transition.* Lovell notes that just prior to the Korean War, nine out of ten commanders in the Seoul metropolitan area were Japanese-trained (p. 155).

[15] See Han, *Failure of Democracy in South Korea*, 15.

and "hesitant public."[16] In terms of functions also, beyond the usual areas of law and order, the police continued to be multitasked with important political and economic responsibilities. One close observer of "police reorganization" noted that, although the Americans disbanded the colonial departments of thought control, intelligence, and economic tasks, the police came to perform similar functions within new structures.[17]

In sum, the infrastructure of the colonial state was maintained. This outcome was largely a product of American political goals in South Korea, though continuity also served Syngman Rhee well. Unlike Germany or Japan after the war, where the need to create pro-American political orders led to a major political reconstruction, including democratization, South Korea was a relatively minor war spoil for the Americans, who saw the main threat as communism. For the Americans, preserving the colonial state, and thus stability, was an effective means to counter that threat. Hence working quickly from the colonial base, the Americans rebuilt a centralized, pervasive, and penetrating bureaucracy. Even though economic development, however understood, was hardly Rhee's priority and despite the fact that personalism and loyalty politics at the top and groupism and factionalism among the rank and file were not uncommon, by developing country standards, South Korea's Japanese legacy left it a bureaucratized state quite sophisticated in its legal and rational development. This task-oriented bureaucracy, like its predecessor, could get things done. Of course, given regime priorities, the tasks that the bureaucracy undertook were not developmental; that would come only later. Political control and resource extraction were instead important regime goals, and, irrespective of one's view of these goals, the South Korean bureaucracy under Rhee performed these and related tasks well.

Before leaving this discussion on state structures, we turn to one other institution that was more or less created anew and that would have long-term significance: the South Korean army. The armed forces were, of course, molded in the American image, but here, too, the Japanese connection was far from insignificant. Senior officers in the early army – including Park Chung Hee – "consisted mainly of [Korean] veterans of the Japanese army."[18] Americans used Korean advisers who had served in the Japanese army to recruit these officers, and even when enlisting men in the provinces, Americans in charge often spoke Japanese and not Korean, which led them

---

[16] See Henderson, *Korea*, 143.

[17] This is from the same account of an American military officer as cited above in note 6. See Meade, *American Military Government in Korea*, 126–29.

[18] Han, *Failure of Democracy*, 50. See also Cumings, *Origins of the Korean War*, vol. 1, p. 173, where he notes that, of the sixty officers in the first class of the constabulary (the predecessor to the army), twenty had served in the Japanese army, twenty in the Japanese Kwangtung army, and another twenty in the Chinese nationalist army.

to men trained by the Japanese.[19] Thus, over time, the army became the "preserve" of officers with a Japanese military background.[20]

The size of the military in South Korea grew tremendously during the Korean War to emerge as a relatively strong institution: from some 5,000 men in 1946 to 50,000 by 1950, and up to some 600,000 by 1953. Officers of this sizable army, however, were divided along quite a few cleavages: "Tokyo group," "Manchurian officers," "northerners versus southerners," and, of course, well-trained, war-hardened officers of the intermediate ranks who considered many of the generals to be less competent and less well trained than they were.[21] As long as the army grew rapidly, ample opportunity existed to accommodate competing ambitions and to mute these cleavages. After the war, however, as opportunities grew fewer and as the country's politics grew more chaotic, the coup coalition of 1961 emerged out of these cleavages and groups, especially out of the rank of frustrated intermediate-level officers. For now, however, that is moving too far ahead in the story.

Rhee's Politics and Politics under Rhee

The Rhee regime in South Korea was largely an American creation, and in retrospect Rhee himself turned out to be an unexceptional right-wing autocrat. By the time the Americans propped him up after the Second World War,[22] he was already in his sixties. Coming out of the landed class, he had struggled against the Japanese in the early part of the century and turned to Christianity while imprisoned.[23] None of Rhee's subsequent American experiences – a Princeton doctorate and association with Woodrow Wilson, repeated visits to Washington to lobby for Korean independence, or an extended stay in Hawaii – turned him into much of a liberal. To the extent that he had any coherent, ruling ideology, it was right-leaning anticommunism in the manner of the neighboring Chinese nationalists. He was essentially a nonpurposive, personalistic autocrat.

In truth, the scope of Rhee's power was quite constrained, given the American military presence, South Korea's dependence on U.S. foreign aid, and a traumatic and threatening division of the country. While Rhee occasionally protested the American emphasis on economic stabilization

---

[19] See Sawyer, *Military Advisors in Korea*, 15, 210. There was no shortage of qualified Koreans because nearly 400,000 had served as policemen and soldiers under the Japanese during the war years. See Lovell, "Military and Politics in Postwar Korea," 156.

[20] Cumings, *Origins of the Korean War*, vol. 1, p. 175.

[21] Han, *Failure of Democracy*, 51–53.

[22] General MacArthur is reported to have instructed General Hodge – the American in charge of U.S. forces in Korea – to greet Rhee on his return to Korea as a "homecoming national hero." See Robert Oliver, *Syngman Rhee: The Man behind the Myth* (New York: Dodd Mead, 1954), 213.

[23] Two political biographies of Syngman Rhee are Oliver, *Syngman Rhee;* and Richard C. Allen, *Korea's Syngman Rhee: An Unauthorized Portrait* (Rutland, Vt.: Charles E. Tuttle, 1960).

(as distinct from economic growth), for the most part he worried about warding off challenges to his personal power. To this end, he was often busy outmaneuvering competing elites and repressing potential personal threats, especially from the left, including the liberal left. When it came to policy priorities, he focused primarily on issues of Korean unification and on maximizing U.S. aid. As to economic development, in the words of one observer, "during the twelve years of Rhee's rule, no developmental program was conceived and no meaningful reform measures were enacted."[24]

I underline this point, that the Rhee regime did not focus on any systematic economic development. The middling economic performance in Rhee's South Korea is often explained in neoclassical terms as resulting from an import-substitution model of development (in contrast, that is, to an export-promotion model associated with very high growth rates in subsequent periods).[25] My dissent from this view emerges in due course. One important ingredient of the disagreement, however, is precisely this: It is more accurate to view the Rhee regime as one in which economic development was simply not a priority than to treat his scattered economic policies as constituting a coherent "model" of development, dubbed "import substitution" or any other type for that matter. While modest economic performance in this period is to be explained with reference to a variety of factors (more on this below), one factor was that the Rhee state – unlike its predecessor, the Japanese colonial state, or Park Chung Hee's state that followed – was simply not a purposive, economistic state. It had no serious involvement in facilitating investment or promoting technology or any of various other economic tasks that cumulatively help economic growth.

---

[24] Se-Jin Kim, *The Politics of Military Revolution in Korea* (Chapel Hill: University of North Carolina Press, 1971), 21. Even if this claim is a little exaggerated, some other serious observers of Rhee's Korea concur. Richard Allen thus notes that "the fact was that South Korea (during Rhee) had no policy-making mechanism as such"; see Allen, *Korea's Syngman Rhee*, esp. 218, but also more generally. Jones and Sakong are more specific and more to the point: "Rhee was preoccupied with political and integrative tasks. . . . Rhee's concerns were not with (economic) growth, but with short term objectives of reconstruction and maintenance of minimum consumption standards, both of which were to be achieved by aid maximization rather than investment and production." See Jones and Sakong, *Government, Business and Entrepreneurship*, 41–42. For one differing account that suggests that there was more "method" to Rhee's "madness" than is readily apparent, see Jung–En Woo, *Race to the Swift: State and Finance in Korea's Industrialization* (New York: Columbia University Press, 1991), esp. 44. Yet another interpretation of the Rhee period that assigns greater "purposiveness" to it is, of course, the one that views it as an import-substitution phase. This is discussed below.

[25] An early formulation along these lines by a group of economists was Charles Frank, Jr., Kwang Suk Kim, and Larry E. Westphal, *Foreign Trade Regimes and Economic Development: South Korea* (New York: National Bureau of Economic Research, 1975). A more recent, more political economy proponent of this view is Haggard, *Pathways from the Periphery*.

Rhee presided over a turbulent polity. Generalizing broadly,[26] Rhee's approach to other Korean elites, both political and economic, was to "buy" the support of as many as possible, to maneuver and outmaneuver challenging factions, and when all else failed to strong-arm these challengers out of the political arena. As to the rest of the society, three trends give some sense of mass politics under Rhee and were economically consequential: repression, deliberate social reorganization, and co-optation. As to repression, state organs and mobilized youth squads both were used in brutal fascist manner against the left.[27] For example, Rhee controlled and used the police and intelligence networks that Korea inherited from the Japanese against his political opponents. Factories, universities, and political groups were all infiltrated by agents looking to weed out "communists." Additionally, neo-Nazi groups – among whom *Mein Kampf* was popular reading and who were often likened to Hitler's Jugend Brigade – were unleashed against leftist forces, especially labor unions.[28]

Such repression and human rights violations must be part of any balance sheet of South Korea's "successful" model of development. For our immediate analytical purposes, however, another important point also follows. With the left, including the liberal left, largely eliminated, the political alternatives in South Korea came to be mainly on the right. The real choice was between the personalistic right and the bureaucratic right, a choice that was finally made in the favor of the latter when Park Chung Hee captured power. Meanwhile, unlike many other developing countries, socialism as a set of legitimizing political and economic ideas was simply not allowed a place on South Korea's political agenda. Of course, in practice, South Korea eventually undertook such socialist programs as pursuing land reform and establishing state-owned enterprises quite vigorously. However, such policies were conceived mainly as actions in defense and/or in support of capitalism and not as interventions aimed at "humanizing" the harshness of market forces. Socialism of the latter variety – and its various modifications and distortions practiced within the developing world – was forcefully eliminated in South Korea early on, paving the way for reestablishing a Japanese-style political economy based instead on close cooperation between a cohesive state and capitalism.

Whereas repression alone may have been sufficient to cow purely political foes – though by no means permanently and not even for too long – dissenting groups that were part of the production system were a tougher

---

[26] For a fuller historical account, see Bruce Cumings's work (note 1) and political biographies of Rhee (note 23). In addition, see Han, *Failure of Democracy in South Korea*; Henderson, *Korea*; John Kie-Chiang Oh, *Korea: Democracy on Trial* (Ithaca, N.Y.: Cornell University Press, 1968); and W. D. Reeve, *The Republic of Korea: A Political and Economic Study* (London: Oxford University Press, 1963).

[27] For a quick overview, see Eckert et al., *Korea Old and New*, chap. 18.

[28] See Han, *Failure of Democracy*, 13–21; Cumings, *Origins of the Korean War*, vol. 2, p. 196; and Allen, *Korea's Syngman Rhee*, 109.

target: They had to be deliberately reorganized and/or co-opted. Labor was thus recorporatized and the peasantry was given some land. Recall that by 1945 Korea had already undergone nearly two decades of rapid industrialization. While still largely an agrarian economy, nearly 20 percent of the population lived off "wages earned in mining, manufacturing, communication and commercial enterprises."[29] With the rapid Japanese departure from Korea, these workers took over the management and daily running of many factories.[30] A left-leaning, national level organization, Chun P'yung (All Korean Labor Council), came to represent the empowered workers during this brief, heady period.

South Korean politics turned rightward fairly quickly, however, and labor came under growing attack. Chun P'yung was destroyed after a general strike in 1946 in which workers demanded higher wages and tenants demanded land – but which the American occupation force treated as a communist-inspired insurrection.[31] Rhee's regime subsequently helped to organize the General Federation of Korean Labor – No Chong – which one astute observer of the Korean scene described as "a regime-controlled organization exercising top-down coordination of workers in the interest of business and the state."[32] While this union was wrapped in American legal trappings, the actual practice was much closer to that of the Japanese: "The ghost of Japanese labor regulation by police was re-incarnated; the use of goons to persuade workers of the 'right way' became systematized, and the manipulation of legal interpretation to favor government became standard action."[33] Once reestablished, this Japanese-style system of control continued – well into the Park Chung Hee era and even beyond – though not without encountering repeated challenges.

Turning to the countryside, land reform went a long way toward taking the steam out of peasant restiveness, so the countryside during the Rhee period was "relatively quiet."[34] While the fact of land redistribution in South Korea is well known, some of the details are not.[35] When the Japanese departed, only about one-third of the land was controlled by owner-operators. The remaining land – nearly 63 percent – was leased out by Japanese and/or

---

[29] See, for example, George Ogle, *South Korea: Dissent within the Economic Miracle* (London: Zed, 1990), 9.

[30] See Meade, *American Military Government in Korea*, 340.

[31] For an excellent discussion of lower-class politics in this early period, see Cumings, *Origins of the Korean War*, vol. 1, chaps. 8–10.

[32] Cumings, *Origins of the Korean War*, vol. 2, chap. 6. Another account of how interest groups in South Korea were "corporatized" under Rhee, see Sang-Ch'o Shin, "Interest Articulation: Pressure Groups," in C. I. Eugene Kim, *A Pattern of Political Development* (Kalamazoo, Mich.: Korean Research and Publications, 1964).

[33] Ogle, *South Korea*, 12.

[34] See Eckert et al., *Korea Old and New*, 353.

[35] The discussion below is based mainly on a useful but a relatively obscure study: Ki Hyuk Pak et al., *A Study of Land Tenure System in Korea* (Seoul: Korea Land Economics Research Center, 1966).

Korean landowners. The Japanese sold a fair amount of the land they owned in a hurry, and the rest of what they owned – nearly 14 percent of the total – came under the direct control of the American military.[36] Rhee and other upper-class politicians opposed the redistribution of this land. American forces, however, worried about land hunger and communism, demonstrated considerable foresight. They stabilized tenancy rents and redistributed most of the land that had formerly been owned by the Japanese.

By the time of the Korean War in 1950 and prior to the formal land reform, the land situation in South Korea had already undergone considerable change: Land controlled by owner-operators had increased from some 36 percent to 73 percent. American attempts to nudge South Korea toward further land redistribution had been repeatedly frustrated by Rhee and his cronies in the parliament. During the Korean War, however, as the northern forces moved down, capturing large parts of the South, they redistributed land behind the lines to build political support among the peasantry. When the northern forces were pushed back, the Americans formalized some of this redistribution and undertook even further redistribution, this time with Rhee's cooperation. This tendered South Korea's formal land reform special in character and limited in extent: It occurred during a civil war and was largely sponsored by occupying forces, but the land so redistributed amounted to no more than 15 percent of the total land under cultivation.[37]

The changing land-tenure situation had several important consequences. First, landownership became quite egalitarian. For example, if smallholders (under 2.5 acres) occupied only 10 percent of the total cultivated land in 1945, by 1955 they occupied nearly half of the total. Although most of this shift resulted from deliberate redistribution, some also occurred when smallholders bought land from the departing Japanese. At the upper end also, by 1955 only 1 percent of the total cultivated land was held in large holdings (over 7.5 acres).[38] While old landlords were by no means eliminated – many of them remained agriculturists with smaller pieces of land and continued to exert considerable influence within village communities well into the 1960s – land-related conflicts declined.[39] Second, the economic impact of land redistribution would come only later, because the Rhee regime did not invest much in agriculture and there were thus no dramatic gains in

---

[36] Ibid., 75.

[37] Ibid., 83–84, esp. 84, table 2.

[38] Ibid., 92, tables 4 and 5.

[39] For discussions of rural society and politics after the land reforms, see Vincent S. R. Brandt, *A Korean Village: Between Farm and Sea* (Cambridge: Harvard University Press, 1971); Sang-Bok Han, "Village Conventions in Korea," in Shin-Yong Chun, ed., *Korean Society* (Seoul: International Cultural Foundation, 1976); Dieter Eikemeier, *Documents from Changjwa-ri: A Further Approach to the Analysis of Korean Villages* (Wiesbaden: Otto Harrassowitz 1980); and Man-Gap Lee, "Politics in a Korean Village," in Man-Gap Lee, *Sociology and Social Change in Korea* (Seoul: Seoul University Press, 1982).

productivity during this period. And finally, the landowners who totally lost out – mostly absentee landowners – took their compensations, savings, and energy and threw them into both industry and education, such that the "education explosion" that followed was financed primarily by these dispossessed landed classes.[40]

To conclude this section, the political sociology of Rhee's regime is best summed up by noting that a sprawling, repressive, but task-oriented colonial state was maintained, while the restiveness of the mass society was tamed, in part by repression but also by deliberate reorganization of the working class and by land redistribution to the peasants. We have seen that economic growth was not Rhee's priority, and thus the colonial state that the Americans remade and that Rhee inherited did not focus on economic goals. Nonetheless, the evidence suggests that the state during this period continued, like its predecessor, to be an effective state; this effectiveness, however, was limited to pursuing such goals as political control and extracting taxes that were important to the leadership. With this as background, we now shift our attention to political economy themes, namely, (1) the interaction of the state and the economic elite and (2) the war-related destruction and subsequent recovery of the South Korean economy with the help of American foreign aid.

II. The State, Economic Policy, and Economic Change

Rapid decolonization and the Korean War wreaked havoc on the South Korean economy. If southern Korea's production in mining and manufacturing in 1940 is taken to be 100, by 1953 these levels were down to about 30–35, or down by nearly two-thirds. Industrial production in South Korea recovered to its prewar levels only in the early 1960s. The economic story of the Rhee period is thus mainly not one of planned development but one of economic destruction and recovery, the latter with the help of considerable U.S. economic aid.

As the Japanese departed, they printed plenty of money, quickly divested themselves of as much of their fixed capital as possible, and nearly destroyed the Korean economy. Since the Japanese owned and operated a very substantial component of the Korean economy and as all of this fell rapidly into Korean hands, the impact could have been disastrous. However, according to Jones and Sakong, "There is some evidence that the enterprises ran quite well for more than a year after the departure of the Japanese."[41] Clearly, Koreans had learned much during the colonial period about running manufacturing plants. The real disruption to the economy came shortly thereafter. The hardening of the division between the north and the south

---

[40] Lee, *Korea*, 47.
[41] Jones and Sakong, *Government, Business and Entrepreneurship*, 36.

caused major market disruptions, including the cutoff of the power supply, which was nearly all generated in the north. In addition, labor and political strife grew, especially as U.S. occupation forces confronted the briefly empowered popular sectors.

That production plummeted sharply in the aftermath of such disruptions is not surprising. What is noteworthy is the considerable economic recovery that followed. After a sharp decline, "the recovery of production (albeit from a low level) was fairly rapid" between 1946 and 1949: Production of cotton cloth increased from 100 to 230, of cement from 100 to 225, of electric power from 100 to 291, and average production "increased about two and a half times."[42] Much of this increase in production was, of course, based on resuscitating capacity that had already been built up. Indirect American help may have been important for this process of recovery, but direct American aid at the early stage was aimed at maintaining minimal consumption rather than at rebuilding the economy. More important was the basic resilience of the economy that South Korea had inherited from colonialism, an economy with a substantial industrial component that could withstand major disruptions caused by rapid changes in ownership and management, severance of established markets, and labor strife.

This nascent recovery was again cut short by the onset of the Korean War in mid-1950. As already noted, the three-year civil war destroyed nearly two-thirds of South Korea's industrial capacity and left nearly one million people dead. It would take South Korea almost a decade to recover from this trauma. The period 1945 to 1953 in South Korea was thus mainly a period of "such turmoil and disruption that no orderly movement toward development [was] discernible."[43] When discussing issues of the state and economic development during the Rhee period, therefore, we are basically discussing a relatively brief period following the Korean War, that is, 1953–60. Given the specific circumstances, moreover, even this brief period was hardly "normal." It was mainly a case of "slow recovery (from war-related destruction) assisted by massive grant aid from the United States"[44] and thus quite atypical of development experiences. What makes South Korea unique as a "developing" country in this early period is that it already possessed significant experience of industrialization.

Table 2.1 outlines the basic dimensions of economic growth during the Rhee period. An annual average increase in national production of some 4 percent is not bad by international standards, though it is modest by the standards of South Korea's subsequent economic progress. One component of this modest economic performance was the sluggish growth

[42] See Frank et al., *South Korea*, 8.
[43] Edward Mason et al., *The Economic and Social Modernization of the Republic of Korea* (Cambridge: Harvard University Press, 1980), 7.
[44] Ibid., 7.

TABLE 2.1 *Economic Growth during the Rhee Period (%)*

Year	GNP	Agriculture	Industry	Services
1954	5.5	7.6	11.2	2.5
1955	5.4	2.6	21.6	5.7
1956	0.4	−5.9	16.2	4.0
1957	7.7	9.1	9.7	5.8
1958	5.2	6.2	8.2	3.5
1959	3.9	−1.2	9.7	7.5
1960	1.9	−1.3	10.4	2.8
Average per year	4.3	2.4	12.4	4.5

Note: Calculations are based on constant 1970 prices. The figures for agriculture include those for forestry and fishery, those for industry include mining and manufacturing, and those for services include social overhead expenditures.

Source: Bank of Korea, *Economic Statistics Yearbook* (Seoul: Bank of Korea, 1973), 298–99.

of the dominant but neglected agricultural sector. More impressive by contrast was growth in industry – most of which consisted of rebuilding war-destroyed mining and manufacturing. Some critics of Rhee's "import substitution" economic strategies criticize the record as if industrial performance in this period were truly dismal, but in fact it was middling by subsequent Korean standards. And this middling performance established the parameters for analyzing the factors that promoted and hindered economic performance.

After decolonization the mines and manufacturing plants once owned by the Japanese rapidly changed ownership several times: Following a brief period of de facto control by Korean workers, the properties were first vested with the U.S. military, then transferred to the South Korean government under Rhee, and eventually sold by Rhee at rock-bottom prices to private Korean entrepreneurs.[45] Several aspects of this substantial property transfer from Japanese to Korean hands are noteworthy. First, the Korean experience of decolonization was unique insofar as it led not only to a shift in power, but also to a large-scale, nonrevolutionary transfer of property from Japanese to Korean capitalists. If the subsequent South Korean economy appeared to be mostly devoid of foreign ownership – and thus of foreign contribution – the roots of this "illusion" go as far back as the nature of decolonization. Second, such a transfer of ownership strengthened emerging

[45] For example, Jung-En Woo estimates that a textile plant worth some 3 billion in 1947 was sold at one-eighth of the price, that is, for 360 million. Fixed yearly payments were stretched over fifteen years and, given high inflation, became meaningless. And finally, the Korean War made collection of payments nearly moot. She thus concludes that the transfer of Japanese properties was nearly a "giveaway." See Woo, *Race to the Swift*, 67.

Korean capitalism. As noted in Chapter 1, a substantial entrepreneurial stratum of Koreans had already emerged during the colonial phase. After decolonization and the division of the country, many entrepreneurs from the north moved south, though most of these entrepreneurs were relatively small operators. Quick transfer of Japanese properties to select individuals within this stratum instantly created potentially bigger capitalists. And finally, the "lucky" ones who actually got the Japanese properties were generally individuals who were somehow well connected to regime authorities and who were willing to contribute illicit resources to the decision makers. A pattern of politically dependent and corrupt crony capitalism was thus established quite early and continued to characterize much of the Rhee period.[46]

Along with the land reforms discussed above, the transfer of Japanese-owned mines and manufacturing plants to Korean entrepreneurs rapidly created a private enterprise economy operated mainly by Korean owners. Economic growth during the Rhee period was built on this base. While issues of investment and the variety of price-regimes during the Rhee period are discussed below, this economy already had some "hidden" strengths. On the agricultural side, land redistribution created positive production incentives for the land tiller and South Korea had inherited fairly advanced agrarian technology from its colonial past, including the improved seeds and plant varieties, chemical fertilizers, and a well-organized irrigation system.[47] Industry was, of course, first severely dislocated and then damaged and even destroyed during the Korean War. Nevertheless, the fairly obvious point that needs to be repeated is that it is easier to rebuild a war-torn, industrializing economy than it is to commence industrialization from scratch in a traditional agrarian society. This assertion, in turn, rests on the claim that "knowledge" plays a significant role in industrialization, a point also mentioned in the last chapter and strongly stressed in the "new" endogenous growth theory.[48] Therefore, even if mines and factories were destroyed during the Korean War, a viable group of entrepreneurs, some knowledge of industrial technology and management, experience of urban living, and an educated, trained, and "disciplined" work force had survived as a positive legacy to undergird subsequent economic recovery and growth.

The economic recovery was largely supported by a massive inflow of foreign aid from the United States. Between 1953 and 1960, U.S. aid to South Korea – nearly all of which was a grant – amounted to some 10 percent of the latter's GNP per year. During these years external resources financed nearly

---

[46] For details, see Kyong-Dong Kim, "Political Factors in the Formation of the Entrepreneurial Elite in South Korea," *Asian Survey 15* (May 1976): 5, 465–77.

[47] See, for example, Mason et al., *Economic and Social Modernization of the Republic of Korea*, 82.

[48] See, for example, Paul Romer, "Idea Gaps and Object Gaps in Economic Development."

70 percent of all imports and 74 percent of the total investment.[49] It should be clear therefore that U.S. aid was central not only to economic survival following decolonization, but also to the post–Korean War reconstruction. The impact of this aid, however, was not always growth-promoting, at least in part because it was premised on Rhee's regime pursuing policies that "emphasized reconstruction and price stabilization more than growth."[50] U.S. policy preferences thus only reinforced Rhee's tendency to assign a low political priority to economic growth.

In spite of the American emphasis on stability, U.S. aid ended up making a substantial contribution to resuscitating South Korea's war-destroyed economy and thus to longer-term growth. Infrastructure was quickly rebuilt, electric power supply was re-created, and a variety of mines and factories were restored and reopened. In the words of one historian of the economy, a major accomplishment was

the resuscitation of the South Korean textile industry. Building on its colonial base, the textile industry experienced its most rapid expansion in history between 1953 and 1957, with growth rates averaging about 24 percent per year; by 1957 the industry had achieved complete import substitution in cotton, woolen, rayon and knitted textiles and was beginning to explore possible export markets.[51]

We know in retrospect that this textile industry would spearhead South Korea's export drive in subsequent years, as is discussed in Chapter 3. What is noteworthy here is the long process that predated the eventual export success in textiles, plywood, footwear, tobacco products, and machine tools.[52] This entailed having a solid colonial base; economic recovery from dislocation and destruction, financed largely by external grants; and a successful phase of production for the domestic market on which the export drive was eventually built. Such "import substitution" as occurred was more de facto than planned and was an important stage in the eventual export-driven model of development.

Another contribution of U.S. foreign aid was in the area of education. The Rhee period experienced considerable expansion of education, with literacy rates climbing up to almost 70 percent. Pushed by growing demand from Korean society, both U.S. foreign aid and domestic Korean resources were important in this development. American funds generally helped to build the infrastructure, such as school buildings, whereas significant private Korean resources, especially from the dispossessed landed elite

---

[49] The details are readily available. The figures quoted are from Mason et al., *Economic and Social Modernization of the Republic of Korea*, 15. See also Anne Kruger, *The Developmental Role of the Foreign Sector and Aid* (Cambridge: Harvard University Press, 1979).

[50] Mason et al., *Economic and Social Modernization of the Republic of Korea*, 95.

[51] See Eckert et al., *Korea Old and New*, 396.

[52] Note that in 1970 these five industries, namely, textiles, plywood, footwear, tobacco products, and machine tools, accounted for nearly 60 percent of all of South Korea's exports.

seeking opportunities for their children, provided complementary inputs. What is also noteworthy, however, is that American efforts to "democratize" Korean education – to mold it along more American lines – did not succeed. Koreans resisted such changes and Korean schools continued with the inherited Japanese traditions: large classes, respect for authority and teachers, a government-managed system of entrance and exams, and a curriculum more oriented to the state and economy than to the liberal arts – all rigidly controlled.[53]

If a colonial base and U.S. foreign aid facilitated some economic growth and recovery, the Rhee regime itself was not very helpful, as we have seen. One important area where the Rhee regime's economic neglect was manifest was the low rates of domestic savings, which averaged close to zero during these years (or, to be precise, 0.3 percent between 1953 and 1960). Gross investment in the period averaged about 9 percent, and nearly all of this came from U.S. foreign grant-in-aid.[54]

Inflation and interest-rate policies are often blamed for the low rates of savings during the Rhee era. However, only household savings were extremely sensitive to these variables and, even at their maximum, constituted only a small portion (under 20 percent) of South Korea's domestic savings.[55] Domestic savings were instead supplied in these years mainly by government and business. While business savings were moderately sensitive to interest rates (elasticity of 0.34), their main determinants were nonagricultural value added and profits (elasticity of 0.67); put differently, business savings, on the one hand, and profitability and growth, on the other hand, mutually reinforced each other. Business savings remained quite low throughout the Rhee period and started climbing mainly under Park, when growth rates picked up. Similarly, government savings remained relatively low during the Rhee era, hemmed in by both the scope and the pattern of public revenues and expenditure. Tax revenues actually grew sharply after the Korean War – from 5 percent of GNP in 1953 to 10 percent of GNP in 1959 – underlining the point made above concerning the bureaucratic capacity of the colonial state inherited by Rhee. However, Park's 1964 tax reform boosted these savings further, to nearly 16 percent of the GNP, also suggesting that Rhee left a lot of resources untapped. Also important during the Rhee period were patterns of government expenditure, where substantial public resources were expended to maintain minimum consumption standards under difficult circumstances and to buy the political support of various groups.

[53] For some of these points, see Mason et al., *Economic and Social Modernization of the Republic of Korea*, 52.

[54] See Frank et al., *South Korea*, 17, table 2–8.

[55] Ibid., 228–30, esp. 229, table 11–4. Most of the comments in this paragraph on the "supply" of savings are based on this material.

That low rates of savings and investment produced relatively low growth rates in Rhee's Korea is an unexceptional point, but it still needs to be made. Some critics of South Korea's early development strategy home in on the price distortions created by the import-substitution regime, implying that resources were misallocated and that the resulting growth was inefficient. While there were plenty of price distortions in Rhee's Korea, how much more growth than 4.3 percent per annum could one expect from an average yearly investment rate of 9.1 percent?[56] These investment and output figures suggest a rough capital-output ratio of 2, which stayed about the same (or worsened) even during the higher growth decade of the 1960s,[57] pointing to the critical role of higher rates of investment for growth in the subsequent period. As a matter of fact, given all the distortions in this period, the growth achieved with the relatively low rates of investment was remarkable. An important explanation for this is that what was afoot was mainly rebuilding of a war-damaged economy; a unit of investment, in other words, went farther in rebuilding an established but war-damaged economy than it would have if industrialization were commencing afresh.

This last point is further supported by disaggregating the growth picture and noting the fairly rapid growth of manufacturing during this period. Agriculture during this period grew at a low annual rate of 2.4 percent (Table 2.1). The Rhee government did not invest much in the agrarian sector. What was impressive about the low rate of agricultural growth, therefore, was that it was mainly productivity-driven, facilitated in part by improved incentives following land reforms and in part by the use of fertilizer and improved seeds that had been introduced during the period.[58] The bulk of the investment thus went into rebuilding infrastructure and the industrial base. As noted in Table 2.1 above, industrial growth during this period averaged 12.4 percent – not as impressive as what was yet to come but nevertheless quite impressive by standards of other developing countries at the time.

Rhee's neglect of economic growth was also manifest in the management of external economic relations. His priority was maximizing the inflow of U.S. foreign aid, and almost all other international economic policies followed from this goal. The Rhee government paid for the U.S. forces in South Korea in won, and the U.S. government, in turn, compensated Koreans at the official exchange rate in American dollars. In spite of the dubiousness of the underlying economic logic, the Rhee government reasoned that an overvalued exchange rate would continuously yield more American dollars.[59] Rhee

---

[56] Ibid., 17, table 2–8, and 11, table 2–4.
[57] Ibid.
[58] See Mason et al., *Economic and Social Modernization of the Republic of Korea*, 82.
[59] See Woo, *Race to the Swift*, 63; and Jones and Sakong, *Government Business and Entrepreneurship in Economic Development*, 92.

thus resisted – often successfully – U.S. demands for devaluation. But the overvalued exchange rate led to a number of other policies.

The U.S. occupation force introduced import quotas and tariffs in South Korea, aimed at minimizing imports. With an overvalued exchange rate, Rhee subsequently increased the tariffs, which averaged some 40 percent under his government. Some of the literature makes much of these tariffs as a distortionary import-substitution regime. While tariffs did protect domestic industry recovering from war-related destruction and some de facto import substitution did occur, two qualifications are in order. First, what is meant by "import substitution" must be clarified. Compare, for example, an average rate of tariffs of some 40 percent in South Korea at the time with India or Brazil at about the same time, where average tariffs tended to be over 100 percent. Second, and more important, there were numerous exchange rates within Rhee's Korea, some that applied to imports and yet others that applied to exports. A variety of subsidies were also provided to exporters, leading Jones and Sakong to conclude that the overvalued exchange rate "emphatically did *not* have the effect of discouraging exports as is widely asserted."[60] It is a curious import-substitution regime indeed where exporters receive close to competitive rates.

Two more related points further underline Rhee's approach to the economy and highlight the fact that his development strategy fell well short of a full-blown import-substituting industrialization (ISI) regime. First, Rhee's government undertook very little economic planning. What passed for planning under Rhee was merely a collection of projects. A serious development plan, with emphasis on "self-reliance," was prepared for South Korea by an American consulting group, Nathan Associates, but was never accepted by the Rhee government.[61] Second, having "privatized" most Japanese-owned mines and factories, Rhee never promoted state enterprises. With communism an ever-present danger, both Rhee and the Americans viewed state ownership of property with suspicion; rapid development of the state sector in South Korea occurred only subsequently, in the Park era. In retrospect, some observers may consider neglect of planning and of state enterprises in a positive light. Whatever one's normative evaluations today, it needs to be remembered that developing country leaders concerned with promoting economic development in the 1950s generally looked to planning and state enterprises. Considering Rhee's neglect of these economic instruments, it is difficult to sustain a view that he systematically pursued a statist development agenda, including ISI. A situation of no planning, no state enterprises, and, most important, a trading regime that did not discourage exporters hardly

---

[60] Ibid., Jones and Sakong, *Government Business and Entrepreneurship in Economic Development*, 92, emphasis in the original.

[61] For details, see David C. Cole and Princeton Lyman, *Korean Development: The Interplay of Politics and Economics* (Cambridge: Harvard University Press, 1971), esp. 210.

adds up to a dirigiste model of development. More persuasive instead is a view that Rhee's approach to the economy was haphazard and that many of his economic policies, including protectionism, followed from his noneconomic priorities.

The final point concerning how Rhee's priorities detracted from systematic pursuit of economic growth is the nature of state-capital relations during this period. The relations between the political and economic elite during Rhee's rule are best described as mutually corrupt. Rhee's legitimacy was relatively shallow and, given the periodic American pressure that he renew his mandate via elections, he constantly needed financial help to buy the political support of real or potential challengers. Control and allocation of scarce foreign exchange, government contracts, and credit enabled Rhee to establish ties with a select group of Korean businessmen. These businessmen, in turn, channeled some of this quick money they made back to Rhee and to the political organization he controlled, that is, the Liberal Party. This pattern of political alliance, in turn, hurt economic growth via two different routes. First, a number of well-connected businessmen found relatively easy ways of making money without really undertaking productive investments. And second, Rhee's dependence on these businessmen sapped any capacity he may have had to prod them into more productive activities, a capacity that became much more evident later during the Park era.

To sum up, the economic story of Rhee's Korea is mainly a story of recovery from postcolonial dislocation and war-related destruction. Industrial recovery was especially impressive between 1953 and 1957, though subsequently an American imposed stabilization program aimed at controlling inflation hurt economic growth and contributed to Rhee's downfall. Viewing the period as a whole, U.S. aid helped to rebuild the colonial infrastructure, mines, and factories and thus helped to generate modest economic growth. It is doubtful, however, that this growth could have been sustained without significant political and policy changes, since U.S. aid had necessarily to decline over time. More important, the Rhee regime was simply not focused on the economy, as is evident in low domestic savings, cumbersome management of the external sector, and the channeling of entrepreneurial energies into less-than-productive activities.

III. Conclusion

Many accounts of South Korea's economic success begin with the Rhee period, broadly suggesting that it represented an unfortunate statist, import-substitution phase that was fortunately followed by the more market-oriented, export-led model adopted by Park Chung Hee. There is some truth in such a view, but the account developed here also diverges in important respects from this standard view. Some of these differences are already clear, others will become evident in the next chapter. Three differences have already emerged. First, the "story" of Korean development is begun more appropriately with the colonial phase. Second, the Rhee interregnum was not as bad as is often suggested, and, more important, a number of developments in this period set the stage for the subsequent high growth of the economy. Third, to the extent the economy under Rhee was lackluster, the explanation lay more in Rhee's neglect of the economy than in his adoption of an inappropriate model of development.

The South Korean state and economy acquired certain important traits during the Rhee period that contributed to the growth "miracle" of the 1960s and beyond. Among these the following are noteworthy:

- An efficacious (though also repressive) colonial state was maintained, if not rebuilt, under American tutelage.
- A fairly dense entrepreneurial strata that had its origins in the colonial period grew stronger and now came into its own.
- Workers were recorporatized, more or less in the same fashion as in the colonial period.
- Agricultural land was redistributed in a fairly egalitarian manner, and, thanks to the technology and institutions inherited from colonialism, agricultural productivity continued to improve.
- Building on a good colonial base, there was rapid spread of education, including basic literacy.
- And the colonial industrial economy was rebuilt, ready for further expansion.

All these developments of the Rhee period were part of the package of "initial conditions" on which the eventual growth "miracle" was built.

Of course, this is not to suggest that the Rhee regime was truly forward-looking. Nothing could be further from the truth. The logic impelling many of these developments was instead the threat of communism, whereby preserving and modifying the colonial political economy provided the shortest route to stability. That important elements of Japanese-style cohesive capitalism survived should thus not be totally surprising.

As to the political economy of the Rhee regime itself, it is a mistake to think of it as mainly another statist experiment centered on import-substituting industrialization. A minimal definition of an ISI regime would include an effective exchange rate that discriminated against exporters. As noted above, this was not the case under Rhee. Moreover, Rhee's dirigisme was highly limited in that he did not undertake systematic economic thinking or planning, did not promote public sector enterprises, and maintained an average tariff rate that was modest by developing country standards. And finally, even though some import substitution occurred behind modest tariffs, the period was short enough that it was never institutionalized.

The Rhee regime was mainly concerned with "politics": maintaining personal power, fighting communism, and constantly negotiating and renegotiating its dependence on the United States. While overwhelmed with such concerns, Rhee tended to ignore the economy, contributing to low domestic savings, a distorted price regime, and corrupt relations with capitalists. A nonpurposive regime was thus the main economic villain of the era. By contrast, the state and the economy inherited from colonialism and then rebuilt with American support ended up providing some of the important building blocks of Korea's future hypergrowth.

3

A Cohesive-Capitalist State Reimposed

Park Chung Hee and
Rapid Industrialization

Park Chung Hee's rule in South Korea lasted for nearly two decades, from May 1961 to October 1979. During this period he put Korea firmly on the route to cohesive-capitalist development, mainly by re-creating an efficacious but brutal state that intervened extensively in the economy. South Korea industrialized rapidly during this period, with growth in mining and manufacturing averaging nearly 15 percent per annum and the overall economic growth averaging some 9 percent per annum. The political economy that produced this rapid transformation has been well studied, even overstudied.[1] The following account repeats some well-known information to facilitate a comparison of South Korea with other cases. My emphasis on the role of the state in promoting rapid economic growth will not come as a surprise to those familiar with the subject. However, my account also differs from some standard accounts, including statist accounts. I focus not only on industrial policy and export promotion, but also on the state's role in generating high rates of investment and in creating a cheap and disciplined labor force. Moreover, it is an analysis that goes deeper into the causal chain, to uncover why the state did what it did. Thus, I find that continuity with colonial institutions helps to explain state efficacy as well as state brutality, that earlier experience with industrialization helps to explain

[1] An incomplete list of some of the more prominent political economy book-length works would include Alice H. Amsden, *Asia's Next Giant: South Korea and Late Industrialization* (New York: Oxford University Press, 1989); Charles R. Frank, Jr., Kwang Suk Kim, and Larry E. Westphal, *Foreign Trade Regimes and Economic Development: South Korea* (New York: National Bureau of Economic Research, 1975); Martin Hart-Landsberg, *The Rush to Development: Economic Change and Political Struggle in South Korea* (New York: Monthly Review Press, 1993); Leroy P. Jones and Il Sakong, *Government, Business, and Entrepreneurship in Economic Development: The Korean Case*, Harvard East Asian Monographs, no. 91 (Cambridge: Council on East Asian Studies, Harvard University, 1980); Il Sakong, *Korea in the World Economy* (Washington, D.C.: Institute for International Economics, 1993); and Jung-En Woo, *Race to the Swift: State and Finance in Korean Industrialization* (New York: Columbia University Press, 1991).

subsequent success, and that reestablishment of close relations with Japan looms large in understanding how the South Korean state secured capital and technology for its miracle. So whereas an activist state indeed drove South Korea's rapid industrialization, it was prolonged contact with Japan that encouraged the development of both the South Korean state and the South Korean economy.

The discussion proceeds in two parts. First, I delineate the nature of the cohesive-capitalist state that Park created, as well as the relations of this state with capital and labor. At the heart of the analysis is the new leadership's commitment to economic growth, often justified as essential for national security, and institutional reforms aimed at controlling and transforming society and often reflecting continuities with the Japanese colonial past. And the relationships this state established with capital were growth-oriented, collaborative, and export-oriented. By the same token, state relations with labor sought to enhance productivity through repressive plans. This cohesive-capitalist state also utilized economic nationalism to mobilize and harness the economic energies of the entire society.

The analysis in the second section attempts to explain the rapid and successful industrialization of the period. The initial conditions that served as the foundation for economic miracle – discussed in detail in Chapters 1 and 2 – were considerably more favorable than in other developing countries. Beyond that, however, South Korea's rapid economic growth, especially manifest in its manufactured exports, was a product of the efficient use of substantial new inputs, mainly new investment, but also labor. The role of the South Korean state and of Japan was critical for mobilizing high rates of savings, harnessing capital and labor, and promoting exports. To this end the state utilized both market and extramarket mechanisms. For example, interest-rate reform was enacted to increase private domestic savings. At the same time, increased taxes and publicly guaranteed foreign loans, especially from Japan, helped to sustain high rates of investment. Similarly, devaluation played a role in export promotion, as did numerous subsidies and nonfinancial political pressures, not to mention the role of Japanese technology, businessmen, and trading companies. But heavy state intervention and dependence on Japan were not unmixed blessings. Yes, they facilitated rapid economic growth, but repression and other social problems were also part of the equation. Important as well were the unresolved, longer-term problems of making the transition to a fully developed country in a globalized economy, issues that are not analyzed below.

I. Reimposing a Cohesive-Capitalist State

By 1960 Rhee's regime was in crisis. On top of having an elderly leader of limited energy, which already made Rhee a remote leader, South Korea was experiencing an economic recession. Rhee, still obsessed with unification and communism, was ill equipped to cope with this shift in national priorities. Charges of corruption at the highest levels of government were also rampant. And finally, the fraudulent 1960 election led to the considerable student-led mobilization that eventually forced Rhee out of power.[2] His successor, Chang Myon, held on to power for less than a year. Though Myon introduced several important policy shifts – improving relations with Japan, introducing a new development plan, and purging the old colonial police – that Park would also eventually adopt, they contributed only to a sense of growing political turmoil in Chang Myon's time. Given a modicum of democratic opening during 1960 and 1961, students and/or labor unions led nearly two thousand demonstrations involving over a million people.[3] They were protesting the reestablishment of contacts with Japan, the continued prominence of old Korean colonial officials in public life, and, of course, corruption in high places. Chang Myon's purging of senior police officials only added to the mood that left-leaning forces might gain significance and that public order might be in jeopardy.

Amidst the growing turmoil in this relatively small country stood one of the world's largest armed forces – nearly 600,000 strong – which sooner or later was bound to play a political role. Certainly in the Korean case, since the end of the Korean War, the swollen barracks had increasingly become "a forum for political discussion, if not for conspiracy."[4] With the end of the war, the rapid growth of the army that had been necessitated by the war came to a halt, blocking opportunities and breeding frustration among junior officers, including Park Chung Hee.[5] Tales of corruption among high-level military officers and politicians fueled the state's crisis of legitimacy. About this time a group of eight lieutenant colonels (all of one army class) initiated a "purification campaign" within the armed forces, thus joining in with the broader societal protest led by the students. These officers tended to be rural and nationalistic, and, like many students, they argued for "Korea first." The coup that brought Park Chung Hee to power in May 1961 was engineered by this group[6] and would have profound long-term consequences for South Korea.

[2] See, for example, John P. Lovell, "The Military and Politics in Postwar Korea," in Edward Reynolds Wright, ed., *Korean Politics in Transition* (Seattle: University of Washington Press, 1975), 153–99.

[3] See John Huer, *Marching Orders: The Role of the Military in South Korea's "Economic Miracle," 1961–1971* (New York: Greenwood Press, 1989), 34.

[4] Lovell, "Military and Politics in Postwar Korea," 167.

[5] See Hahn-Been Lee, *Korea: Time, Change and Administration* (Honolulu: East-West Center Press, University of Hawaii, 1968), 152.

[6] For a good account, see Se-Jin Kim, *The Politics of Military Revolution in Korea* (Chapel Hill: University of North Carolina Press, 1971).

The Political Apex Transformed

The emergence of Park Chung Hee and his colleagues as South Korea's new rulers marked a dramatic change in the nature of the country's leadership. Most obviously, elected civilian leaders were forcibly replaced by military men. In their thirties and forties, this group represented a new generation: admiration for Japan replaced pro-Americanism. Park, for example, had experienced rapid career success in the Japanese colonial army. Educated at the Japanese military academy in Manchuria, he graduated at the top of his class, then went for two years to the Tokyo Military Academy, and subsequently served in the colonial army in Manchuria. Unlike Rhee, therefore, Park was very comfortable working with the Japanese. As several observers have pointed out, his "experience in (colonial) Manchuria was to remain a dominant factor in his thinking."[7] It was in the 1930s that Park saw firsthand how the Japanese colonial state – which was essentially a cohesive-capitalist state – could organize capitalism from above. This may well have influenced him later on. (As noted in Chapter 1, the colonial state worked closely with large organizations, such as the South Manchurian Railway Company, to build large dams, factories, and power stations.)[8] Park, too, admired Meiji Japan for its state-led nationalist revolution and fancied himself and his coup colleagues as something akin to the "young samurai" of the Meiji era.[9]

What is clear is that while Park was a strong anticommunist,[10] he was also no political or economic liberal. He justified the coup in terms of the "Asian masses" who preferred "bread to freedom" and as an act necessary to "save the nation." He believed that the solution to both the communist threat and economic development was a state-guided "great national awakening."[11] As to economic liberalism, in his own words: "We know of no instance where strife did not emanate from the exclusive pursuit of individual profit."[12] Characterizing the Rhee period as a failure of "laissez-faire," Park argued that following the coup it was important for "the state to directly and positively participate in economic activities."[13] Eschewing both communism and free-market capitalism, Park proposed that "the case of

---

[7] Ibid., 90. Also see Mark L. Clifford, *Troubled Tiger: Businessmen, Bureaucrats and Generals in South Korea* (Armonk, N.Y.: M. E. Sharpe, 1994), 35–37.

[8] Ibid., 35.

[9] See Robert A. Scalapino, "Which Route for Korea?," *Asian Survey* 2, no. 7 (September 1962): 11–12.

[10] Park flirted with communism in the 1940s and was even court-martialed for his "subversive" activities within the armed forces. Not much is known about this phase of Park's life. What is clear, nevertheless, is that by the time he came to power in 1961, he was a strong anticommunist. Among other sources, see Hak-Kyn Sohn, *Authoritarianism and Opposition in South Korea* (London: Routledge, 1989), esp. 19.

[11] Park Chung Hee, *Our Nation's Path: Ideology of Social Construction*, rev. ed. (Seoul: Hollym, 1970), 20.

[12] Ibid., 21.

[13] Ibid., 38.

Meiji imperial restoration will be of great help to the performance of our own revolution."[14]

Park Chung Hee and the military junta that came to power in 1961 set as a priority the "restoration of political order" and "promotion of economic growth." Of course, many military rulers in developing countries have at one time or another similarly espoused such goals, too, but without the same results as in South Korea; the shift in leadership was therefore not the main explanatory variable in the shift in development strategy. The Brazilian military, for example, not to mention the Nigerian military that captured power only a few years later in 1964, also defined its priorities similarly. What was distinctive about Korea was both the intensity of the commitment and the organizational capacities that were available (or were constructed) to achieve these goals. Given South Korea's geo-political situation, the threat of communism was real. Restoring political order and promoting economic development were thus seen as essential for preserving national security. Even as the American "security umbrella" remained in place, foreign aid from the United States was starting to decline. Park's own values and real-world pressures combined to facilitate a highly purposive leadership that reinforced inherited state institutions and exploited nationalism as a mechanism for legitimizing repression and for harnessing the energies of various social groups for economic development.

Park helped to reconstruct a militarized, top-down, repressive, growth-oriented state. A cohesive-capitalist state modeled after its predecessor, the Japanese colonial state, its defining features were an authoritarian apex that minimized intraelite divisions, a variety of top-down institutions that incorporated major social groups, and a commitment to promoting capitalist growth. The apex of this state came to be dominated by many of Park's close military associates.[15] Decision making was relatively centralized within this top group, and several factors facilitated intraelite cohesion. Many of these military men shared a common geographic background, coming from the southeastern province of Kyong-Sang. Quite a few of them had also studied together in the same officer's program at the military academy. Since decision making reflected "the military staff system," the military seniority system further minimized disagreements. And finally, whatever cohesion did not emerge naturally was facilitated instead by fear of an effective intelligence service, to which we now turn.

Among Park's earliest organizational initiatives was the creation of the Korean Central Intelligence Agency (KCIA). Details of how the agency

---

[14] Park Chung Hee, *The Country, the Revolution and I*, rev. ed. (Seoul: Hollym, 1970), 120.

[15] This account is drawn from Se-Jin Kim, *Politics of Military Revolution*, esp. 118 and 165. See also Wan Ki Paik, "The Formation of the Governing Elites in Korean Society," in Gerald E. Caiden and Bun Woong Kim, eds., *A Dragon's Progress: Development Administration in Korea* (West Hartford, Conn.: Kumarian Press, 1991), 43–57.

operated are scanty; what is known is that it very quickly became an all-pervasive and powerful organization, a "state within the state." Both Park and his relative Kim Jong-Pil, who came to head the KCIA, had backgrounds in the intelligence service; both were also very familiar with how the Japanese colonial state used its vast intelligence network to penetrate and control Korean society. With the police force in disarray in the postcoup period and needing an organization to impose power, Park came to depend heavily on the KCIA.

The KCIA very quickly gained "unlimited powers," becoming not only an "elaborate and effective security apparatus," but also "the eyes and the ears" of Park Chung Hee.[16] The KCIA did loyalty checks on all major political figures, placed a network of informers throughout private companies, and maintained constant surveillance over the press, students, and labor unions.[17] One observer notes that "almost no Korean was beyond the reach literally of the KCIA,"[18] and another suggests that the KCIA "emerged as the group to be feared most"[19] during the Park era. This enhanced capacity to penetrate society is what set Korean authoritarianism apart from many of its less-effective relatives elsewhere in the developing world. This cohesive, disciplining state, I argue below, was, in turn, economically consequential in numerous ways because the regime was able to focus narrowly on economic goals without needing to respond to the demands of various groups.

The military rulers also undertook important bureaucratic reforms that led to changes in both the size of the bureaucracy and the way it operated. The size of the government budget rose sharply in the first ten years of the junta's rule and the bureaucracy nearly doubled in size, from some 240,000 employees in 1960 to nearly 425,000 in 1970.[20] The departments that grew most attest to the priorities of the new government: The export department grew from one to six divisions; taxation from one bureau and seven divisions to five bureaus and fourteen divisions; and the department of industrial development from one bureau and seven divisions to two bureaus, twelve divisions, and thirty-nine subdivisions.[21] Park also established an Economic Planning Board (EPB) and a powerful economic secretariat within the Blue House, the presidential residence.

Details of who staffed this expanded bureaucracy, the training and values the new bureaucrats shared, and how the bureaucracy operated are not readily available – a surprising scholarly gap, considering how many

---

[16] Kim, *Politics of Military Revolution*, 111.
[17] See Scalapino, "Which Route for Korea," 7; and Clifford, *Troubled Tiger*, 81.
[18] Clifford, *Troubled Tiger*, 81.
[19] See Kim, *Politics of Military Revolution*, 112.
[20] See Huer, *Marching Orders*, 117.
[21] Ibid., 118.

observers point to the South Korean "state" as a crucial economic actor. Sifting through the scanty evidence leads to the following preliminary account. The main point is that the reconstructed bureaucracy continued to be based on the Japanese model. In the words of a former correspondent of the *Far Eastern Economic Review* in Seoul, Park "grafted the powerful growth-oriented bureaucratic structure of the Japanese colonial era onto the Korean political structure. He did this by drawing on what he knew best of Japan; the militarized, top-down approach."[22]

How did this approach manifest itself? First, important bureaus and ministries, especially such economic ones as the EPB, the Ministry of Trade and Industry, and the South Korean central bank, were either built on a colonial base or modeled on their Japanese counterparts, such as the well-known Ministry of Trade and Industry (MITI).[23] Second, the civil service exam and training of recruits under Park also continued to be modeled along Japanese lines.[24] And third, Japanese-trained Korean civil servants remained in senior positions such that, as late as 1968, some 75 percent of senior civil servants (including subsection chiefs and above) still had a background in the colonial civil service.[25] This is not to say that the Americans were no longer a visible influence on the South Korean bureaucracy; for example, American-trained South Korean economists occupied some prominent positions during the Park era. Their influence was not substantial, however, since, as one observer notes, American-trained social scientists were more "advisers" than "policy makers."[26] Moreover, Park "despised American-trained economists," whose role certainly declined in the 1970s as Korea's growth strategy shifted toward heavy industry.[27]

The sizable bureaucracy under Park was thus economically oriented, well educated, and quite professional. And it was far superior to what we will encounter in Nigeria. When compared with India or Brazil, however, it is not obvious that the level of education, talent, and public-spiritedness of the South Korean bureaucracy was markedly superior. It follows that, while an educated and professional bureaucracy is clearly important for the story of economic growth, what is really critical is the role of the political leaders who dominate the bureaucrats, because with clear priorities they can utilize that bureaucracy to achieve many goals. These leaders both create and represent new ruling coalitions, following development routes that play out

[22] Clifford, *Troubled Tiger*, 41.

[23] See Hart-Landsberg, *Rush to Development*, esp. 139.

[24] See Lee, *Korea*, chap. 5.

[25] See Suk-Choon Cho, "The Bureaucracy," in Wright, *Korean Politics in Transition*, 72–73.

[26] Dal-Joong Chang, *Economic Control and Political Authoritarianism: The Role of Japanese Corporations in Korean Politics, 1965–1979* (Seoul: Sogang University Press, 1985), 82.

[27] Clifford, *Troubled Tiger*, 59. See also Byng Sun Choi, "The Structure of the Economic Policy-Making Institutions in Korea and the Strategic Role of the Economic Planning Boards," in Caiden and Kim, *Dragon's Progress*, 95–106.

via a process of trial and error, and thus reflect some synthesis of a leader's own values and society's broader structural constraints.

Further support for the general observation that the quality of the bureaucracy was not the main factor explaining the South Korean state's developmental effectiveness derives from the fact that South Korean bureaucracy exhibited many traits common to other bureaucracies. Groups based around patrons and factionalism were common,[28] for example, detracting from what an ideal-typical Weberian bureaucracy may look like. Moreover, recent research has documented that Rhee's bureaucracy was not sharply different from Park's bureaucracy.[29] And finally, a variety of interest groups, especially business groups, lobbied the bureaucracy secretly and used bribes to buy influence.[30]

The focus in trying to understand the economic role of the South Korean state thus needs to remain on the role of the state and politics as a whole, that is, on its cohesive-capitalist characteristics. I find that what really changed between the Rhee and the Park periods was not so much the nature of the bureaucracy as the nature of the state itself, considerably more fragmented in the former and considerably more cohesive and purposeful in the latter.

Park Chung Hee set industrialization and economic growth as a singular priority.[31] Having clarified his goals, Park put many of his military associates in charge of important bureaus and ministries, especially the economic ones. In good military tradition, these men not only obeyed Park but also pressured the bureaucracy to perform. Indeed, observers have noted that this "managerial approach" helped to rejuvenate the sluggish bureaucracy.[32] Others have pointed out that policy making, especially in the economic sphere, and its implementation increasingly came to be executed as if it were a "war plan."[33] Determined leadership goals and pressure from above were thus the key variables in transforming a competent bureaucracy into an efficacious economic actor.

Politics of the Cohesive-Capitalist State

Besides engaging in institutional reform, the new regime was active in other areas: repressing the opposition, building political support with some groups, imposing the will of the new state on the society as a whole, undertaking significant top-down mobilization, and reopening relations with

---

[28] See Cho, "Bureaucracy," 81.

[29] David Kang, *Crony Capitalism: Corruption and Development in South Korea and the Philippines* (New York: Cambridge University Press), 2002.

[30] See Cho, "Bureaucracy," 81.

[31] One of the best and the most original accounts of South Korea's rapid economic growth, one that also assigns considerable significance to leadership goals as a variable, is Jones and Sakong, *Government, Business and Entrepreneurship*, passim.

[32] Ibid., 48, and Lee, *Korea*, 169.

[33] See Kim, *Politics of Military Revolution*, 164.

Japan. Further, under a modified constitution instituted in 1971, politics became even more repressive than it had been in the 1960s.

Shortly after coming to power, the new junta "summarily dismissed" some two thousand military officers, including fifty-five generals deemed to be "corrupt."[34] Dissent became very costly. Numerous politicians and left-leaning activists were arrested or barred from political activity. Moreover, KCIA undertook regular "loyalty checks" on active politicians. And a number of businessmen, arrested for corruption, were fined but later released. While Park was nominally an elected leader between 1963 and 1971 and while he never succeeded in quashing all opposition, he always pursued a strategy of rule based on instilling fear and repressing opposition.

Since fear and repression are seldom sufficient, the short-term political strategy also involved building support, for example, among urban groups. Imprisoning corrupt politicians, army officers, and businessmen was enormously popular with students, intellectuals, and workers. Smugglers, black marketers, and usurers were marched through cities with placards around their necks. Park also engineered another significant, though less noted, political shift: a "rural tilt." In the early years, he employed a populist-style, procurable rhetoric and backed it up with substantial new agricultural investments. These actions not only won political support in the countryside, but were also economically consequential: Agricultural growth proceeded at a higher rate than during the Rhee period.[35]

Park's longer-term ruling strategy also involved sustained imposition of the state's will on the society and selective, controlled mobilization from below. Reminiscent of the colonial period – when General Terauchi Masatake sought to "impress the Korean people with the weight of the new regime" – was Park's effort to penetrate and control the entire society. To track citizens, everyone was registered, with an address and a file. Corporate elites were admonished to fall in line with state-defined national priorities. And workers' attempts at unionization were attacked as communist-inspired and brutally repressed as being a threat to national security. The KCIA was the omnipresent reminder of the new state.

Park's military authoritarianism relied on the controlled mobilization of social groups via the systematic utilization of propaganda and campaigns, a technique reminiscent more of interwar fascist regimes and/or

---

[34] Huer, *Marching Orders*, 97.

[35] Scholars of agricultural development in South Korea have noted that agriculture did not so much contribute to that country's industrial growth as follow it. See, for example, Sung Hwan Ban et al., *Studies in the Modernization of Korea 1945–1975: Rural Development* (Cambridge: Council on East Asian Studies, Harvard University, 1980). Nevertheless, it is hard to imagine an appropriate "supply response" to the "demand pull" without increased public investment. For a more micro study of rural changes during the period, see Clark W. Sorensen, *Over the Mountains Are Mountains: Korean Peasant Households and Their Adaptations to Rapid Industrialization* (Seattle: University of Washington Press, 1988).

of neighboring communist China than the military rule of the Brazilian variety, where the main goal was political control and the main strategy was demobilization. Early in Park's rule, some twenty thousand transistor radios and one thousand loudspeakers were distributed for free. The massive propaganda drive involved broadcasting Park's speeches and films, especially to rural audiences and to underprivileged urban groups. Then there were specific campaigns in which the "junta's efficiency was prodigious":[36] The Saemaul Undong movement, for example, was a massive social mobilization experiment from above. First focused on the countryside, it then moved to the cities, exhorting citizens in mass rallies and in the workplace to sacrifice and increase production for the sake of national security. The goals ranged from vague and general to quite specific, for example, national reconstruction, land reclamation, or building new villages. Besides accomplishing specific tasks, the campaigns aimed to cultivate group work habits and inculcate obedience to the state and the nation.

The motivation behind these campaigns is the same as that which drove other "mobilization regimes" of the left or the right, communist or fascist, namely, to utilize ideology – in this case, nationalism – to generate new political attitudes aimed at enhancing legitimacy and accomplishing tasks. But it is very difficult to estimate the effectiveness of such ruling strategies. Park certainly never succeeded in eliminating opposition to his rule. Whereas his propaganda and campaigns may have influenced some groups – probably the less literate rural groups – they did not succeed with others, notably students and workers. The economic impact of such a political strategy is even more difficult to assess. Nevertheless, what is clear is that this was no simple authoritarian regime that just restored "political order" and then let markets do their work. It was also more complicated than implied by the model of a "developmental state," namely, insulated bureaucrats and businessmen happily colluding to promote growth and profits. Rather, Park's cohesive-capitalist regime was more reminiscent of interwar fascism, with its twin emphases on nationalism and mobilization. Park looked to the Japanese colonial past and to "modernizing" Japan as his models.

Political changes under Park also involved important changes in South Korea's external relations, especially noteworthy being the reopening to Japan. As noted above, Park and his colleagues were already Japanophiles. Moreover, the United States, South Korea's main patron, was concerned about its aid burden and saw value in enhancing the ties between Japan and South Korea. Given the American security umbrella, the political and

---

[36] Huer, *Marching Orders*, 93. Also of interest in this context is a collection of speeches by Park's daughter, Keun Hae Park, *The New Spirit Movement* (Seoul: Naeway Business Journal and Korea Herald, 1979). For a comparison of this political system with that of Japan in the 1930s, see Jai-Hyup Kim, *The Garrison State in Pre-War Japan and Post-War Korea: A Comparative Analysis of Military Politics* (Washington, D.C.: University Press of America, 1978).

economic elites in both South Korea and Japan saw significant opportunities for economic collaboration in postcoup Korea.

The Korean leadership looked to normalization of diplomatic and trade relations with Japan to compensate for declining U.S. aid and to promote new economic development. Korean business interests also favored economic opening, mainly because the domestic market was relatively small and already saturated. Inspired by their own past, they saw a potential to win export markets by combining Korea's cheap and "disciplined" labor with Japan's capital, technology, and marketing skills.[37] This political attitude of South Korean businessmen distinguishes them from business groups in many other developing countries, such as India, who in the early stages of industrialization often preferred protectionism and limiting the role of foreign capital. South Korea's industrialization, however, especially in such products as textiles, was already far enough along that import substitution in the domestic market was nearly complete. Moreover, collaboration between Korean and Japanese business to promote exports was part of the recent historical memory. But the type of collaboration they sought differed, say, from what Brazil was after. The Koreans were not looking for a large influx of Japanese direct foreign investment because that could have inhibited the development of Korean business houses. Instead, both Korean businessmen and the Park regime were looking for commercial loans and technology transfer aimed at export promotion – a pattern of collaboration that would open the way for businessmen to flourish.

For their part, Japanese businessmen who had old colonial links with Korea and who had financial connections to prominent Japanese politicians founded a "Korea lobby" and argued for closer links with South Korea and for economic transfers.[38] Their motivation – combining some of their capital and industrial goods with cheaper Korean labor to promote exports – complemented South Korean needs well. These attitudes of Japanese businessmen were also distinctive. Western corporations investing in developing countries in the 1960s and the 1970s often did so to make "technological rents," that is, to make profits mainly by using well-developed technology with which they did not want to part and by producing goods for the protected domestic markets of the countries in which they invested; this pattern will be quite clear, for example, in the case of Brazil. As late industrializers, Japanese corporations, in contrast to Western counterparts, were keen constantly to move up in the global division of labor by producing higher value-added exports. But this created the problem of what to do with capital and technology associated with lower-value-added goods, such as textiles. One solution was to transfer this technology to a familiar neighboring country,

---

[37] See Kwan Bong Kim, *The Korea-Japan Treaty Crisis and the Instability of the Korean System* (New York: Praeger, 1971), 88.

[38] Ibid., 88–89. Some of the factual information in this and the next paragraph is also taken from this source.

such as South Korea, so as to continue to sell exported goods to a country like the United States.

Large sums of money were spent within Japan by the "Korea lobby" and by Liberal party politicians to build support for reestablishing closer ties with Korea. Several Japanese survey missions visited Korea between 1962 and 1965 to explore opportunities for Japanese investment. Prior to the formal normalization of relations in 1965, some sixty leading Japanese firms had already opened offices in Seoul. Business pressure for renewed relations was thus patently manifest. On the Korean side, however, popular sentiment remained strongly anti-Japanese. Reestablishment of closer ties with Japan thus posed serious management problems for the political leadership. Nationalist mobilization harped on the North Korean and communist threat as the authoritarian South Korean regime marshaled all its resources to control society and keep popular sentiment at bay so as to push through its rapprochement with Japan.

The die of the Park regime was thus pretty well cast by the mid-1960s. The essential features of the cohesive-capitalist state included a cohesive military apex in which power came to reside more and more with the president; a strong commitment to economic growth and to working with big business groups; a sprawling bureaucracy, also with an economic tilt; nationalist mobilization; renewed links with old colonial masters; and a powerful intelligence agency to secure control and to deter dissent at the bottom of the society. Nonetheless, dissent never really died out in Park's Korea – and given continued American influence, Park needed to relegitimize his rule via elections, however nominal. The 1971 election exposed deep resentment toward Park, with more than half the population voting for opposition candidates, including Kim Dae Jung, who eventually became South Korea's president in the late 1990s. Aimed at quashing this opposition, as well as at dealing with shifts in the international environment, Park further tightened his regime by creating what came to be known as the "Yushin system," which lasted until his assassination toward the end of the decade.

The word "Yushin," meaning "restoration," was borrowed by Park from Japanese history to invoke "a new beginning," similar to that initiated by the Meiji restoration. In practice, however, there was not much of a new beginning, certainly not in the political sphere. The political system of the 1970s represented continuity more than any substantial departure from the 1960s; it was mostly a "systematic consolidation" of an authoritarian system that was already "substantially established."[39] In fact, the main change was a further tightening of the system: more widespread use of the KCIA and more frequent state-orchestrated rallies, aimed at whipping up nationalist hysteria among some groups and simultaneously quelling dissent among others.[40]

---

[39] See Sohn, *Authoritarianism and Opposition in South Korea*, 44.
[40] Ibid., 204 and 51, respectively.

In tightening his control, Park was responding to both domestic and external pressures. In addition to the general dissent reflected by the electoral results, labor disputes increased sharply in 1971, mainly because the political system had opened up a little to deal with elections. These disputes again declined sharply after the postelection tightening,[41] which was justified as necessary for dealing with issues of production efficiency and the security threat posed by communism. Moreover, the Nixon doctrine implied greater self-reliance for East Asian countries. This occurred politically because of a decline of the cold war hostilities in the region and because of the steady American withdrawal from Vietnam and improving relations with China. Economically, the period saw growing protectionism in the United States, especially toward Korean textiles.[42] Park thus further tightened the state's authoritarian control over both the society and the economy. He argued for greater national self-sufficiency and shifted the country's development strategy substantially.

State and Business

One needs to examine the nature of the cohesive-capitalist state's relation with such critical economic groups as business and labor within the framework of reinvigorated authoritarian institutions and politics. The relationship between the state and business, especially big business, was so close under Park that scholarly observers found the Western distinction between public and private to be "misleading"; rather, the "public" and the "private" were instead "rolled into one."[43] Often referred to as "Korea incorporated" and again reminiscent of Japan, the state-business alliance was the product of a number of structural and personal factors and, in turn, was consequential for how the state managed the South Korean economy.

Right after coming to power, Park imprisoned some prominent businessmen on charges of corruption. But as he needed businessmen, not so much for maintaining power – which depended on coercion and other political techniques – but as growth producers, their release was inevitable. This early action nevertheless established a direction of influence – from the state to business – that remained fundamentally unchanged throughout the Park era.[44] The fact that business was highly concentrated facilitated governmental control and collaboration. Two aspects of this business concentration are

---

[41] Ibid., 42.

[42] See Woo, *Race to the Swift*, esp. 119.

[43] Ibid., 175. This blurring of the public and private in South Korea is quite distinct from what we see in the case of Nigeria, below, where such distinctions never really emerged. In Korea, by contrast, a distinct public realm had emerged, and the conflation of the public and the private realms occurred at the behest of public authorities, who were in command.

[44] A major study thus notes that the state in the state-business alliance was "unequivocally the dominant partner." See Jones and Sakong, *Government, Business, and Entrepreneurship*, 67. Over time, of course, the stronger business became, the more the power balance altered in favor of business groups.

striking. First, as is well known, large Korean business houses, the chaebols, were "beyond immense." By the end of the Park era, for example, sales by the top ten chaebols accounted for nearly two-thirds of South Korea's GNP.[45] Fostered by deliberate state policies, this concentration grew throughout the Park era: Thus between 1962 and 1974, output per business establishment grew ninefold, whereas the number of establishments increased only 40 percent, underlining that growth resulted not so much from the emergence of new entrepreneurs as from the success of older ones.[46] Second, Park forced all businesses into a number of top-down business associations that were assigned, in turn, to various ministries, thus enhancing government's capacity to regulate and monitor.[47]

Economic, political, and personal ties bound government and business together. As in the colonial period, the Park regime used periodic economic plans to set the direction in which the state intended to move the economy; this "announcement effect" was a major factor in guiding private decisions.[48] More directly, credit control in the hands of government was an important political tool for influencing business behavior, especially considering that the debt-equity ratio of the large chaebols tended to be about 5 to 1. The government was also not shy about making strategic use of political tools to influence business: Most prominently, the Park regime set export targets for sectors and firms. It rewarded those who complied with easy credit, tax benefits, and the prestige of being named national heroes. And it punished those who failed with tax audits and a credit squeeze. Personal ties also facilitated state-business relations. Given a relatively small country with a concentrated political and economic elite, bureaucrats and business often shared cultural and educational backgrounds, leading to highly interconnected personal networks. At the highest level, Park was a personal friend of the heads of two of the largest chaebols, Hyundai and Daewoo, occasionally enjoying a casual dinner with Chung Ju Yung, the owner of Hyundai.[49]

State-business ties in Park's South Korea were thus so intertwined that it is difficult at times to disentangle the role of the state-defined public purpose of growth of GNP from the role of private profit motives and/or of cronyism. That the state was in command, though, seems to be supported by the evidence. Jones and Sakong found in their survey during the period that businessmen experienced the state's compulsions as pervasive and real.[50]

---

[45] Robert P. Kearney, *The Warrior Worker: The Challenge of the Korean Way of Working* (New York: Henry Holt, 1991), 39; and Amsden, *Asia's Next Giant*, 116.

[46] Jones and Sakong, *Government, Business, and Entrepreneurship*, 170.

[47] Clifford, *Troubled Tiger*, 63.

[48] Jones and Sakong, *Government, Business, and Entrepreneurship*, chap. 3.

[49] For a good anecdotal account of such personal links, see Clifford, *Troubled Tiger*, chap. 8; and Kearney, *Warrior Worker*, 189–212. For more scholarly case studies of five chaebols, see Jones and Sakong, *Government, Business, and Entrepreneurship*, appendix B.

[50] Ibid., 132–39.

Others have pointed to the fact that the larger chaebols – which graduated into Japanese-style general trading companies in the 1970s – often
exported at fairly low profits, apparently as a national and public service.[51]
These business groups, however, were also handsomely compensated for
their low-profit export prowess by subsidized public credit and access to numerous other publicly controlled profitable opportunities. Businesses were
also not lacking in power at critical moments, especially on issues that truly
mattered to them; in 1974, for example, 76 percent of the Korean Trader's
Association's representations were accepted by the government.[52] The best
that one can then suggest is that a dominant state worked closely with large
business groups to promote economic growth and profits. By contrast, a less
well organized state in close alliance with business – but with goals other
than economic growth – could have readily moved the national political
economy away from concerns of investment and efficiency and toward such
outcomes as are found in many African economies, including conspicuous
consumption, mutual corruption, and even predatory plunder.

State and Labor
Labor, which played a critical role in South Korea's rapid economic growth,
has remained an understudied topic. We know that at the heart of the export
prowess were long hours of work and relatively low wages. Again reminiscent of the colonial era, deliberate political control and economic mobilization were the main strategies, and the cohesive-capitalist state was the main
agent.

During the Park era employment in manufacturing as a proportion of the
total employed grew sharply, from some 8 percent in 1963 to 23 percent in
1979, while that in agriculture dropped from 63 to 36 percent.[53] The majority of workers in manufacturing were employed not by the chaebols but by
small- and medium-size firms. Within the chaebols that spearheaded Korea's
exports and industrialization, women were concentrated in the main export
industries of textiles and electronics, contributing 70 and 60 percent of the
total work force of these two industries, respectively, during the 1970s.[54]
These women tended to be quite young (aged fourteen to twenty-four),

---

[51] See Doug-Sung Cho, *The General Trading Company: Concept and Strategy* (Lexington, Mass.:
Lexington Books, 1987), 57.

[52] Jones and Sakong, *Government, Business, and Entrepreneurship*, chap. 3.

[53] Jang Jip Choi, *Labor and the Authoritarian State: Labor Unions in South Korean Manufacturing
Industries, 1961–1980* (Seoul: Korea University Press, 1989), 44. This University of Chicago
doctoral thesis turned into a book is a rare and useful scholarly treatment devoted exclusively
to labor issues in South Korea. I have depended quite heavily on this account. Also relevant
here are Yoong-Ki Park, *Labor and Industrial Relations in Korea: System and Practice* (Seoul:
Sogang University Press, 1979); and Moon Kyu Park, "Interest Representation in South
Korea. The Limits of Corporatist Control," *Asian Survey* 27, no. 8 (August 1987): 903–17.

[54] Choi, *Labor and the Authoritarian State*, 53.

worked long hours (ten to twelve hours a day, with one day a week off), and were generally paid half of the average wage of male workers. Workers overall, male or female, gave South Korea its export edge.[55] The question is how such a work force was created – with its habits of "punctuality, discipline, regulation, hard work, conformity, and obedience to the instructions of superiors."[56]

I begin by discounting the view that the South Korean work ethic was mainly a product of cultural habits. While inherited traditions may have played some role and the fact that workers were educated was of considerable consequence, the fact is that a deliberate, coercive effort of enormous proportions was deployed and redeployed continually to produce a "disciplined" work force that would work hard for low wages. Nevertheless, despite these efforts, South Korea's rulers and businessmen never succeeded in creating a fully docile work force. Against tremendous odds, South Korean workers continued through this period and beyond to protest their difficult work conditions – a testament to the human spirit.[57]

Once Park established the KCIA, the intelligence agency was early on assigned the task of reorganizing labor. One may recall that Japanese-style labor management practices were imposed in Rhee's Korea but rapidly came undone toward the end of his reign. Park set out to rebuild the system. Viewed over the period as a whole, state control of labor was a little more relaxed in the 1960s than in the 1970s, with some scope in the first decade for collective bargaining and for open labor-management conflict.

The KCIA basically set out to reproduce the rigid, top-down Japanese-style *sampo* system of labor-management relations in South Korea. The KCIA trained top labor leaders and installed them in power for the purpose of demobilizing labor politically.[58] Below the apex the system was characterized as follows: (1) Union officials were paid by the company; (2) union decisions were made without much contact with the rank and file; and (3) companies owned union furniture and utilities and generally had easy access to the union.[59] Such a formal structure allowed ready penetration and control of labor by both the state and the business elite. The aim was, of course, to keep the unions' economic activity to a minimum and to repress their political ambitions.

---

[55] While I will return to economic issues in the next section, for such an economic argument, see Rudiger Dornbusch and Yung Chul Park, "Korean Growth Policy," *Brookings Papers on Economic Activity*, no. 2 (Washington, D.C.: Brookings Institution, 1987), esp. 397–401.

[56] The quote is from Choi, *Labor and the Authoritarian State*, 175.

[57] For some case-study material, especially concerning activism of women workers under difficult circumstances, see George E. Ogle, *South Korea: Dissent within the Economic Miracle* (London: Zed, 1990), esp. 80–90. See also Fredric C. Deyo, *Beneath the Miracle: Labor Subordination in the New Asian Industrialism* (Berkeley: University of California Press, 1989).

[58] Choi, *Labor and the Authoritarian State*, 30.

[59] Ogle, *South Korea*, chap. 1.

The formal and macrocorporatist structures were buttressed by crude, firm-level intimidation by police and intelligence agents. Consider these firsthand observations of an American missionary:

[Police's] reputation for brutality comes down unchanged from their Japanese mentors.... They still retain the job of keeping labor under surveillance. Each police precinct in an industrial area has an office in charge of labor. It works in close conjunction with the management of the companies. If management reports that there is a troublemaker among its employees, an investigation is begun. The [trouble]maker, his family, friends, co-workers, neighbors, supervisor and co-unionists are visited, questions are asked and suggestions of impending catastrophe are scattered about. The police seldom work by themselves.... They enjoy full consultation with, and receive orders from, the labor department, the department of public order, the prosecutor's office and the KCIA.[60]

As one might expect, such surveillance and control were applied unevenly. Big chaebols close to the Park regime received a lot of political help in keeping unions at bay. Foreign companies in the free trade zones were similarly supervised closely. The overall level of control, moreover, was heightened in the 1970s, when the political system turned more authoritarian. The role of the KCIA thus increased in the 1970s, both in controlling labor leaders and in torturing and intimidating "troublemakers."

In the face of these structures and controls aimed at demobilizing labor politically, what methods were used to inculcate a work ethic and motivate productive labor in South Korea? The fact that the labor force was well educated certainly played a role in labor's productivity, as did the long working hours imposed by the government. Economic incentives alone would not have been a major determinant in facilitating a productive labor force. For example, wages in South Korea were influenced by politics: Every year the EPB would publish the rates at which wages next year could increase. Unable to bargain for more, the result was that throughout the Park era workers' wages grew more slowly than gains in productivity and were fairly low by international standards.[61] Though difficult to assess in any definitive way, it seems that military-like organization of the work force and nationalist mobilization played some role in the high level of productivity.

Park's Korea was a peacetime economy with a warlike mentality, especially in the workplace. Following a military style reminiscent of colonial Korea, an employee's life was closely tied to the workplace.[62] Workers in many factories wore uniforms, had short haircuts, and displayed their rank on tags.

[60] Ibid., 60.

[61] On wages lagging behind productivity, see Hart-Landsberg, *Rush to Development*, 200, table 9.4. For international comparisons, see Dornbusch and Park, "Korean Growth Policy," 401, table 10.

[62] The following comments on the "militarization" of the workplace draw on Kearney, *Warrior Worker*, esp. 8–11.

They would arrive at work early and were checked at the gates; prior to the beginning of the workday, they would march to martial music blaring from loudspeakers. Employees saluted their superiors and were subject to strict regulations and orders. Lunch was served at the factory cafeteria, which was itself organized by rank. Deviant behavior, laziness, and political dissent were not tolerated. While it may be difficult to estimate precisely the economic contribution of such an organizational form, there can be little doubt that it must have contributed to both transforming peasants into workers and, more important, rationalizing the work collective and thus maximizing the impact of a group effort.

In return, workers got job security – most factory jobs came with lifetime "contracts," if not explicitly then certainly implicitly. Additionally, the state periodically attempted to motivate the workers with nationalist exhortations. Unlike in Japan, in Korea, the idea of an "enterprise family" did not resonate. Nationalism in terms of an imminent threat to national security was, by contrast, a much more potent rallying cry. The state rather than corporations thus took the lead in ideological mobilization,[63] especially with the Factory Saemaul Movement launched by the Park regime.

Top company managers were recruited to run the Saemaul Movement in factories. Factories were divided into Saemaul teams with the aim of promoting "management rationalization programs to improve productivity." Team leaders took classes on the "spirit of the movement," especially on the threat of North Korea, the need to export for national survival, and on the need for intrafactory harmony, sacrifice, and hard work. They would then convey these ideas to workers with a "strong sense of mission." Once again, it is difficult to assess the impact of such state-led efforts. After detailed fieldwork in textile, metal, and chemical industries, one scholar concluded that the state-led Saemaul Movement contributed importantly to the creation of a "compliant, hard working labor force."[64] I have not found anything to lead me to question this conclusion. In any case, what is minimally clear is that for a period Park put together a fairly successful strategy to control labor, even if not to motivate workers to work hard for low wages. Labor control, in turn, freed Park to focus on a national development strategy with economic growth as its main goal.

II. The Cohesive-Capitalist State and Rapid Industrialization

No simple, parsimonious explanation quite explicates South Korea's phenomenal economic growth – which resulted from a confluence of circumstances and deliberate policy actions. Economists comparing numerous

---

[63] The discussion on the state's role in nationalist mobilization within factories and on the Saemaul Movement draws on Choi, *Labor and the Authoritarian State*, passim, esp. 188.

[64] Ibid., 43.

high- and- low growth cases, including South Korea, have concluded that no single factor explains varying economic performance; between 1965 and 1978, for example, one authoritative cross-national study concludes that the main underlying factors were probably "high rates of investment and favorable domestic preconditions."[65] Growth-accounting studies for South Korea itself have similarly concluded that about half of the economic growth (say, between 1963 and 1982) "resulted" from increases in factor inputs (that is, from more capital and "more work done") and the other half from improvements in factor productivity.[66] The task for a political economy study of the present type is thus to identify and analyze the building blocks of South Korea's impressive economic performance. This, in turn, is best done by focusing on such distant causal factors as the state's role in facilitating high rates of investment and labor input, on the one hand, and in allocating that investment, including toward export promotion, on the other hand. The critical role of South Korea's "Japan connection" is also an important background condition.

In retrospect it is clear that by the time Park came to power, South Korea's economy already possessed a number of favorable traits. First, a growing colonial economy with a significant industrial base, though destroyed between 1945 and 1953, had been rebuilt and was ready for further expansion. Related to this, a fairly dense entrepreneurial stratum that was used to looking to the state for help was in place, as was an educated work force with a tradition of Japanese-style controls. Third, the spread of education also yielded cadres of engineers and other technocrats. And finally, agricultural land had already been distributed in a fairly egalitarian manner and, thanks to the technology and institutions inherited from colonialism, agricultural productivity had improved steadily. Very few developing countries embarked on their quest for industrialization with such favorable conditions already in place.

---

[65] See Kemal Derns and Peter A. Petri, "The Macroeconomics of Successful Development: What are the Lessons?," in Stanley Fischer, ed., *NBER Macroeconomics Annual, 1987* (Cambridge: MIT Press, 1987), 211–54. For the inconclusiveness of "proximate variables" to explain variations in developing country growth rates, see also Dani Rodrik, "Introduction," in Rodrik, ed., *In Search of Prosperity: Analytic Narratives on Economic Growth* (Princeton, N.J.: Princeton University Press, 2003), 1–19.

[66] See Kwan-Suk Kim and Joon-Kyung Park, *Sources of Economic Growth in Korea, 1963–1982* (Seoul: Korea Development Institute, 1985), 169, table 8-1. This study builds on the work of E. Denison and uses the growth accounting method associated with his name. Subsequent studies have, by contrast, found that the role of "growth in productivity" may have been smaller. See, for example, Alwyn Young, "The Tyranny of Numbers: Confronting the Statistical Realities of the East Asian Growth Experience," *Quarterly Journal of Economics* 110, no. 3 (1995): 641–80. As both Gustav Ranis and William Branson explained to me, such discrepancy arises mainly because of how one defines the production function, and for a political economy analysis, it is pretty safe to accept the earlier rough claim that growth in both factor inputs and productivity contributed to the overall growth.

TABLE 3.1 *Savings and Investment Ratios, 1961–1980 (as percentage of GNP)*

Annual average	Private savings	Government savings	Foreign savings	Gross domestic capital formation
1961–65	6.8	0.0	8.1	14.9
1966–70	10.3	5.5	9.8	25.6
1971–75	15.5	3.7	9.1	28.3
1976–80	18.0	6.2	6.4	30.6

Source: Calculated from Bank of Korea, *National Income in Korea*, various issues.

High Rates of Investment

After consolidating power, Park Chung Hee focused his government's attention on promoting economic growth, guided more by broad instincts and preferences than by any detailed blueprint. While the general model was the Japanese-inspired state and capital collaboration, specific policies were a series of improvisations guided by a process of trial and error. We know from those who worked closely with Park at the time that he modeled his efforts at industrialization explicitly on the Meiji system.[67] But scholars of Korean policy making also note that Park and his colleagues were less ideological in style than they were "pragmatic," "improvisational," and "results oriented." Moreover, these policy makers were often surprised by how positively the economy responded to such changes as interest-rate reform or devaluation or even changed levels of investment.[68] This trial-and-error view of policy making, to which I subscribe, also underlines the earlier theoretical claim that one should not overemphasize the role of individual leaders; rather, policy trajectories reflect some synthesis of leaders' preferences and broader structural constraints.

Early in Park's rule, declining aid from the United States threatened the availability of both investment and foreign-exchange resources in South Korea. The regime responded by a concerted effort to mobilize domestic and foreign savings and to promote exports. The success in mobilizing savings and investments is evident in the figures in Table 3.1. If gross capital formation during the Rhee period averaged below 10 percent, it climbed steadily during the Park period, averaging nearly 25 percent annually over the two decades. How did the Park regime encourage such high rates of savings and investment? The answer to this question has several parts: significant increase in domestic savings, both public and private, and a significant

[67] Mark Clifford's interview with Yoo Chang Soon, who participated in drafting the first five-year plan. See Clifford, *Troubled Tiger*, 50.

[68] See, for example, Jones and Sakong, *Government, Business, and Entrepreneurship*, 46; David C. Cole and Princeton N. Lyman, *Korean Development: The Interplay of Politics and Economics* (Cambridge: Harvard University Press, 1971), 159; and Chang, *Economic Control and Political Authoritarianism*, 104.

shift in the origin and type of foreign savings, mainly from American grants-in-aid to Japanese commercial loans.

Park took the government's intent to collect taxes seriously. A series of political reforms – in 1960, 1964, 1966, and again in 1967 – was responsible for both broadening the tax base and improving tax collection.[69] The tax bureaucracy was revamped and expanded in the early 1960s, with the Office of National Taxation being established in 1966. To collect taxes, the government allocated quotas to regions, districts, and even individual tax officials. Consistent with the cohesive, disciplining nature of the new state, it used an incentive system of strict rewards and penalties. The result was that tax revenues as a percentage of GNP went up from their low point of some 7 percent in 1964 to nearly 11 percent in 1966, and averaged close to 16 percent during the rest of Park Chung Hee's reign. The share of direct taxes in overall taxes also increased, from some 34 percent during the Rhee period (already quite high by developing country standards) to some 46 percent between 1966 and 1976.

On the expenditure side of the ledger, it is important to reiterate that the South Korean state did not follow a program of austerity. It took in large amounts and it spent even more – investing in wise, long-term projects – making up the difference by borrowing. Welfare spending, however, did not increase as a share of available resources in Park's Korea. Thus, for example, health and social welfare expenditures remained at about 2 percent of the central government expenditures, and social security expenditure stayed close to 1 percent of GNP between 1966 and 1973.[70] At the same time, however, overall expenditures grew sharply, the lion's share being absorbed by defense, a growing bureaucracy, and a rapidly growing public sector.

The government's investments in public enterprises are especially noteworthy. While the overall economy during the Park era grew at an annual, average rate of some 9 percent, public enterprises grew at nearly 11 percent. Moreover, some 13 percent of the nonagricultural GDP in South Korea in 1972 originated in public sector enterprises, about the same share as in India. The key difference between South Korea and many other developing countries was, of course, that public enterprises in South Korea were generally efficient by global standards and did not become a sinkhole for public monies.[71] Why this may have been so remains an understudied question. But the following factors were probably consequential: A disciplined emphasis on economic performance may have minimized shoddy management and

[69] The discussion in this paragraph draws on several sources, including Cole and Lyman, *Korean Development*, 176–77; and Frank et al., *South Korea*, chap. 2.

[70] See Yong-Duck Jung, "Distributive Justice and Redistributive Policy in Korea," *Korean Social Science Journal* 5, no. 11 (1984): 143–62, esp. 146, table 2.

[71] See Il Sakong, "Macroeconomic Aspects of the Public Enterprise Sector," in Chong Kee Park, ed., *Macroeconomic and Industrial Development in Korea* (Seoul: Korea Development Institute, 1980), esp. 103 and 115. Also see Leroy P. Jones, *Public Enterprise and Economic Development: The Korean Case* (Seoul: Korea Development Institute, 1975).

rent seeking; after a brief start-up period, some public sector enterprises were made to compete with private enterprises; and in some very large public sector projects, such as Pohang Steel, the latest Japanese technology and management practices were adopted and periodically updated.

Domestic private savings also grew steadily in Park's Korea, though corporate savings during the Park era contributed nearly 50 percent to the overall savings and investment. The savings habits of individual households were thus also a part of the Korean story. It is best, however, to not think of these habits as a product of some cultural givens; they were rather deliberately promoted. The role of the state was thus also important. In the early years of the Park regime, an officially sanctioned increase in interest rates was associated with a jump in private savings. Should one then conclude that interest rate change was the main underlying variable? Even this conclusion is not necessarily accurate because it is difficult to disentangle the impact of renewed political stability from that of higher interest rates, especially in light of the fact that the association between high interest rates and rates of household savings in subsequent years was far from perfect. As important, therefore, were the numerous Japanese-style campaigns undertaken by Park to promote thrift and savings.[72]

With the large amount of corporate savings, the relationship of higher savings and higher economic growth was mutually reinforcing in a regime that facilitated domestic corporate investments. The regime also assured the availability of high-quality cheap labor. And finally, it provided numerous public services to support new business ventures and open new markets, especially export markets. All of this served to enhance business confidence in a profitable future and contributed to the mutual relationship between profitability, savings, and investment.

Finally, foreign savings, especially Japanese public and commercial loans, played a critical role in the high-growth "miracle." Foreign savings in the Park period averaged nearly 9 percent of the GDP per annum. Assuming a capital-output ratio of 2.5, foreign savings contributed 3 to 4 percent of the overall annual economic growth. It is no exaggeration to suggest, therefore, that minus the foreign savings, South Korea would have grown at 5 to 6 percent per annum, which would still have been high by international standards but would not have been a "miracle." How did South Korea attract such large resource inflows on a regular basis?

The substantial inflow of foreign resources into South Korea, especially Japanese public and commercial loans,[73] reflected the economic needs of

---

[72] For a good discussion, see Sheldon Garon, "The Transnational Promotion of Saving in Asia: 'Asian Values' or the 'Japanese Model'?," paper presented to the Abe Fellows Workshop on "Consumer Culture and Its Discontents," Harriman, New York, April 9–11, 2003.

[73] Besides benefiting from Japanese resources, South Korea also continued to benefit from American resources, especially during the Vietnam War. Between 1966 and 1969, for example, nearly 30 percent of South Korea's total foreign exchange earnings were derived

both Japan and Korea, as well as deliberate policy efforts, especially of the Park regime. On the Japanese side, the government and business were both keen to transfer some capital and technology overseas. By the early 1960s Japan's balance of payment was becoming favorable, and in 1965 the Bank of Japan removed important restrictions on foreign investment.[74] With domestic wages on the rise in Japan, the availability of skilled, disciplined, and cheap labor across the narrow Korea Strait was very attractive. Japanese businessmen understood Korea's potential as a platform for labor-intensive exports, following a prolonged historical record of such successful collaboration.[75] Thus Korea and not, say, the Philippines received the lion's share of Japanese monies. Moreover, as Japanese corporations moved to produce higher-value-added goods at home, they were eager to unload the technology associated with the production of lower-value-added goods. Capital, trade, and technology transfer policies thus became intertwined. It is not surprising that MITI reports from the period argued explicitly for the need to move capital overseas so as to shift low-value-added manufacturing to cheap wage countries (read South Korea) with the hope of promoting labor-intensive exports to "third" countries (read the United States).[76]

The Park regime was obviously keen to promote economic growth, by whatever strategy. Given Korean nationalism and the considerable anti-Japanese sentiment of the population, however, the regime discouraged direct foreign investment. Instead, the preferred strategy was to attract foreign loans, both public and private, and to channel them in ways that would sustain the government's commanding position in economic management. The government did this by guaranteeing overseas loans, both against default and against foreign-exchange depreciation, which also reassured Japanese corporations about moving their capital to South Korea. Within South Korea, the government created a multiple-interest-rate regime to cheapen external borrowing and to make it attractive to domestic borrowers.[77] However, the government was also likely to sanction these loans mainly for successful exporters, often the large chaebols. Investment and trade policies thus became closely intertwined in Korea as well. As a result the big chaebols grew even bigger, mostly on borrowed money. While chaebols

---

from a variety of goods and services Koreans provided to Americans in Vietnam. Since such war-related earnings were more fortuitous than systematic, they are not discussed here. For details, see Hart-Landsberg, *Rush to Development*, esp. 148.

[74] See, for example, Nakano Kenji, "Japan's Overseas Investment Patterns and FTZs," *AMPO: Japan Asia Quarterly Review* 8, no. 4, and 9, nos. 1–2 (1977): 33–50, esp. 39. See also Kiyoshi Kojima, *Japan and a New World Economic Order* (Boulder, Colo.: Westview Press, 1977), esp. chap. 1.

[75] See Woo, *Race to the Swift*, 100.

[76] See Nakano Kenji, "Japan's Overseas Investment Patterns," 40, 44.

[77] See Amsden, *Asia's Next Giant*, 74.

became a source of economic growth via exports, they also became highly indebted and hence potentially vulnerable.

The basic process of collaboration between Japan and Korea worked something like this.[78] Japanese corporations, often with past connections to Korea, would explore investment opportunities in South Korea, as well as the possibilities for working with specific South Korean firms. Having identified worthwhile projects, Japanese corporations would lobby their government for public support, often in the form of "supplier's credit" for South Korean firms that would enable those firms to purchase Japanese capital goods. On the South Korean side, both Japanese and Korean firms would lobby for loan guarantees, including bribing senior government officials to smooth the process.[79] With loan guarantees in place, commercial loans from Japan poured in; these were also "tied" in the sense that loans were for specific purposes, such as to buy industrial plants from the loan-providing zaibatsus, or business conglomerates. It was in this way, for example, that Mitsubishi, Mitsui, and C. Itoh provided more than half of Japan's total commercial loans to South Korea in the 1960s. These loans were concentrated in manufacturing, primarily in textiles and fertilizer during the 1960s and, subsequently during the 1970s, more and more in the heavier industries.

In sum, the Park regime played a critical role in mobilizing both domestic and foreign savings, and these resulting high rates of investment, in turn, contributed significantly to Korea's rapid industrialization and economic growth. But the state did not always act alone. Broadly defined public purposes had to be made to fit the private calculations of profitability before a dynamic public-private collaboration could work. Businessmen, both Korean and Japanese, thus remained major actors, especially in deciding what to produce and how to produce it. Nevertheless, the cohesive-capitalist state of South Korea was in command: collecting taxes; establishing multiple-interest-rate regimes – with high rates of interest for savers and cheaper ones for borrowers; providing loan guarantees to foreign lenders; and most important of all, facilitating the availability of the cheap, repressed, and hard-working labor that attracted ongoing investment.

Deliberate Industrialization

The Park regime intervened deliberately and systematically to channel high rates of savings into rapid industrialization. The instruments of intervention included economic planning, credit control, manipulation of the foreign trade regime, licensing of technology transfers, and control of labor and

---

[78] Among other sources, this discussion draws directly on Woo, *Race to the Swift*, esp. 87. See also Hosup Kim, "Policy-Making of Japanese Development Assistance to the Republic of Korea, 1965–1983," Ph.D. diss., University of Michigan, 1987.

[79] Chang, *Economic Control and Political Authoritarianism*, esp. 110. See also Cole and Lyman, *Korean Development*, esp. 194.

education policies. The focus below is on interventions that influenced the economy as a whole. In the next subsection I analyze the role of the government in the more specific area of export promotion.

Economic planning in Park's South Korea served mainly a "guiding" function. Jones and Sakong suggest that each five-year plan provided an "economic topographic survey" of sorts that facilitated private corporate planning and also educated economic officials, whose short-run decisions drove the economy.[80] The first two plans, especially the second one (1967–71) sought to liberalize the economy – at least, somewhat – to promote labor-intensive exports. By contrast, the third and fourth plans shifted the direction of the economy fairly sharply toward heavy industry and toward a greater degree of import substitution.

The impact of planning in South Korea is difficult to assess, however, because the plans were only one component of a much wider array of government interventions. In general, the earlier plans were less consequential. For example, close observers of the political economy noted that when the Economic and Planning Board (EPB) came out with the second plan, it essentially reinforced the direction of policies that had already been emerging from other branches of the government.[81] With a deliberate shift to heavy industry, the third and fourth plans in the 1970s may have played more of a greater guiding role, though again the evidence is mixed. The main evidence against such an interpretation is the better-known fact that the locus of economic decision making in the 1970s shifted away from the EPB and toward the economic secretariat within the President's Office.[82] Moreover, throughout the four five-year plans that roughly corresponded with the Park era, economic growth always exceeded what was projected. Economic planning in South Korea thus provided no more than a broad framework, within which government interventions of a much more specific and forceful type were regularly undertaken.

Critical short-term economic policy decisions were molded, if not made, by the powerful economic secretariat in the President's Office.[83] Economic bureaucrats and select businessmen would meet frequently within the Blue House – as often as two to three times a week – to assess the current economic situation and to take quick decisions to remove production bottlenecks and solve other problems. The main criteria for decisions was what would facilitate economic growth: If markets worked, fine, but if they did not, the government was more than willing to get involved, directly or indirectly.

---

[80] See Jones and Sakong, *Government, Business, and Entrepreneurship*, chap. 3.

[81] See Cole and Lyman, *Korean Development*, 193.

[82] See Clifford, *Troubled Tiger*, 59. See also Choi, "Structure of the Economic Policy-Making Institutions in Korea."

[83] This account of how policies were made is taken from various sources, but especially from Jones and Sakong, *Government, Business, and Entrepreneurship*, chap. 3.

According to close observers, bureaucrats vied with each other for better growth ideas, and businessmen looked to them to get a sense of what was permitted and what was not.[84] While some corruption and cronyism existed, most observers conclude that the decision making was highly effective in facilitating state-business collaboration for economic growth. Notice, however, the broader political and economic context that facilitated such "flexible" and "pragmatic" decision making: tremendous concentration of power in the executive; a clear commitment to economic growth; and close collaboration between government and business – to the exclusion of all other interest groups, especially labor.

Credit control was a powerful tool in the hands of the government to influence business activities – especially broad patterns of investment but also microbehavior at the firm level.[85] Park nationalized all the banks so as to steer the nation's economic goals. He also revived such specialized banking institutions with colonial roots as agricultural credit institutions, a bank for small industries, and, of course, the Korea Development Bank to manage foreign borrowing. According to Jung-En Woo, the bureaucrats who ran these credit institutions thought in terms of GNP and not profits.[86] Park maintained pressure on the bureaucrats to minimize corruption and to steer credit mainly to "qualified users."[87] Those who "qualified," in turn, were not only creditworthy in the narrow banking sense but also accepting of government priorities about what to produce and for whom to produce it.

The Park regime used its control over credit to accomplish a variety of goals, including export promotion. The two other goals of note are economic adjustment and, of course, broad patterns of investment. As an example of the former, cheap foreign loans led South Korea to borrow heavily and thus led to a serious debt crisis in 1971.[88] The debt service ratio rose from some 8 percent of export earnings in 1965 to 28 percent in 1971. For a solution, the government called for a moratorium on all domestic debt payments, relieving both domestic private firms and their foreign creditors. This move hurt small investors, while dramatically benefiting Korean businessmen. Such adjustments clearly could not have been made without public control of credit, not to mention without authoritarian control over potential political protest.

As to broad investment patterns, the two decades of the Park era divide neatly into two, with the 1960s dominated by labor-intensive, light consumer goods, and the 1970s, by a push toward heavy industry. Credit control was

[84] Ibid.

[85] The best political economy account of South Korea's financial system remains Woo, *Race to the Swift*. I draw on her analysis in the following two paragraphs.

[86] Ibid., 84.

[87] See Jones and Sakong, *Government, Business, and Entrepreneurship*, 109.

[88] For a fuller discussion of this episode, see Woo, *Race to the Swift*, 120.

one of a number of policy instruments the regime used to engineer this dramatic example of deliberate industrialization. The regime openly channeled cheaper credit to many industries, thus promoting their growth during the 1970s. Of course, other policy instruments were also used to promote heavy industry, as is discussed in due course.

The shift from light to heavy industry during the Park era stands as an exemplary case of deliberate industrialization. As is often the case in early stages of industrialization, textiles dominated, along with other light manufacturing. These were encouraged by a number of factors: historical patterns, cheap labor, a favorable exchange rate, and the nature of available technology, especially from Japanese firms, which often ensured that investment resources in the form of loans and technology were linked. Since this pattern of investment was broadly consistent with the factors of production readily available and was encouraged by market-approximating prices, some scholars have characterized this rapid industrialization as a market-driven phenomenon. But these marketlike tendencies prevailed, to the extent they did, mainly in the 1960s, though the overall picture was certainly more complex. For example, even textile manufacturing was politically promoted with the help of preferential loans, tax and tariff exemptions, export subsidies, wastage allowances, and other social overhead and administrative supports.[89]

The Park regime intervened much more deliberately in the 1970s, to promote such heavy industries as steel, chemicals, metals, machines, electrical goods and electronics, and shipbuilding. Known in the literature as the Heavy Chemicals and Industry (HCI) drive, the motives behind this effort were mixed. Some have suggested that the shift was stimulated by the Nixon doctrine in 1971, which implied a withdrawal of the United States from East Asia and the need for countries such as South Korea to handle their own national security. This international shift, the argument continues, led Park to worry more about "self-sufficiency" and to promote defense-related heavy industries by accelerating import substitution.[90] But the idea of the HCI was being discussed as early as 1970, predating the Nixon doctrine. Moreover the pursuit of HCI led less to self-sufficiency than to growing dependence on Japan. Others have provided a more domestic political explanation, suggesting that the more authoritarian Yushin system enabled Park to pursue his nationalism more vigorously in the economic sphere.[91] More persuasive,

[89] See, for example, Amsden, *Asia's Next Giant*, 14. For a detailed discussion of Korean textile industry, see Yung Bong Kim, "The Growth and Structural Change of Textile Industry," in Chong Kee Park, ed., *Macroeconomic and Industrial Development in Korea* (Seoul: Korea Development Institute, 1980), 185–276.

[90] See Woo, *Race to the Swift*, 120.

[91] This argument is implicit in Sohn, *Authoritarianism and Opposition in South Korea*, passim, but esp. 51 and 176.

however, is a third argument, namely, that the HCI drive was actually supported by Japan.

During the late 1960s and the early 1970s economic reports in Japan, as well as joint reports between Korea and Japan – for example, the Yatsugi Kazuo Plan in 1970 and subsequent MITI documents – argued for the transfer of certain Japanese industries to South Korea: steel, aluminum, oil and zinc refining, chemicals, plastics, electronics, and even shipbuilding.[92] The underlying rationale was the need to boost exports of capital goods and to push those pollution-generating industries offshore. These were precisely the industries that Park's HCI targeted in 1973, suggesting that Japan's prior approval and support were important for the eventual policy shift. The evidence on policy making provides further support for this view. One analyst notes that the Japanese were directly involved in Korean policy making, helping to draft both the third and the fourth five-year plans.[93] Another concludes that the HCI drive evolved with such close Korean and Japanese cooperation that "it is difficult to tell whether [it was] Korea's or Japan's."[94]

Even this line of argument needs to be qualified, however. While generally supportive, Japanese corporations were occasionally hesitant to transfer heavy industry to South Korea, concerned as they were about the possibility that Korean products could end up competing with Japanese exports. The cases of Mitsubishi and of Pohang Steel are instructive.[95] Park's efforts to build Korea's steel industry, especially with a significant public sector involvement, ran into considerable opposition from Western countries, as well as from international development institutions. Within Japan, large corporations such as Mitsubishi hesitated to get involved for reasons of economic feasibility. Park, however, pushed hard, and the Japanese government tried to persuade its corporations that such projects needed to be viewed from the larger perspective of regional security. Mitsubishi signed on. Park was so pleased that even if returns on this specific investment were not significant, he eventually gave Mitsubishi a large share of a much more lucrative project, namely, the construction of the Seoul subway system.

Central among the factors that pushed South Korea toward the HCI drive then were the state's commitment and the willingness of the Japanese to provide the necessary capital and technology. Widely considered as an

---

[92] See, for example, Kenji, "Japan's Overseas Investment Patterns," 44; and Hart-Landsberg, *Rush to Development*, 152. See also Chang, *Economic Control and Political Authoritarianism*, esp. 130–31.

[93] Hart-Landsberg, *The Rush to Development*, 152.

[94] Kenji, "Japan's Overseas Investment Patterns," 48.

[95] Among the studies of the HCI drive, see Ji Hong Kim, "Korean Industrial Policy in the 1970s: The Heavy and Chemical Industry Drive," working paper 9015 (Seoul: Korea Development Institute, 1990); and S. C. Lee, "The Heavy and Chemical Industries Promotion Plan (1973–1979)," in Lee-Jey Cho and Yoon Hyung Kim, eds., *Economic Development in the Republic of Korea: A Policy Perspective* (Honolulu: University of Hawaii Press, 1991).

audacious (and by some a foolish) move, the Park regime committed an enormous amount of public support to ensure the success of the select new industries – steel, chemicals, electronics, automobiles, and shipbuilding (hence the somewhat misleading phrase, "picking the winners"). The government protected these industries to help them get established. But these protections were timebound, the goal being to help them to graduate quickly into the ranks of successful exporters. As in earlier time periods, therefore, the strategies of import substitution and export promotion were interconnected.

Besides channeling cheap credit to these select heavy industries, the Park regime offered them various other supports as well. For example, there was no pressure for repayment, infrastructure support was given, administrative obstacles were removed, and discounted fees were applied for freight harbor use, water, electricity, and gas.[96] Moreover, a number of private corporations that were centrally involved in promoting these industries were allowed to grow into monopolies. The biggest of these corporations became general trading companies, which received further support from South Korean embassies and other public overseas organizational networks that helped them to strategize and discover new export markets.

South Korea's HCI drive was not an unqualified success. In the short run the concerted push contributed to inflation, foreign indebtedness, current account deficits, and the crowding out of light industries – problems that slowed South Korea's economic growth in the early 1980s (although growth resumed again after some macroeconomic policy adjustments). Over the longer term the HCI drive promoted industrial concentration and a more skewed income distribution. Moreover, the government's pressure on corporations to diversify led them to borrow heavily from public banks. This strategy of indebted growth served South Korea well for a while, but it also saddled this East Asian "miracle" with such longer-term structural problems as highly indebted firms and vulnerable loans.

Despite these problems, South Korea's HCI was a phenomenal success as judged by many other conventional measures of economic success. Manufacturing industries during the 1970s grew at an impressive 16 percent per annum, contributing to an annual GDP growth rate of nearly 9 percent. The government succeeded in channeling the majority of investment into HCI industries – as high as 75 percent of all manufacturing investment in some years – and the share of heavy versus light manufacturing in manufacturing as a whole shifted decisively toward the former with heavy industrial goods crossing the targeted 50 percent mark by 1983. Most impressive, in particular, was South Korea's success in exporting such products as steel, electronic goods, and even ships.

---

[96] Lee, "The Heavy and Chemical Industries Promotion Plan."

Steel provides a good example of the success of the HCI drive.[97] As noted above, Western countries, international development institutions, and even Japanese corporations were skeptical of South Korea's push into steel production, aimed mainly at the export market, as steel was already a crowded international market in the early 1970s. Park Chung Hee pressed hard, however, and eventually won over the Japanese. Taking a personal interest in the project, he assigned a loyal military technocrat with strong Japanese connections to supervise it. The result was the Pohang Iron and Steel Company (POSCO). As a public sector undertaking, POSCO was largely built with Japanese commercial loans and cutting-edge Japanese technology. Between 1972 and 1982 the annual steel-making capacity of Korea multiplied fourteenfold, and it grew into one of the world's largest and most efficient steel producers and exporters.

Some forays into heavy industry were more successful than others, and there was many a false start. For example, the petrochemical and some of the machine-building industries were not all that successful, certainly not when compared with steel. The record in electronics and shipbuilding, by contrast, was remarkable. Though the shipbuilding industry was repeatedly rescued at early stages by government interventions,[98] large chaebols such as Hyundai and Daewoo eventually succeeded, outpacing even the Japanese shipbuilders in terms of international orders by the early 1990s.

South Korea's dramatic success with heavy industries sets it apart not only from many less successful developing countries, but also from other "Asian tigers" that focused mainly on labor-intensive, light-manufacturing exports and often relied heavily on foreign direct investment. South Korea is thus a remarkable example of successful state-driven, deliberate industrialization in a developing country. Among the salient underlying factors in this success were

- a cohesive, disciplined, and competent state that prioritized economic growth and channeled substantial capital into select industries
- a historical legacy of governments and entrepreneurs working together and well attuned to capturing foreign markets
- a driven set of entrepreneurs who were willing to align their profit ambitions with publicly defined plans for national economic growth
- an educated and controlled labor force, and
- the availability of state-of-the-art technology and management from its former colonial master, Japan.

[97] I have drawn this material from a fine essay written by one of my former graduate students who now works for the World Bank. See Dolgor Solongo, "Heavy and Chemical Industry Plan of Korea, 1973–1979," manuscript, Woodrow Wilson School, Princeton University, 1995. A good case study of decisions leading to POSCO is Hosup Kim, "Policy Making of Japanese Development Assistance," chap. 4.

[98] For a good account, see Amsden, *Asia's Next Giant*, chap. 11.

Some of these factors, such as a highly committed state and the Japanese connection, were unique to South Korea; others, like high rates of investment, state-capital alliance, and an educated but controlled labor force, may be more generalizable. At a minimum, South Korea's successful HCI drive challenges simplistic claims that state intervention is always bad for economic development.

Besides generating high rates of savings and guiding investment patterns, the South Korean state also played an important role in promoting productivity growth. Some of these governmental influences were indirect and worked mainly through the price mechanism. Well-known examples of such market-enhancing governmental intervention in South Korea would include the following factors: important prices (exchange and interest rates), though "distorted," were not as distorted as in many other developing countries; protections to facilitate import substitution often tended to be timebound; and public sector enterprises often had to compete with private enterprises. As a result, resources were allocated relatively efficiently; there were marketlike competitive pressures, especially for well-established firms; and productivity was boosted.

The relationship of productivity to growth in a developing country such as South Korea was not unidirectional. Rather, as Alice Amsden has persuasively demonstrated, the relationship was mutual, constituting nearly a "closed loop" that, in turn, required a state push to maintain an upward spiral.[99] Economic growth itself helped to improve productivity in South Korea through a variety of mechanisms. High growth used up excess capacity, high rates of exports that accompanied the high growth enabled continuous import of new technology, and the very large production firms, the chaebols, generated economies of scale. Thus, the state contributed to productivity growth by facilitating technology transfers and by maintaining competitive pressures on the large chaebols.

South Korea's rapid industrialization depended heavily on Japanese technology, most of which – anything from blueprints to standard operating procedures to turnkey projects – was closely tied to commercial loans from Japan, which, in turn, were guaranteed by the South Korean government. Between 1962 and 1981, for example, nearly 60 percent of all technology licensing arrangements in Korea were with Japan.[100] Given the colonial heritage and the cultural and geographical proximity, moreover, there was a significant flow of manpower across the borders: South Korean managers, engineers, and skilled workers regularly went to Japan for training; and similarly, Japanese businessmen and consultants became a regular feature of South Korea's industrial landscape.

[99] Ibid., chap. 4.
[100] Calculated from Sakong, *Korea in the World Economy*, 276, table A.48.

The Japanese, of course, were unloading technology mainly in those industries they were looking to leave. The technology was thus often a "decade behind the frontier."[101] But when the technology was cutting-edge, as in the case of steel, the negotiations were tough and often involved Park's direct intervention. Whether cutting-edge or "a decade behind," South Korea mainly imported capital goods from Japan during these years, regularly running a trade deficit that was paid for in part by commercial loans from Japan as well as from exporting to "third countries," including the United States. So significant was South Korea's technological dependence that one analyst notes that "more than half of textile, chemical and civil engineering industries have been Japan-made,"[102] and another concludes that, over time, "the Koreans could not build or operate new plants without Japanese approval and cooperation."[103]

Technology here has to be understood not only narrowly in terms of machinery and production know-how but more broadly in terms of organization and management of production. South Korea, then, directly or indirectly, imported Japanese technical knowledge and production practices,[104] with the South Korean government intervening regularly to facilitate this technology transfer. In this way efficient Japanese technical and organizational practices became an integral part of South Korea's industrial production. Economists studying the phenomenon have concluded that these technology transfers contributed importantly to South Korea's productivity growth and industrialization.[105]

Finally, in this discussion of the state's role in productivity growth, there is the issue of industrial concentration. Given high concentration, how did the chaebols stay competitive? Part of the answer, of course, is that large size facilitated some economies of scale. For the rest, the large chaebols were constantly under political pressure to perform well, especially to meet their export quotas. While nominally private business groups, many of the large chaebols were highly indebted to government-controlled banks. A government committed to economic growth, in turn, used this power to intervene, even down to the microlevel of a firm, to monitor performance and to reward and punish firms accordingly.[106] Moreover, the chaebols often competed with each other along nonprice lines, for example, for government favors, for technical licenses from international firms, for best work force,

[101] Chang, *Economic Control and Political Authoritarianism,* 195.

[102] Ibid., 163.

[103] Chong Sik Lee, *Japan and Korea: The Political Dimension* (Stanford, Calif.: Hoover Institution Press, 1985), 66.

[104] Amsden, *Asia's Next Giant,* 234.

[105] See, for example, Howard Pack and Larry E. Westphal, "Industrial Strategy and Technological Change: Theory versus Reality," *Journal of Development Economics* 22 (1986): 87–128.

[106] See Jones and Sakong, *Government, Business and Entrepreneurship in Economic Development,* 109. See also Cho, *General Trading Company,* 8.

and over quality and delivery.[107] A cohesive state and large chaebols were thus close partners, not only in ensuring firm profits, but also, and more important from the standpoint of continuous production growth, in fostering productivity growth.

Export Promotion

South Korea's rapid industrialization was accompanied by rapid growth in exports. From this well-known association some have extrapolated that export promotion is an appropriate strategy for rapid industrialization and growth.[108] Such an analytical leap from association to causation and policy prescription is surely too simple, even misleading. The relationship of growth and exports must instead be viewed as mutual because, as noted above, production growth in South Korea itself contributed to productivity growth and thus to competitiveness of its exports. The question, then, is why did the South Korean state choose to promote exports, and, more important, how did it achieve such remarkable success?

Park Chung Hee did not start out committed to export promotion. His initial political preferences veered instead toward national self-sufficiency. The Meiji development model appealed to him at least in part because of its state-led, nationalist character. Nonetheless, while Park adopted and pursued a state-led model with a vengeance, concrete pressures eventually chipped away at his ambitions to impart economic self-sufficiency to South Korea. Over time South Korea came to be deeply integrated into the regional economy, developing considerable economic dependency on Japan, even during Park Chung Hee's own lifetime.

Committed to rapid economic growth, the Park regime faced the prospect of shrinking U.S. aid and therefore the need to find alternative foreign resources, especially foreign exchange. One could thus suggest that this was the motivation for Park's interest in exports. While not incorrect, such an argument would leave an important puzzle unresolved. When developing countries periodically faced foreign-exchange bottlenecks in the 1950s and the 1960s, a common response was not export promotion but rather import substitution. Why then did the Park regime choose to focus on export promotion?

The answer here – as with so many other questions about South Korea's economic success – has to do with South Korea's Japan connection, two aspects of which are especially noteworthy. First, Japan was not only willing but keen to invest in South Korea – to unload its "surplus" technology and capital, combine it with South Korea's cheap labor, and thus boost regional exports, mainly to the United States. As noted above, Japan's

---

[107] Amsden, *Asia's Next Giant*, chap. 5, esp. 130.
[108] See, for example, World Bank, *World Development Report* 1987 and 1991 (Washington, D.C.: Oxford University Press, 1987 and 1991, respectively), where this was a central theme.

foreign-investment-for-exports need was somewhat distinctive in comparison with other advanced industrial countries whose investors also sought foreign locales, but mainly as protected markets, not as export platforms. There was an elective affinity then between many American and European overseas investors and the import-substitution regimes that existed at the time in, say, Brazil and other Latin American countries. By contrast, as late developers themselves, Japanese companies in the 1960s and the 1970s were constantly moving up the value-added scale, creating the problem of what to do with technology and capital associated with the production of lower-value-added goods. The solution that emerged was a different pattern of elective affinity: Japanese firms would invest in those countries where the policy regime ensured cheap, competent, and disciplined labor, as well as conditions supportive of export promotion. Colonial, cultural, and geographical links made South Korea additionally attractive. Needing Japanese capital and technology for growth, therefore, it was prudent for the South Korean state to give vigorous support to an export drive.

South Korea's Japan connection influenced its export proclivities further via a second, more cognitive variable: South Korea did not share the "export pessimism" of other developing countries, such as India and Brazil, at least not to the same degree. Colonial Korea experienced considerable industrialization, including success in manufactured exports. This historical experience contrasted sharply with that of India, Nigeria, and, to an extent, Brazil, which did undergo early industrialization but remained mainly an exporter of coffee well past the Second World War. India and Nigeria emerged from colonialism believing – based at least in part on their own past – that open economies hurt indigenous industrialization and that the best route to rapid industrialization was via import substitution. Many Brazilians after the war similarly interpreted their failure to industrialize in the pre-1930 period as a result of booms and busts associated with an open economy, and they saw the modicum of industrialization in the post-1930 period as a result of de facto import substitution. The conclusion then was that state-led import substitution provided a ready path to rapid industrialization. By contrast, early success with manufactured exports and rapid industrialization in the context of an "open" imperial economy bequeathed a more complex set of lessons to the South Korean elite, providing them some confidence that they could export successfully or at least inclining them to experiment with a variety of paths. With Japan as a model, moreover, South Korean decision makers understood well that an export push did not necessarily require a fully open "liberal" economy. This was probably critical; ideological alternatives in South Korea were not limited to a laissez-faire, open economy, on the one hand, and a statist, closed economy, on the other hand. Instead, South Korea learned readily from Japan that state intervention, selective import restrictions, and an export push could be combined successfully within the framework of a cohesive-capitalist state.

Following a policy commitment to promote exports, South Korea's exports grew rapidly, even phenomenally. For example, between 1962 and 1981, the rate of export and import growth averaged some 38 percent and 27 percent per annum, respectively.[109] The role of foreign trade in the overall economy during the same years grew from some 20 percent to nearly 65 percent. During the 1960s South Korea's exports were mainly light manufactured goods. Major early exports included products of industries first established during the colonial period: textiles and garments, plywood, footwear, and tobacco products. Following the HCI drive, the export mix became more diversified to include heavy industrial goods; by 1980, for example, Korea's top five exports were textiles, electronic products, steel products, footwear, and ships. This export drive was also import-intensive: South Korea imported most of the machinery and synthetic inputs that fueled the export drive and ran a continuous trade deficit for the two decades under consideration, especially vis-à-vis Japan but also the United States. The foreign-exchange gap was, in turn, made up by various inflows of foreign resources, including commercial loans, public transfers, some direct foreign investment, and earnings from South Korea's involvement in the Vietnam War.

South Korea's export drive was helped by some fortuitous factors. Thus, for example, the circumstance-driven decision in the 1960s to push exports was followed by a period of growing global trade, a development that was not anticipated by most developing countries.[110] Moreover, the import intensity of South Korea's export drive and ready availability of foreign resources to cover the trade deficit – some of which had more to do with the cold war than with strictly economic issues – also takes some of the bloom off the "miracle." Leaving such fortuitous factors aside, however, the export boom in South Korea was in fact remarkable and systematic. How South Korea achieved this success is a subject that has received considerable scholarly scrutiny and aroused a lot of controversy.[111] What follows is a synoptic overview of this

[109] These and the other data cited in this paragraph are widely available. I have taken them from Sakong, *Korea in the World Economy*, esp. 226–34, tables A–4 to A–10.

[110] See, for example, Arthur Lewis, "The Slowing Down of the Engine of Growth," *American Economic Review* 70 (September 1980): 555–64.

[111] Prominent scholars who have suggested that export success of South Korea and of other East Asian countries was mainly a market-driven phenomena include Bela Balassa, "The Lessons of East Asian Development: An Overview," *Economic Development and Cultural Change* 36 (April 1988 supplement): 3; and Anne Kruger, *The Developmental Role of the Foreign Sector and Aid* (Cambridge: Harvard University Press, 1979). Important studies that disagree with this view and suggest instead that the state's role was as important or more important include Jones and Sakong, *Government, Business, and Entrepreneurship*; and Amsden, *Asia's Next Giant*. A recent restatement of these debates is World Bank, *The East Asian Miracle* (Oxford: Oxford University Press, 1993), and a series of critical responses to this World Bank study is Albert Fishlow et al., *Miracle or Design? Lessons from the East Asian Experience*, Overseas Development Council, Policy Essay no. 11 (Washington, D.C., 1994). A flurry of

issue that takes sides in the existing scholarly debates in a manner that is consistent with the focus of this study.

The South Korean state intervened heavily to promote exports, using both market and nonmarket tools to achieve its goals.[112] On the market side, devaluation was the main instrument. The Park regime undertook a series of devaluations in hopes of encouraging exports. As in the case of interest-rate reforms aimed at boosting savings, however, these measures did not prove to be sufficient, even if they were necessary. The timing of devaluations and of sharp increases in exports, for example, do not coincide in a manner to support the view that only devaluations boosted exports.[113] Devaluation was thus supplemented by numerous government subsidies. As noted above, these subsidies came in such various forms as cheap and ready credit, tax exemptions, infrastructure support, and discounted transportation and other costs. Dozens of such public programs existed at any given time to support the exporters.

Scholars who have quantified the impact of subsidies have concluded that the "effective exchange rate" was close to "neutral" (i.e., it did not bias the incentives to produce either for the domestic market or for exports) or, more likely, that it imparted a modest "proexport bias."[114] It is evidence of this type that lends some credibility to the promarket analyses of the South Korean export drive that suggest that trade was facilitated by a neutral trade regime. Two important qualifications are necessary, however. First, to the extent that the trade regime was neutral, it was mainly on the export side. The import side of the trade regime was, by contrast, highly regulated. Even during the more "liberal" 1960s, some 300 to 600 items were "prohibited" from being imported.[115] Whenever balance-of-payment problems emerged during the Park period – as, for example, in 1967 – the response was to promote import substitution and exports simultaneously.[116] Tariffs and other detailed import controls were created periodically and even imposed somewhat arbitrarily.[117] By contrast, imports that were necessary for exports – for example, capital goods and synthetic imports – were, if not free of all controls, certainly much easier to bring into the country. During the HCI drive of the 1970s, protection of new and targeted industries was, of course, even

---

interpretations and reinterpretations again followed the "Asian financial crisis" in the late 1990s, though South Korea's fairly rapid recovery seems to have stopped that flurry. One sensible discussion of related issues is Robert Wade, "Wheels within Wheels: Rethinking the Asian Crisis and the Asian Model," *Annual Review of Political Science* 3 (2000): 85–115.

[112] As I wind my way through this controversial terrain, I rely heavily on the balanced judgments of Jones and Sakong, *Government, Business, and Entrepreneurship.*

[113] See, for example, Amsden, *Asia's Next Giant,* esp. 67, table 3.4.

[114] For a quick review of these studies, see Pack and Westphal, "Industrial Strategy and Technological Change," esp. 93–95.

[115] See, for example, Frank et al., *Foreign Trade Regimes and Economic Development,* 45, table 4.1.

[116] Ibid., 120.

[117] See Cole and Lyman, *Korean Development,* 189.

an explicit part of the development strategy. So whatever claims one may make for South Korea's trade regime during the Park era, it was not fully neutral. A more balanced conclusion is that the Park regime intervened heavily, utilizing both market and nonmarket mechanisms to facilitate exports and to discriminate selectively against imports.

A second qualification is even more important. The question remains, given that the cumulative impact of devaluation and of subsidies was mainly to "neutralize" barriers against exports, were these financial incentives sufficient to promote exports? A balanced answer again has to be "no"; financial incentives may have been necessary, but they were not sufficient. An important piece of evidence supporting this conclusion is that the effective exchange rate for exports during the Park era was not all that different from what it had been in the Rhee period.[118] Jones and Sakong thus conclude that exchange rate and subsidies were not the whole story behind exports because "the effective direct return to exporters – was as high (or higher) in the 1950s as in the 1960s and 1970s."[119] A full explanation of the export boom during the Park period then must take into account additional nonfinancial, institutional factors.

The additional factors that need to be underlined here are those suggested all along, namely, the impact of the South Korean state and of the "Japanese connection." Committed to growth via exports, the Park regime utilized all the political and economic tools it could muster to push exports. Clear government priorities, announced via formal plans and speeches, facilitated private planning; private companies understood clearly that a variety of public supports would be forthcoming. Moreover, starting in 1967, the government began offering monopoly rights on export markets to successful exporters. Public help was further provided through an export-promotion agency, the Korea Trade Association (KDA), which operated through South Korean embassies to discover markets, to train Korean salesmen, and to provide lessons on how to prepare samples, packaged goods, and presentations and how to steer products to customers.[120]

Export promotion was managed by setting targets akin to public quotas – countries to which exports would go were targeted, as were sectors and even firms within South Korea that would meet these targets. As one scholar notes, "The export targets agreed upon between the government and individual firms were taken by businessmen as equivalent to compulsory orders."[121] Firms were scrutinized directly from the president's office. Successful exporters – even if they "succeeded" while making very little profit

---

[118] An earlier study that reached this conclusion and that in retrospect must be deemed pioneering was Frank et al., *Foreign Trade Regimes and Economic Development*, table 5–8, 70–1.

[119] Jones and Sakong, *Government, Business, and Entrepreneurship*, 92, see also table 14.

[120] See Clifford, *Troubled Tiger*, 57.

[121] See Byung-Nak Song, *The Rise of the Korean Economy* (New York: Oxford University Press, 1990), 91.

over the short run – were much more likely to receive public support and thus more likely to profit over the long run. Conversely, those who failed at exports were allowed to go bankrupt. In addition to administrative support, successful exporters were also accorded great national visibility and status: The government celebrated a national export day when the most successful firms were given prizes and treated as national heroes who were contributing to the struggle for national survival.

Many of these public supports for exporters were formally institutionalized in the mid-1970s, when the largest chaebols were accorded the formal status of general trading companies (GTCs). Modeled closely on highly successful Japanese GTCs, large Korean business houses such as Samsung, Hyundai, and Daewoo graduated into the ranks of GTCs, qualifying them for national prestige and a variety of special preferences. A "winner take all" system was thus created in which every large Korean corporation wanted to grow into a GTC. These GTCs were not only modeled on their Japanese counterparts, but also worked closely with them. The cooperation included capital and technology transfers, as well as promotion of South Korean exports. One scholar estimates that Japanese GTCs working in Korea were responsible for nearly 20 percent of South Korea's worldwide trade and nearly 30 percent of Korea's exports to Japan.[122]

Finally in this discussion of the institutional setting of Korea's trade regime, we should take note of the free trading zones (FTZs). From the mid-1960s onward the Korean government created several FTZs – such as the well-known one in Masan – to attract foreign investment, especially from Japan.[123] The idea was to combine South Korean labor with Japanese capital, technology, management, and market connections to promote exports to third countries. Besides all the subsidies discussed above, foreign investors were also lured by duty-free imports for raw materials and political help in ensuring a supply of cheap, disciplined labor. Just across the narrow Korea Strait, both direct Japanese foreign investment and commercial loans tied to technology and management poured into these exclusive territories. Already experienced exporters, Japanese corporations thus also became significant players in export promotion from the FTZs. Besides the role of the Japanese GTCs noted above, by the mid-1970s Japanese companies operating from Masan and other FTZs were responsible for nearly one-quarter of Korea's exports.[124]

Unlike the impact of exchange rates on exports, or even of financial subsidies, the influence of the institutional variables just outlined is difficult

---

[122] Chang, *Economic Control and Political Authoritarianism*, 160.
[123] See, for example, a special issue on "Free Trade Zones and Industrialization in Asia," *AMPO: Japan Asia Quarterly Review* 8, no. 4, 9, nos. 1 and 2 (1977), esp. the "Introduction" by Tsuchiya Takeo, 1–6.
[124] Ibid., 60.

to quantify. One thing is clear: The financial incentives alone do not fully explain the rapid growth of South Korean exports. To sum up, besides setting appropriate exchange rates and numerous subsidies, the Park regime mobilized all parts of the Korean government that could be of help to promote exports. Moreover, exploiting its considerable reach into the society, the Korean state cajoled its businessmen to fall in line with its export plans, while ensuring a ready supply of cheap but disciplined labor. Given their own economic and political needs, the Japanese state and corporations became willing partners in South Korea's export drive. The rapid export growth that accompanied South Korea's rapid industrialization and production growth was thus a result of deliberate state design, involving both market and non-market mechanisms.

III. Conclusion

As records of developing countries go, South Korea is a great economic success story of the twentieth century. Starting from a war-destroyed, impoverished economy in the mid-1950s, South Korea industrialized rapidly for four decades and in 1996 joined the "rich man's club," the Organization for Economic Cooperation and Development. Thanks to land reform and labor-intensive exports, income inequality in South Korea (though not wealth inequality) was also relatively modest, enabling the fruits of economic growth to be shared. When democracy was finally achieved in the 1990s, South Koreans could genuinely take pride in all that they had achieved.

The successes, however, came at a high cost. Rapid industrialization occurred within the framework of a highly authoritarian state characterized by overtones of fascism, a state that I have labeled cohesive-capitalist. Political dissent was not tolerated. Many opposing the regime were repressed, and labor was corporatized and state-controlled. Income, wealth, and power inequalities in the society also became more skewed, especially starting in the 1970s, as the government deliberately encouraged economic concentration in the hands of the big chaebols. Even the economic strategy of rapid industrialization was not without its faults. The focus on heavy industries exacerbated such problems as highly indebted chaebols, a vulnerable banking sector, and a significant dependence on foreign economic flows, especially vis-à-vis Japan. These difficult problems continued to fester, demanding solutions in subsequent periods, especially when a serious financial crisis and economic slowdown enveloped the East Asian region toward the end of the century.

When economic success comes at a serious political cost, there is no easy moral calculus available to provide a net balance. The best that one can do is to clearly recognize the costs, even underline them, while focusing on how the rapid industrialization was achieved. The explanation of the latter developed over the last three chapters has taken a long historical view of the evolving political economy. The central argument throughout has been that the character and the role of the Korean state decisively molded economic patterns on the peninsula.

At the turn of the twentieth century Japanese colonialists conquered Korea and rapidly transformed the ineffective indigenous monarchy into a modern, cohesive, disciplining state capable of generating economic growth. Following imperial needs, the colonial state intervened heavily, facilitating considerable new economic activity. As a result Korean agriculture grew steadily throughout the colonial period, including growth in productivity. From the 1930s on significant industrialization also occurred, making Korea a unique colony.

Following the Second World War, the Japanese departure and a civil war wreaked havoc on the Korean people. When the dust settled, the Rhee regime that emerged in the American-controlled South remained preoccupied with the politics of survival. The disciplining state constructed by the Japanese survived within the shell of this nominally democratic regime. Rhee, however, seldom focused on the economy. Significant American foreign aid facilitated the rapid rebuilding of the war-torn colonial economy. Given the state's lack of a focus on the economy, however, South Korean economic progress remained lackluster during this period.

By the time Park came to power, South Korea possessed a set of conditions quite favorable for rapid industrialization, especially a post–land reform productive agriculture, an industrial base, a dense entrepreneurial stratum, and an educated population. Park re-created the cohesive-capitalist state inherited from a colonial past and used it with a vengeance to push industrialization. Renewed contacts with Japan and the availability of Japanese capital and technology proved indispensable for these efforts. Within this framework, Park engineered a growth-oriented alliance of state and capital, recorporatized labor, and used economic nationalism to exhort the entire society into the service of economic advancement. South Korea's industry and exports grew at phenomenal rates, contributing to rapid economic growth. This basic state-led model of development survived Park and more or less continued throughout the 1980s. Over time some "liberalizing" reforms occurred, first in the economy, then in the polity, and then again some more in the economy. It is too early to tell whether the "new" South Korea with democracy and freer markets will also grow rapidly or not. The story told here is mainly one of illiberal politics, a state-directed economy, and rapid economic growth. The subsequent story of a more "liberal" South Korea, as well as of a potentially united Korea, will be told by others, probably a few decades from now.

TWO STEPS FORWARD, ONE STEP BACK

Brazil

Like Korea, Brazil by the end of the twentieth century was a middle-income country. Industry in Brazil had grown for much of the century, but at a pace that was often not as rapid as that of Korea. And more important, periods of growth were punctuated by periods of stagnation and even decline, especially toward the end of the century. The political underpinnings of this mixed economic record are analyzed in the next two chapters, focusing on the state's effective guidance of industrialization, as well as on the state's limitations. Among the political factors that enabled the Brazilian state to facilitate industrialization were early sovereignty, stability, rule by a narrow coalition of political and economic elite, and the relative competence and public-spiritedness of that elite. The Brazilian state thus shared some characteristics of cohesive-capitalist states and provided a secure and protected environment for capital, especially foreign capital, to make profits while generating industrial growth. Conversely, state power in Brazil was fragmented along the lines of the center versus regions and elites versus the masses; the ruling elite was not very nationalistic; and class politics occasionally emerged, forcing leaders to adopt populist economic programs. These tendencies of fragmented-multiclass states limited the capacity of the Brazilian state to mobilize domestic resources for economic development, often leaving the country dependent on foreign actors and resources for its development. As long as foreign resources were available, therefore, Brazil did well; when they dried up, Brazilian development went awry. A tight alliance between the state and foreign capital has thus been a key source of both strength and weakness in Brazil's industrial development. The patterns of state construction and early industrialization are analyzed in Chapter 4, and state-led "dependent development" is discussed in Chapter 5. Consistent with the design of the study, the more recent, neoliberal phase is not analyzed below.

4

Invited Dependency

Fragmented State and Foreign Resources in Brazil's Early Industrialization

Unlike the more extreme cases of developmental success and failure in this study, namely, South Korea and Nigeria, respectively, both Brazil and India represent mixed cases. The case of Brazil is closer to the success end of the performance continuum, at least as far as industrial growth is concerned, and at least as manifest in its middle-income status. However, Brazil's industrialization also began in the late nineteenth century. While industrial development in the twentieth century was far from steady, Brazil's industry grew for much of the period. The gains were impressive, though coupled with significant periods of slower growth and even decline, especially after 1980. At a per capita income of more than $7,000 – albeit distributed highly unevenly – Brazil at the end of the century was a middle-income country, with a diversified industrial base. It was well ahead of India, which had less than a third of Brazil's per capita income, though it was also well behind Korea with close to double its per capita income (see Table 1 above; all of these per capita income figures are at purchasing power parity adjusted). In analyzing the case of Brazil, then, the puzzle is thus not only why it has done as well as it has, but also why, despite its early start, industrial development there has been relatively crisis-prone, limiting its overall achievements.

The focus of this inquiry is on the role of the state in generating this mixed economic outcome, as a moderately effective developmental actor for much of the twentieth century, though not without important limitations. Among the political factors that enabled the Brazilian state to facilitate industrialization was a growth-oriented political leadership in a narrow ruling coalition with the economic elite. In this respect, the Brazilian state approximated a cohesive-capitalist state. It also provided a secure and protected environment for capital, especially foreign capital, to make profits while generating industrial growth.

Conversely, it took a long time before the decentralized and fragmented Brazilian polity coalesced into a semblance of a centralized, modern state. Moreover, Brazil's ruling elites often identified more with their counterparts in Europe and the United States than with the people they governed – hence their narrow conception of the "public." This reinforced the limited downward reach of the Brazilian state into its own society, as well as the state's limited commitment to enhance national sovereignty. And finally, as economic development proceeded, class politics emerged, occasionally forcing leaders to adopt populist economic programs to hold together multiclass coalitions. These tendencies toward political fragmentation and multiclass politics, in turn, limited the capacity of the Brazilian state to mobilize domestic resources for economic development. This left Brazil repeatedly dependent on foreign actors and resources, with the result that as long as foreign resources were available, Brazil did well, but when they dried up, Brazilian development went awry. A tight alliance between the state and foreign capital has thus been a key to both strength and weakness in Brazil's industrial development.

Within the frame of this argument, the chapter analyzes the related processes of state construction and industrialization in the Brazil of the first half of the twentieth century. The discussion is divided into two periods: the old republic, which lasted from 1889 to 1930, when industrialization began; and Brazil under Vargas, from 1930 to 1945, the crucible of modern Brazil. Three themes are developed in the chapter. First, some regional states within the radically decentralized polity of the old republic provided a favorable context for early industrialization, though with some important limitations. This role was both indirect and direct. Most indirectly, the regional state of São Paulo especially played a key role in supporting the coffee economy. Booming coffee incomes, in turn, helped to generate the "movement on a broad front" necessary for an industrial economy to take root: development of infrastructure, rise of demand for industrial goods, availability of capital for investment, and the growing attractiveness of the economy to foreign investors.

Less indirectly, the federal and also some regional states subsidized substantial immigration from Europe; from these ranks there emerged not only a semiskilled working class but also numerous pioneering entrepreneurs. And even more directly, the federal state supported significant protectionist tariffs, which allowed such consumer industries as textiles to flourish. Of course, the state during the old republic was not much of a national or a cohesive state at all: The sense of nation was weak; the armed forces were fragmented; there were few, if any, effective national political organizations; and the state elite aped European ideas of laissez-faire. The result was that economic dynamism was restricted to a few commodity-exporting regions, while the rest of the country languished, dominated by large, low-productivity agrarian estates.

A second theme concerns patterns of state construction in Brazil. The puzzle here is twofold. Why, despite becoming a sovereign state in the early nineteenth century, did a centralized, modern state not emerge until the

1930s? And relatedly, how and why was this centralized, modern state eventually constructed in the 1930s? As for the first question, I suggest that the failure to create a centralized, modern state was in part a political legacy of the decentralized pattern of colonial rule and in part a result of the nearly accidental manner in which sovereignty was acquired, leaving both national sentiments and political organizations fragmented. This failure was further reinforced by rule of agrarian oligarchs, whose economic interests were well served by a fragmented polity. The eventual process of constructing a modern state was mainly a political process, though, and as is often the case, it was well supported by underlying shifts in class power. Significant contributing factors were the emergence of new middle-class elements and the depression-related weakening of the power of the old coffee oligarchy in 1929. The more obvious drama of state construction, however, involved warring political factions and their armed supporters, with the highest officers of the armed forces playing a decisive role in helping to avoid a civil war, in bringing the old republic to an end, and in placing Vargas at the helm.

The final issue discussed in this chapter is the nature of the state created by Vargas and the impact of this state on industrialization. That Vargas presided over the creation of a cohesive-capitalist state of sorts, tinged with shades of fascism, and that this state inaugurated an era of more dirigiste economic development are propositions accepted by many Brazilian specialists. While repeating some of this analysis, I nonetheless suggest that Vargas's state remained fragmented and limited in important ways, especially in terms of its penetration of the vast agrarian periphery, as well as in its relatively superficial commitment to economic nationalism. Patterns of economic intervention reflected these mixed-state characteristics. On the one hand, the new state created favorable conditions for industrial development. It supported the coffee economy and related incomes, provided protection and subsidies to industrial production, and eventually involved itself directly in the production of such "national security" industries as steel. Industrial growth between 1930 and 1945 was rapid, building in part on past capacity but also responding to governmental initiatives and policies that helped to generate demand and provided a variety of supports. On the other hand, given the limitations of Vargas's state, indigenous capacity to mobilize capital or to create new technology did not improve significantly during these years. Following the Second World War Brazil thus emerged with a substantial industrial base. But it was a base also characterized by capital scarcity and outdated and overused technology, requiring the support of either the state or foreign actors for sustained development.

I. Historical Background

Although Brazil was a colony of Portugal for nearly three centuries, it has been a sovereign state since the early nineteenth century. Two historical issues demand attention: why a coherent, centralized state did not emerge throughout the nineteenth century, and why the economy, despite some successful commodity exports, remained sluggish throughout this period, characterized by limited productivity growth in agriculture and by a near absence of industry until the last decades of the century. Of course, most parts of the non-Western world that are now considered the developing world shared with Brazil limited development of a modern state and industry in the nineteenth century; that is, after all, why the non-West was left behind and remains the "developing world." But what makes the situation specially poignant for nineteenth-century Brazil is that, unlike large parts of Asia and Africa (though similar to other parts of Latin America), Brazil was a post-colonial, sovereign country in this period. Settled by European immigrants, it possessed numerous potential advantages that could have been realized through close contacts with Europe and the United States. And yet, unlike Japan or even the United States, Brazil was unable to translate these early advantages into a dynamic political economy.

Feeling pressure from Spain and other European countries, Portugal colonized Brazil mainly for political purposes.[1] Brazil at that time was neither an organized state nor rich in readily available minerals. The scarcity of manpower and materials to plunder made Brazil economically unattractive, at least initially.[2] Settling the colony was thus rather difficult, and Portugal expended few resources in establishing a state and central control. The main strategy was therefore to grant giant pieces of unexplored territory to military men or other court favorites – the so-called captaincies. The original twelve or so of them sought to attract a variety of colonists, in hopes of establishing decentralized, agriculture-based political economies; among the colonists were their personal militias, which would secure order. Indigenous Indians were devastated by their contact with the Europeans. As in the rest of the Americas, it was also devastating for the Indians here – as many as half of them may have died in the sixteenth century from disease. The primary source of labor, following the early attempts to coerce the Indians, was thus African slaves, who worked the land for subsistence and for producing exports.

The main Portuguese efforts at creating a bureaucracy or an army in Brazil occurred when other external powers threatened Portugal's hold over

---

[1] For basic details about Portuguese colonialism in Brazil, see Gilberto Freyre, *The Masters and the Slaves* (New York: Alfred A. Knopf, 1946); Leslie Bethell, ed., *The Cambridge History of Latin America* (hereafter *CHLA*), 2nd ed. (Cambridge: Cambridge University Press, 1984), vol. 1, chaps. 12 and 13, and vol. 2, pt. 3; and Celso Furtado, *The Economic Growth of Brazil: A Survey from Colonial to Modern Times* (Berkeley: University of California Press, 1963). A useful textbook-style authoritative overview that situates Brazil within the broader Latin American context is Thomas Skidmore and Peter Smith, *Modern Latin America*, 4th ed. (New York: Oxford University Press, 1997), chaps. 1, 2, and 5.

[2] See Furtado, *Economic Growth of Brazil*, 3–6.

Brazil, and even these were limited to coastal cities, where exports could be readily taxed. For the rest, the use of coercion to maintain control, though pervasive, was localized and privatized.[3] The main agents of order were local *ordinances* (militias of sorts). While the organization of these groups varied from area to area, they were often part of local power structures headed by land-controlling colonists, and served both civilian and military functions. As towns and cities grew, regional militias performed similar functions in coastal areas, though they could also support or come in conflict with local *ordinances*. By contrast, the more centralized, regular colonial army was rather rudimentary – or, in the words of one analyst, "most problematic" – reflecting the broader neglect of state construction in colonial Brazil. This army was not at all professional, made up as it was of the "dregs of society," and it "lacked respect" in the Brazilian society.[4]

Over time, commodity exports from Brazil grew, so much so that the economy of colonial Brazil came to be known as "the King's plantation."[5] During the late sixteenth and much of the seventeenth century, for example, Brazil experienced a sugar export boom, centered mainly in the northeast, especially in the state of Pernambuca. The production and marketing problems were resolved not so much by the Portuguese colonial state as by Flemish capital and technology and African slaves.[6] Local Portuguese colonists, of course, benefited handsomely, but their incomes – spent mainly on imports – also declined when the Dutch started exporting sugar from the Caribbean. Brazil, losing its monopoly and watching prices decline, was in no position to counter these powerful market trends. Gold was discovered in Minas Gerais ("general mines") in 1690s, and as a result this southern region and a few others again benefited through the first half of the eighteenth century.[7] Once again, however, as gold mining declined in the late eighteenth century, the old boom-and-bust pattern of an uncontrolled commodity export economy repeated itself, leaving Brazil in the lurch.

As long as the boom in commodity exports lasted, taxes on exports – readily collected in port cities – were an important source of revenue for the Portuguese monarchy. Given Brazil's growing economic importance for Portugal, one might have expected a greater effort to create a modern state machinery within Brazil. This was not the case, however. Such efforts as were made to increase central authority in the eighteenth century were

---

[3] See, for example, Robert Hayes, *The Armed Nation: The Brazilian Corporate Mystique* (Tempe: Center for Latin American Studies, Arizona State University, 1989), chap. 1.

[4] Ibid., 33.

[5] See Skidmore and Smith, *Modern Latin America*, 25.

[6] This information on the sugar-exporting economy is drawn from Furtado, *Economic Growth of Brazil*, chaps. 2–6. For details, see also Stuart B. Schwartz, "Colonial Brazil, c. 1580–1750: Plantations and Peripheries," in Bethell, *CHLA*, vol. 2, chap. 12.

[7] For details, see A. J. R. Russell-Wood, "Colonial Brazil: The Gold Cycle, c. 1690–c. 1750," in Bethell, *CHLA*, vol. 2, chap. 14.

feeble and produced only modest results. Underlying this approach was the fact that the localized, personalistic political economies worked fine from the standpoint of facilitating commodity exports. Portugal would have had to make a significant political and economic commitment to impose a new centralized order on this working arrangement, a commitment for which it had neither the incentives nor the capacity. Portugal was, after all, a small, preindustrial European state at this time, a laggard within Europe and governed by a traditional monarch. Modernizing reforms for its giant colony of Brazil were simply not in the cards.

The governmental apparatus within Brazil therefore remained rather rudimentary throughout the colonial period with public power often subordinated to private power. At the apex of the colonial administration were representatives of Portugal, often soldiers or lawyers by training. Though probably quite professional, their powers were circumscribed: Not only was the writ of the government limited to coastal cities, but the governors of captaincies reported directly to Lisbon. Below the apex, much of the countryside was governed quite autonomously by landowning militia officers, and towns and cities were governed by municipal governments. Attempts to create a centralized armed force – often with the help of foreign military officers – encountered the reality of armed militias throughout the country. And whatever royal presence existed in parts of Brazil was also further co-opted by colonists for their own use. Hence the colonial government was "often ineffective, sometimes oppressive, and usually corrupt."[8]

Brazil at the turn of the nineteenth century was thus a peculiar political economy, a settler colony of sorts, inhabited by some three and a half to four million people total, less than a fifth of whom were indigenous and about half of whom were African slaves. Power and wealth were highly concentrated in the hands of a relatively small but dispersed European elite, which traced its origins mainly to Portugal. Some had arrived several generations back, others were of more recent vintage. Besides subsistence production, the main economic activity was commodity production for exports; resulting incomes were spent either on imported consumer goods or on export-producing investments such as buying slaves, acquiring lands, and maintaining private government.[9] The reach of the colonial central government, being quite limited, did little else but provide a framework for a slave economy and collect taxes on export incomes. The lives of most people were therefore governed by local elites, who wielded combined economic, military, and political powers.

When pressed by intra-European conflicts in the early nineteenth century, the Portuguese emperor moved his court to Brazil under British protection.

---

[8] See Schwartz, "Colonial Brazil, c. 1580–c. 1750," 498.

[9] As a qualification, it should be added that in the case of sugar exports, processing of sugar could also require considerable investment in establishing processing plants.

As local elites – whether planters born in Brazil or Portuguese-born merchants and government appointees – seldom viewed colonial government as an alien imposition, the emperor was welcomed and eventually even stayed at the request of Brazilian elites, in particular, those of the capital city. With an independent monarchy declared in 1822, Brazilian independence was nearly accidental and occurred considerably more peacefully than in Spanish America. At the same time, however, the "swift" and "painless" process of gaining sovereignty implied that "the nation came into existence without any need to define itself."[10] Independence in Brazil thus implied considerable political continuity with its past. Except for the Portuguese court moving to Brazil, neither Brazil's dominant political ideas – a weak sense of national purpose – nor its political structures – especially, the prevalence of limited central control – underwent any significant shift during the process.

Brazil was formally a sovereign country with an imperial government for much of the nineteenth century.[11] The beginning of a coffee economy in São Paulo in the second half of the century and the emergence of a sizable but frustrated military, especially following the war with Paraguay (1865–70), were the key factors that eventually pushed aside the monarchy in 1889, also helping to end slavery and to establish a radically decentralized republic, the old republic (1889–1930). The fact that the monarchy was unable to accommodate fairly minimal economic and political changes underlined its relative fragility: It provided a semblance of central government, as well as a framework of relative peace and stability in its heyday, especially the 1850s and the 1860s, but it did not govern Brazil effectively. In the words of one scholar: "The emperor might rule in Rio de Janeiro . . . but for the *fazendeiro* and his dependents on his estate, often weeks away from the capital, politics remained essentially a local issue."[12] Such power as the monarch exercised was, moreover, rather constrained: "The oligarchies, not the emperor, ruled the country."[13] The imperial governments also presided over a fairly sluggish economy in Brazil during much of the nineteenth century.

After independence the monarch sought to centralize power, but the effort backfired. While the monarchy may have been welcomed as a source of legitimacy by a faction-ridden, highly elitist political class, encroachments

[10] See Bradford E. Burns, *Nationalism in Brazil: A Historical Survey* (New York: Praeger, 1968), 30.

[11] Among the sources that I consulted for an understanding of the political situation in nineteenth-century Brazil were Bethell, *CHLA*, vol. 3, section on Brazil, and vol. 5, chap. 20; Bradford E. Burns, *A History of Brazil*, 2nd ed. (New York: Columbia University Press, 1980); and Gilberto Freyre, *The Mansions and the Shanties: The Making of Modern Brazil* (New York: Alfred A. Knopf, 1963).

[12] See Peter Flynn, *Brazil: A Political Analysis* (Boulder, Colo.: Westview Press, 1979), 8.

[13] See Emilia Viotti Da Costa, "Brazil: The Age of Reform, 1870–1899," in Bethell, *CHLA*, 5: 736.

on local power and privilege were not. A variety of regions asserted their rights of self-determination, especially economic rights, and the state of Pernambuca went so far as to declare sovereignty. The emperor crushed such revolts, mainly with the help of British and French troops. These power struggles underlined both the monarchy's considerable dependence on European powers, especially on Britain, and the continued significance of a number of regions as the real locus of power. It was local rural bosses – as part of the system of *coronelismo* – who were simultaneously landowners, patrons, and agents of coercion and order, who exercised power in those areas. As nominal elections were introduced to a highly restricted electorate, these rural bosses also delivered votes to the regional overlords who, in turn, exercised considerable power, even in Rio de Janeiro.

Regional representatives in Rio and the monarchy butted heads often. Some of the conflicts were mainly about political turf, but over time numerous policy disagreements also emerged. For example, when the monarchy needed to raise taxes to run the state, the landowning elites successfully resisted the encroachments. When the monarchy raised tariffs instead as a source of public revenue, landowning elites – many of whom were involved in international trade – and importing merchants protested but more or less accepted these as a lesser evil than direct taxation. Over time, especially by 1850 or so, some balance of power emerged and a fairly constrained monarchy – constrained by its dependency on external powers such as Britain and by various regional and local economic elites – settled down to rule. Brazilian historiography generally considers the 1850s and the 1860s to be the monarchy's "golden years," which were then gradually undermined by emerging changes in the export economy and in the army.

For much of the nineteenth century the Brazilian state was committed to the ideology of laissez-faire. From a comparative standpoint, this is somewhat of a puzzle: Why should a sovereign state, presiding over an agrarian economy in the nineteenth century, choose not to promote industry? Not only do such late state-led developers as Germany or Japan present sharply contrasting cases, but even the free-market United States in this period was using tariffs to promote the Hamiltonian vision of an "industrial empire." Why not Brazil? The puzzle is less of a puzzle, however, if we focus on the highly constrained nature of the Brazilian state. Though formally sovereign, Brazil had no national political class at its helm. Instead, power was fragmented among various actors, none of whom privileged a modernizing, industrializing Brazil. And the monarchy, a foreign import, preferred until the end to appoint Portuguese-born men to senior military and bureaucratic positions. The monarch's dependency on Britain, moreover, was translated into economic privileges for the latter, so much so that Britain enjoyed very low tariffs and its manufactured goods dominated the Brazilian market during the period. Powerful Brazilian elites also championed laissez-faire, reflecting an early lack of confidence and an absence of national assertiveness that has continued to cast a long shadow on how Brazil is ruled. Brazilian elites were never willing to join hands with the masses and carve out a real national polity. More important, laissez-faire was consistent with the narrow, short-term economic interests of the powerful: Agrarian elites were exporters and preferred an open trading system, and urban merchants were mainly importers who preferred cheap manufactured goods.

Two developments in the second half of the nineteenth century eventually helped to topple this monarchial system: changes in the armed forces and the emergence of a coffee economy. A border war with Paraguay forced the monarchy and other powerful elites to cooperate in order to rapidly build up the army, which grew from some 16,000 men in 1863 to 36,000 in 1865.[14] From 1850 the officer corps, though remaining racially white, became more merit-oriented. As the rank and file became increasingly nonwhite, however, officer corps came in contact with broader elements of the society. The military officers were also more "positivistic" in ideology, drawing inspiration from the French thinker Auguste Comte and emphasizing science and technology as the basis for progress. Both in their social dealings and in their ideas, then, military officers were at odds with the much more traditional monarchy and its supporters. During the war with Paraguay, moreover, the landed elite often chose not to fight and thus came to be viewed by the military as unpatriotic. And finally, following the war, the monarchy again reduced the army (for example, to 19,000 men in 1871), creating a sense of alienation among officers who came to feel that they had gotten a raw deal. The military increasingly sided with the emerging coffee-based "republicans" and eventually withdrew its support from the monarchy.

The other critical area of change was the shifting nature of the commodity-exporting economy. While sugar exports regained growth early in the nineteenth century and rubber exports boomed in the early twentieth century, the locus of the exporting economy increasingly shifted away from the Northeast to the South. The gold cycle of Minas has already been noted. Starting around the mid-nineteenth century coffee exports started increasing, first around Rio and then from São Paulo. While the real drama of coffee was still to come – after 1890 – the growth of coffee exports set in motion a broad set of changes that would be politically consequential, most obviously in the growing political power of an economically dynamic region such as São Paulo. Also significant was the need for labor generated by the new coffee economy. It being rather late in history for a fresh infusion of slaves, coffee growers preferred and encouraged immigration from Europe, spelling an end to the slave economy, the locus of which was the northeast. Less obvious changes included ideological changes, such as the growing preference for a "modern" republic among the more monied and such middle-class elements as the lawyers and intellectuals of São Paulo.

The power of the monarchy, which rested on a slave-based, sugar-exporting economy of the northeast, was undercut by the coffee oligarchs of

[14] These details on the army in this period are from Hayes, *Armed Nation*, 53.

São Paulo. The old system finally collapsed when the army shifted its support away from the monarchy and toward the "republicans." The fall of Brazil's monarchy was almost an anticlimax, as the monarch and his entourage quietly sailed off for Portugal without struggle.

What had been the impact of this monarchial state on the nineteenth-century economy? Most generally, one can say that this poorly constructed state was neither willing to make significant economic interventions nor capable of doing so. As a result, despite numerous market led booms and busts of commodity exports, nineteenth-century Brazil experienced very little productivity growth in agriculture and nearly no industrial development until very late in the century.

Revisionist accounts of Brazil's economic history have established that Brazil's economy indeed did not grow in the second half of the nineteenth century.[15] On the contrary, "Brazil experienced only a relatively modest increase in per capita income between 1822 and 1913."[16] Why? The more proximate causal variables can be conveniently thought of in terms of demand and supply-side obstacles. On the demand side, Furtado's classic analysis still rings true: A slave economy did not readily generate money demand for mass goods, and elite incomes quickly became a part of an international economic stream insofar as they were spent on acquiring either slaves or imported consumer goods.[17] These demand constraints must have been significant because, when industrialization eventually began in the late nineteenth century, a significant underlying change was precisely the growing demand for mass goods by recently immigrated free labor. Beyond the structure of demand, however, as Leff emphasizes, supply constraints were also significant.[18] Persistent inflationary tendencies underlined that the supply response was not always forthcoming; both capital and technology were scarce.

Since handsome profits were being made during export booms, why were these not invested in anything but acquisition of more land and slaves? The simple answer is that, assuming export demand, such extensive growth was hugely profitable. Additionally, however, the possibility of making profits elsewhere was limited, especially because the state was not doing its job: "An inelastic supply of high return investment projects, perhaps due to an absence of social overhead capital and publicly supplied externalities, lay at

[15] Celso Furtado had originally claimed that per capita income in the second half of the nineteenth century grew at some 1.5 percent per annum. See Furtado, *Economic Growth of Brazil*, chap. 25, esp. 163. The revisionist account to which I refer and from which I draw heavily in this discussion is Nathaniel H. Leff, *Underdevelopment and Development in Brazil*, vol. 1: *Economic Structure and Change, 1822–1947* (London: George Allen and Unwin, 1982); and idem, *Underdevelopment and Development in Brazil*, vol. 2: *Reassessing the Obstacles to Economic Development* (London: George Allen and Unwin, 1982).

[16] Leff, *Underdevelopment and Development in Brazil*, 1: 38.

[17] See Furtado, *Economic Growth of Brazil*, pts. 2, 3, 4.

[18] See Leff, *Underdevelopment and Development in Brazil*, vol. 1, chap. 4.

the heart of Brazil's low aggregate rate of accumulation during most of the nineteenth century."[19] In principle, the state could have readily invested in infrastructure and in other supportive areas, but, as already noted, it was neither willing nor capable in that regard. This was a hands-off state, not interested in deliberate development. The state's financial resources were also meager, as public authorities were not capable of directly taxing elite incomes. Such limited public revenues as there were – mostly collected by taxing foreign trade – were spent primarily on supporting a minimal army and bureaucracy, as well as on paying off foreign debt.[20]

The level of technology in nineteenth-century Brazilian society was also very low. The aristocratic values of the elite placed a premium on acquiring nontechnical educational skills, especially legal training. As a matter of fact, it was the attachment of new middle-class elements, especially in the military, to a more positivistic world-view that further undermined the legitimacy of traditional classes to rule. The levels of mass education were also dismal. For example, in contrast to some 40 percent of the population of Japan enrolled in primary education about 1868, only 1 percent of Brazil's population was so enrolled in 1857, and 3 percent in 1907. Brazil was of course a slave society. At the same time, however, illiteracy was quite widespread even among the free population; for example, in 1887 four out of five free Brazilians remained illiterate.[21] Without engineers, skilled manpower, or an educated work force, this society was not readily capable of absorbing technology and responding quickly to new demand, even if it wanted to – which it did not.

The result of all this is that both agriculture and industry languished in nineteenth-century Brazil. Agriculture remained stagnant because of low levels of technology, poor transportation, and a highly skewed, inefficient land-tenure system. On the industry side, low levels of technology were also a problem. Although capital could have been mobilized for industrial investment – while buying technology from elsewhere – that would have required protection and a variety of public supports. Those, however, were mostly not forthcoming. It is thus hard not to agree with Leff's conclusion that, among the factors that acted as obstacles to growth in the nineteenth century, "the country's politics were of paramount importance."[22] An ineffective state and a sluggish economy went hand in hand.

II. The Old Republic (1889–1930)

Industrial growth in Brazil picked up in the late nineteenth century and grew at an average rate of some 5 percent per annum for the next three

---

[19] Ibid., 137.
[20] See Leff, *Underdevelopment and Development in Brazil*, 2: 107, table 5.2.
[21] This data are from ibid., 1: 19.
[22] See ibid., 2: 131.

decades, picking up steam again in the 1930s and growing at an average rate of 9 percent per annum between 1930 and 1947.[23] By the end of the Second World War, more than 20 percent of Brazil's national product originated in industry, a level close to that of Korea just prior to the abrupt departure of the Japanese but much higher than in most developing countries around midcentury, including India and Nigeria. The role of state intervention in molding the rate and pattern of industrialization during old republic Brazil is analyzed in this section.

The Old Republican State

The politics of the old republican state is often described in Brazilian historiography as "politics of governors," suggesting that real power lay not with the central government but with the regional governors, especially those of the three powerful southern states of São Paulo, Minas Gerais, and Rio Grande do Sul. Below the governors, the majority of politically disenfranchised citizens lived in rural areas, their political lives controlled by a variety of bosses. The institution of *coronelismo* discussed above did not undergo any dramatic changes. While this view is more or less accurate, it calls for some qualification, in that the central government was not as feeble and ineffective as is often suggested.

This political economy analysis of the old republic state begins with the question of why it was relatively decentralized. The answer has two related components. First, there were no national-level political organizations, except possibly the military, that could wield effective power. But even the military, which had played a central role in toppling the monarchy, was not unified enough to take the lead in constructing the new state: It was divided politically between the army and the navy, and the army itself was factionalized along personalistic lines, as well as along the lines of more or less apolitical officers.[24] The size of the central military was also not huge in comparison with the various local and regional armed militias found throughout the country. And second, in the absence of viable national political organizations, power naturally devolved to the wealthier and politically better organized regions. São Paulo was increasingly the most dynamic coffee-exporting region, Minas Gerais was the center of cattle breeding and of a variety of other commodity exports, and Rio Grande do Sul was politically mobilized. Together these three states were also home to nearly half of the eligible voters (under 14 percent of the total population) of the republic; São Paulo and Minas Gerais – in that order – basically steered the old republican state.

The constitution of 1891 gave enormous powers to the regional states, including the power to tax exports, raise loans abroad, and raise local armies.

---

[23] The figures are from ibid., 1: 165–68.
[24] See, for example, Flynn, *Brazil*, 28–34.

States such as São Paulo used this power to keep most economic profits within the state for the benefit of Paulista elites. By the end of the old republic in 1930, for example, the per capita income of the three southern states was nearly three times the national average.[25] At the same time the central state was relatively weak. Not only was there no centralized army, but the central state had almost no political and bureaucratic capacity to collect direct taxes. In 1928, for example, only 3 percent of the national budget originated in income tax, whereas 42 percent of it was derived from taxing imports.[26]

This is not to say the central state was irrelevant.[27] First, this was a sovereign state that took numerous economically consequential decisions, such as setting tariff policies. Second, because controlling the central state was not easy, the important constituent units put enormous political energy into ensuring this control. Third, the threat of actual armed intervention by the central state is what kept the Brazilian political unit together, even facilitating a modicum of political stability. And finally, federal spending increased at a rate of 5 percent per annum through the life of the old republic; at its peak, federal spending in the old republic averaged nearly 11 percent of the GDP, which is about the same as during Vargas's first term in power.[28]

The old republic was described by Cardoso and Faletto in their classic formulation as mainly a "system of local alliances" under the domination of agrarian oligarchs, especially "the agro-exporting capitalists of the center-south."[29] Subsequent research has suggested that although this view is more right than not, it requires qualification. Coffee exports were central to the economy of the old republic, and coffee planters and exporters indeed wielded enormous political power in the old republic, especially in states such as São Paulo. In fact, the old republic comes fairly close to a classic Marxist view of government as an "executive committee of the ruling class." But even here there is doubt whether agroexporters were truly hegemonic. First, they were not very well organized politically; what passed for political parties were little more than a collection of personalistic machines. Second, from the very beginning of the old republic, the agrarian oligarchs had to take account of the military's preferences in politics. Third, those who controlled the governmental machine exhibited some political autonomy, even within the state of São Paulo.[30] And finally, over time, there emerged

[25] See Steven Topik, *The Political Economy of the Brazilian State, 1889–1930* (Austin: University of Texas Press, 1987), 16.

[26] Flynn, *Brazil*, 34.

[27] For this discussion, I draw on Topik, *Political Economy of the Brazilian State*, passim.

[28] Ibid., 20.

[29] Fernando Henrique Cardoso and Enzo Faletto, *Dependency and Development in Latin America* (Berkeley: University of California Press, 1979), 91.

[30] Mauricio A. Font, *Coffee, Contention and Change in the Making of Modern Brazil* (Cambridge, Mass.: Basil Blackwell, 1990), esp. chap. 3.

a number of other politically significant groups having their own preferences. By the 1920s, for example, small and medium farmers, industrialists,
workers, and a variety of middle-class elements had pluralized the politically
relevant class scene, paving the way for significant political changes toward
the end of the decade.[31]

As to the ruling ideas of the old republic, laissez-faire was the dominant
ideology, the sense of nationalism remained weak, and just below the veneer of liberalism, emerging elites increasingly embraced positivism. It is
doubtful, however, that this commitment to laissez-faire and nonintervention, adopted from other Western powers, truly served the material interests
of the ruling classes. Thus, for example, coffee exporters repeatedly needed
state intervention to maintain their incomes. And over time political practice
and prevailing ideological commitments were so much in conflict that they
eventually contributed to the crisis of the old republic.[32] Of course, commitment to laissez-faire was also consistent with the desire of agro-exporting
elites to keep the central state weak. These elites were not very nationalistic at
all, preferring instead to preside over their local wealth and to manage their
regions. They viewed Europe and the United States as their recreational and
cultural areas.[33]

Whatever nationalism began to emerge was mainly a product of the new
middle classes, including the intelligentsia and elements in the military.
A burst of nationalism that followed the First World War was related in
particular to the centenary of independence, and its content was of the
romantic sort: idealization of Brazilian Indians, or a search for the Brazilian
soul. Economic nationalism and related demands for state intervention were
not prominent at the time,[34] but the few that were beginning to emerge
were rooted in the growing embrace of positivist ideas. Also European in
origin, though more French than Anglo-American, positivism stressed the
role of science in progress and was consistent with a conservative, statist, and
technocratic economic leadership. One analyst goes so far as to suggest that
emerging industrialists and the political elite shared the positivist motto of
"order and progress."[35]

The core of the central state – the armed forces and the bureaucracy –
operated within the broad political context just described. As already noted,
the military's political importance increased in the late nineteenth century,

---

[31] Ibid., passim.
[32] For such an analysis, see Topik, *Political Economy of the Brazilian State*, esp. introduction.
[33] See Bradford E. Burns, *Nationalism in Brazil: A Historical Survey* (New York: Praeger, 1968),
   chap. 3.
[34] Ibid., 69.
[35] See Stanley Stein, *The Brazilian Cotton Manufacture: Textile Enterprise in an Underdeveloped Area,
   1850–1950* (Cambridge: Harvard University Press, 1957), 94. For a brief but useful summary
   of the content of positivist ideology, see William P. Glade, *The Latin American Economies: A
   Study of Their Institutional Evolution* (Van Nostrand, N.Y.: American Book, 1969), 232–36.

especially from 1887, when the Military Club was formed and provided officers a platform for their views.[36] After contributing to the toppling of the monarchy, however, the army took a back seat in politics, at least until the First World War. For one thing, the military suffered from internal disunity. Moreover, oligarchic rulers maintained some control over the armed forces by promoting those who demonstrated their loyalty. The central leadership also used the military to intervene in the affairs of most states during the life of the old republic – except, of course, in the three powerful southern states. These pretty well controlled the central state itself.[37]

As wars often are, the First World War was catalyst for change in the nature of the armed force and its political role. For starters, the number of men in arms doubled from some 20,000 in 1910 to 43,000 in 1920.[38] The movement to professionalize the army also picked up speed. First Russian and then French military officers were used to train the Brazilian military. These developments made emerging officers more politically conscious. Following the war, attempts were made to subordinate the national guard and various militias under the control of the federal army. While a truly centralized army did not emerge until later, the beginnings lay here. Military ideology was also increasingly more nationalist, centralizing, and interventionist than that of the ruling elite. While military preferences were far from decisive politically at this stage, the direction of the military's influence is noteworthy. Younger officers – the *tenentes*, or lieutenants – were increasingly at odds with the old guard, including their own senior officers. During the 1920s these junior officers staged several unsuccessful revolts against the old republic and won considerable sympathy from the middle classes and other urban critics of the old republic. Here then was the emerging coalition of the army and urban classes that would eventually help to topple the old republic and bring Vargas to power.

Developments in the civilian bureaucracy of the old republic occurred along two tracks, a more professional and competent track at the apex of the federal government and in the governments of some of the more developed states, but with a second track characterized by a vast understructure of inefficiency, nepotism, and corruption in much of the formal bureaucracy, as well as in the less formal local ruling structures at the political periphery.[39] Fueled by a growing economy and growing public resources, the size of the

---

[36] See, for example, Robert E. Hayes, "The Military Club and National Politics in Brazil," in Henry H. Keith and Robert A. Hayes, eds., *Perspectives on Armed Politics in Brazil* (Tempe: Center for Latin American Studies, Arizona State University, 1976), 139–76.

[37] See Henry H. Keith, "Armed Federal Interventions in the States during the Old Republic," in Keith and Hayes, eds., *Perspectives on Armed Politics*, 51–77.

[38] See Hayes, *Armed Nation*, 123.

[39] For one such discussion of the historical development of Brazilian bureaucracy along two tracks, see Robert T. Daland, *Exploring Brazilian Bureaucracy: Performance and Pathology* (Washington, D.C.: University Press of America, 1981), chap. 2.

bureaucracy during the old republic grew considerably, with the number of employees increasing by some 25 percent between 1890 and 1930.[40] By 1930 the federal government employed nearly 150,000 bureaucrats in a country of some 35 million people. Most of these were blue-collar workers, and even among the more senior civil servants, "there was no civil service examination or institutionalized career pattern."[41] Nevertheless, senior civil servants were relatively "professional"; while they generally gained "positions of power because of whom they knew, what they knew was also important." Unlike in Nigeria, this bureaucracy may have been patrimonial but it was not incompetent. Moreover, "The highest echelons of administration were concerned with carrying out their duties professionally and efficiently. Reasons of state appealed to them as much as the desires of their civil protectors. . . . In Rio bureaucrats came to recognize . . . a federal ethos . . . and to defend national interest."[42] A similar public-spiritedness and competence also characterized the highest echelons of the state bureaucracy of São Paulo. The level of professionalism and skill in the highest bureaucracy, in turn, contributed to a modest degree of effectiveness in the state's economic interventions.

Finally, given the highly decentralized nature of the old republican state, it may be useful to describe briefly the nature of politics in at least the most important constituent unit of the federation, namely, São Paulo.[43] São Paulo during the old republic grew rapidly in terms of population (including a large inflow of European immigrants), coffee exports, and eventually even industry, to emerge as the federation's most economically dynamic and politically significant state. While a fair amount of the economic dynamism was rooted in international market conditions, the role of state-level politics in stimulating and sustaining economic dynamism was not insignificant. The driving force behind the state's politics was clearly coffee. Coffee interests lobbied for the early involvement of the state in building railroads and in subsidizing European immigration of labor from Europe. They also repeatedly argued for public support for coffee exports. Nevertheless, coffee interests never fully controlled state politics and felt especially threatened in the

---

[40] See Topik, *Political Economy of the Brazilian State*, 21.
[41] Ibid., 23.
[42] Ibid., 24.
[43] São Paulo's political and economic significance is reflected in the fact that, even in the English language, there exist three good book-length studies of the state's political economy in this early period. See Warren Dean, *The Industrialization of São Paulo, 1880–1945* (Austin: University of Texas Press, 1969); Joseph L. Love, *São Paulo in the Brazilian Federation* (Stanford, Calif.: Stanford University Press, 1980); and Font, *Coffee, Contention and Change.* Comparison volumes on other important states include John D. Wirth, *Minas Gerais in the Brazilian Federation, 1889–1937* (Stanford, Calif.: Stanford University Press, 1977); and Robert M. Levine, *Pernambuco in the Brazilian Federation, 1889–1937* (Stanford, Calif.: Stanford University Press, 1978).

1920s, when a variety of other economic interests, especially smaller farmers and industrialists, emerged as politically significant within São Paulo.[44]

São Paulo's state government was run by a single party (Partido Republicano Paulista, or PRP) from 1892 to 1930. While the 1920s were politically turbulent within the state, when compared with other Brazilian states, São Paulo was relatively stable for much of the life of the old republic. Flush with coffee money, public authorities created their own "army" – the Forca Publica – of some seven thousand armed men, trained and equipped by the French. This army maintained order within the state and enhanced the state's political standing within the federation. The political elite of the state were relatively homogenous. Love's detailed study of 263 elites led him to conclude that they were well educated (90 percent had university degrees, mostly in law), were of Portuguese background (underlining the limited inroads that other immigrants made into the state's politics), embraced European values, were often interconnected, and had an "elaborate network of foreign ties."[45] While these political elites were clearly tied to coffee interests, Font adds that "over time, important politicians appeared to have embraced an economic philosophy different from that of the established large coffee estate."[46] Whereas coffee interests continued to embrace their increasingly strained commitment to laissez-faire, many of the region's political elites were growing more concerned about what was good for the regional economy as a whole and did not shy away from intervening and pursuing with "impunity" objectives that were at variance with those of "mobilized Big Coffee."[47] State-level bureaucrats, moreover, were quite competent and public-spirited, at least in the sense of not being only personalistic, though their conception of the "public" remained limited to fellow Paulista elites. Elements of a more cohesive-capitalist state thus came to characterize the politics of at least one significant region of Brazil.

To sum up, the old republican state in Brazil, viewed as a developmental actor, was a paradoxical formation. On the one hand, it was sovereign, relatively stable, manned by moderately competetent bureaucrats at the apex of both the federal and the more significant regional governments; and power within it was heavily concentrated in a narrow political and economic elite. These characteristics facilitated some significant economic state interventions that eventually helped to begin the process of industrialization. On the other hand, the old republican state was not much of a state. State power was fragmented regionally, the national horizons of the ruling elite were limited, and the central government, including the central army, remained feeble actors. The majority of the population, which remained politically

---

[44] This argument is developed in detail in Font, *Coffee, Contention and Change*, passim.
[45] See Love, *São Paulo*, 138–52.
[46] Font, *Coffee, Contention and Change*, 30.
[47] Ibid., 77.

disenfranchised, found itself mired in a variety of personalistic, patron-client political structures. With such limited developmental ambitions and capacities, the central state accomplished little in terms of the rate and pattern of early industrialization.

State Intervention in the Economy

The old republican state was overtly committed to laissez-faire, and the economy during this period was influenced mainly by national and international market stimuli. And yet political decisions were significant factors in molding the pattern of economic change, including the pattern of industrial development. Most state interventions during the period were rooted either in the demands of the dominant economic groups or in the partially autonomous actions of the political elite, who enjoyed some room to maneuver in the midst of competing economic pressures. It barely needs to be added that the highly elitist state never intervened on behalf of the masses. Moreover, the elites who ran the state had no strong commitment to sovereignty: "Rather than viewing foreigners as threats to national sovereignty . . . Brazil's dominant class and state administration . . . wanted to Europeanize Brazil and believed reliance on world markets was the best way to achieve that."[48] State intervention during the old republic is thus best understood as a product of the needs and perceptions of a narrow economic and political elite.

This old republican state influenced the process of industrialization both indirectly and directly. The most important indirect interventions aimed at supporting the coffee economy but also ended up influencing industrial development. Coffee exports had emerged as significant by the mid-nineteenth century and grew rapidly after 1890: There was growing demand for coffee in industrializing Europe and the United States, a decline in transportation costs, and a new, decentralized republican government that encouraged this trade and also enabled powerful regions such as São Paulo to keep the incomes within their borders.[49] Coffee interests seeking to expand production pressed for the opening of new lands and the ready availability of labor. Both the regional government of São Paulo and the federal government obliged, facilitating railroad construction to open up interior lands, and publicly subsidizing immigration of the necessary labor.

Coffee planters, who took the lead in railway construction even before 1891, looked to foreign investors for both capital and technology. After 1891, when the new government guaranteed profits to foreign investors, foreign capital, mainly British, but also from the United States, poured in. Slavery was abolished in 1888, but Paulista elites in every instance preferred European labor to the indigenous labor of African slave background,[50] mainly because

---

[48] See Topik, *Political Economy of the Brazilian State*, 130.
[49] See Dean, *Industrialization of São Paulo*, 3–4.
[50] See Skidmore and Smith, *Modern Latin America*, 45.

of racist attitudes but also perhaps because of related perceptions of productivity. The Paulista elite opted to subsidize white European immigration, rather than investing the same resources to improve the productivity of indigenous black labor via education. Between 1900 and 1920 nearly two million immigrants entered Brazil, with more than one million being subsidized by the government of São Paulo alone. Both the infrastructure that developed in the context of the coffee economy and European immigration eventually proved to be significant factors in early industrialization.

Over time the political elite of the Brazilian state nationalized most of the railways; by the Second World War, for example, nearly two-thirds of the railway system was owned and operated by the government.[51] The ruling elite eventually concluded that paying off the guaranteed profits to private investors was proving to be far too expensive. Calculating that the cost of public debt was less onerous than that of paying guaranteed profits, the government borrowed money abroad to buy and nationalize the railways. Viewed comparatively, this is a good example of sovereignty as a developmental asset. Although many Brazilians and Brazilianists bemoan the neocolonial status of Brazil in this and subsequent periods, the issue should be kept in perspective. The contrast with India is instructive. Indian railways were also built with British capital and technology and with rates of profits guaranteed by the British colonial government. Over the years, especially in the first half of the twentieth century, Indian nationalists argued angrily that paying off these guaranteed profits was a source of "national economic drain." However, given a formally colonial government, they were unable to alter the terms, whereas the Brazilian state succeeded in rewriting the basis on which the railways operated within Brazil.

The public role in the economy was especially significant during this period in the state management of coffee exports.[52] Overproduction and related fluctuations in the international price of coffee posed periodic problems. In response, the state of São Paulo designed *valorization* (or support) schemes – an early historical example of buffer stock schemes – by which the government bought and stored excess production, to be released later on. Financed by foreign loans that were paid off by taxing coffee exports, the intervention was relatively successful in terms of stabilizing international prices and maintaining coffee incomes, with far-reaching impact on Brazilian economy. Once successful in São Paulo, the federal government was forced to take over the scheme, though it did so only reluctantly and related responsibilities shifted back and forth between São Paulo and the federal government. Coffee barons, though supportive of the schemes, were not able to

---

[51] This discussion on railways is based on Topik, *Political Economy of the Brazilian State*, chap. 4.
[52] A good and brief synthetic account of the public management of the coffee economy is available in Love, *São Paulo*, chap. 2. See also Furtado, *Economic Growth of Brazil*, chap. 30; and Topik, *Political Economy of the Brazilian State*, chap. 3.

control the entire policy process; they failed, for example, to control the Coffee Institute in the 1920s. The ruling elite thus enjoyed some political autonomy from powerful economic interests.[53]

Ironically, although the political management of the coffee economy aimed at reducing dependence on the international economy, it increased Brazil's dependence on nonnationals.[54] Dependence on foreign resources only grew over time, as much of the international trade of coffee, including the infrastructure, was managed by foreign firms in Brazil, especially migrant merchants in port cities. Many of these trading firms got involved in the business of credit and ended up owning substantial numbers of coffee plantations. Since public involvement in coffee marketing was based on foreign loans, this contributed to an "unprecedented degree of foreign control of federal finances,"[55] with the result that an international syndicate of bankers determined when and how Brazilian coffee could be sold: São Paulo's government could not enact any coffee-related legislation without the "syndicate's approval,"[56] and even the coffee export tax was collected by foreign firms. Charges of neocolonialism on the part of some scholars are thus clearly not without substance.

Why did Brazil's political elite invite such a situation? Although it could have intervened to reduce the vulnerability of the coffee economy to the global economy, it did not, and instead made the national economy even further dependent on foreigners. The answer to this paradox lies with the highly elitist and narrow conception of "nation" held by the rulers, who literally equated what was good for elite incomes with the good of the nation and worried about little else.

In spite of growing dependence, public intervention did succeed in maintaining coffee incomes, which, in turn, provided the broad context within which Brazil's early industrialization took root. Coffee, however, which contributed about 25 percent of the GDP in the 1890s, contributed only about 10 percent by 1930, indicating that the significance of coffee for industrialization declined over time. Since the bulk of industrialization occurred in the post-1930 period, Fishlow is probably more right than not in concluding that the Brazilian coffee economy was not an example of a "classic export engine of growth."[57] Nevertheless, coffee exports and incomes were central in this period for maintaining internal demand, generating public revenues, financing imports, and, less directly, attracting foreign investors – all factors

---

[53] For a blow-by-blow account of the failure of coffee interests to control the Coffee Institute, see Font, *Coffee, Contention and Change*, pt. 2.

[54] See Love, *São Paulo*, chap. 2.

[55] Ibid., 38.

[56] Ibid., 47.

[57] See Albert Fishlow, "Brazilian Development in Long-Term Perspective," *American Economic Review* 70, no. 2 (May 1980): 103. For a contrary argument, see Dean, *Industrialization of São Paulo*, passim.

that were important for industrialization. While the state in the old republic may not have been consciously interventionist or developmental, it indeed ended up providing indirect support to the process of early industrialization by supporting the coffee economy.

The state's role in imposing tariffs on imports during this period helped the process of industrialization more directly. Some revenue-oriented tariffs were imposed as early as 1844, when treaty obligations with Great Britain terminated, and remained in place for much of the second half of the nineteenth century. Major upward revisions occurred in 1900, 1905, and 1913. While the average tariff from 1900 on was about 25 percent, specific tariffs on such critical early industries as textiles and shoes were over 100 percent.[58] There is essentially a consensus in the literature that most of these tariffs originated in the government's need for revenue. Because the capacity of this state to collect direct income taxes was limited, it was forced to depend on such easier-to-collect taxes as that on foreign trade. There is also some evidence, however, that early industrialists valued tariffs as protection and lobbied politicians for it, at times successfully. Stein demonstrates in his detailed study of the textile industry that as early as 1892, textile entrepreneurs successfully argued for "markedly protective" tariffs as being good for "national progress."[59] Another analyst provides evidence that, besides revenue, tariffs during the old republic "also had the objective of protecting certain industries."[60]

More controversial is how protective and thus how helpful these tariffs really were for early industrialists. There is an absence of reliable data on such other variables as exchange rates and inflation that might have diluted the impact of tariffs during the old republic.[61] Nonetheless, the available evidence and the weight of scholarly opinion tend toward the view that tariffs did provide effective protection. Exchange-rate fluctuation was an important issue in the period, but it went up and down. A falling exchange rate enhanced the effects of tariffs, and the opposite tendency was often countered by governments imposing additional tariffs on specific industries, such as textiles.[62] Wilson Suzigan, who is otherwise critical of the government's role in this period for its insufficient promotion of industry, suggests that

[58] See Leff, *Underdevelopment and Development in Brazil*, 1: 174–75.
[59] See Stein, *Brazilian Cotton Manufacture*, 85, 82.
[60] See Topik, *Political Economy of the Brazilian State*, 142.
[61] Among the scholars who doubt that tariffs were all that effective are Albert Fishlow, "Origins and Consequences of Import Substitution in Brazil," in Luis Eugenio Di Marco, ed., *International Economics and Development* (New York: Academic Press, 1972), 311–65, esp. 319; and Werner Baer and Annibal V. Villela, "Industrial Growth and Industrialization: Revisions in the Stages of Brazil's Economic Development," *Journal of Developing Areas* 7 (January 1973): 217–34, esp. 221. It should be added that the evidence these scholars provide for this position, especially Baer and Villela, is pretty meager.
[62] See, for example, Stein, *Brazilian Cotton Manufacture*, 88.

tariffs during the old republic "offered strong effective protection."[63] Leff concludes, similarly, that industry in this period was protected by fairly high tariffs.[64] And finally, based on a detailed study of the most important industry of the period, namely, textiles, Stein argues that tariffs, while enhancing government revenues, also provided industrialists with a "prolonged period of excellent returns."[65]

Aside from indirect public support for industrialization via the development of infrastructure, subsidized immigration, and maintaining coffee incomes during the life of the old republic, as well as more direct support via tariffs, there were also other areas of state intervention in support of industry: maintaining an expansionist monetary and fiscal policy, the creation of Banco do Brazil, and the establishment of engineering schools in several cities. This is still not to say that the old republic was a highly interventionist, developmental state. It was not. Moreover, dominant power within it was wielded by agro-exporters and not by a nationalist elite or by industrialists.

One has only to think of Japan, another late-developing sovereign state of the period, to underline all that the Brazilian state could have done to promote industry in the early 1900s but did not; there was no conscious industrial policy in Brazil, no economic coordination between state and industry, no mobilization of society's internal economic resources for industrial promotion, no attempt to develop the indigenous labor force via mass education, and no attempt to build up a national technological base. And yet, in comparison with most of the colonized parts of the developing world – except for Korea and maybe a few other cases – the sovereign Brazilian state undertook some significant economic interventions. For example, it is hard to imagine a colonized state nationalizing railways, supporting native commodity exporters, or imposing tariffs to keep out manufactured imports and support local industrialization. These are precisely the type of interventions the state in old republic Brazil undertook, with consequences that we investigate next.

The Pattern of Industrialization

Industry grew steadily during the old republic, but the growth was not without its drawbacks. On the positive side, industrial growth in this period averaged between 4 and 5 percent per annum. By the end of the old republic, Brazil was more or less self-sufficient in textiles, shoes, and processed food. Much of this industrialization was of the import-substitution variety and flourished in the context of the growing coffee exports. Less positively,

---

[63] See Wilson Suzigan, "Industrialization and Economic Policy in Historical Perspective," in Fernando Rezende, ed., *Brazilian Economic Studies*, no. 2 (Rio de Janeiro: Institute of Social and Economic Planning, 1976), 13.

[64] See Leff, *Underdevelopment and Development in Brazil*, 1: 174–76.

[65] See Stein, *Brazilian Cotton Manufacture*, 85.

industry was import-intensive, productivity growth in it was limited, and it remained dependent on external sources for capital, technology, and entrepreneurship. The old republic state set the broad parameters that defined both achievements and limitations of industrialization in the pre-1930 period.

The earliest industries to take root in Brazil were textiles and food processing. While the latter enjoyed the "tariff of distance," growth of textiles was especially robust in the post-1890 period. Growing demand and tariff protections both played a role in this development. Other industries that took root in the early twentieth century, especially after 1910, included such light industries as shoes, flour mills, beer, cigarettes, metalworks, lumber, and paper. Major industrialists after the Second World War, such as Matarrazzo, Jafet, Klabin, Votorontim, and Lundrgren had begun their operations in the pre-1914 period.[66] The early successes of some of them attracted new entrepreneurs, created infrastructure and a labor force, and strengthened industrialists as a significant political force, thus paving the way for further industrial development.

The process of industrialization in Brazil was heavily dependent from the outset on linkages with the global economy. For example, "foreign investors" – especially start-ups by European immigrants but also foreign companies – dominated the consumer manufacturing sector in the main home of industry, São Paulo.[67] Foreign investment during the life of the old republic grew fourfold. While most of this was concentrated in public utilities, infrastructure, and export trade, some of it also went into consumer manufacturing. Of the some 1,000 new companies started in this period, twice as many companies were foreign – 619 to be precise – as were indigenous.[68] As will become clear in due course, this dependence was a double-edged sword, both facilitating production and limiting self-sustained growth.

What happened to Brazilian industry during the First World War similarly underlines the double-edged nature of extensive trade linkages.[69] Industrial growth prior to that war depended on imported machinery and inputs that were financed by coffee exports. Coffee incomes, in spite of tariffs, also attracted high-end consumer imports. But the war interrupted

---

[66] See Leff, *Underdevelopment and Development in Brazil*, 1: 173.

[67] See Dean, *Industrialization of São Paulo*, chap. 4.

[68] See Topik, *Political Economy of the Brazilian State*, 12.

[69] The role of the First World War, as of the Great Depression, is quite controversial in the Brazilian literature, mainly because it goes to the heart of the disagreements between the more dependency-oriented and the more orthodox types of scholars concerning the impact of "delinking" on industrialization and development. The statist argument pursued here sidesteps this debate by building on such more nuanced arguments as those developed in Fishlow, "Origins and Consequences," passim. Put simply, this nuanced position suggests that links with the global economy offered both opportunities and constraints.

this trading pattern. Diminished capacity to import, however, was a mixed blessing: While it increased the demand for industrial goods within Brazil, it also reduced the capacity to build industry. The result was growth in production based mainly on fuller utilization of existing capacity. The resulting profits were invested again in the 1920s, even though production growth decelerated as imports resumed again. This stop-and-go process repeated itself again in the 1930s, during the Great Depression.

The extent of industrial development prior to 1930 ought not to be exaggerated. While industry had grown since the late nineteenth century, the base from which it started was extremely low and the pace was modest. It is thus not surprising that by 1920 only 4 percent of Brazil's labor force was employed in manufacturing proper (the figures for industry as a whole are not readily available), and even in the leading state of São Paulo the urban work force constituted only 16 percent of the working population.[70] Most of this industry produced light consumer goods for the low end of the market, with very little production of either sophisticated consumer goods or of intermediate and capital goods. Industry was also highly concentrated geographically, with nearly half the industrial product originating in the state of São Paulo alone. And finally, industry was highly dependent on immigrants and on resident and nonresident foreigners for capital, technology, and entrepreneurship.

What factors help to explain the achievements and limitations of industrialization in the old republic? Industrial growth responded in part to growing demand for industrial goods and in part to a protected environment in which entrepreneurs were more likely to make profits. Although coffee exports and incomes were the main motor behind growing demand, it was not the resulting incomes of coffee elites that were critical for the process of industrialization – Brazilian elites preferred more sophisticated imports for their own consumption. The growth in demand was instead for low-end consumer goods on the part of immigrant workers and peasants drawn to Brazil by the coffee economy, though, once again, with generous help from the state.[71] Specifically, the main source of growing demand was growth in the size of the labor force, since workers' incomes did not rise. This pattern of demand was not without limits, however; once basic needs were satisfied, there was little demand for more sophisticated goods. The pattern of industry that developed reflected this demand structure.

In addition to growing demand, fairly high tariffs on crucial industries such as textiles and shoes promoted new start-ups and the growth of established industry. A leading student of the subject concludes on this point: "Protective tariffs provided early Brazilian industrialists with the assurance

---

[70] The nationwide figures are from Fishlow, "Origins and Consequences," 325. The São Paulo figure is from Love, *São Paulo*, 19.
[71] For details, especially in São Paulo, see Dean, *Industrialization of São Paulo*, chap. 4.

that they would be able to compete with imports. . . . Without the protective tariff, it is inconceivable that Brazilian industrialization would have been launched and proceeded at the rapid pace" that it did.[72] The role of the state in facilitating early industrialization thus ought by now to be clear.

While demand for industrial goods and protection from imports were necessary for industrialization to begin, they were not sufficient. Other ingredients were needed, and, once again, the state's facilitating role was far from insignificant. First, there is the broad political context. The old republican state was investor-friendly. Coffee barons may not always have welcomed state support for industry, but they themselves were aggressive entrepreneurs. Their political influence helped to create a probusiness environment. Critical states such as São Paulo were thus relatively stable politically, especially prior to the 1920s. Moreover, the state maintained low taxes, guaranteed the sanctity of foreign capital and of property, and had no labor laws to protect the emerging working class.

There was also the state's indirect role in facilitating the availability of entrepreneurship, an adequate labor force, and technology. Public support for immigration, mainly from Europe, was critical in resolving all of these potential bottlenecks. It is a phenomenon difficult to imagine in any other sovereign developing country of Asia and Africa that was not a settler colony. But sovereign Brazil's ruling classes were mainly European settlers who were happy to invite more of their own.

Indeed, most consumer industries were started by immigrant entrepreneurs. While native Brazilians of the planter class played an important role in some early industrial ventures such as railways, they generally shied away from consumer manufacturing.[73] Those who moved into producing consumer goods tended either to be migrant importers – who already knew the local markets – or fresh immigrants, who came to Brazil with some capital, technology, and/or experience and could also raise further capital from their connections in Europe.[74] The latter group also had the advantage of knowing the tastes of working European immigrants, for whom they generally produced the low-end mass consumer goods. In a telling piece of evidence, a 1962 survey of industries documented that fewer than 16 percent of existing firms were started by individuals whose grandparents were native Brazilians.[75] This role of immigrants and foreigners in Brazil's early industrialization has few parallels in the developing world outside Latin America – the role of the Japanese in Korea is one, and South Africa may be another.

---

[72] See Leff, *Underdevelopment and Development in Brazil*, 1: 176.
[73] On the early role of planter elites in Brazil's industrialization, see Dean, *Industrialization of São Paulo*, chap. 3.
[74] Ibid., chaps. 2 and 4.
[75] See Love, *São Paulo*, 19–20.

Immigrant labor was also a key ingredient in early industrialization. Some of this labor moved from plantations and was already socialized in the work culture of capitalist enterprises. Others fresh from Europe, most of whom were Italians, brought with them basic education and a variety of skills. And over time indigenous people of slave background also joined the labor force. The relatively low wages paid to these workers were, in turn, another key ingredient in the success of industry.[76] But what the state elite may not have anticipated was the political impact of this migrant labor force. It brought with it ideologies of communist and fascist politics and supported a variety of political movements in the 1920s, paving the way for a much harsher authoritarian response in the 1930s.

To sum up this discussion, the old republic state provided the broad framework within which early industrialization took root. Yet it was committed to laissez-faire and, in any case, relatively feeble in terms of undertaking developmental tasks. So how does one then explain its positive role in promoting industry? The answer emerges by focusing on the fact that the real power in the old republic lay in the regional states, especially in such powerful southern states as São Paulo. Aimed mainly at protecting elite economic interests, the more powerful states of the federation undertook a variety of economic interventions, either directly or by utilizing their significant influence over the federal government. Cumulatively, these interventions supported the growth of industry. These were relatively "easy" interventions that depended mainly on foreign resources to solve national problems. Thus public support of the coffee economy built infrastructure and maintained incomes and demand in the economy. But this public support was also financed by foreign loans and growing financial dependency on foreign creditors. Publicly subsidized immigration helped to attract new entrepreneurs and a semiskilled labor force, even as there were only minimal efforts to build up indigenous capacity. And finally, while tariffs indeed helped industries to take root, they also perpetuated the state's relative disconnect with its own society by providing a ready source of public revenue that substituted one type of economic dependence for another, that is, instead of importing all manufactured goods, Brazil now manufactured many of them by importing entrepreneurs, labor, technology, and even capital. A long-term pattern was being established.

III. State and Industry under Vargas

Getulio Vargas came to power in 1930 and dominated Brazilian politics at least until the end of the Second World War, and then some. Vargas's first continuous fifteen-year rule is notable both for what it achieved and for what it did not. Viewed from a developmental angle, most significant was

---

[76] See Fishlow, "Origins and Consequences," 319–20.

the creation of a centralized modern Brazilian state. This state embraced economic nationalism as a developmental ideology of sorts and intervened more and more in the economy to promote industry. Industrial growth during this period was also rapid, averaging nearly 9 percent per annum. At the same time, however, the central state that emerged was relatively limited in its developmental capacities: A serious disconnect remained between the state and the vast agrarian periphery – and hence between the state and the majority of the population; and relatedly, the commitment to economic nationalism was more rhetorical than substantive. Despite the fascist overtones of the Vargista state, its organizational and mobilization skills were not all that great. Though aiming to be a cohesive-capitalist state, it retained some of the characteristics of fragmented-multiclass states with significant pockets of personalistic politics. State intervention in the economy remained focused on supporting the coffee economy and on inviting foreign resources and technology for further industrialization. The political capacity to mobilize indigenous capital and build national technology remained limited.

Politics and the State
How leaders capture power usually has implications for their subsequent ruling strategies and capacities. While Brazilian historiography often labels Vargas's emergence to power as a "revolution," it was nothing of the sort. His rise instead was mainly an intraelite political affair, with a strong military component; peasants and workers played a minimal role. If the focus is mainly on the propertied classes, it is the case that, with the decline of the old republic, the agrarian oligarchs and agro-exporters lost further power. But whether decisive class winners and losers emerged from the "revolution" is far from clear in the historical evidence. What is clear is that Vargas was a skillful politician. A man who was at the right place at the right time, he emerged as the leader of a variety of forces that were opposed to the old republic, favored a more centralized state, and eventually captured power with the help of the military. This was the main achievement of Vargas's rule. In the economic realm, however, he had to balance a variety of competing pressures: the interests of the coffee economy, the perceived need to promote industry, the need to attract foreign resources, the need of the emerging middle and working classes in the cities, and, of course, the needs and demands of the military.

Vargas was born to a military family, and, as was often the case in Brazil at that time, his father had also served as a rural political boss – in this case in the most southern, cattle-breeding state of Rio Grande do Sul.[77] Vargas

---

[77] I draw on three good studies of Vargas and his rule: Robert M. Levine, *The Vargas Regime: The Critical Years, 1934–1939* (New York: Columbia University Press, 1970); Jordan M. Young, *The Brazilian Revolution of 1930 and the Aftermath* (New Brunswick, N.J.: Rutgers University Press, 1967); and John W. F. Dulles, *Vargas of Brazil: A Political Biography* (Austin: University of

was trained as a lawyer and rose quickly in politics thanks to his political connections and his strong personal skills. While at law school in the state capital, he formed enduring ties with fellow *gauchos* who would remain his lifelong political associates. There was a strong commitment to positivist values among the political elite of Rio Grande, and the values to which Vargas was exposed emphasized centralist and statist traditions. Rio Grande was also well known for its strong militarist traditions in which the dividing line between civilian and military affairs was thin. Within this milieu, Vargas entered politics at the age of twenty-six, when he was elected to the state assembly. He eventually got a chance to be a state representative in Rio in 1923, quickly became the finance minister of the old republic, returned to his home state as governor, and then again quickly found himself the presidential candidate of the "liberal alliance" that opposed the dominant "republican" forces of the old republic, including the leading state of São Paulo.

As noted above, throughout the 1920s a variety of new political forces emerged to challenge the dominance of agro-exporters over Brazilian politics. Significant among these challengers were younger military officers, the *tenentes*, often from the northeast; urban middle classes in the South, with roots in the professions, who were often nationalist; emerging industrialists; and a variety of state-level political elite who felt excluded from the cozy alliances of the old republic. Vargas in the end helped to consolidate this new emerging Brazil, at least a part of which was ironically a product of the coffee economy itself. Yet Vargas never fully excluded the old coffee interests. For example, during his presidential bid in 1930, his electoral platform included promises to give amnesty to rebel army officers, help for the northeast, new equipment for the army, and aid for coffee interests hurt severely by the decline in prices in 1929.[78] The platform said nothing about support for industry. Those who argue that Vargas's "revolution" was a "bourgeois revolution" of sorts thus have to concede that such was certainly not Vargas's early intent and that the process of state formation preceded the emergence of a national bourgeoisie.[79]

Texas Press, 1967). For a brief but clear and useful overview, see also Thomas E. Skidmore, *Politics in Brazil, 1930–1964: An Experiment in Democracy* (New York: Oxford University Press, 1967), chap. 1.

[78] See Young, *Brazilian Revolution of 1930*, 46.

[79] Among those who argue that Vargas's rise represented a "bourgeois" movement, see Flynn, *Brazil*, esp. 61. A more plausible class analysis of Vargas's power base is in Cardoso and Faletto, *Dependency and Development*. They suggest (p. 91) that Vargas represented ranch owners of the south, sugar plantation owners in the northeast, and "urban middle class sectors." They also argue (pp. 39–40) that Vargas's subsequent proindustrialization policies were influenced more by "political than by economic considerations." This emphasis on the "political" as driving state-led industrialization is of course quite consistent with the themes of this study.

Vargas's loss in the 1930 elections was widely perceived by his supporters as fraudulent. His core supporters in his home state then organized a political-cum-military challenge to the electoral verdict, which was joined by a variety of forces opposed to the old republic and which eventually succeeded in placing Vargas at the helm.[80] Two issues requiring further attention concern the decisive role of armed forces in assuring Vargas's victory and the apparent capitulation of the coffee interests.

The fact that the old republic never created a centralized armed force contributed heavily to its own undoing. A variety of regional armed forces, especially those of Rio Grande do Sul and of the northeast, where the rebel *tenentes* held sway, sided with Vargas, successfully challenging the federal army.[81] Any real challenge to the pro-Vargas armed units was likely to come from the well-armed militia of São Paulo, but such a challenge never materialized. Fearing a civil war, the generals of the federal army deposed Washington Luis, the outgoing president of the old republic, and delivered power instead to Vargas.[82] Vargas, in turn, never forgot this political debt to the armed forces. As to why the coffee interests of São Paulo did not mobilize effectively against Vargas, several factors ought to be noted. First, big coffee had increasingly become suspicious of the federal government of the old republic, especially in 1929, when Washington Luis failed to provide adequate support against the catastrophic decline in prices.[83] Second, given Vargas's electoral commitment to aid the coffee economy, the agro-exporters had no reason to think they had much to fear from him.[84] Third, the sharp decline in coffee prices had in any case undermined the political efficacy of coffee barons in São Paulo and elsewhere. And finally, of course, São Paulo did challenge Vargas's growing centralization in 1932, but failed.

For purposes of political analysis, Vargas's fifteen-year rule is best considered as two phases: the period between 1930 and 1937, a mildly liberal phase where the focus was on creating and consolidating a centralized state; and the period from 1937 to 1945, the period of Estado Novo (the "new state"), during which the Brazilian state became more of a cohesive-capitalist state along the lines of the fascist states. Once in power, Vargas worked hand in hand with the military to achieve both political and military centralization. Vargas also threw his political weight behind creating a more coherent and

---

[80] See any of the references cited in note 77 for details of this "revolution."

[81] See Young, *Brazilian Revolution of 1930*, chap. 4. See also Levine, *Vargas Regime*, introduction.

[82] Young, *Brazilian Revolution of 1930*, chap. 4.

[83] One historian notes that coffee interests in 1930 were so alienated from the federal government that they "probably gave their tacit approval to the armed rebellion." Young, *Brazilian Revolution of 1930*, 80.

[84] Mauricio Font in a revisionist interpretation goes as far as to suggest that coffee interests actively supported Vargas's ascent to power. See Font, *Coffee, Contention and Change*, esp. chap. 7.

centralized armed force out of the relatively factionalized, rebellious, and disorganized military he had inherited. The military, in turn, helped Vargas to consolidate a centralized state, including forcefully crushing dissenting regional political forces.

Scholars often note that Vargas was no "ideologue" and that he had no clear plans or policies in his early years.[85] While this is true insofar as Vargas was neither a committed communist nor a committed fascist, he did have clear political preferences, and these were politically consequential. As we saw above in the case of Park Chung Hee in Korea, the process of trial and error reveals both the leader's preferred goals and the structural constraints within which these goals must be pursued. Viewed in this manner, we see that Vargas was a conservative state builder. He was certainly no democrat, and despite some pro-working-class rhetorical flourishes, he was no socialist, either. Given his positivist inclinations, his conservative tendencies were also distinct from what the term generally implies in Anglo-American political discourse. This elitist state builder considered his rule "profoundly nationalist." He was committed to state-led progress on both the industrial front and on the "social question"; the latter for Vargas – as for Juan Peron in Argentina and for a variety of fascists and protofascists in Europe at the time – meant channeling some economic benefits to the working class, without giving them rights to organize and to participate politically.[86]

Guided by these diffuse but real political preferences, Vargas assiduously pursued the building of state and industry in Brazil and left a deep imprint on the making of modern Brazil. Vargas's centralizing moves were resented by the powerful states of the old republic, especially São Paulo. That the political and the military leaders of São Paulo threw down the gauntlet is not all that surprising. More surprising is the relative ease with which São Paulo was contained. While the decisive factor in the historical record here was the loyalty to Vargas of the federal army, which brought São Paulo's rebels to their knees, both an element of chance and deeper economic issues were also important: The fact that Minas Gerais chose to stay neutral in the confrontation was far from foreordained and clearly consequential; also consequential was the fact that many of São Paulo's economic elite were not

---

[85] See, for example, Young, *Brazilian Revolution of 1930*, 82; and Levine, *Vargas Regime*, 5. Later in his study, however, Levine argues (p. 176) – and more appropriately to my mind – that changes between 1930 and 1937 were "planned" and "came from above."

[86] On Vargas's nationalism, see Burns, *Nationalism in Brazil*, 74; and John D. Wirth, *The Politics of Brazilian Development, 1930–1954* (Stanford, Calif.: Stanford University Press, 1970), 217. On the positivist roots of Vargas's political outlook, see Dulles, *Vargas of Brazil*, 17. Vargas's attitude and actions toward the working class are discussed below. For a good discussion of the "organic statist" political tradition of Latin America – of which Vargas would certainly be a part – and which is distinct from both liberal and Marxist worldviews, see Alfred Stepan, *The State and Society: Peru in Comparative Perspective* (Princeton, N.J.: Princeton University Press, 1978), chap. 1.

always hostile to Vargas and were eventually well accommodated by the new centralized political arrangement.[87] After that, Vargas's centralizing push progressed steadily, and he encountered no further organized opposition on this issue. The power of states was thus steadily eroded, and the constitution of 1934 formally eliminated the states' critical rights to tax exports and to maintain their own armed forces.

A new type of political challenge for Brazil came in the 1930s and was posed by organized urban political movements of the left and the right. The vast agrarian periphery remained enmeshed in personalistic networks of domination and was largely excluded – except for the elite, of course – from national politics. A variety of urban groups, however, became quite active politically. Considering that many in the cities were of recent European origin, it is not surprising that competing European ideologies of the time, especially communism and fascism, appealed to these immigrants in the 1930s. Fascism in particular flourished.[88] The communists tried to organize the working class with the help of the Comintern and were easily crushed, but often without much imaginaton by Vargas. The fascists, by contrast, especially the so-called Integralist movement, gained wide support. By 1937, for example, before the imposition of Estado Novo, the Integralists boasted a membership, with a middle-class base, of some 250,000, with 4,000 organized cells in 700 districts; and this in a country of some 40 million people with an electorate of only 2 million.[89] Moreover, the fascists had support and sympathy in high places, including the military and the church. While the fascists were also forcefully disbanded after 1937, many of the goals and values of the Integralists were eventually adopted by the Estado Novo; it is important to note that the communists in fact were treated much more harshly.

Satisfied with neither the scope nor the depth of authority they had already created, Vargas and his senior army supporters pulled off a constitutional coup in 1937 that led to the creation of a much more authoritarian, corporatist, and cohesive state, the Estado Novo. Vargas and his associates acted out of fear that even a highly limited electoral arena might enable the elites of the old republic to reassert themselves politically. Additionally, they faced new urban political challenges from both the left and the right. And finally, working through an elected Congress had frustrated a variety of Vargas's state-building efforts such as creating a more rational bureaucracy. But, knowing that he had the full support of such military leaders as Goes Monteiro and Eurico Gaspar Dutra – not to mention that right-wing authoritarianism was the order of the day in some of Brazil's main reference

---

[87] For a fine and succinct analysis of these political developments, see Flynn, *Brazil*, chap. 4, esp. 62–66.

[88] Ibid., 71–84.

[89] Ibid., 73.

societies, such as Portugal, Italy, and Germany of the 1930s – Vargas successfully led the move to establish a right-wing dictatorship in Brazil.

Although Brazil's Estado Novo resembled European fascist states, it was not quite fascist. In the words of one analyst, it lacked the "ideological unity" and the "totalitarian perseverance" of real fascism.[90] Still, the ideology and politics of Estado Novo shared much with European fascism. According to an ideologue of the new state, Azevedo Amaral, Vargas's authoritarian state was "a harmonious collaboration between the army and the State, which is the organic expression of the Nation itself."[91] Much of the Integralists' emphasis on "patriotism" was "borrowed by the Estado Novo's Brasilidade campaign for patriotism, national unity, and cultural integration."[92] Vargas, moreover, consciously used education to promote "national consciousness" and to "excite the imagination of the masses."[93] Political participation within Estado Novo was, of course, very limited. The right to organize politically became illegal, and the limited elections that had existed were eliminated. Media were censored, security forces enjoyed a near free hand, and an enlarged Department of Press and Propaganda mobilized broad patriotic support for the new regime.

The manner in which Vargas's new state linked itself to a variety of interest groups, especially urban economic groups, also betrayed its fascist inspiration and its ambition to create a cohesive-capitalist state. For example, at the apex, Vargas created a National Economic Council, which included representatives of all the major occupational groups and whose task it was to oversee the national economy. There are clear echoes of fascist Italy here.[94] At least as important because of its long-term endurance were the successful efforts to "incorporate" labor unions as an extended arm of the state, thus initiating the construction of the well-known structures of corporatism. A key player here was Vargas's associate Lindolfo Collor, who successfully tamed the emerging labor movement. He helped to create legal structures that not only precluded efforts at building free labor unions, but also successfully organized labor under state auspices.[95]

The class and other social bases of the Estado Novo are also important. The emerging industrial class of Brazil was initially wary of Vargas, especially given his opposition to protecting "artificial industries," as well as his pro-working-class rhetoric and the related creation of a new labor ministry. By 1934, however, the growing coincidence of interest between the

[90] See Levine, *Vargas Regime*, 182.
[91] Quoted in Keith and Hayes, *Perspectives on Armed Politics*, 167.
[92] Levine, *Vargas Regime*, 181.
[93] Burns, *Nationalism*, 85.
[94] See Flynn, *Brazil*, 104.
[95] For details, see Kenneth Paul Erickson, *The Brazilian Corporative State and Working-Class Politics* (Berkeley: University of California Press, 1977), esp. chaps. 2 and 3.

Vargista state and industrialists was evident: Vargas increasingly talked about economic nationalism and about the need to promote indigenous industry; protectionist tariffs were forthcoming; support for the coffee economy was viewed as necessary for overall economic health rather than as a support for one class-faction over another; and it was clear that the proworker rhetoric was precisely that. The Estado Novo actually institutionalized the growing state and industry alliance by incorporating industrialists in the highest policy-making bodies, on the one hand, and by limiting the rights of labor to unionize freely against the industrialists, on the other hand. Industrial capital thus became very much a part of the ruling arrangement dominated by the state elite, and thus integral to the design of the more cohesive and procapitalist state that Vargas hoped to construct.[96]

As to the role of other social forces, agrarian elites more or less accommodated themselves to Vargas.[97] While the coffee elites might have bemoaned their diminished political significance in the new centralized state, Vargas's steady support of the coffee economy helped them to preserve their core economic interests. Other agrarian elites also found the situation acceptable as long as the new state did not interfere with their respective local hegemonies. Many among the urban middle classes, of course, viewed Vargas as their own candidate. Urban workers were also generally pro-Vargas, drawn to him at least in part by his occasional populist rhetoric and in part by some real economic benefits channeled to them by the new state. Given this fairly broad support, or at least acquiescence, one might wonder, what was the need for a highly authoritarian state? Vargas's authoritarianism has to be understood more as a political and less as a social or class-based phenomenon. Opposition to Vargas could have come from the marginalized political elite of the old republic, from his own former supporters whom he slowly squeezed, or from emerging new groups that favored democracy and were suspicious of Vargas's nationalist and populist rhetoric. Estado Novo was constructed in part to ward off any such potential challenges and in part as a perceived necessity to undertake the critical tasks of state building and industrialization.

During the Vargas era, especially during the life of the Estado Novo, the core of the state was further centralized and rationalized. The federal army disbanded various regional armies and private militias throughout the 1930s. From 1937 on, a semblance of centralized order emerged in the military.[98] The size and professionalization of the military also increased. For example, the army grew from 48,000 in 1930 to 80,000 in 1936 to 171,000 in 1945.[99] The military's share of the budget also grew from 19.4 percent

[96] See Dean, *Industrialization of São Paulo*, chap. 11.
[97] See Levine, *Vargas Regime*, esp. 177–78.
[98] See Hayes, *Armed Nation*, chap. 5.
[99] Ibid., 168.

in 1931 to 30.4 percent in 1938.[100] The officer corps became increasingly native-born, and the military was "depoliticized" in the sense that the rank and file were excluded from any direct and overt participation in politics. Of course, senior officers remained very much part of the ruling alliance. Similar attempts were made to create a more rational civil bureaucracy, with some success. The basic two-track structure, with a large patrimonial component, and a smaller but more competent and professional group at the apex, continued to characterize the overall bureaucracy. The size of the more professionally competent group grew, however. Vargas created a "superministry" of sorts – the Departmento Administrativo do Servico Publico (DASP) – whose aim was to create a modern national bureaucracy. Civil service exams were instituted, as was a merit system for promotions. While the results fell far short of transforming a patrimonial public organization into a modern bureaucracy, a significant segment of highly professional and competent bureaucrats came to control the main policy levers.[101]

The Estado Novo has been rightly described by one analyst as "the kernel of modern Brazil."[102] A modern state – modern in the Weberian and not in a democratic sense – with centralized control over Brazilian territory was finally established for the first time. More substantively, a narrow alliance of the political and economic elite, with the critical support of the military, emerged as the core ruling alliance. Also of long-term significance were the corporatist structures established to control labor. When compared with governmental arrangements only a decade earlier, the Vargas era in Brazil, especially the period of Estado Novo, was marked by an "increasing authority and the capacity of the national government." This new state also mobilized a sense of "national purpose" that has been rightly dubbed "developmental nationalism"[103] and that in turn influenced the changing role of the national state in the economy, especially support for an emerging capitalist economy. Estado Novo was thus clearly a cohesive-capitalist state in the making.

In its way, however, the Vargista state also departs from a fully developed, cohesive-capitalist state. First, neither Vargas's developmental mission nor his commitment to economic nationalism was well developed. The latter especially was more rhetorical than real and led to continued reliance on foreign resources for national development. Second, as to political capacities to pursue goals, Vargas's regime lacked any coherent political party or other relevant organizations that could help to cement the underlying coalition. Given the heterogeneous and multiclass nature of this coalition,

---

[100] Levine, *Vargas Regime*, 177.

[101] For such a favorable assessment, see Barbara Geddes, "Building State Autonomy in Brazil, 1930–1964," *Comparative Politics* 22 (January 1990): 217–35. For details about the working of DASP, see Gilbert B. Siegel, "The Vicissitudes of Government Reform in Brazil: A Study of DASP," Ph.D. dissertation, University of Southern California, 1966.

[102] See Flynn, *Brazil*, 96.

[103] See Wirth, *The Politics of Brazilian Development*, 217.

creating coherence would have been difficult in any case. But the lack of such a fascist party or other organizations distinguished Vargas's Brazil from its more totalitarian cousins in Europe or even Japan during this period. And finally, there were underlying social arrangements that limited the efficacy of Vargas's state, especially the failure to penetrate and incorporate the vast agrarian periphery. A variety of decentralized despotisms thus dotted the countryside, fragmenting state authority and limiting the scope and the reach of the state to direct economic development. A cohesive-capitalist state in ambition and in much of its design, then, the Estado Novo also shared some of the characteristics associated with fragmented-multiclass states.

State Intervention and Industrialization
In spite of some of its limits, Vargas's new cohesive-capitalist state took over the economic tasks hitherto performed by state governments and used its enhanced authority and capability to intervene in new areas. Conscious intervention to promote industry picked up only after 1934 and especially after the establishment of the Estado Novo in 1937. Even prior to that, however, the growing trend was toward increased state intervention in the economy, with important consequences for industrial growth. The most significant early example is, of course, Vargas's continued support of the coffee economy. Shortly after coming to power, his government initiated a coffee support program – or, more precisely, took it over from such state governments as that of São Paulo – aimed at countering the impact of the severe price decline triggered by the economic depression in importing countries. To help to maintain domestic incomes and employment, the new state bought up excess coffee supplies – storing some and destroying the rest. The program was financed by external credit that was, in turn, to be paid by taxing coffee incomes. The "pump-priming" impact of this "Keynesianism before Keynes," though debated, has been credited with maintaining demand in the economy and thus facilitating industrial growth during this period.[104]

Besides coffee, the new state intervened in a number of other areas in its early years. Marketing cartels were set up not only for coffee, but also for cocoa and sugar. Given a sharp decline in foreign-exchange earnings, foreign exchange was rationed, and this helped industrial growth indirectly by providing protection.[105] The new state established a number of *autarqutas* (institutes) to institutionalize cooperation between the public sector and such private industries as salt, sugar, and pinewood.[106] Also significant

---

[104] For the original argument, see Furtado, *Economic Growth of Brazil*, chap. 31. For a balanced review of the debate surrounding this argument that concludes that Furtado was more right than wrong, see Fishlow, "Origins and Consequences," esp. 329.

[105] See Suzigan, "Industrialization and Economic Policy," esp. 16.

[106] See Werner Baer, Issac Kerstenetzky, and Annibal E. Villela, "The Changing Role of the State in the Brazilian Economy," *World Development* 1, no. 11 (1973): 23–34, esp. 24.

was the Tariff Act of 1934. As a result, tariffs reflected more of a logic of deliberate industrialization than of revenue collection; tariffs were raised on domestically produced products requiring protection and decreased on items deemed as necessary imports. The role of the Bank of Brazil was also strengthened in order to provide credit to domestic producers.

Although the impact on industrialization was favorable, these early efforts were not always conceived of in terms of industrial promotion; this was not a case of self-conscious import-substituting industrialization. The first such real effort came instead in 1934, when a new constitution firmed up Vargas's hold on power, and industrialists increasingly became part of the core ruling arrangement. The misnamed Foreign Trade Council brought together policy makers and industrialists to promote trade and develop industry. This was probably the first effort within Brazil to undertake some sort of industrial policy. The basic idea was that industrialization would be led by the private sector, with the government providing finance and protection. The exchange controls, establishment of *autarquias*, and strengthening of Bank of Brazil's credit capacities all pointed in this direction.[107]

Vargas's willingness to intervene directly for the promotion of industry increased significantly after 1937. Not only was his political control firmer, but the competence of the bureaucracy was improving, workers were corporatized, and even employers were organized. The army made more and more demands for industrial promotion in the name of national security. Vargas responded but there were limits on his capacities as well. His initial inclination was to let the private sector take the lead. Only subsequently, when the private sector was not forthcoming, did the state feel compelled to develop infrastructure and heavy industries. For its part, the Brazilian private sector in this period faced serious foreign-exchange constraints – and hence limited capacity to import machinery – as well as domestic constraints of capital and technology. State intervention for industrial promotion was still at a relatively early stage, and the state had not done much to alleviate the constraints faced by the private sector on capital and technology. At the same time the state's resource base was limited. While public spending grew throughout this period – by as much as 7.5 percent per annum between 1932 and 1939 – public debt was also growing, leading Vargas to call a moratorium on foreign debt in 1938. This limitation on public revenues underlined the state's dependence on taxing foreign trade and on indirect taxes; the political and the bureaucratic capacity to tax growing incomes directly remained limited, however.

Within these constraints, Vargas's strategies for industrial promotion included supporting Brazilian industrialists, attracting foreign investors, and,

---

[107] Ibid., 25. For a good discussion of the impact of changing ideologies on economic policies in Latin America, including Brazil, see Albert Hirschman, *A Bias for Hope: Essays on Development in Latin America* (New Haven: Yale University Press, 1971).

when both of those failed, involving the state directly in production by creating public sector enterprises. The main instruments to support indigenous capitalists included expansionist fiscal and monetary policies that helped to maintain demand and facilitated credit, tariffs, foreign-exchange controls that additionally protected the domestic market, and some government subsidies. At times, the Vargista state went even further, exhibiting shades of cohesive-capitalism of the East Asian variety. A good example here is from the paper industry. Aimed at saving foreign exchange expended on importing paper, Vargas wanted to encourage domestic paper manufacturing. He approached the owner of Brazil's largest newspaper chain. Although this businessman refused, he worked with Vargas to identify and to approach another business family in a position to undertake the venture. Vargas offered credit, foreign exchange, and monopoly rights to the family. When older family members refused, Vargas persuaded younger members by offering more: the state's help in providing a railroad spur and a guaranteed market.[108]

Foreign investment continued to grow in Vargas's Brazil, but less so in consumer manufacturing than in public utilities, infrastructure, and after the depression-related hiatus again in the export trade. The United States slowly but surely surpassed Britain as the country of origin for most Brazilian foreign investment. These new investors were reluctant, however, to invest in manufacturing or heavy industry – but not for lack of trying on the part of Vargas and his associates. A good example here is Vargas's keen interest in building Brazil's steel industry.[109] Concerned about both saving foreign exchange on steel imports and responding to the military's demand for autonomy in a national security industry, Vargas examined various alternatives during the 1930s to produce steel within Brazil. Proposals from indigenous capitalists were entertained, but never went very far. Since both capital and technology were lacking in Brazil, a domestic private sector effort would have required enormous support from the government, support that Vargas was reluctant to provide. Instead, he eagerly pursued the possibility of bringing in U.S. Steel, underlining both the limits of Brazilian nationalism and the limits of the capacity of the Brazilian state to mobilize capital and borrow technology. It was only when U.S. Steel pulled out and other private foreign resources were not forthcoming that Vargas seriously turned to a public sector solution. Importing to rather than manufacturing in the "developing" world was still the order of the day. The U.S. government, influenced by realpolitik considerations of keeping Brazil out of the German orbit, eventually provided a loan through the Export-Import Bank, and an American

---

[108] This account is drawn from Dean, *Industrialization of São Paulo,* 215–16.

[109] For this account of the steel industry, I draw mainly on Wirth, *Politics of Brazilian Development,* chaps. 4–6. See also Werner Baer, *The Development of the Brazilian Steel Industry* (Nashville, Tenn.: Vanderbilt University Press, 1969).

company provided the technology for the construction of a publicly owned steel plant at Volte Redonda in 1946.

Between 1930 and 1947 the Brazilian economy grew nearly 6 percent per annum and industrial growth averaged about 9 percent per annum.[110] Irrespective of the numerous problems that remained unresolved, this was a phenomenal growth record, especially in the context of the Great Depression. It is tempting to suggest that interventions of a more efficacious state were mainly responsible for this growth performance, especially in industrial production. Any such suggestion, however, would be as misleading as the argument of early dependency scholars, namely, that rapid industrialization of the depression and war years reflected "delinking" from the global capitalist economy.[111] While delinking indeed contributed to industrial growth by limiting manufactured imports, limits on imports also impeded the building of new industrial capacity in Brazilian industry. Similarly, state intervention during the Vargas years did indeed foster industrial growth, but it was not without limits.

Much of the industrial growth during this time was geared toward the domestic market and thus mainly of the import-substitution variety. One standard interpretation of this process stresses that it was a product of both a decline in consumer imports and the maintenance of demand in the economy.[112] The fact that most of this growth was achieved by fuller capacity utilization rather than by building new productive capacity further underlines the point. Nonetheless, this line of thinking is incomplete. The role of government in this interpretation is limited mainly to supporting the coffee economy, but while this was clearly important, the coffee sector by this time accounted for only some 10 percent of the national income.[113] Moreover, imports had to be deliberately regulated by government intervention, which discouraged those that could be produced nationally and encouraged others necessary for sustained industrial growth. And finally, many new products came to be produced during this period, and the structure of industry diversified to include intermediate and capital goods. None of this would have been possible without active government support.

The entire period was thus characterized by an expansionist fiscal and monetary policy, which initially may not have been aimed at facilitating industrial growth but over time did just that. As already noted, government deficits were a norm under Vargas, and real federal expenditure grew at some 7.5 percent per annum. Monetary policy was also expansionist, with

---

[110] I am relying here as before for my figures on Leff, *Underdevelopment and Development in Brazil*, vol. 1, chap. 8.

[111] See, for example, Andre Gunder Frank, *On Capitalist Underdevelopment* (New York: Oxford University Press, 1975).

[112] See, for example, Baer et al., "Industrial Growth and Industrialization," 225.

[113] See Fishlow, "Brazilian Development," 104.

money supply doubling during the 1930s.[114] Moreover, tariffs and other types of protections existed during much of the period, and from 1934 onward tariff policy was more consciously aimed at promoting industry. Maintaining demand and protectionism probably help to explain the phenomenal growth in such sectors as textiles. During the 1920s, for example, swollen profits were invested in the textile industry, even though production growth was hurt in that decade by the resumption of imports. This excess capacity in turn came in handy in the 1930s: Textile production increased some 150 percent over the decade.

Investments in new products and diversification into heavier industry, however, required more than generalized government support of maintaining demand and offering protection. Economic depression was a mixed blessing for a country such as Brazil: Yes, it supported industrial growth by limiting imports; at the same time, however, it drastically reduced Brazil's export earnings. And this reduced availability of foreign exchange cut the capacity of industrialists to import new machinery. Investments into totally new areas – difficult under the best of circumstances in late-late-developing countries – were therefore especially difficult during the period under consideration. That so much industrial growth resulted from producing new products and from industrial deepening (as in paper and steel) speaks to the important supportive role of a cohesive-capitalist state.

The basic limitation of industrial growth in this period was that private domestic capital resources and technology remained underdeveloped; that is, Brazil's domestic capitalism remained weak. The consumer products produced by indigenous industrialists were often heavily dependent on imports. The inability to import new machinery or other inputs during the depression years only compounded the weaknesses of indigenous capitalism. The pattern of state intervention to maintain demand and provide protectionism encouraged domestic production but did nothing to alter the economy's profound dependence on external resources and technology. A move into heavier industries such as steel would mitigate such problems, but only over time. Meanwhile, the Brazilian version of cohesive-capitalist development was pushed by a state with limited penetration in its own society, some commitment to incorporate classes other than emerging capitalists, and a restricted understanding of nationalism. There was an elective affinity between such a state and a pattern of intervention that produced industrial growth, but it did not create conditions for self-sustained national economic development. The domestic capacity to mobilize savings and technology remained limited, but both Brazilian entrepreneurs and the state elite were satisfied that Brazil produced low-value-added goods behind protectionist walls that depended on imports and foreign technology.

---

[114] See Leff, *Underdevelopment and Development in Brazil,* 1: 206.

IV. Conclusion

At the end of the Second World War, Brazil was among the most indus-trialized countries in the group of countries that would later come to be known as the developing world. But the Brazilian economy was character-ized by a number of problems: It was geographically concentrated; pro-duction was often of low-value-added type; and it remained dependent on foreign resources and technology. Nevertheless, by midcentury Brazil had already been industrializing for nearly five decades, with industrial growth rates averaging over 6 percent per annum. More than 20 percent of the na-tional product originated in industry at the end of the Second World War. Indigenous production provided most consumer goods, and industry was increasingly diversifying, including into such heavy industries as steel. Un-like most other developing countries – with a handful of exceptions such as Korea – Brazil was no agrarian backwater at the midcentury. From a compar-ative standpoint, Brazil's middle-income stature at the end of the twentieth century owes much to this early start. Why, in spite of this early start, Brazil did not do as well as other early starters such as Korea is an important issue that is discussed in the next chapter.

The discussion has focused on the role of the Brazilian state in molding the rate and pattern of Brazil's early industrialization, including an anal-ysis of the nature of the Brazilian state itself. We have seen that factors other than state intervention, especially global market forces, were impor-tant influences on Brazilian industrialization. Still the state's role, though not decisive, was significant. The pre-1930 state of the old republic was rela-tively decentralized and overtly committed to laissez-faire. Moreover, given the political influence of agro-exporters, this was not a state that one would readily expect to support industrialization. Yet states in the old republic, especially the political elite of São Paulo, facilitated industrialization. By supporting a vibrant coffee economy, regional political elites avoided the earlier boom-and-bust pattern of commodity exports and thus provided the broad framework within which industry took root. A conscious policy of at-tracting European immigrants brought to Brazil a semi-skilled working class and entrepreneurs with experience and European links. And finally, tariffs, albeit imposed for revenue purposes, provided the protection necessary for new firms to risk investment. The fact that the resulting pattern of industrial growth was heavily dependent on linkages with the external economy was an important limitation. This too was a product of the nature of the state that was ruled by a settler elite, who shared more with their counterparts in Europe and the United States than with the former slaves and the others they governed.

A centralized and modern state emerged in Brazil only in the 1930s, more than a century after formal sovereignty was achieved. This long delay was reflected in the continuity with decentralized colonial political patterns, which were further reinforced by the nature of regionally concentrated economic development led by agro-exporters in the late nineteenth and early twentieth century. As usual, the process of state formation required a break with the past: As new middle-class groups emerged and old dominant classes weakened due to changed global economic circumstances, the social situation was conducive to the emergence of a new political arrangement. The more direct task of creating a new state was, as one might expect, led by political and military elites. Vargas led the coalition of centralizers and was decisively helped by the military in the drawn-out process of creating one Brazil out of many.

Vargas presided over an economy in which industrial production grew rapidly at an average rate of 9 percent per annum. While the more cohesive-capitalist state clearly provided the framework for this growth, the state's role ought to be kept in perspective. Economic depression in the West limited imports, thus opening the way for import-substituting production. Some of this growth was also produced by utilizing the full capacity of existing plants. Within this context, the state's role in facilitating industrial growth was also quite significant. The more cohesive and interventionist state played a critical role in maintaining demand in the economy, including by supporting the coffee economy. Tariffs and various exchange controls enhanced the prospects of private profitability, creating incentives for increased production. The state, especially the Estado Novo, became much more directly involved in industry promotion. While dependence on foreign resources and technology continued to be the Achilles heel of the model, the trend in this period was for a cohesive-capitalist state to try to enhance national autonomy by both supporting indigenous capitalists and taking on production directly.

A few more comparative observations are in order. Industry in both Brazil and Korea had developed considerably more in the first half of the twentieth century than it did in India or Nigeria, discussed below. A brief comparison of Brazil with Korea, however, already points toward some general conclusions. On the face of it, Korea's and Brazil's early industrial development occurred under very different political circumstances, propelled by a colonial state in the one case and by a sovereign state in the other case that varied from highly fragmented to more cohesive and interventionist. Any simple suggestion that colonialism thwarts industrialization and sovereign states promote it is clearly unwarranted.

What Korea and Brazil shared was a state that promoted industrial growth, if for different reasons. The limited generalization supported by the evidence is that without state support it is unlikely that these economies would have undergone as much industrialization as they did by the end of the Second World War. The parallels in the role of the state are especially striking after 1930, when cohesive-capitalist states of sorts emerged in both countries, whether colonial or sovereign, and when rapid and diversified industrial growth occurred. In both cases national security considerations emerged, and economic nationalism guided policy, especially the prioritizing of state-guided industrialization. Authoritarian states institutionalized close working relations between narrow groups of political and economic elites, and workers were tamed by force in both cases. Foreign capital, technology, and resources played a significant role in both cases. While the specific policy instruments used in the two cases varied, they shared the use of protectionism, public subsidies, and some direct government participation aimed at promoting industrial growth. There were differences across the two cases also; for example, the Japanese colonial state in Korea was in greater command of the society and the economy than was the Brazilian state under Vargas. The long-term significance of such contrasts is noted in due course. For now we can say that prior to the Second World War cohesive-capitalist states helped both Korea and Brazil to develop a significant industrial base, a base that in turn helps to explain why both were middle-income countries by the end of the twentieth century, but India and Nigeria were not.

5

Grow Now, Pay Later

State and Indebted Industrialization in Modern Brazil

In the decades following the Second World War, Brazil experienced two prolonged periods of rapid industrialization, both followed by stagnation and even decline. The first of these periods began right after the war and lasted until the early 1960s. Industry during this period grew at an annual rate of more than 9 percent. A nominally democratic state pursued import substitution vigorously and was largely responsible not only for facilitating rapid industrialization, but also for bringing about considerable diversification and deepening of industry. After several slow years associated with inflation, deficits, and balance-of-payment problems, industry again grew rapidly, from 1968 to 1980. This time a harsh authoritarian regime continued the interventionist strategy but modified it to be more outward-looking. Import substitution was now combined with deliberate export promotion, and the role of foreign capital, especially of foreign borrowing, increased dramatically. This economic expansion again came to an end as external shocks combined with policy-related problems propelled Brazil into the "lost decade" of the 1980s. The era of state-led development essentially came to an end in the early 1990s, when pressed Brazilian leaders embraced a more neoliberal model of development.

This chapter analyzes the role of the Brazilian state in promoting industrialization in the era of state-led development, from about 1950 into the 1980s. As noted in the last chapter, Brazil by the end of the Second World War had already undergone significant industrialization. The contribution of industry to the overall national product by 1945 was about 20 percent, nearly the same as that of agriculture, and by then Brazil was more or less self-sufficient in manufactured consumer products. Building on this base, conscious state intervention facilitated rapid industrialization over the next several decades, but often by transferring its costs to future generations. For example, on the positive side, industry by 1980 had grown at over 8 percent per annum for three decades, contributed 35 percent of the GDP, and employed some 24 percent of the labor force. Between 1950 and 1980 Brazil was thus transformed from a low-income economy to a middle-income economy. At the same time, however, not only was this growth interrupted by a troubled phase in the mid-1960s, but, more important, it was also followed by a period of significant stagnation beginning in the 1980s that was at least in part related to the very borrowing excesses that had produced the earlier growth success.

I argue in this chapter that mixed economic outcomes reflect the mixed character of the Brazilian state, part cohesive-capitalist and part not. On the one hand, various modern Brazilian governments prior to 1985, whether nominally democratic or authoritarian, shared important traits of cohesive-capitalist states. For example, the state set a high priority on industrial growth, represented narrow coalitions of political and economic elites who shared this priority, and, as far as the economy was concerned, depended on competent and technocratic bureaucrats who were empowered to execute the will of the state. These developmental coalitions, in turn, utilized all the means at their disposal to pursue rapid industrialization, including state enterprises, foreign capital, and indigenous entrepreneurs. On the other hand, the developmental commitments of various governments, whether democratic or authoritarian, were thwarted by a variety of political pressures: The downward reach of the state was limited, fragmenting state power; class politics and related legitimacy concerns were never too far from the surface; and there remained a patrimonial underbelly that characterized both part of the central state and the politics of the vast, unincorporated agrarian periphery. The Brazilian state was thus part Korea, but also part India and Nigeria. The latter traits led Brazilian governments to abandon their growth commitment, occasionally to spend more than they could collect, to fail to mobilize various indigenous resources for development, and, relatedly, to grant enormous concessions to foreigners to help to promote national development, a strategy that sometimes worked but just as readily backfired under adverse global conditions.

Within the frame of this general argument, the more specific nature of the Brazilian state and its impact on economic outcomes is discussed in two separate historical phases: the import-substitution phase, between 1946 and 1964; and the more mixed phase, with a greater outward orientation, that began with the military government in 1964 and continued well into the 1980s, even after redemocratization. I argue that Brazil during the first phase was ruled by a nominal democracy that resembled a cohesive-capitalist state. Such important leaders as Vargas and Kubitschek set industrialization as a priority. While under their leadership the state supported indigenous capital, their main development strategy involved state-directed productive activities and dependence on foreign capital to take the lead in producing manufactured goods for a protected domestic market.

Heavy reliance on direct foreign investment reflected shallow and half-hearted nationalism. This reliance, in turn, was a source of both economic strength and weakness: On the one hand, it facilitated rapid and fairly efficient industrialization, but on the other hand, given that the main interest of foreign investors was the protected domestic market, it led to exports lagging behind growing imports, causing serious balance-of-payment strains. A related strain emerged from heavy public spending that also contributed significantly to industrial growth. State fragmentation prevented the mobilization of ample domestic resources, leading to deficits, borrowing, and inflation. Internal and external financial strains were manageable as long as the nominal, highly elitist democracy remained relatively unchallenged. The first signs of democratic stirrings, however, especially from labor, disturbed the precarious equilibrium. The emergence of class politics diverted leaders' attention to issues other than industrial growth. Attempts to incorporate labor and the related politics of populism were particularly threatening to entrenched interests, such as the military, which in turn brought the whole experiment to a forced end in 1964.

Judged from the values of democratic participation and/or of equity – issues that are not central to the present study – the harsh military regime that followed was a dismal failure. Even from the standpoint of industrial growth, the regime's role and legacy were ambiguous. The military regime was cohesive-capitalist insofar as it equated national security with state-imposed order and rapid industrialization, facilitated by an alliance of the state and private investors. At the same time, however, the developmental capacities of the military regime were limited. Internalizing many of the society's political cleavages, it also failed to penetrate many of the regions and the countryside. And since it had no procedural legitimacy, it periodically worried about its performance-based legitimacy, leading it to such poor economic decisions as the pursuit of rapid growth even under adverse global conditions.

In its early stages the new military regime was able to overcome some of the developmental bottlenecks that the democratic regime could not. The state-led "dependent development" model continued as before to depend on public enterprises and on both Brazilian and foreign private enterprises. Unlike the earlier experience, however, manufactured exports were now also deliberately pushed, making for a new economy that was considerably more open. The rapid industrialization that resulted was hailed by many contemporaries as a "miracle." The increase in oil prices in 1974 and again in 1981, however, created great difficulties for the industrialization strategy. Instead of adjusting downward, the political compulsions of the military regime, especially of maintaining some performance-based legitimacy, led it to borrow heavily abroad and to continue to grow rapidly, hoping to pay off debts with growing exports. It was a bold and risky gambit that might even have worked, had global economic circumstances not turned the tide against such a strategy. Instead, the early 1980s plunged Brazil into a prolonged period of economic stagnation.

I. Nominal Democracy and Import Substitution

From the standpoint of this study, the main analytical puzzle posed by Brazil during the period 1945–64 is how to explain rapid industrialization and its decline under the auspices of a democratic, interventionist state. The analysis begins with a focus on the nature of the Brazilian state in this period by considering the broad political context as well as the role of such institutions as parties, the military, and the bureaucracy. The key is that Brazilian democracy was highly limited. Many of the cohesive-capitalist traits acquired prior to the Second World War endured. These characteristics enabled the leaders in the 1950s to prioritize economic growth as a goal, to direct public resources toward private investors, both domestic and foreign, and to mobilize scarce bureaucratic resources to implement these limited goals. The results included rapid industrialization. Economic changes and growing political consciousness in society brought new political forces to the fore. The emergence of new demands, especially from the lower strata, combined with an unfocused leadership, led to poor policies and a decline in economic growth in the early 1960s and precipitated a political crisis that brought the military to power in 1964.

The State

As Brazil emerged from the Second World War, it made a fairly quick transition from the semi-fascist Estado Novo to a formal electoral democracy.[1] This first transition to democracy, like the second one in the 1980s, was rooted ironically in the decisions of the armed forces and came at a time when there was not much popular demand for a democracy. Brazil's decision to fight alongside the Allies in Europe during the war led senior Brazilian military officers to emulate the United States ideologically. These officers thus distanced themselves from fascism and sought to embrace democracy. They pressed these political preferences on Vargas, who vacillated but was eventually forced by the military to step down and call elections. Brazil's postwar democracy, then, was a "gift" of sorts of its pro-U.S. military. The resulting "birth defects" were far from minor, however. The electorate was limited to the literate and excluded more than half the population; the armed forces retained a veto over the direction of politics; such old fascistic political institutions and practices as corporatized labor, institutionalized state-business cooperation in policy making, and the repression of the left

[1] Though I consulted numerous sources for a general understanding of Brazilian politics in this period, I have depended heavily on two books: Thomas E. Skidmore, *Politics in Brazil, 1930–1964: An Experiment in Democracy* (New York: Oxford University Press, 1967); and Peter Flynn, *Brazil: A Political Analysis* (Boulder, Colo.: Westview Press, 1979). For an understanding of the military's role in Brazilian politics, the indispensable source remains Alfred Stepan, *The Military in Politics: Changing Patterns in Brazil* (Princeton, N.J.: Princeton University Press, 1971).

continued; and new institutions, such as political parties and the parliament, remained weak, with a great concentration of power in the office of the president.[2] While illiberal, this limited democracy with significant traits of cohesive-capitalist states also enabled the leadership to concentrate state power and to use it to facilitate rapid industrialization, at least until the early 1960s.

The constitution of 1946 granted the vote to less than half the population. Since literacy was the main criteria for inclusion, large segments of the poor illiterate rural population, especially in the north and the northeast, remained politically marginal. And no major political figure during the 1950s argued for a more inclusive democracy.[3] This limited suffrage is also in sharp contrast to a case such as India, where full adult suffrage was granted at about the same time and where the inclusion of many poor voters gave the polity a "socialistic" tilt fairly early on. Among those who were enfranchised in Brazil, the main interest groups remained relatively fragmented and exercised their influence partly through electoral channels but mainly in a variety of alternative ways.

Emerging Brazilian industrialists, for example, though politically quite significant in such states as São Paulo, remained relatively "timid" and were not politically well organized in national politics, at least until late in this period.[4] Labor's political significance was growing through much of this period, though the autonomous left had already been brutally repressed right after the war, and state-controlled labor could not (or would not) act as a class force. As elsewhere, the urban middle classes were politically fragmented and supported a variety of political positions. The political clout of the old landed classes, whether coffee exporters or food producers, continued to decline with rapid industrialization; however, their entrenched interests were never really threatened during this period, as indicated by the fact that neither mass suffrage for the rural illiterates nor land redistribution was ever seriously proposed by the ruling political elite.

The political parties that sought to represent these interests remained more patronage machines than class- or issue-oriented organizations with clear ideologies. The Social Democratic Party (PSD), which was anything but social democratic, continued to represent the old elite, both landed and bureaucratic, but also enjoyed the support of some business groups, especially in São Paulo. Vargas created the Worker's Party (PTB), in hopes of harnessing the support of noncommunist labor; over time, this party came to represent the more co-opted elements within labor, especially the

---

[2] The theme of the limited nature of the Brazilian democracy in this period is often emphasized by Flynn, *Brazil,* esp. chaps. 6, 7, and 8.

[3] See Skidmore, *Politics in Brazil,* esp. 86.

[4] Ibid., 82. Flynn's analysis in *Brazil* differs on this point, but Skidmore's evidence is more persuasive.

state-appointed labor elite. And finally, the Democratic Party (UDN) was the classic liberal party that championed democracy, laissez-faire, and close relations with the United States and often attracted the support of the urban middle classes. To simplify a fairly complex and shifting political reality, the PSD and the PTB generally lined up behind Vargas and other Vargas-type leaders, including Kubitschek, to generate electoral majorities. The UDN, by contrast, remained mostly an opposition party through most of this period, often frustrated by its inability to stop the old dictator Vargas and his associates from reemerging as popularly elected leaders; the party often sought to mobilize military opinion in its favor.

With interest groups and parties relatively inchoate and legislative institutions such as the elected assembly relatively weak by design, enormous powers came to be concentrated in the president. During the 1950s, moreover, such Brazilian presidents as Vargas and Kubitschek focused this power on matters developmental, especially industrialization. The main check on presidential powers and goals was exercised not by other democratic forces, or at least not directly, but by the military, which generally set the parameters within which political power was exercised.[5] Transfers of power from one president to another, for example, were moments of great national drama, if not trauma. The underinstitutionalized quality of Brazilian democracy is highlighted by the fact that, except for Dutra and Kubitschek, all of the other main presidents in this period – Getúlio Dorneles Vargas, Jânio Quadros, and João Belchior Goulart – met their ends by military pressure or intervention. Military interventions were triggered on occasion by constitutional concerns and at other times by what the military perceived to be leadership transgressions of both political style and substance.

It is not too much of an oversimplification to suggest that a basic political cleavage in Brazil at the time was defined by Vargas and his supporters, on the one side, and by the anti-Getúlio forces, on the other side. Getúlio Vargas generally came to be associated with nationalism, anti-imperialism, and a pro-working-class rhetoric. But as we see below, the developmental policy implications of Vargas's rhetorical flourishes were hardly straightforward. His support for state intervention and import substitution was a position that came to be embraced and more clearly defined by his successor, Kubitschek, who also encouraged foreign investors. Both Kubitschek and Goulart were considered to take after Vargas, though Kubitschek was more "moderate" and presided over a stable polity and a growing economy, whereas Goulart accentuated the "populist" elements and paid for it dearly. The anti-Vargas forces included middle-class elements, especially in the UDN, and growing numbers within the more pro-U.S. Brazilian military. While a distinct

---

[5] Alfred Stepan calls this a "moderating" role. While I find the phrase a tad too approving of the military's actions, the deeper analytic point about the military setting the parameters of political behavior is clearly well taken. See Stepan, *Military in Politics*.

electoral minority, these opposition groups exercised considerable power, mainly through the military's boundary-setting interventions. Many in the opposition were deeply suspicious of the proworker, anti-U.S. rhetoric and preferred a more orthodox economic approach to such pressing issues as inflation and balance-of-payment problems.

If the enormously powerful presidency was the central focus of Brazilian political enthusiasm and ire, the other key political institution in Brazil was, of course, the military, especially the army, with its direct control of the state's coercive force. The role of the military in politics generally reflects how well the civilian polity itself is constructed. This principle is well highlighted by juxtaposing the Brazilian case or, for that matter, the cases of South Korea and Nigeria, also with significant military participation in politics, against India's well-consolidated civilian democracy, with minimum military participation. Nevertheless, some characteristics of the military also help to explain its political behavior. The Brazilian military, for example, grew significantly during the Second World War, from some 93,000 men with 6,000 officers in 1940 to 170,000 men with 10,000 officers in 1944. And the growth continued in the postwar period: By the 1960s the Brazilian military employed some quarter of a million soldiers with 20,000 officers. The military budget during the 1950s hovered between 10 and 15 percent of GDP, though it declined sharply in the early 1960s under Quadros and Goulart, contributing to a growing alienation of the military from the executive.[6] While the size of the military per se may not be predictive of its political proclivities,[7] the sizable Brazilian armed force – lacking any real external enemies and lacking much of a combat role – was an institution in search of a mission.

The officer corps of the Brazilian military continued to be recruited not from the upper stratum but from the middle classes.[8] Thus the pro-upper-class political role that the military has played in the Brazilian political economy was more a function of its ideological proclivities than of its social origins. The highly politicized officer corps weighed in openly on important issues of the day and often disagreed with each other. These internal political divisions were most evident in the very competitive elections among senior officers in the Military Club. Nevertheless, one should not exaggerate the internal divisions within the military.

It is true that a regional recruitment pattern, relatively decentralized command structure, and political differences among officers that paralleled the

---

[6] For the budgetary data, see Robert A. Hayes, *The Armed Nation: The Brazilian Corporate Mystique* (Tempe: Center for Latin American Studies, Arizona State University, 1989), 200.

[7] This thesis is persuasively argued by Stepan, in *Military in Politics*, chap. 2.

[8] For basic information I draw heavily on ibid in this and the next paragraph. The information on social origins is in chap. 3. Brazil specialists may notice that some of my interpretations and emphases vary from Stepan's. See ibid., esp. pt. 2.

broader political divides in the society limited the military's capacity to act as a unified political force. When some senior officers sought to oust Goulart in 1961, for example, other officers, especially fellow *gaucho* officers from Rio Grande do Sul, threatened civil war, and the military ended up reinforcing the constitutional right of Goulart to succeed Quadros. Nevertheless, the Brazilian military was by now a modern military with a corporate identity: well educated and imbued with professional norms of hierarchy and internal promotions according to recognized criteria. In terms of values, this was a conservative military, where the officers' values generally reflected an antipathy toward the lower classes. Over the 1950s, moreover, growing numbers of officers were becoming suspicious of the Vargas style of nationalist-populism and tending toward a right-leaning, pro-U.S. political position.

This political shift within the military was facilitated by the common educational experience of many officers at the War College (ESG),[9] which was established with the help of the United States. Officers who trained there were inculcated with a shared ideology of sorts that equated national security with orderly rule and rapid economic development: "national security," accordingly, required "maximizing the output of the economy and minimizing all sources of cleavage and disunity within the country."[10] This corporatist and semi-fascist developmental world-view, central to cohesive-capitalist states and also encountered in South Korea under Park Chung Hee, would eventually become hegemonic after the military came to power in 1964. Meanwhile, the influence of these ideas grew throughout the 1950s. Sharing their educational experience at the War College with civilian elites (who also attended the college) under American tutelage, many officers came to believe in their entitlement to positions of political power. This perception, along with ideological cohesion, was important in 1964, when the military moved beyond its earlier limited, boundary-setting role in the polity to one that usurped and maintained power.

A strong presidency, reined in by the military, pursued its developmental goals mainly via a relatively competent economic bureaucracy – though the bureaucracy as a whole was anything but a rational, legal meritocracy. The economic bureaucracy constituted a small but deeply consequential "pocket of efficiency" within a broader morass of nepotism and patronage.[11] As noted in Chapter 4, Vargas during the Estado Novo initiated a major effort to create a meritocratic, exam-based civil service in Brazil. The superministry

---

[9] Ibid., chap. 8.
[10] Ibid., 179.
[11] For the argument that the economic bureaucracy was relatively competent, see Nathaniel H. Leff, *Economic Policy-Making and Development in Brazil, 1947–1964* (New York: John Wiley, 1968), esp. 143–53. See also Barbara Geddes, "Building State Autonomy in Brazil, 1930–1964," *Comparative Politics* 22 (January 1990): 217–35. For some general information on the Brazilian bureaucracy in this period, see Robert T. Daland, *Exploring Brazilian Bureaucracy: Performance and Pathology* (Washington, D.C.: University Press of America, 1981).

established to pursue this goal, namely, Administrative Department of Public Service (DASP), was more or less dismantled after the Second World War. While it has been suggested quite persuasively that this move reflected the patronage needs of a more democratic leadership,[12] it is also important to remember that a wholesale restructuring of the state from within is never easy. Committed to state-led industrialization but with limited political capacities, including a patrimonial bureaucracy, Vargas and Kubitschek did what any sensible leader would have done in their position: They recruited a small group of some forty to fifty competent technocrats and created a superbureaucracy that came to control the most significant, economically consequential positions.

Who were these economic bureaucrats and how did they fit into the state structure?[13] They were mainly economists and engineers, some of whom were recruited early and trained earlier by DASP and others of whom were brought in from such semi-public, semi-research institutions as the Vargas Foundation or the Higher Institute of Brazilian Studies (ISEB). Although these *tecnicos* often engaged in heated public debates on the issues of the day, especially issues concerning inflation, balance-of-payment problems, and/or the role of foreign investment, the majority of them generally shared the leadership's commitment to state-led industrialization, import substitution, and the promotion of basic industries. In the 1950s the group included well-known public intellectuals and policy makers as diverse as the "structuralist" Celso Furtado (and his followers) and the "monetarist" Roberto Campos (and his followers). These technocrats, with their reputation for honesty and public commitment, served in such influential positions as directing the Monetary Authority (SUMOC), the Development Bank (BNDE), the foreign-exchange and credit departments of the Bank of Brazil, the various *autarqutas* and executive groups that brought state and private sectors together to make important economic decisions, and some such critical public enterprises as Petrobras (for petroleum). These technocratic elites took charge of various economic functions that the state undertook.

State Intervention in the Economy

The model of development pursued in Brazil between 1945 and 1964 was characterized by conscious state intervention aimed at import-substituting industrialization (ISI). Import substitution in Brazil had of course begun much earlier: By the Second World War, Brazil was already more or less self-sufficient in nondurable consumer goods. What changed after the war was the newly self-conscious quality of state intervention, along with a shift to consumer durables, intermediate goods, and even capital goods. In spite

---

[12] See Geddes, "Building State Autonomy."
[13] I am relying here on Leff, *Economic Policy-Making,* 143–53.

of the early industrial beginning, indigenous capitalism was still not well enough developed to move into the "deeper" phase of industrialization that required large investments and superior technological and managerial know-how. Deliberate ISI was thus pushed mainly by public sector enterprises and by foreign investors. Government spending increased rapidly during this phase, often outpacing revenues, and public policies created numerous favorable incentives for foreign investors, including tariffs to create a protected domestic market and overvalued exchange rates that cheapened necessary imports. The results included rapid industrial growth, on the one hand, and inflation, neglect of exports, and related balance-of-payment difficulties, on the other hand.

The industrialization strategy developed and changed over the nearly two decades under consideration.[14] In brief, following the war, Brazil started out with an open trading economy, though with an overvalued exchange rate; it did not have a full-blown plan for import substitution. Dependent on ample war-related foreign-exchange reserves, this policy aimed at facilitating cheap imports to satisfy the pent-up demand of powerful economic groups while dampening inflation. The resulting pressure on balance of payments emerged almost immediately and remained a significant consideration from then on. In turn, exchange controls and import restrictions that followed aimed at solving balance-of-payment problems, but also had a protectionist impact, facilitating industrial investment and growth. Conscious state intervention for industry promotion began only with Vargas in the 1950s and then became a full-fledged development strategy under Kubitschek. These were also the years of rapid industrialization and growth. Following Kubitschek, however, the political situation became less stable and less focused on matters economic; the cohesive-capitalist elements of the state declined and the more fragmented-multiclass characteristics came to the fore. Quadros's brief tenure as president was followed by Goulart, who was not keenly interested in Brazil's industrialization.[15] Economic policies under him became relatively incoherent, which further accentuated the problems, especially the financial problems of internal and external debt, and helped to precipitate a political crisis.

The nature of the state helps to illuminate the policy choices in this period. Given the concentration of power at the apex, especially during the Vargas and Kubitschek years, the policy choices were less a reflection of

---

[14] For details, see Joel Bergsman, *Brazil: Industrialization and Trade Policies* (London: Oxford University Press, 1970); Werner Baer, *Industrialization and Economic Development in Brazil* (Homewood, Ill.: Richard D. Irwin, 1965); and Leff, *Economic Policy-Making*.

[15] Skidmore thus notes that, "bored and confused by briefings over the financial crisis," Goulart essentially abandoned "any coherent policy combining development and an attack on inflation." See Skidmore, *Politics in Brazil*, 217, 256. Bergsman also suggests that, starting about 1961, the political situation changed so that "economic growth and industrialization lost their top priorities." See Bergsman, *Brazil*, 60.

interest-group pressures than they were elite responses to concrete problems as viewed through their doctrinal prisms. The president and his technocratic policy makers certainly took account of the broad political context, especially the views of the military, but also the interests of such significant economic groups as the emerging industrialists, coffee exporters, and other landed elite. Of all these groups, however, only the military could impress its political preferences on the policy makers in any direct, organized manner. Policy makers also had to keep a sharp eye on foreign interests, especially financial interests, to which Brazil was nearly continually indebted, and on the political sensibilities of the United States, which was increasingly embroiled in cold war politics and which was increasingly the point of origin for most of Brazil's foreign investment. By the same token, the policy makers could and did largely ignore the interests of the lower strata, most of whom remained disenfranchised and enmeshed in coercive patronage networks in the countryside. Within this broad context, then, policy choices mainly reflected elite commitment to "modernize" Brazil by state-guided industrialization.[16]

As noted in the last chapter, laissez-faire was the dominant economic ideology of Brazil's ruling elite prior to the Second World War. This was true even though practices often diverged from the beliefs. More important, the beliefs themselves started to change, especially during the Estado Novo. A number of influences combined after the war to shift Brazilian policy makers even further in a statist direction:

- embrace of state intervention in the form of Keynesianism seen in most Western countries with which Brazil identified
- economic analyses of Brazil by such organizations as the Economic Commission of Latin America (ECLA or CEPAL) that proposed state-guided import substitution as a route to rapid development
- memory of economic successes achieved via state support of coffee programs in the 1930s, including rapid industrialization, and
- a growing convergence of views among the highest Brazilian political leaders, military elite, and business groups that state intervention was necessary for "nation building."[17]

The emerging consensus around "developmentalism" took nearly a decade to gel following the war and came to emphasize deliberate state intervention to promote economic development, import substitution, and industrialization, including basic industries.

---

[16] For a good account of the role of "developmental" ideas in guiding the economic role of the Brazilian state in this period, see Kathryn Sikkink, *Ideas and Institutions: Developmentalism in Brazil and Argentina* (Ithaca, N.Y.: Cornell University Press, 1991). See also Skidmore, *Politics in Brazil*, esp. 82–99; and Leff, *Economic Policy-Making*, chaps. 7, 8, and 11.

[17] Some such factors are analyzed in detail in Sikkink, *Ideas and Institutions*, chap. 4.

It is important to note that though such political commitments to "developmentalism" also emerged in other countries, such as South Korea and India, nationalism in Brazil continued to be relatively shallow. The transition to a nominally democratic regime following the Second World War also did not involve any nationalist mobilization to create new values. Unlike the statism of South Korea or of India, therefore, the Brazilian political elite – their occasional nationalist flourishes notwithstanding – remained much more open to foreign investors in their pursuit of state-led development. Moreover, the Brazilian ruling groups had little interest in including the lower strata politically or economically. The contrast with India on this issue is sharp. There a prolonged struggle for independence from Britain necessitated a mass nationalist movement, leading to a much broader-based polity following the war. I am not suggesting here that developmentalism that is more nationalist or mass-based is necessarily to be preferred; much depends on what one values and what one hopes to achieve. But Brazil's highly elitist developmentalism, with its shallow nationalist roots, was instrumental in promoting rapid industrialization – at the cost of creating new problems and failing to solve old ones.

Guided by Brazil's own brand of developmentalism and facing concrete problems, Brazilian policy makers sought to promote import-substituting industries by attracting foreign investors and building state enterprises. ISI as a conscious development strategy was adopted only from the mid-1950s onward. Even prior to that, however, various policies facilitated protection and the growth of import-substituting industries. For example, following the disastrous 1946 experiment with unrestricted imports with an overvalued exchange rate that rapidly drained all the foreign-exchange reserves, Brazilian policy makers imposed foreign-exchange controls and import restrictions.[18] Devaluation, however, was not pursued, for reasons that were probably both doctrinal and political, in the sense that overvalued exchange rates served important economic interests.[19] As to prevailing doctrines, policy makers were "export pessimists" who believed, probably rightly, that such commodity exports as coffee were not likely to increase by devaluing currency and also, more questionably, that Brazil could not succeed in exporting manufactured goods. Absent the goal of encouraging exports, the political case for devaluation was weak: An overvalued exchange rate served important interests by cheapening imports, enabling profit remittances abroad, and reducing the cost of external debt in domestic currency.

Although the policies on exchange controls and import restrictions fluctuated over time, they generally supported import substitution. The main

---

[18] For details, see Bergsman, *Brazil*, chap. 3.
[19] For further discussion of this issue, see Werner Baer, *The Brazilian Economy: Growth and Development*, 4th ed. (Westport, Conn.: Praeger, 1995), 52; and Leff, *Economic Policy-Making*, 14–20.

legal statute that enabled import restrictions until 1957 was the "law of similars," under which products already produced in Brazil could be protected from foreign competition. Not only did this law benefit numerous established Brazilian firms, but it also became a major incentive for foreign firms to produce within Brazil. With Kubitschek's full embrace of developmentalism, an elaborate tariff structure was established in 1957 that more or less remained in place for a decade. Effective protection provided by tariffs and exchange-rate restrictions averaged between 80 and 90 percent, and exports were "taxed" at the rate of nearly 30 percent.[20] Protection, which varied considerably, was highest for consumer goods and lowest for capital goods. The imports that eventually made it into Brazil were in fact cheaper than they would have been under a free-market regime, and clearly subsidized manufacturing in Brazil.[21]

This import substitution was pursued within the framework of expansionist economic policies: Both fiscal and monetary policy, including short-term external credit, was used to create buoyancy. Public expenditures rose sharply, reflecting the government's commitment to state-led development, funding expansion of the bureaucracy and the army, development of infrastructure, and numerous new public enterprises. Tax revenues also grew but remained behind expenditures. At some 23 percent of the GDP in 1960 (from a base of 15 percent in 1950), Brazil collected ample new taxes, but most of them were indirect, underlining the limited capacity of the state to tax directly.[22] Deficit financing was the order of the day and contributed to demand-led inflation, although inflation during the 1950s remained under 20 percent per annum and also had other structural and supply side causes besides excess demand.[23] Expansionist credit policy was also used through the BNDE to support private Brazilian entrepreneurs. Both fiscal and monetary policies were thus growth-oriented and probably contributed to some inflation, which certainly had adverse distributional consequences; they may also have distorted the pattern of industrialization by discouraging the development of private financial markets within Brazil.[24]

Given a policy framework designed to encourage import-substituting industries, decision makers faced the question of who would build all the new industries. Unlike in India, there was no prior ideological commitment to

---

[20] See Bergsman, *Brazil*, 46.

[21] Ibid., 50–56.

[22] Taxation data are from ibid., 57, table 4.3.

[23] For a brief summary of the views of Brazilian "structuralists" such as Celso Furtado on inflation as an aspect of the broader political economy, see Skidmore, *Politics in Brazil*, esp. 234–43.

[24] For this argument, see Wilson Suzigan, "Industrialization and Economic Policy in Historical Perspective," in Fernando Rezende, ed., *Brazilian Economic Studies*, no. 2 (Rio de Janeiro: Institute of Social and Economic Planning, 1976), 20.

the state controlling the "commanding heights" of the economy in Brazil. Rather, this was a highly elitist, right-of-center state that shared important traits with a cohesive-capitalist state and maintained some key institutions of the semi-fascist Estado Novo. Brazilian policy makers preferred to work with and through the private sector. Lacking a strong and dynamic indigenous capitalist sector, however, limited the policy options. Brazilian indigenous capital, for example, was concentrated in such consumer industries (mainly nondurables) as textiles, food, clothing, beverages, furniture, cement, glass, plastics, and paper.

Most of these industries were already established prior to the Second World War, and after the war the government ensured their continued growth, affording them high rates of protection, enabling them to import necessary inputs readily, and channeling some credit to them via the BNDE. While indigenous capital made use of such incentives and did grow, it seldom moved into bigger and more complex industries. For one thing, state support for indigenous capitalism was modest in comparison with support for foreign investors. Additionally, Brazilian capital itself was organized as family businesses, and owners were reluctant to grow at the cost of decentralizing and losing control. Inflationary conditions and the limited development of private financial markets were also constraining; and many businessmen exhibited a preference for leisure.[25]

Fearful that private domestic response would not be adequate, Brazil in 1953 adopted policies that were extremely favorable to foreign investors. Given that national capitalism in Brazil in the 1950s was not much weaker than in either Korea or India, one concludes that heavy reliance on foreign capital in Brazil was more likely a political decision aimed at integrating economy with global capital. By contrast, Korea and India chose to build indigenous developmental capacities.

A number of factors help to explain these choices. Decolonization was a distant memory in postwar Brazil, and, indeed, nationalism had never been a strong political force. There was also considerable continuity in the nature of the political economy following the war, notably, in the ongoing presence of foreign capital. Moreover, the Brazilian political class continued to identify more with counterparts in Europe and the United States than with the people they governed. Economic nationalism in Brazil, to repeat, was thus a relatively shallow force, despite the occasional flourish of anti-imperial nationalism, especially under Vargas (as manifest in the establishment of Petrobras and in some inconsequential legislation to limit profit remittances of foreign firms).

[25] These were Fernando Henrique Cardoso's research findings (available only in a book in Portuguese); they are summarized in Samuel A. Morley and Gordon W. Smith, "Import Substitution and Foreign Investment in Brazil," *Oxford Economic Papers* (March 1971), 130–31.

Following Vargas's suicide, the interim government of Café Filho quietly adopted policies highly favorable to foreign investors, policies that were later fully embraced by Kubitschek. In any case, foreign investors found Brazil attractive because of its prior economic growth, its sizable elite and middle class, and its large, protected internal market. Their fear of losing their share of the Brazilian market following the implementation of the "law of similars" was also a significant factor in the decision to move production to Brazil.[26] The additional new incentives introduced in 1953 included preferential foreign-exchange rates for profit remittance, tariff reductions and liberal foreign-exchange availability for importing capital goods, favorable rules for registration of foreign capital, and internal tax and credit benefits.[27] If foreign capital inflows totaled some $150 million (U.S.) between 1947 and 1955, they averaged nearly that amount annually afterward, contributing nearly 10 percent of total manufacturing investment until about 1960, when another shift in policy led to limiting the inflows. Moreover, much of this new foreign investment was concentrated in such large industrial enterprises as automobiles, chemicals, and machinery and equipment.[28]

This rapid import-substituting industrial growth, including consumer durables, intermediate goods, and capital goods, is hard to imagine without the substantial role of foreign investment. By one estimate more than 40 percent of the total import substitution was generated by foreign firms.[29] Brazil's import substitution was also relatively efficient, say, in comparison with that of India, with foreign technology and know-how important contributors to this outcome. And finally, on the benefit side of the ledger, by legislating the procurement of indigenous inputs whenever they were available, the Brazilian state also ensured that foreign investment grew in tandem with indigenous capitalism.[30] Much can be added on the negative side of the ledger as well, including political and distributive consequences of the enormous dependence on foreign investment. The main point to be emphasized here, however, is the impact on balance of payments. Foreign investors imported inputs heavily, often providing "suppliers' credit" to

---

[26] For a discussion of various factors that attracted foreign investors, especially U.S. investors, see Lincoln Gordon and Engebert Grommers, *United States Manufacturing Investment in Brazil* (Cambridge: Harvard University Press, 1962), esp. 148.

[27] See Regis de Castro Andrade, "Brazil: The Economics of Savage Capitalism," in Manfred Bienfeld and Martin Godrey, eds., *The Struggle for Development: National Strategies in an International Context* (New York: John Wiley, 1982), 168.

[28] See Bergsman, *Brazil*, 76–77.

[29] See Morley and Smith, "Import Substitution," 160.

[30] The classic statement on how the state, private, and foreign capital all played their respective roles in Brazil's industrialization is, of course, Peter Evans, *Dependent Development: The Alliance of Multinational, State, and Local Capital in Brazil* (Princeton, N.J.: Princeton University Press, 1979). While Evans's study is concerned mainly with the post-1964 model of development, much can be learned from it, even about this earlier phase.

Brazil on "hard terms."[31] Profit remittances also added a significant burden, especially as political instability grew in the early 1960s, when remittances may have amounted to as much as one-third of the export incomes.[32] And last, given that the main interest of foreign investors was in Brazil's protected internal market, it is hard to imagine how exports could have also been promoted simultaneously at this early stage without discouraging the foreign investors.

Besides domestic private and foreign capital, the third major agent of industrialization in Brazil in this period was the state itself. With a few exceptions, the general pattern was that whenever private capital was not willing or available to undertake investment, the state often stepped in, as a last resort. Public investments grew rapidly throughout this period, increasing from some one-quarter of total investments in the early 1950s to more than one-third of the same toward the end of the decade. Investments into public sector enterprises in the same period grew from some 3 to 7 percent of total investments[33] and were concentrated in infrastructure, public utilities, and such public sector manufacturing enterprises as steel, chemicals, transportation equipment, and mining. The public sector investment in public utilities reflected a shift from the past, as the government sought to secure some legitimacy by controlling consumer prices in such areas as electricity and communications. As these controls made public utilities unattractive for the private sector, the government stepped in.[34] And when private sector efforts in some basic industries such as steel fell short, the BNDE, which had provided credit support, ended up owning large equity shares nearly by default.[35]

Capital formation in the public sector was an important component of Brazil's rapid industrialization in this period. By the standards of the developing world, moreover, the Brazilian public sector was relatively efficient because of the degree of insulation its firms enjoyed from the more vulgar forms of politicization that is common in a country such as India and that runs rampant in a case such as Nigeria. On the down side, public sector expenditures in Brazil often outpaced public revenues, with the resulting

---

[31] Milan and Bonelli estimate that some three-quarters of capital inflows were medium-term suppliers' credit on hard terms, contributing to growing indebtedness. See Pedro Milan and Regis Bonelli, "The Success of Growth Policies in Brazil," in Simon Teitel, ed., *Towards a New Development Strategy for Latin America* (Washington, D.C.: Inter American Development Bank, 1992), 74–75.

[32] See Morley and Smith, "Import Substitution," 133.

[33] For the data on total public sector investments, see Andrade, "Brazil," and for the figures on investments in public sector enterprises, Bergsman, *Brazil*, 69 (who in turn cites data from Annibal Villela).

[34] See Werner Baer, Isaac Kerstenetzky, and Annibal V. Villela, "The Changing Role of the State in the Brazilian Economy," *World Development* 1, no. 2 (1973): 27.

[35] Ibid., 26–27.

deficits, funded by printing new money, contributing to inflation. But other factors fueled inflation as well: the limited capacity of the state to collect new taxes and the enormous public expenditures devoted to constructing the new capital city of Brasilia.

In addition to reflecting policy choices, the relative success of ISI in Brazil in the 1950s also resulted from the manner in which the policies were implemented. Notable on this score were the quality of economic bureaucracy, as well as the political arrangements among the state, business, and labor. We have already noted that Presidents Vargas and Kubitschek, in setting economic growth as a political goal, created "pockets of efficiency" within the bureaucracy to pursue that end. The leaders also delegated enormous powers to a technocratic elite to run critical offices such as the Bank of Brazil, BNDE, economic ministries, important public enterprises, and various "institutes" and "groups" created especially to implement economic policies. State intervention in the economy was aimed at creating a favorable environment for business, but unlike, say, in India, the design was to "help" and not to "control" business[36] – a critical difference between more cohesive-capitalist Brazil and fragmented-multiclass India.

Close observers of Brazil generally agree that economic policy making and implementation in this period were relatively sound: The technocratic elite "raised the quality of Brazilian economic policy" and dealt "creatively" with Brazil's economic problems;[37] policy implementation was "flexible" and "efficient";[38] and, more broadly, "of the efficacy of [policy-generated] incentives, there can be no doubt."[39] None of this of course negates the fact that policy-induced problems of balance of payments and inflation were also building through this period, that the noneconomic bureaucracy was a morass of patronage, and that in the early 1960s the political priorities of the leadership shifted again, leading to significant economic slowdown. Any balanced picture needs to take account of these contradictory trends; for now, however, I focus on more specific examples of what the Brazilian economic bureaucracy did right. These included an efficient management of the import-control system that after 1953 eliminated licenses; a leading analyst comments that the Tariff Council generally worked "well" in implementing tariff policy.[40] Unlike the Indian efforts, Brazilian attempts to guide investment never included licenses, but instead relied on a variety of other incentives, including credit, varying rates of protection, and administrative conveniences for priority sectors. As another example, the BNDE, which

[36] Bergsman, *Brazil*, 79.

[37] See Leff, *Economic Policy-Making*, 152–53.

[38] See Bergsman, *Brazil*, 80–82.

[39] See Albert Fishlow, "Origins and Consequences of Import Substitution in Brazil," in Luis Eugenio Di Marco, ed., *International Economics and Development* (New York: Academic Press, 1972), 345.

[40] Bergsman, *Brazil*, 80–81.

"had a first class staff with a strong sense of mission," made loans mostly on economic criteria, and enforced "performance" and "efficiency" standards, especially in "public enterprises."[41]

Some of the state's institutionalized links with business and labor, though quite undemocratic, also helped state elites to implement economic policy. The state generally controlled interest-group activities, including those of the emerging business groups. This continuity from the semi-fascist Estado Novo entailed controlling the "financing and leadership of the Confederation of Industries."[42] State-business relations were thus state-driven and fairly typical of cohesive-capitalist states. How this was turned into a developmental asset is best exemplified by the operation of Executive Groups, created under Kubitschek. These groups, "in charge of setting guidelines and standards for the development of the main industrial sectors and in charge of granting or recommending incentives to particular investment projects,"[43] brought together managers of domestic and foreign private industry and senior economic bureaucrats from various ministries, the Tariff Council, BNDE, and the Bank of Brazil. These groups planned the output and investment strategy of prioritized sectors and concomitantly created appropriate public policies to support private sector needs for credit, imports, and domestic inputs. A fine example of what Peter Evans has dubbed "embedded autonomy," the state elite worked closely with business to direct and facilitate private production.[44] These groups worked very well – "competent and very useful," in the assessment of one economist – especially in such key new industries as automobiles, because planners and implementers were the same people.[45]

Finally, state-labor relations were yet another aspect of state-created societal cohesion from above. The corporatist arrangements created during the Estado Novo, especially the labor laws created in 1943, essentially continued to provide the framework of labor control in the democratic period. Even the apparently "liberal" political party, the UDN, seldom opposed these semi-fascist institutional arrangements. Within this arrangement, labor did not have the right to create autonomous unions. Unions were instead recognized, founded, and controlled by the state, typically by appointing pliable individuals as leaders.[46] Unlike South Korea, however, labor management in Brazil was aimed mainly at political control and not at mobilization for productivity gains. Even as many workers could increasingly vote in elections,

[41] Geddes, "Building State Autonomy," 226–27.

[42] Leff, *Economic Policy-Making*, 183.

[43] Andrade, "Brazil," 167.

[44] See Peter Evans, *Embedded Autonomy: States and Industrial Transformation* (Princeton, N.J.: Princeton University Press, 1995), esp. chap. 1.

[45] Bergsman, *Brazil*, 81–83.

[46] For details, see Kenneth Paul Erickson, *The Brazilian Corporative State and Working-Class Politics* (Berkeley: University of California Press, 1977), esp. chap. 3.

the state often managed to prevent them from freely organizing, striking, and demanding wage increases until the end of the 1950s, with the result that productivity gains far surpassed gains in wages.[47] Between 1949 and 1959, for example, output per worker increased some 90 percent, whereas real wages increased only 26 percent.[48] State repression and discipline of the working class was thus integral to the rapid and relatively efficient ISI of Brazil.

The Pattern of Industrialization

The Brazilian economy grew at some 6 percent per annum between 1947 and 1962, and industrial growth in the same period averaged between 9 and 10 percent per anum – an impressive performance by any standard. Growth declined in 1962, however, only to recover again in 1968, under a harsh authoritarian regime. Nonetheless, the state's policy choices succeeded in producing rapid industrial growth for nearly fifteen years. How was this managed? The industry that developed during this period continued to move into new areas, from already well-developed consumer goods to such durables as automobiles and on to intermediate and capital goods, including machinery, electrical equipment, and steel. The fastest growing industries, such as automobiles, were precisely those that the government targeted for growth, not only via substantial tariff protection, but also via credit, subsidies, liberal imports of inputs, and special administrative arrangements such as the Executive Groups. Industrial growth was driven mainly by import substitution: About one-third of the growth was associated with a decline in the import coefficient.[49]

Within this broad pattern, some industries did better than others, and the import-substitution strategy, even at its most successful, was not without pitfalls. Old consumer industries – textiles, for example – received the highest protection but did not grow as fast as industries with more modest protection.[50] But it was also the case that established industries such as textiles did not receive favorable treatment from public authorities, which limited their access to credit and foreign exchange. Automobiles, by contrast, enjoyed very high rates of protection – up to 200 percent. Foreign investors took the lead in this sector, although they were also forced to procure many Brazilian inputs, which encouraged domestic industry but raised the costs of production. In spite of heavy protection and cost-push policies,

---

[47] For the much more strike-prone behavior of the working classes during 1960–64 that eventually contributed to the military coup in 1964, see Erickson, *Brazilian Corporative State*, esp. pt. 3.

[48] See Bergsman, *Brazil*, 58.

[49] See Fishlow, "Origins and Consequences," 351.

[50] For this argument, see Bergsman, *Brazil*, esp. pt. 3. Some of the information on specific industries that follows is also drawn from this study, esp. chap. 6.

the automobile industry was relatively efficient, with at least one firm close to being globally competitive.[51]

The steel industry is particularly instructive, because it was mainly a public sector endeavor that remained relatively "competitive in a comparative cost sense."[52] Following Volte Redonda, two new mills, Usimas and Cosipa, were established in the early 1960s, with considerable private initiative. Eventually, however, the BNDE ended up with the majority ownership. Among the factors that helped Brazilian steel to be cost-efficient were support and supervision from the BNDE, relative insulation from patronage, growing domestic demand that enabled economies of scale, and such fortuitous factors as ready availability of high-grade iron ore. Finally, there were some capital goods industries that also grew in this period with only modest protection. Most of these new ventures were undertaken by foreign investors attracted by the strong market.[53] At the same time, however, state support for such initiatives was substantial: The BNDE provided loans on easy terms, and targeted policies enabled import of equipment; in addition, profits could be remitted abroad with relative ease.

Let us reiterate several general aspects of the Brazilian pattern of industrialization in this period. First is the ironic heavy dependence of new industries on foreign investors – ironic because the strategy of import substitution was often justified in terms of building a national industrial capacity. It would seem that the real reason for pursuing import substitution was somewhat different: The ruling elite, with only a shallow sense of nationalism, sought a growing economy and growing incomes via industrialization. Given the limited capital and technology readily available within Brazil and given the balance-of-payment constraints, elites invited foreigners to handle the industrialization, which otherwise would not have been possible. State and foreign investors cooperated to develop chemicals, machinery, transport equipment, shipbuilding, electrical equipment, and engineering goods, all rapidly growing industries of the period. Of course, dependence on foreign capital and technology could be readily withdrawn and could create potential strains on the balance of payments, especially when capital inflows slowed and profit remittances increased.

Also noteworthy in Brazil's ISI was its relative efficiency. Thus, the Brazilian economy grew at a rate some 50 percent higher (6 instead of 4 percent per annum, say, in the 1950s) than India's, with an investment rate of 14 to 15 percent, about the same as that of India, which was around 13 to 14 percent. India's industry in the period grew at some 7 percent per annum and that of Brazil grew at nearly 10 percent per annum. Capital-output ratios

---

[51] Ibid., 120–30.

[52] Ibid., 119. For details of the steel industry, see also Werner Baer, *The Development of the Brazilian Steel Industry* (Nashville, Tenn.: Vanderbilt University Press, 1969).

[53] Bergsman, *Brazil*, 132–33.

were thus generally lower in Brazil and, quite remarkably, did not grow over the period, despite the shift to heavier industries. The microevidence for several such specific industries as steel and automobiles is consistent with this macroview. Productivity per worker also grew at some 6 percent per annum in this period, and overall productivity growth averaged 2.4 percent per annum.[54] The rapid growth of manufacturing exports a few years later also suggests that industry must have been relatively efficient. How does one explain this?

There is no single comprehensive answer. In comparison with India during the same period, for example, we find several factors contributing to a somewhat superior performance in Brazil. First, a state committed to economic growth focused policy making on matters that affected production, even at the expense of such other considerations as national sovereignty, political liberties, or better distribution. Second, the large role of foreign investors brought superior technology and management to production processes. Third, close cooperation between state and business enhanced the confidence of business in state intervention and facilitated policy implementation. Fourth, with labor strictly controlled, productivity gains outpaced wages. And finally, Brazil's advanced prior industrialization provided a stronger knowledge base for industrialization, a trained work force, infrastructure, dense supplier networks, demand for goods, and a tax base for further supportive public spending.

The final general comment concerns the negative aspects, especially negative financial aspects, of Brazil's import-substitution drive. We have noticed all along that inflation and balance-of-payment pressures plagued Brazilian decision makers throughout this period. These problems were integral to the model. Regarding inflation, had the Brazilian state been more efficacious, it could have collected more taxes and reduced the demand-led inflationary pressures generated by deficit spending, and it could also have alleviated such supply constraints as ready availability of food items by investing more in the agricultural sector. As it was, however, demand-led inflation was a persistent problem, contributing to various distortions, especially limiting the growth of private savings. And second, as to balance-of-payment problems, the root cause was limited growth of exports. While it is easy in retrospect to blame overvalued exchange rates for this outcome, an important counterfactual ought to be kept in mind: Devaluation, though helpful for exports, "probably would not have produced the desired growth in income, industrialization, and modernization."[55] The role of foreign investors was a source of tension, as their main interest in Brazil was the protected internal market and not the possibility of using Brazil as a base for exports.

[54] See Albert Fishlow, "Brazilian Development in Long-Term Perspective," *American Economic Review* 70, no. 2 (May 1980): 106.
[55] Bergsman, *Brazil*, 99.

This marriage of state and foreign investors, within the frame of import substitution, therefore made it very difficult to push manufactured exports simultaneously.

It is also important to remember that both balance-of-payment and inflationary pressures had existed throughout the 1950s, but were manageable. Inflation remained under 20 percent. Balance-of-payment problems could be tamed by a finance minister's visit to Washington, D.C., and/or to the International Monetary Fund (IMF), promising "good behavior" in return for loans and a signal of "good health" to foreign investors. Thus, the crisis in the early 1960s was sparked by political changes and not by economic problems intrinsic to Brazil's import-substitution model of development. While both the "right" and the "left" criticized the strategy as "exhausted," Wilson Suzigan's conclusion is more persuasive: In the early 1960s, "import substitution [in Brazil] still had a long way to go."[56]

What caused the economic and political crisis, then, was the emergence of new social forces, on the one hand, and of such new leaders as Quadros and Goulart, who were not as focused on economic growth as Vargas or Kubitschek, on the other hand. A ready shift toward greater state fragmentation and multiclass politics, in turn, underlined the fact that the developmental coalition in Brazil was relatively underinstitutionalized. Growing working-class restiveness and new populist leaders in power reinforced each other, throwing developmental policies off their trajectory. A sharp rise in wages produced inflation rates of near 100 percent. Populist rhetoric and some political instability in terms of growing incidence of strikes discouraged both foreign investors and foreign loans needing the sanction of the United States. Internal and external financial pressures thus added to what was mainly a political crisis. And a military concerned about internal security, in turn, felt threatened by what was perceived to be a leftward drift in the Brazilian political economy. Moreover, the cold war atmosphere was supportive of Brazilian military leaders, who deposed elected leaders and imposed a right-wing military authoritarian regime in power in 1964.

II. Military Rule, Economic "Miracle," and Beyond

The military government that came to power in 1964 ruled for more than two decades, until it yielded power to an elected government in 1985. During this period Brazilian industry at first grew rapidly, then slowed in the context of enormous foreign debt. The political economy puzzle posed by this record concerns the role of the military government in facilitating rapid industrial growth and in paving the way for its eventual deceleration. As usual, such other factors as cyclical conditions and the changing

---

[56] Suzigan, "Industrialization and Economic Policy," 22.

global economy were also important. Nevertheless, the state's role looms large in the mixed economic story. The state under military control became highly authoritarian, acquiring more characteristics of a cohesive-capitalist state, and it was able to overcome some important obstacles to growth in the 1960s, triggering a decade-long economic "miracle." This much is well known. At the same time, however, and unlike the South Korean cohesive-capitalist state under Park Chung Hee, the developmental capacities of the Brazilian military state were also limited: The military elite was divided; the downward penetration of state authority into various regions and the agrarian periphery remained circumscribed; the state's social support from the middle and upper classes had dwindled over time as opposition to military rule grew; and the state's capacities were dependent on a variety of external resources, especially foreign capital, for sustained growth. The Brazilian political context thus encouraged a debt-led growth strategy that eventually became unsustainable, especially when global economic conditions turned adverse.

The Militarized State

The military coup of 1964 terminated Brazil's limited experiment with democracy and reestablished a harsh, right-wing authoritarian regime.[57] This regime exhibited a fair amount of continuity with the Estado Novo.[58] As under Vargas, the presidency now, too, was the locus of an enormous concentration of power; competitive politics was not allowed; the state controlled urban groups via corporatist structures; the patronage-based agrarian periphery was left intact; substantial state intervention in the economy continued; the interests of the upper classes were defended; and repressive anticommunism was the order of the day. The past clearly cast a long shadow on the present, which is not all that surprising considering the relative brevity of the democratic interlude. There were some important differences from the Estado Novo, too: The military was now explicitly in power; the role of foreign capital in the economy changed; and the ideology of the military rulers was more individualistic and pro–free enterprise than it

---

[57] An important source on the nature of the military government on which I have drawn heavily is Thomas E. Skidmore, *The Politics of Military Rule in Brazil, 1964–1985* (New York: Oxford University Press, 1988). Other important sources include Frances Hagopian, *Traditional Politics and Regime Change in Brazil* (New York: Cambridge University Press, 1996); Flynn, *Brazil*; Ronald M. Schneider, *The Political System of Brazil: Emergence of a "Modernizing" Authoritarian Regime, 1964–1970* (New York: Columbia University Press, 1971); Stepan, *Military in Politics*; Alfred Stepan, ed., *Authoritarian Brazil: Origins, Policies and Future* (New Haven: Yale University Press, 1973); and idem, ed., *Democratizing Brazil: Problems of Transition and Consolidation* (New York: Oxford University Press, 1989).

[58] For this argument, see Flynn, *Brazil*, esp. 325; and Thomas Skidmore, "Politics and Economic Policy Making in Authoritarian Brazil, 1937–1939," in Stepan, *Authoritarian Brazil*, esp. 37–43.

was fascistic.[59] These differences, however, were more apparent than real. For example, the practices of the new military regime often varied from the regime's pro-American-sounding ideology. The real differences between the Estado Novo and the new militarized state thus reflected less how power within Brazil was organized and used than the obvious fact that the world had changed; whereas Brazil in the 1930s identified with growth of fascism in Europe, Brazil in the 1960s and the 1970s was eager to join the Western alliance led by the United States.[60]

Between 1964 and 1985 Brazil was ruled by a succession of four-star generals. The officer corps that forcibly ousted Goulart from power in 1964 had been relatively united on the need for the coup, mainly because of their shared antipathy to what they perceived to be the growing threat of left-leaning populism. The avowed purpose of the coup was thus to restore political order, stabilize the economy and put it on a growth trajectory, build the confidence of foreign lenders and investors, and facilitate development in a manner that would enhance national security.[61] This was a classic battle between cohesive-capitalist and fragmented-multiclass political tendencies. According to the military, "the means by which all branches of national life can be brought together and subsumed under the broad direction of national security is the power of the state."[62] Despite their explicit commitment to authoritarian, exclusionary politics, the military rulers initially enjoyed support from such social groups as the church, business groups, old right-leaning political parties such as the UDN, and select technocrats and policy makers – all groups that themselves were also wary of what they perceived to be emerging political and economic instability under the prior democratic regime. Over time civilian support dwindled, occasionally hardening into open opposition and defiance, especially on the part of labor.

The momentary political unity among the officer corps that emerged around the coup also turned out to be precisely that, momentary. Divisions that had divided military officers prior to the coup reemerged shortly afterward. On the one side were the more hard-line officers who tended to be more nationalistic on economic questions, more illiberal in political orientation, and generally more "indigenous" and less "cosmopolitan" in

---

[59] For the argument that the new regime was really a sharp break from the past, see Alfred Stepan, "The New Professionalism of Internal Warfare and Military Role Expansion"; and Fernando Henrique Cardoso, "Associated-Dependent Development: Theoretical and Practical Implications," both in Stepan, *Authoritarian Brazil*, 47–68 and 142–78, respectively. These arguments are fully persuasive only if one believes, which I do not, that the essence of a regime lies either in its ideology (for Stepan) or in its underlying class alliances (for Cardoso).

[60] See Skidmore, "Politics and Economic Policy Making," 42.

[61] For a good discussion of the military's ruling ideology, especially its emphasis on promoting internal national security via economic development, see Stepan, *Military in Politics*, chap. 8.

[62] See Flynn, *Brazil*, 322.

their outlooks. On the other side were "moderates," generally associated with the ESG, who were strongly anticommunist, pro-U.S. in political and economic orientation, and inclined toward restoring democracy after the polity had been "cleansed." The first military president, Castello Branco, was associated with the moderate faction. Both Arturda Costa e Silva and Emílio Garrastazú Medici, who followed Castello Branco, were more hard-line, and Ernesto Geisel and João Batista de Oliveira Figueiredo, who ruled after them, were in turn more moderate.[63]

These divisions within the officer corps were politically consequential insofar as they periodically created greater room for "politics," even in an authoritarian setting. Thus, dissent and opposition remained a feature of cohesive-capitalist rule in Brazil and eventually contributed to redemocratization. Despite the political divisions, however, the military elite were relatively united on broad economic goals – committed to "developmentalism," in the Brazilian sense of that term, meaning economic growth, industrialization, statism, close collaboration with foreign capital, and a near total neglect of the welfare needs of the lower strata.[64] The broad economic goals of the military rulers were thus not all that different from those of Kubitschek. Where the military rulers differed was in their unyielding commitment to economic growth as a priority, as well as to the ruthless use of political and policy instruments to achieve this goal.

The Brazilian military justified its extreme level of intervention in politics – both to itself and to relevant "publics" both within and outside Brazil – on the grounds of its superior capacity to restore political order and facilitate rapid development. Whatever minimal legitimacy and support the military enjoyed thus rested on its performance. Any reduction in growth performance was thus deemed politically undesirable and even dangerous by the military rulers; business profit and the incomes of the middle and working classes depended on sustained growth. As numerous policy decisions were influenced by this growth commitment, when stabilization efforts in the early postcoup period did not produce immediate growth, the military rulers adopted a much more activist stance. More important, after the Organization of Petroleum Exporting Countries (OPEC) increased oil prices in 1973 and again in 1979, when economic prudence might have dictated an economic slowdown, Brazilian rulers chose to swim upstream, maintaining their commitment to high growth. A planning minister subsequently explained the underlying logic: "If in August of 1974 we had set our growth target at 4 to 6 percent, the disappointment would have been widespread."[65]

---

[63] See, for example, Skidmore, *Politics of Military Rule*, passim.

[64] See Antonio Barros de Castro, "Renegade Development: Rise and Demise of State-Led Development in Brazil," in William Smith et al., eds., *Democracy, Markets, and Structural Reform in Latin America* (New Brunswick: Transaction, 1994), 183–213, esp. 188; and Flynn, *Brazil*, 382–83.

[65] Quoted in Barros de Castro, "Renegade Development," 189.

Other notable and important aspects of the military rule at its apex included a commitment to constitutionalism and an affinity for technocratic solutions. Even in coming to power the military violated the most basic norm of the existing constitutional democracy, namely, gaining office by winning an election. The military's subsequent rule, nevertheless, was relatively legalistic. It passed a series of constitutional amendments, tersely called "institutional acts," that further curtailed political freedoms and even legalized repression, including torture, against political foes. While observers cannot be blamed for making light of the legal cover that masked a right-wing authoritarian dictatorship, the practice of constitutionalism was not without significance. The product of a long tradition, its continued practice not only preserved the norms of constitutionalism for the future but also curbed the personalistic, corrupt, and arbitrary government common in other dictatorships, such as Nigeria. Brazil's military rulers, though harsh dictators, were thus also committed to what they conceived to be a "greater public good," rather than to personalistic ends; they pursued this public good ruthlessly but within a constitutional framework.

The military also had considerable faith in technocracy as a problem solver. It is difficult to disentangle whether this faith was a product of the military's belief that it stood "above" politics, or reflected the broader Brazilian political culture of respect for specialists, or whether it reflected the legacy of the much earlier Comtean positivism that permeated the mindset of some military elites. The embrace of technocrats may also have been influenced by the military's "new professionalism," a set of norms that the senior officers internalized at U.S.-influenced institutions such as the ESG, where military officers and civilians trained together in matters political and economic.[66] Whatever the root cause, the fact is that the military elite ruled in close alliance with technocratic civilian policy makers. While very much the dominant partner, the military often left it to the technocrats to turn vague goals into specific targets and concrete policies. The choice of specific technocrats very much reflected the military's right-wing political and economic goals and was thus hardly above politics. Nevertheless, military rulers delegated power in critical policy areas, such as in the economy, to policy specialists, adding efficiency to their otherwise brutal political program.

Politics during the two decades of military rule, while always authoritarian, was not static. Following a brief consolidation phase, the first decade was generally harsher than the second decade, when the regime decompressed, and as is often the case, opposition reemerged from below.[67] The early pattern during the consolidation phase – under the "moderate" Castello Branco – was to repress and purge political enemies and permit some

---

[66] For a discussion of military's "new professionalism," see Stepan, *Military in Politics*, esp. chap. 8.

[67] I draw especially on Skidmore, *Politics of Military Rule*; and Flynn, *Brazil*.

opposition. But when the opposition pressed its case, the more hard-line officers would demand harsher rule, leading to newer institutional acts that in turn broadened the definition of "political enemies." The repressed, purged, and even tortured were initially leftists and a variety of pro-Vargas types, but the category rapidly broadened to include much of the political class and even some military officers, eventually including the Congress, as well as a variety of real or potential opposition groups and figures in the civil society. The constraints of a legalistic tradition were stretched, especially in the northeast, far from the centers of power, where arbitrary government – settling of scores – and torture were more prevalent. Reflecting the political logic of cohesive-capitalist states, the harsh authoritarian rule was justified in terms of developmental needs: In the words of Roberto Campos, the economic czar under Castello Branco: "We need the maintenance of social discipline to go on with the urgent business of growth."[68]

The consolidation phase more or less ended by 1967, when the military rulers adopted a new, authoritarian constitution. Armed with their legal, bureaucratic, and coercive apparatus, they settled down to rule, repressing all opposition. The military rulers also created an intelligence service that penetrated various walks of urban life, especially labor and the state apparatus, which helped with screening appointments and promotions in the ministries.[69] While the military thus achieved some direct control over elements in the state and society, and probably frightened many others into acquiescence, if not acceptance, there are some qualifications concerning the cohesive and disciplining nature of military power in Brazil. First, given the nominal nature of the democracy that the military rulers had usurped, "many (perhaps most) middle sector Brazilians were not greatly disturbed at their loss of political options";[70] much of the middle class really did not need to be disciplined. Second, military rule did not reach much beyond the major cities; unlike in South Korea, for example, important regions and the vast agrarian periphery remained insulated from the military rule.[71] And third, military rule in Brazil, again unlike in South Korea, was aimed mainly at depoliticizing and not at mobilizing and incorporating various socioeconomic actors along nationalist or other lines. The organizational base of the military thus remained relatively narrow and dwindled over time.

Costa e Silva (1967–69) and Medici (1970–73) were both hard-line presidents who presided over Brazil's economic miracle. In spite of the repressive rule, opposition did not vanish. Labor strife was brutally put down, but other groups such as students, radical workers, the church, and some politicians

[68] Cited in Flynn, *Brazil*, 331.
[69] See Skidmore, *Politics of Military Rule*, 57.
[70] Skidmore, "Politics and Economic Policy Making," 16.
[71] See, for example, the important case study of Minas Gerais, hardly an outlying state, in Hagopian, *Traditional Politics*.

kept up their demands and criticism. All authoritarian regimes face the options of imposing further repression or making concessions and accommodating political opposition. Both methods were tried in Brazil, but serially. During the rule of Costa e Silva and Medici, further repression was the order of the day. As far as the economy was concerned, a division of labor of sorts emerged between the military rulers and the technocratic policy makers: The military imposed its repressive political order and the technocrats pursued economic growth, without paying undue attention to interest-group demands.

Rapid economic growth generated some support for the military rulers, both among the Brazilian upper and middle strata and among key supporters in the United States. However, the repressive politics that accompanied high growth and the resulting maldistribution of income became major sources of regime criticism. Subsequent presidents such as Geisel (1974–78) and Figueiredo (1979–85), representing the more moderate officer opinion, thus sought to accommodate these growing pressures using political and economic strategies. Examples of political concessions included limited elections, restoration of habeas corpus, return of political refugees, revocation of some harsher constitutional amendments, and limited scope for reformulated political parties to emerge. Similarly, examples of economic concessions entailed allowing labor to negotiate higher wages, adopting policies that would help to reverse the decline in real wages, and responding to the demands of business for looser credit and other concessions.

This more politicized phase of authoritarian rule provided the context in which critical economic decisions were taken by the highest ruling elite to continue the pursuit of rapid economic growth despite the worsening international economic conditions. With the sharp rise in global oil prices in 1973, Brazil, as a significant oil importer, experienced a deterioration in its terms of trade. When oil prices rose for the second time in the late 1970s, the military rulers again entertained the option of adjusting their growth ambitions downward but decided against it. What are the political underpinnings of these economic decisions?

As already suggested, a commitment to rapid growth and industrialization was part and parcel of the regime's legitimacy formula, which rested not on matters procedural but on substantive economic achievements. The more accommodationist phase of politics that began in 1974 made it even more difficult for the regime to accept lower economic growth as a viable political goal. Limited elections in 1974 revealed the significant support enjoyed by opposition parties, who stood for redistribution, democracy, and national autonomy. Since the military was not prepared to embrace these goals, continuing rapid growth was believed to be the main avenue for generating support. Jimmy Carter, who became president of the United States in 1977, emphasized human rights as a foreign policy goal, constraining Brazilian military rulers from becoming even more authoritarian. When oil prices rose again in 1979, the regime contemplated slowing the economy but rejected that option, fearing the wrath such a policy might evoke among business groups, the middle classes, and the more vocal labor groups. This decision to pursue high growth in the face of deteriorating terms of trade was an important cause of the growing indebtedness that eventually brought the growth miracle to a crashing halt in the 1980s.

Within this broad political context, military rulers and the technocratic policy makers sought to implement their developmental agenda by working through the bureaucracy and by establishing ties with such critical economic groups as business and labor. Although the military rulers attempted to transform the bureaucracy, they failed to make any significant headway.[72] After some interruptions, the basic pattern of creating and maintaining pockets of efficiency within a politicized and patronage-based bureaucracy continued. The interruptions occurred first under Goulart, when even the limited pockets of efficiency were threatened by leftist political zeal, and then again under early military rule, when neoliberal efforts unsuccessfully attempted to rationalize the entire bureaucracy. The military rulers did, however, succeed in insulating the bureaucracy from a variety of social pressures, but again, only at the highest levels and only for a while. By the mid-1970s, when politics reemerged, bureaucratic appointments again became a vehicle for satisfying political interests, especially regional interests, and the main strategy for steering the economy reverted to the ad hoc appointment of experienced bureaucrats to positions of responsibility.

Brazil's economic bureaucracy was thus underinstitutionalized, yet relatively efficient. This paradox is comprehensible if one keeps the following in mind. First, Brazil's system of higher education continued to produce a large number of qualified engineers, economists, and other professionals who generally staffed the growing state apparatus at the upper and upper-middle levels. To get a good position in the Brazilian state, whom you knew mattered, but what you knew also mattered. Second, in addition to being well qualified, Brazil's highest civil servants were also public-spirited or at least not overtly personalistic and corrupt. How they acquired this ethos without a highly institutionalized and professional civil service is something of a puzzle. Socialization within long-standing traditions is probably the main reason. Even though underinstitutionalized, senior civil servants within Brazil are a stable group who maintained employment in one form or another

---

[72] See, for example, Ben Ross Schneider, *Politics within the State: Elite Bureaucrats and Industrial Policy in Authoritarian Brazil* (Pittsburgh, Pa.: University of Pittsburgh Press, 1991), esp. chap. 10. See also Alexandre Barros, "The Brazilian Military: Professional Socialization, Political Performance, and State Building," Ph.D. dissertation, University of Chicago, 1978; and Edison de Oliveria Nunes, "Bureaucratic Insulation and Clientelism in Contemporary Brazil: Uneven State Building and the Taming of Modernity," Ph.D. dissertation, University of California, Berkeley, 1984.

in the bureaucracy.[73] Brazilian civil servants were also extremely well paid, near the top of the income pyramid, which probably insulated them somewhat from temptations of corruption, at least petty corruption. One analyst thus argues persuasively: "Direct, immediate, material self-interest was not a major factor" in molding the policy behavior of upper-level economic bureaucrats.[74] Finally, and probably most important, the military leadership of the state was developmental, having a keen interest in the success of the state's economic interventions, whether indirectly through various economic policies or directly through state enterprises. In an authoritarian state with cohesion and discipline, these priorities trickled down, molding the behavior of economic bureaucrats in a manner that contributed to the state's effectiveness.

The militarized state of Brazil was a procapitalist state par excellence.[75] Regime ideology was explicit on this issue, as were the regime's anticommunist and antileft attitudes. Considering that military officers were generally not recruited from the upper classes, their procapitalist orientation was probably a function of their developmental ideology, with its emphasis on the role of the private sector.[76] That developmental ideology was the prime moving force is clear, because even a strongly procapitalist outlook did not stop the military elite from expanding the state sector; on the contrary, the state sector grew in partnership with capital, both foreign and private.[77] The political links between the state and private capital are thus an essential part of the story.

These political relations between state and capital were both formal and informal. Formal representation of business groups in the top policy-making bodies was welcomed more by some military presidents and less by others. More common were other types of networks. Sectoral or industry-specific groups that brought together policy makers and businessmen continued as before, though their significance varied with the prioritizing policy makers. Informal collaboration between policy makers and businessmen was widespread. Also prevalent were networks of businessmen and midlevel bureaucrats aimed at facilitating policy implementation in such areas as foreign exchange, licenses, tariffs, and credit.[78] And finally, while corporatist structures linking state and private capital continued, there emerged during the 1970s a number of more or less independent

---

[73] Schneider, *Politics within the State,* 220.

[74] Ibid., 197.

[75] Albert Fishlow, hardly a flaming Marxist, thus noted in the *American Economic Review* that the military regime had a "frank commitment to capitalism." See Fishlow, "Brazilian Development," 106.

[76] For discussion of the social origins of the military, see Stepan, *Military in Politics,* chap. 3.

[77] See Evans, *Dependent Development.*

[78] Schneider uses Cardoso's concept of "bureaucratic rings" to underline such patterns of influence; see his *Politics within the State,* 227.

business associations that gained influence by collecting their own data, generating research, and arguing their case with relatively sophisticated analyses.

It is well known that the military government welcomed foreign capital to push its agenda of rapid growth and industrialization. Less well known is why the military rulers and their policy makers chose this path. When juxtaposed against the case of South Korea, for example, it becomes clear that dependence on foreign capital does not follow inevitably from a commitment to rapid industrialization: Park Chung Hee and his policy makers successfully decoupled technology from foreign capital, inviting the former and paying for it by high rates of domestic savings, investments, and rapid growth. Brazil, by contrast, continued to invite direct foreign investment as a source of new investments. Why?

The choice is probably best understood as a continuation of past trends. Dependence on foreign capital for growth is really the Brazilian way of development: It was the case in the heyday of coffee, it was true for Kubitschek, and it was not much of a departure from the norm for the military rulers. As in earlier epochs – but unlike in such countries as Korea or India – Brazilian military rulers were part and parcel of a colonial mindset that identified as much or more with their counterparts in Europe and the United States than with those they governed. Growing economic dependence on outsiders and a sharp elite-mass gap were thus inextricably bound up in Brazil, and both reflected the fact that the nationalism of the ruling elite was relatively shallow.

This is not to deny that there was the occasional show of nationalism, just as there were cleavages dividing more or less nationalist military rulers. Surveys of elite bureaucrats, moreover, often found a preference for indigenous private enterprise over both foreign and state enterprises.[79] However, when, at bottom, it became clear that reducing dependence on foreign capital required a more egalitarian and nationalistic political economy – a political economy that the military rulers were neither willing nor capable of creating – then the choice of continued dependence, even growing dependence, became nearly obvious. In addition, many military rulers were favorably inclined toward close relations with the United States. Irrespective of their hesitations on the economic implications of such closeness – and some of these hesitations were strong enough in security-oriented industries to lead to more nationalist choices – most officers happily went along with an economic strategy that depended on close collaboration with foreign capital.

If the state and private capital, whether indigenous or foreign, were in a close developmental alliance, the relationship of the state with labor, by

[79] Ibid., 222, for the survey results of Luciano Martins.

contrast, was mainly one of control and repression.[80] This too was an aspect of the internal political logic of cohesive-capitalist states. The formal corporatist structures were created during the Estado Novo and remained more or less intact even during the more democratic interregnum. The corporatist legal framework, involving state agencies controlling the process, functioning, and leadership of labor unions, continued during the military period. Informal politics, however, was more complex. Labor activism had emerged toward the end of the democratic period and was a key target of military authoritarian angst. Military repression succeeded, but only for a while. Labor strikes again became a feature of Brazilian politics in the second half of the 1970s, especially in 1979, when nearly 400 strikes occurred across the country.[81] As a result, new labor leaders, independent of the state-controlled leadership, started to emerge. The political ascendancy of Luís Inácio Lula da Silva, or Lula (now the president of Brazil), for example, dates from this period. New patterns involving labor bargaining directly with industry also emerged in this period.

The political strategy of the Brazilian state toward labor, mainly to control and depoliticize, was only partially successful. The contrast with South Korea is again instructive. The South Korean state sought not only to control labor, but also to mobilize and incorporate it in a way that would transform laborers into economic soldiers of nationalism. That the South Korean state also eventually failed to mold labor completely in its image is, of course, a testament to the human spirit, which tends to resist subjugation and manipulation. Nevertheless, the labor strategies of Brazil and South Korea, though similar, also had some important differences, with significant political and economic consequences.

To sum up, the nuanced character of the post-1964 military-controlled cohesive-capitalist state in Brazil can be underlined by juxtaposing it to both Brazil's own past and to the cohesive-capitalist state of South Korea. The popular depiction of the post-1964 military governments in Brazil as "bureaucratic authoritarian," though not inaccurate, especially in the sense of being more bureaucratic than personalistic, does create a sense of sharp discontinuity with Brazil's own past.[82] Both the Estado Novo and the post-1964 military rule were defined by such core characteristics as enormous concentration of power in the presidency, corporatist control of urban society and groups, patronage politics in both large portions of the state and the

---

[80] See Erickson, *Brazilian Corporative State.* See also Youssef Cohen, *The Manipulation of Consent: The State and Working Class Consciousness in Brazil* (Pittsburgh, Pa.: University of Pittsburgh Press, 1989).

[81] Skidmore, *Politics of Military Rule,* 214.

[82] The reference here is obviously to Guillermo A. O'Donnell's justly famous formulation; O'Donnell, *Modernization and Bureaucratic Authoritarianism* (Berkeley: Institute of International Studies, University of California, 1973).

agrarian periphery, prohibition of competitive politics and the related use of repression, state intervention to promote economic development, and close working relations between the state and economic elites. The nominal democracy in the period after the Second World War thus appears in retrospect to have been a brief but unsuccessful departure from a more continuous, political history of cohesive-capitalist rule, at least until the more serious democratization of the 1990s.

As in the case of the Estado Novo, however, the developmental capacities of the militarized state were also mixed. To repeat, the sharp concentration of power, state control of select social groups, close collaboration with private capital, and a commitment to state intervention and growth promotion as a near exclusive priority all helped military rulers to promote rapid industrialization. In contrast to a case such as South Korea, however, the developmental capacities of the Brazilian state have always been more limited. The nationalism of the military rulers, as with others, was shallow: Their dependence on foreign capital was enormous. They were also unable (or unwilling) to incorporate the vast agrarian periphery, and they were internally divided. How this militarized state, mostly cohesive-capitalist, but also characterized by distinctive national traits that limited its developmental capacities, sought to promote industry and the economy is the subject to which we now turn.

State Intervention in the Economy
In spite of its avowed neoliberalism, the militarized state in Brazil was highly interventionist.[83] Military leaders prioritized economic growth, especially industrial, as a state goal. The development strategy to achieve this goal involved both import substitution and deliberate export promotion. The state's role as a direct investor and producer grew throughout this period, as did its indirect role in collaborating with indigenous capitalists and in welcoming foreign enterprise, including by repressing wages and the working class. Increasing production depended heavily on foreign savings, technology, and imports. Growing exports paid for part of the enormous import bill, but for the rest, the growth strategy rested on growing foreign debt and keeping cheap foreign money available.

During the first phase of military rule (1964–74), foreign debt was manageable and results included sustained industrial growth. The economy grew for the most part during the second phase (1974–85), too, but only under

---

[83] Among the useful overviews of patterns of state economic interventions during the military period, I draw especially on the following: Baer, *Brazilian Economy*; Milan and Bonelli, "Success of Growth Policies"; Milan and Bonelli, "Brazilian Economy"; Barros de Castro, "Renegade Development"; Suzigan, "Industrialization and Economic Policy"; Andrade, "Brazil"; Fishlow, "Brazilian Development"; Bela Balassa, "Incentive Policies in Brazil," *World Development* 7 (November 1979): 1023–42; and William G. Tyler, "Brazilian Industrialization," *World Development* 4, nos. 10–11 (1976): 863–82.

adverse global economic circumstances. Brazil's debt grew tremendously during this period, as the military rulers essentially transferred the burden of paying for current growth to future generations. Changing international economic conditions were thus an important component of the Brazilian economic story during the military rule, but an even deeper determinant of the rise and decline of the miracle was the pattern of Brazil's international economic integration, which was based more on foreign capital than on trade.

The military inherited a troubled economy when it grabbed power in 1964. Both budgetary and balance-of-payment deficits were high, public and foreign investment had declined, inflation was approaching 100 percent, and economic growth was down significantly. Castello Branco appointed a well-known monetarist, Roberto Campos, as the economic czar. Campos in turn prioritized controlling inflation and restoring confidence of foreign creditors and investors as the primary economic goals. We will never know whether the government believed that such changes would automatically lead to renewed growth. But the following three to four years saw considerable success in controlling inflation and restoring confidence of foreigners, though not in promoting investment and growth. The latter had to wait until a new government adopted a more activist stance, including an expansionist fiscal and monetary policy. We turn now to some of the state's stabilizing interventions in 1964–67, to see not only how they achieved their immediate goals but also how they laid the foundation for future growth.

Campos held a fairly standard assessment of Brazilian inflation, namely, that it was demand-led, but the policies to control it were implemented gradually and included concerns for future growth. Brazilian decision makers, even those who sounded like orthodox economic liberals, remained growth-oriented interventionists. The new leaders sought to curtail demand sharply by restrictive fiscal and monetary policy. The slow but steady progress in achieving this goal – inflation came down to 40 percent in 1966 and 25 percent in 1967 – underlined both the enhanced political capacity of the military state and its anti-working-class bias. On the fiscal side, for example, the government sought to cut expenditures but not in the areas of productive investment. Strategies to cut expenditure instead included prohibiting state governments from issuing bonds that often led to patronage-oriented expenditures. In a polity with strong regionalist traditions, sharp centralization of power under the military was essential to the pursuit of such a policy. In addition to cutting expenditures, the government – mindful of future growth needs – also focused on increasing revenue. Examples here include the sharp, market-oriented upward revision of prices of public utilities, a revision that in the short term contributed to inflation but was considered a necessary corrective to both make the public sector more efficient and to reduce the state's fiscal burden. Given potential opposition to such a move, authoritarian powers were again required for its implementation.

Another important example of curtailing demand while increasing public revenues was a significant improvement in tax collection, at least during the first phase of military rule. Both indirect and direct taxes went up significantly. The improvement in the indirect tax base – from some 13 percent of the GDP in 1960 to 18 percent in 1970 – resulted primarily from restructuring the existing consumption tax into a more rational value-added tax.[84] More important from the standpoint of assessing the enhanced political capacity of the cohesive-capitalist state was the increase in direct taxes: The number of taxpayers increased from some half a million in 1963 to four million in 1967, and the contribution of direct taxes went up from 5 percent of the GDP in 1960 to 10 percent in 1970.[85] Delfim Netto, a key architect of the economic miracle, subsequently suggested that the miracle owed a lot to these tax increases and the resulting increase in public investments and other expenditures.[86] The underlying political change involved centralizing various state-level taxes, rationalizing the federal tax-collection bureaucracy, and instilling the fear of an authoritarian state. Of course, there were limits to this enhanced political capacity. First, the class bias of the cohesive-capitalist state was evident in tax collection, too: Tax exemptions to corporations amounted to nearly 50 percent of total direct taxes, and the burden of income tax fell mainly on urban wage laborers.[87] Second, this enhanced political capacity to collect taxes declined over time, as regions reemerged stronger in the post-1974 period and as inflation cut into the real tax base toward the end of the 1970s and into the 1980s.

A significant element of the military's program to stabilize the economy and to lay the basis for future growth was repression of wages and of the working class more generally. Real wages fell sharply in the early years of military rule but started to rise again in later stages, as politics reemerged and military rulers became more defensive. Some economists have sought to explain the resulting maldistribution of income as inevitable, given the higher rates of return on scarce specialized skills in a rapidly industrializing economy. Others have suggested more convincingly that the process was a

---

[84] See, for example, Michele Guerard, "The Brazilian State Value-Added Tax," *International Monetary Fund Staff Papers* 20, no. 1 (March 1973): 118–69.

[85] The figures for the number of taxpayers are taken from Skidmore, "Politics and Economic Policy Making," 22; figures for the share of taxes in the GDP are from Baer et al., "Changing Role of the State," 28.

[86] Cited in Evan S. Lieberman, *Race and Regionalism in the Politics of Taxation in Brazil and South Africa* (New York: Cambridge University Press, 2003), 162. For a general discussion of the role of public investments in the Brazilian miracle, see Jonathan Krieckhaus, "The Politics of Economic Growth in the Third World: Brazilian Developmentalism in Comparative Perspective," Ph.D. dissertation, Princeton University, 2000.

[87] See Baer et al., "Changing Role of the State," 28, and Lieberman, *Race and Regionalism*, 161–6.

highly politicized one, driven by the deliberate antiworker policies of the military government.[88] The wages of workers were first repressed in the public sector, where the government had direct control, and subsequently also in the private sector via such policy measures as excepting working-class wages from the indexing of various prices against inflation. Authoritarian corporatist control was essential for imposing such policies, though over time even that proved to be insufficient. Meanwhile, repressed wages contributed to cutting demand and thus to reducing inflationary pressures in the economy. Holding wages behind productivity also eventually provided incentives for private investors, especially foreign investors, who might have worried about working-class activism.

On the monetary side, the military government created a new central bank in 1965 and pursued a tight money policy for a few years, reducing inflation but not impeding the recession. Business groups expressed their displeasure over tight credit in various ways. Whereas foreign corporations could borrow elsewhere – though during 1964–70, direct foreign investment in Brazil remained limited, picking up only around 1970 – domestic business was heavily dependent on public sources of credit. Contributing to the new government's success in curtailing demand and in bringing down inflation were a tight monetary policy and the political capacity to resist business pressure and to influence the supply of credit directly.

In addition to controlling inflation, the new military government also sought to restore the confidence of foreign creditors and investors in its effort to restructure short-term debt and invite foreign capital for long-term industrialization. The military government was again relatively successful, though not so much in immediately attracting foreign business as in winning the cooperation of the government of the United States. The American government was embarrassingly quick to congratulate the military rulers on pulling off a coup and subsequently threw its support behind the new government.[89] American foreign aid was the source of nearly 80 percent of capital inflows into Brazil between 1964 and 1967.[90] The support of the United States was also influential with the World Bank and the IMF, which helped to restructure foreign debt and provided loans. In addition, the Brazilian government took direct policy measures, such as repealing the limits on profit remittances by multinational corporations (MNCs) that had been put in place by Goulart, and created various other incentives, including labor discipline, to attract foreign capital. While foreign investors waited a while before risking new investments, the Castello Branco government laid the groundwork for a future boom in foreign capital.

---

[88] See, for example, the contributions of Albert Fishlow and of Fernando Henrique Cardoso, in Stepan, *Authoritarian Brazil.*
[89] For an excellent discussion, see Skidmore, *Politics of Military Rule*, 35–39.
[90] Ibid., 39.

Yet new investments and growth did not result automatically, even though inflation was brought down and the confidence of foreign governments and business was restored. The onset of the economic miracle had to await a much more activist policy stance by the more repressive government of Costa e Silva. A more expansionist fiscal and monetary policy, along with numerous other policy incentives cataloged below, eventually set the stage for sharp increases in industrial production. In the late 1960s these increases resulted mainly from a full utilization of existing industrial capacity.[91] New investments from the public sector, as well as from domestic and foreign private funds, started around 1970 and surged thereafter.

Public sector revenues had begun to surpass government consumption expenditures by now, thanks to improved tax collection, higher prices for public utilities, and "forced savings" from workers, in the form of dues collected for social security and deposited in public sector banks. These new revenues in turn funded significant new public investments. Private domestic savings and investments also increased, partially as a result of indexing interest rates against inflation and thereby encouraging greater private savings. And finally, new foreign investment started pouring in, helped by a number of factors, including the government's visible commitment to labor discipline, realistic prices, freedom to repatriate profits, high growth, and generally pro–foreign investor political economy.

The activism on the part of the military government was both indirect and direct. The more indirect role, aimed at manipulating the incentives and behavior of private agents, can be viewed in terms of its influence on supply and demand.[92] On the supply side, the pattern of holding wages behind productivity gains continued. Government also invested heavily in infrastructure, easing conditions for private investment. For investors calculating costs and benefits, the government offered ample cheap credit – often available through public institutions – as well as tax credits. The balance-of-payment situation had also improved by now, at least in part because several years of low growth had reduced the import bill. The favorable foreign-exchange situation in turn enabled the government to provide tariff exemptions for capital equipment and raw materials. And finally, to ensure implementation of its policies, the cohesive-capitalist state continued the practice of more or less institutionalized cooperation of policy makers/implementors and businessmen in various *colegiados*, or policy councils.[93]

On the demand side, the government encouraged new production for the domestic market and for export. Some scholars continue to insist that Brazil's development strategy under the military was mainly of the import-substitution type and attribute eventual failures to misguided state

---

[91] See Milan and Bonelli, "Success of Growth Policies."
[92] I am especially drawing here on ibid., 80–84.
[93] See Suzigan, "Industrialization and Economic Policy," 31.

intervention and to the distortion of market prices. The reality, however, was rather more complex. The Brazilian economy actually opened up quite significantly under the military, especially prior to the increase in the price of oil in 1973. The average tariff rate, for example, came down during the first phase from some 48 percent in 1967 to 27 percent in 1973. Even when these rates increased again in 1974, they never averaged more than 50 percent during the entire military period.[94] Of course, these average rates hide quite a bit of planned variation that simultaneously enabled cheap imports of capital goods and raw materials and the protection of manufactured consumer goods to encourage new investments. On the export side, too, Brazil's manufactured exports soared during the 1970s, averaging a growth rate of some 30 percent per annum.[95] This then was hardly a simple import-substitution model of development. Very much like South Korea under Park Chung Hee, Brazil combined elements of both import substitution and export promotion. The Achilles heel of the Brazilian experiment was thus not its excessive import substitution but the import intensity of its growth strategy; every 1 percent of economic growth in Brazil during this period required some 2 percent increase in imports. So while exports grew substantially, imports grew even faster, financed by growing debt that eventually became unsustainable.

To return to the issue of how government stimulated demand, expansionist fiscal and monetary policy provided the broad framework. More specifically, a key element of domestic demand was the deliberate effort to skew income distribution in favor of upper-income groups and thus to stimulate production aimed at satisfying their enhanced buying power. (By contrast, working-class wages were not indexed against inflation for the most part and thus fell behind.) Not only were the fruits of the new growth earmarked for upper-income groups, but the government also channeled publicly controlled credit to bolster their consumption. This, in combination with protection of consumer goods, attracted new investments to produce such durables as automobiles. It is no surprise then that foreign-investment-led increases in automobile production became a centerpiece of the military government's growth strategy, which turned out to be quite import-intensive, especially because of the resulting growth in demand for imported petroleum.

The new military government also sought to promote export of manufactured goods in an economy that had long been dependent on coffee and other commodity exports. The shift reflected in part a changing global economy in which it was becoming easier to export manufactured goods, in part the growing sophistication of the industrial base within Brazil, and in part the necessity of enhancing foreign exchange to meet the needs of

94 See Eva Paus, "Political Economy of Manufactured Export Growth," *Journal of Developing Areas* 23 (January 1989): 186–87.
95 Ibid., 179, table 2. See also Milan and Bonelli, "Success of Growth Policies," 80.

rapid import-intensive growth. The government instituted a series of mini-devaluations of the exchange rate – called the "crawling peg" – that was in practice politically controlled. As in South Korea, exchange-rate adjustment, while necessary, was not sufficient to promote exports.[96] In addition, the government provided a variety of subsidies in the form of tax benefits, cheap credit, and administrative support. By one estimate, the subsidies enabled exporters to sell products overseas at nearly 50 percent below their domestic price.[97] Multinational companies within Brazil especially took advantage of these new incentives. While such incentives may not have been sufficient to entice new investment in Brazil, they did appeal to those already well established and producing within the country. By the end of the 1970s nearly half of Brazil's manufactured exports were thus produced by the MNCs.[98]

Besides altering the supply-and-demand conditions of the economy, the militarized Brazilian state also continued to be an important economic actor in its own right. In spite of a neoliberal ideology, the economic role of the Brazilian state grew throughout this period. This growth was also not opposed by private investors or by U.S. policy makers, who often worked closely with their Brazilian counterparts. If one wonders why, the main reason was that state intervention in Brazil was aimed at boosting private profits: Growing state interventions "were accepted and indeed welcomed so long as they were consistent with rapidly increasing profits."[99] This is the heart of the matter: The state-led alliance for growth between state and private capital is the driving force of these right-wing authoritarian models of development. The Brazilian military state was not quite cohesive-capitalist in the same way as was the South Korean state, but the core similarity was very real.

Two areas of direct government economic activity that are especially notable are public sector production activities and public control over savings and credit. The share of public sector investments in overall investments increased throughout the 1970s, approaching some 43 percent in 1978.[100] A survey of Brazil's largest firms in 1981 revealed that half of them were owned by the state, with private Brazilian and foreign companies owning some 40 and 10 percent, respectively.[101] The state's industrial activities were concentrated in such basic areas as mining, metals, chemicals, steel, petroleum, and public utilities. These were generally areas that were not particularly appealing to the private sector or that were deemed too important for "national security" to be left in private hands, especially foreign ownership. The state's

---

[96] See Paus, "Political Economy of Manufactured Export Growth," esp. 193; and Milan and Bonelli, "Success of Growth Policies," 80.

[97] See Andrade, "Brazil," 180.

[98] Paus, "Political Economy of Manufactured Export Growth," 187.

[99] See Fishlow, "Brazilian Development in Long Term Perspective," 106.

[100] Andrade, "Brazil," 171.

[101] Cited in Werner Baer, "Brazil: Political Determinants of Development," in Robert Wesson, ed., *Politics, Policies and Economic Development in Latin America* (Palo Alto, Calif.: 1984), 67.

productive role in Brazil thus grew less out of an ideological preference than out of a commitment to rapid industrialization, filling the gaps that national capital was not willing to fill, and stepping into areas either where foreign capital would not go or that were undesirable. Creating a fair amount of autonomy for public sector firms, including technocratic management, and allowing them to charge market-approaching prices also ensured that this large public sector was not a drag on the growth process.

The other significant area of government presence was the financial sector. Despite government efforts, the private equity market did not improve significantly in this period; most Brazilian firms continued to prefer family ownership and control to listing firms publicly and raising private funds. Savings in public institutions – that of the government and such "forced savings" as social security deposits – constituted nearly 70 percent of all savings in the early 1980s.[102] Credit from these public institutions, in turn, was a main source of private investment, giving the government considerable leverage in shaping production patterns. A firm commitment to rapid industrialization, discipline, absence of corruption at the apex, and competent technocratic personnel working closely with businessmen ensured that government control over credit did not readily translate into excessive cronyism and waste.

The indirect and the direct patterns of state intervention discussed so far provided the framework for rapid industrialization between 1968 and 1974. If 1974 marked a turning point of sorts in Brazil's development pattern, it was not because of any major shift in the pattern of state intervention. The basic pattern, with some modifications, was maintained for the duration of military rule. What changed instead in 1974, of course, were international economic circumstances, namely, a sharp rise in the price of oil orchestrated by OPEC. Brazil imported most of its oil and was thus forced to adjust to the altered terms of trade. Nevertheless, for political reasons Brazil's rulers chose not to adjust downward but to remain committed to high growth. The question then became one of how to sustain rapid industrialization in the face of worsening terms of trade and in the context of a development strategy that was already import-intensive. This was especially so because of automobiles, whose consumption required an even higher import bill.

The Brazilian decision makers, especially Delfim Netto and his colleagues, reasoned that Brazil could essentially borrow and grow fast enough to pay back its debt. The only realistic alternative to debt-led growth – besides low growth, that is – was enhanced mobilization of domestic resources and their transformation somehow into enhanced foreign exchange. It was nearly impossible to expand the tax base into the periphery; the urban tax base had shrunk with inflation; and private equity markets had not developed. Given these constraints, Brazilian decision makers decided to shift the

---

[102] Ibid., 69.

costs of growth: If during the first phase the lower strata paid a dispropor-
tionate share of the costs of rapid industrialization, during the second phase
the strategy was to let future generations pay the growing debt. Whether deliberate or not, this was certainly the consequence.

The avowed reasoning behind the debt-led growth strategy was that it
was rational to borrow, given the low cost of debt on the international
market at the time. The borrowed money, in turn, could be invested in
both import-substituting and export-promoting industries, thus alleviating
foreign-exchange constraints. Netto also argued that the nature of inflation in Brazil – which was again creeping up – had changed: Instead of
being demand-led, the new inflation was now cost-induced. Hence the aim
of public policy was to cheapen credit and to maintain low wages – both of
which would attract investors and facilitate growth. Based on these uncon-
ventional ideas, Netto created a debt-led, high-growth strategy that almost
worked.

Government policies sought simultaneously to substitute for imports and
to promote exports. Import substitution was intensified in both capital goods
and raw materials. Manufactured exports were also promoted, with continuing public subsidies to exporters via taxes, credit, and administrative support. The resulting high-production growth and rapidly growing debt were
inevitably related insofar as foreign borrowing helped to maintain domestic
demand, the main source of growth, and at the firm level growing costs of
necessary imports could not have been met without foreign borrowing. To
facilitate growth, the government relaxed the conditions for firms to borrow abroad: For example, the firms could now borrow without the required
40 percent deposit, and could take out five-year instead of ten-year loans.
Public sector firms were the main borrowers, though both indigenous and
foreign private firms also contributed their shares. Cumulative foreign debt
grew enormously, multiplying fivefold between 1973 and 1978.

In spite of this high debt, it is arguable that prior to the second oil
shock and the U.S.-triggered increase in interest rates in 1979 and 1980,
the Brazilian economy had more or less adjusted.[103] Economic growth in
1979, for example, was respectable, inflation was down, the investment rate
was close to 25 percent, the current account deficit was reduced, and the
trade deficit had been eliminated. Can one conclude that Netto's bold gambit of debt-led growth was really working and might even have worked over
the long term, were it not for worsening international economic conditions?
This intriguing and ultimately unanswerable question is unfortunately also
misleading because it separates national and international conditions in a
way that may satisfy nationalist emotions but is analytically unsustainable, especially in the case of Brazil, where the internal and the external economies
were deeply interconnected. The Brazilian state sustained growth in the

[103] For this argument, I draw on Milan and Bonelli, "Brazilian Economy," esp. 85–87.

post-1974 period by borrowing abroad heavily, thus increasing its vulnerability to shifts in international economic circumstances. The subsequent debacle, then, was part and parcel of the growth strategy.

The second oil price hike, in 1979, more than doubled the price of oil. With nearly 80 percent of its oil imported, Brazil's cost of oil imports as a share of total imports increased from some 30 to nearly 50 percent. Monetary and fiscal policy changes in the United States led to sharp increases in interest rates, peaking in 1981 at some 17 to 18 percent. The cost of the import-intensive, debt-led growth strategy had now become prohibitive and the game was nearly over. The new government of Figueiredo debated slowing the economy. As noted above, however, politics by now was moving in a more open direction, with both business and labor groups pressing their demands. Attempts to contract the economy led to the firing of one finance minister, Mário Henrique Simonsen, and to the reappointment of Delfim Netto, in the hopes of pulling a rabbit out of the hat. Netto continued the high-growth strategy for a couple of years, but by 1982, with the scare of default on debt in Mexico, global capital flows into Brazil dried up and the bold gambit of debt-led high growth crashed. Brazil's policy makers would spend more than a decade trying to cope with their enormous debt. Simply put, the political capacity to deal with truly difficult economic conditions was lacking, especially in the late military and postmilitary democratic period. The experiment of state-led growth essentially came to an end in the early 1990s, when Brazilian rulers were pressed from the outside to embrace a more neoliberal economic program.[104]

Pattern of Industrialization
Brazil industrialized rapidly under military rule, especially until 1980, when production declined for two to three years, turning positive again in 1984, a year before the military handed over power to an elected leadership. Manufacturing grew at a rate of nearly 13 percent between 1968 and 1974 and at some 7 percent between 1975 and 1980; it stagnated or declined between 1981 and 1983. By 1980 nearly one-third of Brazilian GNP originated in industry. The industrial structure, moreover, was relatively diverse and efficient by developing country standards, and exports of manufactured goods grew rapidly throughout the period. The costs of this growth were also considerable: skewed benefits, future debt burdens, and repressive rule. Nevertheless, rapid industrialization steered by a cohesive-capitalist state was impressive. Both the developmental successes and failures reflected the Brazilian state's capacities and choices.

---

[104] For one good comparison of the state's economic role in the military and the postmilitary periods, especially with respect to public investments, see Jonathan Krieckhaus, "Reconceptualizing the Developmental State: Public Savings and Economic Growth," *World Development* 30, no. 10 (2002): 1697–1712.

This basic thesis can be further exemplified by focusing on several specific aspects of the overall pattern of Brazilian industrialization during this period. First, there is the issue of how the industrial growth was financed. While the overall rate of investment in the 1950s averaged some 16 percent, during the military period this climbed and stayed at nearly 23 percent until 1981. Public and foreign investments were the key components of overall investment, and variations in their availability correlated with growth.[105] One may recall that during the economic downturn in the early 1960s, both public and foreign investments had declined; public investment because of a meager tax base, growing expenditures, and inflation, and foreign investment due to growing balance-of-payment problems, anti-investor policies, and lack of confidence bred by populist politics. The military government reversed both of these trends, helping to resume production growth. Tax reforms were important in reversing the public finances, and restoring the confidence of foreign investors led to new foreign investment. As suggested above, it is hard to imagine these policy shifts without a prior political change.

Both public and foreign investments declined again toward the end of the military period, contributing to the end of the miracle. The sharp increase in public revenues over expenditure that military rulers were able to bring about during the first phase turned out to be a temporary blip that coincided with the increased power enjoyed by the military rulers during this phase. Subsequently, as the military worried about its lack of legitimacy and sought support from various quarters, the political capacity to extract new resources from the society declined. Many of the old political limitations to the Brazilian state reemerged, including the inability to expand the tax base beyond the main urban centers, the inability to collect more taxes from the well-off, and, of course, the inability to further reduce expenditures. Foreign investors were scared off by the growing foreign debt and the related potential instabilities that a liberalizing regime may not be able to manage. The combined decline of public and foreign investment, in turn, led to a sharp reduction in growth, starting in the early 1980s.

Industrial growth in Brazil was financed mainly by public and foreign investment. Domestic private investors played their role but remained a junior partner, given the weaknesses in financial institutions. Brazil's financial dependency on external resources is not at all surprising, though, in light of the overall inadequacy of the tax system. Also noteworthy is that, seen in a comparative context, Brazil's investment to output ratios were quite impressive. Brazil's investment rates in the low twenties (as a percent of the GNP) were similar to that of India, but much lower than that of South Korea. The relatively high rate of growth in production in Brazil suggests in a rough way that this growth was probably quite efficient. This is also borne

---

[105] Milan and Bonelli, "Brazilian Economy," 59–60.

out by such other evidence as high rates of growth in labor productivity and manufactured exports and increased rate of return on capital.[106]

A second noteworthy aspect of Brazilian industrialization was the respective shares of the state-owned, indigenous private, and foreign private firms. One prevalent interpretation, namely, the model of "dependent development," leaves one with the impression that all three actors – the Brazilian state and indigenous and foreign private firms – grew more or less in tandem.[107] This model, while insightful, exaggerates the role of Brazilian private capital. During the military period, both state-owned and foreign enterprises in manufacturing grew faster than local capital. Among the largest 300 firms, for example, private Brazilian firms declined from 156 to 139 between 1966 and 1972.[108] Yet one might have expected the role of Brazilian private capital to grow rather than decline. In fact, it is something of a puzzle as to why the Brazilian state did not do more to promote indigenous capitalism. One proposition suggested by comparative materials analyzed here concerns Brazil's relatively shallow nationalism. The state's motivation in promoting rapid economic growth in Brazil was more to enhance elite incomes than to promote nation building in the sense of creating a powerful, autonomous political economy. The economic results were both positive and negative, so there was relatively efficient growth, even as the state did little to enhance control over its own financial and technological future.

Brazilian industrialization also focused on consumer durables. Automobiles, for example, remained a leading sector throughout the period. This growing production of consumer durables catered to elite, upper-income consumers, whose consumption preferences resembled those of their counterparts in the United States and Europe. The military government's policy provided elites with credit and subsidized producers of such goods. The down side of this seemingly ingenious pattern of elitist production and consumption, aside from its exclusionary character, was its dependence on external capital and technology, especially imports. Automobile consumption, for example, led to increased oil imports, which, in turn, were a growing source of foreign indebtedness.

Finally, one must take note of the foreign sector, including trade and finance. Exports, as already noted, grew throughout this period, experiencing about a 15 percent rate of growth per annum. This, then, to repeat, was hardly a standard import-substituting economy that ultimately collapsed because of a failure of export promotion. Of course, more exports might have helped to stave off the eventual debt crisis. But it is not obvious how exports could have grown faster without damaging such other governmental goals as protecting indebted firms from the costs of devaluation. In fact, the real

---

[106] See Tyler, "Brazilian Industrialization," 866–67.
[107] The reference is to Evans, *Dependent Development*.
[108] Andrade, "Brazil," 174.

problem on the trade front was the rapid growth of imports, which increased at some 26 percent per annum throughout this period.

Why was it, however, that the Brazilian pattern of industrialization in this period was so import-intensive? There are only partial answers, many of which reflect governmental policy choices. First, rapid industrialization under even the best of circumstances requires growing imports, especially of capital goods. Under adverse circumstances, such as those faced by Brazil after 1974, a strategy of slower growth might have been more prudent, as it would have spread out the costs of downward adjustment over time. But as we have seen, this was politically unacceptable. Second, Brazilian industrialization catered to elites whose tastes for such items as automobiles increased the import bill, especially for oil imports. And finally, both state and foreign firms tended to import more than domestic private firms in relation to what they exported.[109] The fact that both public sector enterprises and foreign enterprises grew faster than domestic private firms thus added to the bias toward import intensity.

To sum up, the military-dominated cohesive-capitalist regime in Brazil was more efficacious a developmental actor than the regime it replaced, but not as efficacious as, say, the South Korean regime under Park Chung Hee. The developmental capacities of the Brazilian military regime also varied over time, more efficacious during the first than the second phase. The military regime pursued rapid industrialization via both import substitution and export promotion and achieved relative success by a number of means:

– boosting public investment
– attracting foreign investors
– creating a demand base for consumer durables
– providing various subsidies to private investors
– maintaining labor discipline
– empowering technocrats both to make policy and to run public sector enterprises, and
– working closely with business groups

The costs of this approach were also heavy, including repression and maldistribution of income. Worse, even the goal of rapid industrialization eventually failed the militarized state: Though cohesive-capitalist at its core, its power did not penetrate downward and it could not mobilize domestic economic resources for industrialization.

---

[109] In a survey of some 17,000 firms in 1980, Willmore thus found that the export/import ratios of state-owned, foreign, and domestic private firms were 0.27, 1.16, and 1.97, respectively. While these results require a number of qualifications, they do broadly indicate the import and export propensities of various types of firms. See Larry Willmore, "Transnationals and Foreign Trade: Evidence from Brazil," *Journal of Development Studies* 28, no. 2 (January 1992): esp. 315.

Policy choices and the pattern of industrialization often reflected these political limitations. The tax base improved at the outset but then deteriorated. With growing subsidies and inflation, public investment declined. Regressive income distribution fed an import-intensive industrialization strategy. In turn, heavy dependence on imported oil took a toll on the Brazilian political economy. One persuasive analysis suggests that the deterioration in terms of trade was the single most important factor triggering the debt crisis, with increases in interest rates and the slowing of world trade being contributing factors.[110] Clearly, the cost of industrializing rapidly while importing heavily and accumulating foreign debt was serious.

The military quit power in 1985, and in 1994 Brazil embraced an IMF-style, neoliberal model of austerity and development under the leadership of the former dependency scholar turned neoliberal president, Fernando Henrique Cardoso.[111] With serious democratization in the mid-1980s, the character of the Brazilian state also started to alter significantly, shifting away from cohesive-capitalism and toward a more fragmented-multiclass state. After 1985 but prior to fully embracing a neoliberal economic model, Brazil's increasingly fragmented and multiclass state coped haphazardly with its serious debt inheritance. The elected governments pursued several goals simultaneously, without much power to follow through on any of them.[112] Suffice it to note here that, though the economic conditions were extremely difficult, the economic costs of the new politics were also significant. The public sector lost its financial capacity and public investments declined. The large foreign debt discouraged foreign investors. Investment rates declined from some 25 percent of the GDP in the mid-1970s to 14 percent of the GDP in the early 1990s. The sluggish growth rate that resulted must be considered part and parcel of the preceding experiment in rapid industrialization.

III. Conclusion

Between 1950 and the late 1990s Brazil was transformed from a low-income economy to a middle-income economy with a diversified industrial base. Both periods of rapid industrial growth, in the 1950s and again in the 1970s, were followed by periods of deceleration and even negative growth. Overall,

---

[110] See Edmar L. Bacha, "External Shocks and Growth Prospects: The Case of Brazil, 1973–89," *World Development* 14, no. 8 (1986): 919–36, esp. 922–23.

[111] A detailed discussion of this more liberal phase in Brazil's development is for others to pursue. The focus here has been on the development and the evolution of Brazil's statist model of development.

[112] For a brief but good account of the Sarney government, see Skidmore, *Authoritarian Politics*, chap. 8. For a quick review of and guide to further readings about the Collor, Itamar, and Cardoso administrations, see Skidmore and Smith, *Modern Latin America*, 185–88. For a discussion and guide to further readings about the various stabilization plans attempted during the late 1980s and the early 1990s, see Barros de Castro, "Renegade Development."

however, enough progress was made to characterize the Brazilian drive to industrialize as more of a success than not. But the cost was high. Brazil, with its repressive politics, was one of the world's most unequal societies. Also part of the balance sheet was an enormous foreign debt passed on to future generations. The burden of the discussion above has been to demonstrate the central role of the state in generating this mixed developmental pattern.

For the most part Brazil has been a highly elitist state, committed to state-led rapid growth and industrialization and welcoming of foreign resources. Even during the nominally democratic phase of the 1950s, when the Brazilian state was less cohesive and less procapitalist than it would be in the military period that followed, political and business elites worked closely together; foreign investors were welcomed, especially under Kubitschek; workers were tamed via corporatist structures; and traditional clientelism fostered the acquiescence of the vast agrarian periphery. The narrow political base enabled ruling elites to prioritize the goal of growth, which they pursued deliberately through state intervention aimed at producing manufactured goods for a domestic market. In spite of considerable success, however, heavy public spending could not be sustained absent an adequate tax base. Dependence on new foreign investors, whose main interest was the protected domestic market, may have been an easy route to growth, but it was not sustainable; sooner rather than later, exports had to be pursued. The continued fiscal and balance-of-payment crises, along with the more fragmented and multiclass politics of the early 1960s, brought an end to the import-substitution experiment of a nominal democracy.

While the more cohesive-capitalist military regime was clearly more capable of taking unpopular economic decisions, eventually its political capacities, too, turned out to be mixed. The military restored the narrow political coalition at the apex, reprioritized rapid industrialization as the main goal, and pursued it vigorously by encouraging public and foreign firms to undertake new production for both domestic and foreign markets. The specific modalities included delegating power to technocrats, providing subsidies to investors, disciplining the labor force, and fostering close administrative cooperation between the state and business. The new priorities and enhanced political control led to higher rates of public and foreign investment, contributing to rapid industrialization.

At the same time, however, the political capacities of the Brazilian version of cohesive-capitalism were constrained. The military rulers were divided, with one faction more concerned about being accepted in society and about restoring democracy. Moreover, the militarized state did not penetrate very far into the more traditionally governed regions. Over time, therefore, the military, too, realized the limits of its capacity to sustain its tax base, let alone to expand it. Dependence on foreign resources grew as industrialization became more import-intensive. And the foreign debt grew. Once again, the twin crises of balance of payments and public finance brought the miracle to an end.

I conclude by briefly situating the Brazilian case in a comparative context. The import-substitution phase under nominal democracy makes for interesting comparisons with India, which are made below in the context of our analysis of the Indian case. For now, consider a comparison with South Korea. Both Brazil and Korea experienced industrialization in the first half of the twentieth century, but Brazil did not undergo any traumatic disruptions of the type experienced in Korea by the rapid departure of the Japanese and the ensuing civil war. If different starting points had been decisive, Brazil at the end of the twentieth century should have been at least at the same level of income and industry as South Korea, if not ahead. As we know, however, Brazil, though a middle-income country like South Korea, has also been left behind. What happened?

The neoliberal and dependency answers to this question stress Brazil's relative failure to promote exports and its excessive reliance on foreign resources. While taking these factors into account, the statist analysis above stressed the importance of a deeper causal variable, namely, the mixed character of the Brazilian state – developmental, yet limited. When viewed from this standpoint, the failure to generate ample exports to cover the costs of imports, as well as the excessive external dependence, have to be viewed as resulting from state choices. These choices, moreover, were not simply a matter of choosing one set of technically appropriate alternatives over another. The choices were constrained. Surely, a better export performance would have helped. There is also no doubt that shifts in international economic conditions played havoc with Brazil. Both limited exports and foreign vulnerabilities, however, were a function of policy choices made under political constraints emanating from the nature of the Brazilian state.

The Brazilian state under military rule resembled the more clearly cohesive-capitalist state in South Korea under Park Chung Hee, but the two were far from identical. Both the similarities and the differences were consequential. Like South Korea, the Brazilian state was highly authoritarian, set industrial growth as its priority, involved technocratic bureaucrats in policy making and implementation, worked closely with business elites, controlled the working class, and intervened regularly to facilitate rapid industrialization via both import substitution and export promotion. As discussed above (in this chapter and in Chapter 3), these characteristics can be associated with policy choices and patterns of implementation that helped to facilitate rapid industrialization in both countries.

The state governed by the Brazilian military, however, also differed from the South Korean state. The Brazilian military was the product of a different history and different circumstances: It was internally more divided, its downward reach in the society often stopped with regional oligarchs, it sat atop a much more unequal society with independent sources of power, it was less nationalistic economically, and, relatedly, it was happy to collaborate with foreign capital, especially direct foreign investors. These characteristics, as we have also seen, limited the Brazilian state's capacities in two very important areas, namely, its ability to tackle the repeated fiscal and balance-of-payment crises that have plagued Brazil. The roots of the fiscal crises were located in the inability to expand the tax base, as well as in the incapacity to say no to various powerful groups when it came to limiting expenditures. Sustained commitment to high growth, even under adverse international economic circumstances, contributed significantly to growing indebtedness; this growth commitment revealed legitimacy concerns that are more characteristic of fragmented-multiclass states than of ideal-type cohesive-capitalist states. And finally, unlike South Korea, heavy dependence on foreign investors made it difficult for the Brazilian state to mobilize the entire nation for export promotion, a hallmark of South Korea's cohesive-capitalist model of development.

PART III

SLOW BUT STEADY

India

India at the end of the twentieth century was a poor economy, though one with a substantial industrial base. In contrast to both Korea and Brazil, India got off to a slow start, developing mainly in the second half of the century. Even then, however, the pace of growth had been relatively slow, picking up speed only toward the end. The state's role in producing this mixed economic outcome is analyzed in the next two chapters. It is proposed in Chapter 6 that the laissez-faire colonial state was partly responsible for India's sluggish economy in the first half of the century. By contrast, the modern, interventionist state that replaced it at midcentury provided a framework for modest economic growth and industrialization. This is analyzed in Chapter 7. A factor that contributed to the state's inefficacy was its fragmented-multiclass character, manifest especially in the considerable gap between the state's ambitions and capacities. A root cause of this state "softness" was the need of the leaders to maintain a stable and legitimate state within a diverse, relatively mobilized political society. State inefficacy, in turn, limited the impact of state interventions and hurt the rate of industrial growth. The origins of both this fragmented-multiclass state and the sluggish economy are analyzed first, followed by a discussion of how the state managed eventually to facilitate slow but steady industrialization.

6

Origins of a Fragmented-Multiclass State and a Sluggish Economy

Colonial India

Like Brazil, India is a case of mixed economic performance in the second half of the twentieth century: more sluggish than rapidly industrializing South Korea but with its diversified industrial base much sounder than Nigeria. Any comparative analysis must therefore ask why India has been as successful as it has been but also why it has not done better. The state has played the central role in producing this mixed economic outcome, the argument being that the modern, interventionist state that replaced the laissez-faire colonial state at midcentury provided a framework for modest economic growth and industrialization, a clear improvement over the nearly stagnant, free-market colonial economy that had preceded it. State intervention also laid the groundwork for the emergence of a more vibrant private economy toward the end of the century. At the same time, however, the fragmented-multiclass state that India inherited and created was relatively inefficacious, characterized by a considerable gap between its ambitions and capacities. This state inefficacy, in turn, limited the impact of state interventions and retarded the rate and pattern of industrialization.

The present chapter analyzes the impact of colonialism on the formation of the Indian state and industrial economy, especially in the first half of the twentieth century. Three lines of argument are developed, two concerning the political situation and one concerning the political economy. First, the state that Indians inherited from their colonial past was modern and democratic yet not all that effective as an economic actor. This state, as I argue, was a product of both colonial construction and nationalist pressures and design. The British in India created the basic state architecture: political unity and centralized authority, a modern civil service and armed forces, the rule of law and an independent judiciary, and rudiments of federalism and democracy, with growing participation by Indians. While the political practices of the colonial state were mainly autocratic, the downward reach of the state's authority was nonetheless very limited, allowing a variety of local and personalistic despotisms to flourish. This state, with its power compromises with traditional elites and its laissez-faire character, was a fragmented, limited state in the making.

Second, India's mass nationalist movement developed in opposition to the colonial state as a vehicle for capturing state power. The political process helped to create a sense of nation in India and generated political values that placed a premium simultaneously on democracy and on statist developmentalism. But while India's nationalist movement was a powerful oppositional force, it never developed a corresponding organizational structure, such as a tightly knit political party or even a coherent political strategy that would allow it to redesign the state in accordance with its developmental ambitions. The multiclass social base also made for a movement that had to reconcile many competing forces as it sought to define its ideology, policies, and political strategies. The political legacy of India's nationalist movement was thus ambiguous. On the one hand, it succeeded in mobilizing effectively against colonial rule, in consolidating the Indian "nation," and in pushing India toward a full democracy. On the other hand, it was not a cohesive political force that could define priorities clearly and see them to completion. Once victorious, an amorphous, multiclass nationalist movement that sought to expand the state's role in the economy came to be grafted onto a modern but fragmented colonial state. The result was a fragmented-multiclass sovereign state, whose developmental inefficacy has remained at the heart of India's lackluster economic performance.

Finally, the subcontinent has for a long time been characterized by a low-technology, low-productivity agrarian economy. The political instability of the eighteenth and early nineteenth centuries also did not augur well for spontaneous economic progress. The British in this nineteenth-century setting provided political unity, a "national" market, and infrastructure, but these developments were insufficient for sustained economic growth of any type, including industrialization. Among the proximate factors militating against industrialization during the colonial phase were considerations of both supply and demand: low rates of savings and investment, primitive technology, and a poor economy with limited internal demand.

At a more distant level of causation, the negative role of the colonial state was significant insofar as it absorbed savings, failed to invest in such growth-promoting activities as technology development, and maintained an open economy that could overwhelm any indigenous dynamism that might have emerged. It is no accident that when indigenous capitalism and industry did emerge – mainly in the 1930s, though there was some earlier as well – it was primarily of the import-substitution variety, encouraged by a set of colonial policies whose rationale was more financial than industry-promoting. The consequences were, nevertheless, significant. While the role of industry in the overall economy at the time of independence was, given India's large size, extremely small – considerably smaller, for example, than in either Korea or Brazil – India emerged from colonialism with a significant group of indigenous capitalists involved in industry. Equally important, these capitalists and India's nationalist political elite agreed that rapid future industrialization would require protection and active state intervention.

These three themes of colonial state construction, the nationalist movement, and the colonial political economy are discussed below, keeping in mind the following points. First, colonialism in India lasted for more than two centuries, up until the middle of the twentieth century. I summarize the first century or more of colonialism as historical background, giving some attention to post-1857 developments, that is, to the period following the establishment of formal British Crown rule in India in 1857, and then focus on the first half of the twentieth century. Second, given the size, complexity, and regional variations of the subcontinent, the national level focus can be misleading, certainly more so than, say, in the case of Korea. But it is impossible to be comprehensive on that score, though I do refer to some of the most obvious internal variations in due course. It is to be hoped that the perspective adopted here is plausible and offers some new insights. Finally, it must be emphasized that the historiography on colonial India is extremely rich, diverse, and abounds with controversies. The broad synthetic account that follows is adequate only for a comparative analysis of the type undertaken in this book. Students of colonial India ought to familiarize themselves with such alternative approaches to the subject as are provided by the Cambridge School, the nationalists, the Marxists, and the subaltern scholars.[1]

I. Historical Background

Prior to the British rule, the geographical space in which now exist the countries of Pakistan, India, and Bangladesh was at times more politically unified and at times less so.[2] The Mughals, who controlled large tracts of northern and central India prior to the British, ruled India quite effectively, especially at the height of the dynasty under Akbar (1556–1605).[3] His empire has been described as "probably the most powerful in the world at the time."[4] Court administration within the empire was relatively systematic; written records were maintained in Persian; a legal system modeled on Persian laws was in place; a bureaucracy of sorts existed, with court-appointed officials spread all the way from the center to the periphery; and, of course, there was considerable capacity to mobilize an armed force. The latter was related to the Mughal state's capacity to extract taxes from the largely agrarian society: For

---

[1] For a brief review of these approaches and for a guide to further reading, see Bipan Chandra et al., *India's Struggle for Independence, 1857–1947* (New Delhi: Penguin, 1988), 16–22.

[2] For a quick overview of Indian history, see Hermann Kulke and Dietmar Rothermund, *A History of India* (London: CroomHelm, 1986).

[3] On the nature of the state and the agrarian economy under the Mughals, see Irfan Habib, *The Agrarian System of Mughal India, 1556–1707* (Bombay: Asia Publishing House, 1963).

[4] Stanley Wolpert, *A New History of India* (New York: Oxford University Press, 1982), 134.

example, it has been estimated that the Mughals may have collected as much as 15 percent of the national income in taxes, whereas the British in India extracted about half of this amount.[5] This substantial revenue base also supported the construction of numerous monuments and a lavish life-style both at the court and among the aristocracy.

Despite this considerable political sophistication, Mughal India was a premodern agrarian bureaucracy. Notwithstanding the claims of some nationalist historiography, it did not demonstrate much of an impulse toward modernity; it was neither on the verge of modern statehood nor on the verge of an industrial revolution. While these are large and controversial historical issues, a few salient observations are relevant for the current discussion. First, the Mughal state was mainly a personalistic and patrimonial state: "the concept of 'public' service . . . had no roots in Indian soil. . . . In fact, under the Mughals, there was nothing like the modern concept of the state. . . . The Mughal king did not become subject of depersonalization."[6] Additionally, in order to maintain political control while securing agrarian surplus, Mughal emperors parceled out land to court favorites and other local influentials, who would extract taxes, keep a share, and pass on some set proportion to higher authorities. These tax farmers in no way owned the lands they controlled; rather, they always faced the possibility of being moved elsewhere. This mechanism aimed to minimize any threats to the emperor from independent centers of power. But the net result was that those with access to agrarian surplus had little incentive to reinvest, leading to minimal improvement in agricultural productivity – and to conspicuous consumption.[7] And finally, while a fairly sophisticated commercial sector existed, including overseas trade in textiles during the sixteenth and seventeenth centuries, this economy was not moving toward a spontaneous industrial revolution for numerous reasons: There had been no prior agricultural revolution; technology was primitive and there was little interest in Western scientific developments; mass demand was limited; and commercial and industrial organization was weak. Moreover, as the seventeenth century wore on, and the Mughal empire declined, India saw growing political instability, warfare, and the fragmentation of the political economy.[8]

The empire disintegrated in the first half of the eighteenth century, as the result of "inter-regional religious wars, court incompetence, greedy

---

5 See Angus Maddison, *Class Structure and Economic Growth: India and Pakistan since the Moghals* (London: George Allen & Unwin, 1971), 45.

6 See B. B. Misra, *The Bureaucracy in India: An Historical Analysis of Development up to 1947* (Delhi: Oxford University Press, 1977), 387.

7 See, for example, W. H. Moreland, *India at the Death of Akbar* (London: Macmillan, 1920).

8 See Tapan Ray Chaudhri, "The Mid-Eighteenth-Century Background," in Dharma Kumar, ed., *The Cambridge Economic History of India*, vol. 2: *C. 1757–c. 1970* (Cambridge: Cambridge University Press, 1983), 35.

factionalism, and traditional invasions."[9] Meanwhile by the end of the seventeenth century the British in the guise of the East India Company were already well established on the two coasts, quietly prospering as traders and local political brokers. The company was a collection of "merchant adventurers," backed since Cromwell's time by the British state, that had come to India for profits and operated as "a virtual state unto themselves."[10] During the second half of the eighteenth century, these traders raised armies and used their superior military technological and organizational skills to conquer one part of India first and then another. By the end of the century they had largely established a Pax Britannia of sorts on the subcontinent.

What is important for understanding longer-term developments is the emerging nature of the state and the economy in India under the maturing company rule, mainly in the first half of the nineteenth century. This state built on a tendency toward centralized and unified rule that had already emerged late in the previous century. The three separate areas of significant company control, namely, the presidencies of Bombay, Madras, and Bengal, were brought under the control of Bengal as early as 1773, with the governor of Bengal designated as the governor general. The influence of the British Crown over the company's administration in India also grew in fits and starts, especially following Pitt's India Act of 1784, which enhanced the powers of the British Parliament over the appointment of the governor-general in India.

Growing British control over India was facilitated and maintained by a sizable army, including British units but made up mainly of Indians recruited and trained locally. Again, for example, the armies of the three presidencies in 1824 included 170 sepoy regiments (sepoy being the Anglo-Indian term for Indian soldiers) and sixteen British regiments, totaling some 200,000 soldiers, the largest army in Asia.[11] A central government of sorts was established in 1833, and revenue administration was centralized. Routine administration at the top was carried on by civil servants who were appointed mainly at the personal recommendation of company bosses in England. While these appointments served a patronage function, there were repeated efforts to increase the salaries of civil servants so as to make them less nepotistic and less prone to corruption. The creation of a more professional, exam-based civil service in 1853 was the culmination of this effort.

If growing political centralization, supported by organized armies and a civil service of sorts, characterized the apex of the emerging colonial state, the political reality just below the apex was considerably more varied. After subduing one area and then another, the British entered into a variety of arrangements with influential "natives" – generally members of traditional

---

[9] Wolpert, *New History of India*, 173.
[10] Ibid., 147.
[11] Ibid., 216–17.

ruling classes – to facilitate the essential tasks of collecting taxes and securing order. In some parts of India (e.g., in the Bengal presidency) this arrangement involved British rulers in alliance with Indian zamindars (landlords). The British created private property in land and introduced British common law to support the sale and inheritance of such property. In exchange for more secure property rights, the "contract" that the Indian landlords entered into obliged them to transfer a set amount of agrarian taxes to the British and to maintain order within their domains.[12]

This ingenious arrangement of indirect rule served the British purpose very well in securing predictable revenues and long-term ruling allies. Indeed, once they perfected the model in India, the British transferred it to such other colonies as Nigeria. At the same time, however, the arrangement also limited the downward reach of state power, leaving much influence in the hands of traditional elites, and it was also detrimental to the development of the agrarian economy. In other parts of India, especially in Western India, for example, British rule was more direct and reached deeper into Indian society, with British civil servants being directly responsible for collecting taxes from peasant proprietors.[13] A hybrid system developed in parts of southern India. And in yet other parts – in as much as two-fifths of India – the British left the local princes in place, allowing them considerable latitude in terms of how they governed as long as they accepted British sovereignty and agreed to pay tribute.

Ensuring profitable trade was a central goal in the British imperial enterprise. Systematic pursuit of profits not only necessitated political control but also initiated economic changes of longer-term consequence. Among the pre-1857 economic developments (or lack thereof), three are especially notable. First, there were minimal changes in methods of agricultural production and thus in agricultural productivity. This was in part a function of the limited role of the laissez-faire colonial state, but it was also related to the perverse incentives faced by potential private investors. Over time, for example, pressures to provide tax revenues in some parts of India proved to be onerous. Failure to meet these demands led to considerable turnover among landowning classes – often bringing to the fore nonagriculturalists as absentee landlords – and in other parts put moneylenders in positions of de facto control of agrarian surplus. In either case, those with access to agricultural savings often found it easier to make profits via activities other

[12] How this "permanent settlement" that the British reached with Bengali zamindars functioned and influenced Bengali society and economy has been subject of lively scholarly debates. See, for example, Ratnalekha Ray, *Change in Bengal Agrarian Society, 1760–1850* (New Delhi: Manohar Publications, 1979).

[13] For a good and brief overview of regional variations within India, as well as a guide to further readings, see Kulke and Rothermund, *History of India*, 256–69. For more details, see Kumar, *Cambridge Economic History of India*, esp. sec. 3, "Regional Economy, 1757–1857."

than investments in agriculture, leading to longer-term problems with agricultural production.

Second, over time, a colonial pattern of exchange developed, as India increasingly exported raw materials and imported manufactured goods from England. As some Indians moved from subsistence food production to commercial production for export, their incomes probably increased. At the same time, however, numerous premodern producers of manufactured goods – such as the household-based textile manufacturers – went under in India in the face of more efficient British producers, now exporting to India within an open economy that India was forced to maintain.[14] These trends accelerated after the 1830s and the 1840s, when British manufacturers emerged ever more dominant within British politics (the Corn Laws were repealed in 1846), and the liberal ideology of an open economy came to be decisive in guiding British imperial ventures.

Finally, given the need to consolidate rule and facilitate trade, the British initiated the development of infrastructure. During the decade before the "mutiny" of 1857, the British established a national postal and telegraph system in India and began constructing the railways, developments that gave India an organic unity. A national market came into being, troops could be moved readily from one part of the subcontinent to another, and news could travel easily from one part of the country to another. Moreover, the Indian elite that had started to emerge from the new educational institutions in Calcutta, Bombay, and Madras could travel to unfamiliar parts of India – stoking the imagination of a potential Indian nation.

In sum, prior to 1857 – that is, prior to formal British Crown rule over India – the East India Company had already established the essentials of empire over the subcontinent: centralized authority, backed by organized armed forces and a civil service. This process of early state formation contrasts sharply with Nigeria, also a British colony, where colonialism came late and had only a short-lived and superficial impact. In any case, the Indian colonial state was financed by Indian revenues, often collected by Indian elites who entered into a variety of ruling alliances with the colonial power. With the development of an infrastructure, a national economy was created and a pattern of colonial exchange was established.

While colonial conquest had always required the use of force, there were limits to how far the British could fiscally squeeze the native authorities and still hope to use them as ruling allies. These limits were finally reached in 1857, when deeply threatened traditional Indian princes and disgruntled soldiers in central India rebelled against British rule with considerable ferocity. Not surprisingly, given the conflicting perspectives, British

---

[14] For the controversy concerning the decline in Indian manufacturing under early colonial rule, see Morris D. Morris et al., *Indian Economy in the Nineteenth Century: A Symposium* (Indian Economic and Social History Association, Delhi School of Economics, Delhi, 1969).

historiography often calls this event in colonial history the "mutiny of 1857," whereas Indian nationalist historiography calls it "the first war of independence."[15] What is important for our purposes is that 1857 marked a turning point in the construction of the colonial state in India. The British won a decisive military victory against the rebelling Indian princes, marking 1857 as something of the last gasp of India's traditional ruling classes. They survived, however, and even flourished in the next century in a new role – as junior partners in the colonial ruling alliance. We now turn to a consideration of how the British used their newly won power to mold the colonial state and economy and how India's emerging elites reacted to colonialism.

II. Colonial State Construction

The state that sovereign India inherited from its colonial past was simultaneously modern and "limited." It was modern in at least two senses. First, the state was centralized. It held a monopoly over the use of coercion in the territory it governed. And, at least at the apex, it was relatively bureaucratized on the basis of a clear separation between the public and various personal realms. And second, it was increasingly constitutional, with elements of a parliamentary government. But then this state was also quite limited: First, the colonial state had by design been essentially laissez-faire. Second, and less obviously but of more profound importance, the British entered into a variety of ruling alliances with traditional Indian elites, limiting the state's downward reach. And third, Indian nationalist leaders mobilized various social classes into politics, which pushed a limited colonial state into a reactive mode. This modern but limited state was India's fragmented-multiclass state in the making, the product of both colonial state construction and pressures from Indians, especially the nationalist elite.

The colonial strategy of state construction in India was essentially incremental, with ground-level realities providing the frame for one set of actions, which then established the conditions for the next set of decisions and innovations. Although it would be difficult to characterize any one moment or set of decisions as the "revolutionary" turning point for India, probably the developments following the "mutiny" of 1857 came closest.

Of course, incrementalism should not be taken to imply a lack of coherent logic in state-building strategies. Coherence derived, however, not so much from a grand plan as from the unity of imperial purpose, namely, to control India as a unified territory for the twin British goals of profit and global power. India – unlike many African colonies, such as Nigeria – was central to Britain's role as a global power in the nineteenth and the first half of the twentieth century: Balance-of-payment surpluses with India enabled Britain

---

[15] See, for example, Ainslie T. Embree, *1857 in India: Mutiny or War of Independence* (Boston: South Asia Books, 1963).

to run deficits elsewhere in the world, and India provided a second military base from which imperial ambitions in East Africa and the Far East could be pursued more economically.[16] This centrality of India in British imperial designs had more in common with the importance the Japanese assigned to Korea than with the relative neglect of early Brazil by Portugal and of Nigeria by Britain in the twentieth century.

The rebellion by Indian soldiers and princes against the British in 1857 was decisively crushed. From here on, certainly over the next few decades, the "British had India at their feet" and were the "driving force in shaping the Indian polity."[17] India formally became a colony, as the British Crown took over control from the East India Company. The company was in any case bankrupt as a result of the costs incurred in crushing the rebellion and was happy to be rid of its burdens. The direct involvement of the British state reflected the growing importance of India for British global ambitions and therefore the need to control it more effectively.

What sort of rule did the British Crown impose on India? Certainly, the mutiny helped to clarify for the British the type of colonial state they wanted in India. First, there were to be no more mutinies – meaning that British rule had to be centralized, efficient, and, if necessary, despotic. As a result, power was increasingly centralized in a single office in London, the Secretary of State for India, and in turn slowly but surely pressed upon India via numerous centralizing reforms, including the reorganization of the army. Second, understanding the limits to being effective despots from afar, the British learned in the aftermath of the mutiny to respect "the strength and tenacity of the traditional institutions of India."[18] The resulting political strategy was to ally with and strengthen the position of traditional Indian elites, especially the gentry and aristocrats. And third, in keeping with the contemporary British understanding of "good government," the colonial state was to be economical: operating without deficits and financed by resources mobilized within India.

Given that the gentry and aristocracy were part of the ruling alliance, there were limits on resources that could be readily mobilized. While precluding any grand public expenditures, the resources were just sufficient to construct a modest laissez-faire state that collected taxes, maintained order, and provided a legal framework for private economic activities. In addition to an effective armed force, a judiciary and a small, professional civil service were needed. British efforts at state construction in India were focused on precisely these areas.

[16] See, for example, Anil Seal, "Imperialism and Nationalism in India," in John Gallagher et al., eds., *Locality, Province and Nation: Essays on Indian Politics, 1870–1940* (Cambridge: Cambridge University Press, 1973), esp. 7.
[17] Thomas R. Metcalf, *The Aftermath of Revolt: India, 1857–1870* (Princeton, N.J.: Princeton University Press, 1964), ix.
[18] Ibid., 323.

British crown rule in India lasted from 1857 to 1947. The pattern of state construction over these nine decades can be conveniently divided into two periods. During the formative period, which lasted until about the turn of the century, the exercise of power by the colonial state was mainly autocratic and despotic. The core, especially the army and the civil service, became increasingly institutionalized during these years. Around the turn of the century, India's viceroy, Lord George Curzon, described the functioning of the colonial state as fairly routinized: "Round and round like the diurnal revolutions of the earth went file after file in the bureaucratic daily dance, stately, solemn, sure and slow."[19] Meanwhile, nationalist opposition to this state began to emerge in the late nineteenth century and came to a head over the British partition of Bengal in 1905. This marked the beginning of a drawn-out, more defensive second phase during which the colonial state alternatively sought to co-opt, repress, and accommodate the growing nationalist opposition until it eventually withdrew altogether in 1947. While the bureaucratic structure of the state did not undergo profound changes during this second phase, the political context of the state altered significantly, leading to constitutional changes and growing numbers of Indians in both elected and appointed political office.

Exercise of Power

The Indian colonial state was essentially bureaucratic, despotic, and backed by coercive force, as is typical of colonial norms. To understand India in particular, one must also look to the specific political context of interests and institutions that shaped colonial control. Control of India in the second half of the nineteenth century was centralized in London or, more specifically, in the colonial office of the Secretary of State for India, which was nominally under the control of Parliament. In truth, however, imperial issues were neither of great interest to members of Parliament nor did they attract broad popular attention. Those British actors who sought to influence British policy toward India were a narrow group: the economic elite with an interest in India, such as the textile manufacturers of Manchester or Lancashire; politicians and bureaucrats who worried about Britain as a global power; missionaries; and British citizens who were in one way or another directly involved in governing India. The main policy task of the Secretary of State for India was then twofold: to balance the interests of the British state and of British capital and to ensure that these interests were prioritized uppermost in the governing of India.

London's will in India was implemented via the office of the viceroy. While a powerful office, the term of individual viceroys lasted only five years – corresponding mainly to the life of each British Parliament – and was too

---

[19] Cited in Wolpert, *New History of India*, 265.

short to be deeply consequential in terms of policy changes. The ruling mood – whether more or less despotic or more or less efficient – varied with individual viceroys. The office was also of great symbolic importance, as it underlined the existence of unified, autocratic, and foreign rule over the subcontinent. The broad substance of policy, however, was mainly designed by the colonial offices in London and then specified and implemented by seasoned civil servants in charge of various departments in Calcutta (or in Delhi after 1911, when the colonial capital was moved) and their junior counterparts, the legendary district officers, who were dispersed throughout India. This network of senior and junior civil servants provided the essential "steel frame" for governing colonial India.

The ideologies that guided British rule in India were, of course, the set of ideas that the British themselves held dear, namely, liberalism, laissez-faire, and free trade. Liberalism, understood as a functioning democracy and adult suffrage, was far from fully practiced even in England in the second half of the nineteenth century and was certainly impossible for the British to practice in a colony such as India. India was to be ruled with British interests in mind and often against the wishes and interests of Indians. This necessitated autocratic rule and serious departures from liberal beliefs, including racism and self-serving perceptions of Indians as "childlike," really not a "nation," and not ready for democracy and self-government.[20] Nevertheless, British beliefs about what constituted "good government" – especially the idea of rule of law – still had an important impact on India, even in the second half of the nineteenth century. A legal system was necessary to protect private property that the British had introduced to India, as well as to facilitate binding contracts required for the pursuit of private economic activities. Independent high courts were thus established in 1861, and a hybrid legal system based on English common law and local precedents emerged slowly but surely.

The ideologies of laissez-faire and free trade reflected both the victorious position of British capital in British political economy and Britain's position as a leading manufacturing nation that benefited from open economies worldwide. These ideas, in turn, influenced the construction of the colonial state in India. The colonial state was always intended to be a limited state, designed to collect just enough taxes to finance orderly alien rule in India. Profit making was to be the province of unaided private individuals. Extraction of revenues or taxes and provision of order were thus important priorities, as was the development of infrastructure to help colonial economic exchange. But while in practice the colonial state often helped

[20] See, for example, Thomas R. Metcalf, *The New Cambridge History of India*, vol. 3: *Ideologies of the Raj* (Cambridge: Cambridge University Press, 1994). See also Uday Mehta, *Liberalism and Empire: A Study in Nineteenth-Century British Liberal Thought* (Chicago: University of Chicago Press, 1999).

British businessmen in India,[21] the basic design of the state did not reflect these considerations.

Thus, British India saw no close, systematic cooperation for economic growth between the colonial state and private producers – in sharp contrast to the case of Japan in Korea. In India, no government departments were created to develop and promote new industrial technologies, no industrial policy was developed, and no or little public subsidies were provided to promote industrial growth. This limited role of the state, in turn, came to be reflected not only in the design of tax collection (mainly indirectly) and expenditures of the limited public monies (mostly on financing an army and bureaucracy), but also in the limited types of activities that the state learned to master and in the generalist nature of state bureaucrats. That a relatively small group of Cambridge- and Oxford-educated elite civil servants – backed by a significant armed force – could run a colony the size of India thus becomes comprehensible.

To govern effectively, a limited state of this type needed local allies to wield influence and provide local knowledge. Prior to 1857 the British had reached a variety of such arrangements with Indian princes, landlords, and other local notables who were turned into landlords. What transpired after the mutiny was essentially a continuation of this trend, but with a difference. The mutiny clarified for the British that they could push the Indian traditional elite only so far and still hope to work with them as allies. While this was a realpolitik conclusion, it was justified in terms of respect for local customs and traditions. And it represented a significant compromise on the part of the British in terms of state construction and activities. The result was considerable fragmenting of state power.

First, in as much as two-fifths of the subcontinent, Indian princes continued to rule under British suzerainty – the result being only limited penetration of the colonial state. Even basic laws, not to mention patterns of tax extraction and public expenditures, were immune to British influence and varied from one princely state to another. Second, even in the majority of areas where British rule was more direct, the need to accommodate the gentry limited the reach of the state, manifested most strikingly in the constraints on the capacity to tax elite agrarian incomes or to pursue any progressive social legislation that might offend traditional interests and sensibilities. The colonial state, then, autocratic and bureaucratic at the apex, was grafted onto India's highly heterogeneous society by compromising with numerous despotic traditional Indian elites.

By the turn of the twentieth century this modern colonial state had been deeply implanted in India on the basis of centralized control over the subcontinent, a bureaucratic apex, and a semblance of rule of law. But it was a

---

[21] See, for example, Amiya Bagchi, *Private Investment in India, 1900–1939* (Cambridge: Cambridge University Press, 1972).

fragmented and limited state authority – limited in its economic scope but also limited in its downward reach into the society. Following the mutiny, moreover, the British ruled India mostly unopposed as the core patterns of the British Raj became deeply institutionalized during the second half of the nineteenth century. Indeed, many of these patterns would survive even the tumultuous rise of nationalism and the coming of a sovereign state in twentieth-century India. Thus the paradox in the words of Anil Seal: The Raj was only "an immensely powerful system of government . . . in terms of policy making [the scope of which was in any case, quite limited]. In practice, many of its efforts were buckled by the hard facts of Indian society."[22]

The opposition to British rule in India – coming this time from the new, educated Indian elite – started growing again in the late nineteenth century. The nationalist opposition first crystallized in 1905 against the British divide-and-rule strategy for splitting the province of Bengal into a more Hindu western half and a more Muslim eastern half, a move that was itself partly aimed at dealing with growing opposition. We can here note that 1905 marks a transition in the strategy of colonial state construction, as political changes in the first half of the twentieth century often reflected growing political opposition to colonial rule by Indians. The British found themselves increasingly on the defensive. Although the core of the state, and in particular the army and the civil service, did not undergo any dramatic transformation during this new phase, the political context and some political institutions changed significantly, including a growing trend toward democracy and federalism, as well as increasing participation by Indians in the colonial state institutions.

The core ruling alliance of British colonialists and Indian gentry remained intact during the first half of the twentieth century, but the value of the gentry within the alliance declined, more or less in proportion to the declining significance of land revenues, as numerous new sources of public revenues became available, especially customs and excise duties.[23] India's ruling classes had in any case by now become dependent on the British for their position, and the British took them for granted.[24] The British had a new concern on their hands, however: Indian nationalists, whose political significance grew in fits and starts, especially after Gandhi entered the picture about 1920 and helped to transform the nationalist opposition into a mass political movement. British hopes of dealing with

---

[22] See Seal, "Imperialism and Nationalism in India," 9, n. 7. The comment in brackets within the quotation is my addition.

[23] See Dharma Kumar, "The Fiscal System," in Kumar, *Cambridge Economic History of India*, 928–29.

[24] That this may be somewhat of an overstatement is made clear in a specific study of one prince who delicately negotiated between the British and his Indian subjects. See Lloyd Rudolph and Susanne Rudolph, *Reversing the Gaze: Amar Singh's Diary: A Colonial Subject's Narrative of Imperial India* (New Delhi: Oxford University Press, 2000).

this nationalist opposition involved a variety of strategies: manipulation, co-optation and accommodation, and repression. Each of these strategies, in turn, left its imprint on the evolving nature of colonial political institutions in India.

Manipulation as a ruling strategy was generally aimed at weakening the unity of the nationalist opposition by exploiting the numerous divisions that already existed in India's heterogeneous society. The most significant of these divisions was the religious divide between Hindus and Muslims, but distinctions of caste and of regional origin also played a role. Numerous institutional expressions of the divide-and-rule strategy that were of longer-term significance included the already mentioned administrative division of Bengal, the creation of separate political offices (both appointed and elected) for Muslims, the formal categorization of people (for purposes of the census, for example) that hardened previously fluid distinctions, and the reorganization of the army along ethnic lines.

When manipulation failed, the British offered Indian elites some genuine positions and power. The growing participation of Indians in the elite civil service would have long-term consequences. The more politicized and mobilized Indian elites, by contrast, were offered the opportunity – which some took and others resisted – to seek elected office in legislative assemblies with limited power and to represent a limited electorate. And finally, when neither manipulation nor accommodation succeeded in muting the nationalist opposition, as increasingly became the case in the interwar period, the colonial state turned to a variety of repressive measures, including constitutionally sanctioned dismissal of elected representatives, a ban on public assemblies and speech, and imprisonment of leaders. Such repressive institutions also became part of sovereign India's political inheritance.

In sum, while the core of the colonial state was institutionalized in the second half of the nineteenth century, the political context within which this state operated changed significantly in the first half of the twentieth century. Instead of a nearly unopposed, bureaucratic, and despotic state with a fragmented authority structure, the state in the interwar years was simultaneously more open and more repressive – reflecting attempts to deal with the growing mass opposition. Despite the nationalist pressures, however, the British never allowed the dilution of the centralized nature of the state: The centralized army was maintained, the elite civil service was not provincialized, and such core state functions as control over public revenues remained the province of the central government. The long-term benefits of such measures for India are especially striking when juxtaposed against developments in Nigeria, where early "decentralization" would later militate against a viable state. Following is a discussion of how the core centralizing institutions of the army and the civil service were constructed and maintained.

The Army

A large, competent, and centralized army was at the heart of the British colonial state in India. Effective civilian control of this professional and apolitical army was also an important legacy of British rule in sovereign India. The construction and evolution of this army is a complex story.[25] For our purposes, an outline will suffice. Following the mutiny, the reorganization of the army – with the aim of avoiding future mutinies – was a pressing concern for the British. The subject was studied and debated, and numerous reforms followed over the next few decades. First, the proportion of British relative to Indian sepoy regiments increased, and officers from then on and well into the twentieth century remained nearly exclusively British. Second, the recruitment of Indian soldiers was generally concentrated in regions and social strata considered to be more loyal to the British – Punjabi Muslims, Sikhs, Gurkhas, and Rajputs, for example.

A fair amount of thought was also given to whether regiments should be ethnically homogeneous or mixed; the former model was often preferred with the proviso that regiments ought to be recruited and maintained in their region of origin. Fourth, the professionalization of the army was made a priority. Nearly all officers were trained at Sandhurst, and soldiers were often isolated from civilian life, living in neat and well-ordered gated communities, the cantonment, on the outskirts of cities. Finally, while the three separate armies of Madras, Bombay, and Bengal were maintained – with "divide and rule" the main rationale – the command of all three was centralized in Calcutta, with policy and financial issues firmly in the control of civilian authorities.

It was an army designed primarily to support internal colonial order. The British Indian army only became a war-fighting machine during and after the First World War. Prior to that – and even after the war – the armed forces were an extremely effective component of British rule in India, so much so that they rarely had to be used to maintain internal order. While the actual "law and order" tasks were performed by a sprawling, armed police force – modeled after the Irish constabulary and established in 1861, also in the aftermath of the mutiny[26] – the mere presence of a sizable armed force helped to contain challenges to state power. With the traditional Indian elites militarily defeated and then incorporated into the ruling alliance, and with the emergence of the new urban elites still several decades away, this armed force enabled the British to rule India comfortably in the second half of the nineteenth century. Even in the first half of the twentieth century, when nationalist opposition to British rule grew significantly, the presence

[25] I have drawn heavily on Stephen P. Cohen, *The Indian Army: Its Contribution to the Development of a Nation* (Berkeley: University of California Press, 1971).

[26] See, for example, D. H. Bayley, *The Police and Political Development in India* (Princeton, N.J.: Princeton University Press, 1969).

of a sizable armed force still loyal to the government molded the political process. Nationalists were forced to choose their political ground carefully, focusing mainly on issues of legitimacy. They shied away from direct, violent confrontation with the colonial state and even adopted nonviolence as a virtuous ideology of protest.

As British imperial activities grew in Asia and Africa, the British Indian army became more externally oriented. The Afghan War and the "Russian threat" in the late nineteenth and early twentieth centuries were catalysts, as was the "scramble for Africa." The importance of the Indian army in British imperial design is reflected in the fact that one-quarter to one-third of the colonial government's budget was allocated to the army every year (and in time of war this share was even higher). This amount was roughly equal to what the British spent on maintaining the rest of the state apparatus, including the highly paid elite civil servants. Moreover, more than half of the nearly 100,000 Britishers employed in India were in the army.[27]

The First World War was, of course, a major turning point, when the size of the Indian army jumped from some 150,000 men to nearly half a million (and again shrank back after the war), and Indian soldiers fought under British officers in Europe, the Middle East, and Africa. Among the important consequences of the war for the army was a slow but steady increase in the number of Indian officers within the armed force. This was both a reward of sorts for the Indian contribution to the war effort and a response to growing nationalist pressures. Unlike the civil service, however, the British were quite reluctant to allow the armed forces to get "Indianized." While Indians could already take a civil service exam in India in 1922, the Indian Military Academy was established only a decade later, in 1932. Prior to that, about ten Indian officers were trained at Sandhurst every year during the 1920s and eligible to receive the King's Commission. Following the establishment of military academies in India, and especially during the Second World War, the number of Indian officers in the colonial Indian army grew rapidly, from some 1,500 prior to the war to some 15,000 during the war (the army itself grew to more than two million men). It was this generation of officers, especially those trained in the interwar years (prior to the emergency commissioning of officers during the Second World War), that was at the helm of Indian armed forces when India became independent and that contributed to India's democratic evolution by staying out of politics.

Unlike many other developing countries, sovereign India is exceptional in both its democratic record and its apolitical armed forces, facts that are intimately related and that owe something to the British legacy. A quick comparison with Pakistan readily underlines, however, that the main factor behind the military staying in the barracks in India – but not in Pakistan,

---

[27] For budgetary data, see Kumar, "Fiscal System," 931–37. For figures on personnel, see Angus Maddison, *Class Structure and Economic Growth*, 44.

which shared with India the same colonial legacy – had less to do with the nature of the armed forces and more to do with the much broader issue of why civilian politics cohered and took a democratic form in India and not in Pakistan. Nevertheless, the British contribution to the apolitical nature of Indian armed forces ought not to be minimized. First, the British left in place both the ideology and the institutions of civilian control over the military.[28] Second, Indian officers who trained under the British were deeply indoctrinated with the ideology of legitimacy of civilian control and took pride in staying above politics.[29] And finally, the Indian armed forces were highly professional, not only in the sense of military competence but also in the sense of being an organization with its own internal norms and hierarchies – its own esprit de corps – and operating at a distance from the broader society.

The Civil Service
Like the army, an elite civil service became relatively well institutionalized in colonial India in the second half of the nineteenth century. The British had introduced an exam-based civil service system to India as early as 1853, before the mutiny, and about the same time as such a system was created in Britain itself. Over the next several decades, this civil service became deeply routinized, formally becoming the Indian Civil Service (ICS) in 1892. The ICS was indeed the heart of the colonial state, collecting revenues, maintaining order, and executing government policies on a daily basis in often remote regions, at least in those regions where the writ of the colonial state was more direct than indirect.[30] For many Indians, an ICS officer, along with the police officer, was the most obvious manifestation of alien power. Feared and respected by most Indians and reviled by the more politically conscious nationalists, the ICS came to be described by many observers as the "steel frame" that held India together. So significant was its role in providing orderly governance that even Indian nationalists – in spite of their often vocal criticism of the ICS – essentially kept this colonial service intact after independence.

Given the size of India, the ICS was a relatively minuscule ruling elite. For example, India's population in 1931 was some 353 million. The colonial state in this setting employed nearly a million people, most of them Indian *babus*, or clerks and petty officials with some minimal education. By

---

[28] Stephen Cohen, for example, considers the general acceptance of the "doctrine of civilian control" by the colonial army in India as a "major accomplishment of the British." See Cohen, *Indian Army*, 31.

[29] Ibid., chap. 5.

[30] The literature on the ICS is substantial, including many memoirs and semi-scholarly treatments by former civil servants who served in India. I have drawn heavily on the following two scholarly accounts: B. B. Misra, *Bureaucracy in India*; and David C. Potter, *India's Political Administrators: From ICS to IAS* (Delhi: Oxford University Press, 1996).

contrast, the ICS during much of its duration consisted only of some 1,000 officers.[31] Nearly half, especially the younger ones, worked as district officers, acting as local "czars," responsible for revenue, law, police, and general administration. The remaining and more senior officers worked either at the provincial level (though each of the provinces also had its own provincial civil services), representing the central government, or in the central government itself (first in Calcutta, then in Delhi), assigned responsibility for policy decisions and their execution.

ICS officers in the second half of the nineteenth century were nearly all British. Most came from upper-middle-class backgrounds, and were educated at Oxford or Cambridge as well as other universities in London or Dublin and joined the career civil service as young men after passing the British Civil Service exam. Between 1904 and 1913, some one-third to one-half of the top twenty candidates of the British Civil Service exam opted to serve in India.[32] The ICS thus attracted considerable talent: "well rounded" men of "intelligence" and "integrity," who chose to serve the empire in faraway places out of a variety of motivations, including patriotism, career and power ambitions, search for adventure, and the promise of extremely lucrative jobs. All were "generalists," men who shared the very British idea that the key requirement of a good civil servant was not to possess specialized knowledge, but rather to be a "gifted layman who, moving frequently from job to job within the service, can take a practical view of any problem, irrespective of subject matter, in the light of his knowledge and experience of the government machine."[33]

The young, talented generalists were socialized, first via special training and then mainly on the job, especially serving in the districts, often under the supervision of a more senior officer. The service was a fairly closed group, with its own esprit de corps. There was very limited upward mobility into the ICS from provincial services, and senior lateral appointments from the outside were also limited. Officers within the ICS thus built on their gentlemanly values – often acquired in British public schools first and afterward in elite British universities – mainly learning from each other on the job and thus perpetuating shared norms: "confident, courageous, and self-disciplined amateur[s] for whom public service for the community was valued over individual achievements."[34]

This was a highly professional civil service with entry based on a competitive exam and an internal merit system that cut through personalism, patronage, and nepotism. An independent Civil Service Commission oversaw assessments and promotion, and informal socialization and shared norms

[31] See Potter, *India's Political Administrators*, 21.
[32] See Misra, *Bureaucracy in India*, 106.
[33] Ibid., 385.
[34] See Potter, *India's Political Administrators*, 75.

within the service fostered a degree of insulation from the broader society, encouraging officers to respond to the imperatives of the government and their superiors. Of course, these "virtues" should not be overstated: The insulation of the ICS was reinforced by the racism of its officers toward Indians; officers often acted against those with nationalist sympathies; and they often allied themselves with local Indian influentials against the majority they sought to govern. All of this was part and parcel of the broader colonial rule in India and should not be taken as defects of a professional civil service. In fact, most students of the ICS assess it as a first-rate civil service. Even historians as sympathetic to Indian nationalists as Bipan Chandra and his colleagues concluded that the ICS was "rule bound, efficient and, at the top, rather honest."[35]

Following the First World War a larger number of Indians were able to join the ICS, for a number of reasons. First, the war itself cut off the supply of qualified Britishers available to serve in India. Moreover, with nationalism growing in India, the ICS became a less attractive job opportunity, because potential British applicants might view it as the arm of a more openly repressive state. To fill the gap created by a declining British supply, educated Indians were increasingly available to fill the positions. And finally, "Indianization" of the ICS was a key demand of the Indian nationalists, one that the British sought to accommodate. As a result, starting in 1922 it became possible to take the ICS exam in India (and not only in London). By 1939, the number of Indians in the ICS more or less reached the quota set by the British, namely, half Britishers and half Indians.[36]

While most Indians who joined the ICS had not been socialized in British public schools and universities, some had been and the rest were often trained in similar institutions established by the British in India. They, too, became an integral part of the service, as entrance exams and merit-based internal promotions applied to them as much as to the Britishers and thus cut through personalism and nepotism.[37] More important, Indian officers internalized ICS norms, especially in the districts.[38] Although the "political" attitudes of Indians in the ICS may well have been different from those of their British counterparts, especially regarding the nationalist cause, in

[35] Bipan Chandra et al., *India after Independence, 1947–2000* (New Delhi: Penguin, 1999), 18. The foremost scholar of the Indian civil service, B. B. Misra, is a lot more enthusiastic in his assessment: "The prestige which members of the Indian Civil Service enjoyed historically was not without justification.... Their sense of honesty and morality... was the result of a superior and liberal education, intellectual and cultural attainments.... They were in fact a *corps d'elite.*" See Misra, *The Bureaucracy in India*, 392.

[36] Ibid., 291.

[37] An important exception to this trend were some Muslim candidates who, failing to qualify in some proportional sense, were then appointed for the sake of "communal balance" within the ICS. What the subsequent impact of this strategy was on the creation of a civil service in Pakistan is an important subject that clearly belongs to a different study.

[38] See Potter, *India's Political Administrators*, 101–20.

terms of competence and honesty, Indians in the ICS were quite similar to
the British officers. Many of these Indian officers would go on to form the
core of the future Indian Administrative Service (IAS), the inheritor of the
ICS in independent India – thus constituting another critical contribution
of British colonialism to state formation in India.

Still, the power of ICS to get things done was not without its limits. First,
these civil servants operated within a laissez-faire state, with a limited focus
on collecting revenues and maintaining order. ICS officers were in any case
generalists, unprepared for such complex and specialized tasks as running
factories, promoting exports, building technical institutions, and promoting
scientific agriculture, tasks that the sovereign Indian state would eventually
expect them to perform. Second, though competent, the elite service was
a minuscule group that sat atop a much larger, less professional, and less
capable group of public servants. And finally in terms of the political context in which the colonial state operated, it had to strike political bargains
with traditional Indian elites and fragment its authority in order to manage rule over the vast population. The presence of ICS officers was thus a
lot thinner in some parts of the country than in others. And as the state
came under increasing challenge from the nationalists, state legitimacy was
further undermined. In these ways, the state's ambitions and capacities to
pursue state-led projects were constrained.

Despite the limitation, however, the ICS made long-term contributions
to state formation in India. First, because the British resisted the provincial-
ization of the service and maintained an all-India program, the ICS helped
to give meaning to the political unity of India. Even the nationalists were
glad to have such civil service at their disposal. The contrast with a case
such as Nigeria could not be more stark. Second, this competent, efficient
civil service enabled limited but good government. And finally, its public-
spiritedness gave substance to the idea that a modern state stands above
private interests and acts in the public interest, however that is defined by
the political elite.

III. The Nationalist Movement

Leaving aside such cases of successful communist revolutions in the developing world as China, India's nationalist movement was probably the
most significant mass movement against colonialism in the first half of the
twentieth century. And the Indian National Congress (INC) was the most
important organized nationalist group within India. Founded in 1885 and
eventually led by the likes of Gandhi and Nehru, the INC not only successfully opposed British rule in India, but also contributed significantly to the
formation of a democracy with broad developmental commitments. And
yet the core of the state that the INC inherited and maintained was essentially the colonial construct discussed above: "The Congress fought against

the Raj, but it was also progressively becoming the Raj, eventually taking over without major change the entire bureaucratic and army structure, the 'heaven born' civil service and all, mainly substituting the brown for the white."[39] While a tad too harsh, this assessment underlines a central point, namely, that the sovereign Indian state is best understood as a product of both colonial construction and nationalist modification.

India's nationalist movement has been extensively studied.[40] My relatively limited focus here aims at stressing the extent to which the nationalist movement modified the colonially constructed state, as well as the limits of these efforts. The INC so fundamentally altered the political context within which the colonial state operated that colonial rule eventually became untenable in India. Three areas of political change were facilitated by the nationalist movement in general and by the INC in particular: a growing national consciousness and a sense of public purpose; the emergence of modern, democratic politics; and a broad embrace of a developmental ideology, including a belief in the constructive role of a national state. In spite of such profound political changes, Indian nationalists also embraced the colonially constructed army, bureaucracy, and judiciary, and much like the colonial state, they eventually even incorporated landowning classes, albeit smaller landowners, into the ruling alliance. The underlying reasons are not difficult to fathom. For one, the INC was a fairly loosely organized, multiclass movement that was often fragmented along intraelite and elite-mass cleavages. While this mass movement succeeded in generating considerable oppositional power, its capacities to undertake basic political and social changes were limited, leaving it dependent on existing structures of state and social power.

During the first half of the twentieth century the INC helped to facilitate the emergence of unifying nationalism in India. We know that the INC's political project of creating national political unity to oppose the British rule was far from perfect: Numerous Muslims felt excluded and eventually opted for Pakistan; select political groups on the left and the right – such as the communists, the Hindu nationalists, or Subhas Bose's Indian National Army – were probably no less champions of the Indian nation than the INC elite but chose not to accept the INC's middle-of-the-road politics; even among Congress elites there was frequent, even bitter discord; and the INC's version of Indian nationalism embraced by peasants and workers was often shallow. For all these qualifications, it is nevertheless the case that the INC was wildly successful in mobilizing a majority of Indians – political

---

[39] See Sumit Sarkar, *Modern India, 1885–1947* (London: Macmillan, 1989), 4.

[40] The two outstanding studies on which I have drawn heavily are Sarkar, *Modern India, 1885–1947*; and Chandra et al., *India's Struggle for Independence*. Notable among others that I consulted were Seal, "Imperialism and Nationalism in India"; Ranajit Guha, ed., *Subaltern Studies*, vols. 1–4 (New Delhi: Oxford University Press, 1982–86); and A. R. Desai, *Social Background of Indian Nationalism* (Bombay: Popular Prakashan, 1959).

elites "representing" various ethnic groups, businessmen, students, workers and peasants, and even some landowning groups, especially the "lower gentry" – into a mass nationalist movement aimed at ousting the British and establishing a sovereign Indian state.

Of concern to us here are the ramifications of this mobilization for the processes of state formation and intervention in India, as viewed from a comparative perspective. In a nutshell, the INC's version of Indian nationalism emerged as a dominant ideology in India, shaping both the polity and the economy. Mobilized nationalism in India also helped to create a public sphere, an arena of thought and action in which some Indians strove to rise above personal and sectarian beliefs and interests. It was in the name of the nation, for example, that leaders asked their followers to suppress their narrow interests and make sacrifices; by the same token they chastised the blatantly ambitious and individualistic. As the nation came to define the public interest in India, the nationalist cause helped to legitimize political and policy choices, again by subordinating the private to the public good. The nation, in other words, came to define what was in the general or public interest in India. This is not to deny that numerous special interests benefited under the aegis of national interests; ideologies mainly mold how interests are pursued, rather than undermining or dissolving interests. But the significance of Indian nationalism in helping to create a larger, legitimate public arena of politics should not be underestimated, especially when juxtaposed to most African cases, for example, Nigeria. Without a sense of national purpose, the sovereign state there was quickly reduced to a neopatrimonial state, a ready vehicle for personal and sectoral gain.

A related impact of nationalist mobilization, especially under the umbrella of the INC, was to generate a degree of civilian consensus about the desired nature and role of the state in sovereign India. The INC was, of course, far from cohesive about such issues; even Gandhi, Nehru, and Patel disagreed with each other, not to mention the various left, right, and other tendencies within the Congress. Nevertheless, many of these differences were politically manageable. For example, revolutionary communism and authoritarian fascism enjoyed only minimal support within the Congress. More positively, over time, especially as Nehru's leadership position became secure, the Congress became committed to such values as democracy, secularism, and state-led developmentalism, with a high premium placed on maintaining national sovereignty. This democratic-nationalist-statist consensus, in turn, helped to generate popular support and legitimacy for the sovereign Indian state. The benign political impact of this modicum of consensus again cannot be underestimated. Recall, by contrast, the Brazilian case, where sharp political divisions between supporters of a "national developmental" position and a more "open internationalist" position sparked repeated political crises. Looking very different, India's prolonged and relatively cohesive nationalist movement generated more shared values and institutions, leading to a more smoothly functioning civilian polity.

Why did such a united and powerful national movement that emerged in India not develop in many other colonies, for example, in Nigeria, which was also under British rule? An obvious factor concerns timing: India was colonized a lot earlier than much of Africa. By the time self-determination had emerged as a global issue in the early part of the twentieth century, an entire political stratum of educated Indians – often educated at institutions started by the British in India in the nineteenth century – was already on the scene, ready to embrace these ideas and use them as tools of political mobilization. By contrast, Nigeria was only being fully colonized around this time and an educated urban stratum that might lead a nationalist movement did not emerge until much later – closer to midcentury, when colonialism was already losing steam – and even then was fairly thin and concentrated in a few parts of the country.

There is also the deeper issue of the relative importance of India in British imperial design. Given India's centrality, the British created a unified colonial state in India that established authority over various regions and localities. Moreover, in spite of nationalist demands to decentralize colonial power, the British never permitted the core power of the centralized state to be diluted. As Anil Seal has argued, Indian nationalism ought to be understood as a reaction to this centralized colonial state.[41] Seal underestimates the emotive powers of nationalism – often reducing it analytically to a "cloak" behind which self-aggrandizing elites pursue their political ambitions – but he is accurate in his suggestion that Indian nationalists unified mainly as a vehicle for fighting a unified opponent – the colonial state.[42] Without such a coherent and centralized colonial state in a case such as Nigeria, the already weak nationalist impulse was diminished and rendered nearly irrelevant. In India, in other words, a centralized colonial apparatus created incentives for varieties of Indians to come together under a moderately cohesive nationalist umbrella aimed at ousting the British.

India's nationalist movement also had an impact on the creation of a more democratic India. The British introduced to India protodemocratic institutions, such as regional legislative assemblies representing a limited electorate and with limited powers. The colonial state, however, remained fairly autocratic until the very end; in truth it could be little else in light of

---

[41] See Seal, "Imperialism and Nationalism in India."

[42] For example, after the bitter split in the Congress in 1907 (at Surat), when Congress reintegrated in 1916 (at the Lucknow session), the more extremist leader, Tilak, argued for unity in the following terms: "When we have to fight against a third party – it is a very important thing that we stand on this platform united, united in race, united in religion, united as regards all different shades of political creed." See Chandra et al., *India's Struggle for Independence*, chap. 13, esp. 166. Gandhi, of course, repeated this message incessantly in subsequent years.

the growing nationalist opposition to it. The nationalist movement, by contrast, not only was organized democratically, but its demands also included full democracy in India, regular elections, mass adult suffrage, and the basic liberal freedoms of speech and association.[43] These demands reflected elite values, themselves a product of the encounter with colonialism, and pragmatic political considerations of mobilizing broad support to undermine the legitimacy of the rulers' avowed British commitment to liberalism. The political process of generating a nationalist opposition thus created an elite committed to democracy. These commitments eventually found concrete expression, first in the creation of a democratic constitution for sovereign India and then in maintaining democratic practices as fragile institutions took root under adverse political circumstances.[44]

Finally, we observe that the commitment to create a highly interventionist state was also a product of ideas and interests that gelled in the nationalist movement. Although the colonial state had already developed some interventionist instruments during the Second World War, these were ad hoc changes and the state remained until the end limited and laissez-faire. The enormous expansion that followed independence – mainly to promote development – was at the behest of nationalists such as Nehru. While criticizing colonialism on economic grounds has a long history in India[45] – a set of ideas whose evolution and "maturation" was unfortunately ignored by "dependency theorists" in the West – the belief that a nationalist, interventionist state was the solution to problems of underdevelopment crystallized only in the 1930s. And in the 1940s it also eventually received considerable support from emerging Indian capitalists. This powerful alliance of Indian nationalists and businessmen was instrumental in the state expansion that followed independence.

The INC, in generating a powerful political movement to oust the British from India, thus helped to create a national consciousness and a strong preference for a democratic and interventionist state within India. The INC's power overall, however, was mainly oppositional and not architectural. In the political and social sphere the powers of the Indian nationalist elite were relatively limited, hamstrung by loose political organization, internal bickering, and the underlying multiclass coalition on which the movement rested.

---

[43] This theme is emphasized in Chandra et al., *India's Struggle for Independence*, and Chandra et al., *India after Independence*. See also Sumit Sarkar, "Indian Democracy: The Historical Inheritance," in Atul Kohli, ed., *The Success of India's Democracy* (Cambridge: Cambridge University Press, 2001).

[44] See Atul Kohli, "Introduction," in Kohli, *Success of India's Democracy*, 23–46.

[45] For example, Bipin Pal argued as early as 1901 that "the introduction of foreign and mostly British capital . . . was in fact, the greatest hindrance to all real improvements in the economic conditions of the people. It is as much a political, as it is an economic danger." For a review of this and other related ideas of such critics as Dadabhai Naoroji, Ranade, and R. C. Dutt, see Chandra et al., *India's Struggle for Independence*, chap. 7, quote on 94.

Thus, the INC itself was a fragmented-multiclass political force, heading a new sovereign state that was British in design and hence more inherited than created anew. This was so for the civil service, the army, the legal system, politically relevant organizations in society, and patterns of labor organization. And, of course, serious elite-mass cleavages continued.

India's nationalist leaders were not revolutionaries, of either left or right. And such revolutionary leaders as had come on the scene were either repressed and marginalized by the British or failed to find much political support within the Indian social structure. The middle-of-the-road elite that finally led the INC were politicians who sought power through nonviolent means, including running for elective office in British-created limited legislatures. Even when the means were unlawful, the mobilizational strategy was to avoid violent confrontation with the colonial state and focus instead on winning hearts and minds, slowly but surely undermining the acceptance of colonial rule in India while simultaneously creating alternative structures of legitimacy.

The resulting mass movement that was the INC was loosely organized and able to mobilize opposition but not able to wield power constructively and decisively. The Congress had a rudimentary democratic political organization, designed by Gandhi in 1920, whereby an open membership could elect local party representatives; they, in turn, elected the upper level. The organizational design also took account of India's linguistic diversity insofar as regional committees often coincided with linguistic boundaries, sowing the seeds of a federal system based on language. But it was Gandhi's concern – his political genius – for transforming an elite nationalist movement into a mass nationalist movement mobilized as an oppositional power that defined the logic of the INC. While Gandhi and the INC were successful at mobilizing, however, they failed to incorporate the mobilized groups into an ideologically disciplined organization in which leaders could expect followers to follow. The result was a fragmented movement that could at times agree on little beyond a shared disdain for colonialism.

The INC cleavages were along intraelite and elite-mass dimensions. The leadership often disagreed on matters of goals and strategies. Disagreements at national meetings could lead, for example, to chairs being hurled and delegates coming to blows.[46] Moreover, the record shows that once in power – Congress formed several provincial ministries in 1935 – Congress leaders could be corrupt, nepotistic, personalistic, and divided along factional and ideological lines.[47]

The gap between elites and masses during the nationalist phase was also often considerable. Scholars studying the "subaltern" groups have prodigiously demonstrated the scope of political activism among India's peasantry

---

[46] Ibid., 140.
[47] Ibid., 339.

and, on occasion, even among the working classes.[48] The INC at times initiated these mobilizational activities but more often sought to exploit them. In either case, local movements with local grievances often got "ahead" of their leadership and forced leaders to try to undermine the growing radicalism of the masses. Examples include the well-known cases of "Chauri Chaura" in 1922 and the "Gandhi-Irwin pact" of 1931, when Gandhi called off mobilizational activities that he had initiated but that seemed to be getting out of control.[49] These compromises underline a considerable elite-mass gap in motives and strategies that sapped the political energies of the INC. For all that, Gandhi and others still managed to hold the movement together and even to create some unifying symbols, themes, and institutions of lasting consequence. The effort, however, consumed a huge amount of political energy, leaving leadership little time to address the great challenge of creating a new state and society.

Finally, it is noteworthy that the INC was a multiclass movement, leading scholars on the left to observe that despite its socialist rhetoric, the Congress eventually betrayed the interests of the lower classes. The Indian multiclass coalition stands in contrast to efficacious states of the left or right in other parts of the world that have tended to rest on relatively narrow coalitions of either the lower or the propertied classes. The cohesive-capitalist state of Korea is one example of such a state on the right; the Chinese communist case, especially under Mao, is an example of a cohesive-lower-class state on the left. Unlike these cases, all of Indian society's diversities and power inequalities came to be mirrored in the INC. The result was difficulty formulating and pursuing clear goals. In trying to be a little of something to everyone, the INC undermined its own capacity to be a decisive political actor. Thus, the INC simultaneously inclined toward populism, making promises to lower classes while quietly protecting the interests of dominant classes.

To sum up the discussion so far, by the middle of the twentieth century the emerging Indian state already displayed characteristics that would continue to define it over the subsequent decades – modern and constitutional, on the one hand, and characterized by a fragmented authority structure, on the other hand. Ironically, both the British colonialists and the Indian nationalists pushed the emerging state in these directions. The British contributed to the state's centralized, bureaucratized, and constitutional character; Indian nationalists furthered this modernizing agenda by broadening the scope of democracy and by creating a public arena of thought and action. The state's limited developmental capacities also derived from the mix of colonial and

---

[48] See, for example, Guha, *Subaltern Studies.* For a rare study of working-class politics, see Rajnarayan Chandavarkar, *The Origins of Industrial Capitalism in India: Business Strategies and the Working Classes in Bombay, 1900–1940* (Cambridge: Cambridge University Press, 1994).

[49] See Chandra et al., *India's Struggle for Independence,* chaps. 15 and 22, respectively.

nationalist politics. Laissez-faire practices were inherited from the British, whose power had rested on compromising with traditional Indian elites, fragmenting state power, and limiting its downward reach. Although Indian nationalists wanted to expand the state and eliminate the Indian collaborators with colonialism, their capacities were limited, as the INC was dependent on a multiclass coalition. In victory, this amorphous movement grafted on to a limited colonial state eventually created a fragmented-multiclass state characterized by a considerable gap between its ambitions and its capacities.

IV. The Political Economy of Limited Industrialization

The laissez-faire colonial state in India presided over a fairly primitive agrarian economy and did little to enhance its productivity, making for a fairly dismal impact after nearly two centuries of British rule: Thus, agrarian productivity in India at independence was probably not much higher than it had been in the Mughal period; nearly 85 percent of the population remained illiterate; factory-based production accounted for a mere 7 percent of the total national product; and even during the first half of the twentieth century, the economy grew at under 1 percent per annum, implying stagnant or declining per capita incomes.[50] One cannot know how the economy might have performed without colonialism, but it can be said that the indigenous conditions inherited by the British were not very conducive to self-propelled growth. Over the course of the nineteenth century the British did impose peace, create a "national" market, invest in some basic infrastructure, and establish an open trading economy. The Indian economy nonetheless did not respond briskly. Consistent with the concerns of this study, the focus of the discussion that follows is on India's industrial economy, mainly in the first half of the twentieth century.

The role of the colonial state in the Indian economy has to be kept in proper perspective in this discussion. Unlike the Japanese interventions in Korea, the direct role of the British in India was relatively modest.[51] Public expenditures during the first half of the twentieth century (excluding war

[50] A number of overviews of the Indian colonial economy are readily available. See, for example, Kumar, *Cambridge Economic History of India*; Dietmar Rothermund, *An Economic History of India: From Pre-colonial Times to 1986* (London: CroomHelm, 1986); Maddison, *Class Structure and Economic Growth*; and B. R. Tomlinson, *The Economy of Modern India, 1860–1970*, The New Cambridge History of India, vol. 3 (Cambridge: Cambridge University Press, 1993). This last volume also has a fine bibliographic essay at the end.

[51] See Dharma Kumar, "The Fiscal System," in Kumar, *Cambridge Economic History of India*, 905; and Morris D. Morris, "Indian Industry and Business in the Age of Laissez-Faire," in Rajat Kanta Ray, ed., *Entrepreneurship and Industry in India, 1800–1947* (Delhi: Oxford University Press, 1992). Morris notes that "there can be no question that in India during the century and a half of British rule the market was given its head. British India was one of the great social experiments in letting self-interest and market forces do virtually everything" (199, n. 4).

years), for example, averaged a mere 10 percent per annum; more than half of this was spent on running the state itself, another 20 percent or so went for infrastructure, and very little was allocated for primary education, for extension and research in agriculture, or for industry.[52] Moreover, the indirect impact of state activities on the economy was often negative. Again, for example, methods of revenue collection created negative incentives for landowners and peasants to invest in agriculture, and the openness of the economy discouraged investments in new industry. More important still is the issue of what the state might have done to promote the economy, but either could not do because of political limitations or chose not to do because of prevailing norms and practices. For example, the state was unable to tax Indian collaborators, the agrarian elite, further, which limited public expenditures. And given the commitment to laissez-faire, there was reluctance to intervene in support of industry in India – even British-owned industry. When focusing on the state's role in industrialization during the colonial period, therefore, one must keep in mind both the direct and indirect roles.

Industrialization in India started in the second half of the nineteenth century, with British businessmen concentrated around Calcutta and investing in such export industries as jute, processed tea, and coal. Indian business, by contrast, was significant in and around Bombay, producing in particular textiles for the domestic market. Hard data on production and growth, available only from about the turn of the century,[53] reveal a sluggish industrial economy: Mining and manufacturing (including cottage industries) grew at about 1.5 percent per annum between 1900 and 1946. This long-term trend, however, hides as much as it reveals: Growth in production between 1900 and 1930 was much slower than between 1930 and 1946. And while cottage and small-scale industries nearly stagnated throughout this period, factory-based manufacturing performed better. Production of manufactured goods, for example, first doubled between 1900 and 1930 and then grew more rapidly, more than doubling again between 1930 and 1946. The share of mining and manufacturing in the overall economy was about 14 percent in 1900 and remained largely steady, ending at about 16 percent in 1946. The share of factory production in the national product at midcentury was a relatively small 7 to 8 percent, well behind, say, the situation at the same time in Korea and Brazil.

What are the factors that impeded more rapid industrialization in colonial India, and what other factors helped to promote the industrialization

[52] Kumar, "The Fiscal System," 926, table 12.6, and 937.

[53] I have relied mainly on Angus Maddison, "Alternative Estimates of the Real Product of India, 1900–46," *Indian Economic and Social History Review* 22, no. 2 (April–June 1985): 201–10. Also useful are S. Sivasubramonian, "Income from the Secondary Sector in India, 1900–1947," *Indian Economic and Social History Review* 14, no. 4 (October–December 1977): 427–92; and Alan Heston, "National Income," in Kumar, *Cambridge Economic History of India*, 376–462.

that actually did take place?[54] There can be little doubt that the basic economic conditions were difficult, replete with supply-and-demand constraints. On the supply side, for example, capital was scarce, labor was inefficient, technical knowledge and energy resources were limited, and banking was not developed.[55] Capital scarcity is evident in the fact that savings in the Indian economy between 1914 and 1946 averaged under 3 percent per annum and capital formation in the same period averaged under 7 percent per annum.[56] This scarcity reflected a poor economy, low growth rates, and absence of institutions to mobilize savings. Such savings as existed were often in the hands of agrarian elites, who could readily secure high rates of return in commerce and moneylending, to the detriment of industrial development. It comes as no surprise, then, that when industry did begin, it was initiated either by the British or by coastal Indians, especially in and around Bombay, who had a history as overseas traders with access to savings. On the labor side, while there was plenty of raw labor, educated and disciplined labor was scarce.[57] Energy resources, such as coal, were concentrated in some parts of the country and could not be readily and economically transported before the advent of the railways. And finally, India had a low-technology economy and a scarcity of knowledge and skills to absorb technology from elsewhere.[58]

On the demand size, too, both the size and the composition of demand were not favorable to industrialization.[59] Low average per capita incomes were an obvious constraint. Some of the demand for manufactured goods was met by cheap imports. Additionally, the economy was regionally fragmented. While the railways alleviated this problem somewhat – for example, by reducing the fluctuation in grain prices – scarcities in one region, especially rural and interior regions, were seldom readily translated into demand in other regions. And finally, wealthier and middle-class Indians who could

[54] The quality of the literature on these issues is uneven. The book that I found most balanced and informative was Rajat K. Ray, *Industrialization in India: Growth and Conflict in the Private Corporate Sector, 1914–47* (Delhi: Oxford University Press, 1979). Also of use were Amiya Bagchi, *Private Investment in India, 1900–1939*; Ray, *Entrepreneurship and Industry in India*; Morris D. Morris, "The Growth of Large-Scale Industry to 1947," in Kumar, *Cambridge Economic History of India*, 553–76; and a much older volume that remains of some significance, namely, D. R. Gadgil, *The Industrial Evolution in India in Recent Times, 1860–1939* (1924; Delhi: Oxford University Press, 1971).

[55] See Gadgil, *Industrial Evolution in India*, 198–203.

[56] See Chandra et al., *India after Independence*, 10.

[57] Gadgil thus noted in 1924 that "with a low and stunted physique, a mind entirely untouched by education, and an extremely low standard of comfort, it is no wonder that the Indian factory worker was inefficient. The low wages, then, were no advantage to Indian industry." See Gadgil, *Industrial Evolution in India*, 200–201.

[58] This factor is rightly emphasized by Ray, *Industrialization in India*, esp. introduction and chap. 3.

[59] See Morris, "Indian Industry and Business," esp. 199–201.

provide some stimulation to indigenous industrialization were concentrated in coastal cities that were more exposed to international competition.

Thus, supply-and-demand constraints on industrialization were serious and mutually reinforcing. Many of these constraints, however, characterize "underdevelopment" more broadly and do not explain more specific puzzles such as why some developing countries industrialized earlier and/or more rapidly than others or why some industrialization eventually did occur, even in colonial India. The role of governments and of other institutional factors is often the key to understanding these more specific variations.

The colonial state impeded industrialization in India until about 1930, when the policy framework altered and began providing some stimulation to industrialization in the subsequent period. But prior to that the state had been committed to openness and nonintervention, which helped the more competitive British manufacturers looking to sell manufactured goods to India in exchange for raw materials. This classic pattern of colonial exchange had been well established in India rather early on and continued more or less unaltered until the First World War. This framework made it difficult – though, as we see below, not impossible – for industry to take root, especially with the lowering of transport costs that followed the opening of the Suez Canal.

Given the laissez-faire ideology of the British, the government did not seek to promote industry directly. The colonial state therefore failed to invest in activities that might have fostered industrialization. Unlike the Japanese colonial state in Korea or even the provincial government of São Paulo in Brazil, the British colonial state did not even help British industrialists to establish themselves in India. Such promotion would have entailed identifying products that would not have been competitors for British imports. But such behavior would have necessitated close cooperation between government and business, a pattern quite alien to the "liberal" British way of doing things, as well as encouragement of investments in such industries via grant of lands, tax concessions, and various other special subsidies – none of which was forthcoming. Indirectly, the state promoted the development of infrastructure, but this was aimed more at helping trade than at industrialization. Also serious was the neglect of primary education, with the expected negative long-term consequences for labor productivity. The contrast with the role of Japan in Korea is again quite stark. The colonial state did invest in higher education, but more to train generalists than to produce engineers, managers, or business professionals.

Other policy choices of the colonial state further highlighted that its priorities were anything but the promotion of industry in India. A case in point is a consistent tendency in the first half of the twentieth century to maintain an overvalued rupee.[60] With the aim of balancing the budget at home and minimizing sterling expenditures, the colonial state maintained a high

---

[60] See Ray, *Industrialization in India*, 245–50.

level of parity between the rupee and the pound. Devaluation would have increased various India-related sterling expenditures within Britain. The rising value of the rupee created deflation within India and encouraged repatriation of profits by British Indian firms. Both of these hurt industrialization, the former indirectly by curtailing demand, and the latter directly by reducing investment.

Finally, there were institutional impediments to industrialization that were somewhat removed from the state's role but not totally unrelated. First, banking was underdeveloped, especially until the First World War, so there were little savings available in the rural sector to be used for industrial investment.[61] Second, British investments in India were managed by "managing agencies," tightly knit small communities of businessmen – often Scottish in origin – that excluded Indians from business opportunities on racial and ethnic gounds and that cooperated informally with the personnel of the colonial state in seeking favors, big and small.[62] And last, there is the entire set of issues concerning the unhelpful ways – unhelpful from the standpoint of industrialization, that is – in which labor institutions developed in India.[63]

By the time of independence, labor in registered factories was minuscule, only some 2 percent of the total labor force. The state adopted a more or less hands-off attitude toward this labor. Labor institutions and practices emerged as working-class initiatives were molded by the strategies of the industrialists, on the one hand, and of middle-class professional politicians, often nationalists and/or communists, on the other hand. Following the British pattern, industrialists did not invest much in worker training – except for some apprenticeship training for more technical workers – and sought labor flexibility rather than employment security. Without the backing of the state, employers were also not in a position to create labor discipline. So no one – not the state and not the capitalists – contributed much to creating a well-trained, productive, and disciplined work force. Labor leaders – who were often full-time politicians – also sought to mobilize labor more for grandiose political goals than for limited goals that could have helped to create viable unions and slow but steady wage gains. Industrial labor in India was thus relatively politicized from its inception. Industrial strikes, though frequent, did not readily yield gains in wages or improve working and living conditions. It should come as no surprise that the longer-term impact was not benign: poor health and education of workers, minimal efforts to improve discipline and productivity, and early politicization of industrialization.

Given these numerous constraints, how can one explain the limited – but far from insignificant – industrialization that did take place in colonial

---

[61] See B. R. Tomlinson, *The Political Economy of the Raj, 1914–1947: The Economics of Decolonization in India* (London: Macmillan, 1979), 11–13.

[62] This is an important theme in Amiya Bagchi, *Private Investment in India, 1900–1939.*

[63] See Morris, "Growth of Large-Scale Industry to 1947," 642–67. A much more detailed study of labor viewed from below is Chandavarkar, *The Origins of Industrial Capitalism in India.*

India? To reiterate, the broad pattern prior to the First World War was that the British owned the jute export industry in eastern India, and Indian entrepreneurs took the lead in textiles, mainly for the domestic market, in western India. A steel industry of sorts was also inaugurated around 1907 by the Indian industrialist family, the Tatas. These industries did rather well during the First World War, but subsequently, without the war-related demand, fell on hard times. During the interwar years, aside from the older textile, jute, and steel industries, such new industries as paper, sugar, glass, and even shipping were established mainly by Indians and came into their own. Many of these industries did rather well during the Second World War, so much so that "at the time of independence . . . [India] possessed a large and fairly sophisticated modern industrial complex," most of which was in the "hands of a strong indigenous capitalist class."[64] In a comparative context, it is this last point that makes the Indian case unique; even though the level of industrialization in India at midcentury was much lower than in a Korea or a Brazil, the significance of indigenous capitalism was substantial, with longer-term consequences.

The early success of the Indian textile industry is something of a puzzle in light of the open economy and the fact that textiles were central to Britain's own industrial revolution. The literature suggests both economic and noneconomic factors by way of explanation. The Indian textile industry initially used a fairly simple technology to focus on low-end cloth of the type the British were not producing; there were no shipping costs, and there was plenty of cheap, unskilled labor necessary for such production.[65] Moreover, British industrialists were reluctant to invest in India directly because it would be considered a "most unfriendly act" by their fellow textile exporters in Manchester and Lancashire.[66] The Indian industrialists who pioneered this industry were instead already textile traders (such as the Parsis) or had extensive knowledge of trading and marketing in the Indian interior (such as the Marwaris). As to why Indians did not enter the jute industry in the East, it has been credibly proposed that the British, who got there first, subsequently excluded Indians by various less-than-free-market techniques.[67] It may also be that the rate of profitability in the jute industry was less than in textiles.[68] And finally, the early emergence of an indigenous steel industry in India was only partly a result of the enterprising abilities of the Tatas; they also got lucky, first in raising the necessary finances in India by appealing

[64] Rajat Ray, "Introduction," in Ray, *Entrepreneurship and Industry in India*, 1 and 10.

[65] See Dietmar Rothermund, *An Economic History of India*, 52–87; and Rajat Ray, *Industrialization in India*, chap. 3.

[66] A. K. Sen, "The Pattern of British Enterprise in India, 1854–1914," in Ray, *Entrepreneurship and Industry in India*, 119.

[67] This is an important theme in Bagchi, *Private Investment in India, 1900–1939*.

[68] See Morris, "Indian Industry and Business," 211.

to nationalist sentiments and then again when, for strategic reasons, the colonial state chose to favor this industry within India.[69]

Specific explanations of why some individual industries got their start in the period before the First World War are not that important for the argument of this study. The broader, important point instead is that there was an indigenous enterprising stratum capable of initiating industry that took advantage of market opportunities as they arose. Profitable opportunities, however, were rare, and the role of the government up until then had not been very supportive. The First World War created improved conditions for growth in production. In the case of textiles, for example, maritime trade and thus imports into India were interrupted, increasing demand that Indian producers met enthusiastically. The same held for steel. Jute was different insofar as it was an export product, but it also benefited from a sharp increase in the war-related demand for gunny bags. Following the war, the coffers of Indian industrialists were full and they invested heavily, only to be disappointed because imports resumed and they could not readily compete. Textile and steel manufacturers lobbied the colonial state furiously for protective tariffs. The colonial state, however, did not readily oblige, certainly not until its policy framework altered for other, nonprotectionist reasons. Meanwhile, the demands of Indian capitalists for government support were increasingly taken up by the nationalists, including Gandhi, initiating a longer-term political alliance between business groups and the Congress.

During the 1920s, the policy framework of the colonial state began to change.[70] The war had enhanced India's strategic importance in British global designs and suggested that continued defense and other public expenditures required new sources of revenue. Since land revenue could not be increased readily – the landlords were, after all, part of the colonial state's ruling alliance – the state sought instead to get revenue by taxing imports, mainly by imposing tariffs. Other motivations for increased tariffs were to keep such non-British imports as those from Japan or Germany out of India. During the 1920s and the 1930s, such industries as cotton textiles, iron and steel, sugar, and paper thus received protection. The average rate of tariff increased from some 5 percent at the turn of the century to 25 percent by 1930. Another significant policy change was motivated by the need to save India-related sterling expenditures. Numerous goods that the colonial state in India needed – for example, supplies to run the railways – were thus increasingly to be bought not from Britain but within India. Both of these policy changes, especially tariff protections, benefited Indian industry.

---

[69] See Rothermund, *Economic History of India*, 67–69, 89, 113.
[70] See Tomlinson, *Political Economy of the Raj*, 57–103; and Ray, *Industrialization in India*, chap. 5.

Indian industry did well from 1934 onward, once the initial impact of the depression had been absorbed. The parallels with the situation in Brazil at about the same time are rather strong. Modest protectionism and increased sales to the government helped to double industrial production between 1934 and 1946. The role of protection in this production growth is clear insofar as the industries that did the best were precisely the ones that were now protected from imports, namely, textiles, iron and steel, cement, paper, and, most of all, sugar.[71] Sovereign India's major business houses, such as Birla, Dalmia, Walchand, Shri Ram, Thapar, and Singhanias, matured during this period and were ready to take advantage of the new opportunities that independence would eventually create.

The Second World War, of course, provided another spurt to Indian industry. Government expenditures rose dramatically, providing numerous contracts to private producers for such goods as engineering products, clothes, food, timber, and woolens. Indian industry grew rapidly by operating closer to full capacity. The wartime needs of the colonial state also led it to abandon its laissez-faire framework. A variety of new interventionist policies and institutions emerged that were aimed at "industrial licensing, controls of investment and price controls of consumer goods." Moreover, a plan of postwar reconstruction was conceived (though not implemented) on the basis of heavy state intervention, including "nationalization of heavy industrial sector if adequate private financing were not forthcoming."[72] So, well before Nehru and his "socialist" colleagues established a state-led developmental model in India, Indian business was profiting handsomely from colonial state interventions, and the official thinking on state management of the economy had moved significantly away from a "night watchman" conception of the state and toward dirigisme.

It is also important to take note finally of the emerging political significance of Indian capitalists.[73] The role of large private industry in the overall GNP was, of course, still very small, only some 7 to 8 percent. India at independence was very much an agrarian economy. Nevertheless, a robust stratum of private Indian industrial entrepreneurs had emerged in the first half of the century. The political impact of this group was also significant, especially in molding nationalist politics. While leftist nationalists were often suspicious of business, rightist groups within the INC established good working relations with businessmen. Gandhi, for example, was an important fundraiser for the Congress, as was Sardar Patel in later years. The business

[71] See B. R. Tomlinson, *Political Economy of the Raj*, 34.

[72] Ibid., 100.

[73] A good study is Claude Markovits, *Indian Business and Nationalist Politics, 1931–39: The Indigenous Capitalist Class and the Rise of the Congress Party* (Cambridge: Cambridge University Press, 1985). A book that came to my attention after this chapter was written is Aditya Mukherjee, *Imperialism, Nationalism and the Making of the Indian Capitalist Class, 1920–1947* (New Delhi: Sage Publications, 2002).

groups also organized as a national chamber of commerce and in 1943 even produced an economic plan for sovereign India, the so-called Bombay Plan, key elements of which – such as planning, mixed economy, protectionism, and public investment in heavy industry – eventually converged with Nehru's preferences for a new statist economy.[74] Given the Congress's need for broad-based legitimacy, Nehru's statism would be expressed in the language of "socialism." Nevertheless, it is important to note that already before independence, emerging business groups and nationalist politicians had established a working relationship of sorts that fluctuated between mutual cooperation and mutual suspicion – if not quite a totally cozy alliance of the Korea Inc. variety.

V. Conclusion

Two central arguments of this book are that variations in the patterns of state authority in the developing world are deeply consequential for rates of industrialization within them and that basic patterns of state authority were in turn often established well before state elites chose to intervene in their respective economies, especially during the colonial phase. Bounded by the more extreme cases of success and failure, such as Korea and Nigeria, India is a mixed case. The central task of this and the next chapter is to explain the mixed outcome: Why has India industrialized as much as it has, but why not more? The argument that emerges is that responsibility for the mixed outcome lies with a fragmented-multiclass state that was modern and interventionist, on the one hand, but that possessed limited capacity to pursue its stated objectives, on the other hand. The present chapter sought to trace the origins of such a state, as well as of the sluggish economy, back to the colonial phase.

To sum up very briefly, the state that the leaders of sovereign India inherited was a product of both colonial initiatives and pressures from the nationalist movement. The British in India created the basic state architecture, including centralized territorial control, a modern rational army and civil service, rule of law, and the beginnings of a constitutional democracy. At the same time, however, these characteristics were often limited to the apex and so constrained the downward penetration of the modern state that state authority was fragmented into numerous despotic pockets of traditional rule. And in terms of economic matters, even the modernized apex was designed to be laissez-faire and so did not achieve much socioeconomic change. Similarly, the nationalist political movement reinforced both the modern and the fragmented quality of the colonial state, while adding a multiclass social base that diluted the capacity of the INC to define clear priorities and then follow through.

[74] See Rothermund, *Economic History of India*, 123–28.

The colonial state had presided over a low-productivity economy and did little to alter that situation. But there are alternative ways for colonial states to "control" and "exploit," with profoundly different long-term consequences. Japanese colonialism in Korea, as we have seen, took a very different path from the British laissez-faire approach in India. This conscious aversion to helping India's industrialization or even to helping British investors was reinforced by the limited availability of public resources. Thus, whatever limited industrialization did take place prior to 1930 was mainly in spite of state neglect, and when industrialization did finally accelerate in the 1930s, it did so in a time of protective legislation motivated by reasons other than deliberate support for industry. There were some beneficial side effects for Indians in the fact that the colonial state did not support British investors, as numerous indigenous capitalists were able to take advantage of market and legislation-induced opportunities. India, in fact, emerged from colonialism with a substantial stratum of experienced indigenous entrepreneurs.

Two broader, comparative observations on the legacy of colonialism are also in order. First, the fragmented-multiclass state that India inherited from the colonial experience was a much better organized state than the neopatrimonial state we encounter in Nigeria, but it was also a lot less efficacious in promoting socioeconomic change than the cohesive-capitalist Korean state discussed above. That these political tendencies originated in the colonial period and more or less continued for decades afterward underlines the profound impact of early patterns of state formation on their future evolution. And second, to repeat, the Indian economy emerged from colonialism with much lower levels of industrialization than Korea or Brazil, though also ahead of most African cases, including Nigeria. While history is not destiny, the fact that both Korea and Brazil at the end of the twentieth century were middle-income countries whereas India and Nigeria were not owes something to their different starting points at midcentury. The impact of the sluggish first half of the twentieth century therefore ought not to be underestimated in analyzing India's relatively slow economic growth in the second half of the century.

7

India's Fragmented-Multiclass State and Protected Industrialization

Sovereign India's experiment with state-led economic growth has produced mixed results. Between 1950 and 1980 the Indian economy grew at a sluggish per annum rate of 3 to 3.5 percent, but accelerated to nearly 6 percent per annum thereafter (see Table 7.1). Nonetheless, this performance of the sovereign state was a considerable improvement over the nearly stagnant colonial economy, especially the pre-1930 period. At the same time, this growth compares unfavorably, especially with that of South Korea but also Brazil, suggesting the need to scrutinize the role of the state in the Indian economy. As for industrial growth, it fluctuated from over 7 percent in the first fifteen years, to below 4 percent during 1965–80 and then back again to nearly 6 percent per annum between 1980 and 2000. There was also considerable structural transformation over the five decades: Whereas agriculture contributed more than half and industry less than 10 percent of the national product at independence in 1947, toward the end of the century a diversified industrial sector contributed nearly one-quarter and the service sector nearly one-half of the whole.

This chapter focuses on the political determinants of economic performance in India, especially rates and patterns of industrialization, raising questions about the design and the capacity of India's highly interventionist state. Given the mixed outcome, the puzzles for analysis are both why the Indian economy has done as well as it has and why it has not done better. In keeping with the central themes of the study, the main concern is with the state's role, specifically, how the dynamics of a fragmented-multiclass state influenced economic choices and performance.

The scholarly scope of this chapter is broad and sweeping in quality, necessarily leading to neglect of nuances and of controversies relevant for a country specialist. I note at the outset that India's political economy can be interpreted from at least two distinct standpoints, only one of which is emphasized below. A more neoliberal interpretation would suggest that India's lackluster performance results from the sluggish economic growth

TABLE 7.1 *Some Basic Growth Data, 1950–2000 (all figures in percentage per annum)*

	1950–64	1965–79	1980–2000
GDP growth	3.7	2.9	5.8
Industrial growth	7.4	3.8	6.2
Agricultural growth	3.1	2.3[a]	3.0
Gross investment/GDP	13	18	23

[a] Figures are for 1967–80. Inclusion of the two drought years 1964–65 and 1965–66 would make this average figure even lower.

Source: Government of India, *Economic Survey* (various issues). Because of numerous statistical complications, these figures should be viewed as broadly indicative rather than as exact or definitive.

that followed from the closed and statist model of development adopted by India's misguided nationalist and socialist leaders. According to this line of thinking, the last two liberalizing decades have led to some improvement – higher rates of economic growth and a lower rate of poverty in India.[1] While there are valuable insights in such a perspective, it is not wholly consistent with the facts and it reflects a world-view that this study does not share.

I argue instead that the Achilles heel of Indian political economy is not so much its statist model of development as the mismatch between that statist model and the limited capacity of the state to guide social and economic change. There have been statist models in other parts of the world that achieved important gains, but they were generally directed by more efficacious states. The cohesive-capitalist cases of South Korea and Brazil both represent models of the right; the cohesive-lower-class model of communist China is a case on the left. Trying to reconcile political preferences of both left and right in the context of a fragmented state, the Indians failed both at radical redistribution and at ruthless capitalism-led economic growth. The socialist commitment of Indian leaders, for example, was rather shallow. While socialist rhetoric was used to try to build political capital, policies in favor of the poor were seldom pursued vigorously. Such socialist commitments as were pursued, albeit ineffectively, also alienated private investors. The associated difficulties in state-business relations also hurt economic growth. The change in India over the last two decades is not so much that it became more liberal as that Indian politics shifted toward the right, allowing for more harmonious state-business relations and a positive impact on growth. But at the same time the politicized political exclusion of the poor made governance more difficult and fed neofascist tendencies, including the mobilization of nationalism against minorities.

[1] One recent collection that broadly reflects this standpoint is Isher Judge Ahluwalia and I. M. D. Little, eds., *India's Economic Reforms and Development: Essays for Manmohan Singh* (New Delhi: Oxford University Press, 1998).

I have divided the discussion of modern India's political economy into three chronological phases: the Nehru era (approximately 1950–64), the era of Indira Gandhi (approximately 1965 to the early 1980s), and the last two decades of the twentieth century, during which numerous governments have come and gone. This division reflects the judgment that political changes have influenced rates and patterns of industrialization. Thus, I suggest that the state's considerable legitimacy and relatively clear economic priorities in the Nehru period facilitated some economic gains. By contrast, Indira Gandhi's populism hurt investment and growth. And finally, the political drift toward the right in the third phase has been accompanied by a growing role of the private sector in the economy and improved economic performance.

I. The Nehru Era

If the 1940s in India are best thought of as the decade in which India marked the transition from colonialism to sovereign democratic republic, the Nehru era that followed is usefully viewed as the crucible of modern India: It is during this era that a stable democracy took root and a statist model of economic development emerged hegemonic.

Indians by now take their democracy for granted, as if it were the most obvious way of organizing state power in a poor, multiethnic, continent-sized country. Viewed comparatively, however, as well as against the most popular theories that treat democracy as a function of economic advancement, India's democracy is a puzzle.[2] At a minimum the survival of democracy in India suggests that, under specific conditions, a country's political structures enjoy some autonomy from the underlying society and economy. The roots of Indian democracy and of its fragmented-multiclass state thus need to be understood in terms of institutional continuities, including the British political inheritance and, in particular, a relatively centralized and coherent state,[3] with its well-developed civil bureaucracy, its limited but real experience of elections and of constitutional, parliamentary government, and its traditions of independent media and freedom of such associations as labor unions.

Since inheritance is seldom destiny, India, like many other postcolonial countries, could readily have squandered these valuable political resources. Yet it did not. Besides colonial inheritance, therefore, one must underline the constructive political role of India's nationalist movement/party, the

---

[2] For a fuller discussion of this puzzle, see Atul Kohli, ed., *The Success of India's Democracy* (Cambridge: Cambridge University Press, 2001), esp. the introduction.

[3] Those who do not see a ready connection between centralized authority and democracy may consider Samuel Huntington's important argument that "order" nearly always precedes "democracy." See Huntington, *Political Order in Changing Societies* (New Haven, Conn.: Yale University Press, 1968).

Indian National Congress, and of India's leaders in the evolution of the democratic state. In its quest for freedom from British rule, the Congress not only brought together a variety of Indian elites but also established numerous links between elites and the masses, which defined the framework within which India's democracy advanced. India's leaders adopted mass suffrage, committed themselves to a parliamentary democracy, permitted the emergence of a variety of political voices and organizations, and conducted the internal affairs of their hegemonic party in a democratic and inclusive manner.[4]

This combination of a protodemocratic colonial inheritance and a democratically inclined mass nationalist movement provided the institutional preconditions for the emergence of democracy in India. But the political preconditions also helped to lay the foundation for the emergence of a fragmented-multiclass state. The Indian case thus raises the important question: Does democracy in a developing country necessarily lead to fragmented state power with a multiclass social base? The Indian case indeed suggests a strong association between democracy and a fragmented-multiclass state. But as no single case tells us all that much about a general relationship, one must be wary of confusing association with causation. For every India, for example, there is also a Malaysia, with less fragmented state authority. And even if democratization in a developing country tends to encourage fragmented-multiclass states, the reverse is certainly not the case: State power in many authoritarian situations can also be fragmented and rest on a plural class base. Most important for the immediate discussion, certain specific political developments during the Nehru period helped to consolidate India's democracy while also reinforcing the state's fragmented-multiclass nature.

The colonial bureaucracy that India's leaders inherited was a fine professional force, especially the elite ICS officers, but it was mainly a law and order bureaucracy, not well suited to implement the leaders' ambitious developmental goals. A major overhaul of the bureaucracy, though contemplated, was never really pursued, mainly because the well-trained elite civil servants were indispensable for governing the new state.[5] The size of the civil service, including the officer ranks, also grew substantially during the Nehru years. Though renamed the Indian Administrative Service (IAS), the new service reflected the structure of the ICS and still relied for staffing on a highly competitive exam that mainly tested general rather than specialist knowledge. The small fraction of candidates who passed the exam were then trained

---

[4] For a good study of how and why the Indian National Congress – even though a single, hegemonic party – facilitated Indian democracy, see Rajni Kothari, *Politics in India* (Boston: Little, Brown, 1970).

[5] For a good study of continuity in the nature and the structure of the pre- and postindependence higher civil service in India, see David C. Potter, *India's Political Administrators: From ICS to IAS* (Delhi: Oxford University Press, 1996). I draw on this study in the next paragraph, especially chaps. 3 and 4.

in more or less the same way as ICS officers had been – first in an institute and then on the job, apprenticing under more senior officers. To keep
up the old esprit de corps, many of the ICS traditions were maintained,
including the idea that elite civil servants constituted the steel frame that
anchored India's political stability. Internal promotions were made on the
basis of merit and seniority, and an independent supervisory body helped to
maintain the level of professionalism, essentially until the late 1960s, when
the IAS became more politicized. The IAS also adopted the core structure
of the old ICS, namely, district officers that were responsible for revenue
and law and order; new development functions were merely add-ons.

Upon independence, India's leaders faced a cruel choice: advancing the
state either as an effective agent of political order or as a successful facilitator
of economic development. They opted for the former, which would become
a longer-term trend – prioritizing political needs over economic ones and
thus initiating what would eventually become a substantial gap between
the state's capacities and its developmental ambitions. A similar mismatch
came to characterize the Congress Party as it sought to be simultaneously a
popular ruling party and an agent of socialist development.[6] The majority of
Indians lived in the countryside, and most of them operated within a variety
of patron-client relationships. One ready way to build political support in
such a social setting was to cultivate the support of the patrons – generally
the highest, landowning elite castes – who, in turn, could sway the political
behavior of their dependent clients, generally poor peasants. And this is
precisely what the party did, building long chains of patronage that extended
from the center to the periphery. This ensured a popular base – at least for a
decade or two – but eventually also led to the capture of the party by society's
powerful. In this way more egalitarian ambitions, such as land redistribution
and the capacity to tax the agrarian sector, were undermined.

Another significant political development concerned the evolution of
Indian federalism.[7] Soon after India won its sovereignty, each of its numerous ethnic groups began demanding a greater share of power. These
struggles came to a head in the late 1950s, when a reluctant Nehru agreed
to a linguistic reorganization of Indian federalism. Although this decision
accommodated ethnic demands and created a more stable political unit, it
also fragmented state power. To the extent that developmental ambitions of

---

[6] For a fuller discussion of some such issues, see Francine Frankel, *India's Political Economy,*
1947–1977: The Gradual Revolution (Princeton, N.J.: Princeton University Press, 1978), esp.
chaps. 5 and 6. A much more detailed treatment of how the early Congress party "succeeded"
is Myron Weiner, *Party Building in a New Nation* (Chicago: University of Chicago Press, 1967),
esp. chap. 22.

[7] A ready and useful overview is Bipan Chandra, Mridula Mukherjee, and Aditya Mukherjee,
India after Independence, 1947–2000 (New Delhi: Penguin, 2000), chaps. 8–10. For Nehru's
views on this and a host of other related issues, the indispensable source remains S. Gopal,
Jawaharlal Nehru: A Biography, vols. 2 and 3 (Delhi: Oxford University Press, 1984).

India's leaders found institutional expressions – such as the Planning Commission – these were nearly all at the center. By contrast, lower-level governments were mainly "machines" with significant powers and resources. While India's central state continued to be quite powerful in relation to its federal units, a federal reorganization of functions also diluted the state's overall capacity to pursue a coherent developmental agenda.

The ruling ideology of the Congress Party provides a final example of the mismatch between capacity and ambitions. Congress committed itself to "nationalism" and "socialism" – Nehru's creed, which won substantial popularity and legitimacy for him and the party. At the same time, however, these ideological commitments made it difficult to pursue vigorous economic growth, a goal that Congress and the state elites also espoused. In spite of the socialist rhetoric, India was mainly a private-enterprise economy. Vigorous economic growth would be feasible only if there were a vigorous private sector. But the Indian version of multiclass statism found itself at odds with its espoused goals: Nationalism discouraged foreign enterprise in India, and the socialist inclination created difficult relations with Indian entrepreneurs.

Taken together, these political developments during the Nehru era suggest two conclusions. First, there was significant continuity between the colonial state and the sovereign Indian state, even as there were many obvious discontinuities – that the new state was sovereign, democratic, and interventionist. The areas of continuity include, most strikingly, the design of the new civil service but also the organization of the legal system and of the armed forces. The latter was especially consequential for helping to ensure civilian control of the relatively apolitical military, a complex story beyond the scope of this study.[8] A more subtle area of continuity was the pattern of the state's alliances with the property-owning elites. The colonial state had rested its power with landowning traditional elites and generally had a good working relationship with Indian business groups. While Nehru clearly had a broader social base, the power alliances of India's new rulers with propertied groups also demonstrated remarkable continuities. While it is true that the megatraditional elites such as the Maharajas and the Zamindars were eliminated, the Congress rulers still based their rural power on landowning elites, albeit smaller landowners, a "lower" gentry of sorts.

Second, Nehru and his colleagues placed a high priority on consolidating Indian democracy. They thus incorporated society's powerful and conceded some power to demanding regional elites, but they also encouraged the hopes of the masses by promising egalitarian development to the poor. Although these strategies helped to institutionalize India's fragile democracy,

---

[8] This is a surprisingly understudied area of scholarship on Indian politics. Perhaps "dogs that do not bark" attract less attention than the ones that do, but probably not justifiably. One study that does address this issue explicitly is Stephen P. Cohen, *The Indian Army: Its Contribution to the Development of a Nation* (Berkeley: University of California Press, 1971).

at the same time, the resulting political developments also institutionalized the fragmented and multiclass political tendencies of the Indian state and undermined its capacity to pursue developmental goals vigorously. Was this outcome inevitable?

This is a difficult question to answer unambiguously. Certainly, the power to undertake some basic changes existed, as there was nothing inevitable in the degree of state fragmentation and in the lack of focus in the state's developmental priorities. At the same time, however, the nationalist movement was already straining and losing its way as it sought to create unity in diversity prior to independence. Nehru's specific decisions aimed at maintaining a stable and legitimate democracy in a heterogeneous society further weakened this potential in the postindependence period. Maintaining a "law and order" bureaucracy hurt the state's capacity to undertake economic tasks directly; a commitment to nationalism and socialism made it difficult to mobilize private capital; and the Congress Party's dependence on regional and rural elites fragmented state power, making it difficult to penetrate the rural society directly.

The economic model adopted during the Nehru era was, of course, the well-known model of state-led, import-substituting industrialization (ISI). Once adopted, it endured, even in the face of significant efforts in recent years toward a different model. At the end of the twentieth century, India still exhibited some of the core characteristics of its statist model of development – thus underlining the political nature of India's early economic choices.[9]

Nehru's political preferences, expressed through the Congress Party, became India's dominant ideas and stressed the following: maintaining national sovereignty, the superiority of the state in steering progressive capitalist development, and the need for India's poor to share in the fruits of development. The nationalist commitments of India's leaders translated into a suspicion of an open economy and a preference for heavy industry. In spite of low domestic savings, foreign investors were by and large discouraged, mainly because they might have threatened hard-won national sovereignty. A variety of interests, including Indian business groups, benefited from these ideological choices over time and helped to sustain them. A suspicion of an open trading regime is more difficult to understand in terms of underlying nationalism. Protectionism was justified mainly in terms of prevailing economic ideas of "export pessimism" and "infant industry."[10]

---

[9] Good studies of this topic include A. H. Hanson, *The Process of Planning* (London: Oxford University Press, 1966); Jagdish N. Bhagwati and Padma Desai, *India: Planning for Industrialization* (London: Oxford University Press, 1970); and Baldev Raj Nayar, *India's Mixed Economy* (Bombay: Popular Prakashan, 1989).

[10] A good discussion of the belief systems that supported India's economic choices can be found in Sukhamoy Chakravarty, *Development Planning: The Indian Experience* (Delhi: Oxford University Press, 1988), chaps. 1 and 2.

In the Indian case, however, there was also something deeply experiential and political about these choices. We have seen that openness during the colonial era had been interpreted by nationalists, not only as killing nascent industries, but also as inhibiting the emergence of indigenous industrial capitalism. Indian businessmen and industrialists, who stood to benefit from a relatively closed economy in which competition would be limited, expressed these preferences openly. Protectionism, as well as an emphasis on heavy industry, was thus seen as serving the interests of nation building. How else, according to India's leaders, could such an enormous country, with its ancient civilization, reemerge as a powerhouse that was not easily subject to manipulation by external powers?

Widespread was the belief in the state's ability to guide social and economic change efficaciously at the middle of the twentieth century. We have seen this in the Korean and Brazilian cases. This view had a left-leaning tilt in India, reinforced by an admiration of the Soviet Union's developmental "successes" and by an affinity for the British Labor Party's type of socialism. These ideological proclivities were also consistent with the concrete interests of the Indian political elite, which could channel some of the fruits of development to themselves and their offspring. The statist model translated into both a direct economic role for the state – as, for example, in the widespread creation of public enterprises – and into a more indirect role in guiding the activities of private capital via the "license permit raj [or regime]."[11] What is surprising in retrospect is not so much India's affinity for statism but how little open discussion took place concerning the type of state that could successfully undertake such ambitious economic tasks. While market imperfections were discussed ad nauseam, there was no parallel discussion of state imperfections from the standpoint of developmental capacity. One wonders whether the discussion was avoided because it would have focused attention on the shortcomings of the rulers.[12]

Finally, a vague commitment to the poor and the downtrodden permeated much of the nationalist political discourse. Gandhi and Nehru in their own ways shared this commitment. It found expression in socialist rhetoric and in policy areas such as land redistribution and the laws governing employment of urban labor. Unlike the commitment to nationalism and statism, however, the commitment to the poor was relatively shallow. India's upper-caste rulers may have meant well, but they were no revolutionaries. Barrington Moore's apt description of Nehru as "the gentle betrayer of

[11] For a highly critical but excellent description of how this policy "regime" operated, see Bhagwati and Desai, *India*, esp. chap. 13.

[12] To be fair, Nehru did on occasion blame developmental failures on the bureaucracy, though this also conveniently exonerated him and his Congress colleagues for the state's shortcomings. See, for example, Potter, *India's Political Administrators*, 2. A number of government reports also analyzed administrative weaknesses of the Indian state, though without much impact. See Bhagwati and Desai, *India*, chap. 8.

masses"[13] probably applies as well to a fairly broad spectrum of India's political class, though not all of them were always as "gentle." How else would one explain the limited political energy devoted to land reform or, for that matter, to promoting widespread access to primary education?[14]

What was the impact of Nehru's economic approach, which was statist in intent and emphasized public investment in heavy industry? The modest economic success of the period brings us back to the twin questions: Why, in spite of India's fragmented-multiclass state, was a statist model able to achieve some success and why was the performance not better?

We begin by situating India's initial conditions in a comparative perspective. India's socioeconomic conditions at midcentury were probably somewhere between the much more favorable starting point of Korea, or even Brazil, and the considerably worse conditions of, say, Nigeria. On the positive side, India had undergone some industrialization; a small but significant group of indigenous entrepreneurs was in place; banking and other financial institutions existed; and technically trained manpower, though not abundant, was not as scarce as it was in many African and Middle Eastern countries. The agrarian economy, by contrast, had not grown much over the previous several decades; internal demand was limited; savings were low; experience with managing complex modern production was relatively scarce; and the health and educational conditions of the working population were abysmal. Given these conditions, how well designed was the developmental approach of sovereign India's leaders?

First, the agricultural sector: Nehru's approach to this sector was mainly "institutional" in the sense that he and India's economic planners hoped that by tinkering with agrarian relations (via land reforms, for example) and by educating the peasantry (via extension programs, for example), India's agricultural production would improve.[15] After some significant initial public investments, especially in irrigation, the agricultural sector was therefore more or less ignored at the expense of industry. The results reflected this neglect. Agricultural growth was barely able to stay ahead of population growth. More serious was that much of this growth was extensive and not intensive; that is, it was the result of bringing more land under cultivation, not of improving productivity.

The modest increases in agricultural production thus reflected increasing labor input – growing population – and the use of additional land facilitated in part by new public investments in irrigation. Beyond this, the repeal of a variety of colonial-era taxes on agriculture may have created some incentives

---

[13] Barrington Moore, Jr., *Social Origins of Dictatorship and Democracy: Lord and Peasant in the Making of the Modern World* (Boston: Beacon Press, 1966).

[14] See, for example, Myron Weiner, *The Child and the State in India* (Princeton, N.J.: Princeton University Press, 1991), chap. 4.

[15] For a good discussion, see Gunnar Myrdal, *Asian Drama* (New York: Pantheon, 1968).

for agrarian producers that contributed somewhat to higher rates of production. Conversely, the state's downward penetration was minimal and, hence, so was its capacity to alter agrarian relations.[16] The relative neglect of public investments in better irrigation and higher use of such other agricultural inputs as fertilizers further undermined the prospects of rapid increases in food production. By the mid-1960s, then, India's agricultural sector was on the verge of crisis.

Heavy industry, by contrast, was emphasized by Nehru, who used the tremendous legitimacy he enjoyed to pursue his priorities and translate goals into outcomes. In truth, constructing heavy industry was more readily influenced from the political apex than, say, agriculture or land redistribution. The imposition of substantial tariffs and quotas provided a protected environment in which industry could take root. The bulk of this growth, facilitated by rapidly growing public savings and investment, was in the public sector: further development of electricity, railways, and communication, and in such areas as machineries and steel.

The main source of growing public revenues was indirect taxation, especially of consumer goods. There were, consistent with India's socialist leanings, progressive income tax laws in place, but the government's capacity to collect them was limited – a problem that, over time, would become quite consequential. Indirect taxation sufficed in this early period because the government's nondevelopmental expenditures were minimal: Nehru's government spent little on health and primary education, underlining the superficial quality of India's socialism. Moreover, his considerable legitimacy minimized the need to throw money at one group or another to buy political support. The levels of political mobilization in India were also relatively low at this early stage, with much of the lower-class population deeply enmeshed in traditional patron-client relationships. Hence, public expenditures could stay focused on Nehru's priorities, especially the development of heavy industry, which generated substantial production growth.[17]

Critics of this strategy have documented that this growth was quite expensive, in the sense of being relatively inefficient.[18] Some of the underlying causes are inherent to the nature of public sectors – for example, investment in industries that are not immediately profitable or below-market social pricing of output. But others were specific to India: the role of generalist bureaucrats, ill equipped to manage public sector industries, and/or the

---

[16] I have analyzed this issue of the state's limited downward reach in detail elsewhere. See Atul Kohli, *The State and Poverty in India: The Politics of Reform* (Cambridge: Cambridge University Press, 1987).

[17] For a good review, see K. N. Raj, *Indian Economic Growth: Performance and Prospects* (Delhi: Allied Publishers, 1966).

[18] See Bhagwati and Desai, *India.* See also Jagdish N. Bhagwati and T. N. Srinivasan, *India* (New York: National Bureau of Economic Research, distributed by Columbia University Press, 1975).

growing political interference by lower-level political elites who treated public sector industries as one more resource in their patronage networks. The highly protected environment within which these industries operated also contributed to the accumulating inefficiencies.

The Indian state's attempts to guide the private sector have also been roundly criticized.[19] These criticisms, however, need to be kept in perspective. Because the role of private capital in industry at this early stage was not all that significant, the prominent role assigned to the public sector is better understood as providing a substitute for a laggard private sector. After all, India's private sector had hardly flourished in the preindependence period under nearly free-market conditions. That said, however, the socialistic Nehruvian state – unlike the South Korean state – sought more to tame than to encourage private sector development. State intervention had a decidedly regulatory cast: Instead of asking business what it could do and how the state could help, the state itemized what private business could not do and then raised numerous barriers to what it could do. Implementation, too, was haphazard and inefficient: For example, priority industries were not always the ones that enjoyed maximum protection, and overbearing bureaucrats in charge of licensing often deterred private investors. The growing maze of bureaucratic obstacles to private sector development led over time to corruption and to inefficient allocation of private sector resources.

The examples of the steel and textile industries help to fill out this broad account of the Nehruvian state's role in promoting public and private sector industries, respectively. We have seen in Chapter 6 that the indigenous steel industry was initiated in the first half of the twentieth century by the Tatas.[20] To advance their nation-building goals, Nehru and his political colleagues prioritized the development of steel in the 1950s.[21] But, as in South Korea and Brazil, state elites found the private sector not forthcoming. It is true that in India some private steel industries, such as that of the Tatas, continued to flourish, but given the size, complexity, and risk involved, other private sector start-ups were not on the horizon.[22] Steel, therefore, emerged as the leading candidate for public sector development.

---

[19] See Bhagwati and Desai, *India*, esp. pt. 6.

[20] I am indebted to my research assistant, Rina Agarwala, for collecting this information on the steel industry.

[21] A useful recent account of the state's role in India's steel industry is Vibha Pinglé, *Rethinking the Developmental State: India's Industry in Comparative Perspective* (Delhi: Oxford University Press, 1999), chap. 3. Earlier accounts include W. A. Johnson, *The Steel Industry of India* (Cambridge: Harvard University Press, 1966); Padma Desai, *The Bokaro Steel Plant: A Study of Soviet Economic Assistance* (Amsterdam: North-Holland, 1972); and Gilbert Etienne, *Asian Crucible: The Steel Industry in China and India* (New Delhi: Sage, 1992).

[22] Vibha Pinglé thus notes that T. T. Krishnamachari, a successful industrialist, Nehru's confidant, and subsequently minister of steel, approached Indian industrialists but in vain. It was only then that he and Nehru were persuaded that the state would have to undertake development of steel in the public sector. See Pinglé, *Rethinking the Developmental State*, 54.

But in India, unlike in South Korea and Brazil, the steel industry grew up relatively inefficient, not very competitive internationally. A blanket condemnation of public sector ownership clearly will not do, as steel in all three cases was developed in the public sector. Rather, the culprit was the differing nature of states and patterns of state intervention. Moreover the problems in India developed only over time. Under Nehru, substantial public investments were devoted to steel, and foreign collaboration was sought to help to establish and manage the steel plants. Competent senior bureaucrats at the Planning Commission were responsible for steel policy, and there were good management practices at the plant level. The overall protected environment generated by the import-substitution policy regime ensured a ready market in an economy in which industrialization had begun in earnest. The result was that steel production in India between 1950 and 1964 grew rapidly at a rate of nearly 11 percent per annum.

The real problems of the steel industry date to the Indira Gandhi period, when it was starved of new investments and thus of new technology and modernization. It was then that the fragmented-multiclass nature of India's developmental state came to the fore to cause problems for the steel industry. First, locational issues that were politicized by India's federal structure were exacerbated during Indira Gandhi's period. Second, policy making was in the hands of generalists, the IAS bureaucrats, whose relations with plant-level management were at best remote and at worst condescending and demoralizing for the technocrats. Third, pricing and distributional policies were politicized, with especially damaging consequences. Steel prices were kept below market price and became a public subsidy to a variety of industries, including private sector industries. Although justified in terms of the needs of rapid industrialization, the policy could be sustained only as long as ample public resources to support such subsidies were available. A critical constraint was the state's limited capacity to undertake direct taxation, especially in the countryside, where formal political penetration was minimal. Controlled prices were also a constraint on steel industry profits, reducing its capacity for self-sustaining investments. As long as steel was a priority sector during the Nehru period, with continuous infusion of new resources, these problems remained manageable, and fairly impressive growth continued.

By contrast, large-scale textile production performed rather poorly in Nehru's India, even though at the time of independence, the textile industry, concentrated in private hands in western India, was not insubstantial. It is possible that with probusiness state intervention and subsidies for exports, India's textile production could have become internationally competitive. This was not to be so, however, and the state's legitimacy-driven policy choices were the root cause.[23] We have seen that Nehru was not especially

---

[23] See, for example, S. R. B. Leadbeater, *The Politics of Textiles: The Indian Cotton Mill Industry and the Legacy of Swadeshi (1900–1985)* (New Delhi: Sage Publications, 1993); and Sanjib Misra,

supportive of private enterprise. And within this framework, textiles faced special obstacles.

Recall that the issue of the destruction of small-scale household-based textile production at the hands of modern textiles played a central role in India's nationalist imagination. Gandhi successfully exploited *khadi*, or hand-spun cotton, as a tool of political mobilization, as witnessed in the symbolism of the Congress elite donning *khadi* uniforms and caps. With this political inheritance it would have been very difficult to unleash modern textile manufacturing against small-scale production. Mahatama Gandhi's populist commitment to "love of the small people" cast a long political shadow on India's textile policy. (While championing *khadi*, however, Gandhi was simultaneously collecting large dues for the Congress from his close friend, textile manufacturer G. D. Birla.) Add to this Nehru's socialist proclivities, which inclined him to argue in favor of producing cheap cloth for mass consumption, and the political factors molding policy choices start to become comprehensible.

Nehru and his colleagues restricted production of textile mills, taxed them highly, and even priced a part of their output below market prices so as to provide cheap cloth for poor consumers. Contrast this pattern of intervention with the one encountered in Korea and Brazil, where state intervention was often supportive of producers, though the political framework necessary for that support was also much narrower and more repressive. This contrast also underlines a central argument of this study, namely, that variations in patterns of state intervention are what matters most when trying to understand varying roles that states play in late-late-development. Thus, Nehru's textile policies undermined private and large-scale textile manufacturing in India but encouraged small-scale textile manufacturing, first with hand looms and then with power looms. Support, that is, went for anything that was less than a modern textile mill, with commensurate consequences: Output of large mills nearly stagnated, while that of smaller producers grew sharply. The latter were suitable for the low-end market consumption but not for competitive exports.

The story of industrialization in Nehru's India is thus mixed, characterized by notable achievements but also stupendous follies. As demonstrated with examples of steel and textiles, both these successes and limitations are explicable in terms of the underlying patterns of state intervention. Thus, India's 7 percent industrial growth rate per annum in this period was respectable. But Brazil in the same period – one of the fastest growers in the world and also a democracy with a strict import-substitution policy

"India's Textile Policy and the Informal Sector," in Stuart Nagel, ed., *India's Development and Public Policy*, Policy Studies Organization (Aldershot: Ashgate, 2000). For analysis of related economic issues, see Howard Pack, *Productivity, Technology and Industrial Development: A Case Study in Textiles* (New York: Oxford University Press, 1987); and Keijiro Otsuka et al., *Comparative Technology Choice in Development* (Basingstoke, Hampshire: Macmillan, 1988).

regime – industrialized at a rate of nearly 10 percent per annum. This somewhat superior performance also reflected underlying political and policy differences. The rate of investment in Brazil and India in this phase was more or less comparable. The real difference thus was in capital-output ratios, or in the relative efficiency with which capital was invested in the two countries. The roots of this difference, in turn, can be traced back to the fact that Brazilian democracy was considerably less nationalist and mass-based than that of India. Brazilian leaders thus worried less than India's leaders about legitimacy issues of nationalism or redistribution. The clearest manifestations of this greater political room for maneuver in Brazil were the closer cooperation between the state and business and the heavy dependence on foreign investment to facilitate import-substitution industrialization. While this strategy was not without its own problems, the advanced technology and management that foreign investors brought to Brazil was an important reason for Brazil's more rapid industrial growth in this early phase.

II. The Indira Gandhi Era

If democracy and a nationalist-statist model of economic development took root in India during the Nehru era, the political economy of the Indira Gandhi era that followed is best viewed as one in which India's democracy became more populist and deinstitutionalized, economic rhetoric moved further to the left, and the gap between the state's developmental capacities and economic goals widened even further, to the detriment of industrial development. Nehru's death in 1964 marked the slow but steady departure of the first generation of nationalist leaders from the political scene. As nationalist legitimacy declined, numerous movements and parties opposing Congress's hegemony emerged. The party's old ruling formula – a mantle of inclusive nationalism and long chains of patronage fed by statism – was increasingly incapable of generating electoral majorities. Either Congress had to come up with a new winning formula or it would give way to other parties. It was Indira Gandhi who stepped in and provided the winning strategy that revived Congress's sagging fortunes. But her populism and top-down deinstitutionalization of the polity further accentuated its fragmented and multiclass character, with significant developmental consequences.

Under Nehru, India had undergone steady industrialization and experienced modest economic growth, but the poor had not benefited very much. Indeed, the spread of commerce and democracy had eroded patron-client ties, making the poor ripe for new forms of political mobilization. A savvy Indira Gandhi understood these changes and capitalized on them,[24] turning

---

[24] Good biographical studies of Indira Gandhi include Mary Carras, *Indira Gandhi: In the Crucible of Leadership: A Political Biography* (Boston: Beacon, 1979); and Pupul Jayakar, *Indira Gandhi: An Intimate Biography* (New York: Pantheon, 1992).

"poverty alleviation" into her central political slogan. This shift to the left in India's political discourse yielded handsome short-term political dividends. Indira Gandhi became a darling of India's downtrodden, but her popularity, unlike her father's, was not institutionalized. Whereas he had presided over a nationalist party, the daughter found herself opposed by the old, entrenched Congress elite. Her solution: Label the old elite enemies of the poor, exploit her popularity to undermine their power, and appoint loyal minions to positions of responsibility. As India's political system thus became increasingly personalistic, well-established patterns of authority within the party were undermined, and the broader process of institutional development in India's democracy was derailed.[25]

The logic of this process of personalization of power was inexorably de-institutionalizing. Challenged in an increasingly contentious polity, Indira Gandhi not only eliminated her challengers but also weakened the institutions that enabled such challengers to emerge: She tampered with appointments in the civil service and the courts, dismissed "troublesome" chief ministers, and demanded absolute loyalty from supporters. As a result, the professionalism of the bureaucracy, the independence of the legal system, the functioning of the national parliament, and the autonomy of the regional units within the national federation were all adversely affected.

The changing nature of the bureaucracy is especially noteworthy. Though slow and not dramatic, the changes were nevertheless significant, mainly in the direction of undermining the professionalism of the civil service that India inherited from the British. The size of the IAS continued to grow throughout this period, quadrupling between 1950 and 1983.[26] This reflected the overall growth of the public sector, in which employment grew from some four million in 1953 to ten million in 1983. By the end of this period, the IAS employed some 4,000 officers, about 15 percent of whom served in New Delhi, 25 percent in the districts, some 10 percent in public sector enterprises, and the remaining 50 percent in various state capitals. The basic structure of the IAS in terms of its size within the overall public service or in terms of its distribution across various types of jobs (with the significant exception of public sector enterprises, of course) did not undergo any dramatic changes from earlier times. What changed instead was the diminishing degree to which the IAS was insulated from the broader society, the erosion of professional criteria for internal promotion, and a

---

[25] This theme of deinstitutionalization of the Indian polity under Indira Gandhi is emphasized and developed in Atul Kohli, *Democracy and Discontent: India's Growing Crisis of Governability* (Cambridge: Cambridge University Press, 1991). See also Atul Kohli, ed., *India's Democracy: An Analysis of Changing State-Society Relations* (Princeton, N.J.: Princeton University Press, 1988). For a somewhat different interpretation, see Lloyd Rudolph and Susanne Rudolph, *In Pursuit of Lakshmi* (Chicago: University of Chicago Press, 1987).

[26] The factual information here is drawn from David Potter, *India's Political Administrators*, chap. 4.

greater premium placed on connections and loyalty to politicians for securing desirable positions. To some extent these changes reflected the expected indigenization of a colonial state, but they also reflected the priorities of the political elite, as holding on to power became an end in itself.

So, too, Indira Gandhi focused less on matters economic and more on maintaining power. Nehru's statist model of economic development thus essentially continued without major change. Within the framework of continuity, economic policy changes during this era were mainly of two types: a major shift in agricultural policy that had a benign long-term impact on food production and a variety of left-leaning changes that reflected Indira Gandhi's political calculus but helped neither economic growth nor redistribution.

Looked at broadly, this was an era of missed economic opportunities in India at a time when other countries exploited such opportunities. From the mid-1960s on, the global economy became more open to manufactured exports from developing countries,[27] and countries as diverse as South Korea and Brazil sought to take advantage of such global shifts. These countries, of course, came to be ruled by military dictators who prioritized economic growth and sought export promotion as an additional strategy. By contrast, India, after a brief flirtation with devaluation in 1966, moved in nearly the opposite direction, becoming more and more obsessed with "politics."[28] Indira Gandhi's personalistic governance led India down a path on which democracy was maintained, though tenuously, but on which economic policies became further politicized. And the gap between the state's economic rhetoric and its capacity to implement grew only wider.

A set of agricultural policies adopted in the mid-1960s eventually produced India's "green revolution." Insofar as these policies sought to concentrate production inputs in the hands of landowning classes in some regions of India, they did not readily fit in with Indira Gandhi's populist designs. Why and how were these policies adopted?[29] First, they were adopted in the mid-1960s, just before Indira Gandhi's full embrace of "poverty alleviation" in the late 1960s. More important, India faced severe food shortages in 1965 and 1966, which made the country more open to seeking ways to boost food production and temporarily more dependent on food aid, especially from the United States. The United States favored green revolution policies and pressured India to adopt them in exchange for aid. But the adoption

---

[27] See, for example, W. Arthur Lewis, *The Evolution of the International Economic Order* (Princeton, N.J.: Princeton University Press, 1977), chap. 6. See also W. Arthur Lewis, *Dynamic Factors in Economic Growth* (Bombay: Orient Longman for the Dorab Tata Memorial Lecture Series, 1974).

[28] For a discussion of the brief experiment with devaluation, see Bhagwati and Srinivasan, *India.*

[29] For a good account, see John P. Lewis, *India's Political Economy: Governance and Reform* (Delhi: Oxford University Press, 1995), chap. 4. See also Frankel, *India's Political Economy*, chap. 7.

of these policies was such a politically sensitive matter, in terms of both external dependence and possible distributional consequences, that policies were essentially adopted by a handful of the political elite as executive decisions rather than through any open political discussion.

Various other social and economic policies adopted by Indira Gandhi in the 1970s were aimed at legitimizing populist politics. While the significance of some of these was more symbolic, others turned out to be quite economically consequential. Among the more symbolic – and thus politically consequential – were the removal of privileges that Indian government hitherto provided to Indian princes. More economically consequential, Indira Gandhi intensified the rhetoric but also to some extent the efforts to implement land reforms. Land redistribution was a fairly central component of the new "poverty alleviation" strategy, though the actual impact was quite limited.[30] Similarly, the nationalization of the banks was supposed to "democratize" lending and so was popular among Indira Gandhi's constituents.

Among the economically most consequential policy developments, the following had an adverse impact on economic growth. First, Indira Gandhi held her populist coalition together by channeling public resources to numerous interest groups – a case of largess that cut into public investment and hurt economic growth.[31] Second, the radical political rhetoric, some seemingly radical policies, and a new level of labor activism alienated private investors, both domestic and foreign. These policies included restricting the growth of private business and industry, nationalization of banks, and threats to nationalize other industries. And third, India's closer political links with the Soviet Union and a parallel distancing from the West made it difficult for the Indian economy to derive benefits that might come from further integration with more dynamic economies.

With Indira Gandhi's addition of populism to the statist model of development, the gap between the state's ambitions and capacities that had already existed in Nehru's India grew even wider, and India's fragmented-multiclass developmental state became even less developmental. For example, Indira Gandhi raised the expectations that her policies would help to alleviate poverty – a demanding task that would have required high rates of economic growth, some effective redistribution, and the capacity to penetrate and reorganize the rural society. This demanding task, in turn, would have required a cohesive political party and bureaucracy. Indira Gandhi, however, achieved the opposite, by further deinstitutionalizing the Congress Party, further fragmenting the state's authority structure, and undermining the professionalism of the bureaucracy. And instead of enhanced public investment in agriculture, infrastructure, public sector industries, and education

---

[30] For an analysis of related failures, see Kohli, *State and Poverty in India.*

[31] See Pranab Bardhan, *The Political Economy of Development in India* (Delhi: Oxford University Press, 1998).

and health, the state's resources were increasingly directed at buying political support. With growing politicization, the bureaucracy and public enterprises simply deteriorated. And finally, the state simply did not support the private sector and became increasingly anticapital, with predictable negative results for investment and growth.

As is evident in the figures in Table 7.1, India's economy did not perform very well between 1965 and 1979. As we have seen, Indira Gandhi's populism especially hurt industrial growth. The intervening links need to be clarified, but first a few comments on the agricultural sector. Indira Gandhi's agricultural strategy, adopted under conditions of crisis and external pressure, concentrated agricultural investment in providing better seeds and fertilizer to regions with assured irrigation, such as the Punjab. Price supports were also provided for food producers, thus shifting the terms of trade somewhat in the favor of the countryside.[32] While the distributional consequences were decidedly mixed, the new policies did help to improve agricultural production.

On the face of it, the aggregate figures in Table 7.1 do not support this view: Agricultural growth between 1965 and 1979 was lower than in the earlier period. However, much of this new growth was based on higher yields. With the possibility of bringing more land under cultivation more or less exhausted – certainly without major public investments in irrigation – productivity-based food growth was essential to feed the growing population. Dramatic increases in wheat production undergirded this new growth, pulling India back from the brink of famine and mass starvation. The state intervened massively to support those property-owning elites who were most likely to generate economic growth, with benign consequences for production. While state intervention was a result of a crisis and though the intervention was concentrated in the agrarian rather than the industrial sector, this alliance of the state and the propertied class is reminiscent of the East Asian cohesive-capitalist state. Over time even the industrial sector moved in this direction but not before a significant populist interregnum and not without being pressed by yet other economic crises.

Industrial growth in India decelerated sharply during 1965–79, leading some observers to dub this an era of "stagnation."[33] The underlying cause was mainly declining investment, but there were also accumulating inefficiencies, and both of these, in turn, can be traced back to growing populism. While the rate of investment for this period (see Table 7.1) was higher than in the earlier period, a more disaggregated picture clarifies the apparent

---

[32] For a useful discussion of the politics of agricultural policy, especially of issues surrounding debates on terms of trade within India, see Ashutosh Varshney, _Democracy, Development, and the Countryside: Urban-Rural Struggles in India_ (New York: Cambridge University Press, 1995).

[33] See, for example, Isher Judge Ahluwalia, _Industrial Growth in India: Stagnation since the Mid-Sixties_ (Delhi: Oxford University Press, 1985).

contradiction. The higher aggregate rate mostly reflected savings (and thus assumed investment) in the household sector, where the majority of non-consumed resources were maintained in the form of physical assets and were therefore not readily translated into investments with high rates of return. More significant was thus the behavior of public and corporate savings in this period, both of which decelerated.

The decline in public investments reflected both a failure to add to the revenue base (for example, by taxing new agricultural incomes or by generating surpluses in public enterprises) and growing public expenditures in such "nondevelopmental" areas as "subsidies" aimed at securing political support.[34] This pattern was a direct function of Indira Gandhi's growing populism: She essentially threw public resources at numerous social classes she sought to mobilize. As public investments declined, industrial growth was hurt on both the supply and the demand side.[35] Infrastructure development suffered, for example, creating serious supply bottlenecks for industrial production. And in the steel industry, reduced public investment hurt production directly. On the demand side also, given the weight of the public sector in India's industrial economy, reduced investment shrank the demand for a variety of industrial outputs, thereby discouraging production.

Since public investments in India have not grown in recent years but industrial growth has, it is also important to consider the role of corporate investments in industrial deceleration during the Indira Gandhi era. Corporate investments also slowed down in this period, especially in fixed capital formation. The underlying causes are difficult to discern but can be traced back to declining profitability. Decline in demand in the overall economy was probably partly responsible. Also at play, however, were more directly political factors. Populist and multiclass politics led to steeper corporate taxes and to labor activism, industrial unrest, and higher wages, probably cutting into profitability. There is also the more diffuse impact of a seemingly leftward turn in national politics on investor behavior. While difficult to document decisively, investors may have been discouraged by the growing talk of nationalizing business (and the reality of nationalizing some banks), by new policies that sought to limit their growth and areas of investment, and by the adoption of a general antibusiness rhetoric.

Finally, whatever investment was taking place was not always efficient. Since there is little evidence that productivity growth in this period was worse than during the Nehru period,[36] much of the industrial deceleration under discussion cannot be attributed to issues of efficiency. Rather,

---

[34] For such an argument, see Bardhan, *Political Economy of Development in India.*
[35] For details, see Ahluwalia, *Industrial Growth in India.*
[36] Ibid., esp. 146, for data; Ahluwalia notes that "productivity growth estimates do not show a worsening of the situation after the mid-sixties."

the main culprit was reduced investment, both public and private. Nevertheless, continuing inefficiencies were certainly at least a part of the overall economic scene. A poorly managed and inefficient public sector repeatedly failed to generate investable surpluses and thus contributed to a slowing down of industrial growth. A policy framework that did not encourage domestic competition led to misallocation of resources, hurting growth. Capital-output ratios, a rough indicator of efficiency, increased during this period, especially in manufacturing, underlining that, besides the slowdown in investment, investment was simply not being utilized efficiently.

The evolution of the steel and textile industries can further clarify the changes under Indira Gandhi. After considerable growth in the earlier period, steel production in the public sector stagnated during her tenure, especially between 1964 and 1971.[37] Levels of efficiency in the steel industry also remained relatively low. Again, the roots of many of these problems grew out of the new populist politics. For example, in addition to suffering from a war with Pakistan and droughts in the mid-1960s, public investment declined as well because of Indira Gandhi's new political priorities. The results included declining investment in established steel plants. In the words of one analyst, the steel industry suffered in this period because of "the state's lack of investment in technological upgrading and plant maintenance and poor plant management."[38] The problems of an investment-starved industry were exacerbated by low, government-imposed steel prices – again justified in terms of "socialism" – that deprived firms of internal savings for investment and modernization. And finally, among the political roots of the problems of steel industry was the power of politicized labor. Well-organized unions affiliated with and empowered by the ruling party essentially squeezed the managers of public sector firms, leading to numerous rigidities and inefficiencies.

The problems in textile production, dominated by the private sector, also continued in this period and were probably exacerbated.[39] Controls on the growth of the organized mill sector persisted and were made even more restrictive in the name of protecting hand looms and small producers. The same logic was extended to power looms, a hitherto growing segment of the industry, that had started filling the production space between mills and hand looms. Large mills, moreover, were obliged to provide a significant portion of their output to poor consumers at controlled prices. When less-efficient producers faltered, Indira Gandhi nationalized them. These mills did not perform better in the public sector, at least in part because

---

[37] See the references in note 21 above.

[38] See Vibha Pinglé, *Rethinking the Developmental State*, 61.

[39] See, for example, D. U. Sastry, *The Cotton Mill Industry in India* (Delhi: Oxford University Press, 1984). See also the references above in note 23.

they were burdened with producing regulated cloth for the low end of the market. Import of new technology was also restricted in order to deal with balance-of-payment problems. The political context for private textile manufacturers was thus discouraging and contributed to limited growth in both productivity and production.

Finally, a comment ought to be made about the continuing "closed" nature of the Indian economy. Irrespective of whether arguments about "export pessimism" or about the need to protect "infant industries" were ever technically supportable or not, such attitudes were understandable during the Nehru period, given the prevailing political values and popular economic doctrines of the time. By the 1970s, however, many of these assumptions were being globally challenged. Countries such as South Korea and Brazil were aggressively turning toward export promotion and trying to attract foreign investors. Indira Gandhi's legitimacy-driven politics led her instead to adopt a sharply anti-Western and nationalist political rhetoric, pushing India's economic policies in nearly the opposite direction. As a result, India continued to embrace its import-substitution regime fiercely, as well as to resist foreign investment, again hurting growth in multiple ways. Limited exports, for example, remained a key vulnerability, creating periodic balance-of-payment crises. Moreover, by not pushing exports India was not taking advantage of its key resource, cheap labor; it also limited imports of new technology and discouraged economies of scale. Enhanced foreign investment might also have facilitated growth, not only via additional investments, but also and more importantly by contributing to better technology, management, and export promotion.

Populism may be politically expedient and, on occasion, even a political necessity to balance conflicting interests under conditions of weak political institutions, but its economic impact on growth is seldom benign. The Indian case fits this broader pattern. A more genuine social democratic tilt in India, one that would have reconciled better growth and modest redistribution, would have required a well-organized social democratic party and a durable ruling coalition at the helm of a more effective state. In other words, it would have required a cohesive-multiclass state rather than a fragmented-multiclass state. Short of that unlikely outcome, a charismatic and popular leader, promising radical redistribution within the context of a fragmented-multiclass state and a largely private-enterprise economy, was a recipe for failure. Populism harmed economic growth doubly: by hurting public and private investments and by further politicizing the statist and closed economic policy regime.

III. The Probusiness Drift

Following Indira Gandhi's return to power in 1980 and especially following her assassination in 1984, Indian democracy entered a new phase, marked by a slow and steady decline of Congress's hegemony and by numerous efforts to find workable alternatives, culminating in the emergence of a right-wing, religious nationalist party at the helm.[40] While the 1980s and the 1990s were characterized by a fair amount of governmental instability and even political instability, especially by ethnic and communal violence, India's economic policies took on a more consistent character, generally tending in a more probusiness direction – a process dubbed by some observers as economic liberalization. During this phase the gap between governmental economic ambitions and capacities narrowed somewhat, not so much due to enhanced state capacities as to the scaling back of ambitions, both in the productive and the redistributive spheres. Over the last two decades of the twentieth century, in other words, India's fragmented-multiclass state became not so much more cohesive as markedly less multiclass.

Indira Gandhi's departure from the political scene left India without a charismatic leader capable of holding together an increasingly mobilized and heterogeneous political society. Her failure to make a dent in India's poverty also clarified to her successors (and even to her in the early 1980s) the limits of class politics in India; without a well-organized social democratic party, appeals to the lower classes in India quickly devolved into irresponsible populism that simultaneously hurt economic growth and failed to achieve effective economic redistribution. Subsequent attempts to discover new formulas for ruling have moved in one of three directions, none totally successful: maintaining the Nehru-Gandhi family rule, forging new caste coalitions, and encouraging ethnic politics, especially mobilizing Hindu nationalism. The Congress Party pursued the first strategy, and a variety of opposition parties followed the second and the third. Since none of these strategies readily translated into enduring national electoral victories, India's regions also gained national political significance by joining coalition governments at the center.

The most significant political development over the last two decades has been the emergence of the Bhartiya Janata Party (BJP), a right-leaning religious nationalist party, as a major alternative to the Congress. The BJP emerged as India's ruling party toward the end of the 1990s and remains in power as this book goes to press (2003). The rise of the BJP needs to be understood in terms of its ability to fill a growing political vacuum. The assassination of Indira Gandhi's son, Rajiv Gandhi, an heir apparent of sorts, deprived Congress of the opportunity to continue to capitalize on "dynastic popularity." With the aim of finding an alternative to the Congress, a series

---

[40] I have analyzed these changes in more detail elsewhere. See Atul Kohli, "Indian Democracy: Stress and Resilience," *Journal of Democracy* 3 (January 1992): 52–65; idem, "Can the Periphery Control the Center? Indian Politics at the Crossroads," *Washington Quarterly* 19, no. 4 (Autumn 1996): 115–27; and idem, "India Defies the Odds: Enduring Another Election," *Journal of Democracy* 9 (July 1998): 7–20.

of opposition parties sought to mobilize hitherto unincorporated middle-caste groups but failed due to factionalism and leadership rivalries, not to mention the absence of any clear political program.

As a better-organized party, the BJP stepped into this vacuum and sought to unite India's Hindu religious majority into a nationalist political block. In a program reminiscent of European fascist movements, this party sought politically convenient enemies, both within India – India's religious minorities, especially Muslims – and beyond India's borders. The reformulation of Indian nationalism along religious lines paid off handsomely for the BJP, but not enough to win a national electoral majority. The party's appeal remained concentrated in those central areas of India where memories and symbols of rule by Muslims remain mobilizable. Coalition alignments, as well as experience with democratic governance, softened the more extreme elements of the BJP, enabling it to provide a viable alternative to the old Congress, at least over the short term. How the BJP will evolve in the future, however, remains an open question.

From the standpoint of this discussion, it is important to note that shifting governments and coalitions of the last two decades have not translated into sharp economic policy instability. While there have been fluctuations, economic policies over the last two decades have generally moved in a liberalizing or, more precisely, probusiness direction, both dismantling some of the inherited state controls on private economic activities and distancing the state from the rhetoric of redistribution and populism. How can one explain this shift, as well as its consistency, in the face of governmental instability? A few comments will help to round out the story.[41]

Neither state-led economic growth nor political efforts at redistribution and poverty alleviation have proved to be especially successful in India. State capacity to push either the Korean type of high economic growth or the Chinese type of radical poverty alleviation has simply been missing. The more this understanding of past failures seeped into the gestalt of India's political class, however, the more it embraced probusiness solutions to its development problems. Even Indira Gandhi in her later years quietly deemphasized poverty alleviation as a slogan and courted the business class she had alienated earlier on. Her son, Rajiv Gandhi, embraced the rhetoric of economic liberalization, though in practice his attempts to dismantle India's statism ran into numerous obstacles.[42] Subsequent national governments have more or less maintained a rhetorical commitment to liberalize the economy, moving in fits and starts to produce an incremental progress that suits a large, complex democracy. When questioned as to why, in spite of its

---

[41] One recent book on politics of India's economic liberalization is Rob Jenkins, *Democratic Politics and Economic Reform in India* (New York: Cambridge University Press, 1999).

[42] For a full discussion, see Atul Kohli, "Politics of Economic Liberalization in India," *World Development* 17, no. 3 (March 1989): 305–28.

nationalist orientation, the BJP sought to liberalize and open India's economy, India's current prime minister, Atal Bihari Vajpayee, replied: "Nehru
Ji's approach was not all that successful. Indira Ji was never sincere. What
else can we do now?"[43]

The growing sense among leaders that past strategies were not enormously successful and that there is no alternative but to liberalize is probably the driving force behind the shift in India's development strategy. A
moment of reflection, however, suggests that past failures could have been
interpreted differently, with different implications for policy. For example,
India's leaders could have embraced more fully the model of East Asian "developmental states," or, less likely but not totally out of question, they could
have embraced a more genuine social democratic model based on what has
been tried in such Indian states as West Bengal and Kerala. The fact that
they did not, in turn, points to another key factor that has pushed India's
new economic choices: The liberalizing trend is consistent with dominant
interests and ideas, both within India and abroad.

In spite of its socialist flourish, India's statism provided a framework for
the emergence of a largely capitalist economy in India. The more Indian
capitalism has matured over the last few decades, the more difficult it has
become for India's leaders to maintain anticapitalist political positions. Even
India's communist parties now accept market realities and seek to attract private investors. The shifting nature of the political economy has thus bounded
the range of economic choices available to India's leaders. International
pressures have further reinforced these boundaries. Just as at midcentury
statism appeared to be a "natural" path to adopt worldwide, toward the end
of the century the virtues of markets appeared nearly hegemonic.[44] India's
leaders could have resisted these national and international constraints, but
that would have required considerable political cohesion around alternative
values. Having not done so, however, nearly all of India's political parties
have sought to work with powerful interests and ideas, especially antistatist,
probusiness ideas, thus narrowing the range of available options in the economic sphere.

Nonetheless, despite a commitment to economic liberalization, India's
political economy still remains quite statist by global standards. Unlike South

---

[43] This is a translation of a conversation in Hindi between Mr. Vajpayee and Atul Kohli in
Oxfordshire, England, June 19–21, 1992. Mr. Vajpayee at the time was a leader of the opposition in the Indian parliament, and both he and the author were attending a conference
on "India: The Future," organized by the Ditchley Foundation.

[44] This sweeping gestalt shift, which has an ideological quality, should give thoughtful observers
a pause. The earlier embrace of statism led to some successes and numerous failures. The
new commitment to markets is also likely to lead to a similar, mixed record that will be
evident only in the future. For one useful account of this shifting economic mind-set, see
Paul Krugman, "Cycles of Conventional Wisdom on Economic Development," *International
Affairs* 72, no. 1 (1996): 717–32.

Korea or Brazil in the 1990s, there was no basic shift in India's development model in the 1990s. Thus, public enterprises remained very significant, tariffs came down but were far from negligible, the role of foreign investment in the economy was minimal, numerous laws governed capital movements in and out of the country, and a variety of labor laws made the economy anything but a model of flexibility. This is neither an endorsement nor a criticism of the state of affairs. The analytical point is that, during the last two decades of the twentieth century, India's leaders sought to liberalize the statist economy they had inherited. This liberalization, while real, was also limited – a mixed result consistent with powerful political forces in India, since a variety of interest groups, especially business, objected to some aspect or another of a radical policy shift. Weak governments, in any case, were reluctant to undertake major policy restructuring. The policy shift in India is thus better understood as a probusiness drift rather than as economic liberalization, but a policy drift that has nonetheless facilitated improved rates of economic growth.

India's rate of economic growth improved between 1980 and 2000 and averaged nearly 6 percent per annum (Table 7.1). This higher rate was in part a statistical artifact insofar as it reflected the growing share in the national economy of the faster-growing industrial and service sectors of the economy. Nevertheless, agricultural growth over the last two decades must be judged satisfactory, and both industry and services grew at some 6 to 7 percent per annum, propelling India into a group of relatively fast growers in the world. How does one explain this improved performance, especially in light of our focus on the role of the state and of state policies? The discussion distinguishes between the higher growth rates in the 1980s and those in the 1990s: Growth in the 1980s was debt-led, especially by a growing public debt, and growth in the 1990s was driven by higher rates of investment in the private corporate sector.

Other underlying factors that may have also contributed to this outcome ought to be noted. During the Nehru period India invested in heavy industry and in higher technological education to feed this industry. Returns on these investments typically take time, and India may now be benefiting from these earlier decisions. Relatedly, entrepreneurial and managerial skills have been slowly but steadily accumulating in India and probably contributed to better economic performance. There is also some evidence that the structure of industry is steadily shifting toward consumer industries where capital-output ratios are generally lower. India may also have just been lucky over the last two decades, with a spate of good weather, growing remittances from overseas Indians, and better international terms of borrowing and trade. And finally, as noted in the case of Brazil as well, prior industrialization creates its own efficiencies for future industrialization by providing a trained work force, dense supplier networks, demand for goods, and a supportive tax base.

TABLE 7.2 *Patterns of Capital Formation, 1980–1998 (percentage of GDP)*

Period	Total gross capital formation	Private corporate sector	Public sector
1980–85	21.9	4.3	10.2
1985–90	23.7	4.5	10.5
1990–95	23.7	6.0	9.1
1995–98	24.0	8.3	7.0

Source: Adapted from Rakesh Mohan, "Fiscal Correction for Economic Growth," *Economic and Political Weekly* (June 10, 2000), 2028, table 4.

In spite of the potential relevance of such nonpolicy variables, there is still something significant to explain. As is clear in Table 7.2, higher growth rates over the last two decades were accompanied by higher rates of investment, increases that originated in the public sector in the 1980s and in the private corporate sector in the 1990s. What explains these higher rates of investment? Also, what role, if any, have attempts to liberalize the economy played in this improved economic performance? The Indira Gandhi who returned to power in 1980 was considerably less populist than she was in the 1970s. She thus initiated an era – especially marked by a more probusiness Industrial Policy Resolution in 1982 – that increasingly came to be characterized by growing silence on issues of deliberate poverty alleviation and by greater public attention directed toward the promotion of economic growth. The appropriate strategy for promoting growth has been evolving. There was a lot of talk of liberalizing the economy in the second half of the 1980s, when Rajiv Gandhi was in power. While some probusiness policy measures – such as a reduction in corporate taxes – were indeed passed, overall liberalization was fairly limited; for example, the average rate of tariffs in India in 1990 was still over 100 percent.

Following a balance-of-payment crisis in 1991, there was some significant liberalization, especially of the internal economy from state controls, but the pace of change, especially of "opening" the economy to the world, slowed in the second half of the decade.[45] Tariff rates in India at the end of the century still averaged close to 40 percent, and foreign investment was minuscule compared, say, with China. What continued steadily throughout the two decades, however, was a move away from populism and toward a focus on economic growth, and relatedly toward a warmer embrace between the state and national business. The argument I am proposing is that this shift in state priorities and alliances is an important ingredient in improved economic performance.

[45] For a discussion of policy changes in the 1990s, see Shankar Acharya, "Macroeconomic Management in the Nineties," *Economic and Political Weekly* (April 20, 2002): 1515–38.

As discussed above, there was substantial evidence in India in the 1970s of a link between declining public investments and deceleration of industrial growth. With changed priorities, subsequent governments decided that one way to improve growth was to boost public sector investments. This is precisely what happened during the 1980s.[46] The government channeled new investments into promoting infrastructure and industries that provided key inputs for intermediate and final goods, which promoted higher rates of growth. While the direct contribution of an increase of some two to three percentage points in public investment to overall growth may be fairly small, given the significance of such bottlenecks as infrastructure, the indirect contribution of this new investment for growth was in all likelihood much more significant.

How was this new public investment financed? Recall that the economic capacities of the Indian state during the Indira Gandhi years had deteriorated, as politicization of the bureaucracy made it difficult to collect more taxes or to improve the performance of public sector enterprises. Some new public resources were found in further taxing international trade (hardly a route to improving economic performance!), but for the most part the role of new resources was limited. The government also did not cut back on the variety of its nondevelopmental expenditures, such as subsidies. Given weak political parties – essentially, personalistic groupings – it was increasingly difficult to hold together ruling coalitions. Public monies continued to play a key role in buying and maintaining political support. The government thus pursued the only option it thought it had, namely, borrowing – mainly internally but also externally. Given that this borrowed money was being invested in areas with low financial returns and often through inefficient public firms, the results included accumulating debt that created the twin crises of internal and external debt in 1991.

Meanwhile, the economy grew at a handsome rate of nearly 6 percent throughout the 1980s. Increasing public sector investment was one component of this growth. Private investments also grew, though not by much. There is, however, evidence of improvements in the productivity of investments, especially in private manufacturing.[47] The underlying causes are not

---

[46] See, for example, Rakesh Mohan, "Fiscal Correction for Economic Growth: Data Analysis and Suggestions," *Economic and Political Weekly*, June 10, 2000. He concludes that "what becomes clear from examination of the data is that the 1980s were characterized by a significant increase in public sector investment as well as other government expenditure" (p. 2028).

[47] See, for example, Vijay Joshi and I. M. D. Little, *India: Macroeconomics and Political Economy* (Washington, D.C.: World Bank, 1994), chap. 13. Joshi and Little argue that increased investments were too small to explain higher growth rates, which is surprising in light of their own evidence (see p. 327) that public sector investments averaged 7.7 percent of the GDP between 1960–61 and 1975–76 and 9.9 percent between 1976–77 and 1989–90. For a discussion of the "multiplier effect" of public investments in India, see Ahluwalia, *Industrial Growth*.

readily evident. Joshi and Little conclude that "the high level of demand in the 1980s" may be an important part of the explanation.[48] As noted, the roots of this were also the debt-led increase in public expenditure.

The Indian economy continued to grow at nearly 6 percent per annum during the 1990s as well. It will be a while before all the relevant data for the most recent period is analyzed and the underlying determinants of the continuing high growth become clear.[49] Some trends are already evident, however. The crisis of 1991 and the related agreements that the Indian government reached with the IMF led to pressure on government deficits. It is difficult for India's fragmented-multiclass state to collect new taxes, to improve the performance of public enterprises, or to cut back on the various supports and services it provides. The main strategy for debt management is thus evident in Table 7.2, namely, in declining public sector investments. This trend may hurt growth and development in the future, especially because of the woeful state of India's infrastructure but also because of the pressing need to invest more in basic education and health.[50]

In spite of a decline in public sector investments, overall economic growth did not suffer, mainly because private sector investments grew and the share of corporate investments in the GDP actually surpassed the share of public sector investments (see Table 7.2). Private sector industrial investment in India was generally quite productive, though new investment was only partly in new industries. And the industrial sector, especially manufacturing, did not perform all that handsomely in the 1990s. The real locus of growth shifted instead to the less regulated service sector, especially to exports of information technology, as India's accumulating manpower resources in this area found a niche in the global market.

The success of India's computer industry, including software exports, presents a good example of these broader, changing patterns of state-business relations.[51] The roots of this success are generally traced to policy changes in the late 1970s and then especially in 1984 under Rajiv Gandhi, who prioritized this sector for growth. Reminiscent of state-business cooperation in Korea, the Indian government during the 1980s and the 1990s reduced regulations and licensing requirements for this industry, reduced import duties, and promoted exports with aggressive marketing in overseas markets. At home, the state helped to create industrial parks and software technology parks with a communications infrastructure, provided core computer facilities, and engaged in a type of intervention generally more

---

[48] Joshi and Little, *India,* 328.

[49] One such preliminary attempt is Acharya, "Macroeconomic Management in the Nineties."

[50] See, for example, Mohan, "Fiscal Correction."

[51] See, for example, Peter Evans, *Embedded Autonomy: States and Industrial Transformation* (Princeton, N.J.: Princeton University Press, 1995); and Pinglé, *Rethinking the Developmental State,* chap. 5.

supportive than regulatory. This strategic state-business alliance was an essential component of the remarkable performance of the software industry, which grew at a rate of more than 50 percent per annum during the 1990s.

Beyond the information-technology industry, the factors that help to explain growing private sector investments and pockets of dynamism more broadly are the state's increasingly probusiness policies. Over the last decade or so, India's various governments have cut corporate taxes, provided a variety of supports to business, especially for exports, sought to tame labor – evident in the substantial decline of man-days lost due to strikes[52] – and relaxed public controls on entry, exit, and expansion. Tax reforms have included across-the-board reductions in rates and simplification of procedures for paying direct and indirect taxes, lowering of import tariffs by almost one-third between 1990 and 1996, dispensing with industrial licensing agreements for most industries, allowing new entrants – private, semiprivate, and foreign – into the banking system and capital markets, and opening up sectors such as power and telecommunications that had previously been limited to the public sector. While champions of liberalization may see all these measures as evidence of a growing free market in India, it remains the case that India's state is still heavily interventionist and that the Indian economy is still relatively closed to external goods, finance, and investors. The policy trend is thus better interpreted as a rightward drift in which the embrace of state and business continues to grow warmer, leaving many others out in the cold.

IV. Conclusion

India's quest for industrialization over the last half-century has produced mixed results. On the one hand, starting from very little, India now has a substantial and diversified industrial base, considerably more sophisticated than, say, that found in much of Africa, the Middle East, or even parts of Latin America. On the other hand, when compared with a South Korea or a Brazil, the progress of industrialization in India has not been all that rapid, and levels of efficiency have generally been low. Industrial performance has also varied over time, moderately satisfactory in both the beginning and the ending periods and punctuated by a fairly lackluster interregnum during Indira Gandhi's rule. This chapter has sought to analyze the political underpinnings of this economic record. Economic outcomes in India, as elsewhere, are of course a product of numerous nonpolitical factors. Nevertheless, the impact of the state's nature and role on the pattern of late-late

---

[52] If the yearly man-days lost due to strikes averaged some 37 million in the 1980s, this average in the 1990s was down to nearly 20 million. See *Yearbook of Labour Statistics* (Geneva: International Labour Office, various years).

industrialization is significant and varies systematically across cases and over time within a case.

The analysis has emphasized the impact of India's fragmented-multiclass state on rates and patterns of industrialization. The Indian state effectively controls the territory it governs, provides moderate political stability, is run at its apex by publicly oriented leaders and bureaucrats, and has always included among its multiple priorities promotion of industry and economic growth. Moreover, the state has intervened heavily in the economy to undertake production directly and to protect its indigenous entrepreneurs from global competition. The state took the lead during the Nehru period and increasingly supported the private sector in the last two decades of the twentieth century.

Conversely, however, the Indian state often lacked the political capacity to translate its enormous economic ambitions into outcomes. Central to this incapacity is its fragmented authority, characterized by both intraelite and elite-mass schisms and ruling coalitions that are generally multiclass. Leaders in such a state worry perennially about their legitimacy, inclining them to adopt economic policies based on whether they can help to consolidate their political position rather than on whether they will necessarily produce rapid industrialization and growth. The impact of these legitimacy concerns was most obvious during the rule of Indira Gandhi.

In conclusion, the impact of India's fragmented-multiclass state on its middling industrial performance may be usefully compared with the other cases analyzed in this study. When juxtaposed against Nigeria, what stands out is the economic importance of a moderately effective state that provides order, protects private property, operates according to the rule of law and procedures, is run by an elite with a modicum of public commitment and competence, and thus focuses some of the state's energies and resources on promoting industry. Absent such minimal capacities, the state in Nigeria has made a mockery of planned economic development, with dismal results. Indeed, Indian specialists have only to imagine all of India being governed in the manner of Bihar – the Africa within India – to understand the positive contribution of the central Indian state to India's industrialization.

Compared with Brazil or South Korea, however, India's economic performance has clearly been inferior, though India's starting point at the midcentury was not as advanced as that of Korea and Brazil – the share of industry in the Indian economy at independence was closer to 10 percent whereas it was nearly 20 percent in both Korea and Brazil following the Second World War. This difference was consequential in two ways. First, to the extent that prior industrialization helps subsequent industrialization, India was disadvantaged. And second, India would have had to industrialize even more rapidly than Korea or Brazil to achieve the levels of prosperity that these countries now enjoy. As it was, however, the pace of India's industrialization was slower. The question, then, is what role the Indian state has played in the process.

Although I have studied the subject extensively, I confess that a firm, parsimonious, and confident answer eludes me. Rather, only fragments of long chains of causation suggest themselves. Taken together, these may constitute a complex answer. A comparison with Brazil is especially instructive. Both India and Brazil pursued import substitution in the 1950s within democratic regimes, and yet Brazil's industry grew faster and more efficiently. Clearly, blaming import-substitution policies per se is not an adequate explanation. Instead, the role of different types of states in the two countries stands out as significant. The Brazilian state in this period was considerably less nationalist and mass-based than that of India, allowing Brazilian leaders to focus more on industrialization, to invite foreigners to lead the way, to cooperate closely with business groups, and to repress labor. All of these political differences were economically consequential, producing more rapid and more efficient import-substitution industrialization in Brazil.

After the mid-1960s Brazil and India of course took very different political paths, with striking economic consequences. Indira Gandhi sharply politicized economic policies in India, with negative impact on industrialization. By contrast, the right-wing military regime in Brazil, much more cohesive-capitalist in its makeup and orientation, emphasized economic growth, repressed labor even further, worked closely with private investors, both domestic and foreign, and borrowed heavily, hoping to boost exports so as to pay off its growing debts. Brazil's strategy ultimately backfired, but not before first achieving "miracle" growth rates in industry.[53] Industry in Indira Gandhi's India, by contrast, nearly stagnated. This economic situation in India changed somewhat in the 1980s and 1990s, but only when national politics also turned more procapitalist, with a greater emphasis on economic growth, closer cooperation with business, and further taming of labor.

Finally, the comparison between India and South Korea is dramatic. South Korea's cohesive-capitalist state contrasted fairly sharply with India's fragmented-multiclass state. This was evident in how state authority in the two countries was organized – cohesive versus fragmented – as well as in the state's relations with various social classes – narrow and procapitalist in one, broad and multiclass in the other. The South Korean state under Park Chung Hee thus concentrated power at the apex, defined rapid industrialization as essential for national security, penetrated downward, instituted close relations with business, controlled and mobilized labor, and cooperated closely

---

53 It may be worth noting that if Brazil's and India's economic growth are compared over the entire period of, say, 1950 to 2000, the economic performance of the two countries starts to converge more than diverge (see Figure 1).

with Japan without creating debilitating dependencies. While Korean citizens paid a heavy price in terms of repression and lack of freedoms, Korea's cohesive-capitalist state intervened heavily in the economy to promote both import substitution and exports of manufactured goods and, judged at least by growth results, did so rather successfully. India's fragmented-multiclass state, by contrast, pursued several goals simultaneously, cooperated with business only sporadically, faced considerable labor activism, resisted integration into the global economy – either for capital, as the Brazilians did, or for trade, as the Koreans did – and has only lately moved in a more developmental direction, but not without a commensurate rise in communal nationalism as the new legitimacy formula. In broad terms, India's middling industrial performance has also reflected these underlying political patterns.

PART IV

DASHED EXPECTATIONS

Nigeria

The Nigerian economy at the end of the twentieth century was poor, with a fairly small industrial base, despite the fact that Nigeria's rulers apparently channeled billions of the country's oil dollars toward industrial development. What happened? The following discussion of the Nigerian political economy emphasizes the negative role of a neopatrimonial state. Whatever the changes in regime and leadership, the Nigerian state repeatedly failed to facilitate economic transformation. While professing a commitment to development, state elites focused their energies instead on maintaining power and on privatizing public resources for personal gain or gain by ethnic communities. Why Nigeria ended up with a neopatrimonial state is best understood by noting what did not happen in Nigeria: A public realm failed to emerge. Under such circumstances – with a façade of a modern state but without the normative and organizational underpinnings of such a state – the defining tendencies of the society, namely, personalism and communalism, came to characterize the state as well, weakening the prospects for effective state intervention. The origins of such a state in the colonial period are analyzed in Chapter 8 and the failed attempts of the state to promote industrialization are discussed in Chapter 9.

8

Colonial Nigeria

Origins of a Neopatrimonial State and a Commodity-Exporting Economy

At the heart of Nigeria's disappointing economic performance lies a poorly functioning state, characterized here as a neopatrimonial state. While the economic impact of this state's actions were manifested mainly in the second half of the twentieth century, the distortions were the product of earlier historical developments. This chapter reconsiders existing historical knowledge with the aim of elucidating, first, the nature of the political economies that the British carved into Nigeria and, second, the state and the economy that emerged in colonial Nigeria, both in the early colonial phase, which lasted until the onset of the Second World War, and in the late colonial phase, which ended with independence in 1960.

Three main themes emerge: one concerning the precolonial situation and two focused on the impact of British rule during the early and the late colonial phases. Although the British brought together highly diverse political economies that became Nigeria, the localized political economies shared some important traits: They were generally small-scale, relatively simple political units, and they were based on rather undeveloped technology. Of note, therefore, is the highly rudimentary quality of the polities and economies that would become Nigeria. While most scholars of development do not usually compare "levels of development" within "premodern" settings, it is important to do so. Nigeria at the turn of the twentieth century was at a much lower level of development than any of the other societies considered in this study. It was characterized by a highly fragmented political structure, abysmally low levels of literacy, even among elites, and a simple agrarian technology. Given this disadvantageous starting point, Nigeria simply had a longer distance to travel in its search for development than, say, Korea or even India.

Within these local constraints it would have taken a fierce determination on the part of the British, as well as considerable resources, to develop a well-functioning state and to promote economic and technological development. The British did nothing of the sort and instead ran Nigeria on the cheap. During the early colonial phase the British fostered indirect rule in Nigeria, resulting in a poorly formed state that reinforced a patrimonial, personalistic, and localized pattern of rule. It failed to centralize authority, to develop an effective civil service, and, relatedly, to develop the capacity to tax the population directly. Moreover, given the lack of resources and an ideological commitment to laissez-faire, the colonial state also failed to develop institutions that could promote socioeconomic development. In sum, the British in Nigeria created a country but not an effective state. The public realm that came into being was barely demarcated from the existing private realms, in terms of both organizations and culture – with long-term, negative consequences.

While the British in Nigeria were relatively less intrusive than, say, the Japanese in Korea, the British impact on Nigeria was still considerable. This apparent tension is resolved if one keeps in mind that the rudimentary local societies were more fragile and susceptible to external impact than the complex systems of large parts of Asia. Besides the political impact of indirect rule, the other main agents of change, especially during the early colonial phase, were trading interests and missionaries. New politics and traders helped to link Nigerian economies to international markets, promoting mainly a commodity-export economy, with its well-known advantages and drawbacks. The missionaries provided some education, especially in southern Nigeria, giving rise to a new class of Africans that, in time, would join the ruling class. The origins of three critical vectors in the period before the Second World War – a distorted state, a commodity-dependent economy, and the nature of the new political class – eventually determined the evolution of Nigeria after the war.

Finally, the onset of the war marked an important turning point. The political economy of the late colonial phase came to be characterized by two nearly opposing tendencies that together proved very damaging for Nigeria's search for development: The state became ever more involved in the economy but state power became increasingly fragmented as it became further entangled in particularistic and personalistic networks. The framework of a weak colonial state encouraged the further fragmentation of what was already a feeble and a divided nationalist movement. The British slowly but surely ceded power to a variety of indigenous forces that were divided along ethnic and tribal lines. These forces, in turn, further divided the minimal colonial state, particularly along regional lines. At the same time, the Second World War initiated a move toward greater state involvement in the economy. From the standpoint of sustained economic growth, state intervention in the Nigerian economy was directed in all the wrong directions – much more at encouraging control, extraction, and populism than at promoting national production. The growing fragmentation of state power along particularistic lines only compounded the problem of misguided state intervention in the economy.

I. Precolonial "Nigeria"

Before the British there was, of course, no Nigeria. What there was instead was the Niger River and, around it, a variety of political settlements: North of the river was the Sokoto Caliphate, southwest of it the Lagos consulate and the Yoruba Kingdoms, and in the southeast numerous small-scale tribal communities.[1] The discussion below outlines the nature of these precolonial political economies, mainly to emphasize their rudimentary quality. Two caveats are in order. First, the historical literature on Nigeria rests on fairly limited documentation, as written records of precolonial Nigerian history are meager. Second, there are significant, unresolved controversies in this literature.[2] I refer to these in passing, but only a few of them have a direct bearing on the argument developed below.

Coastal Nigeria participated in the slave trade for several centuries, giving rise to small city-states on the coast that were often controlled by local strongmen who profited from the trade. The area between coastal settlements and the Niger was, in turn, dotted with what historians call the Yoruba Kingdoms, some two dozen more or less autonomous political collectivities of varying sizes.[3] These kingdoms did not refer to themselves as Yoruba Kingdoms; the main sense of common identity instead derived from some shared elements in the spoken language and, more importantly, from a shared allegiance to Ife, a traditional center of Yoruba power and creativity. A modicum of stability was maintained among these kingdoms in the eighteenth century, mainly because of the preponderant role of the most powerful kingdom among them, Oyo.[4] The abolition of the slave trade and the subsequent emergence of "legitimate trade" in the nineteenth century, along with such other external pressures as growing military and religious expeditions from the Islamic north, precipitated significant changes in western Nigeria. Whereas the British established a formal foothold in Lagos and the activities of overseas traders increased, the Yoruba Kingdoms disintegrated over the course of prolonged and mutual warfare. This conflict characterized much of the second half of the nineteenth century and ended only when the British annexed the area in 1893 and imposed a peace.

Viewed from a comparative standpoint, one is prompted to ask why the Yoruba Kingdoms did not produce a larger-scale, more centralized

---

[1] For a good overview, see Michael Crowder, *The Story of Nigeria*, 4th ed. (London: Faber and Faber, 1978), esp. chaps. 2–11.

[2] See, for example, Toyin Falola, ed., *African Historiography: Essays in Honour of Jacob Ade Ajayi* (London: Longman, 1993), especially the historiographical essays by Robin Law and Paul E. Lovejoy.

[3] For example, see Robert S. Smith, *Kingdoms of the Yoruba*, 2nd ed. (London: Methuen, 1976).

[4] See J. F. A. Ajayi, "The Aftermath of the Fall of Old Oyo," in J. F. A. Ajayi and Michael Crowder, eds., *History of West Africa* (New York: Columbia University Press, 1973), 2: 136.

polity.[5] But given the paucity of historical information, the answers are necessarily speculative. First, only low-level technology was available. Given the near absence of written language, it is hard to imagine how records could have been kept and how a permanent administration could have developed. The main modes of communication across tribal units were also fairly "crude" and often "nonverbal" – via drums, flutes, and objects identified with special events.[6] And finally, the technology of warfare, too, was primitive. Bows and spears were the main weapons; firearms were known, as was cavalry, but these came into use mainly in the second half of the nineteenth century.[7] Moreover, given resource limitations, well-organized standing armies were rare.

A second set of factors that may help to explain the failure of large-scale, centralized monarchies to emerge concerns the nature of power distribution within local political societies.[8] The basic social unit in the region was the tribe – or what some anthropologists call patrilineal descent groups or lineage groups – whose members shared a belief in a common ancestry and whose property was owned communally. While tribal chiefs were powerful because they controlled the mobilization of manpower for warfare, their capacity to extract surplus was limited because they did not personally own property. Kingdoms, in turn, were generally a collection of tribes in which relatively weak kings shared power with tribal chiefs, who not only controlled the manpower for war making but also often constituted the king's "cabinet." Power in the Yoruba kingdoms was thus relatively diffuse. In combination with the low levels of technology, the obstacles to creating large-scale, complex political units would surely have been formidable.

Finally, and most speculatively, one wonders whether there was some functional congruence between a slave-trading economy and fragmented, small-scale political units. Since communities were defined by lineage groups, there must have been a reluctance to sell members of one's own descent group. And indeed we do know from the historical evidence that raiding, enslaving, and selling members of other communities or tribes was the common pattern. This makes intuitive sense because it is hard to imagine a monarch allowing his "citizens" to be sold to others as slaves – internal slavery being a totally different matter – without losing legitimacy. Moreover, slave raiding and selling was a fairly decentralized activity, controlled not by monarchs but by numerous traditional chiefs and traders.[9] Wealth from a

---

[5] This question informs a useful monograph by Peter C. Lloyd, *The Political Development of Yoruba Kingdoms in the Eighteenth and Nineteenth Centuries*, Occasional Paper no. 31 (London: Royal Anthropological Institute, 1971).

[6] See R. Olufemi Ekundare, *An Economic History of Nigeria, 1880–1960* (New York: Africana Publishing Company (Holmes and Meir), 1973), 47.

[7] See Smith, *Kingdoms of the Yoruba*, chap. 9.

[8] This discussion is based on ibid., chap. 7; and Lloyd, *Political Development of Yoruba Kingdoms*.

[9] Lloyd, *Political Development of Yoruba Kingdoms*, 12–15.

slave-trading economy must therefore have strengthened chiefs and traders at the expense of the palace, further decentering power.

For whatever reason, city-states on the coast and the Yoruba Kingdoms remained more or less autonomous political collectivities well into the nineteenth century. Relative peace was maintained among the kingdoms, mainly because of a balance-of-power type of politics in which a dominant kingdom – Oyo – played a stabilizing role. By the mid-nineteenth century, however, Oyo was disintegrating and warfare had emerged among the Yoruba Kingdoms. Heated debate has characterized the discussions regarding which factors were critical in spurring these changes. Some scholars emphasize the shift from the slave trade to "legitimate trade" in the nineteenth century, on the grounds that new economic activities encouraged new men of power and undermined the stability of the old system.[10] Others argue that the old elites came to control the legitimate trade as well and that the significance of international economic activities for distribution of wealth and power within the Yoruba kingdoms was limited in any case.[11] In this view, the Yoruba Kingdoms disintegrated as a result of internal power conflicts; and to the extent that external pressures were a factor, these were more the military and ideological pressures from the Islamic north and less the economic stimuli from the coast.[12] For our purposes, an overview will suffice: Internal and external changes contributed to growing warfare among the Yoruba Kingdoms, warfare that came to an end only when the British annexed the area and imposed an imperial peace.[13]

A few comments on the region's economy are also in order. As already noted, the region had participated in the international slave trade from the sixteenth century on. While the full impact of the slave trade on Nigerian society and economy will probably never be known, some of its general effects are obvious. First, the "energies and talents of the people

[10] This view was originally proposed in a brilliant, pioneering study by Onwuka K. Dike, *Trade and Politics in the Niger Delta, 1830–1885: An Introduction to the Economic and Political History of Nigeria* (London: Oxford University Press, 1956). While Dike's study was focused on one area, the logic of his argument was subsequently generalized by A. G. Hopkins, *An Economic History of West Africa* (London: Longman, 1973).

[11] For a summary of related debates, see Robin Law, "The Historiography of the Commercial Transition in Nineteenth Century West Africa," in Falola, *African Historiography*, chap. 8, pp. 91–115; Robin Law, "Introduction," in Robin Law, ed., *From Slave Trade to "Legitimate" Commerce: The Commercial Transition in Nineteenth-Century West Africa* (Cambridge: Cambridge University Press, 1995), 1–29; and Martin Lynn, "The West African Palm Oil Trade in the Nineteenth Century and the Crisis of Adaptation," in Law, *From Slave Trade to "Legitimate" Commerce*, 57–77.

[12] This view is especially associated with the scholarship of J. F. A. Ajayi. For example, see Ajayi, "Aftermath of the Fall of Old Oyo."

[13] For such a useful synthetic overview, see A. I. Asiwaja, "Dahomey, Yorubaland, Bargu and Benin in the Nineteenth Century," in J. F. A. Ajayi, ed., *UNESCO General History of Africa*, vol. 1: *Africa in the Nineteenth Century until the 1880s* (Berkeley: University of California Press, 1989), esp. 706.

were either consumed by raiding or being raided" and "hundreds of thousands of the most virile members" of the society were forcibly removed.[14] Second, those who profited from the slave trade often spent those profits on imports. Thus, the impact of the trade on local economic and technological development was negative insofar as for centuries "the slave trade provided an effective barrier against the development of agriculture and industry."[15] Even on strict economic grounds, putting aside the moral repugnancy of slavery, the slave-trading era constituted "a barren three centuries."[16] The turn to exports of palm oil and groundnuts in the nineteenth century had a more positive impact on incomes. But this shift, too, did not contribute much either to technological development or to reduction in the practice of slavery. Illegal slave exports continued, and domestic slavery, especially female slavery, increased, in part to meet the new labor demand to provide exports of palm oil.[17]

Nonetheless, the bulk of economic production was aimed at the domestic market. While there were some crafts and mining, the main economic activity was food production, especially agriculture, which was striking for its "small" and "primitive" quality.[18] While property was owned communally, land could be held in perpetuity, with family farming the primary mode of agriculture, though slave labor was also common. Given the abundance of land, shifting cultivation – that is, moving from one piece of land to another – was widely practiced. "Ploughing was completely unknown,"[19] and the hand hoe was the primary agricultural tool, as draft animals were not used. Even the potter's wheel was still not part of the agrarian economy at the turn of the twentieth century.[20]

Political and economic life north of the river Niger may have been somewhat more sophisticated in the nineteenth century, but not by much. The Sokoto Caliphate was a collection of some fifteen to twenty emirates under the loose suzerainty of an Islamic ruler, the caliph. The caliphate, initiated via an Islamic jihad early in the nineteenth century, struggled for much of the century to establish a semblance of control and stability and eventually came under British control following the Berlin Conference of 1884. There is a lively literature on Sokoto, especially on its politics – on the nature of the jihad, on the manner in which it was governed, and on how it was eventually

---

[14] James S. Coleman, *Nigeria: Background to Nationalism* (Berkeley: University of California Press, 1958), 40–41.
[15] See Ekundare, *Economic History of Nigeria*, 35.
[16] See Crowder, *Story of Nigeria*, 68.
[17] For a quick overview of the relevant debates, see Law, *From Slave Trade to "Legitimate" Commerce*, 6–9.
[18] See Ekundare, *Economic History of Nigeria*, 40.
[19] Ibid., 41.
[20] See Gerald K. Helleiner, *Peasant Agriculture, Government, and Economic Growth in Nigeria* (Homewood, Ill.: Richard D. Irwin, 1966), 2.

colonized – but, once again, claims often rest on fairly modest evidence.[21] The following is a brief outline of the degree of Sokoto's "stateness" and the nature of its economy.

By the standard of political units in precolonial sub-Saharan Africa, Sokoto would rank among the most centralized, stable, and sizable.[22] The rulers of the caliphate exercised some semblance of control over large parts of what is now northern Nigeria, with political units sharing a common religion, Islam. Over time, norms and practices developed to govern the relationship between the caliphs and the emirs, the underlings who exercised actual power over smaller territories.[23] Political organization was inspired by the more complex political units of northern Africa, and written language was used to maintain records. The resulting political stability allowed for economic expansion, including the production of some luxury goods for export across the Sahara to North Africa.

The political structure of the Sokoto Caliphate was nevertheless rudimentary, especially when compared with other non-Western agrarian monarchies of the period, say, the Yi dynasty in Korea, the Mughals in India, or the Manchus in China, not to mention the Ottomans in Turkey. Sokoto attained high levels of neither political stability nor stateness: There was no central army; centralized civil administration was weak, if not nonexistent; the quality of rule varied across emirates, as well as over time; and jihads, mutual warfare, and slave raids remained common themes throughout the century.

The jihad that brought Sokoto into being was led mainly by an Islamic Fulani elite, who managed to mobilize Fulani and other peasants and pastoralists against the incumbent Hausa kings.[24] While the Fulani leaders owed allegiance to the caliph at Sokoto, especially early in the century, it was

---

[21] Two overviews that I found most useful are R. A. Adeleye and C. C. Stewart, "The Sokoto Caliphate in the Nineteenth Century," in J. F. A. Ajayi and Michael Crowder, eds., *History of West Africa*, 2nd ed. (London: Longman, 1987), 2: 86–131; and Murray Last, "The Sokoto Caliphate and Borno," in *UNESCO General History of Africa*, 1: 555–99.

[22] Michael Watts thus writes: "The Sokoto Caliphate was to become the largest, most heavily populated, most complexly organized, and wealthiest state system in the nineteenth century West Africa, if not sub-Saharan Africa as a whole." See Watts, *Silent Violence: Food, Famine and Peasantry in Northern Nigeria* (Berkeley: University of California Press, 1983), 49.

[23] The issue of how much control central leaders actually exercised over the heads of peripheral units remains unresolved in the literature. The safest conclusion is that, while this control varied over time and from emirate to emirate, even under the best of circumstances the emirates were quite autonomous. For a variety of views, see Victor Low, *Three Nigerian Emirates: A Study in Oral History* (Evanston, Ill.: Northwestern University Press, 1972); Murray Last, *The Sokoto Caliphate* (London: Longmans, 1967), esp. chaps. 4–6; R. A. Adeleye, *Power and Diplomacy in Northern Nigeria, 1804–1900* (New York: Humanities Press, 1971); and M. G. Smith, *The Economy of Hausa Communities of Zaria* (London: Colonial Social Science Research Council, 1955).

[24] For a discussion of how the jihad was conducted, see Last, *Sokoto Caliphate*, chap. 2. For a somewhat different set of views on the jihad, especially those that emphasize its Islamic and

always only legitimacy that was centralized. Real power, by contrast, was always more decentralized. Indeed, at no time in the history of Sokoto was there ever a centralized army.[25] And as the legitimacy of the original jihad eventually declined, power increasingly came to rest within individual emirates. Factors contributing to the difficulty of establishing any sort of centralized polity, then, were the primitive technology of warfare and administration, the lack of stable economic and manpower resources, and the great distances between Sokoto and the emirates in the context of slow means of communication.

For much of its existence, the Sokoto Caliphate was managed as a dyarchy, with the eastern emirates under the loose suzerainty of Sokoto and the western ones under another center of power, Gwandu. Political stability and quality of rule varied across emirates, with larger, better organized ones generally hegemonized by one tribe or another, whose leader often secured hereditary rights to the position of emir. These emirs paid tribute to their superiors at Sokoto or Gwandu and provided periodic support for warfare, but for the most part they were relatively free to run their emirates as they saw fit. Rule in other emirates was considerably more contentious, with members of various lineage groups and factions jockeying for position. Under such circumstances the caliphs could intervene to mediate and help to resolve the conflicts, but overall their capacity to impose their will remained rather nebulous.

Although sacred authority increasingly came to rest in Islamic institutions, the emirs were secular rulers who generally ran their domains as an extension of the household, with the help of both kith and kin – often fellow Fulani clan members – and household retainers. Many Fulani clans became rather powerful, giving rise to a Fulani aristocracy of sorts. The personalistic, patronage-type relationship of the emirs with this aristocracy was thus central to the smooth functioning of the emirates as the Fulani aristocrats were assigned rights to property and slaves in exchange for collecting taxes and sharing them with the emir. Since land was plentiful, there was a need for substantial amounts of labor, especially slaves. Slave raids were therefore a regular feature of the local political economies.

The historical literature is not clear on the structure of taxation: the rates, the stability of the system, and the specifics of the actual assignment

revolutionary qualities, see a collection of essays in Y. B. Usman, ed., *Studies in the History of the Sokoto Caliphate* (New York: Third Press International, 1979).

[25] Adeleye thus writes: "The Caliphate was not a militarily powerful polity even when religious enthusiasm was its height. Largely for this reason, and partly because of a lack of a centrally directed permanent or regular military force, the presence of hostile enclaves within the Caliphate persisted throughout the century." See R. A. Adeleye, "The Sokoto Caliphate in the Nineteenth Century," in J. F. A. Ajayi and Michael Crowder, eds., *History of West Africa* (New York: Columbia University Press, 1973), 2: 72. See also Last, "Sokoto Caliphate and Borno," 568.

and collection within these emirates.[26] The safest conclusion seems to be that taxation was relatively uneven – though enough to sustain a substantial, parasitic ruling class – and its collection was based on customary obligations, in the guise of the Islamic ideology of *zakat*, and on confiscation by armed raids. Since slavery was widespread – various estimates range from one-third to one-half the population being enslaved[27] – the picture is even more confused. Slaves were, of course, being "taxed" by the virtue of being slaves. Taxation proper was thus aimed at family farmers, plantation owners, pastoralists, and traders, both local and long-distance.[28]

In spite of a relatively low level of centralization and with warfare a constant theme, the Sokoto Caliphate did provide a degree of political stability – especially compared with what existed in the Yoruba Kingdoms in the period. This stability, in turn, begat some economic expansion built on the fairly crude, agrarian economy. Unlike the south, which is thick with forests and mangroves, Sokoto lay in a dry savannah that slowly but surely trailed northward into the Sahara Desert. Besides cereals, groundnut was an important food crop, and cotton and indigo were important nonfood crops. While the evidence is scanty, it seems that jihad and the establishment of Sokoto led to further enslavement, the addition of new lands, and the establishment of some large plantations run by gangs of enslaved labor.[29] Both food and nonfood crops increased, and the latter, especially cotton and indigo, fed into a vibrant textile "industry" around Kano that produced luxury cloth for export across the Sahara, mainly on donkeys and with the help of slave labor, to North Africa. Leather goods, too, were produced for export. Overall, however, contact with European economies was minimal – evidenced by the survival of Kano textiles – and there were hardly any technological changes or innovations throughout the century.

To sum up, a key characteristic of precolonial Nigeria was the rudimentary quality of the local political economies. The Yoruba Kingdoms remained

[26] Watts thus paints a picture of fairly effective tax collection ("surplus appropriation") that was systematically backed by state coercion. See Watts, *Silent Violence*, chap. 2. Given the low level of stateness in Sokoto in general, this view is not persuasive. Polly Hill's characterization of Kano's emir as an "apex" with no "proper substructure" (or with no proper ruling administration) strikes me as closer to the truth for the whole caliphate. See Polly Hill, *Population, Prosperity and Poverty: Rural Kano, 1900 and 1970* (Cambridge: Cambridge University Press, 1970), 10. Hill's view on the nature of power and administration would also be consistent with Ekundare's suggestion that the level of taxation in Sokoto was "arbitrary – imposed on no recognized basis" and often collected by raids. See Ekundare, *Economic History of Nigeria*, 39. Both R. A. Adeleye and Murray Last (see note 21 above) also paint a picture of the taxation system as rather uneven and unsystematic.

[27] See, for example, Polly Hill, "From Slavery to Freedom: The Case of Farm-Slavery in Nigerian Hausaland," *Comparative Studies in Society and History* 18, no. 3 (1976): 395–426.

[28] See Last, "Sokoto Caliphate and Borno," 578–79.

[29] See Paul E. Lovejoy, "Plantations in the Economy of the Sokoto Caliphate," *Journal of African History* 19, no. 3 (1978): 341–68.

more or less autonomous units for much of the century. Agriculture proceeded without a plow and slave raids across these units were a commonplace. Toward the second half of the century these kingdoms fell into constant warring with each other. The coast was dotted by city-states that had originated with the slave trade.[30] I have not discussed the tribal communities of the southeast, mainly because there was not even a semblance of large-scale organized political and economic life in that region. The north, by contrast, was a more complex political society, inspired by Arabs and Islam. But even there state consolidation was minimal, slave raids were a common occurrence, and the economy was fairly backward.

The Nigerian political economy at the turn of the twentieth century was thus at a considerably lower level of development than the political economies we have encountered so far in this study. The well-known colonial scholar of Nigeria, Margery Perham, contrasted African and Asian realities: "Here in place of large units of Asia was the multicellular issue of tribalism; instead of an ancient civilization, the largest area of primitive poverty enduring into the modern age. Until colonialism the greater part of the continent was without the wheel, the plough or the transport animal; almost without stone horses or clothes, except for the skin."[31] A somewhat later account of precolonial Nigeria by Gerald Helleiner differs little in substance: "a collection of communities, essentially isolated from one another and from the rest of the world, engaged primarily with 'traditional' activities... of subsistence.... The level of technology... was very low. The principal instrument of cultivation was the hand hoe... and local handicraft were of quite backward nature."[32]

One of my central themes is that this relative backwardness was consequential for Nigeria's long-term development because it presented a formidable obstacle to the emergence of either entrepreneurship or an effective state, two potential agents of economic change. For now, I offer a more general observation. Scholars of comparative development often do not assign significant weight to different starting points when assessing development performance across countries or regions. Instead, there is a tendency to treat all preindustrial, low-income developing countries – especially since the Second World War – as having been at a more or less similar starting point. The analytical puzzle for many thus looks to be why some regions have grown so much more rapidly than others. But such a perspective is ahistorical and misleading. We will see that a Nigeria at the end of the war had little in common with a Korea, save for their low-income status.

[30] Besides the marvelous study of Dike, *Trade and Politics*, other useful studies of coastal settlements include Kannan K. Nair, *Politics and Society in South East Nigeria, 1841–1906* (London: Frank Cass, 1972); and Kalu E. Ume, *The Rise of British Colonialism in Southern Nigeria, 1700–1900: A Study of the Bights of Benin and Bonny* (Smithtown, N.Y.: Exposition Press, 1980).

[31] See Margery Perham, "British Problem in Africa," *Foreign Affairs* (July 1951): 638.

[32] See Gerald K. Helleiner, *Peasant Agriculture*, 2.

Pushing the issue of starting points even farther back – to the turn of the century – the collectivities that eventually became Nigeria were sharply distinguishable from, say, their contemporary counterpoints in East Asia. Many in East Asia, for example, already had a lengthy experience with centralized states, professional armies, exam-based civil bureaucracies, and aristocratic civilizations. They had already seen elaborate attempts to innovate – from large organizational tasks (as, for example, the construction of the Great Wall in China) to productivity-enhancing development of irrigation systems. Korea and Nigeria may thus have both been preindustrial, but that is all that they had in common. Scholars of development generally lack a vocabulary and indicators to measure such distances across preindustrial societies and to assess the significance of these distances for future developmental prospects. I continue to demonstrate the relevance of this distance for Nigeria.

II. Early Colonial Phase: State Construction

The British sought to run Nigeria on the cheap and expended little energy to transform the rudimentary political economies they had colonized into a modern state. Instead, they ran the state as three to four separate regions – demarcated along the northern and the southern divides – and utilized traditional chiefs as their agents. The British in Nigeria reinforced weak centralization, indirect, personal rule, and subordination rather than assimilation – the opposite of what was needed to create a modernizing state.[33] This minimal state was organized along laissez-faire lines, responsible for little more than preserving law and order and for promoting infrastructure and commodity exports. Beyond that it promoted no significant economic or technological progress. The following discussion focuses on the origins and nature of this limited colonial state.[34]

---

[33] From Max Weber to Charles Tilly, scholars of modern states have understood these issues well. Tilly thus describes the transition from "premodern" to "modern" states in Europe as involving a shift "from tribute to tax, from indirect to direct rule, [and] from subordination to assimilation." See Tilly, *Coercion, Capital and European States* (Cambridge: Blackwell, 1990), 100.

[34] Recent literature on the impact of colonialism in Africa has shifted away from both the earlier colonial apologia and the subsequent dependency anger that stressed themes of economic exploitation. Two important recent volumes that instead lay the blame for Africa's underdevelopment on the nature of the colonial state are Crawford Young, *The African Colonial State in Comparative Perspective* (New Haven: Yale University Press, 1994); and Mahmood Mamdani, *Citizen and Subject: Contemporary Africa and the Legacy of Late Colonialism* (Princeton, N.J.: Princeton University Press, 1996). Another volume that stresses greater continuity between precolonial and postcolonial politics, thus suggesting that the impact of colonialism may be easily exaggerated, is Jeffrey Herbst, *States and Power in Africa: Comparative Lessons in Authority and Control* (Princeton, N.J.: Princeton University Press, 2000). My more limited focus on Nigeria draws on these studies insofar as my focus is also mainly on the political impact of colonialism. However, I depend more heavily on specific historical literature on Nigeria and

The British came to Africa late in the colonial game, having already been
in India and elsewhere for decades, and this prior experience influenced
the ruling strategy adopted in Africa. The motives in colonizing Africa, as
elsewhere, were mixed: in part to ensure that other European powers did
not get there first, in part to make profits, and in part to save souls.[35] Since
making a profit was mainly the business of traders and saving souls that
of the missionaries, the direct role of the colonial state was understood as
minimal: to establish territorial control.[36] The consensus therefore – both
within the British government and among the local colonial rulers – was
that Nigeria would operate with little funding from London.[37] The critical
decision to run Nigeria cheaply was further reinforced by a lesson that the
British were quickly learning in India, Egypt, and elsewhere, namely, that
"educated natives" were trouble.[38] And since the potential for collecting
taxes from the very backward local economies was always questionable, the
Indian option of creating a significant centralized state, staffed by both
British and educated native civil servants, was never seriously pursued in
Nigeria.[39] Instead, the British sought to use – especially in the north, but

tread a line somewhere in between the two positions that suggest that colonial impact was
either decisive or superficial.

[35] Debates on colonial motives in Africa are, of course, long-standing and often divisive; these
vary from those who emphasize economic motives to those focusing on intra-European
realpolitik considerations. Two recent volumes that stress mixed motives are Thomas
Pakenham, *The Scramble for Africa, 1876–1912* (New York: Random House, 1991); and H. L.
Wesseling, *Divide and Rule: The Partition of Africa, 1880–1914*, trans. Arnold J. Pomerans
(Westport, Conn.: Praeger, 1996).

[36] Over time, of course, in Nigeria, as elsewhere, given the needs of taxation, security, and
helping traders and missionaries, the colonial state expanded its mission and role. See, for
example, D. K. Fieldhouse, *Colonialism, 1870–1945: An Introduction* (London: Weidenfeld
and Nicolson, 1981), 16–20. I return to this issue.

[37] I do not mean to create a distorted impression here that there was complete consensus
on such issues or that related issues were not vigorously debated. For an overview of such
debates, see Andrew Roberts, "The Imperial Mind," in A. D. Roberts, ed., *The Cambridge
History of Africa*, vol. 7: *From 1905 to 1940* (Cambridge: Cambridge University Press, 1986),
24–76. It is especially interesting to note that the idea of investing in and transforming
"Hausa lands" was debated in London among colonial officials but vetoed on budgetary
grounds. See ibid., 44. One wonders why the possible returns on investments were not
considered an adequate compensation for budgetary expenditures. Also the mere fact that
this debate occurred underlines the tortuous process of historical change that is dotted by
paths that could have been taken but were not, and relatedly, that it would be far too easy
to attribute policy choices to underlying "interests," both because "interests" are not always
obvious and because there is always more than one way to pursue "interests."

[38] Ibid., 33–42, 53.

[39] That this model was not a totally preposterous option is underlined by the fact that it was
the mode of rule in the Lagos Consulate in the second half of the nineteenth century.
See, for example, I. F. Nicolson, *The Administration of Nigeria, 1900–1960: Men, Methods,
and Myths* (Oxford: Clarendon, 1969), esp. 51–52. The idea of excluding educated Africans
from government, along with the rise of more explicit racist ideologies, were early-twentieth-
century developments.

also in parts of the south – existing authority structures and cloaked this expedient path in the ideology of "indirect rule," a strategy with significant and mostly negative consequences for state building in Nigeria.

Different regions of Nigeria came to be ruled differently and over time came to develop fairly distinct socioeconomic characteristics. British trading interests were significant on the coast and, with the opening of the Niger, even in parts of the southern interior. Prior to 1900, when Nigeria officially came into being, a fairly sophisticated local colonial government was already functioning in the Lagos Consulate.[40] The British expanded their control over Yorubaland from Lagos, often working through missionaries. They made treaties with one traditional chief after another, threatened others into submission, and when all else failed, resorted to military force. Warring Yoruba chiefs were no match for the well-organized British and generally succumbed without much resistance.[41] The movement eastward from Lagos was trickier because there were very few sizable kingdoms that could be readily incorporated by treaty or by force. Where powerful "houses" existed, as they did in the city-states that dotted the delta, the British often subdued house leaders. Other than that, the process was slow: incorporating tribes in a given area, establishing a district with a magistrate in charge, creating a revenue base while dealing with slavery and warring tribes, and then moving further into the interior.[42]

By contrast, the colonization of the north that the British "acquired" at the Berlin Conference required more military force. The attempt to establish real control in the north, with its more complex political units, involved not only negotiations with the caliph and individual emirs, but also the utilization of the British West African Frontier Force to defeat the various emirates militarily if they did not readily capitulate. Central to this whole process was Lord Lugard, one of the numerous eccentric British colonialists whose names dot British colonial history. Lugard's name is nearly synonymous with the establishment of indirect rule in large parts of Nigeria.[43]

The colonial conquest of Nigeria essentially left traditional authority structures intact, especially in Yorubaland and in the North. The British opted not to establish a centralized state that would supplant the power of

---

[40] For early history of the Lagos Consulate, see Robert Smith, "The Lagos Consulate, 1851–1861: An Outline," *Journal of African History* 15, no. 3 (1974): 393–416. For a discussion of how the Lagos Consulate was administered, see Nicolson, *Administration of Nigeria*, esp. 51–79.

[41] See M'baye Gueye and A. Adu Boahen, "African Initiatives and Resistance in West Africa, 1880–1914," in A. Adu Boahen, ed., *General History of Africa*, vol. 7: *Africa under Colonial Domination, 1880–1935* (Berkeley: University of California Press for UNESCO, 1985), 114–48.

[42] See I. F. Nicolson, *Administration of Nigeria*, esp. 85.

[43] For two very different views on Lugard's "contributions," see Margery Perham, *Lugard: The Years of Authority, 1898–1945* (London: Oxford University Press, 1960); and Nicolson, *Administration of Nigeria*, esp. chap. 6.

traditional chiefs because they were simply not prepared to commit the human and material resources necessary for creating an effective central state.[44] In the north, Lord Lugard decided instead to strengthen the hands of former emirs or would-be emirs (often individuals from dominant lineage groups with some hereditary claim to leadership), mainly in exchange for maintaining order and collecting and sharing taxes. While British civil servants supervised these traditional rulers, especially in the important area of revenue collection, the role of established traditional authority in local areas was critical for the functioning of the empire.[45] Reminiscent of Bengali zamindars and pockets of rule by maharajas, indirect rule became the main system of colonial administration north of the Niger and Benue Rivers and essentially remained in place until independence and even beyond.

British rule in southern Nigeria had more of an appearance of direct rule, though this was somewhat deceptive. Given the paucity of British civil servants and the racist reluctance to train and incorporate "natives," colonial rule had to depend on traditional chiefs. Within the Yoruba areas, such chiefs either existed or could be created. The respective lieutenant governors in Lagos encouraged working through such chiefs, again creating an indirect rule of sorts. The south differed from the north, however, in the significant role played there by traders and missionaries. Education and commerce in the south gave rise to "new men" who eventually challenged the authority of the traditional chiefs. A similar process unfolded in the Southern Protectorate, where in contrast to the Yoruba areas, there were no traditional chiefs to be found. The British sought to create "indirect rule" in the Southern Protectorate as well but with uneven success.[46]

The idea of amalgamating these various regions of Nigeria into one central state was debated seriously on several occasions but never really acted on. The first attempt in 1914 was quite superficial and aimed to create a single treasury so as to use the sizable revenues collected in the south to subsidize administration in the north.[47] What started out as an expedient organization for economic purposes subsequently gained an institutional logic, with strong vested interests in maintaining political fragmentation. The next major reorganization did not occur until the late 1930s, but it was not a move toward further centralization; rather, it formally divided Nigeria

---

[44] Related debates are well reviewed in Jeremy White, *Central Administration in Nigeria, 1914–1948* (Dublin: Irish Academic Press, 1981); and in Nicolson, *Administration of Nigeria.* Also relevant here is Lord Lugard's own thinking on these issues; see Lord F. J. D. Lugard, *The Dual Mandate in British Tropical Africa* (London: W. Blackwood and Sons, 1922).

[45] For details, see White, *Central Administration in Nigeria,* esp. 33–40.

[46] See D. C. Dorward, "British West Africa and Liberia," in Roberts, *Cambridge History of Africa,* vol. 7, esp. 403.

[47] See White, *Central Administration in Nigeria,* 41.

into three regions, the west and the east below the rivers, and the north. This administrative grid, in turn, intensified regional identity struggles, which would eventually prove lethal for the functioning of the Nigerian state.

Besides the failure to create a central authority, the thinness of the colonial state was further evident in the fragmented nature of the police and in the weak civil bureaucracy constructed by the British. Once its supremacy was established, Britain maintained a fairly small armed force within Nigeria, numbering some 3,000 soldiers. The size of this military grew during the two world wars but declined in peacetime; most of the time internal governance was managed by police and civil servants.

The police forces were generally of two types: the colonial or civil police and native police.[48] The former was based in Lagos and over time came to be divided into a northern and a southern component. The colonial police force in the north, however, was relatively small: During the 1930s, for example, there were only some 1,200 colonial policemen for the entire region.[49] This police force, controlled directly by the British, was used mainly to enforce political order. The real, day-to-day policing in the north was done by a native police. These numbered some 3,000 in 1939 and were generally an ill-trained force under the command of numerous native chiefs.[50] Within the context of indirect rule, crimes were defined according to Islamic law, as consistent with the British ideology of "respecting native rights and customs." Traditional chiefs were thus given the primary responsibility for raising and managing a native police force to deal with petty crimes and to maintain law and order within the units they governed.

The police force in the South resembled the police force the British had created in other colonies. The British generally sought out ethnic "outsiders," whom they often dubbed "martial races" and trained them for police work. In the case of southern Nigeria, these were the northern Hausas. The officers were exclusively British, often trained in Ireland, where the art of dealing with a colonized people was already well developed. Before the northern and southern colonial police forces were amalgamated in Nigeria in the 1930s, there were about 3,000 policemen in the southern force. After the amalgamation, the number was closer to 4,000 for the entire country – the largest country in Africa – with some eighty British officers.[51] That the British could rule a vast country of twenty million with such a thin coercive presence underlines several factors: the well-honed skills of the British for organizing colonial rule, the vast cultural and technological distance

[48] See Philip Terdoo Ahire, *Imperial Policing: The Emergence and Role of the Police in Colonial Nigeria, 1860–1960* (Philadelphia: Open University Press, Milton Keynes, 1991), chaps. 1 and 2.

[49] Ibid., 93.

[50] Ibid., 47.

[51] See Roberts, "Imperial Mind," 49.

between the British and the people they ruled, and, most important, the cooperation of native elites, who held sway over their own people and who often benefited from the strategy of indirect rule.

In stark contrast to India, the civil service the British created in Nigeria reflected the minimal goals of British colonialism in that county and therefore was not very good: The numbers were relatively small; they were not well trained; and very few Nigerians were incorporated. Once the territory was controlled, a basis for taxation established, and a framework to facilitate trade erected, there was simply no perceived need to improve governance.[52] With indirect rule in place in the north, only a handful of British civil servants were required per emirate, mainly to supervise the emirs, primarily in the area of tax collection and expenditure. At the height of colonial rule in the interwar years, there was only one British administrator per 100,000 Africans in the North. The density of civil servants in the South was naturally a little higher, but not by much, especially in areas distant from Lagos. There were some 430 British officers in all of Nigeria in 1930 and the ratio of officers to the people they ruled was approximately one to 50,000.[53] This ratio improved during the 1930s, but even at its peak in 1938 there was still only one British officer for every 20,000 Nigerians.[54] This figure contrasts – for around the same time – with colonial rule in Korea, where there was one Japanese officer for every 400 Koreans, making colonial Korea fifty times more densely bureaucratized than Nigeria. In and of itself, of course, bureaucratic density is neither a virtue nor a folly. But the relevant point here is that when leaders of sovereign Nigeria eventually sought to utilize the state to stimulate economic development, the state at their disposal was relatively ineffective – which followed from the poor bureaucracy they had inherited from their colonial experience.

Not only were the numbers of civil servants in colonial Nigeria relatively small but the quality was relatively low. Unlike in India, recruitment for service in Nigeria was not exam-based. Rather it was fairly personalistic – in the hands of one individual, Ralph Furse, who interviewed candidates, looking not for "brainpower" but for "force of character," especially among recent Oxford or Cambridge graduates.[55] The ethos of an exam-based, well-trained civil service was thus never really transmitted to Nigeria. Instead, after recruitment, training required to prepare for service in Nigeria was minimal. In the words of one observer, "As late as 1940, out of 110 administrative officers empowered to act as magistrates only thirteen were professionally

---

[52] Or in the words of Andrew Roberts: "Once the foundations of an export economy had been laid and the financial basis of British over-rule secured," there was no need to "innovate" in either government or in the economy. See ibid., 49.

[53] See Nicolson, *Administration of Nigeria*, 228.

[54] See Coleman, *Nigeria*, 33.

[55] See Nicolson, *Administration of Nigeria*, 230; and Roberts, "Imperial Mind," 48–89.

qualified."[56] Moreover, again unlike India, very few Nigerians were incorporated into the civil service, at least until the Second World War.

Colonial government in Nigeria thus developed without unified rule and without such other components of an effective state as a well-organized army, police, and civil bureaucracy. Much of this did not pose any overt problems for the British because their goals for the Nigerian colonial state were minimal. For example, consider the issue of taxation, or, as the British called it, revenue collection. The British made do with a fairly low rate of taxation: Prior to the Second World War tax revenues accounted for no more than 2 to 3 percent of the GDP.[57] Of that, close to 60 percent of the total tax revenues originated in the foreign trade sector, especially from taxing imported liquor.[58] These revenues were the easiest to collect because the points of entry and exit for imports and exports were relatively centralized. By contrast, collecting direct taxes is generally difficult within very poor agrarian economies, and the British also expended minimal effort to that end. They mainly left taxation in the hands of the emirs in the north, where in the early colonial years "tax collection" often resembled "plunder."[59] As the tax system in the north was systematized over the years, it often brought British civil servants fairly deep into the social hierarchy. Nevertheless, these contacts were fleeting and reserved for no more than an occasional encounter between the state and the citizen.

Collection of direct taxes in the south posed real problems. While the Yoruba areas were somewhat easier because they had a tradition of direct taxes and traditional chiefs could be utilized to do some of the collecting, when direct taxes were introduced in the southeast, the local population rebelled and the British were forced to cancel the plan. Over time some direct taxes were collected regularly but with great difficulty: Most of those being taxed were self-employed; large parts of the economy were not monetized; accounting practices were nonexistent; and the ranks of civil servants were far too thin to establish any form of systematic taxation.[60]

---

[56] Nicolson, *Administration of Nigeria*, 49. I do not mean to suggest that there were no skillful and professional administrators. Well-known individuals such as Anthony Kirk-Greene, who served in Nigeria after the Second World War, would qualify any such blanket generalization. I am indebted to Crawford Young for this qualification.

[57] See Helleiner, *Peasant Agriculture*, 296–97.

[58] Ibid., table 50, see also Ekundare, *Economic History of Nigeria*, 106–17.

[59] See Watts, *Silent Violence*, 160–66.

[60] See Helleiner, *Peasant Agriculture*, 206; Ekundare, *Economic History of Nigeria*, 116; and A. W. Pim, "Public Finance," in Margery Perham, ed., *Mining Commerce and Finance in Nigeria* (London: Faber and Faber Limited, 1948), 225–79. Another interesting source, a diary of sorts of a British civil servant, is Walter R. Crocker, *Nigeria: A Critique of British Colonial Administration* (Freeport, N.Y.: Books for Libraries Press, 1971). This "diary" gives a good feel for how remote the colonial government was from many areas supposedly governed, even in the south, and how difficult it was to collect taxes.

A modest tax base and a poorly formed state did not detract from the minimal economic role the British expected governments to play at this time,
both at home and in the colonies. From the middle of the nineteenth century until the Great Depression, Britain championed a free-trading, laissez-
faire empire. Fieldhouse's generalization about the British in much of Africa
applies well to Nigeria: The imperial officialdom had "a very restricted concept of economic management in the colonies . . . . They normally assumed
that the economic development of tropical colonies would follow a 'natural' course. . . . It was not until the 1940s that any colonial ministry began seriously to think of economic development in terms of . . . inadequate
industrialization."[61]

The hands-off policy implied by the ideology of laissez-faire was not always
practiced. The British colonial government in Nigeria intervened where it
was deemed necessary, in particular, in areas essential to British trading interests. The "basic objective" of colonial economic policy, according to Ajayi
and Crowder, was "to stimulate the production and export of cash crops . . . to
encourage the importation of European manufactured goods, and, above
all, to ensure that [this trade] was conducted with the metropolitan country."[62] Following these general objectives, the colonial government in
Nigeria introduced a new currency pegged to the British pound, established
banking, and put custom regulations in place. A major area of intervention
was infrastructure: railways, roads, communications, and a system of naviga-
tion. To be evenhanded, the British also invested in health and education,
areas that were related only peripherally to British trading interests.

The actual data on public expenditures by Nigeria's colonial government
broadly support this discussion of the state's economic role.[63] During the
interwar years the colonial state generally followed a conservative fiscal policy, keeping expenditures in line with revenues. The largest chunk of public
revenues was spent on running the colonial government itself: Civil and police administration absorbed nearly one-third of the total. Expenditures on
health and education, at approximately 15 percent of the total, were also
sizable, an outcome reflecting the active role of missionaries in the making
of colonial policy. Besides public administration, investment in infrastructure (or "public works," as the British called it) was the largest single area of
public expenditure, at approximately 10 percent. The importance of roads,
ports, and railways for trade hardly needs mentioning. What ought to be
noted, however, is that the British encouraged public ownership of utilities,

---

[61] See Fieldhouse, *Colonialism*, 27–28.

[62] See J. F. A. Ajayi and Michael Crowder, "West Africa, 1919–1939: The Colonial Situation,"
in J. F. A. Ajayi and Michael Crowder, eds., *History of West Africa*, 2nd ed. (Harlow, England:
Longman, 1987), 2: 593–94.

[63] I am drawing here on the data presented in Gerald Helleiner, *Peasant Agriculture*, 232–34,
esp. 223, table 55.

setting a pattern with long-term consequences. And finally, also noteworthy is the negligible amount the colonial government spent on agricultural or industrial production.

Thus the British colonial state played a minimal role in promoting production in Nigeria. The government did play some role in promoting agriculture, but mainly in cash-crop production for export. Even this did not lead to any significant changes in agrarian technology, however; for example, the hand hoe was the main agricultural implement when the British arrived in Nigeria and it was still the main one toward the Second World War. Industry was totally ignored. British manufacturers preferred exporting their manufactured goods to establishing industries in the colonies, and the British colonial government actually reinforced these preferences. Moreover, the colonial state "almost never actively encouraged indigenous entrepreneurs to invest in local import-substituting industrial production. The government did not provide medium or long-term loans. . . . There were very few technical schools capable of training men to become managers or businessmen."[64] One has only to recall the contrasting role of the Japanese in Korea to realize that there was nothing inevitable about these outcomes; they were the result of choices the British made. The choices, in turn, had long-term implications, both for the manner in which Nigeria's economy developed and for the nature of the limited colonial state that was developed in that country.

To sum up, Britain in Nigeria created a fragmented and ineffective state on a social base hardly suited for ready transformation into a modern state. Given their minimal goals and the related need to economize, the British simply did not try very hard. Even from a "liberal" standpoint of what constitutes a good, minimal state – something that the British came closer to devising in colonial India – the colonial state in Nigeria left much to be desired. So while the colonial state served the minimal needs of the British, it was also a distorted developmental state in the making.

III. Early Colonial Phase: Economy and Society

Between 1900 and 1930, Nigeria's average per capita income grew at about half a percent per annum and then essentially stagnated until the end of the war.[65] Economic growth in the first three decades was mainly a result of growth in exports of palm oil, groundnuts, cotton, and cocoa: Export output of these and other commodities jumped some fivefold and export value jumped sevenfold. The underlying dynamic has often been explained with reference to Myint's classic model of "vent for surplus," which suggests that, given international demand, such unused or "underused" factors of

[64] Fieldhouse, *Colonialism*, 68.
[65] Helleiner, *Peasant Agriculture*, chap. 1.

production as land and labor were brought into use, facilitating increases in production.[66] This model is consistent with the evidence that colonialism linked a variety of Nigerian markets to the world market. However, Sara Berry's important corrective is also noteworthy: Supply response was not all that "automatic," but required important institutional changes, such as in the organization of landownership patterns and especially in modes of coercive labor organization.[67] Behind such institutional changes were new laws enacted by the colonial state and the not-so-indirect role of the same state in mobilizing labor.

The principal items that were imported in this period were spirits (gin and rum), cotton goods, building materials (cement, iron, steel), railway items, motorcars, bicycles, and various daily consumer goods. These items were either mainly for consumption or to facilitate the colonial state's infrastructural activities. The trade of both imports and exports was controlled by a handful of British companies: In 1949, for example, 66 percent of Nigeria's imports and 70 percent of its exports were controlled by the Association of West Africa Merchants, an association of United Africa Company and five other European firms.[68] This was the classic colonial pattern: exports of commodities and imports of manufactured goods. Moreover, British authorities discouraged Nigerian exports to countries other than the United Kingdom and imposed import quotas to keep out competitive German and Japanese goods.[69] We see once again that the free-trade ideology was often observed in the breach.

British demand for Nigerian products collapsed with the onset of the Great Depression, and foreign trade suffered from 1930 until about the end of the Second World War, with the result that production more or less stagnated and incomes declined.[70] Following the decline in foreign trade, government revenues, which had been dependent on taxing this trade, declined as well. With its resource base so diminished, the colonial state in Nigeria was in no position to provide a Keynesian response of "demand management." Unlike the other cases, especially the Brazilian case, therefore, Nigeria of the 1930s was not marked by the beginnings of governmental intervention to stimulate the economy.

Both the growth and the decline in foreign trade have to be kept in perspective: Nearly 85 percent of the total production was in the subsistence

---

[66] Ibid., 12.

[67] Sara Berry, "Cocoa and Economic Development in Western Nigeria," in Carl K. Liedholm and Carl Eicher, eds., *Growth and Development of the Nigerian Economy* (East Lansing: Michigan State University Press, 1970), 16–27.

[68] See Coleman, *Nigeria*, 81.

[69] See Ekundare, *Economic History of Nigeria*, 214–16.

[70] Dorward thus notes that "the net barter and income terms of trade were to remain below levels of the 1920s until after the Second World War." See Dorward, "British West Africa and Liberia," 443.

or traditional sector, so the local economy was largely insulated from global trends.[71] Both production and productivity therefore probably changed little during this period. A number of factors help explain this stagnation. First, growth of agricultural production for exports had been mainly extensive, facilitating very little technological change or productivity growth.[72] There was thus no technological learning or "spillover" from one sector to the other. Second, colonial land laws made it almost impossible for foreigners to own land and to initiate large-scale plantation agriculture. And finally, the government undertook little or no investment to promote new agrarian technology. Cumulatively, then, in the words of an African economist, "the system and techniques of [agricultural] production remained largely primitive."[73]

Finally, in this brief discussion of the colonial economy, we note the near absence of manufacturing or industry in colonial Nigeria. The special obstacles in the Nigerian case are a mix of factors in the local economy and society combined with factors related to the colonial framework.

We have seen that British manufacturers were more interested at this early stage in selling their products to Nigeria than in setting up industry locally, mainly for economic reasons. But local conditions and colonial institutions were also relevant: Skilled labor was scarce and the costs of importing it rather prohibitive; infrastructure was poor; the domestic market was very small; major trading companies had a strong local foothold and a vested interest in protecting profits from foreign trade; and the empire's open-door policy was well suited to the needs of manufacturers in Lancashire or Manchester.[74] Local, would-be entrepreneurs faced all these same economic problems, plus more. First, there were few indigenous entrepreneurs with experience in risk taking and organizing large-scale industrial production. Second, those that existed faced serious competition from foreign products. And third, the colonial state certainly did not encourage and may even have consciously discouraged industrial growth in Nigeria.

The colonial government, as noted above, did not undertake even the most minimal government activities to promote industry: provide loans, facilitate technology transfer and protect "infant industry," invest in technical and business schools, and/or initiate some direct public investment that would feed industrial efforts. More serious, the colonial state on occasion violated the norms of a laissez-faire state when it "actively discouraged" certain types of local "manufacturing activities."[75] The underlying rationale was

---

[71] See Helleiner, *Peasant Agriculture*, 6–7.

[72] See Ekundare, *Economic History of Nigeria*, 156, 200.

[73] Ibid., 157.

[74] See, for example, the related discussion in Helleiner, *Peasant Agriculture*, 16; and for broader generalization on the subject, see Fieldhouse, *Colonialism*, esp. 90.

[75] See Carl Liedholm, "The Influence of Colonial Policy on the Growth and Development of Nigeria's Industrial Sector," in Liedholm and Eicher, eds., *Growth and Development*, 57.

mainly to protect the interests of British manufacturers, but it also, especially in the case of Lord Lugard and few others in the north, reflected an anti-industrial bias rooted in their own aristocratic backgrounds and in their sympathy for the local rulers.[76] Thus, the colonial state discouraged local textile manufacturing by imposing tolls on caravans carrying local goods but not on those carrying British goods;[77] it levied freight charges that discriminated against African and smaller companies;[78] and it "enforce[d] ... stringent regulations" and "exact[ed] ... heavy trade licenses" on the marketing of African produce.[79]

In spite of the economic and political obstacles, there were some private efforts to initiate manufacturing in colonial Nigeria. Some of these failed; a few succeeded. Early efforts at establishing crushing mills to process palm kernels ran into problems of unreliable supply of inputs, incompetent labor, high costs of supervisory personnel, and a limited market for by-products. Similar problems plagued subsequent efforts. African entrepreneurs also faced a shortage of medium- or long-term capital. Eventually, prior to the Second World War, a few manufacturing plants were established, but mainly by foreign entrepreneurs: a few soap factories in the east by Unilever, a few sawmills and cotton gins in the west, and one cigarette manufacturing plant by the British American Tobacco Company. Even by the standards of developing countries, this was an abysmally low level of industrial development for the middle of the twentieth century.

Shifting the discussion from the economy to the social structure, three sets of changes are noteworthy for their long-term impact on the politics of Nigeria's economic development: the role of missionaries and of the newly educated, the impact of land policy, and the importance of growing regional identities. Missionaries in southern Nigeria penetrated the local society much more deeply than the colonial state ever did. They succeeded in mass conversions, first in Yoruba areas and then in the southeast.[80] Among those who embraced Christianity, a significant proportion belonged to the lower strata, especially former slaves. Moreover, missionaries offered access to education, mainly in English, and this helped to create an English-speaking educated elite in the south. By contrast, as part of the deal Lugard struck with the northern emirs, missionaries were essentially kept out of the

---

[76] One gets a sense in the historical literature that, on occasion, British rulers in the colonies were still fighting out their own proxy "class war" (aristocracy vs. the bourgeoisie) in the colonies, and this long after the battle over the Corn Laws had been lost. This certainly seems to have been the case with Lord Lugard. See, for example, Nicolson, *Administration of Nigeria*, esp. 125–26.

[77] See Carl Liedholm, "The Influence of Colonial Policy," 57; and Dorward, "British West Africa," 410.

[78] See Ajayi and Crowder, "West Africa, 1919–39," 594–97.

[79] See Coleman, *Nigeria*, 83.

[80] For a good overview, see ibid., chap. 4.

north, where Islam was part and parcel of the traditional authority structures that indirect rule sought to preserve. These northern hierarchies would have been profoundly threatened by missionaries, conversion of slaves, and Western education. Thus, Nigeria saw a differential process of social change: spread of Christianity and education in the south and the preservation of traditional authority and Islam in the north.

Even with the introduction of English education by the missionaries, however, the level of education and literacy in Nigeria was still low; at the time of the Second World War, for example, only 12 percent of Nigerian children of school age were receiving instruction.[81] Certainly, the colonial state did not promote education on its own, as there was no perceived need for trained manpower. Missionary education thus focused on "morals," "character," and "religion" but not on vocational training. Moreover, higher education was minimal. By the early 1950s Nigeria had 1,000 university graduates in the entire country, and the majority of them were Yorubas.[82] This differentiation at the higher level reflected a much deeper and growing divide: By the early 1940s literacy in the Roman script was about 18 percent in the west, 16 percent in the east, and 2 percent in the north.[83] The north was thus basically without an English-speaking middle class.

Given the low level of literacy in precolonial Nigeria, the introduction of even a thin layer of educated people was bound to have important consequences. The educated professionals in the south often challenged and undermined the authority of traditional chiefs. Had it not been for colonial support and for the land policy, tribal chiefs would have lost even more of their legitimacy than they did. Moreover, the newly educated slowly but surely challenged the colonial state and eventually sought control of that state. Unlike in other cases such as India, however, the nationalist impulse in Nigeria was relatively weak, especially prior to the war, for several reasons related to education: The number of educated was small; education was introduced late and the educated were just beginning to come of age; and, from the very beginning, the educated were divided along ethnic lines. According to Coleman, "The interwar period was largely one of nationalist gestation, when new influences were being felt, new associations were being formed, and a new generation was coming of age."[84]

Colonial land policy varied from region to region and imparted lasting legacies. These were especially significant in the north, where, for example, Lugard interpreted past practices as implying that land was not really "owned" by the emirs but was "communal property."[85] This, in turn, led to a

---

[81] Ibid., 126.

[82] Ibid., 141.

[83] For details, see White, *Central Administration in Nigeria*, esp. 118.

[84] See Coleman, *Nigeria*, 202. See also J. B. Webster, "African Political Activity in British West Africa, 1900–1940," in Ajayi and Crowder, *History of West Africa*, vol. 2, chap. 17.

[85] This discussion draws on Watts, *Silent Violence*, esp. 158–78.

policy whereby much landownership came to be vested in the colonial state. Since land could not be readily sold, a landlord class did not develop and the white settler option was essentially eliminated. In practice, taxpaying peasant smallholders came to dominate agriculture. The status of traditional chiefs was also diminished, insofar as they appeared more and more to be doing the bidding of colonial masters. Indirect rule thus led to several perverse outcomes: a real landlord class that might have had an interest in developing agriculture never came into being, and a rational-legal authority structure, with rule by competent civil servants, never really emerged. What continued instead was a traditional, hierarchical society, more or less frozen in time, in which governance below the thin colonial structure was mainly in the hands of personalistic, often corrupt, and despotic rulers.

Finally, as a result of various political and economic changes discussed above, social distinctions across the regions of Nigeria were beginning to be further accentuated. Foreign trade, for example, was differentially concentrated: The western region traded four times more than the northern region, with the eastern region somewhere in between. It comes as no surprise therefore that per capita income in the west was twice that of the north around the Second World War. As we have seen, education was unevenly distributed. In turn, the nature of elites and their aspirations varied across regions: Whereas the northern elite wanted to minimize socioeconomic change so as to protect their political position, those in the south were a product of such changes and wanted even more change, including access to state power. These deepening differences would create additional problems for future collective action. Given the framework of an already weak central state, a fragmented indigenous elite was thus a serious political problem in the making. Prior to the war, however, British rule still appeared secure and the fault lines of future problems were difficult to detect, though they were only a decade or two off.

IV. Late Colonial Phase: State and Politics

The Second World War marked a turning point in the evolution of the political economy of colonial Nigeria. Britain mobilized the resources of many of its colonies, including Nigeria, to pursue its war efforts. The colonial state in Nigeria thus became more statist, initiating new polices to control the economy and ensure a steady supply of resources. This trend toward statism was maintained and intensified in the postwar period, with the goal not so much to promote production as to extract and distribute existing resources. These political economy trends were sustained by underlying political forces: a colonial state that was increasingly on the defensive, willing to appease and to concede power to demanding indigenous groups, and a fragmented nationalist leadership more concerned with building patronage networks and shoring up its power base than with promoting some broader conception of the "national" or "public" good. A commodity boom that started during the war and continued afterward sustained this perverse political economy for a period. In retrospect, however, it is also evident that the outlines of a distorted state were by now clear, a state that in due course would prove incapable of either governing or stimulating industrialization in Nigeria's commodity-dependent economy. The following discussion of the late colonial phase focuses first on emerging political trends and then on the patterns of state intervention in the economy.

Northern and southern Nigeria were more or less ruled as separate political entities until the war. For administrative convenience, southern Nigeria was further divided into west and east in 1939. While this division was really not well thought through – although it did reflect Britain's continuing penchant for the easy way out in its African colonies – it did mark the formal beginning of what would eventually turn out to be a deep and bitter three-way political division of Nigeria. The onset of the war created a shortage of British civil servants. As a result, power and administration further devolved from the minimal center to the three regions, such that by the end of the war the regions came to be endowed "with an individuality."[86]

As if to confirm these growing trends, Britain in 1945 announced a new constitution for Nigeria – known in the literature as the Richards Constitution – that came into effect in 1947. This constitution created a central legislature in which, for the first time, the northern and the two southern regions were supposed to participate. James Coleman's observation is pertinent: "Prior to 1947, there really was no central government in Nigeria."[87] But this constitution turned out to be too little, too late. For one thing it was widely opposed by Nigeria's emerging political class. And in addition to creating a central legislature, it also created regional councils that became the focus of regional identities. By means of a revised constitution in 1954, formal and substantive powers essentially devolved to the three regions, leading a major newspaper to editorialize that henceforth "economically as well as politically there will be three Nigerias."[88] Any move toward a proper centralized government that may thus have begun in 1947 – however doubtful – was certainly reversed by 1954, continuing instead the longer-term trend toward a fragmented, ill-formed colonial state.

The weak and fragmented impulse of Nigeria's anticolonial movement has to be understood at least in part against this background. Initially shaped by a fragmented colonial state, Nigeria's nationalist movement during the interwar years, especially compared with India's, was not a very significant political force. Over time the divided movement further disunited an already weak central state. Over the next two decades there were spurts of nationalist

---

[86] Coleman, *Nigeria*, chap. 11.
[87] Ibid., 50.
[88] The editorial from *West Africa* is cited in Crowder, *Story of Nigeria*, 236.

activity,[89] but by 1960, when a weakened Britain granted independence to Nigeria, the nationalist movement was still largely elitist and divided along personalistic, tribal, ethnic, and regional lines.

Further, the Nigerian anticolonial movement had been confined mainly to the south, as the traditional elite in the north ruled in alliance with the colonial power and had little incentive to oppose it. Moreover, since the British ruling strategy had kept missionaries and Western education out of the north, the usual developing-country intelligentsia – barristers, doctors, educators, and other professionals – that has often spearheaded nationalist movements elsewhere was simply missing.

By contrast, the colonial state had fostered different types of societies in the south. Commerce and education gave rise both to an intelligentsia and to urban workers. Some of the educated went overseas and, as elsewhere, came back imbued with ideas of self-determination and national sovereignty. The Second World War also provided fertile ground for political activism, especially because Britain was now ruling Nigeria with fewer civil servants but had an even greater need to control the society and the economy. In practice, growing wartime statism meant wage controls, lower producer prices for exported commodities, and further limits on credit. Nationalist politicians such as Nnamdi Azikiwe mobilized not only workers unhappy with wage controls but also other dissatisfied elements in the society. Nigerian soldiers who had participated in the war also came back less intimidated by white superiority and feeling a greater sense of empowerment. Nonetheless, all this did not form the basis for a significant nationalist movement, as intraelite divisions sapped the movement's political energy.

James Coleman identified several factors that help to explain the weakness of Nigeria's nationalist movement: a divided elite, resulting from a prior weak sense of a nation; the absence of a transtribal, transregional commercial class; the absence of a coherent colonial state; and the fact that the British increasingly conceded the demands of indigenous elites.[90] While essentially correct, these points can be restated more parsimoniously: The framework of the colonial state conditioned the nature of the nationalist movement. One can then identify two sets of causal mechanisms. First, the varying ruling strategies adopted by the fragmented colonial state for different regions created diverse regional societies, with different elite interests. The problem was therefore not some antecedent "primordial" tribal affinities per se. After all, basic ethnic divisions characterized Indian nationalist elites as well,

---

[89] The best study remains Coleman, *Nigeria.* Also of related interest is Richard Sklar, *Nigerian Political Parties: Power in an Emergent African Nation* (Princeton, N.J.: Princeton University Press, 1963). A quick overview of the subject is to be found in Olajide Aluko, "Politics of Decolonization in British West Africa, 1945–1960," in Ajayi and Crowder, *History of West Africa,* esp. 2: 706–16.

[90] Coleman, *Nigeria,* conclusion, esp. 411–13.

but they were able to overcome them in the process of forging a nationalist movement. A second factor was probably at work as well: There was no coherent powerful colonial state to inspire the development of a unified nationalist movement. The underlying logic here is that a powerful enemy enables opposing elites to overcome their fragmented identities to forge a united front. Moreover, the object of a powerful colonial state also generates a sense that the end of the struggle will yield significant rewards of power and privilege. But the postwar colonial state in Nigeria was neither coherent nor powerful, and by then, the British were more interested in concessions and accommodation than in confrontation. That a Nigerian nationalist movement never really developed thus becomes comprehensible.

The Richards Constitution of 1947 was opposed by many Nigerians, not so much on its substance but on the grounds that it was imposed without consultation. Yet the so-called nationalists did not oppose the significant devolution of power to the regions implied by the constitution.[91] And when the British agreed to consult – taking the steam out of any possible unified struggle – the Nigerians turned upon each other with suspicion. The tripartite administrative division of the country had already begun to provide a focus for political entrepreneurs to mobilize communal "imaginations" into ethnic politics. The fact that each of the regions was dominated by different tribal groups – Yorubas in the west, Ibos in the east, and Hausa-Fulanis in the north – provided the raw material for this mobilization. Instead of focusing on the British, Nigerian politics increasingly concerned itself with real or imagined threats of "Fulani domination," of "rising power of the Ibos," or of the "plans of the more educated and commercially advanced Yorubas to run post-independence Nigeria."[92]

Competing ethnic political tendencies found expression in the emergence of political parties that quickly became identified with the dominant groups of each of the three regions.[93] As in other colonies, the British conducted limited elections. The results of the 1951 elections confirmed that there was no national political party in Nigeria; instead, the outlines of a polity fractured along tribal-ethnic-regional lines were already emerging. The British were also by now in no mood to undertake any significant political engineering. In the aftermath of the bloody division of the Indian subcontinent into India and Pakistan, they were mainly looking for graceful exit strategies in Africa. Aimed at preparing Nigeria for "self-rule," the new constitution of 1954 decentralized real political power into the three regions, essentially marking the end of any nationalist impulse in Nigeria, however limited. According to the new arrangements, national revenues were

[91] Ibid., chap. 12. For a somewhat different interpretation that tends to view Nigerian nationalists as more concerned about national unity, see Crowder, *Story of Nigeria*, chap. 16.
[92] See, for example, Aluko, "Politics of Decolonization," 710.
[93] For details, see Sklar, *Nigerian Political Parties*, passim.

to be divided among the regions in the same proportion as their original contribution to the whole (the principle of "derivation" instead of "need"); marketing boards, established during the war and by now critical sources of public revenue, were increasingly to be brought under regional control; elections in different regions were to be conducted under different rules; and both the civil service and the judiciary were regionalized. Nigeria was ruled under this constitution through independence and until the military coup of 1966, when a different government was forcibly established and a bloody civil war ensued.

Although the question of how power and resources would be distributed in a sovereign Nigeria became a dominant issue, there was a fundamental problem: National power, like national wealth, has to exist before it can be distributed. The failure to understand and act on this key political insight by both the British and the Nigerians was the essence of the tragedy of state construction in colonial Nigeria, as well as in many other parts of Africa. We have seen that the colonial authorities did not construct a centralized state. A coherent nationalist movement that could have overcome the collective action problem of creating centralized authority never materialized. And finally, regionalization of the civil service in 1950s precluded the possibility of a national civil service that could have provided a functional substitute of sorts for missing centralized authority.

On this last critical point, at the end of the Second World War, Nigeria was run by some 1,400 senior civil servants, of whom only seventy-five were Africans.[94] As noted above, this was not a very high quality civil service, with even the British members chosen rather personalistically. The civil servants primarily managed the infrastructure (thus, Railways, Marine, and Public Works Departments employed nearly 800 of the total) and provided general administration (with nearly 500 senior employees). A few civil servants also served in agriculture, education, and police. Those employed were mainly generalists who focused their energies on the minimal tasks necessary for the functioning of the colonial state.

Nigerian politicians had increasingly demanded "Nigerianization" of the civil service: the employment of large numbers of Africans at higher levels. This process was relatively slow until about 1954, when the British obliged by hiring more Africans. But the process of Nigerianization of the civil service also coincided with the growing three-part regionalization of Nigeria, as outlined in the 1954 constitution. Educated Africans were readily available in the west, where with Lagos as a base, there was also a tradition of a better civil service. Nigerianization there proceeded fairly rapidly and smoothly, at least in the early years. The north, by contrast, had very few qualified indigenous personnel but, fearful of southern domination, preferred expatriates to southern Nigerians. The attempt to create their own civil service

---

[94] This discussion draws on Nicolson, *Administration of Nigeria*, 256–300.

was hurried and superficial. Quick training courses focused on how to wear uniforms, on etiquette and mores, and more generally on ceremonial rather than on problem-solving roles.[95] The problems faced in the east were somewhere between those of the west and the north, with the quality of the resulting civil service closer to that of the west.

Meanwhile, the Federal Civil Service was also expanded and filled rapidly with Nigerians. Between 1955 and 1960, the number of Nigerian senior civil servants grew from 550 to 2,308. Many expatriates also left around this time. According to a close observer of the situation, the growth and rapid Nigerianization of the Federal Civil Service was "haphazard," "confused," and driven by considerable "political interference." The resulting bureaucracy thus lacked "confidence, leadership, decision, and initiative."[96]

To sum up the discussion so far, the interaction of a weakened Britain and assertive Nigerians served to concretize the fragmentation of the colonial state, led to a poor-quality, regionalized civil service, and produced a weak anticolonial impulse that readily fractured along particularistic lines – not a good beginning for a new state. Most obviously, these problems would contribute to continuing problems of political instability in Nigeria, as political elites focused more on securing their respective power bases than on pursuing any larger public good. To put it in a different way, the British colonial impact on Nigeria produced a weak public realm, both in terms of organizations and in terms of a cultural ethos, that encouraged the appropriation of governmental functions and resources by private actors. This pattern of state-economy interaction during the late colonial phase in Nigeria became much more pronounced in the postindependence period.

V. Late Colonial Phase: State and Economy

The Nigerian economy performed moderately well in terms of growth in the late colonial phase. Since the colonial state also intervened more heavily in the economy in this period, it would be tempting to propose some connection between the growing statism and higher economic growth. However, the proposition linking statism to economic growth does not hold for the Nigerian materials. While state intervention in the economy did facilitate some growth, especially in manufacturing, Nigerian economic growth in this phase was driven for the most part by an international boom in commodity markets. Moreover, from the onset state intervention in the economy exhibited trends with problematic long-term implications: near exclusive reliance on taxing foreign trade for public revenues, wasteful "social" expenditures, and an inability of the state to promote indigenous capitalism and manufacturing.

[95] Ibid., 294.
[96] Ibid., 297–300.

Conceding that Nigerian statistics are not always reliable, we can nonetheless say that the Nigerian economy appears to have grown at about 4 percent per annum during the 1950s.[97] With an annual population growth rate of some 2 to 2.5 percent, the per capita income grew at 1.5 to 2 percent per year.[98] This was a marked improvement over the prewar per capita growth of approximately half a percent per year. Underlying this growth was increasing investment that grew from some 7 percent of the GDP in 1950 to 15 percent in 1960. Also notable, however, is that the domestic savings rate in the same period actually fell from 9.5 percent in 1950 to 7.5 percent in 1960.[99] Clearly, neither the more activist state nor private actors were saving more than before. The gap between domestic savings and overall investment was made up by foreign resources: direct foreign investment and Nigeria's newly empowered regional governments drawing down Nigeria's own "foreign reserves," which had been built up during the pre-1954 commodity booms, related first to the Second World War and then to the Korean War.

Within these macro trends, the Nigerian economy during this phase continued to be dominated by traditional agriculture (about half of the total production), produced mainly for domestic food consumption. Growth in this sector, at approximately 2 percent per annum, barely kept up with population growth.[100] Underlying this sluggish growth was the relative neglect of this sector by the government, an issue to which I return below. Production growth was thus mainly extensive. It continued to depend on low-level technology and was propelled for the most part by a growing labor force and the cultivation of additional land.

The main source of economic growth throughout this late colonial period was foreign trade. The demand for such Nigerian commodities as palm products, groundnuts, and cocoa increased during the war and stayed high until about 1955. Prices for some of these products rose sharply, especially during the Korean War. Nigeria imported mainly consumer products, as little effort was devoted to developing industrialization. And growth in export-oriented agriculture was also mainly extensive. While the colonial state devoted some resources to technological development in cash crops, the overall level of technology remained low: As late as the mid-1960s, the main instruments of agricultural production continued to be "hoes, cutlasses, axes and knives"; the use of fertilizers, too, was limited.[101]

Manufacturing also grew rapidly during this period, but from a very low base. If manufacturing constituted about 0.5 percent of the GDP at the

---

97 The factual economic information in the account that follows is drawn mainly from three sources: Helleiner, *Peasant Agriculture;* Ekundare, *Economic History;* and Sayre P. Schatz, *Nigerian Capitalism* (Berkeley: University of California Press, 1977).

98 See Ekundare, *Economic History,* 250.

99 Helleiner, *Peasant Agriculture,* 26.

100 Ibid., 28.

101 Ibid., 45; and Ekundare, *Economic History,* 280.

beginning of this period, toward the end, after significant growth, its over-all share was still only some 3 percent. Most of this growth, moreover, was generated by foreign investors who produced such consumer products for the growing local market as textiles, cement, rubber products, beer and soft drinks, and oil products.[102] Manufacturing was first encouraged during the war years, when incomes started to grow, but scarcity of shipping discouraged imports and some de facto import substitution took place. Nigerian nationalists drew the same policy lesson from this temporary delinking from the global economy as did nationalists elsewhere in the developing world, namely, that it is protectionism and not laissez-faire that supports national industry. These policy lessons, however, were not put into practice until the late 1950s, and then mostly after independence. The colonial state also raised tariffs on imports, but the logic was more to collect revenues than to promote domestic manufacturing. Nevertheless, foreign investors took advantage of these tariffs and produced for the protected market; indigenous entrepreneurs, however, failed to respond to the same incentives.

Economic growth, fed mainly by a commodity export boom, was paralleled by growing state intervention in the Nigerian economy. A number of factors promoted this growing statism. First, Britain's wartime needs encouraged greater political control of the economy. Second, following the war, with the growing significance of Keynesian economics and welfare state politics in Britain and elsewhere in the West, statism was by now in the air. This Western ideology focused more on state intervention for "welfare provision" and relatedly for "demand management" than it did on the direct stimulation of production. Third, growing participation of Nigerians in the colonial state further encouraged a greater role for the state, to some extent by stimulating manufacturing but mostly by building infrastructure and encouraging education and other "welfare" expenditures. And finally, resources were increasingly available to fuel an activist state, and taxation of growing foreign trade filled the public coffers.

What is notable about the pattern of state intervention in the Nigerian economy is that it got off to a perverse start, and over time, such perversities only intensified. A central task here and in the next chapter is to identify these perversities and then connect them to state distortions and to the ensuing poor economic performance. If persuasive, this claim will strengthen one of the major arguments of this study, namely, that it is the type and not the degree of state intervention that determines the patterns of economic progress in low-income countries.

Patterns of state intervention in late colonial Nigeria were influenced both by British needs and by the growing political impact of Nigerian

---

[102] Ibid., 295. See also Schatz, *Nigerian Capitalism*, chaps. 1 and 6. While Schatz's focus is mainly on the postindependence period, one can still glean important insights from his work about the late colonial phase.

political forces. Three areas of intervention are especially important: patterns of revenue extraction, patterns of spending, especially on education, and attempts to stimulate indigenous manufacturing. It is also important to note what the state neglected, namely, traditional agriculture. This simply continued the existing British political neglect of production activities in their African colonies. Emerging Nigerian elites reinforced this tendency, and because peasant farmers were never really mobilized as part of the anti-colonial struggle, they did not constitute a vital constituency for the emerging leaders. Thus, the political neglect of agriculture and its unfortunate outcome reflected the interests of both the British and the new elites. Since food production probably constituted half or more of the total national production at this time, this neglect was an early and costly mistake.

In trying to understand the emerging nature of the Nigerian state as an economic actor, we turn first to revenue extraction, or taxation, while emphasizing that the role of the Nigerian public sector in the economy during the late colonial phase was not all that great. At this stage it generated only one-third of the gross capital formation, which was low even by Africa's standards. Nearly 70 percent of all public revenues were generated by taxing foreign trade.[103] At the same time direct taxes contributed only about 20 percent of total revenues,[104] because of the relatively superficial downward reach of the colonial state. The trend of taxing foreign trade began in the interwar years and continued in the postwar years, as foreign trade grew sharply. One of the major sources of public revenue was custom duties on imports, averaging some 20 to 30 percent at this early stage – and this was well before there was any talk of infant industries or import substitution. Exports were also taxed, both directly and indirectly. This indirect taxation through the institution of marketing boards (MBs) was substantial, with long-term harmful consequences.

To ensure a steady supply of industrial inputs within planned expenditures, British authorities during the Second World War started purchasing Nigerian exports at fixed prices. From there it was only a short step to "the introduction after the war of permanent marketing boards to control prices paid to peasant producers."[105] While the main rationale for MBs was price stabilization, their main utility over time became revenue collection. The crude underlying mechanism was just one more means of appropriating agrarian surplus: MBs would buy exportable commodities from peasants at a fixed price and then sell them internationally, often at a higher price, and keep the difference. Helleiner's excellent work on the subject suggests the following conclusions. During the war, Nigerian peasants were certainly taxed through this mechanism and thus supported the war effort; between

[103] Ekundare, *Economic History*, 233.
[104] Helleiner, *Peasant Agriculture*, 210–11, table 50.
[105] Michael Crowder, "The 1939–45 War and West Africa," in J. F. F. Ajayi and Michael Crowder, eds., *History of West Africa*, vol. 2, 2nd ed. (England: Longman, 1987), 679.

1947 and 1954 the earnings of MBs were kept mainly in low-yield British securities, thus again benefiting the colonial rulers; and from 1954 on revenues of MBs became a major source of funding expenditures by newly empowered regional governments, aimed at development, but with mixed results.[106]

The colonial state's heavy dependence on taxing foreign trade led to various perverse trends. First, not only the economy, but also governmental resources were heavily dependent on international commodity demand. This classic colonial situation, in which the government's capacity to intervene remained a function of commodity exports, continued in Nigeria well into the oil-boom period and beyond, when oil prices declined. Second, the pernicious MBs not only squeezed the already poor peasantry but over time also generated incentives against agricultural production. After 1954, moreover, the resources in the hands of the regionalized MBs further eroded the capacity of a national state to function effectively. And finally, the MB resources also became a source of corrupt and irregular public spending by the new regional elites.

A second problematic area of state intervention concerned an inclination toward social spending, as exemplified by the significant public expenditures in primary education that Nigerian federal and regional governments undertook in the post-1955 period. In principle, such expenditures should be desirable not only as an end in themselves but also as a valuable investment in human capital and thus in development. Unfortunately, the Nigerian project failed to achieve its stated goals and ended up an exercise in massive waste. Public energies to expand primary education were expended mainly in the South, where the new nationalist elites were concentrated; the northern elite, by contrast, remained wary of rapid socioeconomic change and continued to resist the expansion of education. As for motives, the emerging southern elite really did not have any long-term, national development project in mind. The elites in both the southwest and the southeast instead viewed education as a route out of backwardness and toward upward mobility within the colonial structure. A focus on promoting mass education also allowed elites to differentiate themselves from the exploitative colonial government that had often ignored education and to establish their own credentials as men of the masses.

In this way universal primary education was proclaimed a goal in much of the south. Despite the enormous resources devoted to this end, the results fell short: Public contracts to construct school buildings often resulted in shoddy or incomplete construction; qualified teachers, books, and supplies were not readily available; and overall follow-through from the new political leadership was missing. As a result, by the late 1950s, "two million primary students . . . were receiving substandard instruction from ill-trained teachers

[106] Helleiner, *Peasant Agriculture*, chap. 6.

in overcrowded and inadequate facilities."[107] Scarce resources were thus utilized ineffectively, mainly to satisfy the short-term political needs of the emerging leadership. This, too, was a longer-term perversity in the making.

Finally, it is important here at least to touch on the emerging role of the state in promoting manufacturing, especially by national entrepreneurs, as these early trends were indicative of future patterns. A fuller discussion follows in the next chapter. It is important again to keep the overall context in mind: While manufacturing grew rapidly in the 1950s, only 3 percent of the GDP originated in manufacturing in 1960. We are thus referring to a preindustrial economy.

The fact that a Department of Commerce and Industry within the government was first established only in 1947 testifies to the minimal role played by the colonial state in early industrialization. As the participation of Nigerians in the government increased, the state came to play a more active role in promoting industry. A series of policy measures to promote industry was adopted, for example, tax reliefs, favorable import rules for producers, and the establishment of industrial estates. Whereas established foreign enterprises responded to these incentives, indigenous entrepreneurs did not. Why not? The simple answer is that such entrepreneurs simply did not exist: "Most Nigerians lacked any knowledge of managerial and technical skills required for industrial development."[108] But this is not the complete explanation. While it is true that one would not expect a significant presence of an experienced, entrepreneurial stratum, the real question is why, given appropriate incentives, were more indigenous entrepreneurs not forthcoming?

Sayre Schatz argues that the real obstacle to industrialization was not so much the "missing entrepreneur" as the obstacles in the "economic environment" that limited profitability: scarce skilled manpower, a shortage of capital equipment, the small size of the local market, poor infrastructure, and limited markets.[109] This argument, too, is incomplete. Many other developing countries also faced situations in which there were few skilled entrepreneurs and numerous "market imperfections" that generated obstacles to profitability and thus to risk-taking enterprise. But this is not so much an explanation as a description of underdevelopment. Why, then, do some countries manage to break out of such low-level traps while others do not? Why was the situation in Nigeria especially precarious?

---

[107] Ibid., 307. Some other analysts qualify this conclusion by suggesting that these problems were indeed real, but they were really short-run problems; on this view, the impact of public spending on education was more benign over the longer run. See, for example, Sara Berry and Carl Liedholm, "Performance of the Nigerian Economy, 1950–1962," in Carl K. Liedholm and Carl Eicher, eds., *Growth and Development of the Nigerian Economy* (East Lansing: Michigan State University Press, 1970), 80. I challenge this position in greater detail in the next chapter.

[108] See Ekundare, *Economic History*, 295. This argument also finds support in Helleiner, *Peasant Agriculture*, 263–65.

[109] See Schatz, *Nigerian Capitalism*, esp. pt. 2.

Analytical consistency demands a restatement of path dependency. Thus, relative levels of backwardness matter, as does the importance of different starting points. Compared with other countries discussed above, Nigeria in the 1950s was simply more backward, having far fewer skilled entrepreneurs and facing far greater environmental obstacles. But other countries have also faced obstacles and overcome them. Among the factors that helped some countries in this regard was the constructive role of nationalist and developmental modern states, whether cohesive-capitalist or fragmented-multiclass. From the beginning this important variable was missing in Nigeria.

The federal government did not play an important, direct role in promoting national industry during this phase. Although it did adopt some important new policies in the 1950s that attracted foreign investors and generated some "easy" import substitution, much more support would have been needed to move nascent national industry to the fore. But this support was not forthcoming, mainly for political reasons.[110] First, the federal government was weak, as was manifest in the fact that total public revenues were shared nearly evenly at this stage between the federal and the regional governments.[111] The impact of Nigerian nationalists, moreover, was felt mainly on regional governments. To the extent that the nationalists helped to direct the federal state as an economic actor, it was mainly toward increasing social expenditures – and not toward industrial development. Nearly one-third was spent on running the government, and the remainder went to infrastructure, education, and health.[112] Had the federal government tried to promote national industry directly, it would have been stymied by the absence of the well-trained manpower necessary for such interventions.

The public bodies that did take on direct promotion of industry at this stage were not so much federal agencies as development corporations (DCs). Their activities were funded mainly from resources accumulated by the MBs, and the functioning of these, in turn, was heavily influenced by the regional governments.[113] The developmental activities of DCs were quite significant, especially in the more advanced western region. Overall the DCs during the 1950s commanded nearly one-third of all the resources available to the regional governments, or nearly 10 percent of the total public investment in Nigeria. Since this expenditure was specifically aimed at stimulating economic development, the role of DCs was potentially vital. They promoted plantations, buying equity in foreign enterprises, owning manufacturing

---

[110] It is important to note here that this discussion is not informed by any implicit dependency type of bias against foreign investment and for national investment. It is, however, informed by a historical view that no sizable country has ever industrialized successfully without significant national participation.

[111] See Ekundare, *Economic History*, 234, table 12.2.

[112] See Helleiner, *Peasant Agriculture*, chap. 9, esp. 233, table 55.

[113] This discussion of the activities of the DCs is heavily informed by ibid., chap. 10.

activities, and supporting (mainly by providing loans and equity participation) small- and medium-sized indigenous entrepreneurs.

While the DCs had some success in promoting plantations and in their activities with foreign enterprise, their record in promoting indigenous enterprise was poor. This was a harbinger of things to come. Publicly owned manufacturing activities in such areas as oil mills, boat yards, and a canning factory were the least successful: "a high proportion of these projects were badly planned and managed."[114] Loans to local entrepreneurs were provided without proper credit checks and were also influenced by "politics" in the sense that the recipients often had personal connections to powerful regional politicians or were politicians themselves. Equity participation in Nigerian-owned firms was similarly corrupt.

Personalism of this kind in state–private sector interactions is common in the developing world. We encountered it even in the successful Korean case. What was distinct about Nigeria, however, was the utter lack of "discipline" and "expertise" within the state sector. Diagnosing the failures of these DCs, Helleiner cites Sir Arthur Lewis to argue that the more appropriate role of the DCs would have been to impart "knowledge and experience" of industrialization.[115] Precisely – but such knowledge and experience were missing, however, reflecting the poor quality of civil service that had come into being. What also would have helped was a keen political commitment on the part of the emerging elite to some larger conception of the public good that could have translated into the political discipline to demand performance from public bodies. As discussed above, however, both the public ethos and the level of expertise were relatively weak in the emerging state. The results included perverse patterns of state intervention in the economy, with detrimental consequences for Nigeria's long-term development.

VI. Conclusion

This chapter has provided the background for understanding the larger puzzle of Nigeria's ineffective state and failed industrialization. The next chapter builds on these materials to provide a fuller solution to the puzzle. For now, we recap the main points developed so far and briefly situate the discussion in a comparative context. First, the various polities and economies that the British incorporated into Nigeria were profoundly backward to begin with: They had not experienced order and prosperity of a centralized state; centuries of slavery had robbed them of their best; they existed in relative isolation, carrying out subsistence agriculture without plows and without draft animals; and they hardly used written language. These rudimentary political economies had a long way to go before they could be transformed

---

[114] Ibid., 260.
[115] Ibid., 265.

even into what the preindustrial world elsewhere recognized as centralized agrarian bureaucracies.

While British colonialists established a semblance of order and authority over these disparate polities, the effort they expended in their African colonial ventures was minimal. Britain's "effortless" colonialism laid the foundations of a distorted state and a commodity-dependent economy. What the British wanted most in Nigeria was a revenue base to finance colonial rule and to use that colonial rule to facilitate trade, and they created the ruling arrangement to satisfy those minimal needs. The result was a fairly poorly formed state without a central authority, without a national civil service, and without any real capacity to reach down into the society to facilitate even such elementary government functions as systematic taxation. Instead, there developed various personalistic and despotic forms of rule, justified by the ideology of indirect rule. The British used this minimal state to promote trade and financed the operation of the colonial state mainly by taxing this trade. Rather than undertaking any significant economic interventions, the colonial state presided over ongoing backwardness and the emergence of a classic colonial economy that exported commodities and imported manufactured goods.

Commerce and missionary-led education propelled new social forces that would eventually challenge these arrangements. Unfortunately, these challengers also never came together in a cohesive and purposive nationalist movement. A fragmented colonial state encouraged the regionalization of the nationalist movement, and new, regional forces further tore apart the weak centralist impulse of the colonial state. Thus, the late colonial phase saw a regionally fragmented Nigeria with a low-quality civil service. As state intervention in the economy grew, this distorted state increasingly imparted new perversities in such areas as dependence on taxing foreign trade for public revenues, premature obsession with social expenditures, and ineffective public promotion of industrial activities. These were long-term trends in the making, with sharply negative consequences for Nigeria's development efforts.

To conclude, it may be useful to juxtapose Nigeria's colonial encounter to that of other cases discussed above, especially Korea and India. At the turn of the twentieth century, Nigeria was already at a much lower level of political and economic development than the other cases discussed in this study. Half a century of colonial rule did little to bridge this gap. On the contrary, the processes of state formation and industrialization had by midcentury proceeded much further in the other cases than in Nigeria. Why? If the relative brevity of colonialism is thought to be a major variable, the contrasting experience of Korea under Japan provides a quick check on that argument. Clearly, the main issue of concern instead is the nature of colonialism. The British in Nigeria sought to pursue their agenda of political control and economic exploitation very differently than the Japanese did in Korea: Japan sought to control and exploit while transforming the traditional Korean society, whereas the British in Nigeria pursued similar goals while squeezing the traditional society. The Japanese in Korea thus left behind the rudiments of a modern state and an industrial economy on which a rapidly industrializing political economy could be built, while Nigeria in 1960 found itself ill-prepared to pursue such a journey.

The comparison of Nigeria and India on the dimension of the "modernizing" impact of colonialism is also useful, especially because both were British colonies. The British in India left behind a considerably more effective state than in Nigeria. Why? The British had ruled India for much longer than they had Nigeria. This was consequential because nineteenth-century British colonialism in India differed from twentieth-century British efforts in Africa. Control of India lay at the heart of British imperial expansion in the nineteenth century. A centralized state in India, including a well-developed armed force, was part and parcel of these global designs. There was also a belief in this early period that such colonial investments would reap economic payoffs. By the time the British colonized Nigeria, however, they were much "wiser." The aim was minimal: to keep other European competitors out. Whatever political arrangement facilitated such political control was deemed sufficient, especially if it could also be financed with local revenues. This approach essentially reinforced the power of existing local despots that enabled the mobilization of some revenues and an economic exchange of manufactured goods for commodities.

The differing patterns of colonial state formation in India and Nigeria were further reinforced by the more and less cohesive nationalist movements that developed in these respective cases. Of course, political entrepreneurs in India could more realistically use their history to create a nationalist imagination than could their counterparts in Nigeria. However, the incentives for nationalists created by more or less centralized colonial states also differed. It made sense for Indian nationalists to unite and undertake mass mobilization against a cohesive enemy, the British colonial state. By contrast, Nigerian nationalists were mostly content to assert control over their own regions and/or ethnic groups. Both the colonial pattern of state formation and the nationalist movement pushed India toward a more coherent, modern state. By contrast, both colonial and nationalist forces moved Nigeria in a fragmented direction, creating the façade of a modern state but enabling various personalistic and sectional interests to gain and maintain control.

9

Sovereign Nigeria

Neopatrimonialism and Failure of Industrialization

Nigeria's attempts to promote industrialization have been a dismal failure. If modern manufacturing contributed some 3 to 4 percent of Nigeria's GNP at independence in 1960, the share of manufacturing toward the end of the century was still under 10 percent. Nigeria's economic performance is clearly the worst of the cases discussed in this study. Especially puzzling is that Nigeria's rulers apparently channeled billions of the country's oil dollars into industrial development, yet reaped no significant gains. What happened? This chapter finds its answer in the negative role of the neopatrimonial state. Whatever the current regime, the Nigerian state has repeatedly lacked the commitment and the capacity to facilitate economic transformation, as state elites focused their energies on maintaining personal power and on privatizing public resources. The result – to restate a theme emphasized by the late Nigerian intellectual Claude Ake – was not so much that development efforts failed but that they were never really made.[1]

A variety of factors, some more and some less persuasive, may be invoked to explain Nigeria's economic failure. The view that Africa's economic woes are rooted in antiagrarian policies pursued by self-seeking, pro-urban rulers, for example, has only limited applicability to Nigeria.[2] Nigerian agriculture has not performed all that poorly; when it has, the reasons have included factors other than pro-urban policies.[3] More important, this tells us nothing about why industrial growth has also been so poor. Another argument – this one miscast – may stress Nigeria's vulnerability to global economic

---

[1] See Claude Ake, *Democracy and Development in Africa* (Washington, D.C.: Brookings Institution, 1996), passim, but esp. 7. Ake is generalizing about all of sub-Saharan Africa, so it is fair to assume that he intends the argument to include his native Nigeria.

[2] This view is associated with Robert H. Bates, *States and Markets in Tropical Africa: The Political Basis of Agricultural Policies* (Berkeley: University of California Press, 1981).

[3] For evidence on agricultural performance, see Tom Forrest, *Politics and Economic Development in Nigeria*, rev. ed. (Boulder, Colo.: Westview Press, 1995), 136–37 and chap. 9.

forces.[4] The relevant question is why Nigeria has been incapable of translating globally fueled economic booms into sustained economic growth. Relatedly, one could also invoke a Dutch disease type of argument, positing that windfall commodity exports overvalue exchange rates and create dependence on cheap imports, a situation that becomes a liability when export earnings decline.[5] But many countries manage such problems – even other oil exporters in the developing world, such as Indonesia, were more successful than Nigeria in utilizing oil wealth. And finally, one may stress such domestic socioeconomic weaknesses as the poor quality of indigenous entrepreneurs, low levels of technical competence, and/or a poorly trained but activist working class.[6] These are important issues that in fact connect the present focus to the earlier emphasis on Nigeria's disadvantageous starting point. But especially prominent among the failures of the neopatrimonial state were the failures to promote entrepreneurship, technology, and a disciplined, productive working class.

The hypothesis that a neopatrimonial state is at the root of a variety of political and economic problems in Nigeria (or, for that matter, in other parts of Africa) is not novel and has received considerable attention in the literature.[7] While I build on this material to situate Nigeria comparatively, it is also the case that important analytical links are not always clear in the literature, which often does not specify exactly how such a state harms economic growth. This analysis looks specifically to the failure of the neopatrimonial state to foster such economic capabilities as entrepreneurship, technology, infrastructure, and a productive working class. Similarly, the literature often fails to address why a neopatrimonial state does what it does, namely, privatize public resources, why the Nigerian state is so neopatrimonial to

---

4 Such a view is commonly expressed in many official documents of the Nigerian government.

5 See, for example, M. Roemer, "Dutch Disease in Developing Countries," Discussion Paper 156 (Cambridge: Harvard Institute of International Development, 1983).

6 For an overview of such subjects, see Paul Kennedy, *African Capitalism: The Struggle for Ascendancy* (Cambridge: Cambridge University Press, 1988); and Paul Lubeck, ed., *African Bourgeoisie: Capitalist Development in Nigeria, Kenya and the Ivory Coast* (Boulder, Colo.: Lynne Rienner, 1987).

7 With reference to Nigeria, see Richard A. Joseph, *Democracy and Prebendal Politics in Nigeria: The Rise and Fall of the Second Republic* (Cambridge: Cambridge University Press, 1987); and Peter M. Lewis, "Economic Statism, Private Capital, and the Dilemmas of Accumulation in Nigeria," *World Development* 22, no. 3 (1994): 437–51. For a generalization of such a view to sub-Saharan Africa, see Thomas M. Callaghy, "The State as Lame Leviathan: The Patrimonial Administrative State in Africa," in Zaki Ergas, ed., *The African State in Transition* (London: Macmillan, 1987), 87–116; and Richard Sandbrook, *The Politics of Africa's Economic Stagnation* (Cambridge: Cambridge University Press, 1986). A useful conceptual essay that goes back to Weber and distinguishes patrimonial from neopatrimonial states (the latter have a façade of a modern state while mainly using public resources for private use) is Jean-François Medard, "The Underdeveloped State in Tropical Africa: Political Clientelism or Neopatrimonialism," in Christopher Clapham, ed., *Private Patronage and Public Power: Political Clientelism in the Modern State* (New York: St. Martin's Press, 1982), 162–92.

begin with, and why a public realm failed to emerge. The inheritance of a sovereign but weakly centralized state with a poor sense of a nation from its colonial past was discussed in the last chapter. The current chapter considers why repeated efforts to create a more effective sovereign state – democratic or authoritarian – also failed and what the economic consequences of this failure were.

An important caveat, the same as for the earlier period, is in order. Factual information about Nigeria remains in short supply. The observation offered by the *Economist* in its 1982 survey of Nigeria still holds: "This is the first survey published by the *Economist* in which every number is probably wrong. There is no accurate information about Nigeria."[8] Given these constraints, I have estimated as best I could, resting the argument more on gross facts and less on nuance and detail.

The discussion is organized chronologically. Discussed first are democratic rule and an open economy that emerged from colonial rule. The sections that follow focus on how and why a variety of governments – military and civilian – squandered oil resources. There is a brief analysis of the half-hearted efforts at structural adjustment in the late 1980s – again with very few positive economic results and therefore again pointing to the continuing centrality of an ineffective state. In sum, neither a variety of regime types nor a range of policies seemed to have mattered much for economic outcomes in Nigeria. The economy remained mainly reactive to shifts in global demand for oil. Underlying this commodity-dependent economy was the absence of both an effective state and indigenous capitalism, which could have laid the groundwork for national industrialization.

I. A Poor Beginning: From Sovereignty to Civil War

The British left Nigeria in 1960 more for their own reasons than because they were pushed out by the nationalist movement, which, as we have seen, was neither cohesive nor mass-based, certainly nothing like what we encountered in India. Following the Second World War, Britain's international position was weakened and colonialism had become profoundly delegitimized. With a belief that friendly regimes in former colonies would facilitate continued economic relations, British rulers began a negotiated retreat from much of Africa, including Nigeria.[9] While sovereignty brought a wave of optimism to Nigeria, the underlying conditions were not auspicious from the standpoint of sustained development. There was simply not an effective state that could help to put Nigeria on an upward trajectory.

---

[8] *Economist* (January 31, 1982): 4.

[9] For a general discussion of decolonization in Africa along these lines, see D. K. Fieldhouse, *Black Africa, 1945–1980: Economic Decolonization and Arrested Development* (London: Allen and Unwin, 1986), esp. 231–33.

The key ingredients of this state were a fragmented and contentious polity with little commitment on the part of leaders to national development; an incompetent bureaucracy that reflected the broader political fragmentation and personalism; and a relatively small armed force that quickly adopted the broader political tendencies of regionalism and patronage politics. All of these issues were continuities from the colonial period, and many of them worsened in the early sovereign phase. The cumulative impact was gross state failure, leading to a military coup and a civil war in 1966.

Within a few years of decolonization, the basic, long-standing fault lines of the Nigerian polity came to the fore and were manifested in the ethnic cleavages that divided the Hausa-Fulani north from the Yorubas in the southwest and the Ibos in the southeast.[10] Each tribal grouping dominated its respective region, which was also home to other tribes. While far from internally homogeneous, these three main groups differed from each other along a number of dimensions: language, a sense of unique historical ancestry and customs, and to an extent religion, with Islam predominant in the north and Christianity widespread in the south.

Power sharing in the central government and sharing related resources were the main sources of conflicts. Moreover, even after independence, the north continued to be organized as a series of emirates controlled by traditional Fulani rulers, whereas in the south a variety of educated and commercially oriented men dominated the political life of both the Yorubas and the Ibos. These differences made for varied policy preferences in what was otherwise a fairly naked ethnic struggle over power and resources. Yorubas and Ibos could mobilize higher levels of education and economic achievement, while nearly half of all Nigerians lived in the poor north. As in cases of ethnic conflict elsewhere, however, prior ethnic differences only hardened as respective political elites mobilized ethnic sentiments to their service.

At independence, modest compromises among the leadership of the main groups enabled the formation of a sovereign central government. In retrospect, however, it is clear that the British presence had been vital for the functioning of the state. Decolonization, therefore, "left Nigeria with no centralized authority with indigenous roots."[11] Thrust into this political vacuum, the main Nigerian contenders fought bitterly, going from crisis to crisis between 1962 and 1966, leading to a military coup and the infamous Biafra War.[12] These were the roots of early state failure.

After independence the educated and commercially advanced Yorubas occupied a prominent political position in Nigeria. Soon enough, however,

---

[10] A good study of ethnic and political conflicts in postindependence Nigeria is Larry Diamond, *Class, Ethnicity and Democracy in Nigeria: The Failure of the First Republic* (Syracuse, N.Y.: Syracuse University Press, 1988).

[11] Forrest, *Politics and Economic Development in Nigeria*, 39.

[12] These crises are ably analyzed in Diamond, *Class, Ethnicity and Democracy in Nigeria*. The discussion of specific political conflicts that follows draws mainly on this study.

factionalism reemerged among Yoruba elites, pitting the two politically prominent chiefs, Awolowo and Akintola, against each other. This conflict was mainly about personalities, intra-Yoruba ethnic tensions, and competing ambitions. Seeking to outmaneuver Akintola, Awolowo sought to trim the patronage rewards within the western region, driving Akintola to forge a winning political alliance with the north. In this seemingly prosaic struggle lay the origins of what was to become an enduring ruling alliance of northern elites and some of the Yoruba factions. One is left to wonder what Nigeria's political trajectory might have been if Awolowo had won the power struggle and succeeded in trimming the patronage politics. Might he have been another Nehru, introducing the necessary political unity and public-spiritedness that would have enabled Nigeria to graduate from dysfunctional neopatrimonialism to a functioning, fragmented-multiclass state? Even in Nigeria, it seems, there were historical beginnings that never came to fruition, cautioning analysts against a view that what happened had to happen, as well as against simplistic notions of continuity or path dependence.

A political alliance of northern elites and Chief Akintola's faction of the Yorubas proved formidable. In 1963–64 after marginalizing Awolowo, they ganged up on the Ibos over control of the results of a national census that would have documented the size of various ethnic groups, thus further fueling power-sharing conflicts. Chief Awolowo responded by mobilizing workers and calling a general strike in 1964. What appeared to be a classic instance of class politics quickly also assumed a regional-ethnic dimension because the central government – now dominated by northern elites and foreign enterprises – joined hands against workers, who were mainly southerners. The army was called in, but not before the workers had gained some significant concessions. And finally, a fraudulent national election in 1964 and an even more fraudulent regional election within the western region in 1965 took the conflict to the streets. As leaders hurled invectives at each other and mobilized ethnic hatreds, the military intervened, bringing the brief democratic beginning to an end – with northern elites and some Yorubas on the winning side and Ibos and other Yorubas on the losing side.

Development was not much of a possibility under these circumstances. For one, the political elite was preoccupied with securing and maintaining power. There was no national vision. In the words of one analyst, Nigerian "politicians had no real commitment to national economic development."[13] And another concludes that "public policies and the general direction of development were not sharply defined."[14] These contentious

---

[13] See James O'Connell, "The Political Class and Economic Growth," reprinted as appendix D in Peter Kilby, *Industrialization in an Open Economy: Nigeria, 1945–1966* (Cambridge: Cambridge University Press, 1969), 378.

[14] Forrest, *Politics and Economic Development in Nigeria*, 39.

beginnings only reinforced the already growing view of the citizenry that the state was a partisan agent of distribution in society and not a neutral umpire or "night watchman" – and even less an agent of national good that might promote economic growth and industrialization.

What about a counterfactual, then? If Nigerian elites had reached some compromises on running the government, could the state have been a more effective agent of development? The answer is: maybe somewhat more, but not by much. The most important piece of evidence for this conclusion is that individual regional governments – which were not as debilitated by ethnic conflicts and which controlled a significant share of developmental resources – were also not very effective at promoting economic growth. The bottom line can thus be stated very simply: Political leaders in Nigeria were more interested in utilizing public resources for personal gain or for the gain of their kin and communities than in pursuing such a public good as economic development. The issue of why this was so is considerably more complex.

Certainly, the issue of developmental commitment of leaders varies widely, as we have seen with Rhee versus Park in Korea, Goulart versus the military rulers that followed in Brazil, and Nehru versus Indira Gandhi in India. Nigeria, however, stands as an extreme case of the absence of such commitment. How and where leaders are socialized appears to be an important underlying variable in any explanation of why some are more developmentally oriented than others.[15] Park and a number of Brazilian military leaders, for example, were socialized in national security–oriented armed forces, and Indian elites in a prolonged nationalist movement. Nigeria had no such national crucible. A colonial state that accentuated ethnic distributional concerns only fed the personalistic and communal yearnings of Nigerian leaders and their quest for relative gains across elite and community lines.

We have seen that the bureaucracy that Nigeria inherited from its colonial past was of poor quality, in stark contrast to India, which reached independence with a civil service that was enormously professional in the Weberian sense – competent, hierarchical, and rule-bound. During the late colonial phase in Nigeria, especially in the 1950s, the quality of this bureaucracy declined further and the trend only continued after independence.

Politicians were very much in command in this early postindependence period in Nigeria. Higher civil servants, in particular, enjoyed great respect and prominence in society, being better educated than most other members of the society, relatively anglicized, and inheritors of offices hitherto occupied by white colonialists. Moreover, they were generally more modern

---

[15] This issue of leadership commitment is slightly different from the issue of why leaders in some places are more corrupt than in others. The latter draws attention to institutional constraints on and public scrutiny of leaders.

and developmentally oriented than the political elite, who were relatively "traditional," "communal," and "patronage-oriented."[16] Nevertheless, these political leaders enjoyed substantial nationalist legitimacy – however shallow and short-lived this proved to be – and were very much in command of their British-style parliamentary democracy. While civil servants thus took decisions on "technical, noncontroversial matters . . . on matters of real interest to politicians . . . policies were actually determined by the politicians, and they ensured that civil servants implemented such policies."[17]

The tendency of political leaders to emphasize personal power and relative gains for their own ethnic communities quickly seeped into the bureaucracy. At independence there were some 70,000 personnel employed by the federal and regional governments (not including the military, local governments, or the parastatals), with some 60 percent of the senior employees being Nigerians. The bureaucracy grew rapidly after independence, employing some 115,000 by 1965.[18] Much of the growth resulted from patronage-oriented political pressures. Several pieces of evidence support this conclusion. First, the political economy in this early period was hardly a classical, state-directed, import-substitution economy; it was rather a relatively open economy, welcoming foreign investors and mainly oriented toward promoting commodity exports. Second, much of the bureaucratic growth occurred at the regional level, where significant attempts to consolidate ethnic bases of power were under way and civil service jobs helped to build support among the more educated. And finally, the resulting jobs went mainly to ethnic kith and kin, with little regard for merit.[19]

The result was bureaucratic development in any direction but a Weberian rational-legal one, though there were important regional variations. The bureaucracy in the Yoruba-dominated western region, for example, was superior to that of the other regions. Indigenization had proceeded the furthest in this region prior to independence, facilitated by the availability of educated Yorubas who demanded jobs.[20] Toward the end of the period under discussion, the Yoruba bureaucracy was considered "efficient"

[16] O'Connell, "Political Class and Economic Growth," 378–79.

[17] See Ladipo Adamolekun, *Politics and Administration in Nigeria* (London: Hutchinson and Company, 1988), 85. For a somewhat different perspective that suggests that civil servants were considerably more powerful, even in the first republic, see Peter M. Koehn, *Public Policy and Administration in Africa: Lessons from Nigeria* (Boulder, Colo.: Westview Press, 1999), 61. As I read the evidence, the power of civil servants grew significantly but mainly in some subsequent periods.

[18] See Ladipo Adamolekun, "Postscript: Notes on Developments in Nigerian Administration since 1970," in D. J. Murray, ed., *Studies in Nigerian Administration* (London: Hutchinson University Library for Africa, 1978), 322.

[19] Koehn, *Public Policy and Administration in Africa*, 18–23.

[20] Ibid., 19.

and characterized by a sense of "esprit de corps."[21] But even this judgment needs to be kept in perspective: Even in the western region the quality of bureaucracy just below the top was relatively poor, manifest most clearly in the repeated failure to collect income tax.[22]

The quality of the bureaucracy in the Hausa-Fulani north was low throughout its ranks. Even as the northern regional government grew, the native authorities of individual emirates continued to exercise control. The personnel of these emirates were recruited according to ascriptive criteria, such that there was not even the façade of a modern state. The regional government of the north also sought to expand and indigenize, however haltingly. But again, given the low level of formal education in the region, there was great scarcity of competent personnel. By 1996, for example, one-third of the senior administrators had essentially been shifted from various native authorities to Kaduna, the regional capital, and quite a few expatriates continued to occupy responsible positions on paid contracts.[23] Any sort of coherent and competent regional bureaucracy thus remained a distant goal.

The growing power of the north at the federal level further impeded the project of building a good national bureaucracy. At the time of independence, only twenty-nine of the 4,398 administrative officers of the federal government were northerners,[24] again reflecting the paucity of well-educated people from the region. As the political power of the north grew, however, northerners came to find this situation unacceptable. There was no ready solution. The needs of a growing state could have been pursued only by employing more southerners – a politically unacceptable solution. So some expatriates were kept on and many unqualified or underqualified northerners were hired, based often on personalistic and ascriptive criteria. This way the national civil service, too, grew in defiance of the basics of a good bureaucracy, and professionalism was repeatedly subverted by political interference. With bureaucratic behavior "greatly influenced by personal preferences, loyalty considerations, and face-to-face interaction," and decisions frequently "reached on an ad hoc basis without reference to written documentation," the foundation was laid for the massive corruption that was to follow in subsequent periods.[25]

Finally, we turn to the third main component of the state: the armed forces. When the British left Nigeria, the military was relatively small – some

[21] See D. J. Murray, "The Impact of Politics on Administration," in Adebayo Adedeji, ed., *Nigerian Administration and Its Political Setting* (London: Hutchinson Educational, 1968), 22.

[22] See George M. Walker, "Personal Income Tax Administration," in Murray, *Studies in Nigerian Administration*, esp. 279–82.

[23] See Murray, "Nigerian Field Administration: A Comparative Analysis," in Murray, *Studies in Nigerian Administration*, 97, n. 2.

[24] See Koehn, *Public Policy and Administration in Africa*, 21.

[25] Ibid., 22.

8,000 armed men – and more of a constabulary force trained for internal security than for military purposes.[26] Moreover, it was already ethnically divided, with mostly northern Hausas recruited by the British to the rank and file, but southerners, especially Ibos, recruited to the officer ranks because of their education and willingness to join. Of the thirty commissioned officers in 1959, for example, six were northerners, ten were Yorubas, and fourteen were Ibos.[27]

Between 1960 and 1966 the armed forces also grew from some 8,000 to 11,000 men, and from 61 to 511 officers.[28] This nearly ninefold growth in the officer corps over six years was rapid, indeed, and with long-term consequences. First, haste brought in individuals without appropriate professional training and experience, leading to "deficiencies in professional experience and organizational cohesion" that seriously affected the "professional efficiency, discipline, and morale of the army."[29] In fact, junior officers were often better educated – creating conflicts in the hierarchy and disciplinary problems. And all this occurred within the first few years of independence.

The armed forces were also plagued by growing ethnic conflict, mainly northerners versus Ibo officers. The increasingly powerful Hausa-Fulani elite found this situation unacceptable and sought to alter it, leading to the establishment of quotas within the armed forces: As many as half of the new officer-rank positions were reserved for northerners. The result was again that unqualified or underqualified officers started filling the ranks, generating hostility between them and the better-qualified Ibo officers. Whereas similar problems in the civil service undermined the professional character of the national bureaucracy, the result in the army was more ominous: This ethnic hostility was a civil war in the making.

The national political situation deteriorated sharply in 1965, with ethnic and regional conflicts on the rise, leading the army to intervene in a bloodless coup in early 1966. Six of the seven majors who organized the coup were Ibos. And so while its leaders proclaimed it a "national coup," there was a widespread sense that it was Ibo-led and that it had dramatically shifted national power away from the northerners.[30] Junior officers from the north reacted sharply, in turn, pulling off a much bloodier countercoup within a few months. Thousands of Ibos and numerous Ibo army leaders were killed, leading others to proclaim Biafra – the Ibo-dominated east – a sovereign country and precipitating the civil war, which the Ibos lost.

In retrospect it is clear that the state that Nigerian leaders inherited from the British was not much of a state. The new leaders, personalistic and

---

[26] See Jimi Peters, *The Nigerian Military and the State* (London: I. B. Tauris, 1997), 76.

[27] Ibid., 79.

[28] See Robin Luckham, *The Nigerian Military: A Sociological Analysis of Authority and Revolt, 1960–1967* (Cambridge: Cambridge University Press, 1971), 90.

[29] See, respectively, ibid., 90, and Peters, *Nigerian Military and the State*, 78.

[30] See Luckham, *Nigerian Military*, chaps. 1 and 2, esp. 43–50.

preoccupied with communal affairs, accentuated these defects by further polarizing ethnic conflicts and by pursuing kinship gains at the expense of national development. Similar tendencies also quickly seeped into the bureaucracy and the armed forces, undermining their professionalism. We turn now to a consideration of the political underpinnings of what would be minimal industrial development.

Nigerian per capita income during this phase grew at the modest rate of some 2 percent per year,[31] most of this growth stimulated by commodity exports. Oil exports contributed nearly 0.5 percent annually to growth in production; the other major exports were palm products, groundnuts, and cocoa.[32] The economy at this stage was mainly agricultural, with agriculture contributing some 50–60 percent of the GDP and manufacturing still under 5 percent. Marketing boards in each of the main regions kept agricultural prices below world prices, probably hurting production. Nevertheless, agricultural production grew during this period, as indicated both by the fact that food imports were minimal despite very low tariffs and by the fact that food prices fell.[33] This growth was facilitated by colonization of new lands and by productivity improvements facilitated by better inputs. But industrial growth – the main subject of the present discussion – was not insignificant: Starting from a very low base, it grew at some 8 percent per annum.[34] This growth, however, was problematic, as neither indigenous entrepreneurs nor public sector enterprises contributed much. Instead, most of this growth originated with foreign corporations, which mainly undertook last-stage-assembly type of production that was import- and foreign-exchange intensive. Only the growing oil revenues kept balance-of-payment crises at bay.

We begin by observing that this was not a planned economy. Such planning documents as were prepared – mostly by expatriate economists – did not receive much political support, as there was no cohesive national economic thinking or direction. As elsewhere in the developing world following independence, there was talk of supporting national capitalism and even of pursuing "socialism," but in Nigeria it was short-lived. These mutterings came mainly from the more nationalist leaders from the south, but they rapidly lost political ground to northerners. Moreover, both indigenous capitalists and public sector enterprises proved ineffective. The less nationalist northern leaders thus turned to foreign economists to create a set of "open" policies that provided the basic macroframework for the economy.

---

[31] See Peter Kilby, *Industrialization in an Open Economy: Nigeria, 1945–1966* (Cambridge: Cambridge University Press, 1969), 9.

[32] See Sayre Schatz, *Nigerian Capitalism* (Berkeley: University of California Press, 1977), 18.

[33] See Kilby, *Industrialization in an Open Economy*, 14.

[34] Manfred Berger, *Industrialization Policies in Nigeria* (Munich: Weltforum Verlag, 1975), 236.

Peter Kilby described the Nigerian economy of the period as essentially "open,"[35] meaning it had a conservative monetary policy and, given the availability of foreign exchange, an open trading regime. Tariff levels averaged 20 to 30 percent, in contrast to the much higher levels of India and Brazil during this period, and the internal price structure was "fairly closely related to world prices – bringing efficiency in domestic resource allocation."[36]

Given the weaknesses of the national center, a fair amount of economic drama unfolded within each region, with some similarities and some variation from one region to the next.[37] They shared considerable dependence on marketing boards for revenues, a widespread pattern of political use of these revenues to build patronage networks and enhance personal wealth, and a focus on such "distributional" activities as education and health. In terms of the variation, the government in the western region – given the influence of nationalists and Fabian socialists – went furthest in its attempts to promote industry directly – a little bit of India in Nigeria. The government in the east, though also activist, was mainly ineffective in its support of the private sector. And the economic attitude in the north, by contrast, ruled as it still was by various emirs, was mainly defensive, that is, it was looking to ensure that the developmental distance between the north and the south did not widen even further. The north was also reluctant to embrace "modernity" out of fear that modern education and new industries would create new centers of power that would threaten traditional power, which was based on the prerogatives of birth and lineage.

How in this context did the key economic actors – foreign and national firms – behave? First, foreign multinational corporations (MNCs) continued to dominate Nigeria's modern manufacturing. A survey in 1963, for example, documented that 68 percent of the equity in large-scale manufacturing was private and foreign, 10 percent was private Nigerian, 3 percent was owned by the federal government, and the remaining 19 percent was owned by regional governments. This trend had originated in the colonial period, and given the weak nationalist impulse, independence did not mark any discontinuity. On the contrary, foreign investors were encouraged – even if quietly – with favorable incentives, especially tariff protections on finished products for the domestic market.[38]

The end of the colonial monopoly and modest tariffs imposed by the sovereign Nigerian government – mainly as a source of revenue rather than as a part of a planned ISI strategy – raised concerns with such foreign

---

[35] See Kilby, *Industrialization in an Open Economy.*
[36] Ibid., 1.
[37] This discussion builds on Forrest, *Politics and Economic Development in Nigeria,* 35–36.
[38] Schatz thus notes that disappointment with both national capital and public sector initiatives quickly set in, leading to an "unacknowledged shift" in the early 1960s toward "increasing reliance upon foreign-owned enterprises." See Schatz, *Nigerian Capitalism,* 6. This shift also corresponded with the growing power of the north within the federation.

companies as the British United African Company that they might lose their Nigerian market.[39] A typical corporate strategy was to increase production locally and then, given the high cost of employing expatriates for management, ask the national government for further protection. Manufacturers of both beer and cigarettes, for example, followed this pattern, and the federal government obliged.[40] Some de facto import-substitution industrialization thus took place, mainly in consumer industries and mainly led by foreign companies.

This new foreign investment was not part of any coherent industrialization strategy advanced by the government, however. The federal government was far too ineffective to have any such strategy, and even the policies to attract foreign investors were not very effective. Interviews with companies revealed, for example, that fiscal incentives offered by the state were not a huge draw.[41] Instead, the main motivation for investors was to protect their Nigerian market. New investment thus remained in existing branches of industry, and there was little industrial diversification.[42] Moreover, much of the production was last-stage production, based largely on imported inputs, including management.[43] This reflected the supply inelasticity of the indigenous economy and the failure of the government to set terms for foreign investors. This was a long-term pattern in the making: Foreign investors were interested in Nigeria only as long as plenty of foreign exchange was available to import nearly all the inputs and then to assemble the products and sell them to Nigerians, often behind some protectionist walls (the exception was the oil sector). This low-value-added import- and foreign-exchange intensive strategy of industrialization would, of course, work as long as oil exports boomed; short of that, this was long-term industrial failure in the making.

If foreign investors did facilitate some industrial growth, indigenous efforts were unsuccessful – not surprising, given an ineffective state. First, a fair amount of what passed for public sector investment was really not in productive sectors but rather was channeled into such symbol-driven expenditures as luxury hotels, airlines, a merchant marine, stadiums, and television stations. Second, ethnic conflict politicized important economic decisions, for example, the building of a steel plant in the late 1950s. After years of wrangling, it was finally decided that each region would have its own steel plant, but in the end none of them was built. Third, public investments were made in such areas as cement, textiles, breweries, and oilseed crushing plants – nearly all of which ran at a loss. The government's own review of their operation concluded that root problems included "nepotism and favoritism, ethnic rivalry over board membership and employment, ministerial

---

39 See Berger, *Industrialization Policies in Nigeria*, 46.

40 Along with cement and textiles, beer and cigarettes constituted nearly half of Nigeria's modern manufacturing at this stage. See Kilby, *Industrialization in an Open Economy*, chap. 4.

41 See Berger, *Industrialization Policies in Nigeria*, 240.

42 Ibid., 236–37.

43 See Kilby, *Industrialization in an Open Economy*, 24.

interference, and poor management and administration."[44] In sum, the state sector contributed little "to rais[ing] indigenous technical capacity from its low level or to accelerat[ing] structural change towards intermediate and basic industry."[45]

Why Nigerian entrepreneurs also failed to respond to economic opportunities, especially those that would have required a medium- or large-scale response, is harder to understand. There are two related and mutually reinforcing components to the puzzle of "missing entrepreneurs." First, indigenous entrepreneurs with managerial and technical skills necessary to undertake large-scale manufacturing were indeed in short supply. Second, and more important, was the failure of the sovereign state to provide an adequate framework for the development of national capitalism.

The issue of scarcity of capable entrepreneurs was examined by Peter Kilby, who in the mid-1960s undertook detailed case studies of public efforts to promote indigenous industry by providing loans, establishing industrial estates, and offering a variety of other incentives. The results, he argued, were generally disappointing, mainly because of inadequate entrepreneurship:

> With few exceptions, Nigerian industrialists are unwilling to provide continuous surveillance of their business operations, in terms of both physical supervision in the factory shop and in utilizing the principal instrument of managerial control, written records. This disposition is combined with a general lack of interest in production efficiency and in possibilities for improving product quality. Nigerian entrepreneurs are generally slow to move when their operations hit a snag. They show little propensity to undertake innovations.[46]

Deeper reasons for such inadequate entrepreneurship, he suggested, were not so much economic – especially because the policy framework was open and facilitated competition – as "traditional socio-cultural factors." And the way out would necessarily require broader social change, including changes in the political, ideological, bureaucratic, and technological spheres.[47] Another survey of small- and medium-sized Nigerian entrepreneurs, conducted at about the same time, concluded similarly that technical and managerial experience and capacities were very low and contributed major obstacles to further growth, that the "ability – rather than willingness" – to respond to economic opportunities was missing, and that the government could play a "strategic role" in helping entrepreneurs.[48]

---

[44] Cited in Forrest, *Politics and Economic Development in Nigeria*, 35.

[45] Ibid., 8.

[46] Kilby, *Industrialization in an Open Economy*, 338.

[47] Ibid., 341–42.

[48] See John Harris, "Nigerian Entrepreneurship," in Carl K. Eicher and Carl Liedholm, eds., *Growth and Development in the Nigerian Economy* (East Lansing: Michigan State University Press, 1970), 319–20. See also E. Wayne Nafziger, *African Capitalism: A Case Study of Nigerian Entrepreneurship* (Stanford, Calif.: Hoover Institution Press, 1972).

"Poor entrepreneurship" is, of course, more a description of underdeveloped capitalism than an explanation of a weak indigenous developmental impulse. It is no surprise, then, that a list of potential explanations that has been offered reads like a list of explanations one could offer for Nigeria's overall failure to industrialize and grow rapidly: the economic power of foreign trading companies, a long history of involvement of compradors, a lack of managerial and organizational experience, the siphoning-off of the most talented individuals into the civil service, the waste of capital by marketing boards, or, most diffusely, the fostering of unproductive use of capital.[49] While there is a grain of truth in several of these explanations, the fact is that well-constructed sovereign states have been able to overcome such obstacles and facilitate the emergence of robust entrepreneurial classes, as we have seen in the other country studies. What was missing in Nigeria all along, however, was precisely such a developmental commitment and capacity on the part of the state.

Some specific examples of what a more effective state in Nigeria might have done to promote national entrepreneurs may help to support the general argument. First, we reiterate that this unstable, neopatrimonial state had no long-term framework for promoting indigenous entrepreneurs: little or no protection for infant industries, no business schools or training for entrepreneurs, no systematic efforts to facilitate the use of advanced technology, and little or no capacity to bargain with foreign corporations to help to indigenize some management and technology. Second, the logic behind the means adopted to promote private economic activities was often personal gain rather than economic effectiveness. Regional governments, for example, generally favored contractor finance to promote projects. As this inevitably brought significant kickbacks to decision makers, it perpetuated both rent seeking and ineffective projects, including poor-quality infrastructure.

Among the more indirect contributions the state might have made was to create and train a more effective working class. Instead, the state often caved in to populist challenges. And finally, given the low level of competence within the state, Nigeria's small entrepreneurial class did not have much faith in it. Thus, a majority of industrial managers surveyed in the 1960s rejected the idea that the government could help to train private sector personnel, mainly because of the low quality of such public-supported programs.[50] Clearly, this state was in no position to promote national capitalism, and any indigenous development here would be in spite of rather than because of state actions.

Given this picture, the limited efforts as were undertaken to promote national entrepreneurs did not amount to much, for example, in trying to

---

[49] For such a summary, see Forrest, *Politics and Economic Development in Nigeria*, 26.
[50] See Berger, *Industrialization Policies in Nigeria*, 152.

promote a private national textile industry.[51] Textiles would have been an ideal import-substitution industry for Nigeria: There was demand; cotton was available; technological requirements were not overly onerous; and textiles tend to be a labor-intensive industry. Early public support of private efforts, however, led to failed firms. In addition to poor-quality entrepreneurship – poor decisions, poor management, petty trader mentality, poor salesmanship, and bad accounting practices – there were failures that could be traced back to politics. Thus, regional elites jockeyed for regional advantage rather than choosing the most economic solutions to production problems; poor infrastructure cost dearly (in one case, for example, imported looms were damaged in transport due to poor road conditions between Lagos and the North); and the quality of labor was poor, because of lack of education, tribal hiring practices, and populist activism. There was also no follow-up by the authorities after providing financial help, especially in terms of technical help, and there was no effort to achieve quality control. When initial efforts to promote national private industry failed, Nigeria's leaders very quickly turned to the more efficient foreign industry in textiles, as well as in other industries, creating additional obstacles for the development of national capitalism.

To sum up this discussion, Nigeria started out as a democracy and an open economy. Under the Nigerian circumstances, however, these turned out not to be suitable conditions for economic development and welfare maximization. Democracy proved rather fragile when it came to accommodating ethnic hostilities; indeed, democratic competition exacerbated such conflicts. Problems of weak central authority were further compounded by the fact that both the normative and the organizational components of an effective public realm – in the political, bureaucratic, and the coercive components of the state – remained diffuse and underdeveloped and encouraged personalism and communalism within the state. Shortcomings in the public sector directly reflected the state's own weaknesses, and the small entrepreneurial class could not count on consistent state support. Whatever industry did develop was mainly foreign and tended to produce low-value-added, last-stage assembly of products for the local market, creating an economy that would remain heavily dependent on imported inputs and the availability of ample foreign exchange for continued growth.

II. The Nature of Military Rule

The Ibo-led military coup of early 1966 was soon followed by another military coup, this time led by northerners. This in turn precipitated a civil war.

---

[51] I am drawing here on Kilby, *Industrialization in an Open Economy*, esp. chap. 10. While Kilby emphasizes poor entrepreneurship as the main cause of failure, he provides enough material to recast the argument. For examples of failure in industries besides textiles (such as in construction), see also Schatz, *Nigerian Capitalism*, chaps. 9–12.

The northern-dominated military eventually prevailed in the Biafra war, but not easily; the civil war lasted more than two years. The victorious military rulers announced with some bravado their commitment to reconstruct the Nigerian state and at last to commence Nigeria's long journey toward economic development. But the military rule lasted until the end of the century, with a brief civilian interregnum during 1979–83 and numerous coups and countercoups during the remaining period. And unfortunately, the results of any reform efforts came up short. Personalistic patrimonialism continued, and efforts to utilize Nigeria's immense natural resources for sustained economic development were miserable failures. By 1991 after two decades of oil boom, bust, and apparent structural adjustment, for example, manufacturing still contributed only 8 percent of the national product (and declined to 5 percent by 1995). And per capita incomes (excluding oil income) were not much higher in the 1990s than they were in the pre–civil war period.[52]

The period 1970–91 corresponds roughly to the years of increase in oil revenues, followed by a decline in oil earnings and a brief experiment with externally imposed neoliberal economic policies that were abandoned in 1991 when oil prices rose again and brought a renewal of the earlier patterns. An important analytical question for the Nigerian case is why – unlike Korea or Brazil – even prolonged military rule failed to provide an alternative to personalistic and patrimonial politics. The answer lies in the nature of the political rule under the military, which had neither a developmental ideology nor the professional talent to offer itself as a distinct political force in the society. The military thus found itself dependent for governance on the very problematic civil service. Instead of creating a cohesive-capitalist alternative to corrupt, civilian politics, therefore, the syncretic rule of military and civil servants in Nigeria reproduced it. Neopatrimonial politics thus continued, leading to waste and developmental failures – but now with a vengeance, given the magnitude of the oil resources.

The military that came to rule was not much of a military, certainly not capable of ruling an ill-formed polity. At the time of the civil war in 1966, for example, there were some 11,000 men in uniform and only 511 officers.[53] The victorious northern officers who came to dominate the national army came mostly from lower-class backgrounds and from the most underdeveloped emirates of the far north. While a handful of these officers had received more advanced training at staff colleges – often abroad in England or India – most officers "were poorly educated and unlikely to have a high level of comprehension of the major political and social issues of the day."[54] Levels of professionalization among officers were also low, as we have seen.

[52] See Lewis, "Economic Statism," 438.
[53] See Luckham, Nigerian Military, 90.
[54] Ibid., 96.

This poorly trained military dominated by northerners came to depend on a handful of British-trained higher civil servants – often southerners – for the running of the government it had captured by force. As the military grew rapidly during the civil war years – up to some 270,000 men by 1970 – its quality deteriorated even further, with most new recruits being less-educated northerners who in turn were hastily trained by their ill-qualified officers.[55] Basic military competence and internal discipline were absent. Lacking an intelligence corps, for example, the Nigerian military could not even undertake what militaries elsewhere do when they enter politics, namely, impose systematic repression. The overall lack of discipline traveled down the hierarchy, even to the rank and file, so that the bloated military in the 1970s was generally marked by "a high level of corruption and fraudulent activities," including soldiers periodically going on "rampage, molesting civilians."[56]

The military elite, though aware of these problems, was unable to address them.[57] For example, during General Gowon's rule (1966–75), efforts were made following the civil war to trim the armed forces and improve their internal discipline. Some demobilization occurred, but the fact that the military had become a major source of employment for poor northerners proved to be a formidable political obstacle. Attempts to improve internal discipline were also not very successful. Similar efforts at reform were made but again with similar failures during the rule by Generals Murtala Mohammed and Obasanjo (1975–79). The political situation in Nigeria, however, was a catch-22: The military was in power precisely because it controlled the use of force and because civilian leaders were fragmented; given the limited legitimacy enjoyed by these military leaders and given their need to maintain the support of those within the armed forces, they had only limited power resources at their disposal to reform the military itself.

Unlike the military rulers that we encountered in the cases of South Korea and Brazil, Nigerian generals had a fairly limited conception of their role as political leaders: They had no independent developmental goals and fairly quickly came to mirror the broader political society around them, especially its personalism and communalism. General Gowon and his colleagues, for example, had no coherent political views, certainly nothing that could be called a developmental ideology.[58] The same was true of General Mohammed and of General Obasanjo, who actually committed the military to withdraw from politics, thus paving the way for a brief civilian interlude in 1979. The Nigerian military in power thus viewed itself more as a "caretaker" or a "corrective" regime and less a "transforming" or a "developmental" one.

[55] See Peters, *Nigerian Military and the State*, chap. 5, esp. 109.
[56] Ibid., 144.
[57] Ibid., chap. 6.
[58] See Luckham, *Nigerian Military*, chap. 12.

Its priorities were mainly political and not economic,[59] the primary goal being the creation of a more centralized and stable Nigeria with the power balance tilted toward the Hausa-Fulani north. Subsequent military leaders during the 1980s, especially Generals Buhari and Babangida, did have some clear economic goals – but these were also primarily responses to an economic crisis and therefore aimed mainly at satisfying international creditors and investors.

Another important characteristic of military rule in Nigeria was that it quickly internalized such societal characteristics as ethnic divisions and the tendency to use public resources for private ends: "the boundary between the military and civil society" in Nigeria proved to be rather "permeable."[60] There are several underlying reasons for why this happened. First, as early as 1962, recruitment into the army was based on regional quotas. Pushed by northern politicians, this struggle for "group representation" weakened professional norms.[61] The civil war, of course, further intensified ethnic consciousness within the armed forces, and the numerous coups and countercoups that followed only reinforced these tendencies in the name of redressing power imbalances across ethnic groups.

Further, there was little effort in Nigeria to foster an esprit de corps, or separate professional identities for military officers. On the contrary, the social distance between the officers and civilians was rather narrow: "On evenings and at weekends, there is constant stream of brothers, kinsmen, acquaintances from the same village or town-ward or the same ethnic group who came to pay respects at an officer's house and to drink his beer and Fanta orange... [bringing] unsolicited gifts... [and seeking] small or big favors."[62] The officer corps was thus highly "vulnerable to corruption and political pressure."[63] And finally, this corruption spread with access to oil wealth, from those at the apex to those below.

If militaries enjoy any legitimacy as rulers, it is often based on their claim to rise above the politics of intergroup conflict and corruption. When militaries in power actually manage to achieve some such goals – as, for example, during Park's rule in South Korea or under military rule in Brazil – they may use their concentrated power to facilitate economic development. In this regard the Nigerian military never really succeeded.

---

[59] For example, Bennett and Kirk-Greene list nine priorities of the Nigerian military regime prior to the Second Republic (1979–83); not one of these involved any direct innovation in the pattern of economic development. See Valerie P. Bennett and A. H. M. Kirk-Greene, "Back to the Barracks: A Decade of Marking Time," in Keith Panter-Brick, ed., *Soldiers and Oil: The Political Transformation of Nigeria* (London: Frank Cass, 1978), 19.

[60] See Joseph, *Democracy and Prebendal Politics in Nigeria*, 70.

[61] Ibid., 71.

[62] Luckham, *Nigerian Military*, 112–14.

[63] Ibid., 113.

We now turn our attention to the evolving nature of the civil service under military rule. In comparison with the other cases in this study, the quality of the Nigerian civil service remained low, as has already been discussed. For much of the period now under discussion, civil servants remained powerful political actors – especially after the First Republic and before the austerity of the late 1980s. They were, for one thing, relatively better educated; most senior civil servants had university degrees, whereas military officers did not.[64] The most senior of these civil servants – the permanent secretaries – were trained by the British and possessed some international experience. Moreover, many of these senior administrators were southerners, especially Yorubas, and thus represented the more advanced south within the state.

Military rulers often depended on civil servants for policy ideas and implementation. This was especially true of the Gowon administration, which forged a close working alliance with the permanent secretaries. Indeed, the relationship placed Gowon under suspicion of being too pro-south and precipitated the coup that brought General Murtala Mohammed to power. General Mohammed, in turn, sought to trim the power of the civil service, purging some 11,000 of them, nominally on charges of corruption. Most of the permanent secretaries survived, however, and returned to their jobs; many of the junior administrators, by contrast, were pushed out.[65] During the civilian interregnum, as well, civil servants remained powerful partners of elected leaders. This situation altered somewhat in the late 1980s during the Babangida regime, when the state as a whole and the state-led development model came under attack.

There was a massive expansion of the civil service between 1970 and 1984, when some retrenchment began. Exact numbers are hard to come by, but the pattern is clear. Federal public employees grew in number from some 65,000 in 1965 to 114,000 in 1974 (the year of oil price increase) to 300,000 in 1984.[66] Employment in regional governments, parastatals, and local governments also grew tremendously during these years; by 1986, for example, Nigeria employed some two million men and women in the public sector.[67] Factors fueling this growth included a huge growth in public

---

[64] For example, approximately 85 percent of the elite civil servants (grade level twelve and above) in 1978 had at least a bachelor's degree. See Koehn, *Public Policy and Administration in Africa*, 16, table 1.1.

[65] See, for example, Stephen O. Olugbemi, "The Civil Service: An Outsider's View," in Oyediran Oyeleye, ed., *Nigerian Government and Politics under Military Rule, 1966–1979* (New York: St. Martin's Press, 1979), 96–109, esp. 99. See also Adamolekun, *Politics and Administration in Nigeria*, chap. 5.

[66] See Ladipo Adamolekun, "Postscript," in Murray, *Studies in Nigerian Administration*, 322; and Alex Gboyega, "The Civil Service Reforms: A Critique," in Said Adejumobi and Abubakar Momoh, eds., *The Political Economy of Nigeria under Military Rule (1984–1993)* (Harare, Zimbabwe: Sapes Books, 1995), 261.

[67] See Koehn, *Public Policy and Administration in Africa*, 17.

revenues from oil, the creation of numerous new states within Nigeria, the growing role of the public sector in the economy, and the pressures of patronage politics.

Unfortunately, this bureaucratic growth did not enhance the quality of the civil service. While it is true that entry into the elite ranks required a basic university education, the quality of education in many schools and universities in Nigeria was poor. And even these low entry requirements were further diluted for political reasons to accommodate candidates from the north.[68] Moreover, the training they then received within the civil service was also limited. Instead of a unified civil service, officers from one state or another came to control various federal ministries and tended to promote their own. Generalist positions were easy to fill this way, but positions requiring specialists often remained vacant or were filled by expatriates on a contract basis.[69] The military administrators often appointed and promoted according to personalistic criteria, further undermining any possibility of a meritocracy.[70] And finally, corruption was rampant throughout the system, as the military rulers repeatedly failed to enforce any discipline.[71]

It comes as no surprise that this low-quality bureaucracy was not an effective agent of economic transformation in Nigeria. Nevertheless, some of the highest civil servants – the permanent secretaries – were quite powerful within the military government and managed to persuade Gowon and his allies to pursue some modest nationalist and statist economic policies. (This is not to say that these secretaries had a unified political position – as a matter of fact, some sharp differences in preferences have been documented.)[72] Among these policies were a decision to join OPEC, indigenization of foreign industry, some import substitution, and the emphasis on a growing role of the public sector in industrialization.[73] This fairly typical "Third World developmentalism" came rather late to Nigeria – in the 1970s, when the world had changed enough from the 1950s so that countries such as South Korea and Brazil were already beginning to move away from it – and came

---

[68] See P. Chiedo Asiodu, "The Civil Service: An Insider's View," in Oyeleye, *Nigerian Government and Politics under Military Rule*, 73–95, esp. 75.

[69] See Koehn, *Public Policy and Administration in Africa*, 20–21.

[70] Ibid., 25.

[71] This is not to suggest that numerous reforms were not attempted. Some of the main attempts were local government reforms in 1970, the Udoji commission report in 1974, 1979 reforms following the installation of the Second Republic, and the attempted nationalization and retrenchment in 1988. Each set of reforms, however, ended up doing little more than raising the salaries of civil servants.

[72] Terisa Turner, for example, notes the conflict between the more "comprador" and the more "technocratic-nationalist" bureaucrats, going so far as to suggest that such conflict may have been a significant factor in the 1975 coup. See Turner, "Commercial Capitalism and the 1975 Coup," in Panter-Brick, *Soldiers and Oil*, 166–200.

[73] See Forrest, *Politics and Economic Development in Nigeria*, 48.

at the behest not so much of politicians but of civil servants and thus, unlike India, without much popular support.

As for the civil service in general, most civil servants did not distinguish sharply between holding public office, controlling public resources, and pursuing personal and sectional interests. One analyst comments that the "concept of public service" was generally absent among Nigerian civil servants;[74] another concludes that there was no "commitment to the public interest";[75] and yet another observes that the behavior of civil servants was "dictated more by veiled sectional interests than consideration for the common good."[76] It is clear that this was not just a problem of "institutional economics"; Nigerian civil servants were often well paid – and yet were still "on the take." This brings us back to the broader political system in which even the military rulers failed to introduce discipline, and the endemic low level of professionalism within the civil service, dating to the colonial period and exacerbated after independence, that persisted. The consequences were sharply negative.

In the nearly three decades during which the military and civil servants ruled Nigeria and sought to reconstruct the state, some of their efforts succeeded, but most did not. One of the main accomplishments was the construction of a somewhat more centralized Nigerian state. Thus the Gowon regime, having prevailed in a civil war, placed a high priority on creating a unified state that could overcome debilitating ethnic conflicts. To this end, they abolished ethnically oriented political parties, redrew the federal map by creating smaller states – up to twelve from four following the civil war, with the addition of another seven in 1976 – and sought to centralize decision making.

The partial success of these policies was reflected in the fact that public expenditures of the federal and state governments were nearly equal in the First Republic, but the federal share rose to some 70 percent during the 1970s.[77] Nevertheless, one ought not to overstate the extent to which such shifts indicated any real shift in relative power. They mainly reflected the large portion of oil revenues controlled by the federal government. And the new, smaller states remained quite autonomous; on at least two occasions during the 1970s the federal government was unable to get them to pay their loan and just wrote them off.[78] For all its limitations, however, a centralized government that controlled the majority of the country's public financial resources and numerous smaller units that would not readily

[74] Adamolekun, *Politics and Administration in Nigeria*, 132.

[75] Koehn, *Public Policy and Administration in Africa*, 272.

[76] Olugbemi, "Civil Service," in Oyeleye, *Nigerian Government and Politics under Military Rule*, 102.

[77] See Forrest, *Politics and Economic Development in Nigeria*, 51.

[78] Ibid., 51. Forrest thus concludes (see p. 54) that, even in the 1970s, the "state's tail was wagging the federal dog."

polarize provided better building blocks for a modern state than the one Nigeria had inherited from its colonial past.

Even if the redrawn federal map – bolstered by oil revenues – was something of an improvement, the limitations of political engineering attempted by the military were also stark. Three important examples will suffice. First, old ethnic cleavages and politics persisted just below the surface. For example, the Gowon effort to create "national consciousness" was opposed by the "Kaduna Mafia," a group of northern intelligentsia with links to the military who feared any move that would strengthen the hands of southerners.[79] The Gowon regime quickly caved in to the opposition, and the Kaduna Mafia went on to become an important political factor in the subsequent coup that overthrew Gowon and brought Murtala Mohammed to power. Moreover, when the military went back to the barracks in 1979, the earlier tripartite ethnic divisions quickly reemerged, helping once again to bring the military back to power.[80]

But the military's penetration of society was also shallow. Provincial units, for example, were quite autonomous, often run like personal fiefdoms of second-tier military officers. Taxes, already quite limited in the premilitary era, were essentially eliminated with the coming of oil revenues.[81] Large parts of the agrarian sector remained beyond the pale of the state.[82] Attempts to incorporate labor during the Obasanjo regime came to naught. And even efforts to improve the state's repressive capacities, for example, by creating an internal intelligence and security agency, did not amount to much.[83] Nigeria thus benefited neither from vigorous citizenship participation nor from an effective top-down state.

The military also failed to reform the personalistic and patronage-oriented politics of Nigeria. To the contrary, the military itself became a major source of privatization of public resources. The rot, in turn, seeped

---

[79] Billy Dudley clarifies that the links between the "Kaduna Mafia" – mostly northern university professors – and northern military elites were forged in such educational institutions as the Government College, Zaria, and Government College, Keffi. See Billy J. Dudley, *Introduction to Nigerian Government and Politics* (Bloomington: Indiana University Press, 1982), 98.

[80] For the argument that the "Second Republic" was also plagued by old ethnic divisions, see Joseph, *Democracy and Prebendal Politics in Nigeria*, pt. 3. Larry Diamond qualifies this argument somewhat, but not by much. See Diamond, "Social Change and Political Conflict in Nigeria's Second Republic," in I. William Zartman, ed., *The Political Economy of Nigeria* (New York: Praeger, 1983), 25–84.

[81] In a personal conversation, General Obasanjo – at that time out of power – told me that he considered abolishing taxation of incomes as one of the more important mistakes of his administration. While he blamed "bad foreign advice" for this policy decision, the fact is that taxation of incomes even prior to his rule was already quite unsystematic and lax.

[82] See Forrest, *Politics and Economic Development in Nigeria*, chap. 9.

[83] Billy Dudley thus notes that "a good many" members of the not very successful National Security Organization were "barely literate." See Dudley, *An Introduction to Nigerian Government*, 103.

downward, infecting governors of states, federal and state civil services, local governments, and parastatals. Even actors in the private sector – who often worked closely with state agents in any case – were part of the nexus of corruption. This massive state failure was the root cause of economic waste and minimal economic development.

III. Squandering Oil Resources

The increase in oil prices during the 1970s spurred sharp growth in the Nigerian economy, which then plummeted just as rapidly in the 1980s when oil prices declined. While precise data is scarce, World Bank figures suggest that between 1971 and 1992 the real per capita GDP declined by some 10 percent.[84] Both the growth and the decline were especially manifest in the industrial sector.[85] During the 1970s industry grew rapidly – at some 13 percent per annum – and then, within the first few years of the sharp decline in oil prices, nearly 50 percent of manufacturing output was lost.[86] The main issue for discussion here is why, despite the enormous oil revenues, Nigeria's efforts at industrialization ultimately amounted to so little.

Oil prices rose steadily in the world market, skyrocketing in 1974 with the OPEC price hike. As a major oil exporter and a member of OPEC, Nigeria benefited handsomely. Most oil exports were extracted and marketed by foreign companies, which accounted for more than 90 percent of total exports during the 1970s and the 1980s. But the national government also gained significant revenues from oil. These jumped five times between 1970 and 1972 and another five times between 1972 and 1974.[87] The share of oil revenues in total government revenues increased from some 25 percent to

---

[84] See World Bank, *Nigeria: Structural Adjustment Program, Policies, Implementation, Impact* (Washington, D.C.: World Bank Press, 1994), 73.

[85] See Forrest, *Politics and Economic Development in Nigeria*, 184. Forrest notes that the World Bank in 1985 changed its estimates, suggesting that instead of the assumed sharp decline of the 1970s, agricultural growth between 1970 and 1982 was 2.7 percent per annum. Forrest endorses this revised estimate. Without reliable data, a study such as the present one can take only the best available estimates. However, considering how limited the state's reach has been in the Nigerian countryside and considering that agricultural taxes were first reduced with the coming of oil revenues, and then even the marketing boards were eventually abolished, this general picture for the 1970s and 1980s appears persuasive. Of course, weather-related fluctuations could still have been serious, and more reliable data in the future could put such a conclusion in doubt. By contrast, agricultural performance, especially production of food crops, was less volatile; both the World Bank and independent observers now agree that, instead of the presumed decline, food production between 1970 and the 1980s probably kept up with population growth.

[86] See Adebayo O. Olukoshi, "The Political Economy of the Structural Adjustment Programme," in Adejumobi and Momoh, eds., *The Political Economy of Nigeria under Military Rule*, 140.

[87] These and the oil statistics that follow are from Forrest, *Politics and Economic Development in Nigeria*, 134, table 7.1. See also Cliff Edogun, "The Structure of State Capitalism in the

nearly 80 percent between 1970 and 1974 and hovered at about 70 percent throughout the remainder of the 1970s and the 1980s. Correspondingly, government expenditures also increased dramatically, doubling in 1970, doubling again in 1974, and yet again in 1975. Of course, oil prices declined in the late 1970s and for much of the 1980s. Nevertheless, these declining oil prices were still higher than their pre-1974 level, so oil, the main export, continued to provide Nigeria with substantial governmental revenues.

What impact did oil revenues have on industrialization and economic growth? Throughout the 1970s GDP increased faster then private consumption, broadly suggesting that oil resources were not simply consumed by the society. While government consumption also rose sharply, so did overall savings and investment: Domestic investment grew from some 12 percent of the GDP in 1950 to 16 percent in the pre–civil war 1960s to over 30 percent in the flush 1970s.[88] By international standards, this is a very high rate of investment, close to that of East Asian countries. What is puzzling is that this substantial capital was apparently invested without yielding long-term growth.

The post–civil war military government's approach to industrialization was a mild form of import substitution, where the main agent of industrialization was to be the public sector. While foreign investment and foreign expertise would still be welcome, the government also hoped to indigenize some of the existing foreign companies. What was new in comparison with the 1960s was a somewhat enhanced sense of nationalism that had emerged from the civil war – hence the emphasis on indigenization. However, as discussed above, even this revived nationalism was not very deep and was short-lived: Thus, indigenization, by transferring some equity of foreign companies into the hands of national entrepreneurs, was supported by some senior civil servants and businessmen (mostly Yoruba in origin) because they were the likely beneficiaries.[89] The emphasis on the public sector was also less a form of nationalistically inclined statism and more a gesture to the underlying interests of the political elite, because it could further help the northern elite to neutralize some regional imbalances.

Aside from the emphasis on indigenization and the public sector, the military government had no coherent approach to industrialization. Macroeconomic policies were thus mainly reactive to what was happening to the oil economy and did not follow any particular logic.[90] As oil revenues grew,

Nigerian Petroleum Industry," in Claude Ake, ed., *Political Economy of Nigeria* (London: Longman, 1985), 89–112.

[88] See I. William Zartman with Sayre Schatz, "Introduction," in Zartman, *The Political Economy of Nigeria* (New York: Praeger, 1983), 13.

[89] See Thomas J. Biersteker, *Multinationals, the State, and Control of the Nigerian Economy* (Princeton, N.J.: Princeton University Press, 1987), chap. 2.

[90] This discussion on economic policies is based on a variety of sources but especially on Forrest, *Politics and Economic Development in Nigeria;* Sayre Schatz, "Private Capitalism and the

so did government expenditures and, with ample foreign exchange, so did imports. With resources readily available to the government, the military rulers eliminated some direct taxes, though without much thought to the long-term financial consequences of such a move. Massive inflow of foreign currencies appreciated the value of the local currency, encouraging not only consumer imports – a function of growing demand and inelasticity of domestic supply – but also a range of production inputs, including imports of primary, intermediate, and capital goods. These policies assumed a ready supply of public revenues and foreign exchange, both of which depended on high prices for oil exports, and there is no evidence that much thought was given to the possibility of a global decline in oil prices.

When in fact oil prices declined in the late 1970s, the government cut some expenditures and restricted some imports but mainly resorted to a two-pronged strategy of deficit financing and external borrowing. In 1979 a civilian government came to power and needed ample patronage resources to maintain its support; its capacity to cut expenditures was even more limited. Continued deficit financing drew down the reserves, and growing demand contributed to inflation. Given the continued inelasticity of domestic supply and a resistance to devaluation, imports continued unabated. For example, between 1980 and 1981, as oil prices plummeted, Nigeria's imports increased by some 45 percent.[91] Hoping that the decline in oil prices was temporary, the government also borrowed heavily from abroad to avoid balance-of-payment problems. Trade imbalances and borrowing contributed to growing indebtedness. The debt service ratio increased from 4.2 percent in 1980 to over 30 percent by 1984, creating a crisis that eventually led to a structural-adjustment agreement with the World Bank and to some related policy shifts.

That enormous inflow of oil resources only contributed to growing indebtedness emphasizes how poor the economic management was and how ineffective the state was. Arriving at a fuller understanding of how an incompetent state squandered its oil resources takes us to more specific arenas of the state's economic intervention, especially management of the foreign sector, national industry, and such other economically consequential areas as education.

As already noted, the Nigerian economy, especially its oil, banking, and modern manufacturing sectors, were largely owned by and dependent on foreign companies. Prior to the civil war, moreover, foreign companies had received a broad array of support from the government, including tax relief

---

Inert Economy of Nigeria," *Journal of Modern African Studies* 22, no. 1 (1984): 45–57; Lewis, "Economic Statism"; Abba, *Nigerian Economic Crisis*; World Bank, *Nigeria: Macro-Economic Policies for Structural Change* (Washington, D.C.: World Bank, 1983); and Adejumobi and Momoh, *Political Economy of Nigeria.*

[91] See Olukoshi, "Political Economy of the Structural Adjustment Programme," 140.

and tariff protection. Starting in the early 1970s, however, the more nationalist government sought to indigenize foreign companies by legislating
enhanced equity shares and managerial positions for Nigerian nationals.[92]
During the first phase of this program (approximately 1972–75), the emphasis was mainly on transfer of some equity (up to 40 percent in select
companies) to Nigerian businessmen. Although foreign companies found
ingenious ways around the legislation, a small group of Nigerians – some
ten to twenty families, mainly in Lagos and mainly Yorubas – managed to
gain some access to profits in foreign companies. While over the long run
this may have contributed to the emergence of a handful of Nigerian entrepreneurs, over the short run such buying of shares in existing foreign
companies also diverted liquid capital from new investment. Moreover, the
fact that the benefits of the policy were extremely concentrated in Yorubas
created ethnic animosities anew, leading to a policy shift.

The 1975 coup that brought an even more pro-north military government to power shifted the focus of indigenization to include more foreign
companies and to enhance the state's direct participation in economic matters. While packaged as "socialism" and "equality," the logic behind the
shift was to ensure that northerners benefited from the program. The main
"success" achieved during this phase was greater national control over banks
and thus over the financial system. Over time, however, political control over
banks became a major source of corruption and mismanagement, contributing to growing indebtedness. And beyond banking, "no real change took
place in the effective control of the vast majority of [foreign] enterprises."[93]
Both foreign and local businesses, unhappy about state encroachment, did
not cooperate and bribed numerous civil servants and middlemen to help
them to evade the laws.[94] In the end Nigeria did not attract new foreign
investors and existing investors maintained most of their control. When
one considers that the government's growing participation in some heavy
industries often turned out to be a disaster, then the attempts to indigenize
industry must in retrospect be considered one more public policy failure in
Nigeria.

On the trade front, too, there is evidence of considerable policy incoher-
ence. On the one hand, the government was encouraging import substitution and allowing foreign investors to produce consumer goods behind tariff
walls (tariffs on textiles, for example, averaged nearly 100 percent during
this period). On the other hand, faced with a massive inflow of oil-related
foreign exchange, the government allowed the currency to appreciate,

---

[92] The best study of the causes and consequences of indigenization remains Biersteker, *Multinationals, the State, and Control of the Nigerian Economy*. The following discussion draws mainly
on this study.

[93] Ibid., 242.

[94] See Koehn, *Public Policy and Administration in Africa*, 275.

discouraging exports (other than oil) and, more importantly, encouraging a variety of imports. Appreciation of the currency made continued industrial growth dependent on cheap, readily available imports. When oil prices declined, the Obasanjo government attempted to impose some austerity measures – some devaluation and some cuts in government expenditures – but encountering protests, it backtracked, even discouraging subsequent governments from pursuing more prudent policies. As imports continued without abatement, the foreign exchange bill continued to grow while oil export earnings were declining – it was a crisis in the making.

Judgments on trade policy could be more sympathetic because the assumption that oil prices would soon rise again was made by other oil exporters as well, for example, Mexico. However, the state remained unable to channel foreign investment into anything with more value-added than last-stage-assembly consumer products – and that behind tariff walls. This was a state incapable of organizing or encouraging large-scale manufacturing.

As noted above, the infusion of oil resources into the economy was mainly mediated by the state. Moreover, a conscious policy decision was made to channel most of these resources into the public sector. Nevertheless, resources were plentiful in the oil-flush 1970s, including in the private sector. Indeed, resource scarcity has never been a major factor in the slow development of Nigerian capitalism. The Nigerian government set up a development bank – something akin to the Brazilian Development Bank encountered above – in hopes of directing credit to the private sector. But in the face of widespread neopatrimonialism, discretionary control over credit in Nigeria became a major source of corruption, and many a fortune was made by those connected to the political elite and even by the elite themselves.

There is very little systematic research on the subject of Nigeria's indigenous private industry.[95] We do know that even after indigenization, nearly 60 percent of equity in manufacturing continued to be in the hands of nonnationals and that the lion's share of the rest was state-owned, with indigenous private entrepreneurs a poor third.[96] Nonetheless, some Nigerian entrepreneurs did continue to mature out of trading and commerce and into manufacturing or, at least, near-manufacturing. Forrest's survey found a growing Nigerian private presence in such areas as organizing sales of frozen fish (the Ibru group), construction (the Modandola group), tire retreading, canneries, auto parts, beverages, plastics, and some textile manufacturing.[97] Most of this growth, moreover, was independent of state support,

[95] An important exception is Tom Forrest, "The Advance of African Capital: The Growth of Nigerian Private Enterprise," in Frances Stewart, Sanjaya Lall, and Samuel Wangwe, eds., *Alternative Development Strategies in Sub-Saharan Africa* (New York: St. Martin's Press, 1992), 368–401.

[96] See Alkasum Abba et al., *The Nigerian Economic Crisis: Causes and Solutions* (Lagos, Nigeria: Academic Staff Union of Universities of Nigeria, 1985).

[97] Forrest, "Advance of African Capital."

with the possible exception of a few cases of indigenization. While none of this is a Hyundai or even a Tata, it does indicate growing sophistication in organizing production and remains one of the few hopeful signs for the future of Nigeria. What might have been achieved with the help of a supportive and effective state will never be known.

The real policy shift under the military government was, of course, the leadership of the public sector. During the flush years and beyond, nearly one-third of the GDP was annually "invested" by the government. Unfortunately, much of this was wasted and had no real long-term impact. First, substantial expenditures were made on "status" projects that were not productive investments, namely, parliaments, stadiums, theaters, and a new capital city, Abuja: The share of construction in the GDP increased from 5.8 percent in 1972 to 16 percent in 1980.[98] Aside from the dubious economic value of these projects, the industry itself was highly inefficient, with one estimate suggesting that the average cost of construction in Nigeria was some 200 percent higher than in Kenya.[99] Moreover, nearly 80 percent of all construction inputs, including cement, had to be imported, as government factories were unreliable suppliers.[100] Scarcities enabled numerous middlemen to rake in huge profits, contributing to cost inefficiencies. Moreover, when foreign exchange became scarce in the 1980s, numerous incomplete projects were abandoned because imported inputs were not readily available.

Overall, then, Nigeria's public sector investments were plagued by numerous problems, including poor planning, political interference, scarcity of managerial and technical personnel, heavy dependence on foreign technology, expertise, and inputs, and lots of old-fashioned corruption. Nigeria is a prime example of how statist development fails when an ineffective and incompetent state is at the helm.

Some examples will help to fill out the picture. Locational conflicts were always present in federal projects, as in steel. This resurfaced in the 1970s, and after numerous redone plans, delay, and political conflicts, five plants were opened in the late 1970s and the 1980s.[101] Planning was so poor that nearly all the inputs – including ore, machinery, and engineers – had to be imported, making the cost of Nigerian steel nearly double the world

[98] Abba et al., *Nigerian Economic Crisis*, 60.

[99] Ibid., 63.

[100] Billy Dudley provides a great example of waste and governmental incompetence in importing cement. In 1973–74, the government ordered twenty million tons of imported cement, ten times more than Nigerian ports could readily handle. When nearly 450 ships had to wait to unload the cement for a prolonged period, the government shelled out $500,000 per day in demurrage charges. See Dudley, *Introduction to Nigerian Government and Politics*, 81.

[101] These remarks on steel are based on Forrest, *Politics and Economic Development in Nigeria*, 151.

market price. Similarly, government-owned sugar and cement factories were plagued by poor planning: Ample sugar cane was not readily available and cement factories were located far from lime deposits, increasing the cost of production.[102]

Foreign consultants and foreign collaborators were omnipresent. Nigerian airlines was thus essentially run by KLM and Nigerian railways by Rail India. Projects would generally begin with paid foreign advisers, who in turn would bring in other foreign companies, until eventually even the day-to-day running of plants – especially technical supervision – was in the hands of highly paid foreigners. This was the real Achilles heel of Nigerian industrialization: very limited indigenous technological capability. Expensive factories and plants could indeed be made to run, but only so long as ample foreign exchange was available and highly paid foreigners could be retained. However, with the twin pressures first of indigenization and second of declining oil earnings, numerous start-ups ended in disarray, at least in part for lack of technical personnel.

One survey of the sugar, cement, and textile industries highlights the technical bottlenecks in Nigeria's public sector firms.[103] Technology-related problems reduced machine and labor productivity and raised the cost of production in the sugar industry. One of the two sugar factories surveyed performed better than the other, mainly because of a better in-house training program for technical personnel that prepared Nigerians to take over from expatriates. With proper training, Nigerians are thus fully capable of managing and operating their factories. In cement, the companies that performed better were those in which "technical partners" were also "investors," underlining the importance of finding the right incentives and creating technical capabilities. Textile firms generally performed well, but they were nearly all managed and operated by nonnationals.[104] The survey concludes that the "absence of experienced indigenous technical staff" has resulted in "much resource wastage and technological underdevelopment in the industrial sector."[105] This conclusion at the end of the 1980s reinforces the one also reached by T. O. Adeboye for the 1970s, namely, that the "federal government in manufacture" was a "weak entrepreneur," tending to produce at very high costs and incapable of absorbing new technology.[106]

Observers have noted that corruption "matured" during this phase, with senior military and civilian officials receiving direct deposits in foreign accounts of such a magnitude that senior officials even acquired private

---

[102] See John F. E. Ohiorhenuan and I. D. Poloamina, "Building Indigenous Technological Capacity in African Industry: The Nigerian Case," in Stewart et al., *Alternative Development Strategies*, 294–320.

[103] Ibid.

[104] Ibid., 302–6.

[105] Ibid., 307.

[106] Cited in Forrest, *Politics and Economic Development in Nigeria*, 140.

jets.[107] On a smaller scale, government-owned factories and other firms became arenas that the political elites manipulated for political advantage, leading to the appointment of loyal supporters to boards and to the provision of employment for members of one's community. Military governors in various states engaged in especially egregious behavior, using state resources such as parastatals as personal fiefdoms. We have seen that top army officers were in no position to discipline their second tier, and the civilian interregnum during 1979–83 came to be regarded as even more corrupt than the military regime, though perhaps this later corruption was simply more widely publicized.

Finally, in this continuing discussion of the Nigerian military governments as economic actors, we must note that oil wealth brought a massive increase in public expenditure on education. The education budget jumped some eightfold in the mid-1970s. Even during the austere 1980s, Nigeria continued to devote nearly 6 percent of total government expenditure to education (in contrast, say, to India's 2 percent). Universal, free primary education was introduced in the mid-1970s, state governments took over missionary-run secondary schools, and seven new universities were opened. Over the 1970s, student enrollment in universities quadrupled. This looks very impressive, but several important qualifications reveal that the economic impact of all this expenditure was not commensurate with the investment.

As measured by enrollment, the major impact of education was on primary education, especially in the north. Under the best of circumstances the economic impact of growing basic literacy will be manifest over the medium to long term. But the circumstances in Nigeria were not favorable. Many of the earlier mistakes – especially, lack of qualified teachers but also corruption and related underestimation of costs[108] – were repeated, leading to "a serious decline in the quality of education."[109] Indeed, the higher up one went on the education ladder, the less impressive were the gains. From the point of view of running and managing industry, the very small numbers of people with university, and especially technical, education continued to be a major drawback. Part of the problem here was, of course, the very low starting point. For example, while university enrollment between 1965 and 1985 grew fifteen times, still only 3 percent of university-age adults were enrolled in higher education in 1985, compared with 32 percent in

---

[107] Corruption is one of those subjects that everyone seems to know about but that is always difficult to document. Major scholarly sources on Nigeria nearly all agree on the widespread character of corruption in Nigeria, especially in the public sector. For a rare collection devoted exclusively to the subject of corruption in Nigeria, see Femi Odekunle, ed., *Nigeria: Corruption in Development* (Ibadan, Nigeria: Ibadan University Press, 1986). For an overview of corruption in the military government, see Dudley, *Introduction to Nigerian Government,* 112–20.

[108] On corruption in education, see Abba et al., *Nigerian Economic Crisis,* chap. 5.

[109] See Forrest, *Politics and Economic Development in Nigeria,* 148.

Korea, 11 percent in Brazil, and 7 percent in India.[110] The absolute numbers were also staggeringly low: For example, in 1980, only some 5,000 students were enrolled in engineering, compared with 164,000 in Brazil, a country of similar population.[111]

To sum up, the oil boom in Nigeria created an illusion of economic dynamism. For all the reasons already discussed, Nigeria missed a significant opportunity to transform oil resources into something more permanent, probably ending up worse off than when it started. The deeper causes of this economic failure were bad politics and Nigeria's relative underdevelopment in terms of national entrepreneurial and technological skills at the time of the oil boom. Since national capital was not in a position to respond to new opportunities and challenges offered by oil wealth, a domineering, military-run state decided to undertake numerous economic tasks directly. Unfortunately, the Nigerian state was also not up to the task, as we have discussed at length. Unlike the other states encountered in this study, the Nigerian state was thus a very poor entrepreneur, wasting resources and appropriating others for personal use. The little that was put to productive use was mainly in the hands of well-paid foreigners, an unsustainable arrangement. So, instead of real industrialization, the Nigerian state created a house of cards that crumbled just as soon as it was built.

IV. A Note on Structural Adjustment

In 1986 Nigeria entered into a loan agreement with the World Bank. This agreement, also endorsed by the IMF, broadly resembled the well-known package of IMF-recommended orthodox policy changes aimed at stabilization and structural adjustment. The Babangida government pressed these policies relatively vigorously for some five years but less consistently following a mini-oil boom in the early 1990s. After a decade of experience under the somewhat modified policy regime, the Nigerian economy had failed to halt the steady decline that began in the early 1980s, especially in manufacturing and industrialization. Whereas manufacturing had contributed some 8 percent of the GDP in 1980, by 1995 its share had declined to 5 percent. Industry as a whole (including manufacturing, mining, construction, and so on) also declined; the average growth rate between 1980 and 1995 was close to 1 percent. Per capita incomes of Nigerians dropped dramatically, from a high of some $800 in 1980 to $260 by 1995.[112] While these figures may

---

[110] See Sanjaya Lall, "Structural Problems of African Industry," in Stewart et al., eds., *Alternative Development Strategies*, 138–39, table A4.5. The data for India are from World Bank, *World Development Report, 1991* (New York: Oxford University Press, 1991).

[111] Lall, "Structural Problems of African Industry," 140–41, table A4.6.

[112] All these figures are from World Bank, *World Development Report, 1997* (New York: Oxford University Press, 1997). Figures for manufacturing are on p. 236, table 12, for industrial growth on p. 234, table 11, and for per capita income on p. 214, table 1.

not always be accurate, this broad picture of steady decline in industry and income is unquestioned. What is debated vigorously instead are the causes of the decline and, relatedly, what ought to come next.

The brief discussion that follows is a comment on structural adjustment that reinforces the central argument developed above.[113] Throughout the discussion I have suggested that the roots of Nigeria's economic malaise are deep – having to do with the mutually reinforcing impact of an ineffective state and weak national capitalism – and not likely to be altered over the short term by any policy change. The implications may not be optimistic, but they help to explain why expectations engendered by the adoption of promarket policies in the mid-1980s have not borne fruit, certainly not over the short term.

Nigeria's balance-of-payment situation deteriorated as early as the first Obasanjo regime – before the oil prices took a dip – underlining the poor quality of policy management that created a highly import-hungry economy. Early efforts to devalue and introduce some fiscal austerity were reversed in response to political opposition. The same pattern continued under the civilian government of Shagari, even though oil prices had declined; the patronage needs of the civilian government were far too high and its legitimacy far too shallow to pursue difficult policies. Even the military governments that followed were reluctant to enter an agreement with the International Financial Institutions, in part due to nationalist sentiments of some senior decision makers, in part because they were not authoritarian enough to impose unpopular policies, and in part because of fluctuating oil prices and the hope that an upswing might be in the offing. Only when the debt service ratio climbed to nearly 40 percent in 1985 did the overwhelming sense of crisis precipitate some action – one of the main goals of the coup that brought Babangida to power was to satisfy international creditors. And it was that government that entered into an agreement with the World Bank in 1986 to secure foreign loans in exchange for changes in domestic policy.[114]

Over the next few years some significant policy reforms were implemented, some domestic but also some influencing external economic relations. The centerpiece of the reform was a devaluation that reduced the real value of the naira by nearly 60 percent over three to four years. Furthermore, import restrictions were relaxed and the indigenization decrees

---

[113] I do not attempt to assess the merits of structural adjustment policies in Nigeria. The neoliberal phase that many developing countries entered toward the end of the twentieth century is a subject that is beyond the scope of this study.

[114] For the following discussion on the structural adjustment program and its consequences, I draw mainly on Lewis, "Economic Statism"; Forrest, *Politics and Economic Development in Nigeria*, chaps. 10 and 11; and Olukoshi, "Political Economy of the Structural Adjustment Programme." I also consulted official Nigerian government and World Bank documents but have relied less on them due to their partisan nature.

that applied to foreign investments were scaled back, creating a more welcoming environment for MNCs. On the domestic front, the government cut
demand by implementing a wage freeze and sought to shrink public expenditures. As labor and some other interest groups opposed these moves, the
government itself became more repressive but also more cautious in implementing policy changes, with the result that attempts to remove subsidies,
trim the bureaucracy, reform the parastatals, and privatize public sector
firms proceeded haltingly. Sensing that a transition to democracy might be
around the corner, even these halting efforts were more or less abandoned
when oil prices increased in 1991. Nevertheless, given the growing size of
the foreign debt, many of the external economic policy reforms were kept in
place.

It is difficult to assess the impact of these policy shifts, because only some
shifts were real and because the economic malaise was fairly serious both before and after they were instituted. Economic growth and industrialization
are also long-term processes. Devaluation of the naira was long overdue,
and it is likely that a favorable impact will be seen over time in terms of increasing agricultural production (by shifting terms of trade) and in terms of
reducing the overwhelming dependence on imports, especially industrial inputs. Devaluation did not, however, engender any significant diversification
or growth of exports; oil remained by far the single most important export.
This failure of a supply response underlines the weakness of domestic manufacturing, especially private sector manufacturing. Foreign investors also
generally stayed away for a variety of reasons: Declining tariffs and declining
demand made the Nigerian market less attractive, and there were numerous other new countries with cheap, readily available, and better-trained
workers, stable economic policies, and decent infrastructure. Without new
exports and new foreign investment, Nigeria's capacity to repay its foreign
debt remained limited to its oil earnings. As these fluctuated, so did the
debt service ratio. With continued rescheduling and further borrowing to
pay back the debt, the size of the debt continued to grow unabated: from
some twenty to thirty-five billion dollars between 1985 and 1995, or from
some 50 percent of the GDP in the mid-1980s to some 140 percent of the
same by the 1990s.

Most important from the standpoint of this study was the impact of the
new policy regime on industrialization, especially on manufacturing. It is
important to reiterate that manufacturing had gone into a tailspin well
before the adoption of structural-adjustment policies. When oil prices declined in the early 1980s, numerous imported inputs became difficult to
obtain, and the heavily import-dependent industries deteriorated sharply:
Tobacco companies could not import filter tips and wrapping paper; cement factories were short of paper sacks; milk factories could not readily
market their product without imported cartons; and even the generally better functioning textile industry suffered due to the scarcity of imported

cotton.[115] Consequently, manufacturing output plummeted nearly 50 percent in the first half of the 1980s. Any fair assessment of the impact of the modified policies on industry must thus ask whether they were able to halt or reverse the decline. This is a difficult task because industrial restructuring that uses more domestic materials is a time-consuming process, and the results may not be evident for some time.

While there was growth and restructuring in some areas,[116] the overall picture was one of steady decline and deterioration. Manufacturing, for example, contributed a meager 5 percent of the GDP by 1995. New foreign investment remained limited. Starved of funds and imports, the already inefficient public sector enterprises were hit the hardest and continued to operate way below capacity. It was not obvious that privatization could solve such problems, at least in part because there were no ready buyers. The northern-controlled government was loathe in any case to push privatization too far because the main buyers would be southerners. Some Nigerian entrepreneurs have managed to grow, even though the overall environment has not been enabling: Infrastructure and a variety of potential public supports have deteriorated; overall demand in the economy has been low; managerial and technical capabilities remain scarce; and it has become much harder to import these as well as other production inputs. Significant capital has simply gone elsewhere. Peter Lewis's conclusion is worth noting: "The SAP [Structural Adjustment Program] has failed to induce a significant response. Non oil sectors of the economy have displayed an anemic performance, and adjustment has fostered deindustrialization in import-intensive activities."[117]

The modest conclusion that seems beyond debate is that the new policy regime has repeated the performance of the old policy regime in failing to facilitate growth of manufacturing and industry. This disappointing outcome, in turn, focuses attention on the deeper and longer-term problems afflicting the Nigerian economy, namely, a weak private sector, low technical skills, and most important, an ineffective, neopatrimonial state.[118] Sanjaya Lall's argument for sub-Saharan Africa as a whole certainly has resonance in Nigeria. He suggests that, beyond the right incentives, what also impedes industrialization are capabilities (both entrepreneurial and technological)

---

[115] These examples are from Abba et al., *Nigerian Economic Crisis*, 53–54.

[116] For example, see Forrest, *Politics and Economic Development in Nigeria*, 219–20; and Lewis, "Economic Statism," 447.

[117] Lewis, "Economic Statism," 447.

[118] For a discussion of how political changes under Babangida and beyond failed to make a dent into the nature of the state, see Larry Diamond, Anthony Kirk-Greene, and Oyeleye Oyediran, eds., *Transition without End: Nigerian Politics, and Civil Society under Babangida* (Boulder, Colo.: Lynne Rienner, 1997). Especially relevant are the introduction by Larry Diamond et al., the chapter on the civil service by Ladipo Adamolekun, and the chapter on the military by J. 'Bayo Adekanye.

and institutions (many of which may be provided by more effective states).[119] Similarly, and more specific to the Nigerian case, Lewis's causal diagnosis of why the halfhearted structural adjustment program in Nigeria failed is consistent with the theoretical themes of this study: "The Nigerian state has failed to provide the institutional underpinnings and economic inducements for productive accumulation."[120] And finally, when Tom Forrest emphasizes the state's "weakness, instability, and lack of direction" as central to Nigeria's continuing economic problems, he, too, provides support for the overall thrust of the present argument.[121]

V. Conclusion

The political economy of sovereign Nigeria constitutes a sad and tragic story. In spite of immense natural resource–based wealth, common Nigerians are probably not much better off early in the twenty-first century than they were at the time of independence. Failure to sustain economic growth, especially in manufacturing and industry, has been an important ingredient of this overall failure. Among the important underlying causes are the mutually reinforcing impact of a fairly backward economy and society at the time of independence, on the one hand, and the role of a neopatrimonial, ineffective state on the other hand. Compared with the other cases discussed in this study, Nigeria's starting point for deliberate industrialization was the least favorable: The level of industrial development at the time of independence was very low and industry was mostly in the hands of foreign firms; the stock of experienced national entrepreneurs was meager; the level of technology and technical competence in the society was underdeveloped; and the working class was not very productive. If history were destiny, however, no underdeveloped country would ever get out of its low-level equilibrium. Since some have and others have not, this study has emphasized the direct and indirect developmental roles played by respective national states. Unfortunately for Nigeria, the problems of relative backwardness were compounded by those of an ineffective state.

Nigeria was simply not much of a state. Behind the façade of a modern state was a personalistic and ethnically fragmented political elite and a bureaucracy and army that not only shared these traits but were also not very competent and professional. These traits were inherited from the colonial period, and the rulers of sovereign Nigeria failed to alter them. Given a weak nationalist movement, the political elite bickered openly about the relative gains of their respective communities and quietly amassed personal

---

[119] See Lall, "Structural Problems of African Industry," in Stewart et al., *Alternative Development Strategies*, 103–44.

[120] Lewis, "Economic Statism," 438.

[121] Forrest, *Politics and Economic Development in Nigeria*, 256.

wealth. When the civilian regime came apart, the military rulers also failed to reform the state. While a more centralized national state was indeed created, the old personalistic and patrimonial tendencies were only accentuated. Military rulers generally hailed from the north, where any sense of nationalism that might place the public interest over private gain was quite weak. Military officers, exhibiting low levels of competence and professionalism, plundered the state while letting the civil servants do most of the policy making and implementation. Even if the civil servants were slightly more competent – especially at the highest levels – they were suspect because many were southerners. And the rest were not immune to the problems of personalism, ethnic favoritism, low levels of professionalization, and corruption.

This neopatrimonial state lacked both the vision and the organizational capacity to promote development. These failures were evident both in state interventions that might influence medium- to long-term economic changes and in short- to medium-term developments. During the period under discussion Nigeria's development strategy shifted from an open economy to a mild form of nationalist import substitution to forced austerity within the same model and, finally, to a halfhearted acceptance of structural adjustment policies championed by international development institutions. Policy shifts were unstable and reactive, mainly driven by circumstances, especially fluctuations in the price of oil.

Lacking a long-term vision, economic actors were subjected to inconsistent incentives. Foreign investors were first tolerated, then discouraged, and finally invited. The government did little to strengthen domestic capitalism over the medium to long term: There were no high-quality business or engineering schools; no or little pressure on foreign firms to train local businessmen; little effort to train and organize a productive working class; and a shifting government attitude toward national business, from lack of confidence to antibusiness to lukewarm attempts at support. And finally, when rich with oil income, much of the money was pumped into the public sector and directed at public projects that rarely reached fruition. Waste and corruption were the order of the day, as most public sector projects operated at a loss and required continuous government subsidies.

With profound weaknesses in the domestic economy, the government came to depend on foreign investors and imported goods – both for consumption and as inputs to last-stage-assembly type of production – to meet the growing demand fed by oil. Short-term mismanagement of such policies as exchange rates further encouraged dependence on imported inputs, a pattern that could be maintained only as long as oil prices stayed high. When they declined, the political capacity to cut back on imports and public expenditures was lacking, leading to an even more serious crisis. Eventually, the state had to bow to the demands of its creditors, slowly paying the debt but again, without much to show for it in terms of national economic development. The combined weaknesses of domestic capitalism and of a neopatrimonial state continued to undermine economic growth, in industry in general and in manufacturing more specifically.

Finally, a few broader comparative observations may be in order. Nigeria's model of development was quite dependent on external resources and expertise. Viewed only on the dimension of relative dependency, Nigeria followed a path that was more akin to the one adopted by Brazil than to the much more nationalist routes pursued by South Korea and India. As in the case of Brazil, Nigeria fell into the debt trap once external resources dried up. However, Brazil used its external dependencies much more effectively than Nigeria and industrialized rapidly for decades. South Korea's and India's relative autonomy from, say, foreign direct investment is also associated with very different rates of industrialization. Clearly, based on the cases examined here, it would be difficult to claim whether greater capital integration into the global economy is an asset or a liability for national development efforts. When viewed comparatively, the Nigerian evidence does not lend itself to a dependency type of analysis.

If the developmental inefficacy of the neopatrimonial state is the main causal variable in Nigeria's dismal economic performance, what might one learn from situating the empirical analysis in a comparative context? Nigeria's ethnic heterogeneity is often blamed for the political fragmentation and subsequent ineffectiveness. The contrast with India on this point is revealing. India has managed its ethnic diversities much better than Nigeria. Why? A critical variable was the inheritance of a relatively centralized state in India, an inheritance that enabled leaders such as Nehru to make concessions to active minorities without raising the specter of the national state itself coming apart. Decentralizing concessions within the frame of a centralized state were possible in India but not in Nigeria. Concessions in the latter threatened the already fragile state, and further repression only heightened the alienation of excluded groups rather than creating a more genuine centralized state. Once again, then, the different legacies of colonialism and of related nationalist politics loom more significant as causal variables than do any givens of Nigerian society.

Last, one may ask why even a military government failed to create a more effective, developmental state. The contrast with Brazil is instructive. If the Brazilian military could move the Brazilian polity in a more effective, cohesive-capitalist direction, why could not the military in Nigeria do the same? Obviously, the societies were of different types, but, more important, the contrast between the two militaries itself was of great significance. The Nigerian military was considerably less professional than the Brazilian one and thus reflected many problematic attributes of Nigerian society, such as ethnic divisions, strong loyalties to kith and kin, and the shared belief that

the main purpose of the state was to pursue personalistic and sectional interests. Once in power, the militarized state in Nigeria was thus incapable of
rising above the society it hoped to transform and of meeting that challenge.
Whether ruled by civilians or by the military, and whether ruled more or
less democratically, the main features of the Nigerian state thus remained
neopatrimonial, contributing to Nigeria's long-term developmental failures.

Conclusion

Understanding States and State Intervention in the Global Periphery

This study has sought to explain why some developing countries have industrialized more rapidly and with more success than other developing countries. There is clearly more to development than industrialization, however. A successful program of development also ought to aim at strengthening a country's agriculture, alleviating poverty, improving income distribution, enhancing political security and civil liberties, and building capabilities that enable individuals and groups to live meaningful lives. Nevertheless, industrial societies are generally wealthier than agricultural societies, so it is not surprising that all leaders of developing countries seek, as well, to build new industry. Yet some peripheral countries have progressed further than others in achieving this goal. How does one best explain the relative success of some late-late industrializers vis-à-vis others?

The answer developed in this study has emphasized the state's role in both promoting and hindering industrialization, while conceding some important qualifications. A variety of other factors have also influenced the rates and patterns of late-late industrialization. Such factors include conditions of the global economy, the functioning of national markets, the role of indigenous entrepreneurs, and differing "starting points," including the availability of knowledge and technology. Second, it has struck me on more than one occasion that the relationship between states and economic development also runs in the opposite direction, with some minimal level of development probably necessary for the construction of modern states. And finally, I am aware of the limitations of the comparative case studies as a method of analysis – neither doing justice to the complexity of individual countries nor analyzing a large enough sample of cases to facilitate statistical results.

Setting aside such doubts for others to pursue, the proposition that seems to fit the puzzle of relative success in late-late industrialization best, both over time and across cases, is that some states have simply proved to be more effective agents of economic development than others. The burden of the

367

discussion above has been first to demonstrate this thesis in select cases, then to describe what constitutes more or less effective states, and, even more important, to explain why some parts of the global periphery acquired such states but others did not. Having presented the detailed empirical materials, I now take stock of what this all adds up to and tease out the implications.

The conclusion is organized in three parts. First, I examine a number of alternative explanations for the greater or lesser success evidenced in late-late industrialization. I then revisit the statist argument developed in this study, reexamining and summarizing the core logic and offering some necessary qualifications. This second part focuses on varying developmental pathways: Why and how did the differing parts of the global periphery acquire their varying state types and how did these, in turn, mold the patterns of industrial transformation? The final section is devoted to generalizing about the nature of state construction and state intervention in the developing world, with a discussion of some normative and prescriptive implications that follow from the study.

I. Alternative Explanations

The transformation of societies from agrarian to industrial political economies has always attracted scholarly attention. For example, the issue of why Western European countries and not others industrialized first has generated numerous contentious propositions. These vary anywhere from Max Weber's emphasis on the religious underpinnings of early capitalism to more proximate economic explanations based on relative per capita incomes, rates of savings and investments, and the availability of technology, all the way to an emphasis on class structures and/or on dependency and imperialism that argue that such gains came at the expense of colonizing and exploiting the nonindustrial world. More recently, it has become clear that there is considerable variation even within the non-Western world. This growing sensibility has reignited new scholarly debates: Why is East Asia industrializing more rapidly than, say, sub-Saharan Africa, or why should a country like Brazil or India not be able to imitate a country like South Korea?

Before resummarizing the answer developed in this book, we review some alternative explanations. Four sets of such explanations have been forcefully advanced by other scholars or otherwise struck me as eminently plausible. These explain the puzzle of greater or lesser success in industrialization with reference mainly to one of the following: the role of social structure, including culture; the significance of ruling regimes, especially that of democracy versus authoritarianism; the importance of free-market conditions; and the degree of dependence on the global economy. I reject only some of these alternative explanations on the grounds of insufficient evidence or unpersuasive logic. For the rest, the real issue is one of proximate causation.

A suggestion, for example, that some developing countries have industrialized more rapidly because of higher rates of investment is not so much wrong as it is unsatisfying because it begs the question of why the investment rates were higher. Such proximate explanations are not so much rejected in this study as they are incorporated into a more complex analysis in which political variables turn out to be the deeper causal variables.

Social Structure

That social structural or societal conditions vary across developing countries and that these variations in turn influence development patterns are important claims. What is really doubtful, however, is that one can build a full and parsimonious explanation for late-late industrialization around such variations. Let us consider at least one characteristic of the premodern social structure, namely, the role of landowning agrarian classes, and several aspects of the more modern social structure that one might expect to have an impact on industrialization, namely, the role of indigenous entrepreneurs, the work ethic of the laboring class, and levels of education in society.

It was Barrington Moore, Jr., who identified the commercialized landed classes as a key force in the turn of premodern agrarian bureaucracies toward a democratic pathway to a modern, industrial society.[1] While some such tendencies are mildly noticeable in the cases discussed above, on the whole the landed agrarian classes turn out to be neither major political nor major economic actors in the drama of late-late industrial transformation. Brazil was the only case where the commercialized coffee oligarchy was a powerful force early in the twentieth century, but its political contribution was hardly democratic and it slowly lost to the centralizing state after 1930 the capacity to influence economic matters. Traditional large landowners lost out in both Korea and India around midcentury, with very different political consequences; the absence of such classes may well have enabled state elites to push their industrializing agendas. Nigerian traditional elites – who are really not landowning classes in the European or Asian sense of that term – survived well into the modern period and may well have been a hindrance to state consolidation, democracy, and industrialization. Even in Nigeria, however, the basic drama of developmental direction was molded by the "new men," including the military. In general then, the twentieth century was too late in history for landowning classes to play the central role that Barrington Moore, Jr., identified in earlier periods. The model of centralized states had by now spread from Europe to the global periphery, and from the mid-twentieth century onward, it was the state elites who commanded economic change.

---

[1] See Barrington Moore, Jr., *Social Origins of Dictatorship and Democracy* (Boston: Beacon, 1966), esp. chap. 7.

Turning to the more modern aspects of the social structure, I was often struck by the fact that the presence or absence of a sizable group of indigenous entrepreneurs might be of major independent significance for the rates and patterns of late-late industrialization.[2] This was especially so because the origins of entrepreneurship prior to the mid-twentieth century had varying roots and could not readily be reduced to state actions. Thus, for example, while indigenous entrepreneurs in Korea were indeed fostered by the colonial state, their significance was also enhanced by the nationalization of colonial firms and by the civil war that led to their concentration in the south. Early entrepreneurs in Brazil were generally immigrants. Indigenous entrepreneurs in India, who had their origins in such minority communities as Parsis, used their commercial and trading traditions to enter manufacturing in the far reaches of the British empire, where the impact of the colonial state was weakest. Nigeria, by contrast, emerged from colonialism without many indigenous entrepreneurs.

This absence of indigenous entrepreneurs was an important part of the Nigerian story of failed industrialization during the second half of the twentieth century. By contrast, South Korea, Brazil, and India, having inherited a respectable stock of national entrepreneurs, went on to industrialize more or less impressively thereafter. Could one then construct a more general explanation of success in late-late industrialization around the independent variable of national entrepreneurship? For several reasons the answer is probably no. First, since South Korea, Brazil, and India all inherited a respectable stock of national entrepreneurs, the differential performance of these countries in subsequent decades would be difficult to explain in terms of the variable of entrepreneurship. Second, and relatedly, it is clear in all the cases discussed above that state policies were a factor in the further development of national entrepreneurship: highly supportive in the case of South Korea, generally supportive but leaning more in the direction of foreign enterprise in the case of Brazil, reluctantly supportive in India, and obstructive and mutually corrupt in the case of Nigeria. And finally, there is an important conceptual issue: The level of entrepreneurship in a society ought to be treated more as a proxy for – or as an indicator of – the level of business and industrial development than as its cause.

The issue of the work ethic and productivity of the working class can be set aside quickly because, despite its importance for industrial output, in all cases it was socially constructed, either by corporations or by state structures and policies. This was most clearly the case in South Korea, where a

---

[2] Following Max Weber, Joseph Schumpeter emphasized the importance of entrepreneurship for capitalist industrialization. See Schumpeter, *Capitalism, Socialism and Democracy* (New York: Harper, 1950). Subsequently, the interest in entrepreneurship as a possible variable in late-late development has waxed and waned, probably deserving more attention than it has received in recent years.

cohesive-capitalist state building on colonial traditions provided the framework for on-the-job training, job security, repression, and the nearly warlike mobilization of labor to create a highly productive work force. The Brazilian state also imposed corporatist control on workers, but, in contrast to South Korea, the aim was more often depoliticization rather than productivity-oriented socialization and mobilization. The context of a fragmented-multiclass state in India encouraged a highly politicized labor force that never amounted to a cohesive political force, so it contributed neither to productivity nor to social democracy. And finally, nothing highlighted the developmental ineffectiveness of the neopatrimonial state in Nigeria better than the inability even of military dictators to penetrate downward and tame a relatively small working class.

Variations in levels of education across societies are deeply consequential for late-late industrialization because they influence not only the productivity of the work force but also the capacity to absorb existing technology and to innovate.[3] This relationship is well evidenced in our cases, especially at the more extreme ends of economic performance. Since an educated population is also desirable from the standpoint of liberal values, one is tempted to highlight education as an important independent variable. This may be misleading, however. First, as evidenced in South Korea, the type of education that enhances individual freedoms may not be the same as that which promotes discipline and improved productivity. Second, as is apparent in both Brazil and India, a focus on higher education can have considerable economic payoffs, even if only after a significant time lag. Third, the Nigerian case underlines the fact that public spending alone is not a reliable guide to how well educated a society's population is likely to become. And fourth, and most important, levels and type of education across cases were deeply influenced by state attitudes and policies.

It is obvious that variations in societal conditions across developing countries influence economic activities. But the real issue is whether one can build parsimonious and satisfactory explanations for patterns of late-late industrialization around such variations. And about this there is real doubt, mainly because most economically relevant societal conditions are themselves regular objects of state policies. Evidence thus suggests that such conditions as density of entrepreneurs, labor's work ethic, and levels of education have been successfully and regularly altered by state intervention; the analytical focus therefore needs to shift to variations in the patterns of state intervention itself. Of course, there are other aspects of the social structure – such as ethnic heterogeneity, patterns of authority in the society, levels of associational life and mobilization, and the development of social classes

---

[3] Different aspects of this theme, for example, are emphasized in A. K. Sen, *Development as Freedom* (New York: Knopf, 1999); and Alice Amsden, *The Rise of the "Rest": Challenges to the West from Late-Industrializing Economies* (New York: Oxford University Press, 2001).

more generally – that are economically relevant because they influence the functioning of the state itself. States, after all, mold their own societies and are molded by them. I return to some such issues below.

Democracy versus Authoritarianism

Is it possible to explain the extent of success in late-late industrialization with reference to the regime type of a developing country – whether a democracy or a dictatorship? While the answer developed in this study is clearly no, the issue merits further discussion, both because the theme is a popular one[4] and because the bare logic of the argument, namely, that patterns of state authority have an impact on economic processes and outcomes, is quite similar to the one underlying the argument of this study. First, the evidence. There is little in the four case studies above that would lead one to conclude that there is any generalizable relationship between regime type and industrial growth. Brazil, for example, was governed democratically between 1945 and 1964, first growing handsomely and then entering a period of crisis. Democratic India's industrial growth was satisfactory in the 1950s, was fairly poor in the 1960s and the 1970s, and then recovered to respectable levels in the 1980s and the 1990s. Conversely, authoritarian South Korea and Brazil may have industrialized rapidly, but authoritarian Nigeria did poorly. It would seem, then, that the gross categories of democracy and dictatorship are inadequate for systematically tracing the impact of regime types on economic outcomes. This comparative case study finding is moreover consistent with the recent findings based on more aggregate quantitative data.[5]

Moving beyond the grossest categories of democracy and dictatorship, the case studies underline that there is considerable variation within both categories and that it is these variations that can be economically consequential. Thus, for example, highly politicized democracies in India under Indira Gandhi and in Brazil under Quadros and Goulart hurt economic growth. As analyzed above, the underlying reasons were that both intraelite and elite-mass conflict in these societies increased during these periods, bringing class politics to the fore. Leadership priorities in such circumstances were directed more at political management than at economic growth and were evidenced in radical mobilization strategies that discouraged investment and investors. By contrast, narrower, more elitist democracies that shared some characteristics of cohesive-capitalist states, such as Nehru's India and Kubitschek's Brazil, set economic growth as a goal and oversaw satisfactory rates of industrialization. However, the fact that Nehru's socialist ideology

---

[4] A good review of some of this literature is in Adam Przeworski and Fernando Limongi, "Political Regimes and Economic Growth," *Journal of Economic Perspectives* 7 (Summer 1993): 51–69. See also Adam Przeworski et al., *Democracy and Development: Political Institutions and Material Well-Being in the World, 1950–1990* (Cambridge: Cambridge University Press, 2002).

[5] See Przeworski and Limongi, "Political Regimes and Economic Growth."

discouraged foreign and domestic private investment, whereas Kubitschek and others in Brazil openly encouraged private capital, further underlines that even narrow, elitist democracies are not necessarily homogeneous.

The economically consequential variations within the so-called authoritarian regimes were even more stark. Looking beyond the subtle but important distinctions between South Korea under Park Chung Hee and Brazil under military rule, we find that the dramatic contrast in the capacity to facilitate economic development is between the military regimes in Nigeria and those in Brazil. Thus, Nigerian rulers were personalistic, Brazilian rulers were not; Nigerian rulers did not prioritize economic growth as a state goal, Brazilian rulers did; Nigerian rulers were unable to mobilize domestic and foreign capital to undertake industrial investments, Brazilian rulers were successful; public sector investments in Brazil were considerably more efficient than in Nigeria; and Brazilian military rulers controlled the workers much more successfully than their counterparts in Nigeria. We must conclude therefore that there is no a priori reason whatsoever for lumping such disparate regimes as the Brazilian and Nigerian military states into one category labeled "authoritarian."

In fact, both democratic and authoritarian regimes in the same country may share important traits. Thus both democractic and authoritarian regimes in Nigeria shared economically consequential traits – both were personalistic and neopatrimonial – just as Brazil's nominal democracy in the 1950s and the subsequent military regime shared consequential traits – both were governed by narrow developmental coalitions that prioritized economic growth, mobilized private capital, and excluded the working class. Given such underlying conceptual realities, it is no surprise that attempts to generalize about the impact of democracy or authoritarianism on economic growth have remained inconclusive.

Is it possible then to conclude that a developing country's status as a democracy or as authoritarian has no bearing on that country's economic processes and outcomes? Such a conclusion would necessarily be based on limited available knowledge and would therefore be an overstatement. The comparative case study materials discussed above suggest that some subtle but important relationships merit further investigation. For example, all the cases of really rapid industrialization tended not to be democratic. Moreover, if one looks at other developing country cases of very rapid economic growth that are not examined in this study – such as Taiwan, post–Cultural Revolution China, and maybe Malaysia and Mexico in some periods – one is struck by the absence of democracy. A variety of underlying reasons may help to explain this correlation, such as the state's need to maintain narrow economic priorities and/or a narrow ruling coalition, to control the working class, and to create a probusiness environment. A more limited hypothesis then may hold up, namely, that certain types of authoritarian states, conceptualized in this study as cohesive-capitalist states, are conducive to rapid industrialization. To the extent that it is hard to imagine how cohesive and disciplined capitalist development could be pursued within the frame of underinstitutionalized democracies – the type of democracy most commonly found in the developing world – it may also be the case that authoritarianism turns out to be a necessary but not a sufficient condition for rapid industrialization in the developing world.

Democratic regimes, too, may have some discernable impact on late-late industrialization that may be drowned out in aggregate studies. The comparative analyses above lead one to suspect that democracies in developing countries are likely to be middling economic performers, at least as long as states remain highly interventionist. Given that this is only a peripheral theme of this study, a brief comment will suffice.[6] Democracies in developing countries are likely to be fragmented-multiclass states that exhibit a considerable gap between political ambitions and promises, on the one hand, and limited capacity to fulfill these goals, on the other hand. This gap, in turn, reflects the difficulty faced by ruling democracies in trying to reconcile the nearly contradictory roles of representing and leading their respective societies, especially when they seek to transform their societies rapidly. Political parties are one set of institutions that, if well developed, may bring together leaders and citizens in coalitions that can help to reconcile their tension-riddled roles of representation and developmental leadership. But political parties in developing countries are generally weak, so leaders tend to make excessive promises to shore up political support. Once in power, however, they find themselves constrained, leading to simultaneous but halfhearted pursuit of multiple goals and a lack of long-term coherence and consistency in policy. While numerous factors contribute to how well an economy may perform in such circumstances, the political context of underinstitutionalized democracies does tend to exclude the "rate busting" performances of South Korea under Park Chung Hee or the "miracle" of a Brazil under military rule.

The Role of Markets

The most serious challenge to the statist argument for late-late industrialization developed in this study comes from the promarket argument, namely, that the free play of market forces best explains why some countries industrialize and grow more rapidly than others. The promarket position is of course articulated at varying levels of sophistication, from popular media to policy advocacy to scholarly theoretical and econometric studies. The *New York Times* summarized the "standard" but popular version: "A nation that

---

[6] I have developed this theme in somewhat greater detail elsewhere. See Atul Kohli, "Democracy in Developing Countries," in Atul Kohli, Chung-In Moon, and George Sorensen, eds., *States, Markets and Just Growth: Development in the Twenty-First Century* (Tokyo: United Nations University Press, 2002), 39–63.

opens its economy and keeps government's role to a minimum invariably experiences more rapid economic growth and rising incomes."[7] Behind the popular view lie important policy documents that seek to propound and legitimize these views.[8] And at a yet deeper level are numerous scholarly studies considered to be a part of the neoclassical revolution that was said to have swept away the old development economics. These studies generally criticized import-substitution strategies, sought to establish the superiority of export-oriented growth, and argued more broadly that state intervention in the economy led more to rent-seeking, corruption, and various distortions than to growth or development.[9]

These are serious arguments that are widely endorsed. How well do they stand up to select comparative and historical materials? It is possible that I have misunderstood or misrepresented the country cases discussed above. It is also possible that examination of additional cases would lead to different conclusions. However, the empirical materials that underlie this comparative analysis raise serious doubts about the general validity of such arguments. Shorn of numerous complexities, two claims are central to this neoclassical body of literature: first, the outward-orientation claim, namely,

---

[7] *New York Times*, February 9, 2002, p. 1. The reporter suggested that this view was shared by most business executives and government leaders attending the World Economic Forum in New York City in February 2002.

[8] See, for example, World Bank, *Development Report* (Oxford University Press, 1987 and 1991). The bank argued that "outward-oriented" and "market friendly" development strategies were superior. For one of many critiques, see Robert Wade, *Governing the Market* (Princeton: Princeton University Press, 1990), chap. 1. Another important essay that summarizes the Washington consensus, or the prevailing orthodoxy shared by Washington policy circles on how to pursue development, is John Williamson, "The Emergent Development Policy Consensus," in Michael R. Carter, Jeffrey Cason, and Frederic Zimmerman, eds., *Development at a Crossroads: Uncertain Paths to Sustainability after the Neoliberal Revolution* (Madison: Global Studies Program, University of Wisconsin, 1998), 33–46. A sharp recent critique of the Washington consensus by a policy insider is Joseph Stiglitz, *Globalization and Its Discontents* (New York: W. W. Norton, 2002).

[9] An incomplete list of some of the more influential such statements would include: Ian M. D. Little, Tibor Scitovsky, and Maurice Scott, *Industry and Trade in Some Developing Countries: A Comparative Study* (London: Oxford University Press, 1970); Bela Balassa, "Trade Policies in Developing Countries," *American Economic Review* 61, Papers and Proceedings (1971): 178–87; Anne O. Krueger, "The Political Economy of the Rent-Seeking Society," *American Economic Review* 64 (1974): 291–303; Deepak Lal, *The Poverty of "Development" Economics*, Institute of Economic Affairs (London: Hobart Paperback no. 16, 1983); Jeffrey Sachs, "External Debt and Macroeconomic Performance in Latin America and East Asia," *Brookings Papers on Economic Activity* 2, no. 2 (1985): 523–73; and Jagdish Bhagwati, "Rethinking Trade Strategy," in John P. Lewis and Valeriana Kallab, eds., *Development Strategies Reconsidered* (New Brunswick, N.J.: Transaction Books, 1986), 91–104. Two good critical reviews of this literature that question the "truth" value of many of the claims are Helen Shapiro and Lance Taylor, "The State and Industrial Strategy," *World Development* 18, no. 6 (1990): 861–78; and Paul Krugman, "Cycles of Conventional Wisdom on Economic Development," *International Affairs* 72 (1996): 717–32.

that greater openness and competitiveness in the economy generates higher rates of production growth via more efficient allocation of scarce resources; and second, the laissez-faire claim, namely, that state intervention in the economy necessarily generates distortions that hurt economic growth. Both claims are plagued by empirical and logical problems.

As to the claim that an outward orientation is superior, numerous quantitative studies have marshaled supportive evidence, but others have raised serious questions about the quality of this aggregate evidence.[10] This leaves considerable room for comparative case studies employing a political economy orientation to take up a position in the debates. Some of the country-specific evidence examined above could be construed as supportive of the outward-orientation claim, but a fair amount of the evidence turns out to be either more complex and ambiguous or downright contradictory. For example, the association between equilibrium exchange rates, rapid export growth, and rapid industrial growth in the South Korean case (say, during the 1960s and the 1970s) could be construed as supporting evidence. A closer examination, however, reveals layers of complexity. Devaluation in South Korea, for example, was far from sufficient to spur exports; rather, numerous state supports, including subsidies, were needed to make exports globally competitive. The causal direction of change was not simply from exports to growth. Rather, a careful tracing of historical processes suggests that a variety of other factors, including well-designed state interventions, were responsible for promoting cost- and quality-efficient production that then facilitated exports.

The historical materials also reveal two more serious problems with the case for the superiority of an outward orientation. First, as others have also noted, import substitution and export promotion turn out not to be mutually exclusive development strategies.[11] Both South Korea and Brazil, for example, simultaneously pursued import substitution and export promotion in the 1970s, with considerable success. Instead of juxtaposing countries along the dimension of relative openness, it therefore makes just as much sense to analyze why countries such as South Korea pursued both import substitution and export promotion successfully, whereas others such as Nigeria attempted and failed at both. And second, a simple but inescapable

---

[10] The "first generation" studies were critiqued in Sebastian Edwards, "Openness, Trade Liberalization, and Growth in Developing Countries," *Journal of Economic Literature* 31, no. 3 (September 1993): 1358–93. A more recent critique is Francisco Rodriguez and Dani Rodrik, "Trade Policy and Economic Growth: A Skeptic's Guide to the Cross-National Evidence," in Ben Bernanke and Kenneth S. Rogoff, eds., *Macroeconomics Annual 2000* (Cambridge: MIT Press for NBER, 2001).

[11] This was noticed fairly early on by Colin Bradford, "Policy Interventions and Markets: Development Strategy Typologies and Policy Options," in Gary Gereffi and Donald Wyman, eds., *Manufacturing Miracles: Paths of Industrialization in Latin America and East Asia* (Princeton: Princeton University Press, 1990), 32–54.

fact that comparative historical analyses have brought home has even more serious implications for the validity of the outward-orientation claim: In all the cases examined above, industrial development began and flourished, especially early on, only when the national economy enjoyed some protection from the global economy.

The neoliberal understanding of the state's role in the process of development, an understanding that leads to a preference for laissez-faire, is even more seriously flawed. There is no doubt that states in some parts of the developing world are grossly corrupt and use state intervention mainly for the self-enrichment of the ruling elite. Nigeria was the clearest such case. At the same time, however, there are hardly any significant examples in the developing world, now or in the recent past, where industrialization has proceeded very far without state intervention. The underlying reason is simple but powerful: Private investors in late-late-developing countries need organized help, help that effective states are most able to provide to overcome such obstacles as capital scarcity, technological backwardness, rigidities in labor markets, and to confront the overwhelming power of foreign corporations and of competitive producers elsewhere. The cases of Korea, Brazil, and India all exemplify this proposition. Specifically, none of the more measurable aspects of state intervention (for example, government expenditure as a proportion of the GNP, public investments, or public sector production; see Table 1) varied in any systematic way with production performance in the cases analyzed above. More quantitative studies have also reached similar conclusions.[12] The general claim that less state intervention is better for economic growth in developing countries is thus hard to sustain. Instead, a central proposition that fits the comparative evidence examined above is that state intervention in more or less successful industrializers varies, not so much by quantity as by type and quality. It is therefore patterns of state intervention in the economy that are key to explaining successful late-late development.

Before leaving this discussion on the role of free markets, I reiterate that what is found wanting here are some of the more extreme arguments and not the more sensible positions that simply underline that governments must respect economic logic to achieve such goals as sustained industrial growth. Thus, when such populist leaders as Indira Gandhi in India or Goulart in Brazil violated economic fundamentals and jeopardized macroeconomic

---

[12] See, for example, D. A. Aschauer, "Is Public Expenditure Productive?," *Journal of Monetary Economics* 23 (1989): 177–200. Aschauer actually finds a positive relationship between public investment and growth. My claim by contrast is relatively limited; I am not arguing that "more" is better but rather that the main issue is the quality of state intervention and not its quantity. For skepticism that is more consistent with the tone of my argument, see D. Renelt and R. Levine, "A Sensitivity Analysis of Cross-Country Growth Regressions," *American Economic Review* 82, no. 4 (1992): 942–63. I am indebted to Jonathan Krieckhaus for bringing these pieces to my attention.

stability, economic growth suffered. More important is the point that private investment responds to the profit motive, and in the cases examined above, robust private initiative was strongly associated with growth success. The argument here is clearly consistent with that position. However, if the neoclassical argument is that free and open economies subject to minimum government intervention are best situated to maximize growth, then supportive evidence is lacking. On the contrary, such conditions were generally found to threaten investors, leading governments to intervene in order to encourage and sustain profitability and thus new investments and growth.

Relative Dependency

Last, one ought to consider the dependency argument, an argument that used to be rather popular but has lost some of its saliency in recent decades. It nonetheless remains a serious argument. Shorn of numerous subtleties and complexities, the dependency argument suggested that the developmental prospects of peripheral countries were hurt by their economic integration into the global capitalist economy.[13] The argument was supposed to be the clearest for the past, especially the colonial past, but was also said to hold for neocolonialism, where partially sovereign states may help to facilitate dependent development but where the ultimate prospects of self-sustaining, egalitarian development remain limited. A number of underlying reasons were proposed for why such expectations should hold, including the "exploitative" nature of foreign investment, the "unequal exchange" manifest in "free trade," foreign control over technology, and the "comprador" nature of the ruling elites who would rather cooperate with Western countries and corporations than advance the interests of the people they governed.

For this study, dependency theory would posit that sovereign strategies of development ought to lead to more rapid industrialization than strategies that entangle peripheral countries in a variety of dependencies, especially dependency on foreign capital and technology.[14] How well do such predictions hold up against the limited empirical materials examined above? While there is some solid historical support for such expectations, there is also a fair amount of contrary evidence. As I review this evidence, the general position I come to is that the global economy offers both opportunities and constraints to developing countries and that much depends on how well state authorities are situated to maneuver.

---

[13] For a good review of the dependency literature, see Gabriel Palma, "Dependency: A Formal Theory of Underdevelopment or a Methodology for the Analysis of Concrete Situations of Underdevelopment," *World Development* 6 (1978): 881–924.

[14] At least one recent, sophisticated study suggests something fairly close, arguing that countries that have successfully built independent stocks of "knowledge," countries such as South Korea and India, are likely to do better in the brave new globalized world than others, such as Brazil, that have chosen to integrate even further in the global capitalist economy. See Amsden, *Rise of the "Rest."*

First, the evidence from comparative colonialism. In the first half of the twentieth century Korea underwent a fair amount of industrialization, India some, and Nigeria very little. Brazil does not readily fit the discussion because it was already sovereign; like Korea, it, too, had experienced steady development of industry prior to midcentury. These outcomes reflected a host of conditioning variables, including the availability of experienced entrepreneurs and technology, and changing global economic conditions. It is also clear that the policies of the colonial state – or of the sovereign state in the case of Brazil – were deeply consequential. These varied anywhere from highly interventionist and supportive of industry in the case of the Japanese colonial state in Korea to the British in Nigeria, who remained committed to laissez-faire and an open economy, while neglecting industry. The extent of industrialization in these countries during the colonial period can then be broadly associated with the pattern of state intervention.

On the basis of such evidence it would be difficult to generalize about the impact of colonialism on peripheral economies, although a dominant tendency was a preference on the part of metropolitan countries to sell their manufactured goods in exchange for commodities. This both reinforced and created new patterns of unequal exchange, hurting the prospects for self-generated industrialization in the periphery. Two important qualifications are in order, however. First, one ought not to push the counterfactual too far, namely, that but for colonialism these countries would have experienced autonomous industrialization. While the nationalist discourse in every country maintains such a proposition, the fact is that "premodern" domestic political and economic structures in every case exhibited traits – for example, political fragmentation, inability to collect taxes and provide public goods, low levels of technology, low levels of productivity, incomes, and demand, and the channeling of economic "surplus" into conspicuous consumption and unproductive investments – that generated significant obstacles to industrialization and even made these countries vulnerable to colonial onslaught. And second, the variety of metropolitan strategies of control and exploitation led to the construction of different types of states in the periphery that, in turn, framed various patterns of economic change. The focus, then, ought to be on types of colonialisms, rather than on colonialism per se, and on such political matters as patterns of state construction.

What about the broad evidence from sovereign developing countries? How well does it fit the expectations generated by the dependency approach? If dependency on foreign capital and technology is of main concern, then India pursued the most autonomous developmental strategy, whereas both Brazil and Nigeria pursued more dependent strategies. South Korea often split the difference by inviting foreign technology but not capital. It would be difficult to generalize from this evidence that the more autonomous a development strategy, the better the prospects of a sustained industrial drive. More nuanced comparisons, however, reveal both strengths and further weaknesses of the dependency propositions. Take, for example, the case of Nigeria. Many in Nigeria, as well as in other parts of Africa, bemoan their dependence on foreign corporations as a major constraint on their prospects for industrialization. Even a cursory comparison with Brazil or with such other Latin American countries as Mexico reveals that considerable industrialization can be achieved even in the presence of dependency on foreign capital and technology and that Nigeria's failure to industrialize is rooted in other factors, especially in a highly ineffective neopatrimonial state.

The case of India's nearly autarkic but sluggish industrialization could be construed as a heavy indictment of the dependency proposition, although this, too, requires a more nuanced approach. There is no denying that the absence of foreign capital and technology contributed to an inefficient and slow pattern of industrial growth in India. This is clearest if one compares the early phases of deliberate import substitution in India with that in Brazil, say, during the 1950s. At the same time, however, India's long-term investments in higher education and national technology began to pay off in the 1980s and the 1990s and may continue to do so in the future. In addition, by minimizing dependence on foreign capital, India avoided the debt trap that now plagues such countries as Brazil and Nigeria.

Finally, a comparison of South Korea and Brazil offers some additional insights. South Korea, unlike Brazil, often avoided capital dependency, while securing and paying for foreign technology. Before touting "buy technology, avoid capital dependency" as the new developmental mantra, however, we offer several qualifications. First, South Korea's capacity to pay for technology imports was heavily dependent on its export prowess, with decoupling of capital and technology part and parcel of the overall developmental strategy. And second, South Korea also got lucky, for example, when Japanese industrial investments in Korea became national property by virtue of the historical "accident" of the Japanese losing the Second World War. There was also rapid rebuilding with the help of foreign aid from the United States. Park Chung Hee's industrial drive was thus propelled from a base largely financed by foreign capital, but without the many burdens of accumulated foreign investment faced by countries such as Brazil.

To sum up, a good explanation of why some developing countries have industrialized more rapidly than others must take account of multiple factors but without sacrificing parsimony. However, it would be difficult to build such an explanation around variables like the social structure, regime type, extent of market freedom, and/or the degree of dependency on foreign capital and technology. I thus now move to resummarize the statist argument.

II. Statism in the Periphery

The central argument of this study is that the role of the state has been decisive for patterns of industrialization in the developing world. As the types of states emerging in the periphery varied, often reflecting institutional continuities with colonialism, so, too, did their developmental effectiveness vary, ranging from rapid industrialization to stalled. What was the nature of the state that propelled countries along these different routes, how were such states acquired, and what exactly did these states do to promote or hinder industrialization?

The Cohesive-Capitalist Route

Cohesive-capitalist states have proved to be the most effective agents of rapid industrialization in the global periphery and efficacious at creating new wealth in poor societies. From the standpoint of liberal political values, these are not desirable states. Rather, they are economistic states that concentrate power at the apex and use state power to discipline their societies. Generally right-wing authoritarian states, they prioritize rapid industrialization as a national goal, are staffed competently, work closely with industrialists, systematically discipline and repress labor, penetrate and control the rural society, and use economic nationalism as a tool of political mobilization. The rulers of these states are able to generate purposive power that can be used to accomplish narrowly defined state purposes. State power in such instances has been used to undertake industrialization directly under public auspices and to channel private initiative into prioritized sectors, especially rapid industrial growth.

Cohesive-capitalist states are characterized by ideological and organizational characteristics that help to define goals narrowly and therefore concentrate resources on a narrow set of priorities. But why should an entire society support such narrow state-defined goals as rapid industrialization? In fact, society often does not, forcing state elites to devise political strategies based on material rewards, coercion, and emotive appeal. A close, cooperative relationship with business and private entrepreneurs, for example, enables state elites to harness the energy of such key groups. Corporatized labor keeps gains in productivity ahead of gains in wages. Similarly, downward penetration of state authority enables state elites to silence various social groups and keep new demands off the political agenda. Successful cohesive-capitalist states are competent states, run by public-spirited rather than personalistic leaders and staffed by well-educated, professional bureaucrats. But a state that defines its priorities narrowly and rests its power on a narrow social base is difficult to sustain, forcing its authoritarian rulers to remake their authority structures periodically. It is thus not surprising that the rulers of cohesive-capitalist states often use nationalism, especially economic nationalism, to mobilize the entire society in the service of developmental goals.

Such cohesive-capitalist states are difficult to construct, even more difficult to institutionalize, and are not found in abundance in the developing world. In the limited materials analyzed above, the purest cases of cohesive-capitalist states were in Korea, first under colonial auspices in the 1930s, and then South Korea under Park Chung Hee during the 1960s and the 1970s. In both instances, ruling elites set rapid industrial growth as a state goal, whether in anticipation of international conflict during the colonial period or later on to cope with the threat of communism. State elites forged cooperative relationships with the business elite, controlled labor, and penetrated downward into the countryside. Both the late colonial period and the Park Chung Hee era saw successful industrialization.

Some of the regimes that governed Brazil also moved the Brazilian state in the cohesive-capitalist direction, though not as "purely" as in the case of Korea. Especially notable are the two periods of rapid industrialization: first, the late Estado Novo period, and second, the early phase of the military rule. Regime authorities in both periods prioritized economic growth and industrialization as state goals, by forging close links with business and by corporatizing labor. The Brazilian state never penetrated the countryside, however, and its strategy toward labor aimed mainly at political control rather than at economic mobilization. In addition, the economic nationalism of the ruling elite remained shallow, which led Brazilian rulers to increasing dependence on foreign capital. Foreign capital, by its very nature, tends to be more difficult to channel into state-defined economic priorities than national capital. Thus, even as dependence on foreign capital can be a source of rapid growth, it can also be a liability – hence, the recurring boom-and-bust quality of Brazilian industrialization.

Finally, hints of cohesive-capitalism were also evident in the occasional democratic regime. This was especially true in Brazil during the 1950s, where key traits of the preceding Estado Novo had survived: the enormous concentration of power in the executive, the prioritization of narrow industrial growth, close institutionalized relations with private capital, and corporatized labor. Such a nominal democracy, with its cohesive-capitalist traits, provided the framework for rapid industrial growth; the entire experiment eventually crumbled when the political arena became more politically fragmented and multiclass. A paler but not insignificant example is also provided by India in the 1980s and especially the late 1990s. India is a genuine, broad-based democracy, whose developmental strengths and weaknesses have been conceptualized here in terms of a fragmented-multiclass state. Nevertheless, in the last decades of the twentieth century India took a conservative turn – setting aside populist goals and reprioritizing economic growth as a state goal, establishing close working relations with business, and promoting religious nationalism. The improvement of economic growth during this period is more than just a coincidence.

It may be useful at this time to take a brief detour and ask how this discussion of cohesive-capitalist states applies to cases other than those analyzed in this study and, relatedly, how other scholars have conceptualized similar relationships between states and economic development. A few other countries may fit the category of cohesive-capitalist states, most obviously Taiwan, which industrialized rapidly for several decades under a right-wing authoritarian-nationalist regime. Taiwan shared some of the core characteristics of cohesive-capitalist states summarized above.[15] A number of other countries in East Asia, especially Thailand, Indonesia, and Malaysia, also shared some of these traits in some periods. Beyond East Asia, such countries as Turkey, Mexico, and South Africa in some periods would be candidates for further examination in light of the argument developed here.

It is also important to distinguish the cohesive-capitalist category developed in this study from such conceptual cousins as mobilization regimes, bureaucratic-authoritarian states, and developmental states. The older category of mobilization regimes was developed mainly to explain the efficacy of communist states in developing countries.[16] It was argued provocatively that communist states, by virtue of their ideology and organization, might be better than democracies at mobilizing and incorporating their citizens and thus better at such "nation building" tasks as creating political order, implementing land reforms, and maybe even achieving rapid industrialization.[17] In the twenty-first century this cold war thinking may appear irrelevant, but the underlying insight is still compelling. It is true that by now most communist countries in the developing world, such as China, have turned to private enterprise for higher rates of economic growth and have taken on in the process many characteristics of cohesive-capitalist states. Nevertheless, even during the 1950s, such communist states as China proved to be highly effective developmental states in the sense that they defined clear and narrow goals, such as land redistribution, and implemented them effectively. Are there insights to be gained by comparing such communist states with the cohesive-capitalist ones that have been the focus of my discussion?

---

[15] Some of these aspects (though not others) of the Taiwanese "model" are stressed in Wade, *Governing the Market*, esp. 370–81; and Thomas Gold, *State and Society in the Taiwan Miracle* (Armonk, N.Y.: M. E. Sharpe, 1986).

[16] See, for example, David Apter, *The Politics of Modernization* (Chicago: University of Chicago Press, 1965).

[17] See, among others, Samuel P. Huntington, *Political Order in Changing Societies* (New Haven, Conn.: Yale University Press, 1968); Franz Schurmann, *Ideology and Organization in Communist China* (Berkeley: University of California Press, 1966); and Kenneth Jowitt, *Revolutionary Breakthrough and National Development: The Case of Romania, 1944–1965* (Berkeley: University of California Press, 1971).

Two insights are especially noteworthy. First, there is an uncanny re-semblance between how communist and cohesive-capitalist states generate power resources to accomplish their respective goals:

- defining their goals narrowly and clearly (land redistribution in 1950s China and rapid industrialization in South Korea under Park Chung Hee)
- forging alliances with those likely to benefit directly from these goals (peasants in China and big business in South Korea)
- repressing those who were likely to oppose such goals (landlords in China and workers in South Korea)
- using state authority to penetrate the far reaches of the society so as to both mobilize and control others, and
- utilizing various emotive appeals, including nationalism, to maintain support.[18]

Of course, because communist and cohesive-capitalist states repress those they govern, they are often incapable of sustaining their narrow goals be-yond short periods. Nevertheless, both types of states have managed to cre-ate powerful and effective states that have achieved such desirable goals as redistribution of wealth and rapid generation of new wealth.

The second insight underlines the contrasts between cohesive-capitalist developmental states and communist states. Whereas the former tend to be allied with property-owning groups, the latter tend to be closer to the propertyless and hence can be conceptualized as cohesive-lower-class states. The general principle is that any state's developmental effectiveness is a function not only of how well the state is organized but also of the underlying class basis of power. If economic growth is the goal, then a close alliance with private investors is called for; if, however, land redistribution is the main goal, then an alliance with the peasants may be necessary. These principles are especially telling for understanding the inefficacy of other states that may define clear goals, such as rapid industrialization, but then balk at clarifying and reorganizing the class basis of the state, maintaining a multiclass base, or, worse, adopting an anti-investor posture so as to build political support in other quarters.

The category of bureaucratic-authoritarian regimes was devised mainly to capture the distinctive nature of Latin American authoritarian regimes in the 1960s. The formulation, extended to areas beyond Latin America, too, eventually came under sharp criticism.[19] I have shied away from adopting

---

[18] For my understanding of 1950s China, I am especially depending here on Schurmann, *Ideology and Organization.* See also Vivienne Shue, *Reach of the State: Sketches of the Chinese Body Politic* (Stanford, Calif.: Stanford University Press, 1988).

[19] The original formulation was in Guillermo O'Donnell, *Modernization and Bureaucratic Author-itarianism* (Berkeley: University of California, Institute of International Studies, 1973), 943.

this category for two reasons. First, as was clear in the discussion of Brazil above, the characterization of the military regime in the 1960s and beyond as bureaucratic-authoritarian suggests more discontinuity from the past than the historical record warrants. And second, I am not comfortable with the underlying functional thinking, namely, that bureaucratic-authoritarian regimes emerged to open up some persistent economic "bottlenecks." While functional logic may yield provocative hypotheses, they ought to be treated only as a starting point of historical analysis. Many countries, for example, face bottlenecks, but no solutions emerge. Moreover, even in such cases as Brazil and Argentina, the "solutions" turned out to be illusory.

The final conceptual category that resembles my discussion of cohesive-capitalist states is that of developmental states.[20] As noted in the introductory chapter, I have found the scholarship on developmental states of great use and have borrowed from it freely and built on its insights. If so, one might wonder, why create a new label or category? The main answer is that my theoretical understanding of the dynamic of cohesive-capitalist states is distinct from that implicit or explicit in the scholarship on developmental states. Take, for example, the important contribution of Peter Evans, who suggests that states that exhibit "embedded autonomy" tend to be successful developmental states.[21] State efficacy, in this formulation, derives from such variables as competent state bureaucrats and the free flow of information between the state and business elite. How well does this hold up against the empirical materials?

My understanding of cohesive-capitalist states, too, stresses the alliance of state and business, but the heart of the matter is the state's capacity to channel private initiative into areas of state priority. This capacity, in turn, depends on the state offering financial incentives to private investors and on its cajoling, if not coercing, to adopt certain behaviors by threatening to punish and/or by appealing to nationalist or other loyalties. Such political capacities are rooted not in the levels of information exchanged between the state and business but in the amount of power the states command to extract resources, to define priority areas of expenditure, and to instill a sense of discipline and purpose in society. Similarly, the competence of state bureaucrats, though consequential, did not appear to be a decisive independent variable in the empirical materials above. Senior bureaucrats in India, for

A useful collection that both celebrates and criticizes O'Donnell's contribution is David Collier, ed., *The New Authoritarianism in Latin America* (Princeton, N.J.: Princeton University Press, 1979), 861.

[20] For various uses of this concept, see Chalmers Johnson, *MITI and the Japanese Miracle: The Growth of Industrial Policy, 1925–1975* (Stanford, Calif.: Stanford University Press, 1982); Wade, *Governing the Market*; Peter Evans, *Embedded Autonomy: State and Industrial Transformation* (Princeton, N.J.: Princeton University Press, 1995); and Meredith Woo-Cumings, ed., *The Developmental State* (Ithaca, N.Y.: Cornell University Press, 1999).

[21] See Evans, *Embedded Autonomy*.

example, are no less competent or professional than are their counterparts in South Korea or Brazil. The key issue, rather, is how elites structure and use state power for development. For this reason my analysis of successful developmental states emphasizes power over competence or information: power to define goals clearly and narrowly and power to pursue those goals effectively. The core research task is to examine states that command more or less power and then to demonstrate that the purposive use of power by state elites is indeed consequential for economic outcomes.

Let us now pursue the twin issues of the origins and the economic impact of cohesive-capitalist states. Getting at a historical answer is easier than constructing a more theoretical one. I will attempt both, beginning with a simple but important observation, namely, that modern states as an organizational form developed within Europe and spread from there to the rest of the world via imposition, diffusion, and emulation. While countries such as Japan and Russia quickly emulated and thus resisted colonialism, much of the peripheral world was otherwise reorganized, first into colonial dependencies and then into near-modern states by such colonizers as England, France, and Japan. In this way modern states were imported into the developing world. Any analysis therefore must begin with the type of ruling arrangements created and left behind by colonial powers.

The Japanese in Korea, as we have seen, arrived to find an already centralized polity and eventually left behind a highly repressive but efficacious cohesive-capitalist state. Korea, as restructured by the Japanese, developed a highly centralized and bureaucratized authority structure that penetrated downward to forge production-oriented alliances with propertied groups and corporatized labor to undertake rapid economic change. This model essentially survived the American occupation of South Korea following the Second World War and was eventually reinforced in the south by the Japanophile Park Chung Hee.

Given this historical background, how much weight can one assign to Japanese colonialism in the construction of South Korea's cohesive-capitalist state? What made the ruling strategies of Japanese colonialists distinct from those of some European colonizers? Japanese colonialism was a necessary but not a sufficient condition for the emergence of a cohesive-capitalist state in Korea, as can be illustrated by pondering two counterfactuals. First, had Japan colonized Nigeria, could it still have created a cohesive-capitalist state? We do not know, of course, but the probable answer is that Nigeria would have been a very different place than it is today, even if it would not quite be like South Korea. One realizes from this exercise that the successful transfer of the cohesive-capitalist model to Korea also owed something to geographical and cultural proximity and to the Korean social structure, including traditions of centralized rule and power hierarchies. And second, had the American occupation forces chosen to restructure Korea the same way that they reordered Japan, or had Syngman Rhee been replaced not by a

Park Chung Hee but by another personalistic leader, would South Korea still have evolved in a cohesive-capitalist direction? The answer is probably no, underlining the importance of conscious decisions to reestablish continuity with historically inherited structures.

While not sufficient, the Japanese colonial background was nonetheless necessary for South Korea to evolve as it did. Absent Japanese colonialism, Korea would probably have gone the same route as China, including political fragmentation, peasant revolts, and eventually a communist revolution leading to the establishment of a cohesive-lower-class state. Whatever the merits of such historical speculation, we do know that the Japanese transformed the Korean state and left an enduring legacy. Beyond Korea, Japanese colonialism also built the foundations of a cohesive-capitalist state in Taiwan. And the Japanese model has spread in other parts of Pacific Asia, if more slowly and less perfectly, by conscious emulation. It is not surprising that these Japanese-style states are to be found mostly in the region that Japan dominates.

As to why Japanese colonialism should have varied from European colonialism, the simple historical answer is that, as a latecomer in the game of nation building and industrialization, Japan had perfected a state-led model of development at home that it transferred to its colonies. A deeper theoretical answer, however, may be that the urge for more power and wealth lies at the core of large-scale historical transformations, but that strategies to acquire these goals vary with the circumstances. We know from European history, for example, that prior to the industrial revolution, landed agrarian classes, pressed for revenues in some parts of Europe, such as England, turned to commerce, and eventually eliminated the peasantry altogether. In other areas, by contrast, generally to the east, landed classes imposed the "second serfdom" in their respective rural societies.[22] These decisions, in turn, were deeply consequential for the subsequent patterns of development within Europe. Something similar probably underlay the different patterns of colonialism pursued by Japan and England.

European and Japanese colonialism were identical in that both sought political control and economic exploitation of other people, using different strategies that resulted in profoundly different long-term consequences for the areas they ruled. The British, given their own needs and values, sought mainly to maintain political control, to collect enough taxes to finance the functioning of a minimal laissez-faire state that facilitated this control, and to trade freely, selling manufactured goods produced by their emerging capitalist classes for commodities from the periphery. There were variations even within this broad pattern, as exemplified by the early and prolonged colonialism in India and the late and relatively superficial colonialism in Nigeria.

---

[22] See, for example, Moore, *Social Origins*, esp. chaps. 7 and 8.

The Japanese, by contrast, were in a hurry to add to their national wealth and power, and they pursued these goals via state-led capitalist industrialization both at home and in their colonies. The Japanese in Korea constructed a new state structure that enabled them to enhance their revenue base not only by squeezing the agrarian society harder but also by pushing landholders to improve productivity and thus enlarging the overall tax base.

The Japanese attitude toward industrialization within its colonies evolved over time, and by a process of trial and error, the logic of state-led capitalism within Japan clarified for the Japanese rulers that growth of industry in the colonies need not be at the expense of Japanese manufacturing and exporting interests. In fact, the rapid growth of state-guided industry both in Japan and in Korea was a recipe for the rapid growth of Japanese imperial power. Instead of imposing a "second serfdom" of sorts, therefore, the Japanese strategy in Korea – both brutal and deeply architectonic – laid the foundations of a cohesive-capitalist pathway to rapid economic transformation.

Besides Korea, the other case with significant cohesive-capitalist traits in the analyses above was Brazil. Since colonialism was a distant memory in the case of Brazil, what analytic lessons might one derive from this case to help to refine our understanding of the origins of a cohesive-capitalist pathway to economic development? First, cohesive-capitalism in Brazil was far from "pure" and differed from that in South Korea in important respects: The downward penetration of the state in Brazil was relatively limited, and the state's capacity to influence the national economy was circumscribed by numerous foreign dependencies. These limitations underline the importance of the legacy of Japanese colonialism for creating cohesive-capitalism in South Korea – it is probably difficult to create such a pattern of state-led development in a developing country without decisive external input. At the same time, however – and this is the second main lesson – Brazil, first under the Estado Novo and then again during the military period, approximated a cohesive-capitalist state, suggesting at least that developing country elites can go quite a ways in molding their own states and that the importance assigned to colonialism in the Korean case above may well be exaggerated. Such a conclusion, while possible, is also not entirely accurate.

The Estado Novo was the formative period of a cohesive-capitalist state of sorts in Brazil. Prior to that, the defining features of the Brazilian polity included strong regions under the oligarchic rule of settler elites with European roots. This was the long-term political legacy of distant colonialism in Brazil. The Estado Novo, in the establishment of which the armed forces played a major role, attempted to counter some of its inherited traits, especially to create a centralized state with a greater sense of a nation. In this important sense, the Estado Novo was very much a homegrown Brazilian affair. As the Estado Novo evolved, however, its German and Italian immigrants supported a strong fascist movement, and the state came to resemble its fascist counterparts in Europe. It took on such cohesive-capitalist traits as enormous concentration of power in the executive, authoritarian politics, close working relations between the state and private capital, incorporation of the working classes, aggressive anticommunism, appeals to nationalism, and growing emphasis on state intervention to promote industrial development.

The second important period when the Brazilian state approximated a cohesive-capitalist state was the military period, from 1964 to 1985. It was "too late" in history by now to make a virtue out of fascism. Nevertheless, just below the veneer of the military's ideology of "developmentalism" and "anticommunism," important traits of the Estado Novo were either maintained or reestablished. Military rulers now derived their inspiration and support not from European fascists but, ironically, from the democratic United States, which, within the context of the cold war, propagated doctrines that equated national security with rapid industrialization and gave legitimacy to the view that efficacious and authoritarian capitalism was preferable to democratic chaos that might breed communism. While not a sufficient condition, it is hard to imagine the reemergence of cohesive capitalism in Brazil without the historical legacy of the Estado Novo and without the support of the world's main superpower. Of course, the right-wing military authoritarianism also served narrow private interests.

To sum up this brief discussion on the origins of the cohesive-capitalist developmental pathway, major formative influences, listed in order of importance, appear to be: colonial legacies or other similar, external impacts; a degree of functional congruence – discovered by trial and error – between the goals of the ruling elite and the state's capacity to achieve these goals; and the pursuit of narrow private interests via an exclusionary state. The role of colonialism seems to loom especially large, most clearly in the case of Japan in Korea. The more general relationship between the nature of colonialism and the types of states that have emerged in a variety of developing countries will become even more apparent in the discussion of state types other than cohesive-capitalist.

Finally, what exactly did cohesive-capitalist states do to promote rapid industrialization? The answer has two broad components: first, the creation of a political context appropriate for the pursuit of economic growth, and second, pursuit of a distinct set of economic policies. The nature of the political context has already been summarized and includes such characteristics as prioritization of economic growth as a state goal, close cooperation between state and business, rule by competent bureaucrats, control of labor, downward penetration of state authority so as to silence opposition and control behavior, and nationalist mobilization so as to put a peacetime economy on a wartime footing. We turn next to the second component, namely, the pattern of state economic intervention that most effectively advances rapid industrialization.

Some prevailing arguments about the nature of state intervention are dubious, given the examination of our case studies. First, such developmental states as South Korea were definitely not "minimalist states" that respected the logic of the market and focused on getting prices right. This point, though by now well understood by many scholars and policy makers, is still advanced in some circles. Second, and relatedly, the claim that export promotion is superior to import substitution as a development strategy appears overstated when viewed in the context of, say, the cohesive-capitalist experiments in South Korea and Brazil. There is no doubt that countries such as South Korea avoided Brazil's "debt trap" because of their relatively high export earnings. The rate of growth of manufactured exports in Brazil during military rule was hardly insignificant, however; the problem was instead that their imports and foreign borrowing grew even more rapidly. Both South Korea and Brazil simultaneously pursued both import substitution and export promotion, with the state intervening to provide a variety of subsidies for both sets of activities. And third, the search for the magic set of policies that will produce rapid industrialization in the developing world may simply be in vain, as the effectiveness with which policies are pursued is deeply consequential. How else would one explain why both import substitution and export promotion worked in South Korea but failed in Nigeria?

Cohesive-capitalist states have succeeded in facilitating rapid industrialization by promoting high rates and efficient allocation of investment and have done this better than other types of developing country states, mainly because they are able to mobilize, concentrate, and utilize power in a highly purposive manner. This then is the "secret" behind the rapid rates of industrial growth achieved in such cases as South Korea under Park Chung Hee and Brazil during the military period. Let me elaborate.

First, why do leaders of cohesive-capitalist states tend to define rapid industrialization of their economies as the state's main priority? There is no easy, general answer, only historically specific ones. In both South Korea and Brazil, national leaders defined national security in terms of rapid industrialization. Whereas the real and/or imagined threat to national security in South Korea was external, in Brazil it was more internal, having more to do with popular sector activism. Since it is easy to think of cases that faced either external threat (for example, Pakistan) or a variety of internal popular pressures (for example, late Sukarno Indonesia), but where leaders did not prioritize rapid industrialization as a goal, it is probably wise not to put too much emphasis on "threat environment" as a necessary precondition for rapid industrialization to emerge as the state's main goal. The more contingent variable of the nature of the leadership is therefore also important. The more limited generalization that is warranted then is that defining rapid industrialization as the state's narrow and main priority requires the state elite to promote such industrial gains as necessary for national salvation – and not as welfare enhancing for all or as good for limited classes.

Keeping the state's energies focused on promoting rapid industrialization is not easy, especially in polities that are either more open or less well organized than cohesive-capitalist ones. Nehru in India in the 1950s, for example, also sought to prioritize industrialization of India as the main goal of economic planners. Soon, however, various other issues required attention: The neglect of agriculture became a major liability in an inflation-sensitive, open polity; organized labor pushed wages and cut into the rates of return on industrial investment; regional politics politicized the issue of location of industry; and patronage needs hurt the efficiency of public sector investments. The Indian state, in other words, was not capable of mobilizing and concentrating power in a manner that enabled it to pursue narrow goals consistently. By contrast, both South Korea and Brazil pursued rapid industrialization ruthlessly and consistently during their cohesive-capitalist phases, with considerable success in the former and with mixed results in the latter.

These cohesive-capitalist states achieved their goals by intervening heavily in the economy, directly and indirectly, for the purpose of removing supply-and-demand constraints and thereby mobilizing capital and labor for industrial production. Let us quickly revisit some of the main interventions, starting with savings and investments. Rapid industrialization of South Korea under Park Chung Hee, as we have seen, was fueled in part by very high rates of investments. The inheritance helped: Japanese colonialism left behind a significant industrial base and its accompaniments, such as a knowledge base, some managers and entrepreneurs, and a trained working class. Although these industrial plants were destroyed during decolonization and the civil war, substantial foreign aid from the United States helped to rebuild the war-torn economy rapidly.

Building on this base, Park's growth-oriented state was able to collect increased taxes and to mobilize high rates of investment. Japanese foreign capital, mainly in the form of commercial loans, was also attracted to the new state, in part because of its renewed commitment to growth and in part because of its authoritarian capacity to limit anti-Japanese nationalist politics. Once growth rates picked up, they fed private indigenous savings. While cultural patterns of frugality helped, the state also provided a variety of supports to encourage private domestic savings, such as positive real interest rates, savings institutions capable of mobilizing resources of small savers, and concentration of ownership in business and industry.

The pattern in Brazil was similar, with the underlying differences often traceable back to the differences between the two cohesive-capitalist states. Once in power, the Brazilian military government also succeeded in boosting tax collection and in focusing expenditures on core investments – an important component of the higher rates of growth of the miracle years, especially during the first decade of the military rule. Over the second decade, however, the military was unable to maintain the high rates of taxation, and its public expenditures increasingly reflected a growing political need to generate support. The military rulers also undertook such regressive but growth-generating actions as shifting the savings of workers within public institutions to support and subsidize private investments. Domestic private savings in Brazil remained relatively low, in part because cycles of high inflation discouraged private equity markets to develop. The second main component of Brazil's higher investment rate during the military period was thus private foreign capital. Much of this, unlike in South Korea, came first in the form of direct foreign investment, and then when the import bill far surpassed exports, in the form of commercial loans. In so doing the Brazilian state again played a key role in maintaining the high levels of economic growth.

In addition to creating the political environment necessary to mobilize high rates of savings and investments, the growth-oriented authoritarian states in South Korea and Brazil also sought to channel private investment into preferred areas. This controversial domain of industrial policy was pursued in both cases, though more effectively in South Korea. The South Korean state soon combined export promotion with a focus on heavy industry and import substitution. These choices were made in such close collaboration with businessmen, including Japanese companies, that it is difficult to disentangle who made them and why. Given these priorities, the public elites in South Korea used a number of instruments to channel private investment, including control over credit, subsidies, administrative supports, punishment for failing to fall in line, and nationalist exhortations. The Brazilian state similarly sought to combine import substitution with export promotion, also devaluing the exchange rate, while maintaining various sorts of protections and providing numerous financial and administrative supports to exporters. Working with direct foreign investors, however, the Brazilian state was not in the same position as the South Korean state to cajole, exhort, and mobilize investors to export as if national survival depended on it. With lower rates of overall investment and with a lesser capacity to channel investment into such preferred areas as export promotion, Brazilian efforts in the end were less successful than those in South Korea.

Finally, leaders of cohesive-capitalist states, cognizant as they were of the need for rapid industrialization, also strove to ensure that their state-led economies grew in a relatively efficient manner. Leaders in both South Korea and Brazil delegated economic policy making to technocrats, who sought to avoid the gross distortions of the price regime often found in other developing countries. First, they pursued systematic labor repression, which generally kept wage gains well behind productivity gains, as workers were mobilized to work hard in the name of the nation. Second, extensive public investments in both South Korea and Brazil were insulated from the most vulgar patronage politics and so were kept in the productive economy. And third, the state played a significant role in both cases to promote technology. This was more successful in South Korea because of the extensive support for education and the deliberate decoupling of foreign technology from foreign capital. But it was also far from insignificant in Brazil, where the state supported higher education and various arrangements with foreign investors to promote local technology and production.

The Neopatrimonial Route

The nearly polar opposite of cohesive-capitalist states along the continuum of state effectiveness at economic development is the neopatrimonial state. Variously described as clientelistic, corrupt, or predatory, they are not modern, rational-legal states. Leaders of such states have generally failed to promote industry or for that matter any other type of economic progress that one may label development. In their ideal-typical form, neopatrimonial states can be identified with reference to a number of characteristics. First, leadership tends to pursue more personal or sectional goals than such public goals as nation building, economic development, or industrialization. Second, neopatrimonial states are generally staffed by individuals whose level of competence and professionalism as civil servants tends to be low. Third, relations of state elites to business in these settings tend to be mutually corrupt, with state resources buttressing private rents, on the one hand, and private rents supporting the power position of the ruling elite, on the other hand. Fourth, the state's downward reach is generally limited. Even if governmental decision making is highly centralized, these states are generally disconnected from a variety of such groups as workers, and especially those who live in rural areas. And finally, even though various views such as socialism or economic nationalism may be espoused by the leadership, ideologies play only a minimal role in guiding policy, in legitimizing the state elite, or in binding the state and society together in a shared project.

Neopatrimonial states then fail to promote development mainly because of their failure to generate purposive power. They may use the rhetoric of development, but often merely to mask their real intent – to use state resources for personal benefit or for the benefit of personal associates. This pattern of behavior is unmistakable and reflective of public institutions that were poorly formed and that over time contributed to further decline in institutional effectiveness.

Even if some political elites within a neopatrimonial state would like to promote development, they find themselves thwarted by a variety of structural constraints. This political incapacity to pursue state-led development is part and parcel of the neopatrimonial political economy. Its critical ingredients are the absence of competent and professional bureaucrats, nearly routinized corruption at the highest levels, a serious political disconnect between the state and the citizenry, and relatedly, the absence of any normative glue to bind rulers and followers in a joint national project. The type of purposive power abundantly available in cohesive-capitalist states to pursue state-led development, including industrialization, is simply missing.

While a "pure" neopatrimonial state is probably rare in the real world, the case of Nigeria comes close, in terms of all the characteristics noted: use of state resources for private aggrandizement, widespread corruption (famously squandering and misusing Nigeria's abundant oil resources), bureaucratic incompetence, and having the state disconnected from society, making it difficult for state elites to mobilize internal resources and in turn enhancing their dependency on the vicissitudes of oil revenues. State-led development lacking purpose or capacity thus repeatedly turned into development disasters.

Neopatrimonial tendencies, especially misuse of public resources for personal or sectional gains, were evident in all the other cases analyzed above. This should not be too surprising, as this type of corruption is widespread and hardly unknown in even the best organized states. But when the state is poorly organized from the top to the bottom, the developmental impact of such misuse increases. Thus, what distinguishes an India or a Brazil from Nigeria is not so much the level of state intervention in the economy as the fact that, at least at their apex, the Indian and Brazilian states are moderately effective. Below the apex, however, they, too, suffer from personalism, patronage politics, and misuse of public resources. These states managed to overcome such neopatrimonial tendencies because they were limited to a few regions and because the better functioning central governments were responsible for the pursuit of planned industrialization.

Neopatrimonial states may be more abundant in the developing world than cohesive-capitalist states. This is because the latter have to be deliberately and carefully constructed, whereas the former reflect the more common failure of state construction and the subsequent evolution of "traditional" politics behind the façade of a "modern" state. Most states in sub-Saharan Africa, with a few important exceptions, probably fit this category. Richard Sandbrook in his prescient study argued that neopatrimonial states were a major cause of Africa's economic stagnation.[23] Strong neopatrimonial tendencies are also evident in many South Asian and Middle Eastern states, as well as in some Latin American polities of the recent past that were run by caudillos and ruling families. Such tendencies were exhibited even in the more developed East Asia, for example, South Korea under Syngman

---

[23] See Richard Sandbrook, *Politics of Africa's Economic Stagnation* (Cambridge: Cambridge University Press, 1985).

Rhee and the Philippines for much of its modern history.[24] In each case, the debilitating impact of neopatrimonialism obviously varies with the degree to which it pervades the state.

Let us now consider the twin issues of the origins and consequences of such states. Answers are again more readily forthcoming from a historical examination than from an attempt to get at a general explanation. Nevertheless, I will attempt both. Neopatrimonial states are best understood as imperfect states, lacking especially an effective public arena. While there are no perfect states as such, the modern states that first emerged in parts of Europe came to share several common characteristics: the centralizing of the legitimate use of coercion and territorial control and the emergence of a public arena that was above and distinct from various private interests. Following Max Weber, numerous scholars have documented the complex pathways by which resources of patrimonial monarchies of Europe became detached from the household of the monarch, how modern central authority was constructed with centralized armies and impersonal public services, and how nations came to be imagined. The development of this normative and organizational political model was protracted and imperfect, even within Europe. Its export to the global periphery, mainly via colonialism, resulted in numerous distortions.[25]

The distortions are most serious in those parts of the developing world, such as in Africa, where traditions of statelike political organizations were historically weak and where colonial powers failed to create effective modern states, having chosen instead to rule by accommodating various "premodern," personalistic, indigenous elites. These are the areas that came to be governed by neopatrimonial states. While sovereign rulers of developing countries have proved quite capable of destroying state institutions they inherited, the reverse, namely, constructing modern states anew, has proved to be remarkably difficult. That is why the legacy of colonialism looms so large for understanding the variety of state types to be found within the developing world.[26] In those areas that eventually turned into neopatrimonial states, colonial rulers had failed to establish full territorial control in

---

[24] For the Philippines, see Paul Hutchcroft, *Booty Capitalism: The Politics of Banking in the Philippines* (Ithaca, N.Y.: Cornell University Press, 1998).

[25] For one such argument, see Bertrand Bradie, *The Imported State: The Westernization of the Political Order* (Stanford, Calif.: Stanford University Press, 2000).

[26] Two important studies that do not necessarily follow the causal logic developed here but nevertheless trace the roots of, say, Africa's state pathologies back to the colonial period are Crawford Young, *The African Colonial State in Comparative Perspective* (New Haven, Conn.: Yale University Press, 1994); and Mahmood Mamdani, *Citizen and Subject: Contemporary Africa and the Legacy of Late Colonialism* (Princeton, N.J.: Princeton University Press, 1996). Another scholar who traces the roots of such pathologies to even earlier demographic variables is Jeffrey Herbst, *States and Power in Africa: Comparative Lessons in Authority and Control* (Princeton, N.J.: Princeton University Press, 2000).

the course of centralizing state authority and concomitantly failed to create effective public arenas.

In terms of political organization, an effective national level public arena would have required the centralization of state authority via the development of professional armies and civil services and simultaneously the elimination or weakening of various traditional intermediaries who exercised personal authority and performed such key governmental functions as collecting taxes and maintaining local law and order. The normative counterpart of such an organizational arrangement would have been the creation of an ethos, shared at least by sections of the indigenous political elite, that sovereign modern states are capable of serving and enhancing a public good that transcends personalistic and sectional interests. In turn, such an organizational and normative frame might have helped to generate nationalistic movements aimed at ousting colonial powers and at utilizing sovereign state power to promote a new type of public good, namely, economic development. What happened in some parts of the developing world instead was that colonial powers created minimum ruling arrangements by either reinforcing or re-creating various intermediate "traditional" elites and by expending little energy and few resources on creating modern states – with the result that indigenous nationalist movements quickly fragmented along a variety of sectional cleavages. The normative and organizational underpinnings of an effective modern state thus remained elusive in parts of the global periphery.

The origins of neopatrimonial states are thus best understood by focusing as much on what did not happen as on what actually happened. The roots of neopatrimonialism lie in the encounter of various peripheral societies devoid of state traditions with powerful, colonizing European states. For their own reasons, European colonizers in some peripheral parts, such as in sub-Saharan Africa, created a façade of a modern state that lacked scope or depth. As indigenous elites mobilized to capture these fragile and imperfectly constructed states, they readily reduced it to a vehicle of personal and sectional aggrandizement. Colonial discourse in Africa and elsewhere often argued that the colonized "natives" did not deserve sovereign control over states because they were not ready for such a responsibility. While self-serving and often racist, the description was also not entirely inaccurate. What was missing from the discourse instead was a consideration of deeper causes of this ill-preparedness, namely, the poorly constructed states left behind by colonial powers that never "prepared" the indigenous elite to run a modern state.

Many of these tendencies were evident in Nigeria. We recap briefly. First, Nigeria lacked state traditions. This was consequential in several ways: It influenced the colonial ruling strategy; leaders of sovereign Nigeria found it difficult to draw on historical symbols and memories to inspire a unifying nationalist imagination; and state elites confronted a citizenry not habituated to obeying and respecting an impersonal, centralized state. Second, although these inherited disadvantages might have been overcome, they were reinforced and even exacerbated by the pattern of colonial rule. For example, instead of creating unified rule, British colonizers chose to rule different parts of Nigeria differently. This reinforced existing differences and encouraged new distinctions, such as the emergence of commerce and modern education in the south but not in the north. Colonial rule also strengthened the position of a variety of traditional elites, especially in the north, paving the way for the eventual capture of a seemingly modern state by personalistic leaders. And at the first sign of regional schisms within nationalist politics, British rulers conceded power and resources to regional elites, strengthening them at the expense of a potential nationalist leadership.

Third, Nigerian nationalism remained superficial and fragmented along tribal lines, in contrast to a case such as India. Nationalism and nationalist movements in the developing world have proven to be crucibles of "publicness," or arenas in which sensibilities and organizations that seek to rise above private and sectional attachments have arisen. Minus such a nationalist movement, which of course was not unrelated to the pattern of colonialism, Nigeria also lacked an indigenous political force that might have helped to construct a coherent state with developmental commitments and capacities. And fourth, within sovereign Nigeria, military rule proved not to be an agent of state construction. That it "might have been" is suggested in part by the fact that states are ultimately agents of centralized coercion, frequently constructed for the sake of exercising coercion – hence Tilly's famous aphorism that "states create wars, and wars create states"[27] – and in part by contrasting the case of Brazil, in which the armed forces indeed played a critical role in both state construction and promoting industrialization. The Nigerian military essentially internalized many of the cleavages and sensibilities of its society and, thus, was more a part of the society than an agent of change capable of undertaking a developmental role.

The final issue in this discussion of the neopatrimonial pathway concerns the modalities neopatrimonial states used to create development failures. We have seen already that such states lack the will and capacity to promote economic development and that they typically squander public resources. What more, if anything, can be said at the general level? Extrapolating some insights from the Nigerian case and examining them against some other cases as well, a few final observations are in order.

First, there is a line of thinking in some scholarly and policy circles that what is really wrong with states identified here as neopatrimonial is that they repeatedly distort markets because of the narrow urban interests they serve; the consequences include serious economic failures, especially low

---

[27] See Charles Tilly, *Coercion, Capital and European States, AD 990–1992* (Oxford: Basil Blackwell, 1990), esp. chap. 3.

agricultural production.[28] Although adjustment policies pursued over the last two decades, say, in sub-Saharan Africa, often rested on such an analysis, several reservations about the diagnosis and proposed remedies ought to be noted. The Nigerian evidence does not fit this line of thinking very well, in part because Nigerian agriculture did not perform all that poorly but, more important, because a focus on the urban bias of the polity hardly helps to explain why urban-based industries did not perform well. Moreover, halfhearted pursuit of more promarket policies in the era of structural adjustment has not improved economic performance in any significant way, either in Nigeria or in many other countries of sub-Saharan Africa. The evidence thus suggests that the culprit was not wrongheaded policies, but that irrespective of policy choices, the broader context, especially the context created by poorly functioning state institutions, is at the root of the economic problems plaguing neopatrimonial states.

Neopatrimonial states are simply not all that seriously committed to promoting economic development, including industrialization. This situation stems from the broader failure of state elites to develop public commitments, which in turn repeatedly leads to the appropriation of the state for personal and sectional enrichment. The results include frequent disregard for macroeconomic stability, short-term policy inconsistencies, and a longer-term failure to initiate changes that may help to build a society's economic and technological capacities. The process of policy implementation is also fraught with problems. Irrespective of the policy regime, therefore, the outcomes are seldom favorable. This is because private agents receive neither consistent signals nor state support to undertake risky investment. Moreover, when the state attempts to undertake economic activity directly, state structures encourage channeling public resources into corrupt private uses. Such a pattern was evident in the analyses above, most clearly in the case of Nigeria but also to an extent in South Korea under Syngman Rhee and in select regions of India and Brazil.

More specifically, neopatrimonial states generally fail to promote new investments and an efficient use of this investment. Shorn of oil resources, in Nigeria it was clear above that the domestic capacity to mobilize new resources for investment and growth was highly limited. This limitation, rooted in the inability to tax and mobilize public resources and in the failure to build appropriate institutions and provide consistent incentives to private agents to save and invest, is common to most patrimonial states. Lest it be believed that high rates of investment alone could solve some critical problems of growth and industrialization in neopatrimonial states, the Nigerian case again provides a sobering check. During periods of high oil prices, Nigeria

---

[28] With reference to Africa, see Robert Bates, *Markets and States in Tropical Africa* (Berkeley: University of California Press, 1981). Several subsequent reports of the World Bank on the developmental problems of sub-Saharan Africa also reflect this general line of thinking.

was "investing" at a very high rate, as high in terms of aggregate figures as in parts of East Asia. And yet we know that sustained industrialization did not result. Why not?

The answer points to the more general developmental failures that emerge when state intervention in the economy is pursued by highly ineffective states. Part of the problem in Nigeria was that much of what passed for public investment was really nothing of the sort: Public resources were devoted instead to building a new capital city, to sharp wage hikes for civil servants, to ineffective pursuit of education, and to building theaters and stadiums. These problems are hardly unique to Nigeria. Even when resources were intended for productive investment in Nigeria, such as for steel production, numerous corrupt practices, delays, and bureaucratic inefficiencies hampered the efficient use of resources. Such problems also plague other neopatrimonial states. And finally, there were the critical policy decisions to promote import substitution of the worst kind, namely, low-value-added, last-stage assembly of manufactured goods. Highly import-intensive, this strategy could be sustained only as long as oil exports provided ample foreign exchange. The deeper failures of a neopatrimonial state at work are clear in the neglect of production of intermediate and capital goods, focusing instead on the easiest form of import substitution that catered primarily to the needs of a narrow, self-serving elite.

Fragmented-Multiclass States at the Helm

In between the two extremes of cohesive-capitalist and neopatrimonial states lie many other developing country states, labeled fragmented-multiclass states. Unlike neopatrimonial states, these are real modern states with a rational-legal structure, at least at the apex. Unlike cohesive-capitalist states, however, state authority in these cases tends to be more fragmented, and the social base of power tends to be more plural. Fragmented-multiclass states are thus typically characterized by a considerable gap between promises by the leadership, on the one hand, and the state's ability to fulfill these promises, on the other hand. The general issues for discussion then are what political traits do fragmented-multiclass states share, what conditions typically account for their emergence, and how do they influence the rates and patterns of late-late industrialization?

Fragmented-multiclass states are modern states in the sense that they indeed centralize the use of coercion in a defined territory and that state structures within them are normatively and organizationally distinguishable from a variety of private interests. Leaders of fragmented-multiclass states are dedicated to pursuing state-led development but, for reasons of legitimacy and political support, tend to define development fairly broadly, including goals of industrialization, redistribution and welfare, and national sovereignty. The quality of both the armed forces and the civilian bureaucracies in such states tends to be uneven – generally superior in areas deemed by leaders to be of great political importance and inferior elsewhere. What truly distinguishes fragmented-multiclass states from other state types within the developing world is the nature of political expectations that link rulers and the various social groups. Whether organized as a democracy or as a dictatorship, the citizenry of fragmented-multiclass states tends to be mobilized – politically aware and active – and at times even organized. The political institutions that systematically link rulers and social groups generally tend to be weak, however, leading to fragmentation of state power. Dispersion of power, mobilized citizenry, and weak political institutions such as parties thus define the broad political matrix within which fragmented-multiclass states seek to promote late-late industrialization.

Leaders of these states attempt to promote industry by supporting private enterprise, but given the political compulsions of maintaining legitimacy, the relationship of state and business tends to be cooperative at times but distant and even conflictual at other times. Similarly ambiguous is the relationship of the state with the working class. In the absence of well-developed parties, leaders may emphasize a pro-working-class rhetoric to shore up political support, but, on balance, they feel obliged to maintain a functioning private economy, including a working class whose gains must not outstrip gains in productivity. The relations between the political elite and the vast numbers of the poor, both in the cities and in the countryside, tend to be unorganized, encouraging both rhetorical populism and, on occasion, sharp conservative reactions to such populism. Populist ideologies and nationalism generally play a significant role in fragmented-multiclass states, helping leadership legitimacy but constraining economic policy choices.

Via their ideology and organization, fragmented-multiclass states are able to generate some purposive power to pursue industrialization – but within limits, as they seek simultaneously to represent and to transform the societies they govern. Trying to reconcile conflicting imperatives, fragmented-multiclass states seek to satisfy rather than maximize and tend to be middling performers on many dimensions, including promotion of industry. A committed leadership, moderate levels of competence and professionalism of the bureaucracy, broad legitimacy, and the ability to establish working relations with a variety of social groups are all political assets that can readily be translated into developmental capacity. At the same time, however, the developmental power of these states is constrained – by fragmenting state authority, simultaneously pursuing multiple goals, treating pockets of bureaucracy as tools of politics and patronage, maintaining political distance from business elite, and tilting the political process in favor of popular groups so as to accommodate multiclass politics. Fragmented-multiclass states are therefore inclined to adopt and implement policies that detract from really rapid industrialization.

These mixed developmental capacities were most apparent in the case of India. It is fair to suggest that the Indian state has been run by leaders committed to industrialization as a significant state goal, that it has been manned at the apex by professional bureaucrats, that it enjoys a fair amount of legitimacy, and that the state and business elite in India, though not in a total embrace, enjoy good working relations. These characteristics, which contributed to moderate success in industrial promotion, were especially evident in Nehru's time and in the last two decades of the twentieth century. At the same time, state authority in India is fragmented along a number of dimensions, including intraelite conflicts, the center versus the regions, and elites versus the masses. Moreover, state power in India tends to rest on a multiclass coalition, generating perennial concerns on the part of leaders about their legitimacy. Legitimacy needs, in turn, have often inclined India's rulers to pursue other goals at the expense of rapid industrialization: Bureaucracy has thus been used as a tool of patronage and political interests; business groups have on occasion been vilified; foreign capital has been kept at a distance; and just as often, the embrace of the popular sectors has been prioritized. While these tendencies have been present in India over the last several decades, they were most apparent during the two decades of Indira Gandhi's rule, to the detriment of industrial growth.

Based on the Indian case it would be misleading to equate fragmented-multiclass states with developing country democracies in general. First, the developmental effectiveness of India's democratic state varied over time. Second, it was evident in the Brazilian case that during the period 1945–64, the narrowness of Brazilian democracy enabled state elites to pursue industrialization quite effectively, at least until the early 1960s, when working-class activism, populist political rhetoric, and ineffective leadership exacerbated state ineffectiveness. Third, authoritarian regimes can also be readily ineffective in the sense of exhibiting a considerable gap between promise and performance. South Korea under Syngman Rhee, for example, was a state where, in spite of the political inheritance, leadership priorities were anything but effectively developmental. The second decade of the Brazilian military rule also moved in the same direction when military rulers troubled by sagging legitimacy became less effective tax collectors and channeled public expenditures to shore up political support.

There is some minimal overlap between the typology of cohesive-capitalist, neopatrimonial, and fragmented-multiclass states, on the one hand, and the regime categories of democracy and authoritarianism, on the other hand; that is, cohesive-capitalist states are likely to be authoritarian, and most developing country democracies are likely to be fragmented-multiclass states. Beyond that, however, what looms is the lack of congruence. Authoritarian regimes can be cohesive-capitalist, neopatrimonial, or fragmented-multiclass states. State characteristics within the developing world thus exhibit institutional traits that often endure a regime shift from authoritarianism to democracy and back. This is especially so with neopatrimonial states, where the comings and goings of democratic and authoritarian regimes do not readily alter the state's developmental effectiveness. The same lack of congruence also holds for fragmented-multiclass states, where the middling developmental effectiveness rarely transcends distinctions of ruling regimes. Imagine for a moment an authoritarian India, much like its neighbor Pakistan. Would it be more effective developmentally? In all probability, the answer is a resounding no.

Many developing country states are fragmented-multiclass states of the type we have seen in India and for brief periods in South Korea and Brazil, including South Asian, many Latin American, and some Southeast Asian countries. As already noted, highly effective cohesive-capitalist states are rare in the developing world and concentrated mostly in East Asia. The grossly dysfunctional neopatrimonial states tend to be concentrated in sub-Saharan Africa. The prevalence of fragmented-multiclass states in the developing world underlines the twin facts that the process of state formation has proceeded quite far in much of the developing world but that such states remain troubled institutions, especially in light of the many tasks they have set for themselves.

Most fragmented-multiclass states seek simultaneously to represent and transform their societies. The former requires responding to social demands, whereas the latter demands a more autonomous leadership agenda. Attempting to reconcile these conflicting imperatives taxes the best of states and puts a high premium on effective political institutions, such as political parties, that can generate more cohesive authority by mitigating intraelite and elite-mass conflicts. The common weakness is the inclination of fragmented-multiclass states to promise more than they can deliver, which makes them middling performers.

What might one say at a general level about the origins of fragmented-multiclass states and about their patterns of economic intervention? To get at answers, one needs to consider why and how these states acquired such modern characteristics as centralized control over territory, professional civil and military bureaucracies, and the emergence of a separate public realm. One also wants to know the conditions that give rise to fragmentation of authority and to multiclass politics that, in turn, create a nearly perpetual mismatch between leadership goals and the capacities to promote development.

It was clear in the Indian case that a modern state emerged as a product of India's encounter with British colonialism. While more or less centralized empires had dotted parts of India for a long time, it was the British who established centralized territorial control, created the beginnings of a modern army and civil service, established an administrative infrastructure, and set the tone for impersonal rule. The Indian nationalist movement reinforced some of these tendencies by pushing for greater Indian participation in the civil service and the army, by generating its own public-spirited leaders at the apex, and by mobilizing along nationalist lines – a process that generated values and organizations that transcended numerous personal and sectional interests. Such were the origins of some of the critical ingredients of a modern state in India.

What also comes out of the historical discussion of India, however, is that the early antecedents of state ineffectiveness in India were also to be found in the colonial phase. Thus, for example, we noted that British rule in India from the mid-nineteenth century onward rested not only on the domination of a modern, repressive state, but also on an alliance with a variety of premodern Indian elites. These arrangements were a logical outcome of the minimal British goals of exercising political control and pursuing economic gain. The result was fragmented state authority, including the inability of the state to penetrate downward or to initiate any meaningful socioeconomic changes in India's vast rural periphery. To this long-term trend, India's nationalist movement contributed an additional dimension of state ineffectiveness. Moved by the main political goal of ousting the British, Gandhi's mobilization strategy created the Indian National Congress (INC), a loosely organized political organization with a multiclass, mass base that spearheaded India's nationalist movement. The tension between leading and representing was well handled within the INC, at least insofar as the main goal of the nationalists was to create a sovereign state with some shared sense of a nation. Viewed from the standpoint of economic development, however, the INC from fairly early on tended to make political promises that it could not readily fulfill. Once in command of a sovereign Indian state, therefore, it reinforced the state ineffectiveness already inherent in the British colonial design.

Sovereign India thus inherited a state that was simultaneously modern but limited in its political capacities. While the die of a fragmented-multiclass state was cast rather early, the direction of future change was far from preordained. Nehru launched a highly ambitious multifaceted developmental program for India in which the state was to play a central guiding role. At the same time, however, he did little to improve the state's developmental capacities. On the contrary, many of Nehru's actions were prudent when viewed from the standpoint of consolidating a stable democracy – maintaining a law and order bureaucracy, aligning the Congress party with the powerful in the society, and accommodating India's ethnic pluralism in a federal structure – but nonetheless further exacerbated the short-term gap between developmental ambitions and state capacities. Still, the nationalist legitimacy and the relatively low levels of political mobilization in India's vast hinterland enabled Nehru to focus the state's resources on the goal of state-led development of heavy industries, with some success. Indira Gandhi's subsequent populism in retrospect appears to have been the logical conclusion of a much earlier trend in Indian nationalist politics, namely, the widening of the gap between promises and performance. India's right-wing nationalist rulers who came to power in the 1990s narrowed some of this gap not by improving state capacities significantly but by cutting back on radical promises, prioritizing economic growth as the state's main goal, and establishing closer ties with indigenous and foreign capital.

South Korea under Syngman Rhee and Brazil in some periods offer evidence of other instances of limited developmental capacities within well-established states. The well-built colonial state that the Japanese left behind in Korea could have readily collapsed in the wake of rapid decolonization but, motivated by the need to maintain order and stability, was just as readily strengthened and reestablished with U.S. help. Instead of moving this state in a developmental direction, however, Rhee used it to pursue corrupt, personalistic ends and such noneconomic priorities as saving South Korea from communism, with the result that the state's developmental capacities were diluted.

The two important instances of state ineffectiveness in Brazil following the Second World War are the period just before the military coup in 1964 and then the second decade of the military rule. Post-1984 Brazil, which I have not analyzed here in any detail, would probably also stand out as a case of a fragmented-multiclass state writ large. Brazil's nominal democracy in the 1950s shared some core characteristics of cohesive-capitalist states and exhibited considerable capacity to define and pursue a high-growth agenda. The first real spread of democracy to the working classes and the related emergence of multiclass politics and populist leaders, however, quickly exposed the contradictions of a nominal democracy and weakened the state's capacity to promote rapid industrialization. The military government in its first decade was, of course, much closer to a real cohesive-capitalist state, with Brazil's rapid industrialization to its credit. During the second decade of its rule, however, the military government worried more about its underlying support and simultaneously made more political concessions and pursued wrongheaded economic policies. Unable to improve rates of tax collection, it channeled public monies to unproductive rural oligarchs and pursued debt-led rapid growth when economic circumstances demanded a less ambitious agenda.

It ought to be clear that though fragmented-multiclass states share some core characteristics, the conditions under which they arise vary enormously. One cannot generalize about the typical path they might follow from origin to maturation, though some limited observations are possible. The question is, are there any general patterns by which peripheral states acquire modern characteristics, on the one hand, and by which the recurring political incapacity to pursue their developmental ambitions fully appears, on the other hand?

The origins of a modern but limited state in many peripheral countries are probably located in their colonial phase. We have already probed the importance of these foundations for subsequent state development. Extrapolating from this, one may suggest that roots of fragmented-multiclass states are located in a pattern of European colonialism, mainly in Asia, that differed from the pattern of both Japanese colonialism and European colonialism in Africa. The typical process by which the rudiments of modern states were created in some peripheral countries involved imposition of political control by centralizing territorial control, establishing modern armies, police, and civil bureaucracy, and, at least at the apex, depersonalizing government rule. This pattern of early colonial rule, found in India, is probably also to be found in such other countries as Sri Lanka, Malaysia, and Indonesia.

Colonial state power needed to be grafted on to existing organized societies. The main choice was either to weaken the political hold of indigenous elites or to incorporate them into a new ruling alliance with the colonial state. The former pattern, followed mainly by the Japanese, led to considerable downward penetration of state power in society. European colonists, however, moved both by ideals of limited government and by self-interest defined in terms of trade rather than economic transformation, often took the easy way out and created alliances with indigenous rulers, strengthening and modifying their hold on power. Colonially constructed modern Weberian states that were grafted on to personalistic despots thus provided the beginnings of fragmented states in the global periphery.

With colonialism a distant memory, the specific historical pattern of state construction differed in most Latin American countries. Elements of the political and class logic evident in the emergence of a fragmented-multiclass state in India, however, were also evident in the case of Brazil. When a modern state finally emerged in Brazil in the 1930s, for example, it was in part driven by shifting class forces but also by politics, in the sense that it involved the coming together of military forces and professional politicians capable of imposing centralized order. The new state then had to accommodate a variety of preexisting centers of power, especially those that did not pose any obvious threat to the centralizers. The hitherto decentralized polity was thus replaced by centralized rule, while leaving numerous landed oligarchs powerful in their local domains. Thus again we see the pattern of a modern state grafted on to the local population of despots.

Over time the power of modern states vis-à-vis landowning oligarchies in all fragmented-multiclass states generally increased. The growth of cities and urban capital wealth as well as the spread of plebiscitarian politics weakened the hold of rural oligarchs. Finally, as states became more professional and centralized, they were able to impose their modern technology of administration and rule. However, none of this strengthened the developmental capacity of fragmented-multiclass states to any remarkable degree because such states were never able to solve a core dilemma: how to promote the narrow interests of private capital, which was essential for rapid industrialization, while simultaneously legitimizing their hold on power in the eyes of the majority of citizens.

The problem facing fragmented-multiclass states was not simply one of "class rule," an issue also central to most advanced industrial countries, where over time a variety of institutional solutions were developed to facilitate the coexistence of economic inequality and plebiscitarian politics. The problem for late-late-developing countries is deeper, in the sense that the state's role in society is pervasive from the outset. Since the life chances of many depend on state actions, the functioning of the state is deeply scrutinized, politicized, and fought over. At the same time, however, promoting state-led industrialization requires narrow collaboration between the political and economic elite. This is the core contradiction facing fragmented-multiclass developmental states – a contradiction that never really emerges in neopatrimonial states because of pervasive personalism and that cohesive-capitalist states resolve by coercion. While the historical pathways through which this core contradiction emerges differs across cases, all such states share the pressures to manage this tension, leading to less than stellar performance as an agent of industrialization.

The final issue concerns the pattern of economic interventions that fragmented-multiclass states typically undertake and that is just as typically associated with middling economic performance. When fragmented-multiclass states intervene in the economy, it is to pursue several state-defined goals simultaneously, with industrialization being only one of many, including rural development, redistribution and welfare provision, maintenance of a broad-based polity, and/or the protection of national sovereignty. The pursuit of several goals might lead to a more "balanced" pattern of development, but it seldom leads to the rate-busting industrial development characteristic of cohesive-capitalist states.

Thus, the relations of state elites with private capital in fragmented-multiclass states tend to be cooperative only some of the time, and systematic control of labor is often difficult. Penetration of the more traditional, rural sector is limited by the power of landholding elites. The organization of the state itself is also likely to be distinctive. If organized democratically, organizations such as political parties are likely to be characterized by weak organizational structures and multiclass alliances. Whether democratic or authoritarian, only part of the state bureaucracy is likely to be effective, the rest being devoted to the distribution of patronage resources in the management of complex polities.

Multiple goals and a relatively fragmented political context influence both the rates and the efficiency of industrial investment within fragmented-multiclass states. Let us first take up the issue of rates of investment. If public, private indigenous, and private foreign capital are the main components of overall investment anywhere, political conditions are likely to push industrial investment rates in fragmented-multiclass states into some middle range, somewhere between the dismal rate of neopatrimonial states and the very high rates of cohesive-capitalist states. Why should this be so?

First, rates of public investment in industry reflect governmental capacity to mobilize public revenues, generally via taxation, and the political ability to direct expenditures on industry. The capacity to mobilize public resources within fragmented-multiclass states, though substantial, is also limited, in part by the uneven quality of the bureaucracy and in part by the inability to penetrate and tax the rural society. Even more important are the perennial pressures in fragmented-multiclass states to channel public monies into various "consumption" activities that help to shore up political support but that do not always maximize return on investment.

Second, fragmented-multiclass states limit the scope of mobilizing private savings. The fact that these states are not committed exclusively to the promotion of high rates of growth and private profitability influences the business climate for private investors. The public resources available to subsidize private risk taking are available but limited. Highly nationalistic leaders of these states are also likely to limit the role of private foreign investors. More significantly, if organized democratically, a periodic tilt toward the left is likely. The resulting economic policies, more likely populist than genuinely social democratic, will in turn discourage both domestic and foreign private investors to the detriment of prospects for rapid industrialization.

Not only rates of investment but also political conditions influence the efficiency of industrial investments. The general point is that economic policy making within these states tends to be subsumed by political concerns that include more than industrial growth in the name of national salvation and that as a result generally undermine the efficiency of industrial investment. First, because decision making is seldom exclusively in the hands of "apolitical" technocrats, political calculus influences all modes of economic decision making – from the overall choice of development strategy, say, import substitution versus export promotion, to the more mundane issues of the location of a public sector industrial plant. Once the development path is chosen, moreover, various interests impede the ability of fragmented-multiclass states to undertake radically new policies.

In addition, the process of economic policy implementation in such states also tends to impose numerous inefficiencies on the process of deliberate industrialization. Management of public enterprises, for example, readily becomes a victim of patronage or other types of politics. What may be less obvious is that a similar logic also pervades state relations with the private sector. Industrial policy interventions that work well in the context of cohesive-capitalist states do not work as well in the context of fragmented-multiclass states. Thus, credit channeled to "future winners" is just as likely to end up in the hands of cronies as in the hands of deserving industrialists. Similarly, other state subsidies, including protection, may shield inefficient but powerful producers instead of promoting new and efficient ones.

To sum up, fragmented-multiclass developmental states are real modern states whose developmental capacity is enhanced by the public commitment of leaders, the moderate professionalism of the bureaucracy, a relatively broad-based legitimacy, and the channeling of public resources and efforts to promote industry. At the same time, however, state authority in these settings tends to be fragmented and the social power base of the state relatively plural. Further, these states pursue multiple goals but none of them all that effectively. Fragmented-multiclass states are thus best understood in juxtaposition to both cohesive-capitalist and neopatrimonial states within the developing world. If cohesive-capitalist states succeed in coercively reorganizing the societies they govern to enhance developmental capacity, and if the inefficacious neopatrimonial states are shells of modern states captured by a variety of personal and sectional interest, then fragmented-multiclass states seek simultaneously to represent and to transform their societies, achieving both to some extent, but excelling at neither.

III. Concluding Reflections

This study explores both how and why developing countries acquired different types of states and how and why these states produced a range of economic outcomes. What remains now is to reflect on some general conclusions. At the risk of some repetition, three sets of issues require final comments. What forces best help to explain the process of state formation in the developing world? How can one best understand the role of states in fostering and hindering economic progress in the developing world? And what, if any, normative and prescriptive lessons can one draw from this study for future development efforts?

State Formation

I have approached the study of developing country states mainly from the standpoint of their effectiveness as economic actors. This concern does not exclude but is also not coterminous with the Weberian focus on territorial control and bureaucratic development or with such issues of power distribution as democracy versus authoritarianism. A concern with the state's developmental effectiveness instead leads me to ask such questions as whether a developing country state is really a modern state or not, that is, whether it is part of a society's public arena that is genuinely demarcated from various private interests, organizations, and loyalties. The failure of such a public realm to emerge generally leads to private and sectional capture of a state, producing highly ineffective neopatrimonial states. Among the more modern, rational-legal states in the developing world, developmental effectiveness seems to vary mainly with the degree to which state authority is cohesive or fragmented and with the extent to which the social base of state power is narrow or plural. Cohesive-capitalist states thus turn out to be more effective economic actors than fragmented-multiclass states, at least assessed in decades. What factors best help to explain the emergence of these various types of states in the developing world?

The process of state formation in the developing world has proceeded in a series of "big bangs," with formative moments few and far between, though incremental changes have certainly altered power configurations within each state type and, at times, even accumulated to yield a basic change in state type. That the latter process is rare and tends to be drawn out and complex is understandable, given that state formation generally requires a preponderance of force in the hands of some to impose their preferred design on others for long enough of a period that basic institutions take root. The comparative historical analysis above suggests that the main political forces capable of creating states and molding basic state forms have been colonialism, nationalist movements, and regime changes, especially militaries moving in and out of power. Incremental shifts in power configurations within states, in turn, have generally been pushed by political parties, by new social classes, or by some combination of the two. As I revisit each of these factors, the main message comes through clearly: Colonialism has proved to be the most significant force in the construction of basic state structures in the developing world, and the emergence of new class forces within these countries, especially the growing power of capitalists, has the greatest potential to alter power configurations of these states.

Much of the developing world was dragged into the modern era by colonialism. However one judges it, this is a historical legacy with which all scholars interested in the political economy of development, especially political economy over the long duration, must come to terms. Colonialism everywhere was a system of direct political control created to enhance the political and economic interests of the ruling power. Armed with a preponderance of power, metropolitan countries created states or statelike structures in the colonies so as to control territories, people, resources, and economic opportunities. These colonially constructed political institutions, in turn, proved to be highly resilient, influencing and molding the shape of sovereign developing country states. Within these shared commonalities, however, the pattern of colonialism varied, as did its long-term legacy.

The sharpest contrast in the pattern of colonialism was evident above in the role of the Japanese and the British in Korea and Nigeria, respectively. Without doubt, Korea and what eventually became Nigeria were already distinct societies in the precolonial period. Nevertheless, it would be difficult to extrapolate long-term patterns of change mainly from these initial differences. Of decisive impact instead was the fact that the Japanese sought to control and exploit Korea while transforming it, whereas the British pursued similar goals while squeezing Nigeria. These contrasting strategies proved to be of considerable long-term significance: The Japanese created and left behind the building blocks of a cohesive-capitalist state, while the British left a legacy that included the rudiments of a neopatrimonial state.

Distinct from both of these extreme cases were the British in India. They left behind a state that was relatively well constructed at the apex but in which power remained highly fragmented just below the apex – the foundation, that is, of the fragmented-multiclass state of India. The process in Brazil shared some similarities. Although colonialism there was a distant memory, it took the Brazilians nearly a century to overcome the Portuguese failure to construct a centralized national state. When such a state was eventually constructed, traditional regional despots obstructed state consolidation, paving the way for a mixed state, mostly cohesive-capitalist but with a fragmented-multiclass underbelly.

If the basic variations in the political impact of colonialism and in their long-term significance for patterns of state formation are clear enough, two explanatory issues deserve a final comment: Why did the impact of colonialism vary and why did this impact prove so enduring? The impact varied because colonizing powers adopted alternative ruling strategies in their respective colonies. These strategies varied not simply because of the different circumstances confronting colonizers but also because the colonizers carried with them different capacities and understandings of how best to control and exploit colonized people. The comparison of Britain and Japan is again instructive.

Whereas the British sought to rule their colonies via limited, laissez-faire states, the Japanese imposed states that were considerably more encompassing. These differences followed logically from the alternative pathways the colonizers had themselves taken to become modern, powerful states. Great Britain, as an early industrializer with a limited laissez-faire state at home, sought to construct similar states in its colonies. Such a strategy fit well with the British interest in trading manufactured goods in exchange for the raw materials of the colonies. Such a limited governance approach also necessitated reaching a variety of arrangements with indigenous, traditional rulers, who mainly squeezed their own low-productivity economies so as to enable colonial rule to be more or less self-financing. By contrast, the Japanese were late developers who on their own had perfected a state-led model of development, well suited to advancing them within the global political economy. This was the model they transmitted to Korea, thus laying the foundations of an effective dirigiste state. A state-led economy at home also enabled the Japanese in Korea to coordinate the interests of those Japanese firms mainly interested in exporting manufactured goods to Korea as well as of those mainly interested in exporting capital and establishing manufacturing in Korea. The Japanese pattern of colonialism was thus considerably more transformative, leaving in its wake a state that was simultaneously brutal and capable of introducing socioeconomic change, on the one hand, and a growing economy with an industrial base, on the other hand.

Why did colonially constructed state institutions prove to be so enduring despite the commitment of nationalist leaders in the developing world to eradicate the colonial legacy, to don traditional attire, to change names of cities, roads, and buildings, to construct new national symbols, and to bring about revolutionary renewal of their states and nations? Of course, one should not exaggerate the continuity of present-day developing country states with the state institutions established by colonial powers. Much has changed, especially the intent of the new rulers and the size of the states in relation to their respective societies. Rather, the institutional continuities that I have drawn attention to concern such basic state characteristics as their autonomy from personalistic forces in society, relative coherence of authority, both at the apex of the state and in the state's relations with various social forces, and the underlying class basis of state power. The claim has been that alternative colonial strategies of rule helped to construct such basic state characteristics and thus laid the foundations for the eventual emergence of neopatrimonial, cohesive-capitalist, and fragmented-multiclass states in the developing world.

While institutions tend to endure, their persistence still requires an explanation. State institutions tend to persist in part because the powerful in society are incapable of designing new institutions to replace the old ones and in part because the existing institutions enable the powerful to pursue their material and ideal interests. The former limitation stems from an inability to mobilize the preponderance of autonomous force that would be required to create and maintain a new state architecture. That is why colonial powers, which are generally well armed with such an architectonic force, end up being the state constructors par excellence. However much nationalist movements and military rulers might seek to fundamentally alter the inherited structures, they rarely succeed. At least as important, state institutions do not always persist by default. Instead, they are made to endure because the powerful in society discover that they can pursue their own interests through them. Institutions thus mold the way in which the political and economic elite pursue their interests; by contrast, institutions that hinder the powerful seldom survive.

Revisiting very briefly some of the main historical instances of institutional continuities that we encountered above may help to place these abstract generalizations into sharper relief. In South Korea, for example, key elements of the cohesive-capitalist state that the Japanese created survived the Rhee period, mainly because they served the interests of the Americans and of Rhee. Park Chung Hee was able to build on this inheritance and, given his preference for rapid growth, was able to institute a Japanese-type model of development in South Korea, including an efficacious cohesive-capitalist state. By contrast, the poorly constructed state left behind by the British in Nigeria was readily co-opted by a variety of personalistic and sectional forces. Repeated efforts generally failed to create a more rational-legal state. The result was the continuity of the neopatrimonial state that, in turn, enabled various elites to appropriate public resources for personal ends.

The elements of continuity were somewhat less pronounced in the cases of India and Brazil, where a nationalist movement and military rulers, respectively, were able to introduce significant political changes. Nevertheless, the element of fragmented state power that characterized colonial India continued into the sovereign period, in part because of the inability of the new rulers to mobilize sufficient cohesive force to penetrate the countryside and in part because the legitimacy of the new rulers depended on allowing different centers of local power to survive and flourish. Brazil is even more complicated. One element of the continuity there is the long legacy of a radically decentralized polity created by the Portuguese. Whatever the nature of subsequent states, this element of regional autonomy and the related state fragmentation have remained integral aspects of Brazilian state design. Equally significant elements of continuity were notable from the Estado Novo in the 1930s to the military period from the 1960s onward. Elements of the cohesive-capitalist state created under Vargas survived and were modified and re-created by the military because they were useful for producing rapid growth that mainly benefited the elites. Overall, then, when judged by the standard of the state's developmental role, the fact that varied colonial inheritance has persisted into statehood turns out to be of great significance. It has meant that those who inherited more effective state institutions have been better situated to propel their economic progress than those who inherited relatively poorly constructed states.

In addition to colonialism, other possible agents that might have had a decisive impact on developing country states were indigenous nationalist movements and militaries coming in and out of power. The historical discussion above noted the role played by these agents in the process of state formation in different settings, while underlining that on balance the role was not all that decisive. India was the most important of the four country cases for assessing the impact of anticolonial nationalist movements on state formation. India's popular nationalist movement proved to be a significant oppositional political force. It can also be argued that its nationalist movement contributed to the establishment of a functioning democracy while also influencing India's choice of development strategies. And yet, when assessed in terms of its contribution to the developmental effectiveness of the state, the nationalist movement turns out not to have played all that positive of a role. Indian nationalists, that is, maintained the colonial law-and-order state, reinforced its fragmented character, and pluralized the state's social base in a manner that helped to institutionalize a fragmented-multiclass state.

In the other cases analyzed in this study, organized nationalist movements were even less of a political force than in India. With colonialism only a distant memory in Brazil, one would not expect such a force to have emerged at midcentury. The absence of the same in Korea is also not much of a puzzle, because Japanese colonial rule – highly authoritarian and nearly fascistic – left little political room for such a movement to emerge and then collapsed suddenly at the end of the Second World War. The failure of a significant and cohesive nationalist movement to emerge in Nigeria, however, is more of a puzzle; it was analyzed above while invoking such variables as the absence of an indigenous state tradition, the late emergence of an educated stratum, and, most important, the fragmented character of the colonial state itself. The absence of popular and organized nationalist movements in all of these cases, in turn, made it unlikely that indigenous nationalist sensibilities could be directed to become a force for state transformation. While nationalist sensibilities, or their absence, could certainly be significant variables in development policy choices, the point here is instead to underline the limited role that developing country nationalists ended up playing in forging their respective states.

Why were these nationalists not more effective state builders? After all, one can imagine that such movements could capture state power and mold state forms decisively. Thus, if one conceives of communist revolutionary movements as extreme nationalist movements, then something very much along these lines came to pass in a country such as China.[29] Yet among the cases discussed in this study, nationalist movements were less effective. Juxtaposing India and China suggests some insights as to why this might have been so. In comparison with China, India's nationalist movement was a multiclass movement, but it was also less well organized than China's Communist Party. As a result of these class and organizational characteristics, the Indian movement better reflected Indian society, meaning that Indian nationalists could represent Indian society well – thus being more effective as agents of democracy – but could not readily rise above it so as to generate the autonomous and cohesive power necessary for a radical redesign of the state. If the Indians, with their relatively successful nationalist movement, could not on their own create a more effective state, it should come as no surprise that nationalists elsewhere in the noncommunist developing world had even more limited capacity.

The role of military rulers as state builders varied substantially in the cases analyzed above, as a quick revisit will show. With a civilian polity well in place, the political role of the military was least significant in the case of India – the analytical lesson being that the direct intervention of the military in politics generally reflects the failure of social and political forces to create a workable civilian polity. In the other three cases discussed above, the military role was significant but not always consequential in terms of state formation, with the Nigerian case the most dramatic. Military regimes

[29] For a discussion of the central role of nationalism in the Chinese revolution, see Chalmers Johnson, *Peasant Nationalism* (Stanford, Calif.: Stanford University Press, 1962). For an argument that Chinese communists were effective state builders, see Schurmann, *Ideology and Organization in China*; and Theda Skocpol, *States and Social Revolutions* (New York: Cambridge University Press, 1979), 97.

have come and gone in Nigeria, but without much success in enabling the state in that country to transcend its neopatrimonial character.

Military rulers, by contrast, were major players in both South Korea and Brazil. Park Chung Hee, for example, was a military man, as were many of his colleagues. They pulled off the coup in the early 1960s, helped to reestablish a cohesive-capitalist state, and put South Korea on a trajectory of rapid industrialization and growth. What is also important to note, however, is that Park Chung Hee built on the Japanese political inheritance that survived the Rhee interregnum and was helped by the U.S.-sponsored land reforms that enabled state penetration of the countryside. And the role of the military in Brazil's political development was the most significant of the four cases discussed. The military was a key actor in the 1930s when Brazil finally constructed a centralized, modern state under Vargas. Throughout the democratic period of the 1950s, moreover, military rulers continued to act as "boundary setters." And finally, in 1964, the military grabbed power directly and set about creating a state that approximated a cohesive-capitalist state. Once again, however, the Brazilian military rulers built on such past inheritances as the state's close working relations with business, the continued role of foreign investors, and state-incorporated labor. The military rulers also derived many of their ideas and support from external actors. Seemingly all-powerful, they were nonetheless ultimately unable to alter such basic traits of the polity as the relative autonomy of patronage-oriented regions. When militaries went out of power in both South Korea and Brazil, they again contributed to a shift in the nature of the state – moving it in the direction of a fragmented-multiclass polity.

Three empirical generalizations about the role of the military as state builders in the developing world thus seem apt. First, militaries intervene mainly when civilians fail. Second, militaries are not very successful at helping states to transcend their neopatrimonial character. And third, among the more modern states, militaries in power can indeed alter the class basis and the organizational character of the state, moving it in a more cohesive-capitalist direction when they come to power and in a more fragmented-multiclass direction when they leave power. Even in these instances, however, one should not exaggerate their transformative power. Military rulers are often supported from the outside, often build on the political structures and patterns that they inherit, and are often incapable of radical political innovation.

How can we explain these descriptive generalizations? The main hypothesis parallels the one developed above with reference to the role of nationalist movements: The more the militaries internalize the core characteristics of the societies in which they exist, the less likely they are to rise above the existing social and political patterns to create effective, modern states. This was clearest in the Nigerian case, where the personalism and sectional loyalties of the Nigerian society came to characterize the Nigerian military as well, limiting its capacity to reform the state. By contrast, where military professionalism helps to create a cohesive political force one degree removed from the immediate social context, and where the values of the military elite incline them to cooperate with producer groups, the military can help states to move in a cohesive-capitalist direction. These tendencies were evident in the externally inspired military rule in both South Korea and Brazil.

Beyond short periods, however, military rule is nearly always contested. As militaries in power negotiate these oppositional tendencies, they often internalize social cleavages. With the organizational cohesion of the military thereby reduced and with class and other cleavages internalized, the military loses the political advantage of being "above" politics, paving the way for its departure from politics. Ironically, therefore, the impact of militaries on state formation may be most striking when they exit from power and leave in their wake a dramatic shift in the direction of a fragmented-multiclass state.

Colonialism, nationalist movements, and militaries coming in and out of power have thus proved to be the main agents capable of transforming developing country states. The die cast by colonialism has proved to be of especial long-term significance. This is not surprising because colonial control was established via preponderant force and because colonizing countries imposed and maintained their preferred models of rule, creating in the process new state organizations and class alliances. Following decolonization, nationalists and indigenous militaries sought a radical reordering of developing country states. The success of these efforts has been mixed, however. Nationalist rulers were not effective state builders in most developing countries. Except for Brazil, where colonialism was in any case a distant memory, the success of militaries in restructuring states was also limited. Thus, the lineage of contemporary neopatrimonial, fragmented-multiclass, and cohesive-capitalist states can generally be traced back to the colonial ancestor.

Within each type of state, incremental political changes of considerable significance have been introduced by a variety of actors. The role of the nationalists and of militaries has already been noted. There is, in addition, the role of political parties and, even more important, of new classes, especially that of emerging capitalists. In the cases analyzed above, political parties proved to be significant state reformers mainly in the case of India. As the number of other countries turning to democracy grows, the role of parties is also likely to grow. In the case of India above, the Congress Party, the nationalist party, took a leading role in establishing India's fragmented-multiclass state. Worth reiterating is the role of the Bhartiya Janata Party (BJP) in India in the recent years – this better organized religious party now in power, with its pro–free enterprise ideology, has shifted the Indian state somewhat in a cohesive-capitalist direction.

A major source of incremental change in the nature of state is the growing power of new social classes, especially that of capital. This, too, is not surprising. State-led development aims to promote new economic activities and, when successful, brings new economic actors to the fore. These newly endowed actors, in turn, demand a political role. Since capital-owning groups tend to be disproportionately powerful, their demands are often respected by state elites, leading to a slow but steady shift in the nature of states. This much was clear in South Korea, Brazil, and India – all cases where real private economies and the power of capital have grown steadily. It was less the case in Nigeria, however, where private capital, especially indigenous capital, is still not a significant political force.

If the direction of a power shift from states to private capital is clear enough in most cases where private economies are growing, what is less clear is the content of this change. What exactly do developing country capitalists want from their states? Can one generalize about this issue? Do they all want less interventionist states that, in turn, leave markets free to guide economic activities? While important questions, the empirical material above really does not provide any ready answers; they must instead be part of a future research agenda. Only a few pertinent observations follow from the comparative materials analyzed above.

State-led development generally begins with states in command. Whether state elites in the early stages ally exclusively with capitalists or more inclusively with various social classes is more likely to reflect the ideology and the organization of the political rulers. As private economic activity grows, however, the class content of politics also grows, as both capital becomes more powerful and an emerging working class is likely to assert its rights. In cohesive-capitalist states this shift brings state and capital closer so they can simultaneously pursue the state's narrow developmental agenda and capital's perennial quest for profits. The incorporation and control of the working class serves both purposes. By contrast, challenged political elites in fragmented-multiclass states may ally with the working class and other lower classes in order to check the growing power of capital. Since well-organized social democratic parties are rare in the developing world, the most frequent outcome is then economically destabilizing populism. After some trial and error, therefore, inclusive elites are also likely to shift the state's role to avoid alienating private producers, on the one hand, and to satisfy the needs and demands of other social groups, on the other hand. With the state involved in the economy and thus heavily implicated in partisan class politics, the political energies of leaders are thus spread thin as they try to manage political conflicts; they find themselves distracted from the single-minded pursuit of rapid economic growth.

There was no evidence in the case materials above to suggest that capitalists use their growing power to demand less state intervention in the economy. At some future date when capitalism becomes hegemonic and capable on its own of removing numerous bottlenecks to sustained profitability in these countries, such may be capital's demands. Meanwhile, the political orientation of capital in the low- and middle-income countries analyzed in this study seems mainly to mold state intervention in its own favor. This was true both in Park Chung Hee's Korea and in Brazil under the military, two cases in which capital-owning groups were politically significant. It was also evident in India after Indira Gandhi, as private capital favored removing "socialistic controls" but not the many other supportive state interventions. One preliminary hypothesis suggested by the empirical materials above, then, is that developing country capitalists seek not so much free markets and laissez-faire as procapitalist state intervention.

In summing up, I offer a cautionary methodological caveat. It is difficult to isolate the relative significance of a number of causal variables via comparative analysis of a few cases. Immersion in the details reveals at best a feel for what might be the most significant causal dynamics at work. I claim no more. Within these parameters the following claims are advanced. Over the last several decades modern states as a form of political organization have spread from Europe to much of the developing world. When trying to understand the process of state formation in the developing world, colonialism has proved to be a major architectonic force. Where colonialism was a distant memory, as in the case of Brazil, militaries and military-supported elites were decisive players instead. Numerous agents have subsequently sought to reorder developing country states, and most significant has been the role of military rulers. Short of successful social revolutions, however, state structures have generally been altered only incrementally. The most consistent force pushing for slow but steady change in the nature and role of the state has been the power of private capital. The more the state succeeds in promoting capitalist development, the more politically potent capitalists become, and the less likely it is that the state will have much choice but to continue to do the same in the future. Developing country states have thus become the midwives assisting in the birth and spread of industrial capitalism in the global periphery.

State Intervention

If explaining why developing countries acquired a variety of states has been a central focus of this study, the other core concern has been to trace the impact of state intervention on economic outcomes, especially on rates and patterns of industrialization. Having discussed the latter subject in depth thoroughly throughout the study, only a few concluding comments are now necessary. These underline again the importance of political power in propelling state-led economic development.

State intervention in developing country economies is often discussed in terms of its technical appropriateness: import substitution versus export promoting, inward versus outward orientation, or market distorting versus market reinforcing. While these matters are far from unimportant, this study has been informed by a different frame of reference. The alternative approach rests on the observation that some countries, such as South Korea, have pursued a variety of policy packages relatively successfully, including import substitution and export promotion, while others, such as Nigeria, have also pursued similar policy packages, with little success. If this observation is acceptable, it follows that the context within which specific sets of policies are pursued matters at least as much as the particular policies.

At a proximate level of causation, the variety of contextual variables that might have influenced the relative success of development efforts included the availability of experienced entrepreneurs, the competence and the work ethic of labor, the capacity of the society to absorb technology, and the general levels of health and education of the populace. A set of institutional factors, moreover, that are well recognized by economists and other social scientists and that often proved to be consequential in the analysis above included the security of property rights, the ability to forge binding contracts, and the availability of banks and of other institutions to mobilize savings. Early success in industrialization and growth itself, we noticed, becomes a basis for future success by creating dense supplier networks, an adequate base for taxation, enhanced private savings, and improved infrastructure. At a deeper level of causation, however, the comparative analysis above highlighted how, over time, more effective states have undertaken sustained actions that alter these and other contextual conditions. States that proved most effective were those that prioritized economic development as a political goal and then promoted and supported entrepreneurs in a manner that helped to sustain high rates of efficient investments.

For those who work within the paradigm of modern economics, the success of state intervention, if admitted at all, is to be explained mainly in terms of the state's role in reducing "market failures." When not bound by these intellectual constraints, the political economy problem of why state intervention helps to promote industrialization in some cases but not in others appears mainly to be a problem of political power. States with a certain type of power at their disposal, and more of it, are able to use it in a sustained way to promote economic growth. They do this by mobilizing resources, channeling them into priority areas, altering the socioeconomic context within which firms operate, and even undertaking direct economic activities. By contrast, other states are incapable of generating developmental power, and their efforts at state-led development are generally failures. The majority of developing country cases lie in between the two extremes of state effectiveness and ineffectiveness.

The key theoretical problems of understanding state intervention in developing country economies are thus to identify how effective state power for development is generated and how this power is used to promote economic change.

Any society has a variety of sources of political power. Among the most important are the power of centralized coercion and of its legitimate use by the state, the power of capital and of other property ownership wielded by the economic elites, and the power of numbers, especially when workers, peasants, and others are well organized. Cohesive-capitalist states harness a variety of these power resources so that they are aggregated or at least do not operate at cross-purposes. The state that is created is disciplined and disciplining, has a close working alliance with capitalists, and systematically incorporates and silences those who might detract from the state's narrow goals of industrialization and rapid growth. But such states are difficult to construct and, mercifully, even more difficult to institutionalize. Many in the society resist the state's close partnership with the economic elite and its social control over the rest. Authoritarian control and ideological mobilization are thus generally part of the ruling strategy of such states, especially those organized along anticommunist and nationalist lines. While such states may not persist beyond a few decades, ruling elites are often tempted to revert to such organizational forms. Meanwhile, when in control, cohesive-capitalist states have proven to be the most effective at amassing and using power to transform their respective economies.

Power resources of a society, by contrast, tend to be more fissiparous in fragmented-multiclass states. State organization itself is less cohesive in these settings, with both intraelite and elite-mass political conflicts more common. The fragmented-multiclass states define their goals more plurally, working closely with capitalists some of the time and at cross-purposes at other times. A variety of lower classes may also be well organized, demanding the state's attention and resources. With power more decentered, liberals find these states less reprehensible than cohesive-capitalist states. Imagining the possibility of reproducing historical patterns of economic development, many are even led to argue that such states are better equipped to facilitate rapid industrialization because they might provide a better framework for the emergence of individual initiative. The historical record of late-late developers, however, does not readily support such expectations. State-led industrialization has generally been less rapid under the auspices of fragmented-multiclass states than under cohesive-capitalist states. This is because successful state-led development requires the focused use of the state's ample powers. Cohesive-capitalist states generally control more of such resources than do fragmented-multiclass states.

As distinct from both cohesive-capitalist and fragmented-multiclass states, neopatrimonial states are relative failures at amassing and using power constructively. That is why state intervention in these settings tends to produce numerous economic failures. These states do not centralize coercion adequately, leaving power dispersed among local despots. The states are also ill formed in the sense that politicians, military men, and bureaucrats do not always differentiate clearly between their public roles and their personal and sectional loyalties. Given low levels of economic development, private capital tends to be weak. Many in the lower stratum also remain embedded in patron-client ties and are not free to mobilize and organize. Unlike the cohesive-capitalist states, therefore, in which power resources of both the state and the society are melded to pursue a unified goal, and also unlike fragmented-multiclass states in which real power resources exist in both the state and the society but often work at cross-purposes, neither the state nor the society in neopatrimonial settings is capable of organizing much national-level power. There may be enough power to plunder or to wreak vengeance on the hated "other," as in the hands of an Idi Amin or a Mobutu. Such "primitive" power, however, is wholly inadequate for sustaining state-led development.

State intervention in the economy, then, does not succeed or fail primarily because some states have more clever policy makers, capable of pursuing technically correct policies. Such sophistication matters, but the deeper reasons for why state intervention succeeds or fails have to do with the politics of the states. Some states are better at organizing power for use in a focused manner, while others are not. The resulting power gap is at the heart of why cohesive-capitalist states have proved to be so much better than neopatrimonial states at facilitating rapid industrialization. The former were able to use their power to boost both the rates and the efficiency of investment. Numerous examples of how this happened in countries such as South Korea and Brazil have been provided above. By contrast, without consistent purpose and power, intervention by neopatrimonial states squandered investable resources; these states, such as in Nigeria, promoted neither higher rates of investment nor more efficient investment. And yet other states with mixed purposes and some power resources, such as India's fragmented-multiclass state, achieved modest economic success by helping to improve rates and efficiency of investment – albeit only in some areas and during some periods.

Normative and Prescriptive Implications
This has been mainly an explanatory study that has amassed historical and contemporary materials to explore a key puzzle in the study of late-late development, namely, why some developing countries industrialize more rapidly than others. I have analyzed the state's role in matters economic, on the one hand, and the factors that might help to explain the emergence of more or less effective states, on the other hand.

A study such as this is bound to have normative implications. Although I am sorely tempted to leave the findings to stand as they are and let readers draw their own implications, I offer a few normative comments in conclusion, to avoid any misunderstandings. Some readers will also want to know the prescriptive or policy implications of the findings. Once again, seeking appropriate prescriptions for developing countries has not been my main concern in this study. To stand the old master Karl Marx on his head, far too many scholars and practitioners have been trying to change the developing world; the point is also to understand it. And yet if a problem has been understood well, it ought to have some implications for how to deal with it in the future.

This study has posited that cohesive-capitalist states have been most effective at facilitating rapid industrialization in the developing world. If correct, this argument raises serious normative dilemmas.[30] While the goal of rapid industrialization is not shared by all, it is at least defensible on the grounds that it contributes to rapid economic growth – and growth in the end is necessary if everyone in a poor society is to become better off. However, what if this growth also comes at the serious political cost of a repressive state that amasses and uses power well in some areas but also curtails the important urge of the many to participate politically and to control their own destinies? While not totalitarian, cohesive-capitalist states of the type discussed above do resemble fascist states of the past. Can one then comfortably recommend such states as desirable on the ground that they are the most likely agents of rapid industrialization and economic growth?

When good things do not go together, there is no easy moral calculus for making choices. Nevertheless, my answer is a clear no. An explanatory study specifies dependent variables and seeks to isolate a few independent variables that may both logically and empirically help to explain the phenomenon of interest. The jump from such an exercise to normative and prescriptive judgments is fraught with problems, the most obvious being that societies value many things other than those under a scholar's microscope. In addition to economic growth, a better income distribution and democracy are goals sought by most societies. It may well be that somewhat lower rates of economic growth are then morally acceptable if that acceptance enhances the likelihood of better distribution and/or of more desirable states. Such trade-offs, of course, are not attained readily in the real world; the discussion here is mainly on a normative plane. Two normative implications of immediate relevance then follow. First, any assessment of economic success in such cases as South Korea, Taiwan, military-ruled Brazil, or contemporary China must be weighed against the serious political costs paid by the citizens of these countries. Second, the somewhat lower economic growth rates achieved by such countries as India or Malaysia ought not always to be judged harshly, at least not without a serious analysis of possible trade-offs.

If it is important to resist the temptation to embrace growth-producing, right-wing authoritarians, it is also important to distance oneself from the fantasy that all good things can be had together, that democracy, equality,

---

[30] When I presented this argument at a seminar in Ann Arbor, Michigan, in 2002, Susanne Rudolph pointedly remarked that I must take the "moral responsibility" for my argument. She was indeed right and I will try my best.

free markets, and rapid economic growth can all be achieved simultaneously in the contemporary developing world. Not only is there no evidence for this in the contemporary developing world, but it also represents a poor reading of how development proceeded in the West. As Barrington Moore, Jr., concluded a while back: "There is no evidence that the mass of population anywhere has wanted an industrial society, and plenty of evidence that they did not. . . . At bottom all forms of industrialization have been . . . the work of a ruthless minority."[31] This element of "ruthlessness" or of coercion in its various forms has also been omnipresent in the most successful cases of rapid industrialization in the contemporary developing world. The normative implication then is to treat with suspicion claims that trade-offs are not necessary and that all good things can readily go together.

The normative challenge posed by the findings of this study flows from the fact that none of the state types analyzed above is unambiguously desirable. Moreover, those states that are the least bad politically, at least when judged against liberal political values of shared power and inclusiveness, namely, the fragmented-multiclass states, turn out not to be the most effective agents of economic growth. Where then is one supposed to turn when searching for appropriate models of development? Again, there are no ready answers. It is not likely that desirable models of the past can be readily emulated by contemporary developing countries, certainly not in their totality; nor do recent experiences of alternative development pathways suggest choices that others necessarily ought to hold up as a beacon.

There is no doubt that many a sub-Saharan African country would rather be like South Korea. The analysis above suggests, however, that neither is this an unambiguously desirable choice nor is such a transformation likely to occur soon, given the long set of historical preconditions that led to that specific pathway and the associated outcomes. What prescriptive options emerge from this study instead are fragments of insights that often challenge existing orthodoxies but that do not add up to a full-blown developmental alternative. And that may be just as well because, as I quickly outline some of these scattered prescriptive implications, the most important implication may well be that developing countries differ enormously from one another, certainly across regions and income levels, and that no one set of prescriptions is likely to apply equally to all.

Within the scope of this caveat, three final observations are in order. First, states and state intervention can be a powerful force for the good insofar

---

[31] See Moore, *Social Origins of Dictatorship and Democracy*, 506. Or in the words of Alexander Gerschenkron: "To break through the barriers of stagnation in a backward country, to ignite the imagination of men, and to place their energies in the service of economic development, a stronger medicine is needed than the promise of better allocation of resources or even of the lower price of bread." See Gerschenkron, *Economic Backwardness in Historical Perspective*, 24.

as they help to promote rapid industrialization and economic growth in the developing world. While this claim may appear to be nearly obvious to some, it does contradict some of the central tenets of the promarket argument for development that emerged nearly hegemonic toward the end of the twentieth century and that lingers as an orthodoxy of sorts at the start of the twentieth-first century. The promarket claims generally rest on two implied or explicit assertions, namely, that state-led development had generally been a failure and that the new globalized world had made states less relevant as development actors. In this study I have not addressed the issue of "globalization" directly.[32] What I have documented in great detail, however, is that the record of state-led development is considerably more nuanced than reflected in promarket critiques. Put even more forcefully, rapid industrialization in the developing world has been a product of effective state intervention. Policy discussions about the developing world thus need to abandon the state versus market dichotomy and need instead to focus on the various ways in which states and markets can work together to promote development.

Second, certain types of states and thus certain types of state interventions have proved to be more successful than others at promoting growth. While it may be neither possible nor desirable to emulate the successful models fully, the less successful countries can learn some things from the more successful cases. This learning can take place both at the level of reforming political institutions and in the choice of development strategies. At the level of institutions, a rapidly developing country underscores the importance of focused and competent states, of established working relations between the state and business, and of the state's role in institutionalizing social discipline. The challenge for the less successful developers, especially for fragmented-multiclass states, is how to acquire some such institutional strengths without embracing the nearly fascistic qualities that often accompany them. Once again, there are no ready answers. It may well be that some movement in the direction of a cohesive-capitalist state does not have to come at the expense of totalizing social control by the state. It may also be the case that the preferred agents of such change are disciplined and inclusionary political parties, such as well-organized social democratic parties, rather than right-wing, nationalist parties or state agents themselves.

The challenge for institutional reform in neopatrimonial states is even more serious. This is not only because so much needs to be done but also

---

[32] For others who have, and whose argument is consistent with the thrust of the argument developed in this study, see Stiglitz, *Globalization and Its Discontents*; Barbara Stallings, *Global Change and Regional Response: The New International Context of Development* (New York: Cambridge University Press, 1995); Wade, *Governing the Market*; Dani Rodrik, *The New Global Economy and Developing Countries* (Baltimore, Md.: Johns Hopkins University Press, 1999); and Robert Gilpin, *Global Political Economy: Understanding the International Economic Order* (Princeton, N.J.: Princeton University Press, 2001).

because it is not even clear who will lead the effort in these settings. A realistic goal of reforms here would be to make Nigeria more like India, or to get neopatrimonial states moving toward becoming somewhat more effective states with centralized authority over their territories, a modest commitment on the part of political actors to public goals, reduced corruption, some pockets of efficiency in the bureaucracy, and the establishment of working relations with key private economic actors in the society. With major political actors deeply embedded in a variety of personalistic and sectional networks, however, it is not at all obvious who the agents of change, even of modest change, would be. It may well be that a slowly emerging stratum of private entrepreneurs will eventually lead such a political effort. It may well be that altruistic external actors, defying the logic of self-interest, will help to initiate some such reforms. Or it may well be that not every problem finds a solution.

Short of institutional reform, less successful developers can learn some policy lessons from more successful developers. While I have often emphasized the importance of the institutional context over that of policy choices, one should not carry that argument too far. Some development strategies and policies work better than others. Between import substitution and export promotion, for example, the experience of import-substituting industrialization has not been as bad as many critics maintain. It is probably best to think of it as a necessary phase in a move toward promoting the exports of manufactured goods. At the same time, it is clear that countries that failed to promote exports, such as India and Brazil, paid dearly, in terms of either growth or foreign indebtedness. Export promotion is thus clearly important. What is also clear, however, is that successful promotion of manufactured exports has required a variety of state supports to enable private producers to compete internationally.

A related policy area in which the less successful developers can learn from more successful experiments regards appropriate strategies for integration into the global economy. The contrasting experiences of South Korea and Brazil suggest that it is better to integrate along the axis of trade than of capital. Relatedly, it may be important to try to decouple capital and technological dependencies. Developing countries need technology imports to industrialize. However, they ought to be willing to pay for it in the first instance and in the second instance to build, slowly but surely, their own capacities to absorb and to innovate. This at least has been the case of South Korea.

The third and final prescriptive observation is not overly optimistic. Even though effective states have been at the heart of rapid development successes, effective states are hard to create. This is especially the case if one thinks of states more holistically and includes the state's political actors. If my analysis of state formation above is persuasive, it suggests that basic state forms alter only rarely and that that, too, happens mainly in big bangs. Forces capable of creating such big bangs, namely, colonialism or a well-organized nationalist movement, are more typically aspects of a historical past that is not likely to reemerge. Regime transitions can be a major source of state reform but mainly if an effective state is already in place. In neopatrimonial states, the emergence of so-called democracies is not likely to be an agent of either effective state creation or of sustained economic development. The main hope for state reform is for incremental reform, and the main agents are likely to be organized indigenous political forces such as parties or, more likely, the slow but steady emergence of indigenous capitalism and capitalists.

None of these brief concluding reflections on possible directions of change in the future ought to detract from what is mainly an explanatory work. I have in this study sought to explain the origins and the economic roles played by a variety of developing country states. While some developing country states have done much harm to their own societies, most have made a positive contribution to improving the societies they govern and a few have been spectacularly successful. States remain the most likely organizations to preserve and enhance the interests of their own citizens. When states perform poorly, the task is to reform them, not to undermine them further. A major source of hope for the numerous poor living in the developing world thus remains effective national states.

Select Bibliography

General

Ake, Claude. *Democracy and Development in Africa*. Washington, D.C.: Brookings Institution, 1996.

Amsden, Alice. *Asia's Next Giant: South Korea and Late Industrialization*. New York: Oxford University Press, 1989.

———. *The Rise of the "Rest": Challenges to the West from Late-Industrializing Economies*. New York: Oxford University Press, 2001.

Apter, David. *The Politics of Modernization*. Chicago: University of Chicago Press, 1965.

Balassa, Bela. "Trade Policies in Developing Countries." *American Economic Review* 61, Papers and Proceedings (1971): 178–87.

Bates, Robert. *Markets and States in Tropical Africa*. Berkeley: University of California Press, 1981.

Bhagwati, Jagdish. "Rethinking Trade Strategy." In John P. Lewis and Valeriana Kallab, eds., *Development Strategies Reconsidered*. New Brunswick: Transaction Books, 1986. Pp. 91–104.

Bradford, Colin. "Policy Interventions and Markets: Development Strategy Typologies and Policy Options." In Gary Gerefi and Donald Wyman, eds., *Manufacturing Miracles: Paths of Industrialization in Latin America and East Asia*. Princeton, N.J.: Princeton University Press, 1990. Pp. 32–54.

Bradie, Bertrand. *The Imported State: The Westernization of the Political Order*. Stanford, Calif.: Stanford University Press, 2000.

Cardoso, Fernando Henrique. "Associated-Dependent Development: Theoretical and Practical Implications." In Alfred Stepan, ed., *Authoritarian Brazil: Origins, Policies and Future*. New Haven, Conn.: Yale University Press, 1973. Pp. 142–78.

Derns, Kemal, and Peter A. Petri. "The Macroeconomics of Successful Development: What are the Lessons?" In Stanley Fischer, ed., *NBER Macroeconomics Annual*. Cambridge, Mass.: MIT Press, 1987. Pp. 211–54.

Edwards, Sebastian. "Openness, Trade Liberalization, and Growth in Developing Countries." *Journal of Economic Literature* 31 (September 1993): 1358–1393.

Evans, Peter. "Class, State and Dependence in East Asia: Lessons for Latin Americanists." In Frederic D. Deyo, ed., *The Political Economy of the New Asian Industrialism*. Ithaca, N.Y.: Cornell University Press, 1987. Pp. 203–26.

——. *Embedded Autonomy: State and Industrial Transformation.* Princeton: Princeton University Press, 1995.

——. "Predatory, Developmental and Other Apparatuses: A Comparative Political Economy Perspective on the Third World State." *Sociological Forum* 4 (Fall 1989): 561–87.

Fieldhouse, D. K. *Colonialism, 1870–1945: An Introduction.* New York: St. Martin's, 1981.

Gerschenkron, Alexander. *Economic Backwardness in Historical Perspective.* Cambridge: Harvard University Press, 1962.

Gold, Thomas. *State and Society in the Taiwan Miracle.* Armonk, N.Y.: M. E. Sharpe, 1986.

Haggard, Stephen. *Pathways from the Periphery: The Politics of Growth in the Newly Developing Countries.* Ithaca, N.Y.: Cornell University Press, 1990.

Halliday, Jon. *A Political History of Japanese Capitalism.* New York: Pantheon, 1975.

Herbst, Jeffrey. *States and Power in Africa: Comparative Lessons in Authority and Control.* Princeton, N.J.: Princeton University Press, 2000.

Hirschman, Albert. *A Bias for Hope: Essays on Development and Latin America.* New Haven, Conn.: Yale University Press, 1971.

——. "Rise and Decline of Development Economics." In Albert O. Hirschman, ed., *Essays in Trespassing: Economic to Politics and Beyond.* Cambridge: Cambridge University Press, 1981. Pp. 1–24.

Huntington, Samuel P. *Political Order in Changing Societies.* New Haven, Conn.: Yale University Press, 1968.

Hutchcroft, Paul. *Booty Capitalism: The Politics of Banking in the Philippines.* Ithaca, N.Y.: Cornell University Press, 1998.

Johnson, Chalmers A. *MITI and the Japanese Miracle: The Growth of Industrial Policy, 1925–1975.* Stanford, Calif.: Stanford University Press, 1982.

——. "Political Institutions and Economic Performance: The Government-Business Relationship in Japan, South Korea and Taiwan." In Frederic C. Deyo, ed., *The Political Economy of the New Asian Industrialism.* Ithaca, N.Y.: Cornell University Press, 1987. Pp. 136–64.

Jowitt, Kenneth. *Revolutionary Breakthrough and National Development: The Case of Romania, 1944–1965.* Berkeley: University of California Press, 1971.

Kohli, Atul. "State, Society, and Development." In Ira Katznelson and Helen Milner, eds., *State of the Discipline.* New York: W. W. Norton, 2002. Pp. 84–117.

Kohli, Atul, Chung-In Moon, and George Sorensen, eds. *States, Markets and Just Growth: Development in the Twenty-first Century.* Tokyo: United Nations University Press, 2002.

Krueger, Anne. "The Political Economy of the Rent Seeking Society." *American Economic Review* 64 (1974): 291–303.

Krugman, Paul. "Cycles of Conventional Wisdom on Economic Development." *International Affairs* 72 (1996): 717–32.

——. "Toward a Counter-counter-revolution in Development Theory." *World Bank Economic Review,* Supplement (Proceedings of the World Bank Annual Conference on Development Economics, 1993): 15–38.

Lal, Deepak. *The Poverty of "Development" Economics.* London: Institute of Economic Affairs, Hobart Paperback No. 16, 1983.

Lewis, W. Arthur. *The Evolution of the International Economic Order.* Princeton, N.J.: Princeton University Press, 1977.

————. "The Slowing Down of the Engine of Growth." *American Economic Review* 70 (September 1980): 555–64.

————. "The State of Development Theory." *American Economic Review* 74 (March 1984): 1–10.

Little, Ian M. D., Tibor Scitovsky, and Maurice Scott. *Industry and Trade in Some Developing Countries: A Comparative Study.* London: Oxford University Press, 1970.

Mamdani, Mahmood. *Citizen and Subject: Contemporary Africa and the Legacy of Late Colonialism.* Princeton, N.J.: Princeton University Press, 1996.

Mann, Michael. *The Sources of Social Power.* 2 vols. New York: Cambridge University Press, 1986.

Migdal, Joel. *Strong Societies and Weak States: State Society Relations and State Capabilities in the Third World.* Princeton, N.J.: Princeton University Press, 1989.

Moore, Barrington, Jr. *Social Origins of Dictatorship and Democracy.* Boston: Beacon, 1966.

O'Donnell, Guillermo A. *Modernization and Bureaucratic Authoritarianism.* Berkeley: Institute of International Studies, University of California, 1973.

Palma, Gabriel. "Dependency: A Formal Theory of Underdevelopment or a Methodology for the Analysis of Concrete Situations of Underdevelopment?" *World Development* 6 (1978): 881–924.

Przeworksi, Adam, and Fernando Limongi. "Political Regimes and Economic Growth." *Journal of Economic Perspectives* 7 (Summer 1993): 51–69.

Przeworski, Adam, et al. *Democracy and Development: Political Institutions and Material Well-Being in the World, 1950–1990.* Cambridge: Cambridge University Press, 2002.

Reynolds, Lloyd G. *Economic Growth in the Third World, 1850–1980.* New Haven, Conn.: Yale University Press, 1985.

Rodriguez, Francisco, and Dani Rodrik. "Trade Policy and Economic Growth: A Skeptic's Guide to the Cross-National Evidence." In Ben Bernanke and Kenneth S. Rogoff, eds., *Macroeconomics Annual 2000.* Cambridge, Mass.: National Bureau of Economic Research, MIT Press, 2001.

Rodrik, Dani, ed. *In Search of Prosperity: Analytic Narratives on Economic Growth.* Princeton, N.J.: Princeton University Press, 2003.

Romer, Paul. "Idea Gaps and Object Gaps in Economic Development." Paper presented at World Bank Conference on "How Do National Policies Affect Long Run Growth?" Washington, D.C., February 7–8, 1993.

Sachs, Jeffrey. "External Debt and Macroeconomic Performance in Latin America and East Asia." *Brookings Papers on Economic Activity* 2 (1985): 523–73.

Sandbrook, Richard. *Politics of Africa's Economic Stagnation.* Cambridge: Cambridge University Press, 1985.

Schumpeter, Joseph. *Capitalism, Socialism and Democracy.* New York: Harper and Brothers, 1950.

Schurmann, Franz. *Ideology and Organization in Communist China.* Berkeley: University of California Press, 1966.

Scott, James C. *Seeing like a State: How Certain Schemes to Improve the Human Condition Have Failed.* New Haven, Conn.: Yale University Press, 1998.

Sen, Amartya K. *Development as Freedom.* New York: Knopf, 1999.

Shapiro, Helen, and Lance Taylor. "The State and Industrial Strategy." *World Development* 18 (1990): 861–78.

Shue, Vivienne. *Reach of the State: Sketches of the Chinese Body Politic.* Stanford, Calif.: Stanford University Press, 1988.

Stepan, Alfred. *The State and Society: Peru in Comparative Perspective.* Princeton, N.J.: Princeton University Press, 1978.

Stiglitz, Joseph. *Globalization and Its Discontents.* New York: W. W. Norton, 2002.

Tilly, Charles. *Coercion, Capital and European States, AD 990–1992.* Oxford: Basil Blackwell, 1990.

Van de Walle, Nicholas. *Politics of Africa's Permanent Economic Crisis.* Cambridge: Cambridge University Press, 2001.

Wade, Robert. *Governing the Market: Economic Theory and the Role of Government in East Asian Industrialization.* Princeton, N.J.: Princeton University Press, 1990.

———. "Wheels within Wheels: Rethinking the Asian Crisis and the Asian Model." *Annual Review of Political Science* 3 (2000): 85–115.

Waterbury, John. *Exposed to Innumerable Delusions: Public Enterprise and State Power in Egypt, India, Mexico, and Turkey.* Cambridge: Cambridge University Press, 1993.

Williamson, John. "The Emergent Development Policy Consensus." In Michael R. Carter, Jeffrey Cason, and Frederic Zimmerman, eds., *Development at a Crossroads: Uncertain Paths to Sustainability after the Neoliberal Revolution.* Madison: Global Studies Program, University of Wisconsin, 1998. Pp. 33–46.

Woo-Cumings, Meredith. *The Developmental State.* Ithaca, N.Y.: Cornell University Press, 1999.

World Bank. *The East Asian Miracle.* New York: Oxford University Press, 1993.

Young, Crawford. *The African Colonial State in Comparative Perspective.* New Haven: Yale University Press, 1994.

Korea

Amsden, Alice H. *Asia's Next Giant: South Korea and Late Industrialization.* New York: Oxford University Press, 1989.

Allen, Richard C. *Korea's Syngman Rhee: An Unauthorized Portrait.* Rutland, Vt.: Charles E. Tuttle, 1960.

Balassa, Bela. "The Lessons of East Asian Development: An Overview." *Economic Development and Cultural Change* 36 (April 1988 Supplement): S273–90.

Ban, Sung Hwan, et al. *Rural Development.* Cambridge: Harvard East Asian Monographs, Harvard University Press, 1980.

Brandt, Vincent S. R. *A Korean Village: Between Farm and Sea.* Cambridge: Harvard University Press, 1971.

Chang, Dal-Joong. *Economic Control and Political Authoritarianism: The Role of Japanese Corporations in Korean Politics, 1965–1979.* Seoul: Sogang University Press, 1985.

Cho, Doug-Sung. *The General Trading Company: Concept and Strategy.* Lexington, Mass.: Lexington Books, 1987.

Choe, Ching Young. *The Rule of the Taewon'gun, 1864–73: Restoration in Yi Korea.* Cambridge: Harvard University Press, 1972.

Choi, Byng Sun. "The Structure of the Economic Policy-Making Institutions in Korea and the Strategic Role of the Economic Planning Boards." In Gerald E. Caiden and Bun Woong Kim, ed., *A Dragon's Progress*. Hartford, Conn.: Kumarian Press, 1991.

Choi, Jang Jip. *Labor and the Authoritarian State: Labor Unions in South Korean Manufacturing Industries, 1961–1980*. Seoul: Korea University Press, 1989.

Chung, Young-Iob. "Japanese Investment in Korea, 1904–45." In Andrew Nahm, ed., *Korea under Japanese Colonial Rule*. Western Michigan University, Center for Korean Studies, 1973. Pp. 89–98.

Clifford, Mark L. *Troubled Tiger: Businessmen, Bureaucrats and Generals in South Korea*. Armonk, N.Y.: M. E. Sharpe, 1994.

Cole, David C., and Princeton Lyman. *Korean Development: The Interplay of Politics and Economics*. Cambridge: Harvard University Press, 1971.

Conroy, Hilary. *The Japanese Seizure of Korea, 1868–1910*. Philadelphia: University of Pennsylvania Press, 1960.

Cumings, Bruce. *The Origins of the Korean War*, vol. 1: *Liberation and the Emergence of Separate Regimes, 1945–1947*. Princeton, N.J.: Princeton University Press, 1979.

———. *The Origins of the Korean War*, vol. 2: *The Roaring of the Cataract*. Princeton, N.J.: Princeton University Press, 1990.

Deyo, Frederic C. *Beneath the Miracle: Labor Subordination in the New Asian Industrialism*. Berkeley: University of California Press, 1989.

Dornbusch, Rudiger, and Yung Chul Park. "Korean Growth Policy." *Brookings Papers on Economic Activity*. Washington, D.C.: Brookings Institution, 1987.

Eckert, Carter. "Economic Development under Japanese Colonial Rule." In *Cambridge History of Korea/"Modern" Volume*. Cambridge: Cambridge University Press, forthcoming.

———. *Offspring of Empire: The Koch'ang Kims and the Colonial Origins of Korean Capitalism, 1876–1945*. Seattle: University of Washington Press, 1991.

Eckert, Carter J., et al. *Korea Old and New: A History*. Cambridge: Cambridge University Press, 1990.

Eikemeier, Dieter. *Documents from Changjwa-ri: A Further Approach to the Analysis of Korean Villages*. Wiesbaden, Germany: Otto Harrassowitz, 1980.

Fairbank, John K., Edwin O. Reischauer, and Albert M. Craig. *East Asia: Tradition and Transformation*. Boston: Houghton Mifflin, 1978.

Fishlow, Albert, et al. *Miracle or Design? Lessons from the East Asian Experience*. Policy Essay No 11. Washington, D.C.: Overseas Development Council, 1994.

Frank, Charles R., Jr., Kwang Suk Kim, and Larry E. Westphal. *Foreign Trade Regimes and Economic Development: South Korea*. New York: National Bureau of Economic Research, 1975.

Government-General of Chosen. *Annual Report on Reforms and Progress in Choson (Korea)*. Keijo (Seoul), 1910–39.

Grajdanzev, Andrew J. *Modern Korea*. New York: John Dey, 1944.

Haggard, Stephan, David Kang, and Chung-In Moon. "Japanese Colonialism and Korean Development: A Critique." *World Development* 25 (June 1997): 867–82.

Han, Sung-Joo. *The Failure of Democracy in South Korea*. Berkeley: University of California Press, 1974.

Hart-Landsberg, Martin. *The Rush to Development: Economic Change and Political Struggle in South Korea*. New York: Monthly Review Press, 1993.

Hee, Park Chung. *The Country, the Revolution and I,* 2nd ed. Seoul, Korea: Hollym Corporation, 1970.

_____. *Our Nation's Path: Ideology of Social Construction,* 2nd ed. Seoul, Korea: Hollym Corporation, 1970.

Henderson, Gregory. *Korea: The Politics of the Vortex.* Cambridge: Harvard University Press, 1968.

Huer, John. *Marching Orders: The Role of the Military in South Korea's "Economic Miracle,"* *1961–1971.* New York: Greenwood Press, 1989.

Ireland, Alleyne. *The New Korea.* New York: E. P. Dutton, 1926.

Ishikawa, Shigeru. *Economic Development in Asian Perspective.* Tokyo: Kinokuniya Bookstore, 1967.

Johnson, Chalmers. "Political Institutions and Economic Performance: The Government-Business Relationship in Japan, South Korea and Taiwan." In Frederic C. Deyo, ed., *The Political Economy of the New Asian Industrialism.* Ithaca, N.Y.: Cornell University Press, 1987. Pp. 136–64.

Jones, Leroy P. *Public Enterprise and Economic Development: The Korean Case.* Seoul: Korea Development Institute, 1975.

Jones, Leroy P., and Il Sakong. *Government, Business and Entrepreneurship in Economic Development: The Korean Case.* Cambridge: Harvard University Press, 1980.

Jung, Yong-Duck. "Distributive Justice and Redistributive Policy in Korea." *Korean Social Science Journal* 11 (1984): 143–62.

Kang, David. *Crony Capitalism: Corruption and Development in South Korea and the Philippines.* New York: Cambridge University Press, 2002.

Kearney, Robert P. *The Warrior Worker: The Challenge of the Korean Way of Working.* New York: Henry Holt, 1991.

Kenji, Nakano. "Japan's Overseas Investment Patterns and FTZs." *AMPO: Japan Asia Quarterly Review* 8 (1977): 33–50.

Kim, Hosup. "Policy-making of Japanese Development Assistance to the Republic of Korea, 1965–1983." Ph.D. dissertation, University of Michigan, 1987.

Kim, Jai-Hyup. *The Garrison State in Pre-war Japan and Post-war Korea: A Comparative Analysis of Military Politics.* Washington, D.C.: University Press of America, 1978.

Kim, Ji Hong. "Korean Industrial Policy in the 1970s: The Heavy and Chemical Industry Drive." Working Paper 9015. Seoul: Korea Development Institute, 1990.

Kim, Kwan Bong. *The Korea-Japan Treaty Crisis and the Instability of the Korean System.* New York: Praeger, 1971.

Kim, Kwan-Suk, and Joon-Kyung Park. *Sources of Economic Growth in Korea: 1963–1982.* Seoul: Korea Development Institute, 1985.

Kim, Kyong-Dong. "Political Factors in the Formation of the Entrepreneurial Elite in South Korea." *Asian Survey* 15 (May 1976): 465–77.

Kim, Se-Jin. *The Politics of Military Revolution in Korea.* Chapel Hill: University of North Carolina Press, 1971.

Kruger, Anne. *The Developmental Role of the Foreign Sector and Aid.* Cambridge: Harvard University Press, 1979.

Kublin, Hyman. "The Evolution of Japanese Colonialism." *Comparative Studies in Society and History* 2 (October 1959): 67–84.

Ladd, George. *In Korea with Marquis Ito.* New York: C. Scribner's Sons, 1908.

Lee, Chong Sik. *Japan and Korea: The Political Dimension.* Stanford, Calif.: Hoover Institution Press, 1985.

———. *The Politics of Korean Nationalism.* Berkeley: University of California Press, 1963.

Lee, Hahn-Been. *Korea, Time, Change and Administration.* Honolulu, Hawaii: East-West Center Press, 1968.

Lee, Ki-Baik. *Korea Old and New: A History.* Seoul: Ilchokak Publishers, 1990.

Lee, Man-Gap. "Politics in a Korean Village." In Man-Gap Lee, ed., *Sociology and Social Change in Korea.* Seoul: Seoul University Press, 1982.

Lee, S. C. "The Heavy and Chemical Industries Promotion Plan (1973–1979)." In Lee-Jey Cho and Yoon Hyung Kim, eds., *Economic Development in the Republic of Korea: A Policy Perspective.* Honolulu: University of Hawaii Press, 1991.

Lovell, John P. "The Military and Politics in Postwar Korea." In Edward Reynolds Wright, ed., *Korean Politics in Transition.* Seattle: University of Washington Press, 1975.

Mason, Edward, et al. *The Economic and Social Modernization of the Republic of Korea.* Cambridge: Harvard University Press, 1980.

McNamara, Dennis. *The Colonial Origins of Korean Enterprise.* New York: Cambridge University Press, 1990.

Meade, Grant E. *American Military Government in Korea.* New York: King's Crown Press, Columbia University, 1951.

Moskowitz, Karl. "The Creation of the Oriental Development Company: Japanese Illusions Meet Korean Reality." In *Occasional Papers on Korea* 2. Seattle: University of Washington, March 1974.

Myers, Ramon H., and Mark R. Peattie, eds. *The Japanese Colonial Empire, 1895–1945.* Princeton, N.J.: Princeton University Press, 1984.

Ogle, George E. *South Korea: Dissent within the Economic Miracle.* London: Zed Books, 1990.

Oh, John Kie-Chiang. *Korea: Democracy on Trial.* Ithaca, N.Y.: Cornell University Press, 1968.

Oliver, Robert. *Syngman Rhee: The Man Behind the Myth.* New York: Dodd Mead, 1954.

Pack, Howard, and Larry E. Westphal. "Industrial Strategy and Technological Change: Theory versus Reality." *Journal of Development Economics* 22 (1986): 87–128.

Paik, Wan Ki. "The Formation of the Governing Elites in Korean Society." In Gerald E. Caiden and Bun Woong Kim, eds., *A Dragon's Progress: Development Administration in Korea.* West Hartford, Conn.: Kumarian Press, 1991.

Pak, Ki Hyuk, et al. *A Study of Land Tenure System in Korea.* Seoul: Korea Land Economics Research Center, 1966.

Palais, James. *Politics and Policy in Traditional Korea.* Cambridge: Harvard University Press, 1975.

Park, Kee, ed. *Macro-economic and Industrial Development in Korea.* Seoul: Korea Development Institute, 1980.

Park, Keun Hae. *The New Spirit Movement.* Seoul: Naeway Business Journal and Korea Herald, 1979.

Park, Moon Kyu. "Interest Representation in South Korea: The Limits of Corporalist Control." *Asian Survey* 27 (August 1987): 903–17.

Park, Soon Won. *Colonial Industrialization and Labor in Korea: The Onada Cement Factory*. Series on Korean Studies. Cambridge: Harvard University Press, 2000.

Park, Yoong-Ki. *Labor and Industrial Relations in Korea: System and Practice*. Seoul: University Press, 1979.

Reeve, W. D. *The Republic of Korea: A Political and Economic Study*. London: Oxford University Press, 1963.

Rosenberg, Hans. *Bureaucracy, Aristocracy and Autocracy: The Prussian Experience, 1660–1815*. Cambridge: Harvard University Press, 1958.

Sakong, Il. *Korea in the World Economy*. Washington, D.C.: Institute for International Economics, 1993.

Sawyer, Robert K. *Military Advisors in Korea: KMAG in Peace and War*. Washington, D.C.: Office of the Chief of Military History, Department of the Army, 1962.

Scalapino, Robert A. "Which Route for Korea?" *Asian Survey* 2 (September 1962): 1–13.

Scalapino, Robert, and Chong-Sik Lee. *Communism in Korea, Part I: The Movement*. Berkeley: University of California Press, 1972.

Schumpeter, E. B. *The Industrialization of Japan and Manchukuo, 1930–40*. New York: Macmillan, 1940.

Shin, Gi-Wook, and Michael Robinson, eds. *Colonial Modernity in Korea*. Harvard-Hallym Series on Korean Studies. Cambridge: Harvard University Press, 2000.

Shin, Susan S. "Some Aspects of Landlord-Tenant Relations in Yi Dynasty Korea." In James B. Palais, ed., *Occasional Papers on Korea*. Seattle: University of Washington, 1975.

Sohn, Hak-Kyn. *Authoritarianism and Opposition in South Korea*. London: Routledge, 1989.

Song, Byung-Nak. *The Rise of the Korean Economy*. New York: Oxford University Press, 1990.

Sorensen, Clark W. *Over the Mountains Are Mountains: Korean Peasant Households and Their Adaptations to Rapid Industrialization*. Seattle: University of Washington Press, 1988.

Suh, Sang-Chul. *Growth and Structural Changes in the Korean Economy, 1910–1940*. Cambridge: Council on East Asian Studies, Harvard University, 1978.

Takeo, Tsuchiya. "Free Trade Zones and Industrialization in Asia." *AMPO: Japan Asia Quarterly Review* 8 and 9 (1977).

Trumbull Ladd, George. *In Korea with Marquis Ito*. New York: Charles Scribner's Sons, 1908.

Wagner, Edward W. "The Ladder of Success in Yi Dynasty Korea." In James B. Palais, ed., *Occasional Papers on Korea*, 1. Seattle: University of Washington, April 1974.

Woo-Cumings, Meredith, ed. *The Developmental State*. Ithaca, N.Y.: Cornell University Press, 1999.

Woo, Jung-en. *Race to the Swift: State and Finance in Korean Industrialization*. New York: Columbia University Press, 1991.

World Bank. *The East Asian Miracle*. New York: Oxford University Press, 1993.

Wright, Edward R., ed. *Korean Politics in Transition*. Seattle: University of Washington Press, 1975.

Young, Alwyn. "The Tyranny of Numbers: Confronting the Statistical Realities of the East Asian Growth Experience." *Quarterly Journal of Economics* 110 (1995): 641–80.

Brazil

Andrade, Regis de Castro. "Brazil: The Economics of Savage Capitalism." In Manfred Bienfeld and Martin Godrey, eds., *The Struggle for Development: National Strategies in an International Context.* New York: John Wiley, 1982. Pp. 165–88.

Bacha, Edmar L. "External Shocks and Growth Prospects: The Case of Brazil, 1973–89." *World Development* 14 (1986): 919–36.

Baer, Werner. *The Brazilian Economy: Growth and Development*, 4th ed. Westport, Conn.: Praeger, 1995.

————. *The Development of the Brazilian Steel Industry.* Nashville, Tenn.: Vanderbilt University Press, 1969.

————. *Industrialization and Economic Development in Brazil.* Homewood, Ill.: Richard D. Irwin, 1965.

Baer, Werner, and Annibal V. Villela. "Industrial Growth and Industrialization: Revisions in the Stages of Brazil's Economic Development." *Journal of Developing Areas* 7 (January 1973): 217–34.

Baer, Werner, Isaac Kerstenetzy, and Annibal V. Villela. "The Changing Role of the State in the Brazilian Economy." *World Development* 1 (1973): 23–34.

Balassa, Bela. "Incentive Policies in Brazil." *World Development* 7 (1979): 1023–42.

Barros, Alexandre. "The Brazilian Military: Professional Socialization, Political Performance, and State Building." Ph.D. dissertation, Department of Political Science, University of Chicago, 1978.

Bergsman, Joel. *Brazil: Industrialization and Trade Policies.* London: Oxford University Press, 1970.

Bethell, Leslie, ed. *The Cambridge History of Latin America.* Cambridge: Cambridge University Press, 1984.

Burns, Bradford E. *Nationalism in Brazil: A Historical Survey.* New York: Praeger, 1968.

Cardoso, Fernando Henrique. "Associated-Dependent Development: Theoretical and Practical Implications." In Alfred Stepan, ed., *Authoritarian Brazil: Origins, Policies and Future.* New Haven, Conn.: Yale University Press, 1973. Pp. 142–78.

Cardoso, Fernando Henrique, and Enzo Faletto. *Dependency and Development in Latin America.* Berkeley: University of California Press, 1979.

Cohen, Youssef. *The Manipulation of Consent: The State and Working Class Consciousness in Brazil.* Pittsburgh, Pa.: University of Pittsburgh Press, 1989.

Daland, Robert T. *Exploring Brazilian Bureaucracy: Performance and Pathology.* Washington, D.C.: University Press of America, 1981.

Dean, Warren. *The Industrialization of São Paulo, 1880–1945.* Austin: University of Texas Press, 1969.

Dulles, John W. F. *Vargas of Brazil: A Political Biography.* Austin: University of Texas Press, 1967.

Erickson, Kenneth Paul. *The Brazilian Corporative State and Working-Class Politics.* Berkeley: University of California Press, 1977.

Evans, Peter. *Dependent Development: The Alliance of Multinational, State, and Local Capital in Brazil.* Princeton, N.J.: Princeton University Press, 1979.

————. *Embedded Autonomy: States and Industrial Transformation.* Princeton, N.J.: Princeton University Press, 1995.

Fishlow, Albert. "Brazilian Development in Long-Term Perspective." *American Economic Review* 70 (May 1980): 102–8.

————. "Origins and Consequences of Import Substitution in Brazil." In Luis Eugenio Di Marco, ed., *International Economics and Development*. New York: Academic Press, 1972. Pp. 311–65.

Flynn, Peter. *Brazil: A Political Analysis*. Boulder: Westview, 1979.

Font, Mauricio A. *Coffee, Contention and Change in the Making of Modern Brazil*. Cambridge: Basil Blackwell, 1990.

Freyre, Gilberto. *The Mansions and the Shanties: The Making of Modern Brazil*. New York: Alfred A. Knopf, 1963.

————. *The Masters and the Slaves*. New York: Alfred A. Knopf, 1946.

Furtado, Celso. *The Economic Growth of Brazil: A Survey from Colonial to Modern Times*. Berkeley: University of California Press, 1963.

Geddes, Barbara. "Building State Autonomy in Brazil, 1930–1964." *Comparative Politics* 22 (January 1990): 217–35.

Glade, William P. *The Latin American Economies: A Study of Their Institutional Evolution*. New York: American Book Company, 1969.

Gordon, Lincoln, and Engebert Grommers. *United States Manufacturing Investment in Brazil*. Cambridge: Harvard University Press, 1962.

Hagopian, Frances. *Traditional Politics and Regime Change in Brazil*. New York: Cambridge University Press, 1996.

Hayes, Robert A. *The Armed Nation: The Brazilian Corporate Mystique*. Tempe: Arizona State University, Center for Latin American Studies, 1989.

Hirschman, Albert. *A Bias for Hope: Essays on Development and Latin America*. New Haven, Conn.: Yale University Press, 1971.

Keith, Henry H., and Robert A. Hayes, eds. *Perspectives on Armed Politics in Brazil*. Tempe: Arizona State University, Center for Latin American Studies, 1976.

Krieckhaus, Jonathan. "The Politics of Economic Growth in the Third World: Brazilian Developmentalism in Comparative Perspective." Ph.D. dissertation, Department of Politics, Princeton University, 2000.

————. "Reconceptualizing the Developmental State: Public Savings and Economic Growth." *World Development* 30 (2002): 1697–712.

Leff, Nathaniel H. *Economic Policy-making and Development in Brazil, 1947–1964*. New York: John Wiley, 1968.

————. *Underdevelopment and Development in Brazil*, vols. 1 and 2. London: George Allen and Unwin, 1982.

Levine, Robert M. *Pernambuco in the Brazilian Federation, 1889–1937*. Stanford, Calif.: Stanford University Press, 1978.

————. *The Vargas Regime: The Critical Years, 1934–1939*. New York: Columbia University Press, 1970.

Lieberman, Evan S. *Race and Regionalism in the Politics of Taxation in Brazil and South Africa*. New York: Cambridge University Press, 2003.

Love, Joseph L. *São Paulo in the Brazilian Federation*. Stanford, Calif.: Stanford University Press, 1980.

Milan, Pedro, and Regis Bonelli. "The Success of Growth Policies in Brazil." In Simon Teitel, ed., *Towards a New Development Strategy for Latin America*. Washington, D.C.: Inter American Development Bank, 1992.

Morley, Samuel A., and Gordon W. Smith. "Import Substitution and Foreign Investment in Brazil." *Oxford Economic Papers* (March 1971): 120–35.

Nunes, Edison de Oliveria. "Bureaucratic Insulation and Clientelism in Contemporary Brazil: Uneven State Building and the Taming of Modernity." Ph.D. dissertation, Department of Political Science, University of California, Berkeley, 1984.

O'Donnell, Guillermo A. *Modernization and Bureaucratic Authoritarianism.* Berkeley: University of California, Institute of International Studies, 1973.

Russell-Wood, A. J. R. "Colonial Brazil: The Gold Cycle, c. 1690– c. 1750." In Leslie Bethell, ed., *The Cambridge History of Latin America.* Cambridge: Cambridge University Press, 1984.

Schneider, Ben Ross. *Politics within the State: Elite Bureaucrats and Industrial Policy in Authoritarian Brazil.* Pittsburgh, Pa.: University of Pittsburgh Press, 1991.

Schneider, Ronald M. *The Political System of Brazil: Emergence of a "Modernizing" Authoritarian Regime, 1964–1970.* New York: Columbia University Press, 1971.

Schwartz, Stuart B. "Colonial Brazil, 1580–1750: Plantations and Peripheries." In Leslie Bethell, ed., *The Cambridge History of Latin America.* Cambridge: Cambridge University Press, 1984.

Siegel, Gilbert B. "The Vicissitudes of Government Reform in Brazil: A Study of DASP." Ph.D. dissertation, University of Southern California, 1966.

Sikkink, Kathryn. *Ideas and Institutions: Developmentalism in Brazil and Argentina.* Ithaca, N.Y.: Cornell University Press, 1991.

Skidmore, Thomas E. *Politics in Brazil, 1930–1964: An Experiment in Democracy.* New York: Oxford University Press, 1967.

———. *The Politics of Military Rule in Brazil, 1964–1985.* New York: Oxford University Press, 1988.

Skidmore, Thomas, and Peter Smith. *Modern Latin America,* 4th ed. New York: Oxford University Press, 1997.

Stepan, Alfred. *The Military in Politics: Changing Patterns in Brazil.* Princeton, N.J.: Princeton University Press, 1971.

Stepan, Alfred, ed. *Authoritarian Brazil: Origins, Policies and Future.* New Haven, Conn.: Yale University Press, 1973.

Suzigan, Wilson. "Industrialization and Economic Policy in Historical Perspective." In Fernando Rezende, ed., *Brazilian Economic Studies.* Rio de Janeiro: Institute of Social and Economic Planning (IPEA), 1976.

Stein, Stanley. *The Brazilian Cotton Manufacture: Textile Enterprise in an Underdeveloped Area, 1850–1950.* Cambridge: Harvard University Press, 1957.

Topik, Steven. *The Political Economy of the Brazilian State, 1889–1930.* Austin: University of Texas Press, 1987.

Tyler, William G. "Brazilian Industrialization and Industrial Policies: A Survey." *World Development* 4 (1976): 863–82.

Viotti Da Costa, Emilia. "Brazil: The Age of Reform, 1870–1899." In Leslie Bethell, ed., *The Cambridge History of Latin America.* Cambridge: Cambridge University Press, 1984.

Willmore, Larry. "Transnationals and Foreign Trade: Evidence from Brazil." *Journal of Development Studies* 28 (January 1992): 314–35.

Wirth, John D. *Minas Gerais in the Brazilian Federation, 1889–1937.* Stanford, Calif.: Stanford University Press, 1977.

———. *The Politics of Brazilian Development, 1930–1954.* Stanford, Calif.: Stanford University Press, 1970.

Young, Jordan M. *The Brazilian Revolution of 1930 and the Aftermath.* New Brunswick, N.J.: Rutgers University Press, 1967.

India

Acharya, Shankar. "Macroeconomic Management in the Nineties." *Economic and Political Weekly* (April 20, 2002): 1515–38.

Ahluwalia, Isher Judge. *Industrial Growth in India: Stagnation since the Mid-Sixties.* Delhi: Oxford University Press, 1985.

Ahluwalia, Isher Judge, and I. M. D. Little, eds. *India's Economic Reforms and Development: Essays for Manmohan Singh.* New Delhi: Oxford University Press, 1998.

Bagchi, Amiya. *Private Investment in India, 1900–1939.* Cambridge: Cambridge University Press, 1972.

Bardhan, Pranab. *The Political Economy of Development in India.* Delhi: Oxford University Press, 1998.

Bayley, D. H. *The Police and Political Development in India.* Princeton: Princeton University Press, 1969.

Bhagwati, Jagdish N., and Padma Desai. *India: Planning for Industrialization.* London: Oxford University Press, 1970.

Bhagwati, Jagdish N., and T. N. Srinivasan. *Foreign Trade Regimes and Economic Development: India,* vol. 6. New York: National Bureau of Economic Research, distributed by Columbia University Press, 1975.

Carras, Mary. *Indira Gandhi: In the Crucible of Leadership: A Political Biography.* Boston: Beacon, 1979.

Chakravarty, Sukhamoy. *Development Planning: The Indian Experience.* Delhi: Oxford University Press, 1988.

Chandavarkar, Rajnarayan. *The Origins of Industrial Capitalism in India: Business Strategies and the Working Classes in Bombay, 1900–1940.* Cambridge: Cambridge University Press, 1994.

Chandra, Bipan, Mridula Mukherjee, and Aditya Mukherjee. *India after Independence, 1947–2000.* New Delhi: Penguin, 1988.

Chandra, Bipan, et al. *India's Struggle for Independence, 1857–1947.* New Delhi: Penguin, 1998.

Chaudhri, Tapan Ray. "The Mid-Eighteenth-Century Background." In Dharma Kumar, ed., *The Cambridge Economic History of India: c. 1757–c. 1970,* vol. 2. Cambridge: Cambridge University Press, 1983. Pp. 3–35.

Cohen, Stephen P. *The Indian Army: Its Contribution to the Development of a Nation.* Berkeley: University of California Press, 1971.

Desai, A. R. *Social Background of Indian Nationalism.* Bombay: Popular Prakashan, 1959.

Desai, Padma. *The Bokaro Steel Plant: A Study of Soviet Economic Assistance.* Amsterdam: North-Holland, 1972.

Embree, Ainslie T. *1857 in India: The Revolt against Foreign Rule.* Boston: South Asia Books, 1988.

Etienne, Gilbert. *Asian Crucible: The Steel Industry in China and India.* New Delhi: Sage, 1992.

Frankel, Francine. *India's Political Economy, 1947–1977: The Gradual Revolution.* Princeton, N.J.: Princeton University Press, 1978.

Gadgil, D. R. *The Industrial Evolution in India in Recent Times, 1860–1939,* 2nd ed. Delhi: Oxford University Press, 1971.

Gopal, S. *Jawaharlal Nehru: A Biography,* vols. 1–3. New Delhi: Oxford University Press, 1984.

Guha, Ranajit, ed. *Subaltern Studies,* vols. 1–4. New Delhi: Oxford University Press, 1982–86.

Habib, Irfan. *The Agrarian System of Mughal India, 1556–1707.* Bombay: Asia Publishing House, 1963.

Hanson, A. H. *The Process of Planning.* London: Oxford University Press, 1966.

Heston, Alan. "National Income." In Dharma Kumar, ed., *The Cambridge Economic History of India.* Cambridge: Cambridge University Press, 1983. Pp. 376–462.

Jayakar, Pupul. *Indira Gandhi: An Intimate Biography.* New York: Pantheon, 1992.

Jenkins, Rob. *Democratic Politics and Economic Reform in India.* New York: Cambridge University Press, 1999.

Johnson, W. A. *The Steel Industry of India.* Cambridge: Harvard University Press, 1966.

Joshi, Vijay, and I. M. D. Little. *India: Macroeconomics and Political Economy.* Washington, D.C.: World Bank, 1994.

Kohli, Atul. *Democracy and Discontent: India's Growing Crisis of Governability.* Cambridge: Cambridge University Press, 1991.

――――. "Politics of Economic Liberalization in India." *World Development* 17 (March 1989): 305–28.

――――. *The State and Poverty in India: The Politics of Reform.* Cambridge: Cambridge University Press, 1987.

Kohli, Atul, ed. *India's Democracy: An Analysis of Changing State-Society Relations.* Princeton, N.J.: Princeton University Press, 1988.

Kohli, Atul, ed. *The Success of India's Democracy.* Cambridge: Cambridge University Press, 2001.

Kothari, Rajni. *Politics in India.* Boston: Little, Brown, 1970.

Kulke, Hermann, and Dietmar Rothermund. *A History of India.* London: CroomHelm, 1986.

Kumar, Dharma, ed. *The Cambridge Economic History of India.* Cambridge: Cambridge University Press, 1983.

Leadbeater, S. R. B. *The Politics of Textiles: The Indian Cotton Mill Industry and the Legacy of Swadeshi (1900–1985).* New Delhi: Sage Publications, 1993.

Lewis, John P. *India's Political Economy: Governance and Reform.* Delhi: Oxford University Press, 1995.

Lewis, W. Arthur. *Dynamic Factors in Economic Growth.* Bombay: Orient Longman for the Dorab Tata Memorial Lecture Series, 1974.

Maddison, Angus. "Alternative Estimates of the Real Product of India, 1900–46." *Indian Economic and Social History Review* 22 (April/June 1985): 201–10.

――――. *Class Structure and Economic Growth: India and Pakistan since the Moghals.* London: George Allen and Unwin, 1971.

Markovits, Claude. *Indian Business and Nationalist Politics, 1931–39: The Indigenous Capitalist Class and the Rise of the Congress Party.* Cambridge: Cambridge University Press, 1985.

Mehta, Uday. *Liberalism and Empire: A Study in Nineteenth-Century British Liberal Thought.* Chicago: University of Chicago Press, 1999.

Metcalf, Thomas R. *The Aftermath of Revolt: India, 1857–1870.* Princeton, N.J.: Princeton University Press, 1964.

————. *Ideologies of the Raj, The New Cambridge History of India,* vol. 3. Cambridge: Cambridge University Press, 1994.

Misra, B. B. *The Bureaucracy in India: A Historical Analysis of Development up to 1947.* Delhi: Oxford University Press, 1977.

Misra, Sanjib. "India's Textile Policy and the Informal Sector." In Stuart Nagel, ed., *India's Development and Public Policy.* Aldershot: Ashgate, Policy Studies Organization, 2000.

Mohan, Rakesh. "Fiscal Correction for Economic Growth: Data Analysis and Suggestions." *Economic and Political Weekly* 35 (June 10, 2000): 2027–36.

Moreland, W. H. *India at the Death of Akbar.* London: Macmillan, 1920.

Morris, Morris D. "Indian Industry and Business in the Age of Laissez-Faire." In Rajat Kanta Ray, ed., *Entrepreneurship and Industry in India, 1800–1947.* New Delhi: Oxford University Press, 1992.

Morris, Morris D., et al. *Indian Economy in the Nineteenth Century: A Symposium.* New Delhi: Indian Economic and Social History Association, Delhi School of Economics, 1969.

Myrdal, Gunnar. *Asian Drama: An Inquiry into the Poverty of Nations.* New York: Pantheon, 1968.

Nayar, Baldev Raj. *India's Mixed Economy.* Bombay: Popular Prakashan, 1989.

Otsuka, Keijiro, et al. *Comparative Technology Choice in Development: The Indian and Japanese Cotton Textile Industries.* Basingstoke, Hampshire: Macmillan, 1988.

Pack, Howard. *Productivity, Technology and Industrial Development: A Case Study in Textiles.* New York: Oxford University Press, 1987.

Pinglé, Vibha. *Rethinking the Developmental State: India's Industry in Comparative Perspective.* New Delhi: Oxford University Press, 1999.

Potter, David C. *India's Political Administrators: From ICS to IAS.* New Delhi: Oxford University Press, 1996.

Raj, K. N. *Indian Economic Growth: Performance and Prospects.* New Delhi: Allied Publishers, 1966.

Ray, Rajat K. *Industrialization in India: Growth and Conflict in the Private Corporate Sector, 1914–47.* New Delhi: Oxford University Press, 1979.

Ray, Ratnalekha. *Change in Bengal Agrarian Society, 1760–1850.* New Delhi: Manohar Publications, 1979.

Rosen, Stephen P. *Societies and Military Power: India and Its Armies.* Ithaca, N.Y.: Cornell University Press, 1996.

Rothermund, Dietmar. *An Economic History of India: From Pre-colonial Times to 1986.* London: CroomHelm, 1986.

Rudolph, Lloyd, and Susanne Rudolph. *In Pursuit of Lakshmi.* Chicago: University of Chicago Press, 1987.

Rudolph, Lloyd, and Susanne Rudolph. *Reversing the Gaze: Amar Singh's Diary: A Colonial Subject's Narrative of Imperial India.* New Delhi: Oxford University Press, 2000.

Sarkar, Sumit. "Indian Democracy: The Historical Inheritance." In Atul Kohli, ed., *The Success of India's Democracy.* Cambridge: Cambridge University Press, 2001.

————. *Modern India, 1885–1947.* London: Macmillan, 1989.

Sastry, D. U. *The Cotton Mill Industry in India.* New Delhi: Oxford University Press, 1984.

Seal, Anil. "Imperialism and Nationalism in India." In John Gallagher et al., eds., *Locality, Province and Nation: Essays on Indian Politics, 1870–1940.* Cambridge: Cambridge University Press, 1973.

Sen, Amartya K. "The Pattern of British Enterprise in India, 1854–1914." In Rajat Ray, ed., *Entrepreneurship and Industry in India, 1800–1947.* New York: Oxford University Press, 1992.

Sivasubramonian, S. "Income from the Secondary Sector in India, 1900–1947." *Indian Economic and Social History Review* 14 (October–December 1977): 427–92.

Tomlinson, B. R. *The Economy of Modern India, 1860–1970.* New Cambridge History of India, vol. 3. Cambridge: Cambridge University Press, 1993.

————. *The Political Economy of the Raj, 1914–1947: The Economics of Decolonization in India.* London: Macmillan, 1979.

Varshney, Ashutosh. *Democracy, Development, and the Countryside: Urban-Rural Struggles in India.* New York: Cambridge University Press, 1995.

Weiner, Myron. *The Child and the State in India.* Princeton, N.J.: Princeton University Press, 1991.

————. *Party Building in a New Nation.* Chicago: University of Chicago Press, 1967.

Wolpert, Stanley. *A New History of India.* New York: Oxford University Press, 1982.

Nigeria

Abba, Alkasum, et al. *The Nigerian Economic Crisis: Causes and Solutions.* Lagos: Academic Staff Union of Universities of Nigeria, 1985.

Adamolekun, Ladipo. *Politics and Administration in Nigeria.* London: Hutchinson and Company, 1988.

————. "Postscript: Notes on Developments in Nigerian Administration since 1970." In D. J. Murray, ed., *Studies in Nigerian Administration.* London: Hutchinson University Library for Africa, 1978. Pp. 310–27.

Adeleye, R. A. *Power and Diplomacy in Northern Nigeria, 1804–1900.* New York: Humanities Press, 1971.

Adeleye, R. A., and C. C. Stewart. "The Sokoto Caliphate in the Nineteenth Century." In J. F. A. Ajayi and Michael Crowder, eds., *History of West Africa,* vol. 2, 2nd ed. London: Longman, 1987. Pp. 86–131.

Ahire, Philip Terdoo. *Imperial Policing: The Emergence and Role of the Police in Colonial Nigeria, 1860–1960.* Philadelphia: Open University Press, Milton Keynes, 1991.

Ajayi, J. F. A. "The Aftermath of the Fall of Old Oyo." In J. F. A. Ajayi and Michael Crowder, eds., *History of West Africa,* 2nd ed. London: Longman, 1987.

Ajayi, J. F. A., and Michael Crowder. "West Africa 1919–1939: The Colonial Situation." In J. F. A. Ajayi and Michael Crowder, eds., *History of West Africa,* vol. 2, 2nd ed. London: Longman, 1987. Pp. 706–31.

Ake, Claude. *Democracy and Development in Africa.* Washington, D.C.: Brookings Institution, 1996.

Ake, Claude, ed. *Political Economy of Nigeria.* London: Longman, 1985.

Aluko, Olajide. "Politics of Decolonization in British West Africa, 1945–1960." In J. F. A. Ajayi and Michael Crowder, eds., *History of West Africa*, 2nd ed. London: Longman, 1987. Pp. 706–31.

Asiwaja, A. I. "Dahomey, Yorubaland, Bargu and Benin in the Nineteenth Century." In J. F. A. Ajayi, ed., *UNESCO General History of Africa*, vol. 6: *Africa in the Nineteenth Century until the 1880s*. Berkeley: University of California Press, 1989. Pp. 669–723.

Bates, Robert H. *States and Markets in Tropical Africa: The Political Basis of Agricultural Policies*. Berkeley: University of California Press, 1981.

Berger, Manfred. *Industrialization Policies in Nigeria*. Munich: Weltforum Verlag, 1975.

Berry, Sara. "Cocoa and Economic Development in Western Nigeria." In Carl K. Liedholm and Carl Eicher, eds., *Growth and Development of the Nigerian Economy*. East Lansing: Michigan State University Press, 1970. Pp. 16–27.

Biersteker, Thomas J. *Multinationals, the State, and Control of the Nigerian Economy*. Princeton, N.J.: Princeton University Press, 1987.

Callaghy, Thomas M. "The State as Lame Leviathan: The Patrimonial Administrative State in Africa." In Zaki Ergas, ed., *The African State in Transition*. London: Macmillan, 1987. Pp. 87–116.

Coleman, James S. *Nigeria: Background to Nationalism*. Berkeley: University of California Press, 1958.

Crocker, Walter R. *Nigeria: A Critique of British Colonial Administration*. Freeport, N.Y.: Books for Libraries Press, 1971.

Crowder, Michael. *The Story of Nigeria*, 4th ed. London: Faber and Faber, 1978.

Diamond, Larry. *Class, Ethnicity and Democracy in Nigeria: The Failure of the First Republic*. Syracuse, N.Y.: Syracuse University Press, 1988.

——. "Social Change and Political Conflict in Nigeria's Second Republic." In I. William Zartman, ed., *The Political Economy of Nigeria*. New York: Praeger, 1983. Pp. 25–84.

Diamond, Larry, Anthony Kirk-Greene, and Oyeleye Oyediran, eds. *Transition without End: Nigerian Politics and Civil Society under Babangida*. Boulder: Lynne Reinner, 1997.

Dike, Onwuka K. *Trade and Politics in the Niger Delta, 1830–1885: An Introduction to the Economic and Political History of Nigeria*. London: Oxford University Press, 1956.

Edogun, Cliff. "The Structure of State Capitalism in the Nigerian Petroleum Industry." In Claude Ake, ed., *Political Economy of Nigeria*. London: Longman, 1985. Pp. 89–112.

Ekundare, Olufemi. *An Economic History of Nigeria, 1880–1960*. New York: Africana Publishing Company, Holmes and Meir Publishers, 1973.

Falola, Toyin, ed. *African Historiography: Essays in Honour of Jacob Ade Ajayi*. London: Longman, 1993.

Fieldhouse, D. K. *Black Africa, 1945–1980: Economic Decolonization and Arrested Development*. London: Allen and Unwin, 1986.

Forrest, Tom. "The Advance of African Capital: The Growth of Nigerian Private Enterprise." In Frances Stewart, Sanjaya Lall, and Samuel Wangwe, eds., *Alternative Development Strategies in Sub-Saharan Africa*. New York: St. Martin's Press, 1992. Pp. 368–401.

——. *Politics and Economic Development in Nigeria*, 2nd ed. Boulder: Westview, 1995.

Gboyega, Alex. "The Civil Service Reforms: A Critique." In Said Adejumobi and Abubakar Momoh, eds., *The Political Economy of Nigeria under Military Rule (1984–1993)*. Harare: Sapes Books, 1995. Pp. 259–81.

Gueye, M'baye, and A. Adu Boahen. "African Initiatives and Resistance in West Africa, 1880–1914." In A. Adu Boahen, ed., *General History of Africa*, vol. 7: *Africa under Colonial Domination, 1880–1935*. Berkeley: University of California Press for UNESCO, 1985. Pp. 114–48.

Harris, John. "Nigerian Entrepreneurship." In Carl K. Eicher and Carl Liedholm, eds., *Growth and Development in the Nigerian Economy*. East Lansing: Michigan State University Press, 1970.

Helleiner, Gerald K. *Peasant Agriculture, Government, and Economic Growth in Nigeria*. Homewood, Ill.: Richard D. Irwin, 1966.

Herbst, Jeffrey. *States and Power in Africa: Comparative Lessons in Authority and Control*. Princeton, N.J.: Princeton University Press, 2000.

Hill, Polly. "From Slavery to Freedom: The Case of Farm-Slavery in Nigerian Hausaland." *Comparative Studies in Society and History* 18 (1976): 395–426.

———. *Population, Prosperity and Poverty: Rural Kano, 1900 and 1970*. Cambridge: Cambridge University Press, 1970.

Hopkins, A. G. *An Economic History of West Africa*. London: Longman, 1973.

Joseph, Richard A. *Democracy and Prebendal Politics in Nigeria: The Rise and Fall of the Second Republic*. Cambridge: Cambridge University Press, 1987.

Koehn, Peter M. *Public Policy and Administration in Africa: Lessons from Nigeria*. Boulder, Colo.: Westview Press, 1999.

Kennedy, Paul. *African Capitalism: The Struggle for Ascendancy*. Cambridge: Cambridge University Press, 1988.

Kilby, Peter. *Industrialization in an Open Economy: Nigeria, 1945–1966*. Cambridge: Cambridge University Press, 1969.

Last, Murray. "The Sokoto Caliphate and Borno." In J. F. Ade Ajayi, ed., *UNESCO General History of Africa*, vol. 1: *Africa in the Nineteenth Century until the 1880s*. Berkeley: University of California Press, 1989. Pp. 555–99.

Law, Robin. "The Historiography of the Commercial Transition in Nineteenth Century West Africa." In Toyin Falola, ed., *African Historiography: Essays in Honour of Jacob Ade Ajayi*. London: Longman, 1993. Pp. 91–115.

Law, Robin, ed. *From Slave Trade to "Legitimate" Commerce: The Commercial Transition in Nineteenth Century West Africa*. Cambridge: Cambridge University Press, 1995.

Lewis, Peter M. "Economic Statism, Private Capital, and the Dilemmas of Accumulation in Nigeria." *World Development* 22 (1994): 437–51.

Liedholm, Carl. "The Influence of Colonial Policy on the Growth and Development of Nigeria's Industrial Sector." In Carl K. Liedholm and Carl Eicher, eds., *Growth and Development of the Nigerian Economy*. East Lansing: Michigan State University Press, 1970. Pp. 52–61.

Lloyd, Peter C. *The Political Development of Yoruba Kingdoms in the Eighteenth and Nineteenth Centuries*. London: Royal Anthropological Institute, Occasional Paper No. 31, 1971.

Lovejoy, Paul E. "Plantations in the Economy of the Sokoto Caliphate." *Journal of African History* 19 (1978): 341–68.

Low, Victor. *Three Nigerian Emirates: A Study in Oral History.* Evanston, Ill.: Northwestern University Press, 1972.

Lubeck, Paul, ed. *African Bourgeoisie: Capitalist Development in Nigeria, Kenya and the Ivory Coast.* Boulder, Colo.: Lynne Rienner, 1987.

Luckham, Robin. *The Nigerian Military: A Sociological Analysis of Authority and Revolt, 1960–1967.* Cambridge: Cambridge University Press, 1971.

Lugard, Lord F. J. D. *The Dual Mandate in British Tropical Africa.* London: W. Blackwood and Sons, 1922.

Lynn, Martin. "The West African Palm Oil Trade in the Nineteenth Century and the Crisis of Adaptation." In Robin Law, ed., *From Slave Trade to "Legitimate" Commerce: The Commercial Transition in Nineteenth Century West Africa.* Cambridge: Cambridge University Press, 1995. Pp. 57–77.

Mamdani, Mahmood. *Citizen and Subject: Contemporary Africa and the Legacy of Late Colonialism.* Princeton, N.J.: Princeton University Press, 1996.

Medard, Jean-François. "The Underdeveloped State in Tropical Africa: Political Clientelism or Neopatrimonialism." In Christopher Clapham, ed., *Private Patronage and Public Power: Political Clientelism in the Modern State.* New York: St. Martin's Press, 1982. Pp. 162–92.

Murray, D. J. "The Impact of Politics on Administration." In Adebayo Adedeji, ed., *Nigerian Administration and Its Political Setting.* London: Hutchinson Educational Ltd., 1968.

Nafziger, E. Wayne. *African Capitalism: A Case Study of Nigerian Entrepreneurship.* Stanford: Hoover Institution Press, 1972.

Nair, Kannan K. *Politics and Society in South East Nigeria, 1841–1906.* London: Frank Cass, 1972.

Nicolson, I. F. *The Administration of Nigeria, 1900–1960: Men, Methods, and Myths.* Oxford: Clarendon, 1969.

Odekunle, Femi, ed. *Nigeria: Corruption in Development.* Ibadan: Ibadan University Press, 1986.

Olugbemi, Stephen O. "The Civil Service: An Outsider's View." In Oyediran Oyeleye, ed., *Nigerian Government and Politics under Military Rule, 1966–1979.* New York: St. Martin's Press, 1979.

Olukoshi, Adebayo O. "The Political Economy of the Structural Adjustment Programme." In Said Adejumobi and Abubaker Momoh, eds., *The Political Economy of Nigeria under Military Rule (1984–1993).* Harare: Sapes Books, 1995.

Pakenham, Thomas. *The Scramble for Africa, 1876–1912.* New York: Random House, 1991.

Panter-Brick, Keith, ed. *Soldiers and Oil: The Political Transformation of Nigeria.* London: Frank Cass, 1978.

Perham, Margery. "British Problem in Africa." *Foreign Affairs* 29 (July 1951): 637–50.

———. *Lugard: The Years of Authority, 1898–1945.* London: Oxford University Press, 1960.

Peters, Jimi. *The Nigerian Military and the State.* London: I. B. Tauris, 1997.

Pim, A. W. "Public Finance." In Margery Perham, ed., *Mining, Commerce and Finance in Nigeria.* London: Faber and Faber, 1948. Pp. 225–79.

Roberts, Andrew. "The Imperial Mind." In A. D. Roberts, ed., *The Cambridge History of Africa,* vol. 7: *From 1905 to 1940.* Cambridge: Cambridge University Press, 1986. Pp. 24–76.

Sandbrook, Richard. *The Politics of Africa's Economic Stagnation.* Cambridge: Cambridge University Press, 1986.

Schatz, Sayre P. *Nigerian Capitalism.* Berkeley: University of California Press, 1977.

———. "Private Capitalism and the Inert Economy of Nigeria." *Journal of Modern African Studies* 22 (1984): 45–57.

Sklar, Richard. *Nigerian Political Parties: Power in an Emergent African Nation.* Princeton, N.J.: Princeton University Press, 1963.

Smith, Michael G. *The Economy of Hausa Communities of Zaria: A Report to the Colonial Social Science Research Council.* London: H. M. Stationery Office for the Colonial Office, 1955.

Smith, Robert. "The Lagos Consulate, 1851–1861: An Outline." *Journal of African History* 15 (1974): 393–416.

Smith, Robert S. *Kingdoms of the Yoruba,* 2nd ed. London: Methuen, 1976.

Tilly, Charles. *Coercion, Capital and European States.* Cambridge: Blackwell, 1990.

Ume, Kalu E. *The Rise of British Colonialism in Southern Nigeria, 1700–1900: A Study of the Bights of Benin and Bonny.* Smithtown, N.Y.: Exposition Press, 1980.

Usman, Y. B., ed. *Studies in the History of the Sokoto Caliphate.* Published by the Sokoto History Bureau. New York: Third Press International, 1979.

Watts, Michael. *Silent Violence: Food, Famine and Peasantry in Northern Nigeria.* Berkeley: University of California Press, 1983.

Webster, J. B. "African Political Activity in British West Africa, 1900–1940." In J. F. A. Ajayi and Michael Crowder, eds., *History of West Africa.* New York: Columbia University Press, 1973.

Wesseling, H. L. *Divide and Rule: The Partition of Africa, 1880–1914.* Translated from Dutch by Arnold J. Pomerans. Westport: Praeger, 1996.

White, Jeremy. *Central Administration in Nigeria, 1914–1948.* Dublin: Irish Academic Press, 1981.

World Bank. *Nigeria: Macro-Economic Policies for Structural Change.* Washington, D.C.: World Bank Press, 1983.

———. *Nigeria: Structural Adjustment Program, Policies, Implementation, Impact.* Washington, D.C.: World Bank Press, 1994.

Young, Crawford. *The African Colonial State in Comparative Perspective.* New Haven, Conn.: Yale University Press, 1994.

Index